ENTHUSIASTIC ENDORSEMENTS FROM *BOTH* FOUNDERS OF THE NIELSEN NORMAN GROUP!

Personas personified. The definitive word on why personas are better than people in guiding your designs. Filled with case histories, sidebars, and helpful, useful guidelines as well as deep, penetrating analyses. A big book, and for a reason. This book is unique in that it is truly for everyone: the practitioner, the researcher, and the teacher. Did I say this was essential reading? Well, it is: if you use personas, if you have thought about using them, but especially if you don't even know what they are, this is the book for you.

—Don Norman, Nielsen Norman group & Northwestern University; author of *Emotional Design*

Personas are powerful design tools, which are that much more dangerous if they are grounded in weak methodology. Pruitt and Adlin show you how to do personas right and how to base them on real user data. Follow their advice or risk disaster.

—Jakob Nielsen, Nielsen Norman group, author of *Usability Engineering*

THE MORGAN KAUFMANN SERIES IN INTERACTIVE TECHNOLOGIES

Series Editors:
Stuart Card, PARC ❖ Jonathan Grudin, Microsoft
Jakob Nielsen, Nielsen Norman Group

THE
PERSONA LIFECYCLE

THE
PERSONA LIFECYCLE

Keeping People in Mind Throughout Product Design

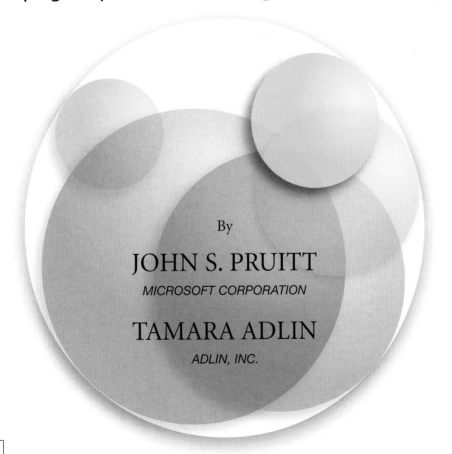

By

JOHN S. PRUITT
MICROSOFT CORPORATION

TAMARA ADLIN
ADLIN, INC.

AMSTERDAM · BOSTON · HEIDELBERG · LONDON
NEW YORK · OXFORD · PARIS · SAN DIEGO
SAN FRANCISCO · SINGAPORE · SYDNEY · TOKYO
Morgan Kaufmann is an imprint of Elsevier

Publishing Director: Diane Cerra
Publishing Services Managers: Andre Cuello, George Morrison
Senior Project Manager: Angela Dooley
Project Manager: Dawnmarie Simpson
Editorial Assistant: Asma Stephan
Cover Design: Yvo Riezebos
Cover and Book Illustrations: Nelson Adlin
Technical Illustrations: Craig Hally
Text Design: Yvo Riezebos
Composition: CEPHA Imaging Pvt Ltd.
Illustration: Dartmouth Publishing, Inc.
Copyeditor: Daril Bentley
Proofreader: Broccoli Information Management
Indexer: Broccoli Information Management
Interior printer: Hing Yip Printing, Co., Ltd.
Cover printer: Hing Yip Printing, Co., Ltd.

Morgan Kaufmann Publishers is an imprint of Elsevier.
500 Sansome Street, Suite 400, San Francisco, CA 94111

This book is printed on acid-free paper.

Library of Congress Cataloging-in-Publication Data

Pruitt, John.
  The persona lifecycle: keeping people in mind throughout product design / John Pruitt, Tamara Adlin.
    p. cm.
  Includes bibliographical references and index.
  ISBN-13: 978-0-12-566251-2 (pbk. : alk. paper)
  ISBN-10: 0-12-566251-3 (pbk. : alk. paper) 1. Product management. 2. New products. 3. Industrial research.
    I. Adlin, Tamara. II. Title.
  HF5415.15.P79 2006
  658.5'03--dc22

                                                                            2006000795

ISBN 13: 978-0-12-566251-2
ISBN 10: 0-12-566251-3

For information on all Morgan Kaufmann publications,
visit our Web site at www.mkp.com or www.books.elsevier.com
Printed in China
06 07 08 09   5 4 3 2 1

DEDICATION

For all the people brave enough to stand up in a room full of smart,
powerful people and say,
"This doesn't make sense. Let's try something new."

And for all the smart, powerful people brave enough to listen.

"KEEP PEOPLE IN MIND"

Be Brave!

CONTENTS

CONTRIBUTED CHAPTERS:

ACKNOWLEDGMENTS

This book has consumed us for several years and we simply couldn't have done it without each other and without the help of dozens of people, including most notably our families, friends, and colleagues who helped us just keep going through what felt like endless months of work. There are a few people we simply must acknowledge by name.

Holly Jamesen-Carr, who was one of the original members of our persona workshop squad and was going to co-author the entire book with us, but got married and ran off to Washington, D.C. instead to pursue her passion for environmental work. Many of her ideas are in this book, and we're thrilled that she decided to co-author the chapter on Mapping with Tamara.

Chauncey Wilson, who was (luckily for us) recruited to be one of the original peer reviewers of our manuscript and kept working with us throughout the revision process. Chauncey, your help was invaluable. Thank you for pushing us to answer difficult questions.

Ginny Redish and Mary Beth Rettger, who have the distinction of both participating in our initial persona workshops and reviewing our draft manuscripts. Ginny, your comments were beyond insightful, and Mary Beth, your enthusiasm carried us through some difficult revisions. Big thanks also to reviewers Sarah Bloomer and Terry Roberts, who provided invaluable suggestions in their reviews of our manuscript in all its many drafts. We thank you for your time and for your encouragement.

We're very proud to include chapters by some of the best usability, HCI, and customer experience experts around: Whitney Quesenbery, Larry Constantine, Jonathan Grudin, Bob Barlow-Busch, and Holly Jamesen. Thanks for spending your non-existent time writing your wonderful chapters.

Thanks to the Nielsen/Norman Group, especially Jacob Nielsen and Don Norman themselves, who helped us polish our ideas by inviting us to participate in their international User Experience conferences. It's been wonderful to have your support and we've loved every minute of your conferences—especially the priceless moments in the "teachers' lounge" listening to Tog tell jokes.

The idea for the 'persona lifecycle' arose quite naturally from two energizing days of workshops in 2001 and 2002 at the Usability Professional's Association (UPA) annual conferences. We want to thank all of our participants; your ideas, experiences, and insights helped us develop the Persona Lifecycle and inspired us to include as many 'stories from the field' as we could. Whether or not you contributed written content directly, all of you contributed the stories and experiences during the workshops that served to bring this book to life. From UPA 2001: Anna Rutgersson, Bryan Kirschner, David Fore, Dawn Taketa, Ginny Redish, Heather McQuaid, Janice James, Julie Nowicki, Karen Eliasen, Mary Beth Rettger, Matthew Lee, Merryl Gross, and Rosa Gudjonsdottir. From UPA 2002: Nathalie Barthe, Len Conte, Brenda D'Angelo, Caroline Jarrett, Rhiannon Jones, Lori Landesman, Sandra Maples, Bob Murata, and Damian Rees. The 'all stars' who participated both years: Robert Barlow-Busch and Judee Humberg.

Dan Gallivan, you inspired Tamara more than she can say. Thanks for pushing her to explore creative solutions and to look past corporate shenanigans. Thanks to Larry Tesler, who went out of his way to ensure that Tamara could continue to work on her book when she joined Amazon.com. We owe our intro paragraphs to you, Larry. Phil Terry, you are responsible for many of the connections that resulted in lots of the sidebars for this book. You are an inspiration, a master connector, and a true leader in the art and science of understanding users.

Thanks to the folks at Morgan Kaufmann who wheedled, prodded, and cajoled us to finish a book we said 'would only take a few months, really!' Diane Cerra, thanks for inviting us to write this book and sticking with the ever expanding deadlines. Asma Stephan, you are a miracle of organization. Julio Esperas, thank you for your design help and for bringing Yvo Riezebos into the project. Yvo, your enthusiasm and creativity are wonderful and we love the look of our book—no one else could have brought all these elements together the way you did. We also thank Jakob Nielsen and Jonathan Grudin again for recommending our work to Morgan Kaufmann in the first place. Finally, thank heavens for Dawnmane Simpson, who flew in like an angel to escort us through the last hectic month of our publishing marathon.

Thanks to Craig Hally and his graphic talents for creating the persona lifecycle illustration concept and for bringing our fictional G4K case study personas to life in expressive example posters.

Thanks to Nelson Adlin and his cavalcade of creatures. They seem to inhabit our manuscript quite happily, and of course Tamara is especially proud to include her daddy's art in the book.

Thanks to Jesica Pruitt for her endless patience and support, and willingness to give up her husband for countless weekends and evenings. Also, thanks to Ms. Madeline Grace Pruitt, who kindly scheduled her own birth to coincide perfectly with the completion of this book.

Thanks to Mark Patterson and Chris Nodder for encouraging John to explore the idea of personas, when the approach seemed so wildly new, ill defined, and untested.

We wrote most of this book during many long saturdays in the Bellevue Public Library. Thanks to the librarians for not noticing our scam, in which we signed up separately so that we could reserve the private study rooms for inordinate amounts of time.

Finally, we'd like to thank Alan Cooper for the inspiration that his book *The Inmates are Running the Asylum* gave us and so many other people interested in designing software that's easy for regular people to use.

FOREWORD

I'm very pleased to see this book published. Not only is it an effective, useful, and thorough treatment of an exciting and relevant new interaction design tool, but it represents a clear recognition of the profound sea change that has swept through the software industry in the last few years. That change, of course, is the shift from post-facto testing as a means of improving software behavior to pre-facto design.

Through our Cooper U division, my company, Cooper, offers training in persona-based interaction design. At a recent session, a senior usability professional at a major software company—obviously apprehensive about directly questioning me—asked me why I "had changed my opinion regarding the effectiveness of usability." What she was referring to was my tendency, a decade ago, to publicly describe traditional usability practices as ineffective and irrelevant, and my more recent stance of detent, or even outright enthusiasm for contemporary usability practitioners.

Although my questioner was bravely asking me a tough question—one that she clearly expected to generate some squirming and backpedaling on my part—the question provoked instead a relaxed smile. She was surprised, but not unhappy, to hear my answer. I replied that I had not changed my opinion at all but rather the practice of usability had changed. It no longer consists primarily of user testing of existing products, but instead now focuses on designing software before construction begins.

In effect, the practice of "usability" has transformed into the practice of "interaction design." In doing so, usability has become far more effective and, as my interlocutor implied, my relationship to it has changed. It is simply that from her point of view, it looks like *I* have moved rather than that an entire profession has shifted.

Arguably, what gave the profession the strongest nudge towards its new-found emphasis on design was Chapter Nine of my book, *The Inmates are Running the Asylum,* published in 1999. In that chapter I wrote for the first time about my invention: personas. I had already been using personas to great effect at my company for four years and had been using them in a primitive form for more than a decade before that.

It is immensely gratifying to see the influence one short chapter has had on the software business. The mere fact that personas have been so widely embraced shows just how extensive the pent-up desire was to make the change from merely evaluating software that programmers had designed to a more proactive stance of designing what those programmers should build.

In *The Inmates,* my intent was to write a manifesto for executives, exhorting them to gain control of their businesses by gaining control of the design of their software. It was never intended to be a how-to book of interaction design. The main purpose of describing personas in Chapter Nine was simply to show that my notions of interaction design were far more rigorous than the word "design" might conjure up in the mind of an exec whose only other exposure to the term was in the context of advertising.

Interaction design is a complex and difficult craft and requires good tools like any other. The popularity of personas has exploded because they are the foundational tool upon which the practice of interaction design rests. Interaction design is about making a particular group of humans effective at achieving a narrow set of goals. Because using personas is a remarkably powerful technique for bringing those humans and their objectives into focus, it becomes the most critical tool for designing the behavior of software.

In this volume, John Pruitt and Tamara Adlin give us the most complete description to date of what personas are, along with useful instructions on how to apply them. While other usability textbooks might devote a chapter to personas, this is the first one to give the topic the full attention it deserves. They unstintingly present the strengths and weaknesses of personas, along with detailed descriptions of how to introduce them to your organization, including particular emphasis on overcoming the wave of protest that is to be expected in any high-tech organization when non-programmers introduce a new idea.

Pruitt and Adlin also demonstrate their talent for unearthing real-world stories of how early adopters have applied personas. In this volume they gather together some of the most useful experiences from the field in applying personas, including voices of our most capable practitioners sharing their own wisdom gained in the heat of battle. These stories are presented as easily digestible sidebars scattered throughout the book.

Any usability professional will find this book indispensable, but you don't have to be a software designer to benefit from its contents. Anybody whose work depends on software quality (and that's about everyone these days) will find personas—and this book—a useful tool for improving the quality of your software and the success of your business.

Alan Cooper
Chairman
Cooper
www.cooper.com
24 August 2005

THE NEXT FRONTIER FOR USER-CENTERED DESIGN

Making User Representations More Usable

Imagine all the people, sharing all the world.
You may say I'm a dreamer, but I'm not the only one...

—John Lennon, lyrics from *Imagine*

We would like to introduce you to Tanner, shown in Figure 1.1. Tanner is a nine-year-old boy who loves to skateboard, play video and computer games, and generally run wild — all of which he prefers to do instead of schoolwork. Tanner doesn't sit still for long, and would rather spend time interactively on the PC than watch TV. Tanner's mom is Laura, who likes to say that Tanner holds the record for most Band-Aids required for a single human being. Tanner is a pretty regular kid, except in two significant ways:

● Tanner is the most influential member of a product development team at a midsize software company.

● Tanner is imaginary.

This book is all about powerful imaginary people — personas — who can help you build products that real people actually like to use. Personas are detailed descriptions of imaginary people constructed out of well-understood, highly specified data about real people. We believe that when

you use data to create personas, and use personas in a thoughtful way during the product development process, you will:

● Increase your products' usability, utility, and general appeal
● Streamline your teams' processes and improve your colleagues' abilities to work together
● Enable your company to make business decisions that help both your company and your customers
● Improve your company's bottom line.

Tanner and personas like him are ready and willing to help you do all of this. All you have to do is bring them to life and give them jobs. This book is here to help you do that.

FIGURE 1.1: *Tanner.*

YOU ARE ALREADY A PROFESSIONAL IMAGINER

Whether you realize it or not, imagining people is already part of your job. If you picked up this book, you are probably paid to participate in the design and development of products for people — consumers, workers, and businesspeople of all sorts. You probably also know how difficult it is to understand who these people are: what they want out of your products, how they get things done, the contexts in which they work and live, and how they differ from you. To build your products and build them well, you have had to become a professional imaginer, someone who builds a relatively concrete mental image of the people you imagine will be using your products. You can imagine things about people all day long, but it is difficult to know if the people you envision using your product bear any resemblance to the people who will actually purchase and use your product.

No matter what we are designing, building, or helping to build, we want our products (including software, hardware, consumer goods, and services) to be useful, appreciated, and profitable. We want to help create products quickly and cost effectively, but with the right set of features and good quality. We want these products to hit the market and instantly inspire demand, desire, and loyalty. We want people to use our products repeatedly and happily, encountering just the right functions at the right times and finding that the products grow with them as they develop expertise. We want our efforts to result in products that delight people, and to delight people we have to have some idea of who these people are and what they want.

In the best of all worlds, everyone working on a product would always be thinking of the needs of every person who will ever use the product. Real information about users would inform every decision and the resulting product would perfectly satisfy everyone who uses it. In practice in the real world, however, it is difficult to get everyone working on a product to think about users at all. To deliver on the promise and benefits of user-centered design

(UCD), we have to find creative ways of injecting accurate information about real users into the chaotic world of product development.

THIS BOOK IS ABOUT BUILDING PRODUCTS FOR PEOPLE

Somehow, we must find again our sense of individual values, lost in this century of enormous technological advance. This very freedom that mechanical aids are giving us has welded us into unmanageable megalopolises, where people are anonymous numbers and where communication with our fellow man seems a minus quantity. We must restore the warmth and spirit we had in the smaller community. I hope that in our leisure time we will once again know our neighbor — and, if everyone knows his neighbor and learns to live with him, the entire world will be at peace.

—Henry Dreyfuss, *Designing for People*
[Dreyfuss 1955, p. 261]

This book is intended for anyone who participates in designing and developing products for people. In particular, it is for those of us who think that understanding people and their environments is the first step in, and the ongoing challenge of, creating good products. The methods described in this book will help you turn data about your users into exemplars of the people who will use your product—into "personas." Personas are clearly defined, memorable representations of users that remain conspicuous in the minds of those who design and build products.

This book addresses the "how" of creating and using personas to design products that people love. Our book doesn't just describe the value of personas; it offers detailed techniques and tools related to conceiving, creating, communicating, and using personas to create great product designs. We provide rich examples, samples, and illustrations for persona practitioners to imitate and model. Perhaps most importantly, the book describes personas as a method complementing other UCD techniques, including user testing, scenario-based design, and cognitive walkthroughs.

WHY DO WE NEED PERSONAS?

It is a rare product indeed that does everything you want it to do in the way you want to do it. Why? Despite the fact that building products based on what real people need and want seems obvious, putting users (i.e., information about users) truly at the center of the design and development process is extremely difficult. Why is it so difficult to be user centered? The problem is threefold.

First, being user centered is just not natural. Our more natural tendency is to be self-centered, which translates to taking an approach to product design based on our own wants and needs (at times even if we are not actually a user of the product). As Bruce Tognazzini points out, we sometimes even seek out users who are just like ourselves to provide feedback on our designs [Tognazzini 1995, p. 230]. Self-centered design is perhaps better than technology-centered design, but most of the time the people on your product development team are not representative of the target audience for your product. Self-centered design results in inadequate products.

The "forever-blinking" VCR clock is a classic example of self-centered design.

> For almost as long as the average American has been alive, people have been driven nuts by the flashing "12:00" of their videocassette recorder's clock. That flashing "12:00" has become a symbol of technology as tyranny, taunt, impotence, ignorance, intimidation, humiliation, stone in the shoe and pain in the butt. It stands for innovation created without humans in mind. Yet humans have grown to live with it. To expect it. To adjust themselves to the selfishness of these machines. Like sheep [Garreau 2001].

Most VCR designers include the clock-setting function in the menu of functions for the VCR because keeping all such functions grouped, and controlled by the same set of buttons and actions, makes sense to the programmer. Evidently, what makes sense to the programmers does *not* make sense to people who have, somehow, managed to set many other types of clocks. Because they are asked to do a familiar task in an unfamiliar and unnecessarily complex way, many VCR owners choose to live with the blinking "12:00." For other examples of self-centered (and otherwise broken) designs, see Mark Hurst's Web site at *www.thisisbroken.com*.

Second, users are complicated and varied. It takes great effort to understand their needs, desires, preferences, and behaviors. And unfortunately, it is sometimes the case that pleasing some users in a given situation necessarily conflicts with pleasing others.

Third, those doing the user and market research to understand who the users are and how they vary (and others who are just more in touch with your users, such as the sales team or the support team) are not typically the people who actually design and build the product. If the important information about users isn't available at the right time, or is difficult to understand or to remember, product teams forge ahead with designing and building features they *think* the users would like (or more likely, what is easiest and least costly to build). We need better methods that put users at the center of our product teams' efforts.

The word "user" isn't very helpful

When UCD was a new idea, simply introducing the word *user* in a design and development process was powerful: it challenged the status quo. Unfortunately, incorporating the word *user* in everyday corporate discourse is not enough to foster effective UCD.

Everyone (we hope) *assumes* that they are building products with users in mind. In most organizations, anyone asked about this would probably answer, "Yes, I think about the user a lot." However, people who talk about the user are almost never asked to further define the term, and it is a sure bet that each person in the organization would describe "users" in a different way. If everyone in the organization does not have a clear and consistent understanding of who they are building the product for, the product is much more likely to fail. It is our contention that the word *user* cannot provide the clarity required. In fact, this is an underlying tenet of our book, as expressed in the following [McGovern 2002].

> *"User" is a catchall and ultimately a mean-nothing word. It reflects a technology-centric, rather than a people-centric, view of the Web. To call someone a user is largely meaningless… The phrase "user-friendly" should never have had to be invented. It implies that technology is inherently hostile and that a new discipline — usability — had to be invented to make it friendlier. After all, we don't refer to cars as "driver-friendly." We don't refer to bicycles as "cyclist-friendly." We don't refer to chairs as "bum-friendly."*

> — Gerry McGovern, *gerrymcgovern.com*

We need to move beyond our habit of referring to "users" and find a better way to communicate about and focus on real people — the people we want using our products. Companies that produce consumer products must become user focused, in the sense that emergency rooms are "injury focused." In an emergency room, it is not enough to convey that a person is injured. Doctors need to know the type of injury, the part of the body injured, the severity of the injury and its effect on vital statistics, and so on before they can identify the critical cases and decide on a course of treatment. Similarly, it is no longer enough to proclaim that something is being built for the user. We need much more information to make the difficult decisions that result in effective products.

When we try to understand users, we collect data

It is necessary to know the class of people who will be using the system…. By knowing the users' work experience, educational level, age, previous computer experience, and so on, it is possible to anticipate their learning difficulties to some extent and to better set appropriate limits for the complexity of the user interface…

—J. Nielsen [Nielsen 1993, p. 74]

Companies routinely conduct many types of user and customer research. They identify likely users of planned products and attempt to make direct contact. They employ interviews, field studies, phone and Web surveys, focus groups, site visits, server log analyses, user testing, support call tracking, and beta program feedback. They collect photographs and artifacts, write up interview notes, perform task analyses, and document observations about the ways people approach and complete tasks.

What do people do after they collect a lot of data? They analyze it, extract information, and write reports — big, long reports. Such reports are full of incredibly useful information. Shouldn't this be enough to establish a company-wide detailed understanding of users and their environments and activities?

Raw data isn't inherently useful, and neither are most reports

What happens to voluminous reports in *your* organization? What do *you* do when given a rich, detailed report? Some of you skim through it, some read it carefully, and some toss it on a pile of other important documents. Reports on users (or customers) and their needs are not always seen as relevant, and even if they are, the reports themselves are often cumbersome, tedious, and difficult to apply in the day-to-day development process. Ironically, many of us create work products (such as reports on users, target customer analysis documents, and even user profiles) that are not very usable for *our* target customers — the members of our teams.

Whether or not data is examined and reports created and read, most people working on a product develop ideas about the product's users. As the product development process continues, people throughout organizations make thousands of decisions related to product planning, design, technical development, and marketing, many of which are based on assumptions about users.

As often as not, even people who have read reports on users end up with an ongoing conception of the user based on a few facts and a loose set of assumptions, all tinted with personal experiences and biases. By the time our colleagues get around to shaping their conceptions of users, the reports that contain insights useful to this process have long been buried under piles of specification documents, design plans, strategic messaging plans, and many other documents related to the product.

Of course, long reports are not the only way to communicate insights about users. Video clips, summary presentations, posters, and other artifacts can convey important data points. These artifacts are products unto themselves, requiring significant effort, creativity, skill, and thoughtful decision making. For example, Sleeswijk Visser et al. [2004] created a "personal cardset" containing illustrative diagrams, narrative, quotes, and photos to facilitate designer insights from user research (see Figure 1.2). The personal cardset (just one of the many design tools the authors have created for context-mapping research) was developed specifically as an aid to the members of a design team in working collaboratively with user data. They even designed using white space to allow designers to write or draw directly on the cards. But even with such rich artifacts to communicate user data, the lion's share of user insights tends to get lost somewhere on the road to a finished product. Why does this happen?

Communicating insights about users is tricky. Insights regarding users suffer the same fate as messages we tried to pass to one another in the childhood game of Telephone. One person starts with what she believes is a clear message and whispers it to her neighbor. The neighbor whispers it to the next person in line, and so on. Inevitably the message, if it is passed on at all, is slowly altered in the process, so that the last person in line hears something radically different from the original message. The same thing happens to information about users as it is passed from person to person. The original message loses clarity, data and assumptions are mixed, and the result is a picture of the user built on random details that vary from person to person.

Understanding your users is necessary, but not sufficient, for good design

Methods for including user information in the design and development process, usually in the form of a "user requirements" section in a specification document, are not very effective (even though such documents are often very detailed and sophisticated). Design and specification documents are not necessarily adhered to. Tiny adjustments are made often — and understandably — as the product developers do their work. Thus, design and specification documents become inaccurate over time. Technologies change, time pressures mount, executives change their minds, the competitive landscape changes, a developer has a pet feature or technology she "just has to work on," and even the "final" specification is slowly abandoned in the day-to-day reality of finishing the product.

Once we do understand the user, and even if we effectively communicate that understanding, we still have to tackle the difficult challenge of incorporating that information in the design of the product. Good designs help people achieve their goals and capitalize on the potential of the technology, and they are not easy to achieve. There is no tried-and-true method that

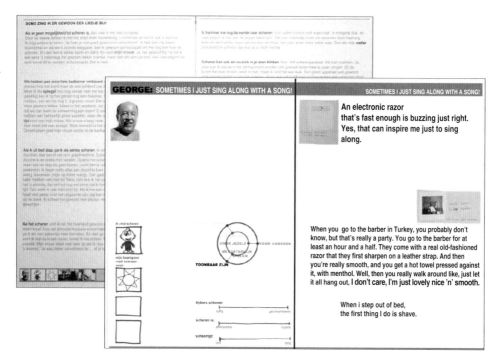

FIGURE 1.2: *The front and back of an example personal card from Sleeswijk Visser et al. [2004]. The focus of these cards is shaving products. Each card represents a single real user. (We've translated these cards from the original to give you a sense of the content.)*

helps us make the leap from existing people, products, and problems to innovations that delight and make a profit.

Much of what we do as user-centered product designers is unsystematic. Our process seems more like alchemy than a structured and dependable methodology and, although there are principles on good interaction design, even the most educated and skilled designer often gets it wrong initially. Moreover, no product is ever built in a day. Even the best design is changed during implementation. Therefore, good designs tend to be those that have been evaluated (by both the product team and the intended users) and iteratively reworked many times according to a consistent and well-maintained vision.

No matter how much work we do to understand our users, we still encounter fairly predictable problems when trying to use data to design great products:

● It is difficult to identify and communicate the information that will help a product team understand its users.

● Even if user information is well communicated, it might not be interpreted consistently. How can you ensure that your team isn't building products in a situation in which "the user" might be interpreted slightly differently by members of the team?

- Once everyone on your team does have a consistent and shared understanding of the user, how do you use this to inform and direct your product design decisions? It is not easy to bridge the chasm between current user roles and tasks and the roles and tasks you want to support in a new way with a new system.
- Once design decisions have been made, how should user information be used to evaluate the design and ensure effective implementation?

As we look to the future, UCD professionals are expanding our vision. Rather than simply creating user interfaces (UIs), we are working to create rich and complete *user experiences*. This ideal is more difficult to achieve than simply creating a usable package, and requires a greater focus on the part of product teams regarding the target audience of those experiences.

PERSONAS HELP MAKE USER-CENTERED DESIGN POSSIBLE

How do you get the people who are designing and making decisions about your product and those who are actually building it to embrace information about users? To take it a step further, how do you get them to empathize with user perspectives and take them as seriously as those elements that affect their own daily development jobs? You need a variety of tools to make this happen. This book offers one such tool that, although immensely popular and frequently discussed, until now has been only loosely described to practitioners. Enter personas.

Personas are fictitious, specific, concrete representations of target users. The notion of *personas* was created by Alan Cooper and popularized in his 1999 book *The Inmates Are Running the Asylum: Why High Tech Products Drive Us Crazy and How To Restore The Sanity* [Cooper 1999]. Personas put a face on the user — a memorable, engaging, and actionable image that serves as a design target. They convey information about users to your product team in ways that other artifacts cannot.

Personas will help you, your team, and your organization become more user focused. Consider the following story by Meg Hourihan regarding her discovery of and experience with personas.

Story from the field

TAKING THE "YOU" OUT OF USER: MY EXPERIENCE USING PERSONAS

—Meg Hourihan, cofounder and former Director of Development, Pyra

The Best-Laid Plans...

In 1999, I cofounded a small San Francisco–based start-up called Pyra. Our plan was to build a web-based project management tool and we chose to focus initially on Web development teams for our target audience since, as Web developers ourselves, we had intimate knowledge of the user group. We considered ourselves to be good all-around developers, competent in both interface and back-end development. We also assumed we were developing our product (called "Pyra" for lack of a better name at the time) for people just like us, so we could make assumptions based on our wants and extrapolate those desires for all users.

At this time, Microsoft had just released Internet Explorer 5 (IE 5) for Windows and we were anxious to use its improved standards support and DHTML in our application to make the interface as whiz-bang as possible. So we set to work building the coolest Web application we could, taking full advantage of the latest wizardry in IE 5 for Windows. Development was chugging along when Alan Cooper's *The Inmates Are Running the Asylum* was released and I picked it up. When I got to the chapter discussing the use of personas, I was intrigued. Though I was confident in our approach, creating personas sounded like a useful exercise and a way to confirm we were on track.

Discovering Personas

Cooper's personas are simply pretend users of the system you're building. You describe them, in a surprising amount of detail, and then design your system for them. Since you can't build everything for every persona (and you wouldn't want to), the establishment of a primary persona is critical in focusing the team's efforts effectively. In our case, the development of personas helped us recognize that the target audience we'd chosen, Web development teams, wasn't as homogenous as we first assumed. Not everyone who's involved in Web development is gaga for DHTML or CSS — some people on the team might not even know what those acronyms stand for, a simple fact we'd failed to consider up until this point.

Our team stopped working to discuss personas and we agreed it sounded important enough to devote some time to it. As we sketched out our various personas (a project manager for a large company whose corporate standard was Netscape 3, a Web designer who worked on a Mac, an independent consultant who worked from home), it became apparent we had made some bad assumptions. Not only were the personas not all like us — our personas wouldn't even be able to use the system we were building for them! We'd been so blinded by our own self-interest we failed to realize we were building a useless team product. We were cutting ourselves off from the people who would most likely make the decision to use the tool — and no project team would sign up for Pyra because an entire project team couldn't use it.

We were a month away from releasing the beta version of Pyra at this point, but we knew what needed to happen. We had to go back and redo our application to work for Netscape and IE, for Windows and Macintosh, and in doing so we needed to reevaluate our tool using our personas (specifically our primary persona) rather than ourselves or the mythical "user" to guide our decisions. So that's what we did, pulling out all our beloved DHTML and remote scripting so that our 37-year-old project manager persona could access the application from her home office in Seattle on a Saturday afternoon. Though the rework delayed our beta release by two months, it resulted in a tool our potential customers could use immediately.

Learning Hard Lessons

Through the process of developing personas, the mistakes we'd made became clear to us:

Mistake 1: We chose flashy technology over broad access.
We allowed the geeky part of our personalities, with its lust for the newest and greatest ways of doing things, to overwhelm the decision-making process. Though there was a sense at the beginning that we needed to support other platforms, we let our desire to use the newest "toys" change the priority of doing so. This is a common mistake programmers and engineers make but one which can be avoided through the use of personas. Interestingly, when we redid Pyra based on our personas' needs we didn't lose any of the previous functionality—we only changed how it was done (e.g., reverting to less elegant page reloads rather than DHTML client-side changes). The previous version had only been impressive to fellow geeks like ourselves, but we hadn't realized that. More importantly, the essential features of the tool were never lost; by redoing the product, we made those features available to many more people.

Mistake 2: We assumed users would be more impressed by a robust interface they couldn't use than by a less elegant application they could use.
Again, our technical hubris blinded us into thinking that potential customers would be impressed by how we built our functionality, not by what the underlying features were. We let our wants come between our product and our users.

Mistake 3: We thought we were the primary persona.
While we shared common goals with some of our personas, and though one of the personas we developed was very similar to the members of our team, none of us was the primary persona. Defining a primary persona prevented us from releasing our original tool with its issues around broad access.

Less than a month after the beta release of Pyra, we released a second tool, Blogger. Though we didn't create formal personas for Blogger users, the experience we gained by using personas infused our company's approach to building Web applications. Any time the word *user* was mentioned, questions flew: "What user? Who is she and what's she trying to do?" Our work with personas increased our awareness of our audience and their varying skill levels and goals when using the application. The use of personas helped move all our discussions about the application, not only those related to the interface, away from the realm of vagaries and into tangible, actionable items (e.g., "It should be easy to create a new blog." "Easy? Easy for whom?" "It should take less than a minute to get started."). We developed a system of familiar, conversational personas on the fly, focusing on the primary persona without going through the formal process.

In retrospect, some of this sounds like common sense, and yet time and time again I find myself looking at an interface and making assumptions based on how I'd like it to work. Like a recovering substance abuser, it's a constant challenge for me to refrain — I can always imagine that I'm the user. I've carried the lessons I've learned through their development with me for the past three years to other projects and engagements. The use of personas resulted in a fundamental shift in the way I approach not only interface design but application architecture as a whole.

As Meg Hourihan's story illustrates, personas have many benefits:

- Personas make assumptions and knowledge about users explicit, creating a common language with which to talk about users meaningfully.
- Personas allow you to focus on and design for a small set of specific users (who are not necessarily like you), helping you make better decisions.
- Personas engender interest and empathy toward users, engaging your team in a way that other representations of user data cannot.

Let's examine each of these benefits in more detail.

Personas make assumptions about users explicit

You have likely heard people in your company say things like "Our customers would never buy that," or "Users won't understand that." Everyone you work with carries assumptions about their customers or users. These assumptions — inevitably full of personal, cultural, or corporate bias — remain individually held, often completely hidden from colleagues, and perhaps even unknown to the people holding them. Whether or not you surface these assumptions, they will affect the design and success of your products.

Story from the field

PERSONAS HIGHLIGHT DIFFERENCES IN ASSUMPTIONS

—Bob Murata, Katja Rimmi, and Sheryl Ehrlich, Adobe Systems

A few years ago, when personas were first coming into vogue, many of the designers on the User Interface Team at Adobe started to generate user profiles and personas to drive discussion with their product team members.

However, as more and more profiles and personas were created it became increasingly evident that there were subtle differences in how the various product teams viewed their core customer bases. For instance, although Photoshop and Illustrator had both created a "Graphic Designer" user profile, the descriptions of the work done by such a user differed between the two teams. Interestingly, about this same time Adobe made a strategic shift to concentrate on creating an integrated suite of products for the "Creative Professional," instead of focusing on individual products. For this strategy to work, it was critical that the product teams share a common understanding of their target customers, so that they could develop the right cross-product workflows. The creation of user profiles and personas helped surface differing assumptions that would have otherwise gone undetected. Those user profiles and personas then served as a basis for discussing which cross-product features and workflow should be pursued and developed.

Simply surfacing assumptions and agreeing on a single set of them can enhance communication and help a team build a better product. However, there is no substitute for data. Our first goal as product designers should be to build a shared, data-driven, well-communicated vision of the user to focus the efforts of the product team.

Personas humanize vast and disparate data sources by capitalizing on our ability to remember details about individual people. In so doing, they provide a usable alternative to referring to the nebulous "user." In other words, personas do the job of creating a concrete, focused, and stable definition of your audience.

Personas place the focus on specific users rather than on "everyone"

Although personas have generated a lot of buzz in the product design community in recent years, and techniques of using abstract representations of users have been around for quite a while, the idea of designing products for a small set of concretely defined users is still a fairly new — and radical — idea for most of us. After all, most of us have a difficult time defining our broad target markets in the first place. We are convinced that we have to build products that will solve problems for, and appeal to, as many customers as possible, so that our products sell well and stay competitive.

We work in a world in which technology changes at an unbelievably fast rate and processing power increases dramatically almost every year. We are used to building products that undergo a process of version development, wherein subsequent versions add features to match those of our competitors, to take advantage of increased technical capacity and to meet the requirements of our customer bases. We live in a corporate culture of "more is more" and tend to build products accordingly. The definition of any target audience tends to be the all-encompassing "everyone."

In limiting our choices, personas help us make better decisions

In *The Inmates Are Running the Asylum*, Alan Cooper states, "To create a product that must satisfy a broad audience of users…you will have far greater success by designing for one single person" [Cooper 1999, p. 124]. The idea of building a product with a single user, or a small selection of users, in mind seems to completely contradict the mind-set of our industry. At face value, it seems to suggest that if you limit the features and functions of the product you design to those that will satisfy just a few very specific people you will somehow build a successful product.

At first, most balk at this idea because it seems unnecessarily restrictive and dangerous. The thought of limiting our product designs to satisfy just a few people is terrifying. What if only those few people we design for purchase our product? Worse, what if we choose the wrong people to design for? Isn't it safer to design a product that the greatest potential number of people will like?

In his book *The Paradox of Choice: Why More Is Less*, Barry Schwartz asserts that having excessive choices can make people feel more trapped, less happy, and less able to make *good* decisions than they would if they had fewer options [Schwartz 2004]. His argument has some interesting implications for the world of product design and may explain why personas, which embody a constrained set of user characteristics and enable (or even force) us to eliminate many choices, can free us to make better decisions and therefore better products.

At the start of a product development cycle, there are typically a lot of ideas for features and someone (or a group of people) has to decide which features are worth developing. Most companies realize that building every possible feature is not an option due to limited resources and, more importantly, the understanding that trying to build every possible feature tends to result in products that satisfy no one. Every time we start a new project we are faced with trade-offs, and "being forced to confront trade-offs in making decisions makes people unhappy and indecisive" [Schwartz 2004, p. 125].

Schwartz describes findings of research studies in which people were forced to make trade-offs similar to those we have to make when designing products. The research found that in being forced to make trade-offs we face the stress of selecting wrongly, the regret of possible missed opportunities, and a natural aversion to loss. For example, Schwartz argues that at some level stakeholders feel that every feature they decide *not* to build could be the reason the product fails (and no one wants to have been the one to have established a low priority for that key feature). When the stakes are high and mistakes are perceived as costly, research finds that the tendency is to avoid making *any* decision. If a stakeholder avoids making the decision

Story from the field

CUSTOMER FOCUS CHANGES THE GAME

—Brian Schlosser, Chief Executive Officer, Attenex Corporation

Competitors lurk at every turn ready to steal the revenue that I need to keep my engineering department in Krispy Kremes and lattes. No matter what new feature my company develops, competitors will tell innocent prospects that they already have it or it will come out in the next release. Then they claim that their new innovations will make our software obsolete. There is no way that my team can outrun their unscrupulous marketers. Feature wars could kill the company.

One way to respond is to change the game. Because the competition can always respond to features, we find it useful to market the things that make *our company* unique. Attenex invests a significant portion of its budget in the development of personas, Maps, and other tools to create a superior user experience. [For more details on "Maps," see Chapter 10: "Reality and Design Maps."] Our user experience group is focused on matching our mature persona's needs with each specification before any code is written. Our understanding of the customer is a competitive advantage that others can't fake.

Competitors who readily claim to have any feature or capability that we release are often flummoxed when called on to explain the process that their company uses to achieve user delight. For Attenex, one key to our success is to do more than talk about *what* we make; we focus on *who* we make our products for.

of which features *not* to build, the result is feature creep and a product that in trying to appeal to everyone satisfies few.

In his final chapter, Schwartz encourages us to "learn to love constraints" because "choice within constraints, freedom within limits, is what enables [us] to imagine a host of marvelous possibilities" [Schwartz 2004, pp. 235–236]. Personas are helpful *because* they are constraining. Personas clearly define who is and who is not the target user (or customer) for the product and thereby make some of the decisions for us. For example, if the primary persona for a product doesn't have broadband access we have no choice: we *cannot* create a design that requires broadband. Every detail we include in our personas limits the number of choices we have to make. Personas define a tight domain within which the product needs to perform. Within that domain, personas free us to explore all of the "marvelous possibilities" for the product we are designing.

From the very beginning of a product development cycle, personas can be there to provide data in the form of the "voice" of the user, which can reduce feature debates and refocus projects. In this regard, personas offer a consistent target-audience vision. Perhaps this is why, paradoxically, designing for just a few well-defined personas increases the likelihood that many people will love your product.

Personas engage the product design and development team

Of course, you could likely obtain the benefits mentioned to this point by invoking other UCD techniques and by using representations of users other than personas. So, what is the overriding benefit of personas compared to similar techniques? We believe it lies in the way personas can engage your team.

Personas are fun. Just like characters in books, TV shows, and movies, personas evoke empathy and inspire the imagination. People on a product development team can relate to personas and become active participants in bringing the personas "to life." We have witnessed team members becoming attached to personas.

As comically illustrated in Figure 1.3, we have seen product teams treat personas as real people, arguing with conviction on the persona's behalf and sometimes even expressing a sense of sorrow when a persona is retired from duty upon release of a product. This happens in part because personas are detailed, specific, and personal. When created from meaningful data, they have a credibility other representations lack.

We provide several case studies throughout the book that discuss this characteristic of engagement. In one of the contributed chapters later in this book ("Why Personas Work"), Jonathan Grudin provides an interesting discussion regarding why personas have this power and

FIGURE 1.3: *Personas make it easy to imagine the real people who will eventually use the product you are designing and building. Personas inspire teams to develop stories about the ways their products will be used, and can even inspire the type of loyalty Janae is enjoying in Tom Chi and Kevin Cheng's cartoon! (Image courtesy of www.ok-cancel.com. Copyright © 2004. Tom Chi and Kevin Cheng. All rights reserved.)*

provides insight on how to exploit it. For our purposes here, suffice it to say that personas can help your product team become user focused in an intense, compelling, memorable, and fun fashion. If personas are created with rigor (i.e., utilizing rich data and a systematic process), the resultant user focus is deep and meaningful, educating your broad team with relevant information about their most important users. For product teams new to UCD, personas can pave the way for other highly beneficial (albeit more costly) methods such as iterative user testing and longitudinal ethnographic research.

Story from the field

PERSONAS ARE ESSENTIAL TO EFFECTIVE DESIGN

—Harley Manning, Forrester Research

As a leading industry analyst, Forrester Research has the unique opportunity to look at the business practices across hundreds of companies. From this perspective, we know that successful design efforts have resulted from the adoption of a disciplined approach called "scenario design." The premise of scenario design is simple: No Web site, IVR system, kiosk, or software application is inherently good or bad; it can only be judged in terms of how well it supports the goals of its intended users. This seems simple (and maybe even obvious),

(Story from the field, continued)

but sadly it is not. That's because many of the firms we study know little about their users and user goals *that are useful to a designer*. Most firms rely on simple customer profiles based on traditional market research to provide user data. But we've found that personas, informed by qualitative research, are a much more useful representation to guide design, particularly when used in conjunction with scenarios.

For example, a typical customer profile at an auto manufacturer might tell you that a prospect is 25 years of age, lives in Chicago, earns $50,000 a year, and is buying her first new car. But it doesn't tell you where she starts her buying process: by talking with friends, reading a consumer magazine, or conducting research online at either a consumer site or a manufacturer site. It also doesn't tell you the information most important to her purchasing decision (price? safety? style? gas mileage?), how she will choose a dealer (proximity? reputation?), or whether her overarching goal is to feel good about her decision or simply tick a chore off her list.

Lacking this information, businesses make bad design choices and often have difficulty making any decisions at all. *Ford.com* is a case in point. That Web site is the corporate portal to all Ford brands, including Ford vehicles, Volvo, and Jaguar. As a result, the site managers have a "steering committee" of almost 100 stakeholders from the individual brand sites that get traffic from the portal. Prior to adopting the practice of personas, even a simple decision could bog down in conflicting agendas. But now the design team uses three personas that represent all new car buyers to create a common view of the customer and win quick approval from the various divisions.

Personas don't just help industries selling high-consideration products, either. The manager of the corporate Web site at a giant consumer-packaged-goods manufacturer told us that she floated over 20 design proposals that were rejected because internal stakeholders couldn't agree. Within days of creating personas, she finally won approval for a design and is very happy with the business results the design produced.

Personas can create cross-company buy-in on who the most important customer segments are and what they want and need, which in turn provides an instant litmus test for whether you are making good design decisions or bad ones. These examples illustrate why creating a shared understanding of customers and their goals by embracing personas is the thing to do if you do nothing else.

USER REPRESENTATIONS ARE NOT NEW AND WE CAN LEARN A LOT FROM THE PAST

Joe and Josephine are austere line drawings of a man and a woman, and they occupy places of honor on the walls of our New York and California offices.... They are part of our staff, representing the millions of consumers for whom we are designing, and they dictate every line we draw. Joe and Josephine did not spring lightly to our walls from the pages of a book on anatomy. They represent many years of research by our office, not merely into their physical aspects but into their psychology as well.

—Henry Dreyfuss [Dreyfuss 1955 (2003 ed.), pp. 26–27]

Industrial designer Henry Dreyfuss calls Joe and Josephine the "heroes" of his book *Designing for People*. Dreyfuss is only one of many who have created representations of users to inform the efforts of product development. Over the years, several methodologies have arisen for consolidating, communicating, and employing user data and information developed via user representations. We believe it is worthwhile to understand and borrow from these representation techniques. Throughout this book we expand on many of the ideas laid out by the pioneers discussed here. The following pages provide a brief chronology and description of the history of user representations in product design.

Representations of users in marketing and branding

Although this book focuses primarily on personas as effective user representations for product design, there is considerable precedent for user representations in marketing and branding.

Sissors' and Weinstein's market definitions

The basic idea of defining a market dates back at least to the 1960s. Although not the first to deal with the topic, Jack Sissors' 1966 article "What Is a Market" is a classic that helped introduce the concept of user representations to the world of business [Sissors 1966]. Sissors discussed how important it is to define *who* you are trying to sell to if you want to have a successful product. Many practitioners have built on this foundation to create increasingly specific representations of target customers. In his 1998 book *Defining Your Market: Winning Strategies for High-tech, Industrial, and Service Firms*, Art Weinstein describes a detailed approach to identifying and using market definitions for product marketing and business strategy. Weinstein's framework for strategic market definition consists of three major steps [Weinstein 1998, pp. 99–107]:

1. Identify the relevant market.
2. Create the defined market.
3. Specify the target market.

Weinstein's "defined markets" in step 2 consist of a series of specific market types (e.g., penetrated versus untapped) that remain impersonal and abstract in form. They refer to groups of customers but do not describe any personal attributes of the individuals who comprise each market. For example, if a certified public accounting (CPA) consulting company were toexplore various markets relevant to their products and services, they might do so as outlined in Figure 1.4.

Defined Market	Composition of this market for a CPA consulting firm
. . .	. . .
Penetrated market	Existing accounting clients
Untapped market	Nonusers (clients and non-clients) of business consulting
Defined market	Growth-oriented, closely held businesses, new IPO companies
Segmented market	Businesses following a growth strategy
. . .	. . .

FIGURE 1.4: *Markets and their composition from the perspective of a CPA consulting firm. (Adapted from Weinstein [1998, p. 106].)*

The argument is that the clearer the definition of the market, the easier it is to target the market with specific messages and value propositions. Note in Figure 1.4, however, that the markets are defined in terms of common characteristics shared by *companies*, not *individuals*. Those of us accustomed to working on products that have user interfaces are more familiar with market segments defined in terms of common characteristics of *people*. A more recognizable representation of target markets is evident in the following examples:

- Single moms between the ages of 25 and 45 who have full-time jobs, earn more than $30,000 annually, and do not enjoy cooking or have time for it
- Retired professionals in metropolitan areas who are interested in traveling and whose children have left the home
- 18- to 24-year-old college students who love music and own a cell phone.

As shown in Figure 1.5, such market segments can be defined along a variety of dimensions.

Type of Market Segment	Shared Group Characteristics
Demographic Segment	Measurable statistics such as age, income, occupation, etc.
Psychographic Segment	Lifestyle preferences such as music lovers, city or urban dwellers, etc.
Use-based Segment	Frequency of usage such as recreational drinking, traveling, etc.
Benefit Segment	Desire to obtain the same product benefits such as luxury, thriftiness, comfort from food, etc.
Geographic Segment	Location such as home address, business address, etc.

FIGURE 1.5: *Market segments can be defined according to multiple sets of related characteristics. (Adapted from FindLaw for Small Businesses [2005]).*

Market segments are representations of groups of users, and such representations can be defined in meticulous detail. However, they do not typically describe specific goals and needs of individuals in a cohesive "whole-person" format. (For a further discussion of this, see the sidebar "Customer Segmentation and Design Personas: What's the Difference?" by Frank Spillers, later in this chapter.) Interestingly, Weinstein notes that customer needs are the most important market definition characteristic for organizations (twice as important as any other single factor).

We see Weinstein's approach (and those like it) as providing a basic foundation for market research and strategic customer definition that is useful, if not critical, in creating personas. In chapter 3, we recommend that you take advantage of familiar terms used to describe your company's users when you create and communicate your personas. If your company has invested in market segmentation, these familiar terms might be the names of the segments. As you will see, you can use the segment names, descriptions, and source data to help you create personas that resonate for your organization.

Moore's "target customer characterizations"

In his book *Crossing the Chasm*, Geoffrey Moore discussed "target customer characterizations" [Moore 1991]. Moore's thesis started with the need for "informed intuition" as opposed to "analytical reason" as the most trustworthy decision tool for the job of targeting specific markets.

Moore argues that market-segment definitions such as "yuppies versus teenyboppers" or "laggards versus early adopters" are too impersonal and abstract. He claims that images of customers, not markets, are the key. According to Moore, "Target Customer Characterization is a formal process for making up these images, getting them out of individual heads and in front of a marketing decision-making group" [Moore 1991, p. 95]. They provide "…something that gives more clues about how to proceed…then, once we have their images in mind, we can let them guide us to developing a truly responsive approach to their needs" [Moore 1991, p. 95].

Moore proposed that one should initially create 20 to 50 of such characterizations and then narrow them down to 8 to 10 distinct alternatives. Each characterization incorporates the following five aspects:

1. **Personal profile and job description**

    Jerome is a 32 year old account executive with Splashi & Splashi, a leading sportswear manufacturer, located in La Jolla, California. He is responsible for placing their new line of Plastique swimwear in sporting goods stores and upscale boutiques, and his territory is northern California. The line is very pricey, and Jerome wants to maintain an upscale, professional image… [Moore 1991, p. 96].

2. **Technical resources**

    Jerome himself has never used a personal computer, but he works in an office that is equipped with several IBM PCs, which are connected to the main computer at the head office. The PCs are equipped with modems and printers [Moore 1991, p. 97].

3. **A "day in the life" dramatization before the introduction of the proposed product**

    Jerome is in the midst of taking an order for the basic line of Plastique swimwear at the Ghirardelli Square Windsurf and Kite Store. He notices that the other sportswear on display features a lot of fluorescent colors. Plastique is coming out with a new line of fluorescent wear, but Jerome… [Moore 1991, pp. 97–98].

4. **Problem or dilemma that motivates the purchase of the proposed product**

    To sell the maximum amount of high-margin product line, Jerome must maintain a highly professional image and be able to reference large amounts of detailed information at a moment's notice. Jerome's inability to do this more efficiently is costing his company sales… [Moore 1991, p. 98].

5. **A "day in the life" after the introduction of the product**

    Having noticed the interest in fluorescent colors, Jerome touches the button on the screen of his pen-based laptop that says "reference materials." This calls up a display of several icons, and he selects "new products" [Moore 1991, pp. 98–99].

Moore further describes a system of employing these characterizations toward product definition and marketing. Note that Moore's characterizations do not include photos or other images, nor do they attempt to describe the person much outside the relevant setting. However, Moore's work does bring us one giant step closer to the idea of personas. While market segments are intended to capture the range of demographics, psychographics, and technographics common to a group of customers, Moore's Target Customer characterizations begin to explore the value of deeply understanding individual customers in the context of their work environment.

Upshaw's customer "indivisualization"

A few years later, but apparently independently, Lynn Upshaw — in his 1995 book *Building Brand Identity: a Strategy for Success in a Hostile Marketplace* — described a similar notion that he called "indivisualizing the customer." "Indivisualizing is the discipline of continuously visualizing the customer or prospect as an individual rather than as part of a mass population, group, or segment," writes Upshaw [Upshaw 1995, p. 97]. Like Moore's characterizations, the purpose of these profiles is to inform and inspire decision making. "The act of indivisualizing itself encourages marketers to create a living, fluid visualization of their individual customers that keeps their personal perspectives uppermost in mind" [Upshaw 1995, p. 98].

Upshaw makes a distinction between descriptive profiles and indivisualized profiles. Descriptive profiles include data that describes the customer as seen by others (i.e., primarily your product or marketing team). Indivisualized profiles portray individuals, within the context of a purchase decision, as they see themselves:

Descriptive Profile — "Middle/upper-middle income, married, children in high school or college, suburban, some discretionary investments" [Upshaw 1995, p. 101].

Indivisualized Profile (abridged) — "I'm Alice. I'm feeling the burden of my responsibilities more than ever. I don't want to waste money on commissions for advice I'll just end up having doubts about. Schwab is run the way I would run a brokerage" [Upshaw 1995, p. 101].

Upshaw's indivisualized customer profiles consist of many paragraphs of first-person text (perhaps several pages) and include a photo. They provide a more general view of the daily life of the target customer than the dilemma-focused before/after characterizations of Moore. Upshaw provides a much tighter and more detailed description than Moore of their creation, which is data oriented, as well as of the process of using them.

Mello's customer image statements

More recently, Sheila Mello — in her 2002 book *Customer-centric Product Definition* — describes a process for understanding users' needs and desires, which is used ultimately for product definition [Mello 2002]. Her book highlights the need for companies to have a clear "Image" of the customer. Mello states that such an image typically does not emerge on its own, despite investments in customer and market research. She provides a method for deriving image statements that answers questions such as the following:

● What is the customer's life like?
● What challenges the customer?
● What motivates the customer?

Although this sounds promising and seems similar to other representations, these images are typically limited to a single sentence describing some essential characteristic of the customer and are meant, according to Mello, to "conjure up a concrete picture of the customer's surroundings." Statements of customer desire and suggestions for solutions do not belong in image statements. For example, the following is an image statement: "I have to get my reading glasses to read the numbers on the remote." The following, however, are not image statements [Mello 2002, p. 80]:

- "I want a system that fits in my suit pocket" (statement of customer desire).
- "I'd like it to make all the adjustments automatically" (customer has suggested a feature).
- "I would like it to weigh less than two pounds and easily fit in my briefcase" (customer has suggested a solution).

Notably, all of these statements are derived directly from customer research, and although useful at a high level, none (even taken together) provides the depth and richness required to truly define a product in all of its complexities. Toward this end, Mello's method involves the extraction of hundreds (if not thousands) of such image statements, reduction of these to the key subset of 20 to 30, and then the organization of them into a format that facilitates deep understanding of what it is like to be a customer. The end result is an "image diagram" (as shown in Figure 1.6) that represents the relationships between image statements both hierarchically and linearly to show common threads (shared concepts) as well as cause and effect. Mello's approach includes the translation of these images into specific, actionable requirements for the product.

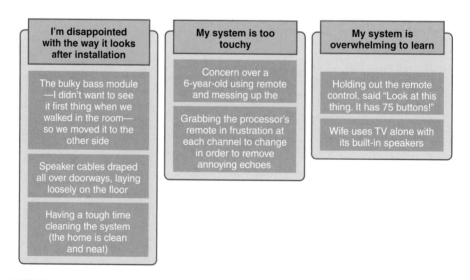

FIGURE 1.6: *Image diagram for a home theater system. (Adapted from Mello [2002, p. 85].)*

Mello's work begins to bridge the gap between marketing and product design, while market segments and target customer characterizations are intended to help build strategies for marketing and sales, Mello's Image Diagrams are built to help designers create desirable products.

Representations of users in usability and interaction design

Designers have long used scenarios and their close relative storyboards to organize, justify, and communicate ideas. More recently, however (dating to the mid 1980s), usability specialists began to use scenarios as aids to system design, product development, and research in human/computer interaction.

Carroll's scenarios

At their core, scenarios are simply stories. They have a setting, actors or agents who have goals or objectives and a plot or sequence of actions and events. John Carroll, a longstanding proponent of scenarios, argues that scenarios can help designers and analysts focus on assumptions about people and tasks — assumptions that are implicit in the software [Carroll 1995]. Scenarios can encourage reflection during design. They are concrete yet flexible, and are easily revised and extended. They can be viewed from multiple perspectives, and can be abstracted and categorized.

Scenarios tend not to focus on users. Scenarios are overviews of entire networks of actions and reactions. Each scenario describes many parts in motion, including the actor, the system, the context, and the specific actions or dialog associated with both actor and system. Scenarios do not depend on the actors that perform in them. The actors are treated as simply another component of the system. For example, the following are examples of scenarios that might have been written at different times for a single project:

Scenario 1 — Harry, a curriculum designer, has just joined a project developing a multimedia information system for engineering education. He browses the project video history. Sets of clips are categorized under major iconically presented headings; under some of these are further menu-driven subcategories.

Scenario 2 — He selects the Lewis icon from the designers, the Vision icon from the issues, and an early point on the project timeline. He then selects Play Clip and views a brief scene in which Lewis describes his vision of the project… [Carroll 1995, p. 4]

Interestingly, the extensive literature on scenario-based design offers little discussion of the agents and actors incorporated in such scenarios (the concept of "actor" was introduced by Ivar Jacobson as part of the use-case approach [Jacobson 1992; *see also* 1995]). After reviewing many of the available books, chapters, and articles on scenario-based design, we found that none provides more than a paragraph or two focused on the procedures for using actors and agents in scenarios. Although seemingly central to the paradigm, little is said about the act of defining an agent or how to use one appropriately once defined.

Mikkelson and Lee argue that most scenario-based design suffers from the lack of a clear and usable representation of the user [Mikkelson and Lee 2000]. They note that, although the scenarios provide specificity in capturing user context and tasks, the author often assumes that the reader knows who the user is and the relevant detail about the user. As such, they leave out critical details about the user regarding motivation, previous actions or events, and preferences — as well as other less critical but perhaps more engaging details that promote insight, credibility, interest, and empathy. Thus, contrary to Carroll's evaluation, scenarios tend to be static and non-generative (i.e., difficult to extend and reuse).

In Chapter 6, we provide recommendations for using personas to enrich scenarios and improve scenario-based design processes.

Hackos and Redish's user profiles

User profiles are a UCD technique that arose from the need to analyze and consolidate rich information about users gained from interviews, site visits, and similar (more qualitative) forms of user research. The technique has been applied to usability engineering since the early 1980s, although the degree of rigor in definition and application of the concept varies somewhat across the discipline (e.g., see Boyle and Clarke [1985], Cushman and Derounian [1988], Gould and Lewis [1985], Mayhew [1992] and [1999], and Nielsen [1992]).

In their book *User and Task Analysis for Interface Design*, Hackos and Redish describe the concept of *user profiles* and provide a detailed methodology for generating and using them [Hackos and Redish 1998]. User profiles are detailed representations of users refined to the point of unique types or classes of users. User profiles tend to be accurate and terse summaries of the data from which they are derived. Typically, they do not tell stories about experiences nor contain fictional components added for the sake of engagement and realism. In some cases, they can actually be devoid of personality, describing only an abstract set of characteristics. Hackos and Redish describe list-based user profiles (see Figure 1.7) and more personal forms of profiles, which include narratives (see Figure 1.8) and illustrations (posters with images).

These representations are only a small part of Hackos and Redish's larger practical guide on planning, analyzing, and using field research. They have not taken the idea to the extreme of

> **User 1 (Al, a pseudonym)**
>
> - Rural Wyoming, county population about 3,500
> - Al told us there are more cows than people around
> - Age 45
> - Doctor of veterinary medicine, specializing in large animals
> - More time spent at client site (farms and ranches) than in office.
> - Prefers outdoor to indoor work in general
> - Office work done mostly by assistants (local teenagers, elderly mother) but all by hand, lots of forms.
> - Frequent computer users, only user in the office (doesn't want anyone else to touch the computers)
> - ...

FIGURE 1.7: *Example of a list-based user profile. (Abridged from Hackos and Redish [1998], p. 307.)*

> User 4, known by our team as Harry, is a 73-year-old large animal veterinarian. Harry practices in a rural community in southern Illinois, about 100 miles from the Southern Illinois University campus where he attended veterinary school. Harry has a computer in his office, but he made a special point of telling us that he doesn't use it very much. He said he really doesn't know much about this Windows stuff. His computer still has DOS. ...

FIGURE 1.8: *Example of a narrative-style user profile. (Abridged from Hackos and Redish [1998], p. 308.)*

creating amalgamated fictional characters based on these profiles, nor have they promoted their user profiles as intense focal points in the design/development process. Hackos and Redish do recognize personas as both a precursor and natural extension of the practices described in their book. Hackos and Redish helped the UCD community understand the value of highly specific information about users in the product design process.

Constantine and Lockwood's User Roles

User roles and use cases are close cousins of actors, scenarios, and personas. According to Constantine and Lockwood:

> A user role, in contrast [to personas], does not look or sound like a real person and is not intended to; it's an abstraction — a relationship, not a person, title, job description, or function. It is defined as a set of characteristic needs, interests, behaviors, and expectations. In its most compact form it is described by the three Cs of Context, Characteristics, and Criteria: (1) the overall responsibilities of the role and the larger context within which it is played; (2) characteristic patterns of interaction, behaviors, and attitudes within the role; and (3) special criteria or design objectives related to the effective support of the role [Constantine and Lockwood 2001, p. 1].

Constantine and Lockwood point out that actors, roles, and personas are highly interrelated and can build on each other to serve different purposes related to product development [Constantine and Lockwood 2002]. For any one product, there are usually a number of possible actors, and for each of those there are multiple roles. For any key role, one may choose to create a detailed persona to help enrich and enliven that role. "The analyst/designer who wants to map out the complete context of use for a particular system must complete a number of activities to identify all the Actors and the Roles they play" [Constantine and Lockwood 2002, p. 1]. They also note, however, that actors and roles should be explored before personas are created. Consider the example of a business-to-business e-commerce application shown in Figure 1.9.

Possible Actors - Customer, Fulfillment, and Credit Approval
Possible Roles of Customer Actor - Regular Buying Role, Incidental Buying Role, and Casual Browsing Role

Casual Browsing Role Description - not necessarily in the industry and buying may not be sole or primary responsibility (CONTEXT), typically intermittent and unpredictable use, often merely for information regarding varied lines and products, driven by curiosity as much as need (CHARACTERISTICS); may need enticements to become customer, linkage to others from same account, access to retail sources and pricing (CRITERIA).

Possible persona of Casual Browsing Role - Brenda Browsefield is a 37-year-old administrative assistant to a manager at a small manufacturer. A New Englander who recently moved to the area, she styles herself as an outsider and independent thinker. A self-starter with a determined look permanently painted on her face, she often does research on her own initiative both to broaden her industry savvy and to be one step ahead of her boss. She has her own office and uses the Web a lot but spends relatively little time on any site (except for Google and the portal of one industry e-zine). Ambitious and impatient, she's smart and likes to use industry jargon although she is not a geek.

FIGURE 1.9: *An example of the interrelated nature of actors, roles, and personas as described by Constantine and Lockwood [2001, p. 1].*

Constantine's approach to user roles, as well as their relation to personas, is provided in detail later in this book (see Chapter 8, "Users, Roles, and Personas," by Larry Constantine).

Hugh Beyer and Karen Holtzblatt also embrace the concept of user roles (defined in a manner similar to Constantine and Lockwood) as a part of their broader UCD technique known as contextual design [Beyer and Holtzblatt 1997]. Their approach embraces qualitative field research through innovative analysis techniques and model-building to understand users in the context of their environments, organizations, and cultures. One critical model in their approach involves mapping roles and their relationships among one another as well as their relationships to the tools and systems involved. It is worth noting that Tahir and, more recently, Holtzblatt make the case that contextual design can serve as a foundation for the creation of personas [Tahir 1997; Holtzblatt 2002].

Understanding user roles (both as they exist today and how they might be changed with new products) is critical for anyone designing a product or creating personas. From our perspective, personas can also serve as a communication medium and additional model-building exercise within the contextual design approach. In Chapter 3, we describe how to use information about user roles in the persona creation process.

Mikkelson and Lee's user archetypes

Norrun Mikkelson and Wai On Lee have promoted the idea of creating user archetypes to supplement scenario-based design [Mikkelson and Lee 2000]. Their user archetypes are similar to Cooper's concept of personas, although the genesis of the archetypes was a desire to improve the existing concept of "user classes" (a concept used quite broadly in traditional usability processes). (See, for example, Nielsen [1992] and [1993] and Bias and Mayhew [1994].) According to Mikkelson and Lee:

> Traditional approaches to representing the user often take the form of defining users by attribute clusters (e.g., age group, job title) and general experience with features of certain systems (e.g., length and frequency of experience using basic features or advanced features). Via profiles, users are then grouped into *user classes*. User classes are of some practical value because knowledge about these classes allows designers to steer the product in a general design direction….

> In design and evaluation, user classes such as first-time users, expert users, elders, etc. are often defined by human-interface specialists based on simple clustering of user attributes such as computer/system experience, age, job type, etc. Elsewhere, for the purpose of marketing, user classes such as reluctant, enthused, pragmatic, etc. are also defined by marketing and product planning based on the clustering of attributes associated with purchase decision and loyalty.

> While user classes may represent the user correctly, designers typically find it difficult to call on them during design. For example, it might be difficult for a designer to imagine what a first-time user is like or how he or she would behave if the designer has never met one. User classes may also lead to inconsistency in mental imaging (e.g., one person's mental image of a first-time user might be entirely different from another person's). Most importantly, representing users as user classes often misses what's important to the users, what their high-level goals are, and fails to capture the "essence" or "spirit" of the user [Mikkelson and Lee 2000, p.1].

Mikkelson and Lee's user archetypes consist of the following [Mikkelson and Lee 2000]:

- *Description:* Name, picture (or audio/video sample), and one-line summary description.
- *Attributes:* Age, family, lifestyle, roles played, and interests.

- *Computer skills:* The user archetype's knowledge of (and lack of knowledge of) the system(s) they use. The users' knowledge is represented in a simple (and granular) form the product team can understand. Two types of user knowledge are represented here: declarative and procedural.

- *Concerns and goals:* Three or four high-level and high-priority concerns and goals important to the user.

- *Market size and influence:* How many of this type of user are in the market we are concerned with, and their role in the purchase decision.

- *Activities:* Task and domain knowledge in context. Usually one-page description of typical activities of the user in the form of a "day/week in the life" of the user archetype. This captures life prior to the introduction of new technology.

Mikkelson and Lee provided a process for deriving user archetypes out of user classes based on a variety of data, as well as a method of employing them in product definition and design (though largely as an adjunct to scenario-based design). However, their approach did not have broad adoption.

Cooper's Personas

In *The Inmates Are Running the Asylum,* Alan Cooper discusses many of the reasons he believes high-tech products are built such that they drive us, their users, crazy [Cooper 1999]. Cooper asserts that the very structure of our organizations fosters a focus on technology where we should instead be focusing on people. He introduces personas as part of a solution that will "restore the sanity" to product design and development. While personas were introduced publicly in 1999, Cooper notes that the genesis of personas was really around 1983 as part of a personal role-playing technique that he used while working through design problems on his own [Cooper 2003]. His first formal personas, which better reflected his ideas around Goal-Directed Design® (his trademarked methodology), appeared in 1995 and were used more collaboratively to communicate different user perspectives regarding a complex design solution for a consulting project.

According to Cooper, "Personas are not real people...they are *hypothetical archetypes* of actual users...defined with significant *rigor and precision*" [Cooper 1999, p. 124]. In other words, personas are imaginary people we create to stand in as concrete target users for our products. By calling personas "hypothetical archetypes," Cooper is likely referring to the fact that there is no way to prove that the personas truly are representative of actual users until after the product is released and is being used. When he says personas must be "defined with significant *rigor and precision*," Cooper is asserting that it is the specificity and detail of the personas that gives them their value.

Brenda Buckner — Primary Shopping Persona

Age 29
Shop2Drop@AOL.com

When Brenda Buckner's 29th birthday arrived, she celebrated by going shopping for herself in the morning. Then, she celebrated in the evening by opening presents from her husband, several of which she had suggested to him; in fact, she told him when she saw that great Ann Taylor sweater for 30% off.

Brenda isn't a selfish shopper, though; she is always on the lookout for that perfect item for a friend or for her husband. Brenda keeps track of birthdays in her day planner, where she also jots down gift ideas and clothing sizes for friends and family. She's been known to buy a birthday gift ten months in advance of the actual day. When it's the right item, she knows it and won't pass up the opportunity to grab it. She feels especially clever when she finds things on sale, though full price won't stop her from buying. Of course, she always has her eyes open for personal purchases and has no qualms about making an impulse buy.

Brenda generally begins shopping with only a vague sense of purpose; she seldom has a specific item in mind. She may go to a store that has items appropriate to someone's taste, but she will look for inspiration once she gets there. She knows what stores or departments are definitely not interesting, so she has little patience for stores that force her to walk past a lot of uninteresting merchandise. She will often pick up a few possible items as she browses, then make a decision among them. She likes to make notes about the items she didn't buy, though, since they may be useful ideas for another occasion.

Brenda's favorite stores are Nordstrom and Neiman Marcus, which carry a good selection of the best designers and brands. She has high expectations when it comes to service; she expects to find a helpful salesperson nearby whenever she has product questions but prefers to have the staff remain unobtrusive until she needs them.

Brenda lives and works in Minneapolis, which gives her access to numerous shops and malls. Sometimes, though, the weather just doesn't allow for a Saturday shopping excursion with her friends. To get a shopping fix on a snowy day, Brenda has learned that browsing online can be even more satisfying than browsing and ordering from the stack of dog-eared catalogs on her mail table. Brenda is reasonably comfortable with a computer—she uses basic Microsoft Office functions at work—but is nervous about configuration or other complex tasks.

Brenda's Goals

- Be entertained. Brenda enjoys shopping for the sake of shopping. She expects a good selection and great service.

- Find the perfect item. Whether shopping for herself or for someone else, Brenda enjoys the challenge of finding exactly the right thing.

- Be a shopping expert. Although she would never admit it, Brenda enjoys her reputation as an expert shopper. Knowing what's available helps her find just what she's looking for, too.

FIGURE 1.10: *An example persona, named Brenda Buckner. (Copyright © Cooper 2002)*

Story from the field

CUSTOMER SEGMENTATION AND DESIGN PERSONAS: WHAT'S THE DIFFERENCE?

—**Frank Spillers,** Principal and Co-CEO, Experience Dynamics

Personas are being created at an astonishing rate by design teams, from interactive agencies to large corporate environments. More often than not, many of the customer representations being used in Web development efforts are driven solely by traditional notions of market segmentation (which are typically quantitative in nature and somewhat disconnected from the user's context of use and real-world behavior). At Experience Dynamics, we've found that marketing profiles (Figure 1.11) are often inadequate as a design aid because they miss the strategic role that behavior, cognition, and context play in the interaction design process.

Segment:	Domestic Affluent Progressive Shopper
Age:	39 to 45 years old
Income:	$75,000 – $110,000
Work:	Educated professional, career oriented
Hobbies:	Health, community, shopping

Female, recently divorced with 2 children living at home.
Lives in metropolitan area (e.g., 15 minutes north of Seattle)

Works full time in white collar industry (e.g., for a manufacturer of healthcare electronics)

Likely to be interested in personal fitness and health.
Active in her local community. Is an avid shopper.

Has been online for six years and feels comfortable with ecommerce.
Favorite Web sites are Amazon, Lands End and Macy's.com.

FIGURE 1.11: *Marketing profile based on segmentation and market research.*

Design personas represent the fruits of labor of more qualitative research [Figure 1.12] and help communicate users' needs and goals. While it is important to start with an inventory of who your target audience is from a demographic perspective, it is extremely valuable to expand demographics and segments into psychographic and behavioral profiles gathered from field research techniques such as an ethnographic (observational) study, contextual inquiry, or task analysis.

(Story from the field, continued)

Name/Tagline:	Comparative Caroline
Priority:	High (Primary Persona)
Type:	Comparative shopper
Goal:	Find the best deal
Cognitive Background:	High level of familiarity with shopping carts, comparative tools; needs to self-justify each purchase or impulse purchases
Tools:	Checks 3–5 sites for each purchase, Google, Pricewatch, consults friends

Comparative Caroline has a pretty good grasp of how the Web works and buys something every month or so online. She likes Web sites to be easy to use and doesn't have a lot of patience with difficult Web sites. At work she uses the Web to shop around for deals she can't get in her local stores.

Caroline is resilient about getting the best price online. She will spend several days shopping for one item and has been known to take up to two weeks "shopping around." Caroline is not shy on the Web and regularly uses Google for her search shopping. She will only click Google Adwords if they have the keyword she is looking for, otherwise she doesn't bother. Caroline wants to be sold on why a product is the best deal. She doesn't always shop on price however, but does look for a reason and a feeling as to why purchasing from one site is better than another. For Caroline, the best deal is not always the cheapest buy.

What gets her attention? Free shipping offers, product guarantees, large product images, fast check outs and polite and concise copy.

FIGURE 1.12: *Design persona based on qualitative data and behavioral profiling.*

(Story from the field, continued)

From the design persona, it is easier to derive what to do to meet the user's needs.

What Caroline would like from our e-commerce Web site:
- *Design tip:* Offer easy access to comparison tool at product level. Use warm invitation and bright colors around compare button.
- *Copy tip:* Use respectful and polite copy that emphasizes benefits, satisfaction guarantee, and customer service. Justify price in the product images and in the body of the copy.
- *Marketing tip:* If using cookies, use time-expires offers with this user (anticipate conversion over multiple visits). Use specific product keywords in search engine ads.

Because the goals of usability are often driven by successful task completion, it is crucial to understand the finite details of user needs/goals, behavioral routines (tasks), rhythms, and expectations of your user population. Marketing profiles should not be confused with behavioral personas, whose focus is to specifically inform design decisions. Personas should help you understand your users more deeply; that is, "what they do" and "why they do it," not simply "who they are."

Key to Cooper's personas is that the representation is based on distinct user goals, in addition to behaviors, tasks, or simple demographic information. Cooper's approach, Goal-Directed Design®, focuses on uncovering, understanding, and designing towards the central needs and motivations of users – goals. Cooper asserts, and we agree, that personas created with goals as the critical centerpiece can inform product design in a profound way; one that can result in elegant, broad reaching and lasting solutions. Figure 1.10 shows an example persona from Cooper, which was derived from and reveals critical user goals.

THE NEXT FRONTIER FOR PERSONAS

Personas and other user representations have been "discovered" and used in various disciplines to infuse user data into other processes. Usually, these user representations are built and communicated as static documents or other artifacts that provide a snapshot of interesting and relevant information about users. These artifacts have proven helpful, largely because they help make information about users highly accessible, engaging, and memorable to people making decisions.

These representations are not alive, however. They are depicted as motionless portraits, usually contained within a single finite and static document. There is no room for growth or development. That is, unlike a character in a book or film, personas do not evolve. Moreover, the team using them is supposed to "get to know them" almost instantly. When we get to know a friend, neighbor, colleague, or even a character in a favorite book or TV show, we *build up* an understanding of them (i.e., we develop a relationship with them). Once we know people, we are able to understand why they do what they do, what they want, and what they need. Engendering this level of understanding is the next frontier for user representation.

We believe you have to enable personas to "come to life," allowing them to develop in the minds of the people using them. To be very clear, we are *not* suggesting that personas change drastically over time, take on new characteristics, or develop new skills (they are not to be moving targets). Instead, we believe that *personas must live in the minds of your colleagues.* Towards this end, we propose that persona practitioners must:

● Embrace the challenge of communicating information about users through narrative and storytelling

● Maintain a lifecycle perspective when educating colleagues about personas

● Allow the people using the personas to extrapolate from and extend them.

In other words, personas should be more than a collection of facts. Personas should be compelling stories that unfold over time in the minds of your product team. We believe that successful personas and persona efforts are built progressively. Just as we get to know people in our lives, we must get to know personas (and the data they contain) by developing a relationship with them. No single document, read in a few minutes or posted on a wall, can promote the type of rich and evolving relationship with information about users that is the cornerstone of good product development. No single document can contain the wave of scenarios and stories your personas will inspire. As long as the personas are well built, data driven, and thoughtfully communicated, the product team can use the personas that come to exist to generate new insights and seek out the right details when they need them.

This book explores ways of bringing personas to life in the minds of product teams. The deep and ongoing focus on well-understood users that results will benefit your product, your team, and your company.

SOUNDS GREAT! LET'S USE PERSONAS! ...IT'S EASIER SAID THAN DONE

If personas are such a good thing, why isn't everyone using them? Perhaps one answer is that creating and using personas is easier said than done (which is why we wrote this book). Although the persona concept has become increasingly well known and used, many practitioners (even experienced ones) hunger for fundamental how-to knowledge about the method. The truth is that little is commonly known or broadly shared about how best to create and use personas in development projects. Even less is commonly known regarding how this technique can benefit from, or be used in concert with, other UCD techniques.

The dearth of detailed guidance on personas

While introducing personas in *The Inmates are Running the Asylum*, Cooper presents the basic ideas behind the creation of personas and their application toward design. Overall, the book does an excellent job of evangelizing the concept of personas as well as Cooper's overarching approach, Goal-Directed Design®. The notion of personas was so compelling that many practitioners began trying it; and as they did so, there was a resounding call for more information on how, exactly, to create and use personas.

In *About Face 2.0*, Cooper and his long-term colleague, Robert Reimann, provide an answer to the call for more information on their approach [Cooper and Reimann 2003]. And while their book incorporates new material on personas, *About Face 2.0* is broader in scope than personas, presenting a more complete description of Goal-Directed Design® and offering commentary on the state of the software industry. Because of this broader focus, Cooper and Reimann provide general guidelines to persona creation, rather than specific procedures, instruction and examples. And while Cooper does provide additional detail on personas on his Web site, www.cooper.com (and regularly offers tutorials on his approach at conferences and via Cooper U™), the requests for more information and guidance have continued.

This need has led other UCD professionals to contribute to the methodology and literature on personas. For example, there are a variety of case studies, examples and revealing discussions available on the Web, some of which we highlight in this book. Perhaps more importantly, there are now several books which cover the topic of personas in a more end-to-end fashion.

Bob Baxley includes a chapter on personas in his book *Making the Web Work* [Baxley 2003]. Although Baxley describes the value of the persona approach, his biggest contribution to this area is a set of five examples of personas, complete with details about their key characteristics. He also includes some information on process, though perhaps not in sufficient detail to enable the reader to create personas without additional support.

In his book *Observing the User Experience*, Mike Kuniavsky also offers a full chapter on personas [Kuniavsky 2003]. His coverage of the method is fairly complete, offering detailed how-to and an example of a profile. Although he seems to purposely avoid the term *persona* (referring to this instead as a user profile), his approach is very much like Cooper's. Kuniavsky provides a very useful list of core attributes of personas, which we refer to in Chapter 4.

One other book, *Information Architecture: Blueprints for the Web* (by Christina Wodtke), offers a perspective on personas that includes some good process information and examples [Wodtke 2002]. One noteworthy part of her coverage is the inclusion of a section on writing scenarios from personas and then moving from the scenario to task analysis and on to wire framing and full design. Wodtke also contributed several "Stories from the field" to this book.

In spite of these resources, until now, there has remained no truly comprehensive and detailed coverage of this topic (i.e., one that provides specific steps, rich examples, and insights on the method in practice). Cooper served as our first inspiration to develop the method we now use as standard; our process has continued to be inspired by the practice of others as well.

As we developed our own approach, we talked to many practitioners and learned from their experiences. We discovered that many were encountering the same kinds of questions and problems. The lessons we learned from experienced persona practitioners helped us isolate several key problems that we set out to solve.

Personas are not always successful

One of the reasons we wrote this book was to provide solutions to some of the common problems practitioners have experienced when trying to use personas. Just creating personas is simply not enough. Many practitioners have had less than stellar experiences with personas. In some cases, the initial attempt has failed to such a degree that the likelihood of further attempts is all but gone. Even well-crafted personas can result in little or no focus on users in the development process, and poorly executed persona can keep the development team from investing in other UCD techniques or other efforts that improve product quality. So, why do some persona efforts fail? We have uncovered the following four common reasons. The sections that follow expand on these reasons based on our research.

1. The effort was not accepted or supported by the leadership team.
2. The personas were not credible and not associated with methodological rigor and data.
3. The personas were poorly communicated.
4. The product design and development team employing personas did not understand how to use them.

Personas failed when the effort was not accepted or supported by the leadership team

Many persona efforts are often grass-roots efforts. A few people learn about personas, decide it would be a great thing to do for their product, and then attempt to employ them without considering the fact that they are potentially introducing a major change in the product development process and culture of their company. In such cases, the impact of the personas is typically minimal (persona use is limited to a select few and typically dies out over time). To do personas well, you need to garner the support of the key leaders on your team or elsewhere in the company. Doing an upfront analysis of your organization and product team needs is critical. But perhaps more important is getting the support of high-level people within your organization. In Chapter 3, we provide some specific approaches to solving this issue. Following these will ensure that you get off on the right foot and have ample resources for completing a persona project with success (e.g., people resources for creating and promoting personas, a budget for posters or other materials to make the personas visible, and a mandate from team leaders for people to actually use the personas).

Personas failed when they were not seen as credible and associated with methodological rigor and data

In some projects, the personas that were created were just not believable. Personas do have a fictitious component to them. Creating a believable, realistic, and credible representation of your target users involves considerable effort and is somewhat of an art. If you are not careful, your personas (or your process) can be perceived as lacking validity or rigor (i.e., that your process was not thorough, precise, or methodical). Sometimes personas are not actually created with data: they are based on loose assumptions or are completely fictional. In those cases, they need to be communicated as such, and the degree to which they can be trusted and used should be kept in check. Even where personas are created rigorously out of carefully analyzed data, if the relationship to that data and process is not clear there is a risk of lost credibility. The perception of rigor is important. In Chapter 4, we provide you with a process and specific suggestions for ensuring that lack of credibility is not a major issue in your persona effort.

Personas failed when they were poorly communicated

If your team is not aware of the personas — and of the method more generally — you will not be successful, even with credible personas supported by your leaders. Moreover, if your team is not reminded of the personas regularly, they will be forgotten. We have been witness to numerous instances of personas simply not being communicated well. Often the main communication method was a résumé-like document that got posted around the office building. Little thought or effort was put into communicating the information in the personas deeply and meaningfully. The result was that most people on the product team didn't really know much about the personas other than their names and photos. There was no sense of a shared understanding or language.

In other cases, even when the team had learned who the personas were, the team's focus on the personas faded over time. Your personas will need refreshing and revitalizing from time to time. Understand that personas will continue to evolve in the minds of the people using them. Your team will need to progressively get to know them, developing an understanding of them over time. In Chapter 5, we provide numerous ideas and examples to make your personas known and to help keep them fresh in the minds of your product team over the potentially long haul of a development cycle.

Personas failed when the team did not understand how to use them

By far the most problematic issue for persona efforts is the lack of understanding of how to use them once they are created and communicated. In many cases, we have found that there were no explicit uses of the personas beyond just using them to aid design discussions in meetings. Using them in discussions is a fine thing do to, but in isolation this keeps the impact of personas to a minimum. In other cases, some persona practitioners have crafted methods of using their personas more directly. Without well thought out uses and explicit instructions on how to involve them, personas can be a distraction instead of an aid. In Chapter 6, we provide an array of tools and techniques for utilizing personas and offer suggestions for integrating these tools with existing practices.

In their article "Personas in Action," Blomquist and Arvola describe issues with the persona method [Blomquist and Arvola 2002]. The personas in their study were not used well by the design team, even though they had the knowledge necessary to do so. This highlights the importance of integrating this method with those that already exist in an organization. Tom Chi and Kevin Cheng reiterate this point in their commentary on the persona method. Clearly, for the persona method to overcome these problems, practitioners need some help.

Story from the field

PERSONAS. LOVE 'EM. HATE 'EM. STRUGGLE TO INTEGRATE THEM. ARE THEY TRULY USEFUL, OR A LITTLE HOKEY?

—Tom Chi and Kevin Cheng, *OK-Cancel.com*

Perhaps one of the more controversial aspects of personas is the colorful narratives created around them. Who could possibly care that Ted the Persona drives a blue Buick LeSabre? Or that he is allergic to shellfish? Even when the stories are centered around work, there is always that nagging voice that questions the relevance and applicability of the information being invented. Are we really modeling users well, or simply creating stereotypical users from unfounded assumptions?

One thing that can be said for these stories is that they are memorable. This is because narratives are excellent mnemonic devices. They create a temporal and causal framework that allows our brains to store quite a bit of data. Mention one detail about Juanita and the rest of the story comes flowing back: Oh. She has two kids and has to work late at her financial services company… and because she stays late she starts tasks that require deep concentration after 5:00 p.m. And so on. Of course, such stories can also get mangled after a generation of retellings — but for the most part personas do a good job of creating a shared vocabulary to call up significant detail about user segments.

While having a shared vocabulary is better than having none, it's quite the tricky endeavor to develop the right vocabulary. Even if you've profiled 100 users to develop your set of personas, often you will still find users who don't quite fit in the categories you've created. And even if you do successfully abstract them it's often not clear how that abstraction should inform design. For example, most persona sets have a user who is the "novice" user. What does this mean, though? Can you assume that said user understands drag and drop? right-click? tabbing through fields? In testing you might see that novice user 1 might understand two of the concepts, and novice user 2 understands the third. They are the same persona in front of the same screen, but the results will be vastly different.

(Story from the field, continued)

There may also be environmental differences that drastically affect how two people rep-rensented by the same persona interact with the software. While Joey and Tina may both be mid-level managers in a large organization, Joey is beset with phone calls every 10 minutes whereas Tina's day is more stable and is structured around meetings. As a result, Joey keeps on timing out on his Web sessions because important calls come in while he is halfway through a task, whereas Tina is able to pick good times to approach these tasks and has no timeout problems.

If personas cannot address these very real interaction design problems, at what level are they useful? Do they only become powerful when paired with use cases, or when buoyed by a certain approach to testing? Should they be written for the designers, the developers, the executives?

THIS BOOK IS DESIGNED TO FILL IN THE GAPS

The dearth of information on how to organize and execute a persona effort, particularly how to do it well, and our frustrations with our own first attempts, led us to organize several work-shops and seminars on personas with other "persona practitioners" in the industry, including participation from Cooper's organization. From these interactions with other practitioners, we were able to gather and explore detailed examples, step-by-step procedures, best practices, and lessons learned. The structure and content of our book is based on the outcome of these workshops as well as our own experiences with the persona method since then. This resulted in an approach based on the following core assertions:

● Building personas from assumptions is good; building personas from data is much, much better.

● Personas are a highly memorable, inherently usable communication tool *if* they are communicated well.

● Personas can be initiated by executives or first used as part of a bottom-up grass-roots experiment, but eventually need support at all levels of an organization.

● Personas are not a standalone UCD process, but should be integrated into existing processes and used to augment existing tools.

● Effective persona efforts require organizational introspection and strategic thinking.

● Personas *can* be created fast and show their value quickly, but if you want to obtain the full value from personas you will have to commit to a significant investment of time and resources.

We understand that the devil is in the details when it comes to launching a persona effort within an organization, and we are excited to share the wealth of knowledge that has been shared with us and developed over time. That is what this book is all about.

We include practical methods, detailed instructions, and examples

This book includes stories, suggestions, and best practices contributed by UCD and other product development professionals from around the world who have experience in using personas for product design and development. It also includes step-by-step instructions for every phase of your persona effort. This book contains:

● A start-to-finish persona lifecycle that breaks down and organizes the elements of a successful persona effort. Each phase of the lifecycle includes rich descriptions of procedures, techniques, and tools. Our goal is to provide enough information and instruction so that you do not need to supplement our book with any additional training or tutorial, or by hiring a consultant.

● Discussions of the issues related to launching and managing a persona effort within an existing software organization or effectively as a consultant. We agree with Cooper's assertion that personas can build communication, consensus, and commitment within a software development organization, and we detail techniques that help make these things happen. We provide a series of strategic discussions on how to use personas to establish the role of UCD professionals as a key element of the product development process. These discussions convey how to do this early (and with a more permanent result) in the process, including frank discussions of product development politics (e.g., how to build communication, consensus, and commitment regarding personas).

● Many examples — describing experiences good and bad — of all tools and artifacts we recommend. During our workshops and seminars, we realized the power of stories and examples and are thrilled to include contributions from many colleagues, including:

Story from the field

We have collected a large number of short case studies, anecdotes, commentary, and opinions from other persona practitioners and user experience professionals in a variety of domains and industries. These stories should give you contextualized ideas about what to do, and what not to do, as you launch and maintain your own persona effort.

Bright Idea

These sidebars are practical techniques, tools, and innovative methods you might want to try. They are recommended best practices. As you develop your own approach as a persona practitioner, refer to these practical tips and insightful suggestions for how to solve problems your colleagues have already encountered. Adopt and adapt the best practices of other practitioners.

Handy Detail

These are important reminders, useful definitions, and fine details we don't want you to miss.

G4K Gigantic for Kids

A running case study with rich examples that connects all of the lifecycle phases, demonstrating more *holistically* how personas can be used in building a product from end to end. A fictional company, Gigantic for Kids Inc., has been generated to serve as the basis for this case study. (Gigantic for Kids, or G4K, has historically produced children's games and educational software and is now trying to further its reach and brand through the Internet.)

This book is for you — no matter what your discipline or role in product development

We set out not so much to write a textbook or scientific document but to create a useful handbook for practitioners. This is primarily a book of practice, not theory (though contributed chapters help provide the rationale and theory behind the practice). We believe our book will make an excellent addition to the collection of books for professionals in usability, interaction design, and user-centered methods. We hope that academic readers (students and professors) involved in research and degree programs in human/computer interaction and related fields (e.g., technical communication, graphical and interactive design, industrial engineering, human factors, applied/workplace anthropology, information science, and cognitive, applied, or industrial/organizational psychology) will find it evocative and useful in preparing for a career in the world of product development. We believe it would be especially useful reading for interns or new graduates moving into industry positions.

Because many user experience teams are actually "one-person teams" with few resources and little time, we include a range of tools and suggested best practices that enable personas to be accomplished on a tight budget. We provide coverage in the book for user interface consultants working outside or independently of the actual development team or company, including those who may not be able to directly impact or be involved in the entire product development cycle. Although the information in this book applies to many industries, most of our examples come from software and Web development.

How to use this book

We hope our book becomes a tattered resource you return to often for useful examples and practical information about the entire persona process. We have designed the book to be read front-to-back and to be consulted as a phase-by-phase reference guide.

The content of our persona method book is structured around a concept we used to organize our persona practitioner workshops. We call it the "persona lifecycle." As you will read in Chapter 2, we make an analogy to the human lifecycle. The persona process goes from family planning, conception, gestation, birth, maturation, and adulthood through to retirement and celebrating lifetime acheivement at the end of the project. For the practitioner, the process of creating and using personas follows this basic, largely serial, cycle. The persona lifecycle requires an end-to-end mind-set on the part of the practitioner and reinforces a basic tenet that any persona effort should be considered an ongoing campaign that does not end when your personas are created and delivered to the development team.

Our book consists of an overview of the persona lifecycle (Chapter 2) and five core chapters (Chapters 3 through 7) which cover the phases of the persona lifecycle. We hope you will keep coming back to the core chapters throughout your own projects for ideas, tips, and techniques for warding off potential hazards (chances are, if you run into a problem, others have been there before you).

We have also included several supplemental chapters by invited experts at the end of the book. These chapters are in-depth explorations of specific topics related to personas:

- Chapter 8: Users, Roles, and Personas (Larry Constantine)
- Chapter 9: Storytelling and Narrative (Whitney Quesenbery)
- Chapter 10: Reality and Design Maps (Tamara Adlin and Holly Jamesen)
- Chapter 11: Marketing Versus Design Personas (Robert Barlow-Busch)
- Chapter 12: Why Personas Work: The Psychological Evidence (Jonathan Grudin).

We think you will find these chapters both interesting and useful as you explore the method.

SUMMARY

We hope you are inspired to begin learning about personas, and more generally about UCD. We know that writing about it and collecting examples and best practices from around the community has inspired us. Personas are not only useful tools but fun to create and use.

As you read this book, you are going to find a great deal of information on the method: many details, tips, tools, and complexities you never expected. Don't let that scare you. Effective persona efforts can range from incredibly simple to fairly complex and involved. As we point out in Chapter 7, there is a cost to doing personas. It is not free and it will take away from other work you could do for your company. We believe that if you are going to do personas you should do it well or not at all, but we don't believe this means you have to spend a tremendous amount of time and money. We hope you will use the ideas in this book to customize your own process — after first understanding your organizational culture as well as your product and business needs.

OVERVIEW OF THE PERSONA LIFECYCLE

Putting the Persona Method into Perspective

THE PHASES OF THE PERSONA LIFECYCLE

The persona lifecycle is a metaphoric framework that breaks the persona process into phases similar to those of human procreation and development. As shown in Figure 2.1, there are five phases in this framework: *family planning, conception and gestation, birth and maturation, adulthood,* and *lifetime achievement and retirement.* The phases of the persona lifecycle framework bring structure to the potentially complicated process of persona creation and highlight critical (yet often overlooked or ignored) aspects of persona use.

As the name indicates, the persona lifecycle is a cyclical, largely serial, process model. As Figure 2.1 indicates, each stage builds on the next, culminating but not ending at the *adulthood* phase. Note also that the illustration shows that the final stage, *lifetime achievement and retirement,* is not immediately followed by a cyclical return to the first stage. This is because different persona efforts culminate and restart in different ways. Personas can be reused, reincarnated, or retired depending on the project.

More importantly, although each phase does build on the previous, some are more important than others, and some you can complete in just an hour or two if need be. *Conception and gestation* and *adulthood* are the vital steps. As you read this book, remember that you can (and should) customize your own persona process in accordance with the amount of time, resources, and data you have.

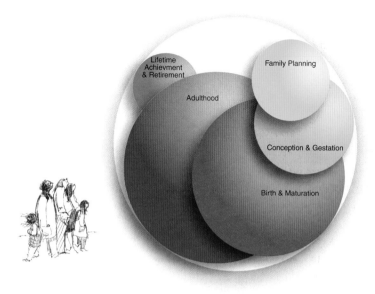

FIGURE 2.1: *The five phases of the persona lifecycle. This diagram is designed to show both the order of the phases (from family planning through conception and gestation, birth and maturation, adulthood, and finally lifetime achievement and retirement) and the relative amount of effort and importance related to each phase. The subsequent five chapters of this book cover each lifecycle phase in detail.*

This is a long book, but the persona lifecycle doesn't have to take a long time. You can, and should, be selective in the techniques you choose to integrate into your persona effort. Although we do not think it is a good idea to skip any of the lifecycle phases completely, we do believe it is completely acceptable to take some shortcuts within any of the phases. Giving some attention to every phase will increase the odds that your persona effort will ultimately be successful. Your overall goal should be to create helpful and well-used personas, not to follow the process described in this book to the letter. Throughout the book, we suggest both complete end-to-end processes and helpful shortcuts. We point out the processes we believe the most important and effective, and you can treat each chapter as a menu of techniques and tools that can be used together or independently.

Phase 1: persona family planning

Persona development begins with family planning. This is the research and analysis phase that precedes the actual creation of personas. During family planning, you will focus on:

● Creating a core team of colleagues to help you with the entire persona effort

● Researching your own organization (which we call "organizational introspection") to evaluate the problems and needs of your company, organization, and/or product. Once you understand the needs you hope the persona effort will address, you can evangelize the persona method and prepare the product development team for the persona effort

● User research and identification of data sources that will provide the raw materials for your personas.

The *family planning* chapter describes the careful resource and needs analysis you should complete before you introduce personas into your organization. We help you put together a core team of people to help you with the personas, and we identify the information you should collect from around your organization to plan an effective persona campaign. Persona *family planning* requires strategic thinking on your part to make sure that your organization will accept and use the personas you create. We suggest strategies for internal evangelism of the persona method that will set the stage for a successful persona effort.

Once this analysis is complete, a persona core team is assembled, and evangelism is underway, it is time to move on to data generation and gathering. In the second half of the *family planning* chapter, we discuss what types of information to glean from a potential user population as you conduct your own user research. We also explore how to access the many existing data sources that surround you, including internal sources (such as market research reports and interviews with product support specialists and other subject-matter experts) and external data sources (such as public Web sites that provide statistical and demographic information).

We believe personas are much more credible and helpful if they incorporate and refer to real-world data. However, we also address what to do if data is simply unavailable and you have no option but to build personas based on assumptions.

Family planning ends at the point at which you have established that personas are right for your organization and current project, have buy-in from key individuals, have completed initial research and data gathering, have a persona core team in place, and have a solid plan for the rest of the persona effort that suits your product team's needs.

Phase 2: persona conception and gestation

In the persona *conception and gestation* chapter we explain how to extract useful information from disparate data sources and use this information to build personas. During the persona *conception and gestation* phase, we will help you decide:

● How many personas you will need to create to communicate the key information your data

● Which qualities and descriptive elements you should include in your persona documents and how to tie these elements back to your original data sources

● How to prioritize and validate your personas

- How to decide when your personas are "complete" and ready to be introduced to your product team.

A lot of the work during the *conception and gestation* phase centers on collaboratively filtering data and organizing information—information that arises out of the data you collect in *family planning* and information that arises from other sources, such as inherent knowledge of how people behave, your business or product strategy, the competitive marketplace, and technological affordances related to your product domain. The information you identify will help you understand the particular user roles, user goals, and user segments that uniquely describe your target users. When you have isolated information about your users' roles, goals, and segments you will be able to determine what personas you should create to capture and communicate the most relevant qualities of (and differences among) target users related to your product domain and business strategy.

Complete personas include concrete facts as well as narrative and storytelling elements. They contain both design-relevant and seemingly extraneous information (e.g., a persona's e-mail activities versus a persona's choice of car or favorite book), which play an important role in communicating who your personas are during persona *birth and maturation* and *adulthood*. We provide examples that show what content makes up a complete persona: how much, and what types, of detail are required to make a persona a persona. We address issues of gender, age, ethnicity, international customers, and accessibility/disabilities. We describe a variety of types of personas, including not only user personas but organizational personas and anti-personas.

When you have completed the process described in the *conception and gestation* chapter, you will have translated raw data and insights into a set of complete, robust personas that are ready to "participate" in the product design process.

Phase 3: persona birth and maturation

Like parents sending young children off to school, you and your core team will send your personas into your organization to interact with other people. The personas are fully formed but may continue to evolve slightly over time. Moreover, throughout the remainder of the development cycle, your personas will continue to develop in the minds of your product team. Problems at this phase might involve a lack of acceptance or visibility and other problems, that lead to personas that "die on the vine" and disappear from the project. More subtly, your personas may come to be misconstrued and misinterpreted. Successful persona *birth and maturation* requires a strong, clear focus on communication to ensure that your personas are not just known and understood but adopted, remembered, and used by the product team. The *birth and maturation* chapter includes:

- Creating a persona campaign plan to organize your work in *birth and maturation* and *adulthood*

- Introducing the personas (and the persona method) to the product team
- Ensuring that the personas are understood, revered, and likely to be used (for example, creating artifacts to progressively disclose persona details)
- Managing the minor changes to the persona descriptions that become necessary after the personas are introduced.

You can use a variety of methods to communicate personas to the members of your product team, including Web sites, posters, illustrations, electronic documents, diagrams, live actors, and videos. We help you decide which of many artifacts to create and when and how to use them to keep the personas (and the data they contain) fresh in the minds of the product team. We also give you pointers on maintaining the delicate balance of sharing ownership of the personas (and the details they contain) while ensuring that new or altered details don't threaten the integrity of the underlying data.

At this phase, you must also be prepared to answer the difficult questions that will inevitably come up as you introduce the personas. You will have to be prepared to discuss the process you used to create the personas, their utility, the ways you would like the product team to use the personas, and the ways you intend to measure the value of the persona effort. We also discuss various considerations and approaches for using personas effectively as a consultant versus as a permanent member of a product team. As a consultant, communicating the information in, value of, and uses for the personas is not easy. Your success will depend on partnering with and educating an internal champion of the personas.

Phase 4: persona adulthood

Personas are "all grown up" in the *adulthood* phase and have a job to do. You have introduced the personas to the product team and have worked to clarify the role and importance of the personas. You have encouraged the product team to embrace the personas and the information they contain, and now it is time to help everyone use the personas to inform the design and development of the product.

In the literature on personas, the primary description of how personas are used is through discussion in design meetings: "Will Sally want to use this feature?" We have found, however, that this is only one of the many ways personas can be involved in the product design and development process. The effective persona practitioner must understand the many other ways personas can be involved in *existing* processes, and ensure that the personas work hard in an organization during the core development phases.

Personas can be used to help you plan, design, evaluate, and release your products. Personas can also inform marketing, advertising, and sales strategy. The adulthood chapter is full of practical tools and suggestions to ensure that your personas have real impact — that they get used in a meaningful way by your product team.

During the *adulthood* phase, maintaining the right amount of control over personas is critical. The product team must feel that their ownership is real, but you have the responsibility of making sure the personas stay true to their source data and purpose. Personas that lose their connection to the data can become feral and can even harm your project. For example, if members of the product team like the idea of using persona names, but several decide to make up their own persona details, your team could end up working against each other even though everyone believes they are using personas correctly.

Phase 5: *persona lifetime achievement, reuse, and retirement*

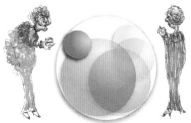

Once the project or product is completed, it is time to think about what has been accomplished and prepare for the next project. You will want to assess how effective the persona method was for your team and product development process. If you are beginning to think about the next product (or next version of the product just released), you will need to decide whether, and how, you will reuse your existing personas and the information they contain.

The end of a product cycle is a good time to assess the effectiveness of personas for the team and to take stock of lessons learned for the next time. How did the development team accept the method? Were your personas useful? To what extent were they accurate and precise? We provide suggestions and tools you can use to validate the use of personas in the development process and to determine if the persona effort was worth the exertion and resources it required. Did personas change the product? Did they change your design and development process? User-centered designers are constantly under pressure to validate the worth and return on investment (ROI) of their activities, and personas can be useful tools for measuring the success of both the product and of the UCD activities as a whole.

Depending on the nature of your products, you might be able to reuse the personas or "reincarnate" some of your persona data in new personas. In this chapter, we help you decide what to do with your "old" personas as you prepare for your next project. Do your personas retire, do they change over time? Do they purchase your product and start using it? Can other product teams utilize your personas or some portion of the information in them (i.e., are they reincarnated)? This section covers the issues and possibilities for making use of your personas after your product has shipped and you are thinking ahead to the next project.

THE PERSONA LIFECYCLE IS DESIGNED TO ENHANCE, NOT REPLACE, YOUR EXISTING PROCESSES

The persona lifecycle is all about early and continuous focus on users' needs and goals. The lifecycle phases are structured to help organize UCD activities that will enhance any product design and development process. The phases are built to help the persona practitioner plan, organize, and execute an end-to-end persona effort.

The persona lifecycle will work for you whether or not you have already incorporated UCD methods into your product development cycle. The persona lifecycle does not *replace* existing processes; rather, the phases of the lifecycle help to structure user-centered thinking throughout whatever design and development process you have in place. In this section, we illustrate the ways the phases of the persona lifecycle will introduce UCD into your organization (if UCD methods have not yet been adopted) or enhance UCD methods already in practice.

Most products start with business plans and basic product definitions. Once the basic vision and requirements are in place, the implementation of the product is planned. For many companies or product teams, this stage is captured in the form of specification documents. Ideally, once the product is specified, developers start building it. At some point after development begins there is enough built to start testing the product for quality. In software, this includes performance (speed), reliability (crashes and bugs), and security (memory leaks, data encryption, and so on). Testing and production often continue in tandem until the product is "complete." Once the product is complete, it goes into production. This general process can be more or less user-centered, depending on the structure of the design and development team and the nature of the product.

The persona lifecycle can introduce user-centered design into your technical development process

There are many models for product design and development. If your company has not yet adopted UCD methods, the product development process probably resembles a classic "waterfall" software development model (see Figure 2.2).

The waterfall model is oriented around technical activities and requirements. UCD requires a focus on users and their needs *before* the technical development activities commence. User-centered designers are constantly swimming upstream in the development process as they try to establish themselves and their methods as critical parts of the very early stages of product development. In fact, many of the user-centered activities built into the persona lifecycle should be completed before the waterfall begins (see Figure 2.3).

If your company does not do user research and user-centered product design, you have some big challenges ahead of you, but personas can still be a valuable tool. Jakob Nielsen describes an evolution of, acceptance of, and reliance on, UCD in organizations in which usability permeates the product development lifecycle [Nielsen 1994b, pp. 267–269]. Discount usability techniques, including personas, can play a major role in

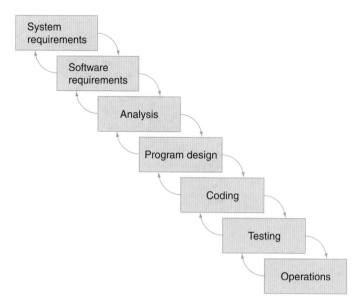

FIGURE 2.2: *Classic "waterfall" model of software development. (Adapted from Max's Project Management Wisdom [2004].)*

driving this evolution. In fact, we have witnessed personas, which in some cases can be considered a discount usability technique, play a major role in driving the evolution towards user-centered design.

If you introduce the persona lifecycle into an organization that is accustomed to a traditional, technically-oriented product development process, you will essentially be asking for time and resources to focus on your users much earlier than anyone in your organization has done so before. This is both beneficial and difficult.

The diagram shown in Figure 2.3 is an ideal scenario if you are starting with a waterfall process. It shows the persona *family planning, conception and gestation,* and *birth and maturation* phases completed before system requirements are drafted. However, in some cases you will find that waterfall activities start before you are finished with the first three phases of the persona lifecycle because no one is willing to wait for the information you are working to provide.

In the chapters that discuss the first three lifecycle phases, we provide advice for how to get the most out of your efforts even if the development process is moving ahead faster than you can create your personas. For example, it is possible to do personas without user research. Creating 'assumption personas' will help to surface assumptions, myths,

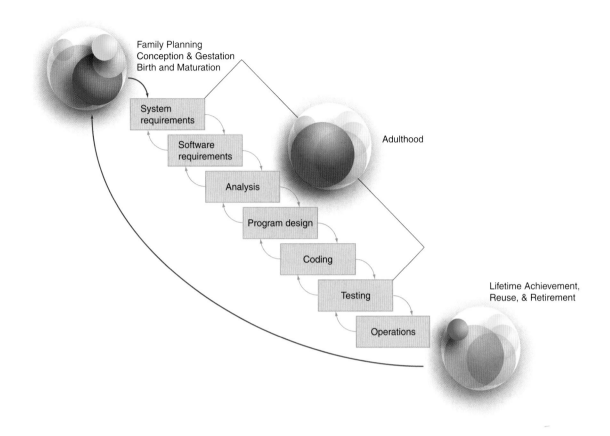

FIGURE 2.3: *The same classic "waterfall" model of software development (shown in Figure 2.2) with persona lifecycle phases added. Note that the persona lifecycle requires customer-focused activities before the "start" of the development process. Adult personas maintain customer focus throughout the requirement-generation and development activities, and the persona ROI and iteration activities (lifetime achievement and retirement) structure the lessons learned for use in the next iteration of the product.*

and fallacies about your target audience shared among your broad team. Personas of this type can actually pave the way to further UCD activities and investment. They can highlight the holes in your teams' knowledge of their customers and motivate research to fill in those holes. We discuss creating these assumption personas in Chapter 3.

Even if your first persona effort isn't perfect (and it is unlikely it will be), the effort will help you move your organization toward a more user-centered design and development process. By producing clear personas that communicate interesting and relevant information about your user base, you can begin to convey the value of understanding users and the importance of considering user needs and goals long before building system requirements. In subsequent projects, you can build on even small successes to introduce additional UCD methods.

The persona lifecycle can enhance user-centered design methods already in place

Many UCD methods and several powerful models for user-centered product design and usability engineering became popular in the 1990s. Both Jacob Nielsen [1994] and Debra Mayhew [1999] described end-to-end "usability engineering" processes for refocusing product design based on user needs above all else. Alan Cooper [1995] introduced his Goal-Directed Design® methods in his book *About Face*. In *User and Task Analysis for Interface Design*, Hackos and Redish [1998] described user research activities that should precede technical design. Vredenburg's *User-Centered Design: An Integrated Approach* [Vredenburg 2001] described the value of understanding and designing for the entire user experience, which depends on applying a cross-disciplinary approach toward integrating an understanding of user needs into the development process.

These and other books by UCD practitioners helped many companies begin to integrate new tools and methods into their existing processes. As more companies recognized the value of designing products users actually enjoyed using, some abandoned technology-driven development cycles in favor of usability engineering processes.

If your company has embraced UCD (to a greater or lesser degree), you probably already use some of the methods and tools listed in Figure 2.4 as part of your development cycle.

Although the phases at the top level of the table shown in Figure 2.4 are not radically different from those in the waterfall model, it is important to note that the first few phases (planning and feasibility, requirements, and design) include many activities related to understanding who users are, what they do, and how they do it—and then translating this into design prototypes. In short, true user-centered product design requires a significant amount of up-front work that should happen well before the development of technical requirements and designs.

No matter how bought-in to UCD a product team is, there never seems to be enough time at the beginning of any project to allow for complete user analysis, prototyping, and testing. Even user-centered designers whose companies have adopted usability engineering still face the challenge of swimming upstream in getting involved early enough in the product development process. It seems that no company feels they have the time to wait for user-centered designers to complete their work before starting to build products.

If your company has already adopted some UCD methods, you should find that the phases of the persona lifecycle (shown in Figure 2.5) augment your existing process and help you get involved earlier in the product development cycle. Again, keep in mind that the persona lifecycle is not meant to replace other UCD tools and is not a complete user-centered

Planning & Feasibility	Requirements	Design	Implementation	Test & Measure	Post Release
Getting started	User surveys	Design guidelines	Style guides	Diagnostic evaluation	Post release testing
Stakeholder meeting	Interviews	Paper prototyping	Rapid prototyping	Performance testing	Subjective assessment
Analyze content	Contextual inquiry	Heuristic evaluation		Subjective evaluation	User surveys
ISO 13407	User observation	Parallel design		Heuristic evaluation	Remote evaluation
Planning	Context	Storyboarding		Critical incidence technique	
Competitor analysis	Focus groups	Evaluate prototype		Pleasure	
	Brainstorming	Wizard of Oz			
	Evaluating existing systems	Interface design patterns			
	Card sorting				
	Affinity diagramming				
	Scenarios of use				
	Task analysis				
	Requirements meeting				

FIGURE 2.4: *UCD tools and methods grouped by product lifecycle phases. (Adapted from Usability Net [2003].)*

product design method on its own. Rather, the persona lifecycle is an organized collection of processes and tools that will complement other familiar methods. You will use personas to enhance these methods, particularly when there exists a need for user definition and reference.

PUTTING IT ALL TOGETHER: THE PERSONA LIFECYCLE IN ACTION

Chapters 3 through 7 of this book describe the phases of the persona lifecycle in depth, but before we begin describing particular methods and tools we want to give you a sense of

Family Planning   Conception & Gestation Birth & Maturation   Adulthood   Lifetime Achievement, Reuse & Retirement

Planning & Feasibility	Requirements	Design	Implementation	Test & Measure	Post Release
Getting started	User surveys	Design guidelines	Style guides	Diagnostic evaluation	Post release testing
Stakeholder meeting	Interviews	Paper prototyping	Rapid prototyping	Performance testing	Subjective assessment
Analyze content	Contextual inquiry	Heuristic evaluation		Subjective evaluation	User surveys
ISO 13407	User observation	Parallel design		Heuristic evaluation	Remote evaluation
Planning	Context	Storyboarding		Critical incidence technique	
Competitor analysis	Focus groups	Evaluate prototype		Pleasure	
	Brainstorming	Wizard of Oz			
	Evaluating existing systems	Interface design patterns			
	Card sorting				
	Affinity diagramming				
	Scenarios of use				
	Task analysis				
	Requirements meeting				

FIGURE 2.5: *The Usability Net tools and methods table with the phases of the persona lifecycle. If you already employ user-centered methods and tools, you will find that the phases of the persona lifecycle complement the work you are already doing.*

how the persona lifecycle can enhance your product design process and your company's focus on UCD. The following case study is a real-life, best-case scenario that describes the way one product team, which was already accustomed to doing UCD, incorporated the persona lifecycle phases into their process.

Story from the field

PERSONAS FOR E-BUSINESS SERVER PRODUCTS: A CASE STUDY

— **Nancy Lincoln, Melroy D'Souza, Tonya Peck, Kaivalya Hanswadkar,** and **Arnie Lund,** Windows Server System, Microsoft Corporation

E-business enterprise servers are complex computer systems that enable businesses of all sizes to be effective, efficient, and successful. They can provide a business with an Internet presence or an automated supply chain management or other key business processes, or enable disparate systems (potentially in legacy systems or on multiple platforms) to communicate and share data. It is essential that these complex server systems be easy to learn, install, configure, use, troubleshoot, and maintain. While personas have often been utilized successfully with consumer products, this story describes our Usability and Design team's experience using a persona-based lifecycle approach to develop complex E-business server systems.

To put things in perspective for other organizations undertaking such an effort, the E-Business line of server products was fairly new, and consisted of three main product lines with a number of individual components within each. These product lines were supported by three different development teams within the E-Business Server division. The ratio of the size of our Usability and Design team to that of the E-Business Server division we supported was 1:60. Further, our team had been in existence for 30 months and had an average UCD experience level of approximately three years.

Family Planning

There were three things to identify before creating the personas: *owners*, *stakeholders*, and *user types*. Our Design and Usability team was the primary owner of these personas, responsible for creating, delivering, maintaining, and ensuring the personas were used appropriately by product teams. Key product team members were also identified as virtual team members to encourage adoption of the personas. Stakeholders are people for whom the personas are created. These people included program managers (responsible for creating the specifications for the product), feature developers, product marketers, user interface designers, technical writers, and high-level product team managers.

(Story from the field, continued)

To identify user types, we tried to determine whether any of the highly successful user personas from other product teams across our company would apply to our products. However, what we found was a distinct difference between the targeting of enterprise products versus consumer products. With no primary research data available on our user types, and no "close match" personas in our organization, we did a meta-analysis of data from a variety of sources available in our company's database. This helped us to identify three main user types: System Administrator, Developer, and Information Worker (or business end user), for which we created a User Roles document. This document became the basis for the creation and validation of our personas.

We validated our assumptions by conducting research on the three user types we identified. Phone interviews and e-mail surveys served to establish users' top tasks and skill sets and integrate them into our initial User Roles document. To further flesh out our personas and key usage scenarios, our team used contextual inquiry techniques of Beyer and Holtzblatt [1997] while conducting field research at multiple e-business companies. We interviewed numerous people from the three user types.

Conception and Gestation

Our interviews during the *family planning* stage yielded a wealth of useful but unstructured data that was not immediately actionable by the product team. A multidisciplinary group consisting of usability engineers, designers, project managers, and technical writers went line-by-line through the detailed site visit reports and recorded significant findings on sticky notes. This was followed by "affinity" grouping of the data to outline the top goals, responsibilities, tasks, skills, and tools per user (Figure 2.6). Patterns then emerged through further data

FIGURE 2.6: *An affinity-diagramming exercise in progress in our hallways.*

analysis, which allowed us to group and identify our main set of personas, or "primary" personas, for which we were designing features.

We documented the key attributes of our primary personas into a bulleted table format ("skeleton" personas) that we then used to validate with our stakeholders and subject matter experts. This initial set of primary personas was validated further with representative users and customers at various customer touch points (on-site customer planning events as well as during company visits) by asking participants to compare the personas to themselves or to similar people within their organizations. Overall, customers were enthusiastic about the personas and how they provided a language for talking about their organizations and their needs.

Birth and Maturation

Even before we had fully created our personas, we ran a "Name Your Persona" contest in order to generate early excitement and buy-in from our product teams. The winning entries were voted on by the entire product team. This activity created a sense of closeness and ownership of the personas. We took this campaign further with the catchphrase "Who Are Your Users?" and released information incrementally to build up excitement. We generated even more interest by strategically placing faceless life-size persona silhouettes made of foam board in hallways and at team meetings. A few weeks later, we created persona silhouette posters with key tag lines for each persona (Figure 2.7).

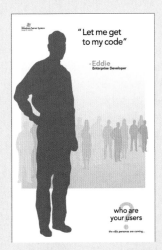 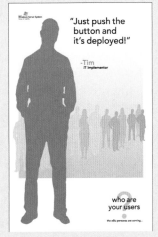 

FIGURE 2.7: *Persona silhouette posters with tag lines.*

(Story from the field, continued)

After collecting sufficient data to build the first version of our personas, we brought the silhouette posters to life by replacing them with pictures of real users. We used internal employees (who did not work on our products) as our persona models. We managed a "model" search and photo shoot internally, which allowed us to reduce our costs and keep our personas looking "natural" and not like professional models. To enhance adoption within our ethnically- and gender-diverse workforce, we felt that it was not critical to use exact demographic characteristics and instead created our personas to reflect that multiculturalism.

In addition to the phased publicity campaign and the creation of a comprehensive persona document, we used other communication methods such as brown bag talks, group meetings, presentations, and e-mail updates to raise awareness and keep the product team interested. Further, a Web site that featured our primary personas was created to serve as a central repository and resource.

Adulthood

Now that personas were created and introduced to the team, it was important that they be put to work. Our first step was to work with marketing to include personas in high-level market requirements documents and vision statements. These documents are generally the starting point for all development work. Thus, making all members of the product group aware of our users through these personas was critical to start the adoption process. We followed this by including personas in the more detailed product requirements document and functional specifications that guide the development of the product. In this way, scenarios that were created to yield product features were based on the primary personas of our products.

Feature creation took shape though iterative prototype design and testing. In the design stages, the personas "stood in" as the users of our product to drive the concept brainstorming, sketching, prototyping, and design recommendations. For example, we took a task-centric approach to our early prototypes versus a feature-centric approach. Persona attributes such as scenarios, tasks, and pain points helped us explore and define potential design opportunities. With additional lab testing, these prototypes provided insights on persona behaviors, task time, and discoverability. The quick turnaround on iterations allowed for a rapid user-centric design process.

We also conducted persona-centric usability baseline studies on specific key tasks in our current E-Business Server products. We organized the studies and tasks by persona and used our persona characteristics to create profile screeners to recruit the appropriate participants. We conducted separate studies for the three user types (System Administrator,

Developer, and Information Worker), and key baselines — such as time to solution and success rate — were reported per persona.

In addition to the usability studies noted previously, the product team conducted several software assurance tests on the product. Here again personas played a role by guiding decisions around how users might be impacted if a particular software issue or "bug" was addressed or not.

Overall, these rich persona attributes guided our UCD approach to the product design concepts, ideas, specs, implementation, and final testing. They allowed us to design an experience that was more targeted toward our users because everyone had a common vision of our users. Using the task-based approach in design, we were able to create a UI [user interface] that allowed the persona to perform key tasks to accomplish his/her main goals.

Lifetime Achievement and Retirement
The adoption of our personas has been fairly widespread across the product group. They were used as a basis for scenarios and use cases, affected feature-based UI design decisions, and influenced strategic planning for the next major product release.

Our E-Business Personas also increased the product team's awareness of our target audience and its goals, skills, tools, and top tasks. Personas helped focus development work, provided a common language for developers and designers, and inspired not just an appreciation for but a buzz around our end users. The vice president in charge of our product cited personas in a kickoff presentation in front of the wider team, they were referenced repeatedly in specifications and scenarios for the new product, and they are mentioned repeatedly in meetings and e-mails. Upper management has even asked the quality assurance team to use the personas in one of their regular "Bug Bash" events.

As we plan for the next version of the product, we are reevaluating the relevance of our primary personas, and looking for finer gaps in our target user audience. Due to product and market changes, we plan to retire three of the seven original personas and create two new personas revealed by our ongoing research. And as we look to grow in global markets, we need to ensure that the needs of our international users are reflected in the personas.

The wealth of customer data and research we have compiled into these personas has also highlighted the most important tasks of our users and the specific pain points they experience performing those tasks with our product. We intend to use this knowledge to drive persona-specific innovations into the product specifications and design of the next release to enable those critical tasks and alleviate the biggest pain points.

Reflections on the Use of Personas

The challenge we faced as a team was to illustrate the value of using personas in the design and development of corporate server products as they are more commonly seen in the consumer product space. By doing so in specific areas of just one product cycle, our team's next challenge is to strengthen their use as a core reference model of our users throughout the next development phase. To do so, we have taken a critical look at what worked well and what needs improvement in our persona process.

Given the small size of our Design and Usability team, and the nontraditional product space, we are very pleased with the overall impact our personas achieved. We are excited about building on them, and continue to find new ways to share persona-based product thinking across the company.

[For lessons learned and best practices from Lincoln and her colleagues, see the sidebar "Story from the field: Personas for E-business Server Products: Lessons Learned and Best Practices" in Chapter 5.]

We believe the E-business Server persona effort worked well because the team was at a strategically good point to introduce personas into their organization. In addition to the persona effort, they simultaneously integrated other UCD methods into the team's product development cycle. Personas were a positive next step in the evolution of their practices. As you probably noted, this case study is primarily descriptive; it does not provide a detailed accounting of *how* they did personas. Instead, it provides the "what" and "why" of one team's persona activities. You will get more of the details on how to do personas in the following chapters.

SUMMARY

The persona process can be thought of in terms of sequential phases that metaphorically map on to the life stages of human reproduction and development. We call this the "persona lifecycle." Framing your persona efforts according to the phases in this lifecycle can help you plan effectively and ultimately succeed in bringing UCD to your product and team.

Each of the following five chapters describes one phase of the lifecycle in detail. For each phase, we cover specific steps, known issues, and common questions — as well as best practices and relevant anecdotes from the field. The persona lifecycle makes it easy to figure out where you are in your persona process and to find the materials that will be most helpful as you move forward. We have designed the next five chapters to provide the right information at the right time as you embark on your own persona effort.

PERSONA FAMILY
PLANNING

3

SETTING THE SCENE: WHAT'S GOING ON IN YOUR ORGANIZATION NOW IF YOU'RE *NOT* USING PERSONAS?

If you are part of a new organization, or if you have yet to launch a product, everyone is likely focusing on how to get started to innovatively fulfill the vision that brought the company together. You can feel the product development cycle wheels starting to turn. Perhaps your new organization is trying to define what is being built and how to design and build it, or perhaps everyone plans on using an established product development process. People in the organization are establishing their roles and territories.

If you have just shipped a product, there is a lot of excitement and relief in the air. The fruits of the team's efforts are finally reaching customers. It feels very satisfying. Congratulations and accolades abound, though there is a bit of anxiety as well. What will happen in the marketplace? Will your product be well received? There is a shift in effort across the team. Some are now moving into high gear to support the product release, whereas others are winding down, having finished the task of building the product. Each team member or stakeholder is focusing on his or her own responsibilities:

- The marketing and sales teams are really busy. The sales team is out there selling the product, and the marketing team is figuring out how the product is doing, looking around to see how the competitive lay of the land is changing and modifying the sales and marketing plans accordingly.

- The executive staff is evangelizing, perhaps on the road meeting with key customers or influential voices in your product space.

- Your customer support team is being barraged with calls, issues, and complaints. Customers are using your product and much is being learned about what works and what does not work in this version.

- Your development team is fixing bugs, working through issues as they arise from the product support team, and supporting the sales engineers.

- The QA team is also focused on aiding the customer support and development teams. They are attempting to reproduce and validate bugs customers are wrangling with.

- The product/project management team—along with the usability, technical writing, and design teams—is either taking a little breather (some much needed downtime) or starting to think about the next big thing. They are also probably doing a bit of process introspection—the so-called "postmortem." They are reevaluating their processes, looking to improve their effectiveness and efficiency the next time around.

If you are part of a smaller organization, many of the same things are happening—the only major difference being that there are fewer people to share the workload and thus many employees wear more than one hat. It is both a perfect and a difficult time to introduce a brand-new method into your organization's product development process.

Before we get started, we would like to introduce you to a fictional company, Gigantic for Kids, Incorporated, or G4K. We will use G4K as a running case study to illustrate some of our main points.

INTRODUCING G4K: A FICTIONAL CASE STUDY

Who Is G4K?

G4K currently specializes in children's software, across the areas of entertainment (games) and education. Their products are distributed through traditional "brick-and-mortar" retail outlets as well as third-party Web retailers.

Why Does G4K Need Personas?

Gigantic has been exploring the viability of the Internet for marketing and distributing their traditional shrink-wrapped software products and for extending their product offerings and business/revenue model. As part of this new strategy, their corporate Web site, *www.G4kids.com*, is soon to become a "destination" site for kids, providing children-oriented entertainment, news, and merchandise primarily related to G4K's existing software offerings.

Although this is not a major departure from their normal business (it is seen simply as an opportunity to build stronger customer loyalty and deeper branding), they are also flirting with the possibility of partnering with other children-focused merchants, potentially offering joint promotions, advertising, and sponsorship (e.g., sponsoring children's events and promoting other noncompeting brands or goods such as clothing, skateboarding equipment, cola companies, and retailers). Although the company does understand their market related to shrink-wrapped software products, which tend to be focused very tightly on specific age groups, they have never dealt with something that potentially spans all of their customers at once. The task is daunting. (For additional information on G4K, including an example persona for their fictitious project, see Appendix A.)

What Does This Case Study Provide?

This case study tells the story of G4K's effort to redefine their existing corporate Web site into a children's destination site. It follows G4K's modest User Experience team, consisting of two people (an interaction designer and a graphic designer, who have recently been moved from a game development team in the company) as they attempt to create and use personas for the first time. Throughout the book, "Meanwhile, at G4K…" case studies provide stories and examples that illustrate major points.

WHAT IS *FAMILY PLANNING* FOR PERSONAS?

Family planning is the first phase in your persona process. It is the time when you will do some investigation and strategic thinking about your organization and its approach to UCD and development. Your personas will not be introduced to the rest of your organization until the *birth and maturation* phase, but the ultimate success you have with them depends a lot on the work you do during the *family planning* phase. It is critical that you use this time to think up front about what happens after the personas are created.

During the *family planning* phase, your first job is to take a realistic look at the problems your team and organization are trying to solve and decide if personas will help. Don't skip this step to save time, even if your team needed personas a month ago. Do a thorough job in examining the personalities and politics that surround you. Only then can you decide if personas are the right way to address the problems facing your organization and product team, and, if so, how you should introduce and maintain the personas to ensure maximum acceptance. If you conclude that personas are appropriate for your team, process, and product needs, you will then be ready to assemble a team, create a plan to ensure that your personas will be used and found helpful, and start collecting data.

We have spent a little time warning you about how much work and time successful personas require. This does not mean, however, that all successful persona efforts require the same amount of work and time. Most organizations cannot afford to dedicate staff members to persona creation and maintenance. As we know all too well, it is tough enough to convince most companies to hire dedicated professionals to pursue user research and UCD. Although we do believe that every persona effort requires a significant amount of attention, we also understand that a full investment in personas is unlikely until the method is proven in your organization, and that you are going to have to explain and justify the work you plan to put into your persona effort. We offer suggestions and identify methods that are particularly helpful—whether your investment in personas is light, moderate, or heavy.

Your level of investment in the persona effort should be directly related to, among other things, the amount of time you can dedicate to the project, the resources beyond your own time you can count on during the effort, the amount of knowledge and focus on users your company already has, and the level of receptivity to new process methods in your organization.

In this chapter we provide many techniques you can use to create your own customized *family planning* process. As with our other chapters, we suggest you approach this chapter as a menu of suggestions rather than a prescribed set of instructions. There are four major activities during the family planning phase.

● Building a core team
● Researching your own organization (organizational introspection)
● Creating an action plan
● Collecting data.

Although we don't recommend that you skip any of the four major activities of the *family planning* phase, we do think you can customize an approach that will allow you to complete these activities given your schedule and resource constraints.

As you begin your persona effort, you should create a persona core team and perform some organizational introspection. The next two sections cover these two activities in detail. Note that core team creation and organizational introspection are, in many ways, highly related and interdependent. For example, creating your core team first is a good idea if you want help in pursuing organizational introspection. However, deciding who to involve in the persona effort might require that you do some of the organizational introspection work before you assemble your core team. Therefore, we suggest that you read both sections before deciding which activity you want to start with.

BUILDING A CORE TEAM

Members of your persona core team will help you complete the *family planning* efforts and work with you throughout the lifecycle. People you invite to join your core team don't necessarily have to understand personas to be helpful. People who are sensitive to the need for user focus in your company will make excellent core team members.

Why do you need a core team?

Your core team members will bring in new perspectives on your organization simply because their jobs are different from yours. Even if your team is just you and one other person, the discussions you will have will provide you with a critical perspective on your work and on the decisions you are making that you simply cannot arrive at by yourself. Without another person to work with, you will have a difficult time isolating your own assumptions and biases and keeping them out of the personas. You need a persona core team because:

- Personas can be a lot of work for just one person.
- Discussion and debate are critical activities in the persona creation process.
- Getting your personas accepted and used requires cross-organizational buy-in.

Although it helps to have people with various talents and experiences, the most important qualifications for participation on a persona core team are a desire to understand users, and be an advocate for them, and a willingness to experiment with new methods. Consider the selection of your persona core team members as an exercise in political and organizational strategy. If certain groups or key individuals are excluded from the process, you may be shut down right out of the gate.

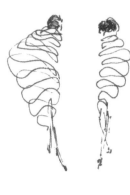

How many people should be on your core team?

This is a question only you can answer, because it depends on the goals you have for the persona effort, the number of people in your organization, the talents and interests of your colleagues, and other factors. In most cases, we have found that effective persona core teams include a minimum of two and a maximum of 10 members. In our experience, teams with over 10 members require too much coordination and quickly become unmanageable. The ideal persona core team has three to five active members and several other members in an advisory or on-call role.

Active persona core team members should be available to come to most meetings and actively participate in all life phases. Advisory (on-call) members might be people such as graphic designers (who can step in to help with posters), a data mining expert (who could do a few specific analyses for your effort), or a friendly software developer (who can give you advice on how best to approach the rest of the software developers). In the following sections we help you identify and recruit colleagues for your core team.

Who should be on your core team?

Your goal is not to create a team that will duplicate research or communication efforts. Rather, it is to consolidate some aspects of these efforts such that they all contribute to the creation of personas. Plan to include the people who are already involved in user research, market research, business analysis, task analysis, or any other user- or customer-focused research or profiling activity. If you have colleagues in any of the following specialties, you should put them on the short list for inclusion on the core team:

- Information architects, interaction designers, and Human-Computer Interaction (HCI) specialists
- Usability specialists, user researchers, and ethnographers
- Technical writers, documentation specialists, and training specialists
- Market researchers, business analysts, and product managers.

These colleagues are likely to understand the value of personas, both for the organization and for their own projects. They bring with them a deep commitment to UCD, experience studying, analyzing, and designing solutions for target users, and an interest in new methods to bring user focus into the entire organization.

PERSONAS CAN HELP YOUR COMPANY INTERNALLY, TOO

—Max Gadney, BBC News Interactive

We have found that personas are useful in uniting different departments in a large company. There are often departments such as marketing, product development, and design that have limited contact with each other—a shame as all are working toward a positive user experience. Different departments often need to gather different types of data, and there can be a little tension and competition. A proper persona effort should involve data from each of these departments, thus bringing their efforts together into a useful whole and validating all their work.

Think strategically as you create your team

Be strategic in your selection of team members. For example, if your marketing team traditionally "owns" the definition of your company's target audience and wields significant power and influence with the executive staff, it would be foolhardy not to include someone from that team. Be wary of the "not invented here" syndrome. Getting broad strategic involvement can help ensure that other teams don't try to redefine the target audience after your personas are in place.

PARTICIPATION FROM ALL CAMPS

—Lene Byskov, Dialog Design

One important lesson we learned regarding persona creation is that you must involve as many parties as possible when creating the personas to ensure that the final result includes thought from all "camps"—developers, tech writers, and usability experts.

To round out your team, approach colleagues from other disciplines. Consider team members who would not traditionally be involved with these types of activities but have team-wide respect or de facto leadership responsibilities. For example, a developer lead, highly respected QA tester, or key program or product manager might be your best ally in getting your persona efforts accepted and assimilated. Remember that you are asking for a scarce resource when you ask for their time. Craft a clear message that expresses why you think their participation in the persona effort will benefit them personally in their jobs (in addition to benefiting the company as a whole). See also "Bright Idea: Create an Elevator Pitch" later in the chapter.

Story from the field

A DIFFERENT POINT OF VIEW ON CORE TEAMS

—Kim Goodwin, VP, Design, Cooper

When people begin bringing personas into their organizations, they have a tendency to build core teams of half a dozen or so people who participate heavily in each stage of the process. This is understandable, since this is one way people attempt to build buy-in.

As consultants whose costs and timelines get scrutinized very carefully, we've found at Cooper that it's entirely possible to do this process with fewer people, more quickly, and at least as well, provided you include the right skill sets and set up specific ways to involve the larger team. (Note that we advocate using personas as part of a larger process called "Goal-Directed Design," which helps translate these useful archetypes into design solutions. Please see www.cooper.com for more information about this method.) This isn't just a useful approach for consultants, though— our clients who have adopted our methods tell us it works well for their internal teams, too.

Start by getting the right mix of skills on the core team

The obvious role to include in the core team is an experienced **interaction designer**. This is someone who not only has a good understanding of human factors, cognition, and good design principles, but who also has strong visualization skills. This doesn't necessarily mean they're graphic designers, though visual literacy is very helpful. It means they can quickly go from understanding the problem to sketching a concrete solution on the whiteboard, then throwing it out and immediately sketching a different solution if the first one breaks. (Many companies don't yet have an interaction designer role. That doesn't mean they can't benefit from using personas. However, I've seen far better success rates in companies that create an explicit designer role and hire skilled people to fill it.)

The other role we routinely involve in our core teams at Cooper is what we call a **design communicator**. The role originated when we decided to hire some strong writers to save the interaction designers' time in documentation. We quickly realized that the right sort of person is not just a scribe, but is an effective partner in the design process. Design communicators often come from technical writing or project management backgrounds. By inclination, they're not usually the people generating the ideas, but they help iterate and improve the design by clarifying fuzzy concepts or behavior, questioning assumptions, and making sure each idea is fully articulated. Whereas interaction designers think visually and spatially, design communicators generally have a strong narrative sense; when an interaction designer draws a sketch, the design communicator insists on seeing what state the screen is in when it starts, what happens next, and what happens after that.

The two roles are full-time on the project. They conduct the research, craft the personas, and generate the design spec. Having these two specific, complementary roles helps us iterate the design very quickly and ensures that the work is thorough. In research and persona creation, having the two complementary roles helps make sure we get the most out of interviews, question one another's assumptions and assertions about the personas, and help each other anticipate the concerns and questions of stakeholders.

In some cases, a third team member will join some of the interviews. This may be the person supervising the project, but could also be a visual designer, industrial designer, or a junior interaction designer or design communicator. This additional person mostly observes the interview or only asks questions at the end, since having three people asking questions can get unwieldy.

Plan on three levels of involvement, rather than two

Rather than having just a "core team" and "everyone else," consider three levels of involve-ment. It's most efficient to have two or three people conduct the interviews and create the per-sonas, since they have all the same first-hand data. However, you do need the expertise and consensus of key stakeholders, so you'll need a somewhat larger team of people who are involved at key points, but aren't actually doing the research, user modeling, or design. The ideal stakeholder group usually consists of managers from development, marketing, and sales; a senior executive or program manager responsible for making trade-off decisions between the ideal product and the timeline or cost; a domain subject matter expert or two if it's a business product; and anyone else whose knowledge or influence are critical to product direction and success. The third level of involvement, of course, is the rest of the project team or company, who meet the personas after you've reached consensus with the stakeholders. The core team of two or three people should first interview each stakeholder to understand their point of view, absorb critical knowledge, and listen to concerns and fears. The core team should draft the research plan with one or two stakeholders (usually from marketing), then conduct all of the research themselves and draft the persona descriptions for stakeholders to review. After that, the personas are introduced to the larger team, and the core team begins the interaction design work.

The people doing the design should do the research and personas

Although user research and personas have many uses, their primary purpose is to help us design successful products. For this reason, it is most effective to have the people who will do the interaction design also drive the research and persona creation.

I've never met a skilled interaction designer who couldn't quickly pick up enough ethnographic techniques to do effective user research; it may not be good enough for a doctoral thesis, but it's exactly what's needed for design later on. Conversely, non-designers who are very skilled in research lack the experience to know what's going to be important later in the process. What's worse is that if the interaction designers aren't doing the firsthand research, they will miss nuance and detail they'll need later in the process; even the most thorough report is less effective than seeing and hearing things in person.

Building consensus another way

The obvious challenge with this small-team approach is building consensus with the stakeholders. At Cooper, we've found there are only a few points where stakeholders really need to be involved (though managing that process is probably worth an entire book in itself). First, get the stakeholders who are most concerned about whether you understand the users and customers to help you craft the research plan. If the amount of time required starts to get excessive, ask a senior executive or other project owner to help make the trade-off choices. Next, meet with stakeholders individually to learn from their knowledge and to understand their goals, concerns, and pet peeves. Do your user research and create the personas, then get all the stakeholders in a room together to review the personas. Make sure they believe these are accurate representations that cover the necessary range of user and customer needs. After that, you need another meeting to get consensus on major requirements, then a few design review meetings as you progress. Once you're past the initial design concept, most of those meetings generally involve just a developer and a subject matter expert, with mediation from the project owner if what's desirable and what's feasible seem to conflict.

Typical objections to this approach

When it comes to having just two or three people do the research, the most common objection is that direct exposure to users and customers helps other team members empathize with them. This is certainly true. However, it's equally possible to build empathy and understanding by showing photos of real workspaces you saw, quoting actual things users said, and publicizing a compelling, realistic set of personas. The fact is that empathy is the only thing most team members need from those user interviews, and that doesn't require attending them. The other problem with too many people doing a few interviews is that even once you have a set of personas, people will tend to focus on the one or two interviewees they saw (along with their associated idiosyncrasies), rather than focusing on the more important pattern.

Many people ask, "But isn't it more efficient to have all the knowledge you need in the room at the same time?" When you're creating personas, the only information that matters is what you saw in the research, not what's in people's heads. That information, if it conflicts with the research, can even be problematic. In addition, the more people you have in the room, the more slowly things progress. When I teach design courses, the groups of two or three people tend to progress at twice the speed of the groups that contain four or more, and their results are at least as good.

As you round out your core team, consider the individuals discussed in the following sections:

Marketing Professionals

- *What they can add:* Perspective and clarity on business goals, insight into your company's outward-facing communication strategies, and clarity in describing "customers and influencers" versus the "users" of your products.

- *Why they benefit from joining the team:* Marketers can bring new insights into the needs and interests of the users of the products they are trying to market, which can help craft messages that appeal to the business goals of customers.

Market Research Professionals

- *What they can add:* Access to and understanding of all internal and external data sources related to identifying and appealing to target customers, and a deep knowledge of your company's existing market segmentation (or other customer classification system).

- *Why they benefit from joining the team:* Personas provide a new vehicle for getting market research data "heard" and used in the organization. The persona effort also identifies where holes in current research lie. As you build the personas, you will find areas of customer and user knowledge that are missing from your current information sources, and can plan future research projects to round out corporate knowledge accordingly.

Business Analysts

- *What they can add:* Understanding of workflow and context in which your product will be used, experience looking at the big picture of user experience, familiarity with users' work environments, and knowledge of competitive and complementary products and distinctions between your product's purchasers, users, and influencers.

- *Why they benefit from joining the team:* Personas reflect the user insights that business analysts uncover and provide a new channel for getting this information integrated into product design and decision making.

Data Mining, Analysis, and Statistics Professionals

- *What they can add:* Access to internal raw data stores, ability to reanalyze existing raw data to extract new information relevant to personas, and ability to translate broad questions into specific, targeted queries that can yield clear answers.

- *Why they benefit from joining the team:* Like market researchers, data miners and analysts find that personas are a new way of humanizing information that arises from data. The persona effort also identifies new and important questions that can turn into fruitful data mining and analysis projects.

Bright Idea

IF THEY JOIN YOU, THEY WON'T TRY TO BEAT YOU

Take a personal inventory of who is going to be the most vocal and influential person against personas and arrange to spend some time with them (e.g., have lunch). Discuss your company's target audience and its ability to identify, communicate, and use this information. See if you can get them interested in, or at least try to agree on, one problem you both think the organization has that personas might help with (perhaps phrased as "Wouldn't you agree that we need a clearer, more useful definition of our target audience?"). Invite them to join the persona team, at least as an advisor. Ask them to help you identify the issues that will be the most difficult for the organization to address.

Product Managers, Program Managers, and Development Managers

● *What they can add:* Key perspective on what product development teams need from the personas, and deep understanding of the interests and resistances of development teams related to new methods.

● *Why they benefit from joining the team:* They can help to produce completed personas that exemplify the target users of the product, whose names and descriptions will serve to clarify product feature discussions and aid in prioritization and documentation.

Customer Support Professionals

● *What they can add:* A close connection to customer issues, needs, and requests, and possibly contact information for good (or unhappy) customers to be interviewed.

● *Why they benefit from joining the team:* Customer support teams have a keen interest in affecting the development team. Participating in the persona effort will allow them to use their knowledge of customer pain points to impact product development and demonstrate their value to the company as a resource.

Sales Professionals

● *What they can add:* Direct connection to customer needs and feature requests, insight into business opportunities, and a resource for potential recruits for interviews.

● *Why they benefit from joining the team:* Sales teams have a vested interest in influencing the development team and the state of the resulting product, which helps ensure that the product contains what their customers are asking for.

Developers

● *What they can add:* Invaluable insight into the needs and issues of the development staff, and service as liaisons to the more technical staff in your organization.

● *Why they benefit from joining the team:* Many developers are interested in creating user-centered products. The persona effort will give them insights into how user data can be collected and communicated. Try to find developers who are interested in moving into management positions, and emphasize the team-building and communication benefits of personas.

Graphics and Interface Designers

● *What they can add:* An array of visual communication talents and ideas, and usually a historical perspective on the difficulties involved in communicating their own understanding of user interests to product teams.

● *Why they benefit from joining the team:* Personas will offer them a handy tool for targeting design explorations and for communicating with the larger product team. Involvement in the persona core team also enables designers to get involved much earlier in the product design process, which is beneficial to the designers and to the finished product.

WE'RE ALL TRYING TO ANSWER THE SAME QUESTION

—**Ken Seiff,** Founder of Bluefly.com and CEO, Glowcast Ventures

One of the common difficulties organizations face is that there are so many well-intentioned team members who are collaborating, each with a slightly different understanding of who the customer is and what they really want. For years now, our efforts to build a customer-centric culture have been measurably slowed as we struggled with these questions. The concept of personas has given us a simple and powerful tool to cut through this knot and achieve a real understanding of what our customers want.

Be ready to ask your colleagues for their time

Time is always at a premium. Before you assemble your team for the first meeting, think through your schedule and estimate how much time you can free up to dedicate to the persona effort. Remember that you and your team will need significantly more time at the beginning of the persona effort (i.e., for the *conception and gestation* and *birth and maturation phases*) than you will need to maintain the personas (e.g., during the *adulthood* phase). Can you create a pocket of time in your calendar to dedicate most of your energy to the persona effort? Is there a time of year when things slow down significantly at your company? Can you block out time during this slow period, perhaps 5 to 10 hours a week for several weeks, to dedicate to personas? If you can't block off entire days or weeks for persona work, can you find at least an hour or two during the week that you can consistently dedicate to this effort?

Note that our sample agenda for your first team meeting (in material to follow) we suggest that you start with an overview of personas and their value. We recommend that you discuss these topics with each of the people you want to invite to your core team well before the first meeting. Garnering individual support will help the group meeting go more smoothly. If this isn't possible, it is a good idea to start off by generating interest and enthusiasm. Once everyone in the room understands the value of the project you are proposing (and understands that all you are really asking for is that they bring insights and interests they probably already have), they will be more likely to adapt their schedules and find the time to participate.

As you start your project, it will be difficult to predict the amount of work and time your team will need to create and maintain effective personas. Plan to meet for at least one hour a week. In addition, agree on a specific date when you want to reach the *birth and maturation* phase (in which you will launch the personas to the organization) and, working backward, how you want to schedule your *conception and gestation* work (for an example schedule, see "Identify milestones and deliverables" later in this chapter).

FIND A WILLING "LUNCHTIME ADVISOR"

Your persona effort will live or die by the quality of thinking and communication associated with it. You need to get used to talking about what personas are, what they are not, why they work, how they will work in your organization, how you made choices about your own persona process, and so on. When it comes to personas, you should take every opportunity to polish your message and your communication techniques, and your lunchtime advisor can help you do this.

If there is someone who would be helpful to you but who does not have the time or willingness to join the core team, ask if he or she is interested enough to sign up to have lunch with you on a regular basis. During your lunchtime conversations, convey your progress and describe the decisions you have been making. Ask your advisor to brainstorm on methods of communicating these decisions to the organization once you "give birth" to the personas. These conversations will help you streamline your story, prepare for the pushback you are bound to encounter, and keep perspective as the persona effort progresses.

Key people don't have to be on the core team to be helpful

If key people don't have time to participate as full members of the core team, ask them if they would be willing to be advisors and serve "on call." Keep in mind that your core team's responsibilities and needs will change as the lifecycle progresses. For example, the *family planning* and *conception and gestation* phases can easily progress without a graphic designer, but the *birth and maturation* phase is much easier with a graphic designer than without one. Similarly, data analysts might lose some interest once the personas are created and leave the major persona communication activities to others (however, it is good to keep them involved in case questions arise regarding specific research findings or data-related characteristics of your personas).

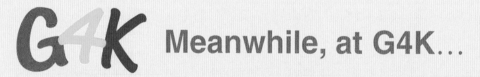

Meanwhile, at G4K...

G4K ASSEMBLES A CORE TEAM TO CREATE PERSONAS

Several people in the games development groups at G4K have been asked to work on the new G4K portal project. Ingrid, an interaction designer and the company's only person responsible for usability testing, is one of these folks. She had heard about personas at a professional conference and recently saw an article on the Web highlighting a persona success story. She thinks the technique would be useful to try here. Ingrid runs the idea past her close colleague Graham (a graphic designer) and together they agree to do it.

(Meanwhile, at G4K...,continued)

The persona technique is brand new to G4K. Not many people at the company have ever heard of it. In addition, although user testing and a few other UCD techniques are sometimes incorporated in the development of G4K products, the notion of doing any type of user profile is simply nonexistent. Ingrid and Graham know they have their work cut out for them.

Their first step is to discuss the technique with the project lead, Paula. She thinks the idea is a bit overboard (not really needed), but it might be useful for some aspects of their work. So, Paula says she will help out a bit with it. Ingrid and Graham know how busy Paula is going to be, so they decide to use her time sparingly. Paula will be both a part-time contributor to the effort and a stakeholder (a key recipient of the end product of the personas).

Ingrid and Graham also approach Michael, the company's only market research professional. Michael has key knowledge of both market trends and customer segments that will be crucial for appropriately defining and prioritizing the personas. He also understands the business better than most people at the company. Although Michael is not directly assigned to the portal project, he will be a key but part-time participant in this effort.

Finally, Ingrid and Graham approach Theo, one of the company's technical writers. Theo has written a range of content for G4K—from user guides to marketing copy and Web site text to storyline content directly in their game products. Theo is no stranger to thinking about target audiences and is intrigued by the notion of personas. The portal project is one of many things on Theo's work list, and thus like several others his involvement will be somewhat limited.

Paula, Michael, and Theo will all be active participants in the persona efforts. However, due to their time limitations and focus they will need to do this on an "on call" basis. Because of this, Ingrid and Graham will be the ones truly responsible for getting everything done, and will likely handle any of the grunt work that needs to happen.

The persona core team consists of:

- *Ingrid:* Interaction-design/usability person from the games group
- *Graham:* Graphic designer.

The persona "on call" team consists of:

- *Paula:* Project lead for the new Web site
- *Michael:* Market research person
- *Theo:* Technical writer.

If you decide to create a core team of three to five members and an extended "on call" team, consider conducting some basic information sessions for the entire group at scheduled milestones and sending notes to the core and "on call" teams. It is helpful to keep everyone on the same page throughout the project, so that you don't have to spend a lot of time getting extended team members up to speed individually. Regularly scheduled full-team review sessions are also helpful for keeping the entire project on schedule and for obtaining reality checks from team members who haven't been steeped in the work to date.

Handy Detail

THE MORE BRAINS THE BETTER

The value of having more than one person creating the personas usually outweighs the value of taking longer to create the personas. Opt for quick collaborations over extended solitary projects when it comes to your persona projects.

Think about your budget

Successful persona efforts don't have to be expensive, but it helps to have some money to dedicate to the effort. How big your budget is will depend on your organization's acceptance of personas and how well funded your project is. Big-ticket items might include:

- Third-party research
- Paying participants for user studies
- Conducting site visits or focus groups
- Give-aways you will distribute during the *birth and maturation* phase
- Designing and creating full-color posters or brochures
- Web development.

If you don't have a large budget, there are some less expensive persona strategies (and there are many in this book) that can provide excellent results. For example, consider using secondary sources of data such as anecdotes and case studies (see the section "Collect data through secondary sources" later in this chapter) if it is difficult to justify the expense of conducting your own research.

What if I can't create a core team?

If you simply can't gather a team of three to five people willing to participate in an ongoing persona effort, don't worry, you can still create effective personas. Consider enlisting *any* enthusiastic person from your team who gets excited about users (and the idea of personas) and can dedicate some time to helping, even if they wouldn't otherwise be your first choice. Consider colleagues who have previously expressed an interest in learning more about UCD or making a career change to UCD.

Read and consider the questions in the "Researching your own organization" section (following) and identify one problem that some basic personas might help to solve and aim specifically for that problem. Limit the scope of your project and your expectations for the personas. You should be able to see benefits even if you end up working alone on persona creation.

If you are working alone, try to find at least one other person to act as a sounding board. Request that they simply review some of the plan, decisions, and materials with you in a series of short, regular meetings. Alternatively, reconsider the scope of your persona effort and approach potential team members with a new plan. For example, perhaps you can create the basic personas over the course of a single week, or even during a one-day offsite effort. (See the section "What are assumption personas and why use them?" later in this chapter. Assumption personas are quick and easy to create and can quickly demonstrate the value of focusing on a well-defined target persona.)

Plan your first persona team meeting

As the coordinator of your new persona core and "on call" teams, it is your job to moderate the first few discussions. The first few meetings can be critical to getting the momentum started in the right direction. Beyond educating your new team on what personas are and the process you will be using to create and maintain the personas, you also have to make sure the core team gels.

Your immediate goal is to build a cohesive, bought-in persona core team. To do this, you are going to have to become an educator and evangelist for the method. This is a great dress-rehearsal opportunity in preparing for the large-scale education and evangelism work you will do during the *birth and maturation* phase. Before you approach prospective team members, think about what they know and don't know about the persona method. If personas are new to your organization, you will need to start with the basics and teach prospective team members enough to understand:

- What personas are and why they are helpful
- The persona lifecycle and how you envision using personas in your organization
- Why you are asking for their help and how they can contribute to the effort.

Bright Idea

CONDUCT A PERSONA POSTMORTEM

If your organization has used personas (or some other profiling technique) for a past product cycle, consider holding a one-hour postmortem meeting with key people involved with that effort, along with your new persona team. During the meeting, you will want to discuss four main topics:

- How the personas were used previously
- What went well
- What did not go well
- What solutions could be put in place to fix the problems.

If you walk away with only two or three items per topic, you will be way ahead of the game this time through. You might find that previous personas suffered an untimely demise (they may have been unceremoniously murdered in one of the darker hallways of your office, for example), and you certainly don't want your fresh new personas to meet similar fates.

If personas have already been used in your organization, your potential team members should understand the basics, but they will probably need more information regarding what worked and what did not work the last time personas were used. They will also need to understand the vision behind this new project. Are you updating existing personas? Are you trying to completely reengineer the persona or development process? Either way, your job is to refresh your colleagues' understanding of personas and give them some context for the upcoming persona effort.

If this is your organization's first foray into persona use, it is unlikely that you will be able to fully explain the theory and process in a single meeting. Instead, plan to present an overview and then

fill in more information in subsequent meetings. Your core team will get more excited about the project if they can get started and see results as soon as possible. The following is a sample agenda for your first core team meeting.

- *20 minutes:* Overview of personas
  - ○ What are personas?
  - ○ How are they different from what we already do?
  - ○ Why do we need them? What problems will they help us solve?
- *20 minutes:* Core team logistics
  - ○ Brief overview of the persona lifecycle
  - ○ Introduction of team members and what each brings to the project
  - ○ Discussion of time and resources; decisions on meeting times
- *10 minutes:* Plan for the next steps
  - ○ Brief overview of organizational introspection

Work to create a solid agenda for every core team meeting, but be aware that questions about the persona method will arise regularly throughout the process. It can take a few meetings to establish a common language around the persona effort and to solidify the long-term plan and goals of the effort. The next three sections (on researching your own organization, creating a plan, and identifying data sources and collecting data) offer actionable suggestions that will help your team get off to a productive start.

RESEARCHING YOUR OWN ORGANIZATION (ORGANIZATIONAL INTROSPECTION)

If you are reading this book, it is likely that some part of your job involves careful analysis of a product's users and the environment or context in which the product will be used. You are probably accustomed to thinking about and evaluating your users' (or customers' or influencers') needs, goals, environment, pressures, and any other information that helps you build products they will love. Those of us who have built careers around being user centered will likely "get" the idea of personas immediately. We can see how great it will be to have exemplary, archetypal people to refer to. Personas can seem obviously worthwhile once you learn about and use them. It can be easy to forget that your colleagues need to be convinced.

Successful personas are those that meet the needs of *their* users and are built to fit seamlessly into their host environments. In the case of personas, the users are your colleagues, and the environment is your workplace with its existing design and development process.

Ironically, it is easy to forget to turn our analytic eyes on our users, the people on our teams and in our organizations who use the products we produce (e.g., research reports, storyboards, scenarios, prototypes, and other artifacts). We forget to carefully consider who our teammates are; what their roles, responsibilities, and goals are; and what is working for them currently and what is not. We launch our bright fresh exciting user-focused ideas into teams who are interested and curious but who ultimately just need to get their jobs done. As far as most product teams are concerned, they already know the fastest and most effective ways of doing their jobs. When push comes to shove and deadlines loom closer, your colleagues will inevitably revert to tried-and-true work habits.

Luckily, you have all the tools you need to understand your colleagues and workplace from this new perspective. That is, you can put your UCD skills to work *on your own colleagues*. If you create personas and push them out to your colleagues without carefully considering these things, your personas will die on the vine. The time to start predicting your organization's reactions to personas is right now. You have probably touched on some of these topics in team discussions of process or in postmortems. Now it is time to dive in and figure out what makes your colleagues tick and how they get their jobs done. This information will help you when it is time to get ready for the persona *birth and maturation* and *adulthood* phases.

We define "organizational introspection" as the process of evaluating the problems and needs of your company, organization, and product team. Organizational introspection is, in simple terms, working to answer the following questions:

- How user focused is your company?
- How do people think and communicate about users?
- How is user information incorporated into the product design and development process?

You will find many answers to these questions by exploring how your company and team currently measure the success of your products and processes. The answers you find to these questions will enable you to plan your persona effort both strategically and tactically as you:

- Decide whether personas will be appropriate and helpful
- Predict the challenges you are likely to encounter as you create, introduce, facilitate use of, and maintain your personas
- Create a plan for your persona effort that will target the application of your personas to appropriate aspects of your development process.

No matter how you gather it, you will use the information about your organization and your personas' audience to create a persona action plan, which will include both strategic and tactical action items you and your core persona team will use throughout the lifecycle.

Question 1: How user-focused is your company?

Every company is different. The best way to ensure the success of your persona effort is to understand the context in which the personas will be used. If you understand the way your company currently operates, you will be able to fully appreciate the changes you will be asking for regarding the persona process. You will also be able to predict when and how you will encounter hurdles and roadblocks.

How can I answer this question?

This question is asking for the big picture of your company when it comes to UCD. In other words, does your company already understand and value UCD? If so, how much and in what ways? If you don't have much time and are planning to start small with your persona effort, you can answer this question by discussing the topics explored in the following sections with your core team.

Does your company *believe* it is user focused?

Look for examples of ways your company describes itself, your products, and your culture. Do these descriptions include reference to customer or user focus? Find copies of your company's business plan, product brochures, Web site, and press releases. In these (and any other) materials:

- Is your *company* described as user or customer focused?
- Does your company describe the *products* it produces in terms of how easy they are to use and/or in terms of how well they satisfy customer needs?
- Is user focus part of your corporate culture?

If you find references to customer or user focus, you can use these references to help you describe the value of the persona effort.

Does your company *act* in a user-focused manner?

It is one thing for a company to describe itself and its products as user focused; it is another thing to "walk the walk" and put resources into UCD. Where does your company put its resources when it comes to product design? For example, does your company engage in the following:

- User research
- Usability evaluation
- Rough prototyping
- Market research

- Product support
- Training
- User-facing documentation
- Design?

If so, are the people who do these activities full-time employees of your company or consultants or contracted employees? Companies fully dedicated to UCD typically hire UCD professionals as full-fledged members of the product team. If your company contracts out some of these activities, you might have a more difficult time helping stakeholders understand why you want to spend resources on personas. Alternatively, if you already have agencies providing one or more of the services listed previously, you might consider adding persona creation to existing contracts and collaborating with these outsourced providers on the best ways to approach persona creation and user focus in your company (see "Decide when and how to involve consultants" in material following). Additional related questions to consider include:

- How does your company decide what products and services to create?
- Do you start with market and user research and build technology to meet the needs you discover, or do you tend to start with interesting technology and work to find ways to make that technology interesting to customers?
- Does your company define target audiences before or after it decides which products to work on?
- How does your company measure the success of its products, services, and internal processes? Specifically, is the success of any product measured in terms of user or customer satisfaction?
- Does your company follow up on promises to customers and users?
- Are product teams judged on how easy their products are to use, or on how fast the products are completed?
- If you were to ask your customers how user focused your company and products are, what would they say? For example, do they love, hate, or simply tolerate your products?

If you have more time or don't think you can answer these questions without some research, your core team's first project could be to create and administer a questionnaire exploring these topics and assessing the knowledge and opinions of your organizational (internal) customers. Whether you administer this questionnaire broadly across your organization or company or limit the respondents to key members of your product team, we expect that you will find convincing evidence to support the need of employing personas and other UCD methods. For examples of questions you might include in your UCD questionnaire, see "Story from the field: Using a Questionnaire to Find Out How User Centered Your Organization Really Is."

Story from the field

USING A QUESTIONNAIRE TO FIND OUT HOW USER CENTERED YOUR ORGANIZATION REALLY IS

—Lisa Mason, Windows eHome PC, Microsoft Corporation

In March of 2002, an article appeared on zdnet on software rage (*http://zdnet.com.com/ 2100-1107-854270.html*). The article stated that users have lost faith in Microsoft because "Computer owners and software developers seem to have fundamentally different visions of who should use programs, and in particular, who's responsible when things go wrong." This article spawned an interesting discussion among members of my product team, Windows eHome PC Division, about what we could be doing better to represent our customers' needs throughout the product cycle. As part of that discussion, we decided to send out a questionnaire to employees across several different but related divisions (for the sake of comparison), to let them voice their opinions on whether they thought their team was doing an adequate job of understanding and addressing their customers' needs. Our goal was to learn:

1. Were the various divisions incorporating UCD principles into their development processes, and if so to what extent?
2. Did the employees understand UCD and what were their attitudes toward UCD in general?
3. Were the divisions working together toward achieving UCD?

We created a Web-based survey that included the following statements, which where to be rated on a three-point scale (I agree, no opinion, I disagree):

1. Cross-Group Collaboration
   - Collaborating with individuals in other divisions is an essential part of my job.
   - It is clear why I need to collaborate with people in other divisions.
   - I know who I need to collaborate with in other divisions.
   - Individuals in other divisions understand why it is important to collaborate with me.
   - Collaborating with individuals in other divisions is difficult.
   - List any projects or situations where you thought the collaboration between Division A and Division B had gone well.
   - List any projects or situations where you thought the collaboration between Division A and Division B had not gone well.
   - What do you believe should happen to make cross-division collaboration more productive? (Verbatim Response)
2. Setting Business Goals
   - I have a good understanding of my product's target market.
   - Information about my product's target market is effectively communicated to me.

- What sources inside the company do you rely on for information about users? (Verbatim Response)
- What suggestions do you have for making information about your target markets more readily available? (Verbatim Response)

3. Understanding Users
   - Visiting customers in their own environment helps me do my job better.
   - My team values observing users in their own environment.
   - My team has identified what users want to accomplish with a product like ours.
   - My team has identified *how* users accomplish tasks with our product.
   - My team has a list of key user scenarios we are trying to address with our product.
   - In the last six months, how many customers have you been out to visit in their own environment? (Verbatim Response)
   - What can be done to give you a better understanding of your customers? (Verbatim Response)

4. Assessing Competitiveness
   - I know my product's primary competition.
   - Information about my product's primary competition is effectively communicated to me.
   - I understand why users choose our competitors' products.
   - I understand both the strengths and weaknesses of my product's competitors.

We allowed two weeks for responses and then collected and evaluated the results. From this, we learned that we were doing some things very well. Across divisions, we were going a good job of:

1. Communicating information about our target markets to our divisions
2. Communicating information about our competitors
3. Instilling the value of customer contact into Microsoft employees
4. Using scenarios to design our user experiences.

However, our team members also had a lot to say about where we could improve. Specifically, they suggested that we:
1. Develop and confirm user scenarios *earlier* in the development process
2. Increase usability and design involvement in the development process, and allow more time for both
3. Improve our cross-group work by clearly defining ownership and responsibilities
4. Change our attitudes toward users by:
   a. Listening to our customers
   b. Not discounting them as being non-savvy
   c. Designing for users, not ourselves
   d. Valuing quality over ship dates
   e. Focusing on users' needs, not technology.

Armed with this information, we set out to improve our processes. We made several changes, which included integrating more UCD methods into our existing processes (including some work with personas), rewarding team members for participating in usability activities, and tracking usability bugs in our bug database. Although we are excited about the progress, we know that these new processes are really just baby steps in the user design process. With each release, we plan to revisit this valuable data and implement processes to address these needs.

How can I use this information?

Through your examination of company documents, discussion with your core team, and employment of a UCD focus questionnaire, you will find some useful information to help you build your persona campaign. The answers you find will help you plan the education and evangelism aspects of your persona effort. At a high level, you might conclude:

- Our company is technically oriented
- Our company is competitor oriented
- Our company is marketing oriented (marketing decides everything)
- Our company is customer or user focused.

If your company is technically or competitor oriented, you will probably have to plan to start small with your persona effort and build understanding and appreciation of the value of UCD over time. When you first try to create personas, you will likely find yourself wanting to use personas for every project and for solving every problem. You won't be able to see how any good work can be done without personas. However, if you try to start big you will increase the already considerable risk that the personas, and everything associated with them, will be rejected wholesale. Consider doing personas for a single product or subset of features. If you can wait to present the personas to larger groups until you have a success story with a single product or small feature set, you will have a much easier time convincing others that personas are worth knowing about.

If your company is marketing, customer, or user focused, you will have to spend less time explaining the value of UCD and more time on the specific ways personas can and should be used as part of a user-centered development process. Consider the conclusions found by Lisa Mason's team (see the previous "Story from the field: Using a Questionnaire to Find Out How User Centered Your Organization Really Is."). Lisa found that there were many ways in which the organizations she queried were already user focused, and that the improvements being asked for had more to do with honing existing methods rather than with starting from scratch. If we were using this information ourselves to plan a persona effort, we would:

- Take advantage of the fact that her organization is already highly invested in being user centered (e.g., plan not to spend a lot of time re-convincing colleagues of the value of UCD, but do plan to help everyone understand the relationship between personas and other UCD methods already in use)

- Identify existing processes that are going well and create personas to complement rather than replace these (e.g., existing communication strategies around target markets and competition)

- Describe personas to stakeholders as essential to improving problematic aspects of the process (e.g., describe the value of personas for facilitating cross-team collaboration and "forcing" user-centered thinking earlier in the development process)

- Build and communicate personas quickly, and plan to continue to develop them over time (to prove that they can help very early in the development process).

Bright Idea

RE-ADMINISTER THE UCD QUESTIONNAIRE AFTER YOUR PROJECT!

In Chapter 7, we provide ideas for how to measure the ROI of your persona effort. One great way to measure the before-and-after difference is to administer the same UCD focus questionnaire at the end of the project. You will be able to point to quantifiable differences in the level of user focus shared by the entire product team.

Question 2: How does your organization think and communicate about users?

Whereas the first question is likely to identify hurdles you will face in your persona effort, this question will help you identify opportunities. You will probably find many inconsistencies in the ways your colleagues currently refer to users, and it should be fairly easy to explain why these inconsistencies could be harming your processes and products.

How can I answer this question?

The easiest way to answer this question is to gather documents and other materials related to a recent release of a product or current project. Feature specification documents, vision documents, use-case collections, and other planning documentation usually contain references to target users. Look back through such documents from a previous product release and collect every reference to users you can find. They will likely occur in association with use cases and scenarios. They may be simple references to user roles or customer segments. However they appear, copy them directly into a spreadsheet or text document and take notes on their use. Consider the following when looking through these artifacts:

- What is the language used to refer to users?
- How are users' characteristics, goals, needs, and behavior described?

Bright Idea

ASK YOUR COLLEAGUES TO DEFINE THE WORDS THEY USE WHEN THEY REFER TO USERS

If your market segments are used as a type of shorthand for the term *user* in your organization, you have a golden opportunity. Ask various people to define what differentiates the various segments from one another. You will probably find that the people walking around saying "We're building this feature for segment X!" won't be able to define who, exactly, constitutes segment X. Ask "What type of people are in segment X?" and "What are their main characteristics?" You will probably find that the answers are quite vague and won't include a useful summary of the demographic, psychographic, or detailed behavioral data at the foundation of the segment. Responses tend to be along the following lines:

- "Segment X are our best customers."
- "Segment X are the people our competitors are ignoring."
- "Segment X are the power users."
- "Let me send you the segmentation report. It's got all of that in it."

None of these answers indicates knowledge of specific characteristics that will be helpful when designing the product. All of the previous definitions are stated in terms easily interpreted in multiple ways. For example, if you get the first answer listed previously, ask the same person to define what, exactly, it means to be a best customer. Is a best customer one who purchases a lot? How much is a lot? Or is a best customer one who purchases infrequently but makes a purchase every time she enters the store? Or is she one who never returns items?

If you record how people define the segments now, you will be able to compare this knowledge (or lack thereof) to the amount of information the same people are able to glean from personas. We believe you will find that personas enable your colleagues to digest, and carry into their daily decision-making tasks, far more salient information about your target users than do market segment descriptions.

- How are users distinguished from customers, if at all?
- How is knowledge about users communicated (e.g., research reports, segmentation analyses, presentations, or other artifacts)?

Create a spreadsheet to record your findings. List the artifact, the specific reference to users or customers, and the purpose of the reference (for an example and additional ideas, see the discussion of the scenario-collection spreadsheet in Chapter 6).

How can I use this information?

In our experience, collections of scenarios and other descriptions of users that appear across such documents have revealed discrepant and haphazard references to target users. That is, each scenario, storyboard, or use case talks about a different user, and each uses a different name, job role, or category. Most are defined without any real data. There will likely be no coherence across such documents. You could find references to:

- No one (a noticeable lack of any reference to users or customers)
- Very high-level, abstract terms such as *users* or *customers*
- Coarse descriptions of customers, such as "segment B folks need it to be easier" or "our target market is people who care about X" or "we're going after people who already use our competitor's product"
- Loosely defined segments or groups of users according to their skill level, such as "novices" and "advanced users"
- Groups of users in terms of their roles, such as "administrators" and "audience members"
- Actual users or customers of your products, such as "Ted, that guy in Boston who is always calling with ideas"
- Reasonably well-defined user profiles and other information about users and their tasks, such as "active organizers" who maintain daily calendars, "to do" lists, and work logs.

If you are finding that the first two bullets describe the user and customer references in your organization, you probably also found that your company isn't terribly user centered yet. If you are already using specific references to users (such as those in the last four bullets), plan to explain how personas are better *product design tools* than any of the existing user references (for suggestions, see "Create a communication strategy" later in the chapter).

Story from the field

DO YOU HAVE A "SHADOW PERSONA"?

—**Kari Rönkkö,** Blekinge Institute of Technology, **Mats Hellman,** UIQ Technology AB, **Britta Kilander,** and **Yvonne Dittrich**

Sometimes existing personas can make your persona effort more difficult. We had this experience at UIQ Technology. UIQ Technology is creating an interface development platform for handheld devices. UIQ's developers all have a good understanding of the platform's history, related applications, guidelines, and standards for the industry. Although this knowledge is good, it does have a downside: the developers are highly engaged and often have strong opinions and suggest many changes to interaction

(Story from the field, continued)

designers' designs. We developed a bad development habit, as we often engaged in time- and energy-consuming arguments over the best way to present functionality on the platform.

These arguments were complicated by the fact that UIQ had a long history of using one particular archetype, or as we labeled it a "shadow persona." The shadow persona was known as the traveling business man (TBM) in the company and had been employed from the very start. In fact, we inherited TBM from our parent company. Everybody knew about the shadow persona, but when asked, few knew how, why, or from where it originated.

With increased usability knowledge and more systematic and extensive user studies, the ID team's understanding of TBM changed. The target group widened to include youths. The widespread usage of Short Message Service (SMS) indicates that they were early adopters of mobile technology and hopefully potential Multimedia Messaging Service (MMS) users. Instead of creating additional personas, everyone allowed TBM to become elastic. Depending who you asked and when you asked them, TBM was both a youth and an adult, male and female, who had any of a number of professions that required them to move around a lot (e.g., plumber, firefighter, doctor on the road, nurse or ambulance paramedic, policeman, salesperson, or veterinarian, to name a few). Even though TBM's meaning had become more elastic, it still was the only widespread and accepted user representative in the company. The developers still thought of TBM as "just like me."

The interaction designers often had to confront developers with such questions as the following. In what way do you constitute a fair representation of the user? From whose perspective do you claim that? How do you know that your opinion is a fair representation of the user's opinions? The interaction design team wanted to remain faithful to the developers' creativity and good intentions, but direct these toward a shared user understanding outside their own personal opinions. We decided to create several end-user representatives from our understanding of different real-world end users. As we created these personas, we realized that the original TBM was never an effective design persona. He was used to argue for a lot of features, but he never was very helpful in providing design input.

We understand why TBM was created: he was a fantasy person whom everyone could imagine using all the features we were building into the platform. He was created with good intentions, and he was an attractive fantasy that could help us sell our products, but he couldn't help us create good, usable designs that would satisfy real people's goals. TBM was created to suit the technology we were building. Technology should be built to suit the needs and goals of personas.

Question 3: How is user information incorporated into the product design and development process?

It is important to understand the design and development processes in use in your organization and the ways user information is (and often isn't) incorporated into these processes. This will help you identify opportunities and scope your effort. If user information is already important in the development process, you need to decide exactly how you hope the personas will enhance user focus. If user information is not integrated into your processes, your personas might have a much larger job to do.

How can I answer this question?

In Chapter 2, we provided two basic product development process diagrams and illustrated how the persona lifecycle affects or integrates with each. What does your product development process look like? If you can, sketch your product design and development process as a diagram and consider the following questions:

- Do you involve users in the design, development, and marketing of your products? If so, how?

- At which stages in your process and in what ways is user information collected and considered?

- When it comes to integrating knowledge and insights about users into the products you create, what processes do your colleagues believe are working well? Which processes are failing, and in what ways?

- How do you measure the success of various processes in your organization?.

- How wedded is your organization to the existing design and development process? Are there any well-known frustrations related to the current processes? Does your organization tend to defend itself from new methods, or has your organization already identified problems with the status quo and decided to make some significant changes?

How can I use this information?

The answers to this question will help you identify ways you can leverage your personas in existing processes. Look for places that are known to be problematic and frustrating to the team. Try to understand what is negotiable and what is not. Perhaps your organization is very protective of activities in the middle of the process but would be open to personas and the information they contain at the beginning of the process, before the major work begins. Also, look for UCD processes where clearer definitions of users could be considered (i.e., scenarios, recruiting profiles). In some cases, so-called user-centered techniques are not very user centered in practice.

PLAN TO MEASURE YOUR PROCESS IMPROVEMENTS

As you analyze your environment and the audience for the personas, you are in a perfect position to think about how you will eventually prove the ROI of your entire persona effort. Your evaluation of your organization will unearth aspects of your current process that are not working as well as they could, which will be easy to identify now and almost impossible to find once the organization has launched full-scale into the next development effort. Look for:

- Process-related documents that have inconsistent or confusing references to target users or to data
- Feedback on aspects of the development process that took too much time or caused your team to have to redo work, including the number of drafts required before a document (such as a spec) was considered complete
- Customer service costs related to bad interface decisions
- The absence of user-related information in places where you believe it is necessary (e.g., members of the product team who are only able to describe users in vague terms or product vision statements that don't include any reference to the target audience)
- Actual times required to get from vision to design to launched product, which may be improved once personas are in place
- Conflicting assumptions about who the target users are and what they need.

Note that one of the biggest benefits you can expect from your persona effort will be consistency and clarity of focus among all the people working on product design and development. After your persona effort, you should be able to compare the documents you collect now to those created using personas. If you are successful, abstract references to users will be replaced by specific references to your personas or (in the case of marketing documents) will describe how the targets are similar to or different from the user personas. At the end of your project you can describe the value of the effort by measuring the before-and-after differences for the previously listed items.

When you craft your persona artifacts and explain their benefits, plan to describe specifically how you see personas working within (or changing) the status quo. You might want to explicitly communicate aspects of existing processes that the personas "won't touch." Work with your team to answer questions and overcome resistance you know will occur. Predicting problems isn't going to be difficult, and overcoming them is easier if you have a plan.

Now you know the problems. Are personas the solution?

Personas are a great tool, but success with them is not guaranteed. Personas are, in the final analysis, just another tool user-centered designers should have in their toolboxes, and not every tool is right for every job. More specifically, personas are powerful communication and design tools, but only if they are applied to the right types of communication and design problems.

*CREATE A PROPOSAL OUTLINING YOUR PLANNED LEVEL OF INVESTMENT
IN THE PERSONA EFFORT*

Consider creating a short (two to four-page) proposal for your supervisor that briefly explains what personas are, specific organizational problems you believe personas will mitigate, and the level of investment you believe is appropriate given your time, resources, and the organizational receptivity to new methods. Your proposal can include:

- A brief definition of personas
- A short description of how you see personas changing the status quo
- Benefits of the effort for your organization
- Milestones and deliverables
- Resources requested.

List the current UCD processes in place and how the persona effort will augment, replace, or perhaps not affect these processes. List the members of your core team and describe the level of effort and amount of time you plan to spend on personas. Explain how you plan to integrate the persona effort into your schedule. It is highly likely that the time and effort you dedicate to personas will enable to you to serve your internal customers more efficiently, but you will have to make a convincing argument to present to your boss.

Your proposal might explain that you plan a persona effort requiring only a light investment, given that you have very limited time to dedicate to the project or perhaps because you believe your organization will be very resistant at first. Alternatively, you might suggest a moderate investment because the organizational issues are pressing, the potential benefits are large, and you have identified many colleagues who are interested in participating. Consider creating a tiered proposal asking for more time and budget in the future as you prove the benefits of personas.

The value of personas is not without cost. Personas require a lot of initial and ongoing work. We can almost guarantee that a significant number of people in your organization will make life difficult for you if you decide to try personas, and that you will have to be ready and willing to answer many questions about what they are, why you are doing them, how and why you created them, and how they should use them. Did you find that your organization:

- Has a fairly solid and shared sense of who the target users of your products are?
- Already makes good and informed decisions about product features?
- Communicates well between various internal teams?

If so, maybe you don't need a huge persona effort, and your time and energy would be better used some other way, with other UCD methods (such as iterative user testing, longitudinal field research, and so on). If there are problems in your organization you think personas *can* solve:

● Which of these problems do you want to focus on first?
● Why does this problem currently exist?
● Is the problem solvable? If so, can you really imagine personas solving it?

Remember that personas are not magical. They don't dissolve deeply entrenched political or organizational problems, they are not immune to resistance, and they are not a complete design process unto themselves.

Building user focus is much more important than building personas

You don't have to embark on a full persona effort to get your organization more focused on users. There are many alternatives. You can customize the level of investment in your persona effort, or you could decide not to start with personas at all but to create some more basic user representations first and build up to personas from there. We provide a lot of information in this book, and we know it can look overwhelming. Remember that doing *anything* to get your organization more focused on users is valuable.

Different user representations suit different needs

What do you hope to accomplish by bringing user representations into your organization? Based on the results of your organizational introspection, why do you think you need personas?

● *Enhance focus:* You need to reduce or expand your possible target/ audience.
● *Guide direction and decision making:* You need to simply articulate user requirements and needs to help determine product goals and features.
● *Promote discovery and understanding:* You need help in uncovering pain points, design opportunities, and hidden truths about your users and customers.
● *Facilitate feature design:* You need to structure design and development activities around user needs and how they should influence design solutions, product flow, and technical implementation.
● *Inspire innovation:* You need to find new ways to inspire creative "outside the box" thinking when imagining or exploring solutions.
● *Promote awareness and empathy:* You need to teach your team more generally about their users and customers and engender a sense of care and concern for their reality and needs.
● *Enhance community:* You want to create a common, shared goal and promote an idea that your entire team can rally around. You want to create a common language and shared understanding that extends throughout your team and across other teams.
● *Overhaul the development process:* You want to completely revamp your development process from end to end to focus on UCD.

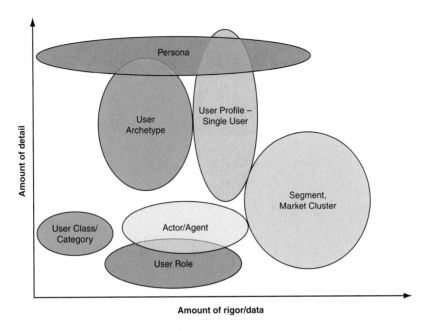

FIGURE 3.1: *User representations may vary in terms of detail and methodological rigor, among other things.*

If your goals align with the first few bullets you may not need the detail and richness of personas; other user representation methods may suffice. If your goals more closely resemble those toward the end of the list, concrete, data-driven personas are likely to be more helpful than other user representations.

As shown in Figure 3.1, different representations of users vary in their degree of abstraction, specificity, and realism, as well as in their adherence to or reliance on data. Given your product team's needs and your available resources, you could use simple user classes or categories of users (e.g., Internet Intenders versus Internet Enthusiasts) that include little detail and are based only on intuitions or logically defined characteristics. With more effort, those simple classes could take the form of narrative scenarios, wherein you begin to see a fuller picture of the user and their behaviors related to your product. Add personal details (e.g., goals, preferences, histories, and peripheral but relevant experiences) and they become personas. Of course, there are clearly exceptions to the definitions of terms listed in our figure (e.g., user classes can be empirically derived and market segments can be highly detailed). The point is that personas are not the only way to enhance user understanding and focus.

CREATE AN ACTION PLAN

Once you determine that personas will help you solve the problems you have identified, you can create an action plan for your team. The action plan is a translation of all of the analysis you have done into a roadmap or spec (specification) for your persona effort.

Your action plan should be based on the insights you have derived from your organizational analysis and serve as a roadmap for all of the persona-related communication you will manage until your product is complete and your personas are ready to retire. Like any good planning document, you will create a substantial portion of the action plan up front. However, as your project progresses you will need to be flexible with your original plans. Effective action plans range from short sets of bulleted points to detailed prose documents. Although they can be of different formats, all persona action plans incorporate the following:

- A definition of the scope of the project and the associated goals for the persona core team
- A description of a communication strategy
- A listing of milestones and deliverables.

Define the scope of your persona effort

If your company is far from user focused, you should definitely start with a small, tightly scoped persona effort and plan not to be discouraged if it takes a while for the value of personas to be felt. If you can succeed with a small project, you will have data that will help you convince more stakeholders at higher levels that the investment in personas is worthwhile for other, larger projects.

If your company is already somewhat user focused, or if you have a lot of influence with the executive staff, it might make more sense to plan a more extensive effort. Rather than starting small and building on your successes, you could decide to drive the adoption of personas from the executive level down. Although insisting that people use personas isn't sufficient to ensure the success of the method (you will still need a solid plan for persona adulthood, for example), this can be a great way to shift corporate culture toward user-centered thinking. For a case study describing a large, executive-driven persona effort, see "Story from the field: Personas to Solve Business Problems: A Top-down Approach to Introducing Personas into an Organization" in material following.

As a rule, if you want to achieve big changes with your persona effort you have to get the executive team involved and bought in. If you want to start with a more localized, grass-roots persona effort to solve smaller problems, your executive team doesn't even have to know about your personas. As you define the appropriate scope for your persona effort, complete the following statements (we have given you some possible endings).

- The personas we build will help the organization to:
  - ○ Create a new product strategy

- ○ Explore new business opportunities
- ○ Make better design decisions
- ○ Communicate more effectively
- ○ Work more effectively as a team
- ○ Understand the desires of the executive staff
- ○ Articulate assumptions that are holding us back
- ○ Identify who we are *not* building this product for.

- ● The personas we build will help the persona core team members by:
  - ○ Evangelizing the notion of UCD to our organization
  - ○ Creating a language to help us communicate our work
  - ○ Helping us to work across departments
  - ○ Delivering detailed information about our users to important stakeholders.

- ● The personas we build will be used by:
  - ○ List the organizations, teams, and people that will use your finished personas.

- ● The personas we build will be used for:
  - ○ All of our company's products
  - ○ A single product
  - ○ A single feature or small set of features
  - ○ Influencing the following decisions: _____
  - ○ Answering the following questions: _____.

- ● The personas we build cannot possibly solve:
  - ○ The fact that the executive team always has the final call
  - ○ Technology-related issues, such as the fact that our UI is limited by the current browser technologies
  - ○ All of our organizational politics.

Story from the field

PERSONAS TO SOLVE BUSINESS PROBLEMS: A TOP-DOWN APPROACH TO INTRODUCING PERSONAS INTO AN ORGANIZATION

—Howard Blumenthal, Former Director, E-Commerce & Database Management, Pfaltzgraff

Pfaltzgraff has been around for 200 years. We are an established company with a tremendous amount of historical data on our customers and our market. But knowing all about a rich and successful history doesn't necessarily make it easy to stay current and in touch with who your customers are today.

We decided to try personas as a tool to get our executive board back on the same page. Many members of our executive staff have been at the company for 10 years or more, and every one of them had a different sense of the customer that had built up over their tenure. These assumptions developed organically, and they had little or nothing to do with the data we have about our current customers (who are very different from our customers of 5, 10, and 20 years ago). Like many executive staffs, we recognized this as a problem and we have been talking about it for years. We were searching for new ways to slice and interpret our data.

We Wanted Personas to Solve Some Well-known Problems

Why weren't our old methods of understanding customers working anymore? As consumer interests continue to fragment, traditional geo-demographics simply cannot give you a clear picture of your customers. Where people live and the recency and frequency of their purchases provide information about groups of consumers, but this information isn't terribly useful. As customers become more niche focused, we have to find some other way to understand consumer groupings and to act on this understanding, and we saw personas as a way to do this.

In addition, we thought personas would help us understand our customers' attitudes, behaviors, and emotions in new ways. Dinnerware is a very emotional product. People associate dinnerware with family events, weddings, and other emotional occasions. Personas promised to give us a new way to find useful commonalities within our range of customers.

We decided to work with a consulting agency to develop our personas. Yankelovich (*www.yankelovich.com*) took on the task of researching and analyzing our customer data and identifying groups of customers that stood out. From this group of rough personas our executive team then collaborated with Yankelovich to identify four groups of customers that had a high purchasing affinity for the particular product we were working on at that time. We built personas to represent each of these four groups and then got to work assessing the similarities and differences between the personas.

Using the Personas

The executive team had selected the personas we felt were important to our business. We knew it was going to be a big step to build the personas into our culture, process, and strategic planning activities. We have a strategy meeting every year and decided to use this meeting as a chance to introduce the personas to the entire company. We also used the personas to organize and contextualize the strategy discussions we had at the meeting.

To do this, we created eight interdisciplinary teams. Half the teams focused on how we could use the personas and the information they contained. The other half focused on other strategic issues. Then we asked them to cross-pollinate to answer some important questions, such as, "How do you address specific strategic issues with respect to the information you have in the personas?" Since the meeting, the executive team has been working hard to prioritize the issues that came up, and everyone else in the company has been thinking about how the personas should influence their activities. For example, product teams have been thinking about *which* persona their products should be built for and will appeal to, and merchandising teams have been considering redesigning entire stores for "Jennifer" or "Cheryl."

Changing the Way You Think About Customers Takes Time

For Pfaltzgraff, we have envisioned the persona effort as a multi-year effort. We got a lot of the bits and pieces in place quickly, but realizing the full benefits is going to take time. First of all, we manufacture dinnerware, and production takes time. Changes we make today may not be visible to our customers for months. We are working on our messaging and marketing materials, many of which take months to produce and publish. We also believe that personas will change many aspects of our internal culture, and that doesn't happen overnight.

Define specific goals for the persona effort

To have a successful persona effort, you must set clear, attainable goals. No persona effort will ever solve all problems you can identify during organizational introspection. The goals you identify now will set expectations regarding your effort throughout the rest of the lifecycle. In addition, the clearer your goals, the easier it will be to measure the success and value of your effort during the *lifetime achievement and retirement* phase. As you define the goals for your persona effort, complete the following statements:

- We will know the persona effort was successful if:
  - ○ Products ship faster
  - ○ Products get better reviews
  - ○ Customer service costs go down

- ○ Overall business strategy changes
- ○ Our development team members can clearly identify and describe our target audience
- ○ The features we end up building are different from those we are planning to build now
- ○ Every feature is designed for and around scenarios with our target personas.

- ● The biggest risks we face with this project are:
  - ○ Complete unwillingness to use the personas
  - ○ Distraction from our other responsibilities, which might delay the product
  - ○ Dedicating time to do it well
  - ○ Finding data
  - ○ Getting everyone to use this method and it not resulting in a better product.

If you are going to create a written action plan, include your scope and goals.

Handy Detail

YOUR ACTION PLAN WILL HELP YOU MEASURE THE ROI OF YOUR WORK

The answers to the "Researching your organization" questions above should help you create a plan for collecting and evaluating ROI-related information as you continue your persona effort. If you know you will need to explain the value of your persona-related work at the end of your project, create your action plan to explicitly answer the questions on the left-hand side of the table shown in Figure 3.2. Figure 3.3 shows a generic action plan and how to detail milestones and deliverables.

Family Planning: Create a plan	Lifetime Achievement: Measure ROI
What resources do we have for personas and other UCD activities?	How much did the persona effort actually cost?
What product problems do we want to solve with personas?	Has the product improved? How much, and in what ways?
What process problems do we want to solve with personas?	Has the process improved? In what ways?

FIGURE 3.2: Measuring the return on your persona-effort investment is much easier if your plan includes specific references to the improvements you hope to realize. If you create your action plan to explicitly cover the questions on the left-hand side of this table above, you will thank yourself during the lifetime achievement and retirement phase.

(Handy detail, continued)

Persona Effort Action Plan	
Elevator Pitch	
	(See materials following for more information on how to create an effective elevator pitch for your persona effort)
Process-related Goals for the Persona Effort (if our work is successful ...)	
	(See chapter 7 for exapmles of measurable process-related improvements you can work towards)
Product-related Goals for the Persona Effort	
	(See chapter 7 for exapmles of measurable product-related improvements you can work towards)
Resources available for our Persona Effort	
	(List: • core team members • person hours available from the core team members • time available from the advisory members of the core team • financial resources, etc.)

Milestones & Deliverables			
Phase	**Activities and Deliverables**	**Timeline**	**Related Development Cycle Milestones**
Family Planning	Include persona-specific work and deliverables during each period (e.g., field research, data assilmilation, skeleton personas, communication activities, etc.)	Include the date of completion or expected duration of the activity	Include the broader product or project milestones here to provide context for the plan (e.g., spec complete date, code complete date, release date)
Conception & Gestation	–	–	–
Birth & Maturation	–	–	–
Adulthood	–	–	–
Lifetime Achievement and Retirement	–	–	–

FIGURE 3.3: *Your action plan should include a mission or vision statement (which we recommend in the form of an "elevator pitch"), overall goals, and resources for completing the work. You will also need to detail the milestones and deliverables for your persona project, which we recommend you complete in terms of the lifecycle phases. (For an example of a completed action plan, see "Meanwhile, at G4K...The G4K core team creates an action plan" later in this chapter.)*

Note that you will be able to use your action plan in measuring the value of your persona effort during the lifetime achievement and retirement phase by measuring the changes that result from your work.

Create a communication strategy

You and your core team will have to educate others in your team and company about the value and use of personas. There are four topics you should be prepared to explain (at varying levels of detail) as you embark on your persona effort:

- What is the persona method, and why does it work?
- Who are your personas?
- How were your personas built, and why did you build them that way?
- How should your personas be used during the design and development of your product?

There are three times during the persona lifecycle you will need to focus your attention on your answers to the questions listed previously and on the best ways to communicate these answers:

- When you taught the members of your core team about personas and why you have decided to undertake this project (you have already done this)
- Now, when you and your core team think about how you will start educating the team leaders and stakeholders in your organization about personas (we call this "method evangelism")
- During the *birth and maturation* phase, when you will be introducing your completed personas to the people who will actually be using them daily.

Create a strategy for method evangelism

Your core team will have to convince the stakeholders and key individuals in your organization that personas are the right thing to do. These key people are the executives, managers, and other formal leaders on your team. They are also the strong individual contributors scattered around your organization—the people who are respected and followed by others. If they buy in to the persona effort, it will be much easier for you to introduce the personas during the *birth and maturation* phase and to support their use during the *adulthood* phase.

Because you have already worked to convince your core team members of the value of personas and the methods you intend to use during the persona lifecycle, you have a head start on planning your method evangelism. You know what messages have been most effective in your core team. If you consider these effective messages and what you know about your organization due to your organizational introspection, you can create an effective plan quickly.

As you get started, think about your recent experiences with your core team. In particular, think about the topics that came up most in conversations. What did you have to repeat as you discussed personas with various colleagues? It is actually a good thing when you have to repeat yourself, because each repetition identifies discussion topics important to your company culture that are bound to arise when you start talking about personas outside your core team. As tedious as it is to discuss these topics over and over, it is important that your answers be solid by the time you are asked the same questions by colleagues who are not on your core team. To help with this, in a core team meeting write down the individual questions or issues and the answers you agree on in an FAQ (frequently asked questions) document.

Prepare a persona "rude Q&A" document

When public relations and marketing people get ready to introduce something—be it a new product, service, or change in your company—they often prepare a document called a "rude Q&A." This document lists all of the difficult questions colleagues are likely to encounter and strategic answers to each. We have prepared a "rude Q&A" for you to use as you introduce the persona method in your organization. We recommend that you use this to craft your own rude Q&A document for your persona core team and other persona stakeholders. We also encourage you to return to this list during the *birth and maturation* phase of the persona lifecycle, when you will enhance and implement your persona communication strategy.

Q: *What are personas?*

A: A persona is a detailed description of an imaginary person that embodies shared assumptions about users of a product, data regarding users of a product, or both. A persona is a design target that helps everyone on a product design and development team focus on user needs and user experience consistency.

Q: *Why do we need this persona stuff? We already know who our target users are.*

A: Answer this question by pointing out discrepancies in the way your colleagues understand and communicate about users:

- Show your collection of user references from previous products or product releases to demonstrate that there really isn't consensus on who your users are.
- Conduct an assumption persona exercise (see "Collecting assumptions to create assumption personas" later in the chapter). Creating assumption personas is quick and easy, and the exercise will make their implicit assumptions explicit and highlight any discrepancies between their expectations, opinions, and experiences and those of target customers. These assumption personas can serve as the starting point for data-based personas, and they can point out holes in your company's knowledge of your users and dictate studies and specific questions that should be researched. In the unlikely event you discover the assumptions about target users are rich, accurate, and shared, you may decide to focus on a UCD method other than personas.

- Emphasize that your finished personas will embody data—sometimes a lot of it. If you have decided to communicate assumption personas (which don't necessarily embody data), your personas will, at the very least, expose and align all of the disparate assumptions about users.

Q: *Why personas? Seems like personas are a lot more work than we need. We can just talk about users more. What's the big deal?*

A: Talking about 'users' is good, but we need to do more than this. The word 'user' does not convey enough real information about the people who will be using our products. Unlike the word 'user,' every persona is as well described and detailed as an individual person. Creating and using personas in our development process will help our entire organization stay clear on who our users actually are and focused on meeting their needs.

Q: *Why don't we just pick a real person and design for them? It's a lot less work.*

A: Designing for a persona isn't really the same thing as designing for a single real person. Real people have quirks. Personas have characteristics that are derived from data. The persona effort will help identify the important and shared characteristics of those people who can benefit from using our product (whether or not they do so today). Personas allow you to focus on the important characteristics across many users, and not be sidetracked by individual preferences and experiences of real people. Personas put a name and face—and set of behaviors, biases, and so on—on top of a much larger set of data. The data-driven characteristics we include in the persona are those we believe relate to and should affect our product.

Q: *Will our personas represent all of our customers/users?*

A: No, personas cannot and should not represent all of our customers or users. Rather, personas are descriptions of people who reside in the "data neighborhood" we have established as important to the success of our product and business. As such, personas are both good examples of typical users and strong strategic targets.

Q: *Will personas really make our product better?*

A: To answer this question, create a list of three to five of the major problems you have identified and a few bulleted items describing ways personas have helped solve these problems for other companies. For inspiration, refer to the many sidebars in Chapter 7 that describe the process and communication improvements other companies have experienced as a result of using personas.

Q: *Our products are for everyone and we need to build something for all of them. Shouldn't we create enough personas to cover them all? Why not create a bunch of personas and create a product they will all love? It doesn't make sense to design anything for just one person!*

A: You are right, it doesn't make sense to design something that only one person will like and use. But it also doesn't make sense to design a product for everyone. When we try to do that, we end up creating a product that probably makes a lot of people only semi-happy. If we can create a product that makes sense and solves real problems for our most important personas, it will make sense and solve problems for many other people as well.

If you are asked this question, remind the questioner that building a product to satisfy a few specific personas does *not* mean that everyone else will hate the product. Remind them that all of the designers and developers have their own definitions of who the users are (some are "designing this so my mom can use it," whereas others are designing it for themselves). Creating personas aligns everyone's thinking and increases the odds that decisions are made on a consistent set of important criteria. We have witnessed several large companies, with very broad audiences for their products, successfully narrow in on a small set of personas to target. You will find multiple examples of this in sidebars throughout this book.

The truth is, no matter what your products are, they aren't really for everyone. They are for a (perhaps large) set of people who share certain characteristics. Personas will help you focus on those critical characteristics. You can create as many personas as you like. In fact, that would be a terrific exercise and help you understand the executive team's thoughts on who your customers are. And over time, yes, it is your goal to make all of your personas and all your customers 100 percent happy. But this has to be done over time and with revisions of the product. If you try to satisfy everyone right now, because of time and other pressures on your product development schedule you are guaranteed to fall short for all of them.

Q: *Does this persona stuff actually work? What other product teams or companies are using personas?*

A: Yes, many companies across a variety of industries have used this method with success.

The case studies we have included in this book, along with the references to other work, provide specific examples to point your colleagues to. See, for example, the "Stories from the field" for Best Buy, Medco Health, and Leo Schachter Diamonds in Chapter 7. Use them to help you create an answer to this question that appeals to your organization.

Consider distributing a few key case studies or published reports on the persona method to your leadership team. We have included several sidebars in this book written by CEOs (e.g., Ken Seiff, former CEO of Bluefly, and Brian Schlosser, CEO of Attenex) and other executives (Howard Blumenthal, former VP Marketing at Pfaltgraff). In addition, the Forrester Group—a leading industry analyst—has several reports on the business benefits of personas that are well worth purchasing and sharing with your leadership team. References to several of these are found in the References at the end of the book.

Q: *What if you create the wrong personas?*

A: This is a concern that comes up all the time for persona practitioners. Remind anyone who asks this question that you are actively involving stakeholders and key contributors in the company. You and your core team will create skeletal personas, and then you will work together to prioritize them according to business objectives. (For more information, see Chapter 4.) As you craft an answer to this question, keep the following in mind:

- Remember that designing for a small set of personas does not imply that you are designing to make all other people *un*happy.

- Your personas either reflect the shared assumptions you all have about your users and/or they reflect the data you have collected. Because you do hope that many people similar to your personas will use your products, all you have to do is pick a persona who is in the right neighborhood to derive the benefits of the persona method.

- The creation of your personas included a review and evaluation process that, at the least, ensures you have made decisions here that are in line with your business strategy. Your validation efforts ensured that your personas do in fact resemble groups of real people you want to target.

- Your "finished" personas are just a starting point. Once your personas are in place, it is important that you both validate them and continue to do user research and employ other UCD techniques to ensure you are on target. (Depending on who asks you this question, this statement can possibly help you make a case for further investment in understanding and designing for your target users.)

- Imagine the worst case: that the assumptions or data behind the persona are completely wrong. If this is the case, you have the larger problem of not being clear on who the audience is for your product. Even if this were the case, picking a single persona to design for—even if this persona turns out not to resemble your actual users in any way at all—still has some benefits. If you create a product that enables the "wrong" persona to achieve a goal, it means that you have made a product that *makes sense* throughout the entire user experience. Consistency across the entire user experience is a by-product of the persona method, and is a benefit your product could gain regardless of which persona you use.

Q: *Won't personas stifle our ability to innovate? We need to be free to explore new ideas and technologies. We are interested in designing for the future, not for today's users.*

A: Personas help clarify where innovation should occur. When personas include goals, needs, aspirations, fears, and "pain points," they help you focus on the way things could be, and the way they should be. They clarify design opportunities.

Q: *Aren't we too far down the development path to start thinking about target users now?*

A: It is much better to think about users as early as possible, and well before product design and development start. However, it's never too late to think about users.

If you are asked this question, tell the questioner that you have assembled a core team to do the difficult work, and that you will create the personas and will show everyone else how they can help. Personas you use now can certainly help on the features you have not finished designing and building yet, and they can help a lot during the inevitable feature triage you will face at one point or another. Using personas will help you make consistent decisions about which projects and features are the most important based on what your users need the product to do.

Q: *It looks like personas are going to make our jobs harder! We don't have time for this!*

A: The personas should help you design it right the first time. In other words, using the personas will help you (and even force you to) make good decisions about your product earlier in the design process, which should eliminate some of the churn and pain of having to undo bad decisions.

Ask everyone to let you know when and if the use of personas interferes with their work, and pledge to remove any difficulties as soon as you hear about them. Remind everyone that your role will continue as the "owner" of the persona effort, and that you are dedicated to using the method only if it turns out to be helpful. Remind your colleagues that it is not your intention to make their jobs more difficult or more complicated. Although you are asking for some time at the beginning to explain the personas and why you are doing them, the actual *use* of the personas should make everyone's jobs a little easier. Because you will share a common perspective on target users, communication and decision making should become quicker and easier.

Q: *So, if we do personas, do we still have to do other things such as usability testing?*

A: Yes, personas can't do everything. Personas can help you focus on data about your users as you make design and development decisions about your product, but using personas doesn't guarantee that you will eliminate the need for other forms of requirements gathering, user testing, and other UCD techniques.

No single UCD method (or software development process) guarantees that a finished product will be perfect or that your product will succeed in the market. Even development processes that include many UCD methods can result in products that have usability problems or fail to meet users' needs and desires. There are many forces that impinge on the development process and the ultimate success of a product in the market (e.g., timing, what your competition does, and so on). Personas will help your organization focus on the right problems and will help you create a better product, but they are not a panacea and there is no guarantee. However, personas are so powerful as communication facilitators, and so good at naturally getting everyone on the same page with respect to their understanding of which users you are all targeting, that a well-executed persona project will both increase the probability of a successful product and have a noticeable positive effect on your development process.

Q: *Target users—isn't that the marketing team's problem?*

A: It's marketing's job to *build interest in* and *sell* the product you create, and the people who actually purchase your product might not be the same people who will be using your product (especially if you build products for businesses). Marketing will have a much easier time selling your product if your product does what your customers need it to do and does it well, solving real problems for real people. Your job is to create a great product, and to create a great product you have to know who you are building the product for, and their goals, needs, and tasks.

For more information on the differences and relationships between personas and marketing, see Chapter 11.

Bright Idea

CREATE AN ELEVATOR PITCH

An "elevator pitch" is a short sales pitch that can be delivered and generate interest in the time it takes to ride an elevator (with, of course, an important executive riding with you!). Elevator pitches or "idea viruses" [Godin and Gladwell 2001] can be written as concise stories that describe how your idea will solve a big problem. For more on writing effective stories related to personas, see Chapter 9.

The following are eight steps for creating an effective elevator pitch (adapted from Hoult [2000]):

1. Assume short buildings (make it short; think 50 to 150 words maximum).
2. Put a tag on it (make it easy to remember with a descriptive phrase or tagline).
3. Solve a problem (be specific and try to name a big, well-known problem).
4. Turn adversity into opportunity (e.g., we have so much research we are drowning in it; personas mean you will never have to read a long research report again).

5. Lay out the benefits (again, be specific).
6. Conclude with a call to action (e.g., "Come to our assumption personas meeting!").
7. Make it tangible (put it in terms that mean something to the listener; don't use jargon).
8. Show your passion.

The G4K elevator pitch is included in "The G4K core team creates an action plan" following. For additional help on creating an elevator pitch, see the article by John Hoult [2000] in the References at the back of the book.

Identify milestones and deliverables

Instead of guessing how much time each phase of your own persona lifecycle should take, figure out how much time you have and work backward. To do this, start by identifying existing deadlines, including:

● The intended "launch" or "live" date for your product or service, including any early 'test' launch dates (e.g., alpha and beta launches, if applicable)

● The "code complete" date (or date when all tweaks must be finished)

● The "design complete" date (or date when coding or development is due to start)

● The "spec complete" date (or date when the plan or design for your product is expected to be complete)

● The "requirements complete" date.

In the best possible scenario, you and your team should aim to:

● Set a date for persona *birth* (e.g., introduction of the personas to the product team) as early as possible in the product lifecycle. In the best circumstances, personas help executives and product managers determine product requirements. If your product has already been specified, try to set a date for persona *birth* before design and development start in earnest.

● Plan for persona *adulthood* to continue from the time you introduce the personas until the product is complete.

● Start *lifetime achievement, reuse*, and *retirement* activities shortly *before* customers are able to purchase and use your product. You will continue aspects of this work as customers use your product, but you can start early to evaluate process improvements and prepare for the next project.

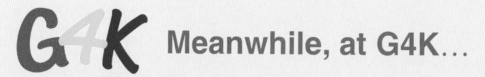

Meanwhile, at G4K...

THE G4K CORE TEAM CREATES AN ACTION PLAN

The G4K core team created the following high-level schedule by working backward from launch date and other significant project milestones. The entire development cycle is extremely aggressive for this team: six months from start to finish.

G4K Persona Effort: Elevator Pitch

G4K creates great games because we know what kids and their parents want from games. The G4K portal can only be great if we know what kids and their parents want from the Internet. We are creating specific descriptions of kids and parents—in personas—to capture everything we know and need to learn to create the G4K portal. Our personas are going to allow all of our data, in the shape of real kids and real parents, to sit in on every meeting, in every office, and influence every decision we make about the portal.

G4K Persona Effort: Action Plan

Resources for our persona effort:

- First two weeks: half-time effort for core team members
- Remaining weeks: 2 hours per week for core team members
- Use of printing facilities in design department (color printer, etc.)
- Permission to expense $200 for persona-related costs.

Product problems we want to solve with personas:

- Other companies have Internet portals for kids. We are behind. How can we create a portal that is world class and worthy of the G4K brand in such a short time?
- How can we recreate some of the key experiences built into our G4K games in an Internet experience? The technologies are very different.

Process problems we want to solve with personas:

- Deal with incredibly fast turnaround required for online portal development (unlike game development schedules)
- We have never done Internet delivery of a product. Personas need to help us understand our existing users in a completely new domain
- Communicate different needs to development staff unfamiliar with Internet-related issues
- Leverage the efforts of our very small team
- Leverage the efforts of people not directly on our team but whose help and expertise is needed.

(Meanwhile, at G4K... continued)

Our milestones and deliverables for the G4K persona project are shown in Figure 3.4.

Phase	Goals for Persona Effort	Timeline	Related Project Milestones
Family Planning	• Organizational introspection • Data collection	Complete 2 weeks from now	Vision complete (business plan, corporate strategy)
Conception & Gestation	• Data organized. • Persona creation complete • Evaluation and prioritization by stakeholders complete • Validation complete • Persona team begins evangelizing persona effort around organization	1 month from now	Requirements complete (system architecture, functional requirements)
Birth and Maturation	• Persona effort introduced to team • Initial posters and communication artifacts delivered to team • Personas used in storyboards, scenarios, design, walkthroughs, etc.	2 months from now	Feature specification complete (Design complete) GOAL: Personas used in feature prioritization decisions
Adulthood	• User testing with personas as recruiting profile • Personas used in Q/A test case selection • Persona knowledge enrichment artifacts delivered	3 months from now	Beta 1 complete (core features intact, but not published)
Adulthood	• Iterative user testing and Q/A testing continues • User Assistance team begins writing documentation based on persona profiles	4 months from now	Beta 2 complete (core features polished; secondary features intact)
Adulthood	• Personas introduced to support team • Marketing begins to explore messaging and advertisement channels considering personas	5 months from now	Release to operations (design complete, no further changes allowed unless they are show-stopper bugs)
Adulthood	• Support team uses personas to categorize customer issues/complaints/requests	6 months from now	Live to Web (site launch)
Lifetime Achievement	• Persona core team measures ROI of persona effort	6–7 months from now	Site Maintenance; planning for next release

FIGURE 3.4: *Milestones and deliverables as part of G4K's persona action plan.*

It is certainly not necessary to list all of your deliverables before you start your persona effort. In fact, we recommend that you wait to decide which specific deliverables you want to create, and their formats, until close to the time you will create them. This way, you will be able to customize your work according to the prevailing circumstances in your company and on the project. However, if you are asked to provide a list of deliverables, include (according to your plans, the scope of your effort, and your preferred methods) some or all of the "basics" listed in the following sections. The sections that follow cover basic deliverables by lifecycle phase:

Family planning deliverables

- Persona core team roster
- Schedule for persona-related work as it fits into the project schedule
- Conclusions from your organizational introspection (usually not shared because they might contain sensitive information)
- Persona action plan
- List of data sources for use in personas
- Plan for additional research (if required)
- Optional:
  - ○ Assumption personas
  - ○ Reality Maps.

Conception and gestation deliverables

- Data assimilation results
- Prioritized persona skeletons
- Persona foundation documents

Birth and maturation deliverables

- Persona communication plan
- Persona communication artifacts

Adulthood deliverables

- Persona-weighted feature matrix
- Design Maps
- Scenario collection spreadsheet
- Mood boards
- Usability test participant screeners
- Usability test results reporting issues per persona
- "Persona Bug Bash" plans for Quality Assurance.

Lifetime achievement and retirement (and ROI) deliverables

- Costs of the persona effort

- Benefits of the persona effort (including a description of how the effort improved your product, your design and development processes, and your company's focus on users)
- A short plan regarding the reuse or retirement of the personas.

DECIDE WHEN AND HOW TO INVOLVE CONSULTANTS

Creating personas can be a lot of work, and finding the time and resources can be difficult. Hiring consultants to perform some of the persona work can help, and more consulting agencies are offering persona-related services every day. If you are a consultant, or plan to hire one, the persona lifecycle will work for you. The challenge will be in figuring out what services the consultant should provide, how involved and integrated the consultants should be with internal teams, and how to maintain the consistent communication successful persona efforts require.

The first problem most consultants encounter is selling the idea of using personas. How can you explain that the time and effort required to create personas will pay off? How can you ensure that the personas will be worth the time and effort required? Consultants cannot fully understand the political environment into which they will try to launch personas, and they are not necessarily paid to spend a lot of time educating clients on the value of personas. Internal teams looking to hire consultants need to figure out how well the consultants understand their product domain, their business goals and strategies, and the challenges of supporting a successful persona effort.

Story from the field

DON'T ASK, JUST DO IT

—Brenda D'Angelo, Information Technology Services

We don't ask for permission to use personas on our consulting efforts. They are simply a part of our process and we involve each project team we work with in the creation of them. We consider personas one of the core UCD methodologies, along with scenarios of use. We tell our clients that if they don't have time for everything we recommend to spend the time on personas and scenarios of use.

Plan to include your consultants throughout the product development process

Personas that are "thrown over the wall" that exists between a consultant and the internal client teams are all but destined to fail. They will be popular for a week or two, the novelty will wear off, and the fancy posters will hang, ignored, on the walls. The undertow that pulls teams

back to familiar development processes is too strong for mere posters to fight. Personas require alert and active champions who have close ties to the development team.

Does this mean it is pointless to try to introduce personas as a consultant, or to hire a consultant to help with the effort? Far from it. But it does mean that a consultant must carefully assess the client's needs, and the relationship he has with the client, to create a customized campaign that will work "across the wall."

Story from the field

WORKING WITH CONSULTANTS

—Howard Blumenthal, Director, E-Commerce & Database Management, Pfaltzgraff

We found that there are two things to consider when choosing consultants: how much and what types of data they can collect or access, and how well they can interpret that data relative to your specific product domain. Consultants must convince me that the data they have is valid and that it includes enough breadth to be meaningful. They also have to convince me that the data they provide is relevant for and specific to my business in particular. I'm not looking for a consultant who has a strong handle on the entire country's demographics. I want a consultant who really understands my industry and the segments of customers who mean something to me.

But relevant data on its own isn't enough either. The reason to hire a consultant is to get their years of experience and expertise using personas and other UCD techniques. I want them to bring ideas on how to message to the personas they create and what I'm doing right and wrong in my current programs. How can they help me build a plan for testing new products and messages with people similar to my personas, because the "old" ways of testing don't really apply when you use personas.

Finally, the consultant has to be able to deliver deep information, but they have to deliver the right amount at the right time. A consultant should be able to create 30 to 60 initial sketches of personas, but then they have to be able to roll them up into six to eight persona profiles to present to the executive staff. If you start too deep in the data at the executive level, you will get bogged down in minutiae and lose focus. I expect them to know the details of the subgroups and even individuals within groups, but they have to be able to craft materials that are at the right level for various audiences in the company.

If you are a consultant: early deliverables will help convey the value of the personas

A consultant's first persona-related deliverable can be a set of assumption personas that provide a consistent set of user referents for everyone on the client's team. Consultants can create these independently or ask the client to participate in an assumption persona exercise. The goal is to show the client that the current descriptions of users are inconsistent and unhelpful *and* that this situation is easily remedied.

If you are a consultant, offer to do a competitive analysis based on the assumption personas: "We all agree that Philip is a great example of our primary user. Let's walk Philip through this latest release from our competitor:

● What will he love about the new release?

● Will he be interested in all these new features?

● What doors did our competitors leave open to us?

When you understand what might make Philip *like* your competitors' offering, you will be able to find ways to make him *love* your product."

Why is this worth your time? Personas are a great way to establish a lasting and iterative relationship with clients. Once you have created basic personas, you can use them to re-approach a client and express the benefits of your services. Drop your clients a note to let them know that your team has been evaluating a lot of market research lately that sheds light on Philip's use of the Internet at home.

Explain how your clients' existing design and development process could be augmented with persona-related tools (such as those described in chapter 6). Hold a free brown-bag seminar for clients to show them how to attach more data to their personas by using free data resources. Offer to analyze your client's usage logs to find out how much more money Philip is spending once the redesign is done. The more your clients know about personas, the more likely they will be to come back and ask you to help them develop real personas.

You can create personas to show to potential clients to express to them the depth of your understanding of their users. Use these provisional personas to show them the distinction between purchasers and users if this is an important distinction. Show them how some of the persona details are drawn from interesting and relevant research available to you.

Finally, make sure you are familiar with the content in the *adulthood* phase. This is where the heavy methodology is and where obvious value can be expressed. You should be able to describe example deliverables you can offer if they opt for personas (e.g., the persona-weighted feature matrix). This is where the real decision-helping value of the persona effort is.

IDENTIFY DATA SOURCES AND COLLECT DATA

You have a core team, you understand the audience for your personas, and you have created an action plan. It is time to start collecting the material you will use to create your personas.

From one-on-one interviews to widely published reports, there are thousands of data resources available to persona practitioners. If warranted and possible, you will do some original user research of your own, though this endeavor tends to be the most time consuming of all. The amount and types of data you will collect will depend on how much time and money you have to spend and your own evaluation of how much data will be necessary to create good personas for your project.

Creating personas from rigorous data is the best option, but it's not the only option

It is difficult to come up with an argument against employing user data in the creation of personas, but it is not impossible. Collecting, analyzing, and translating insights generated from data into personas takes time and energy. If you simply don't have time to create data-driven personas, there are alternatives that require less of an investment. We strongly believe that any focus on users is better than no focus on users. You could choose to use some other representation method instead of personas (such as any of those listed in the previous section, "Different user representations suit different needs"), which might require less data than what we suggest here for persona creation. Alternatively, you could choose to use "secondary" data sources to create personas, as described later in this chapter.

There are different types of data sources you will be able to collect, and different types of information that will be contained in these sources. Data sources are either primary or secondary:

- *Primary data sources:* Primary data is any data collected by directly observing users' behaviors or asking users about their actions, thoughts, or feelings. Primary data sources available to you include research done by your group, by other departments in your company, and by other companies who have published their findings. The "primary-ness" of the data refers to the proximity of the data collector to the people being studied. This means that data sources don't have to be created by you or your company to be primary for your personas.

- *Secondary data sources:* Secondary data comes via a third party, usually a distant teammate who has some contact with users but is drawing upon memory and experience to make "factual" statements or inferences about those users.

Data itself is either quantitative or qualitative:

- *Quantitative data:* Quantitative data usually comes from large numbers of users and is collected via a method that promotes both efficiency and rigor (e.g., a questionnaire, structured phone interview, or analysis of server logs). It is often expressed numerically (e.g., 47% of our users spend $50–$60 a year on our products).

- *Qualitative data:* Qualitative data usually comes from smaller numbers of users and is collected via a method that promotes deep understanding. The "why" behind the facts is answered by qualitative data (e.g., observational site visits or ethnographic research, one-on-one semistructured or unstructured interviews, and journal keeping or a diary study).

Some research methods (e.g., focus groups) can produce qualitative data, quantitative data, or both, depending on how the research is conducted.

Story from the field

USE THE RIGHT COMBINATION OF DATA TO CREATE PERSONAS FOR TARGET MARKETS

—Matthew Lee, Usability Engineer, InfoSpace, Incorporated

We have been very concerned with making sure that the personas we create represent our target market. Some in the company argue that the only way to do this is to use hard quantitative data and statistical analysis to identify the correct target market. Others argue that we need to talk to individual people to find out if they are in our target market. If they are, we should create personas out of the rich information we get from talking directly with them (i.e., personas should be created from qualitative data). Both perspectives are valid, but the true answer lies in a combination of the two approaches: going out on field studies to really understand the people who would use the product, but at the same time bringing in statistical data to give credibility and broad perspective to your answers.

During the *family planning* phase, your goal is to figure out what your data sources should be and to collect the raw data. We believe that the best personas come from a variety of sources, especially including both quantitative and qualitative data. Further, although we have seen great personas created after an extensive data collection and analysis effort, we have also seen useful personas based completely on assumptions.

Given the sheer volume of information available on the Internet, and the amount of information available for free, it is likely that you will always find some data relevant to a persona project. It is also likely that you will feel you don't have enough time or help to ferret out the available data. However, if you do have trouble finding data you can consider creating assumption personas—personas based on the intuition of you and your teammates regarding your target audience. We consider assumptions a type of secondary data. Assumptions are really educated guesses often based on real-world experience as well as knowledge of your domain and business. Assumption-based personas, if created and used carefully, can deliver some of the benefits of data-based personas with less initial effort. (See "What are assumption personas and why use them" later in the chapter.) The sections that follow discuss data collection from various sources, primary and secondary, and describe several techniques to help you get the most out of your own research, particularly qualitative research, toward persona creation.

Identifying data sources

...Note one of the most important attractions of capitalizing on customer data: it's creating value from something you already have. As every industry consolidates and becomes more competitive, the pressure to create value only increases, and it isn't going to let up. Every company needs help. In these circumstances it feels like a gift to discover that you have a valuable "new" asset that in fact has been sitting there all along.

—Larry Selden and Geoffrey Colvin [Selden and Covin 2003, p. 26]

During the *family planning* phase, your goal is to identify and collect as much data as you can. However, the amount and types of data you collect will depend on how much time and money you have to spend and your own evaluation of how much data will be necessary to create good personas for your project.

As we have stated, there is likely to be data already in existence that you can utilize for your personas. Before you do any original research on your own, meet with your core team and use the following questions to discuss and/or brainstorm ways to identify and collect persona-relevant data efficiently:

- Existing primary data sources (internal)
  - ○ What sources of user and customer data are readily available to you? What are the central and peripheral topics or domains that would be pertinent to your project?
  - ○ What are the other possible sources of data in your company? Who currently owns each data source?
- Existing primary data sources (external)
  - ○ What are the possible external sources of data relevant to your domain, company, or product? Are there institutions or other companies that might have conducted

research related to your domain? If you need to purchase these sources, do you have money to do so?

- ○ What types of data or specific types of information do you think you will need to create effective personas? (See the section "Create a 'data by topic' spreadsheet," following.)
- ● Original primary data sources (doing your own research)
  - ○ After seeking out existing data sources, what information is missing? What do you really need to learn? Who do you need to study?
  - ○ What techniques best elicit the type of information you need in order to create personas?
- ● Secondary data sources
  - ○ Who are the subject matter experts in your company? Who has the most contact with existing customers?
  - ○ How can you gather educated guesses (assumptions) from your team in a meaningful and useful way?

The following sections include ideas and suggestions to help you answer these questions.

Finding primary data sources internally

The first place to look for data is within your organization or company. In many cases, there are previous user or market research studies you can capitalize on. Look for field studies, surveys, and focus group reports. Ask around to see if there are reports by consultants or contractors that were brought in previously. Even if the research is several years old, there is likely to be useful information. Get out there and find copies (preferably both electronic and paper) of any research that has something remotely to do with the customers or users of your product.

Story from the field

PERSONA CREATION CONNECTS PEOPLE

—Christina Wodtke, author of *Information Architecture: Blueprints for the Web*

Building personas is like making stone soup. We assigned homework for each group to bring in their own data. Marketing had to bring market research, QA had to bring their test documents, Customer Service had to bring the materials they use to answer customer problems, and so on. Because everyone contributed data, everyone had a stake in the personas. There was also an unexpected (but very cool) side effect: Customer Service and Marketing had never talked to each other before.

A typical internal data source: market segmentation analysis

In the best of all worlds, your business strategy, product planning, or market research team has completed a market *segmentation analysis*. Segmentation analysis is a well-accepted method of breaking down a large mass of possible customers into understandable chunks. Such research can serve as a very strong "data backbone" for your personas. In fact, a segmentation analysis is probably the first data source you should look for. It will help you begin to answer the tough question of how many personas to create. If used as the starting point for personas, it will also satisfy the need for quantitative rigor that many persona naysayers argue for. Either way, if your company does use market segmentation analyses, you will likely need to be prepared to describe the relationship between your personas and the market segments. In most cases, the eventual answer will be "our personas are concrete instances (specific design targets) within each of the critical segments." If you find a segmentation study that was conducted for your company or specific products, you should make sure you ask several key questions about it:

- When was this research conducted? Many segmentation studies hang around for years after they are completed, and consequently grow stale.

- How heavily used is this segmentation by your company? That is, are the segments well known and entrenched in the company culture?

- When does your organization plan to re-segment the market? Be wary if re-segmenting is going to happen during your upcoming product cycle. You will likely need to align your personas with this segmentation after they are created.

The next chapter covers a little more on market segmentation, particularly how to use it toward persona creation. If you would like to get in-depth information about what a market segmentation is and how to do market segmentation, we recommend the books by Clancy and Krieg [2000], Rao et al. [1995], and Weinstein [1998] (see the References at the back of the book). Some additional existing internal data sources and research artifacts to look for include the following:

From UCD specialists:

- Ethnographic and field research
- Usability test results
- Participant recruiting screeners for usability tests
- Results of usability tests (for more on using usability test results to create personas, see "Story from the field: Using Personas to Report Usability Test Results," by Bryan Stapp, in Chapter 6)
- User profiles (rich descriptions of real users).

From product management and business analysts:

- ○ Competitive analyses
- ○ Customer/account briefings (background information on major customers)
- ○ Target audience and market descriptions
- ○ Descriptions of the actors in use cases from previous versions of the product (use cases often have some minimal descriptions of users).

From marketing and product planning:

- ○ Focus group reports
- ○ Results from surveys/questionnaires
- ○ Interviews
- ○ Segmentation studies
- ○ Creative briefs
- ○ Participant recruiting profiles and screeners for market research.

From customer service, sales support, and account management:

- ○ Lists of observations or notes from contacts with customers
- ○ User comments (direct quotes) and feature requests
- ○ Customer service records and support logs
- ○ Product evaluation forms and surveys.

From sales:

- ○ Sales data and strategy documents
- ○ Account profiles, "backgrounders," and customer briefings for training new sales personnel.

From documentation and training:

- ○ Anything they have that describes the audience for the materials they create
- ○ Training materials.

From engineering and operations:

- ○ Web server logs
- ○ Usability-related bugs logged against any previous releases
- ○ "Read Me" documents that were released with the final product (what had to be solved with words after the product was completed).

From the executive staff:

- ○ Business plans
- ○ Product vision documents.

From human resources and internal training (if your target audience is your own employees, such as when creating or redesigning an intranet site):

○ Employee surveys

○ Internal demographics and employee statistics

○ Current and past job descriptions

○ Resumes of people who have applied for work at your company through the years (resumes of those who have been hired may be confidential or otherwise sensitive).

After you collect any of these resources, evaluate them to identify which are important, credible, and useful. Then prioritize them. You should also identify areas where you need more data or data of a different type.

Finding primary data sources externally

We have found an enormous amount of useful data for our own persona efforts that was collected by other companies, research institutes, university professors, and graduate students. Usually, such research is done for some other purpose than informing profiles of users toward software design, but it is surprising how often it can be repurposed toward this end. The sheer wealth of rich and detailed data available for free is astounding. Less hidden and surprising, there are research firms that make their living from conducting and selling market- and customer-related research.

It is not difficult to find external data, but it can be difficult to find truly *relevant* external data. Before you look for external data sources, create a list of keywords or search criteria to help pinpoint your search efforts. It is easy to become overwhelmed with data and sidetracked with articles you find on interesting, but not really relevant, topics. As you perform your searches (for example, using a Web search engine), follow links, read bibliographies, and note additional keywords and search terms that will help you zero in on the resources most relevant to your project. As you hunt down these findings, it is important to look for the primary data source. That is, if possible, do not settle for the interpretation or brief summary. Some external data sources and research artifacts to look for include:

● Research articles in conference proceedings

● Domain-relevant articles in professional, academic, industry, and business journals or trade magazines (see, for example, *www.hcibib.org* or *www.hoovers.com/free*)

- Newspaper or magazine articles about your product or domain
- Articles about the competition and competitive product analysis
- Government and institutional research on specific domains and people (the population), such as the United States Census Bureau at *http://www.census.gov, http://www.freedemographics.com* or the University of Florida, International Demographics and Statistics, at *http://web. uflib.ufl.edu/docs/guides/internationalstats.html.*
- Research reports available for purchase from professional research companies (e.g., Forrester, JD Power, Jupiter Research, or the Markle Foundation at *www.markle.org*).
- Relevant blogs, newsgroups, and bulletin boards
- Resume posting services (see "Bright Idea: Resumes are Great Data Sources" following).

Handy Detail

CLUSTERING SEARCH ENGINES

When performing Internet searches for data sources, we have found it useful to use search services that cluster results from several engines. For example:

http://www.clusty.com
http://www.a9.com

Bright Idea

RESUMES MAKE GREAT DATA SOURCES

For one persona project that had to get done quickly, we were at a loss for finding data for one of the target roles. We needed to create a persona for a graphic designer and had no research available to us. We ended up doing a Web search for online résumés of graphic artists, interaction designers, and the like. We found a lot of great material to help us understand that audience. The résumés had much more information in them than we expected to find, including goals, work activities, interests, education and special training, specific tools, skills, and knowledge. They even gave us a sense of style, culture, and language (common terms, slang, and jargon). Of course, we were careful to omit any names, addresses, or other personal information we found on posted résumés. The resulting persona in this domain was amazingly rich and well supported given the speed of creation and lack of formal data available to us.

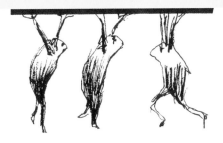

G4K   Meanwhile, at G4K…

THE G4K CORE TEAM FINDS WEB-BASED DATA SOURCES

When G4K set out to find data relevant to the development of their project domain, they did not know quite where to start. They had all sorts of information about kids, parents, and shrink-wrapped games, but nothing except assumptions when it came to kids and the Internet. So, they opened a Web browser and searched on entries such as *Internet behavior*, *PCs and kids*, *statistics software usage*, and so on (because they were primarily interested in children's Internet behaviors). They discovered there was an ocean of data waiting for them. Here are a few of the key resources they found that helped them identify specific studies and larger collections of data:

- U.S. Census Bureau: "Computer Use and Ownership":
  http://www.census.gov/population/ www/socdemo/computer.html
- Pew Internet & American Life Project:
  http://www.pewinternet.org
- Cyberatlas: "The World's Leading Resource for Internet Trends & Internet Statistics":
  http://cyberatlas.internet.com (Also known as NUA, *http://www.nua.com/surveys*)
- Internet Demographics Directory: "Complete guide to Internet statistics and research":
  http://internet-statistics-guide.netfirms.com
- Consumer Internet Barometer: "Trends in Usage and Attitudes":
  http://www.consumerinternetbarometer.us/index.htm
- Galileo Internet Resources: "Demographics and Census Data":
  http://www.usg.edu/galileo/internet/census/demograp.html
- InfoQuest! Information Services: "Internet Surveys and Statistics":
  http://www.tbchad.com/stats1.html
- Websense: "Internet Use Statistics":
  http://www.websense.com/management/stats.cfm.

From these sources and others (see Figure 3.5), the G4K core team found 30 relevant research studies. Many of these were available on the Web for free. Some had to be purchased from a research firm. They made printed copies of each report, distributed them among their core team members, and created a numbered list so that each study could easily be referred to as they used these resources in the *conception and gestation* phase.

G4K Kids Portal project: Data resources

1. The Internet Consumer: Online Children. (December 1999). Interactive Consumers. Cyber Dialogue. http://www.cyberdialogue.com/
2. Cyberfacts: Teenagers on the Internet (summary data sheet in pdf format; based on data from the American Internet User Survey). http://www.cyberdialogue.com/, (internal MS - http://msli
3. Children on the internet,
4. Children's Internet Use (
5. Curiosity: Five to Eleven http://www.sesameworks
6. Why Net Marketers love
7. The Internet Consumer I http://www.cyberdialogue
8. Home Computers and Ir http://www.census.gov/,
9. Gamers Growing Up. Th
10. Computer use in the Uni http://www.census.gov/p

1. The Internet Consumer: Online Children. (December 1999). Interactive Consumers. Cyber Dialogue. http://www.cyberdialogue.com/
2. Cyberfacts: Teenagers on the Internet (summary data sheet in pdf format; based on data from the American Internet User Survey). http://www.cyberdialogue.com/
3. Children on the internet, http://www.otal.umd.edu/UUPractice/children/

11. The America Online/Rop http://www.corp.aol.com/press/study/youthstudy.pdf
12. Student Computer Use – Indicator of the Month, National Center for Educational Statistics (August, 1999). http://nces.ed.gov/pubsearch/pubsinfo.asp?pubid=1999011
13. Children and Interactive Media. Wartell, Lee, and Caplovitz (Nov 2002). Markle Foundation.
14. Teachers say internet improves quality of education. Cyberatlas. http://cyberatlas.internet.com/
15. The social context of home computing. Frohlich and Kraut (April 2002).
16. More Kids say internet is the medium they can't live without. http://www.sriresearch.com/press/pr040402.htm
17. Teenage Life Online: The rise of the instant-message generation and the Internet's impact on friendships and family relationships. (June 20, 2001). Pew Internet & American Life Project. http://www.pewinternet.org/reports/toc.asp?Report=36
18. Targeting Teens is a gender game (August 2000). Jupiter Communications.
19. Teacher Use of Computers and the Internet in Public Schools, Education Statistics Quarterly – National Center for Education Statistics. http://nces.ed.gov/pubsearch/pubsinfo.asp?pubid=2000090
20. Parents Online. (November 17, 2002). Pew Internet & American Life Project. http://www.pewinternet.org/reports/toc.asp?Report=75
21. America's Online Pursuits: The changing picture of who's online and what they do. (December 22, 2003). Pew Internet & American Life Project. http://www.pewinternet.org/reports/toc.asp?Report=106
22. The Ever-Shifting Internet Population: A new look at Internet access and the digital divide (April 16, 2003). Pew Internet & American Life Project. http://www.pewinternet.org/reports/toc.asp?Report=88
23. The Music Downloading Deluge: 37 million American adults and youths have retrieved music files on the Internet (April 24, 2001). Pew Internet & American Life Project. http://www.pewinternet.org/reports/toc.asp?Report=33
24. The Digital Disconnect: The widening gap between Internet-savvy students and their schools (August 14, 2002). Pew Internet & American Life Project. http://www.pewinternet.org/reports/toc.asp?Report=67
25. Zero to Six: Electronic Media in the Lives of Infants, Toddlers and Preschoolers (Fall 2003). Kaiser Family Foundation. http://www.kff.org/entmedia/3378.cfm
26. Online Parents: Gateway to a New Generation, Cyber Dialogue, The Internet Consumer, Year 2000, Vol.7. http://www.cyberdialogue.com/index.html. (internal MS - http://mslibrary/research/mktresearch/FindSVP/indbriefs/ic-ib-2000-07.pdf)

FIGURE 3.5: *A list of some of the external data sources G4K found.*

PLAN AND EXECUTE YOUR OWN PRIMARY USER RESEARCH

…find out who the people are, what they do now, and what the new system is expected to do for them.… It is important to spend some time watching users do their jobs with their current tools, whatever they may be. The closer you are to the prospective users and the more you know about them, the more likely you are to produce a system that meets their needs.

—Richard Rubinstein and Harry Hersh [Rubinstein and Hersh 1984]

It is not unusual to find so much existing data that you can create very effective personas without having to undertake very much, if any, original research. However, the internal and external data sources we have listed so far for the most part tend to provide quantitative data. You will also need to identify qualitative data to create realistic and effective personas. Qualitative data is perhaps the most useful type of information for creating "full" personas that seem like real people. Qualitative research generally provides source material for the elements of personas that help make them seem like real people. Such elements include work and home context, motivation, goals, and fears.

For most products and persona efforts, there will be specific behavioral and environmental information you will want to observe firsthand, in the context of where people will use your product. Moreover, you may want to understand their attitudes, thoughts, and feelings in these contexts. For example, you might have to do your own qualitative research to find out answers to the following:

● What goals do users have?

● What roles or actions do users take to achieve their various goals?

● What specific tasks or activities are associated with the various roles? What motivates these tasks or roles? What are their attitudes and feelings toward these activities?

● How do users interact with each other and with existing products?

- What do users like and dislike about their current products and systems?
- What is the environment and context in which users work (or play) and in which your product will have to function?
- What personality characteristics seem common across these users? Is there an obvious culture or language (terms, ways of speaking) present?

You can use the findings of this qualitative research to enrich your persona descriptions and include specific information about the ways people act and think today, without the help of the product you are building.

There are many ways to observe, interact with, and collect data on users, and it is beyond the scope of this book to cover them all. If you have methods that have worked for you in the past, we suggest you use them, but also consider some of the techniques we describe in the material following, which includes qualitative research activities that help bring out the information you will need in creating personas.

If you find that you need to do *quantitative* research to help complete your sources of data, there are many good books to consult on this topic. See Blankenship et al. [1998], Hague [2000], Jensen [2002], and Maxim [1999] in the References at the back of the book. If you feel you have all the data you need, or have qualitative data collection methods that work well for you and your team, feel free to move on to Chapter 4.

CONDUCT FIELD STUDIES TO GATHER QUALITATIVE DATA

If you have done a good job of tracking down third-party and other existing data sources, you will most likely come to the point at which basic field observation or some other type of ethnographic research (in which you get out of the office and learn about your target users by observing them in their own environments) will best serve your additional data needs.

A field study is any activity that involves researchers observing, interviewing, and directly interacting with users in the users' own environments. Planning and conducting your own field research can be very involved. As such, a detailed coverage of data collection and analysis

---

Bright Idea

STRUCTURE YOUR DATA GATHERING TO LEARN ABOUT A PRESELECTED SET OF PERSONA CHARACTERISTICS

Not sure what additional data you should collect to create effective personas? Look at the section "Choosing persona characteristics to include in the foundation document" in Chapter 4. Select or create a set of characteristics that will be important to the people who will use your personas. Evaluate your existing data sources to determine which characteristics you have enough information on and which you need to research further. Structure your additional research to collect the information you are missing. For example, the G4K team could decide that their personas really should include information about the varying levels of typing skills among children of different ages. If they don't find any in their existing data sources, they could decide to search specifically for typing-skill data to complete their personas.

Handy Detail

APPROACH FIRSTHAND DATA SOURCES THOUGHTFULLY!

Our 2001 and 2002 workshop participants talked about best practices related to asking for the time and input of members of your target user group. These people might be your current customers or subject matter experts in fields related to your product plans. In either case, it is important to think carefully about what you are asking from these people and how you are going to compensate them for their time. If there is some reason the subjects cannot accept money or gifts, offer to make a donation in their name or their company's name. Overtly acknowledge that you understand you are asking for a significant favor in asking for their time and attention. Promise that you will follow up on your research visits after the product is developed to let the subjects know how their input affected the product.

Also remember that the quickest way to exhaust research participants is to ask them to repeat the same things over and over again. Have your process well defined before you do your field research. Ensure that everyone on your data collection team knows how the collected data will be organized and access. Consider creating Reality Maps (see "Bright Idea: Reality Mapping" in material following) during your research sessions so that the information provided by the participants is immediately accessible by your entire team. Reality Maps provide an enduring, highly visible record of your time spent with participants. They minimize the possibility that your participant will be asked the same questions over and over again.

Finally, make sure that your participants feel heard and feel that their time is respected. If your records of the session are not objectionable or critical, and you are sure that sharing the notes won't cause your managers or company any difficulties, consider sharing your notes or summary with the participant. Let them know how this information is going to be used—ideally, to create a better product for all users.

methods is beyond the scope of this book. Although we provide some basic guidance and insights for conducting field research toward persona development, we also recommend that you take a look at the excellent books on field research by Beyer and Holtzblatt [1998], Holtzblatt [2002], Holtzblatt, Wendell, and Wood [2004], Hackos and Redish [1998], and Kuniavsky [2003]. (Full references for these are found in the References at the back of the book.)

Create a list of the things you want to find out

It is possible that the existing data reports you collected are more focused on the domain of your product and the general market (e.g., "children's Web portals" or "gaming") than on the actual users of those portals. That is fine and will likely be useful for your personas. However, for your original research, make sure your key questions include understanding important aspects of the target users themselves:

- What are they like?
- What other interests do they have?
- What activities do they engage in, what behaviors do they demonstrate, and what actions do they take?
- What are their goals, aspirations, and fears?
- What knowledge and skills do they appear to have?

After you collect your list of possible topics and questions, spend some time prioritizing it. What topics are "must have" versus "nice to know" in order to create your personas? You will use these priorities in a bit as you write a site visit script.

Decide who you want to visit and train your team

You can create basic profiles of the types of people you want to observe based on the data you have gathered so far and the questions you need to answer. If there are many different people you would like to observe, prioritize your time according to what types of data you are missing for your personas. If the people you plan to send out to collect data are not familiar with interviewing and data collection techniques, it is important to take the time to do some training. Do practice interviews and share tips about conducting user observations.

Recruit participants

If possible, you should attempt to piggyback with other research efforts in your organization, if they exist. Your first step is simply to find out if there is a Marketing or Market Research team already planning a customer survey, focus group, or some other study. If you can, you will want to influence that research so that it produces the types of data that best supports persona creation—providing insight into behaviors, goals, needs, fears, and aspirations.

As you recruit participants, ask them if you can record the visit and/or collect additional information and artifacts while you are there (e.g., photos of the site and participants, screenshots of key applications or trouble spots, printouts of key documents, drawings of room layouts, and so on). Make sure you have appropriate permission for photos and for making any recordings.

Bright Idea

TRY A "BRAINWRITING" EXERCISE

—Chauncey Wilson, WilDesign Consulting

During a "brainwriting" exercise, you ask members of the product team and other stakeholders to write down questions, topics, or issues they would like to find out more about. They write these on cards and hand them to the persona advocate. I have done this at project and development meetings and it is a simple exercise to get people to think about what they would like to know. You can conduct brainwriting individually, whereby you ask people to list as many topics of interest as they can in two to three minutes and just hand the cards in. Alternatively, you can do several rounds in which you collect the cards, shuffle them, and pass them out and ask people to add an item to the new card. Seeing what other people write often helps generate additional questions. I have done this with teams of 8 to 15 people and easily generated 30 to 50 questions. You can even repeat this exercise with different groups to see what questions emerge (this can be useful in understanding the culture, in that the question might reveal various biases).

Create a script for the visit

You will never have as much time for your field observations as you would like. Create a script or a plan to ensure you cover all of the critical questions you have identified. We recommend that you prepare two lists of topics and questions. The first list is the set of topics you *must* collect data for. The second list is the set of topics that are nice to know about but not critical for each visit. For a two-hour visit, your script could be broken down into roughly 30-minute intervals. For example:

- *30 minutes:* Introductions, setting expectations, and generally building rapport with the participants. If possible, do an introduction session with all of the participants you plan to talk to during the day. This will set a consistent tone and allow more time for gathering data during the individual interviews.

- *30 minutes:* Focus on participants' backgrounds, their job role or main interests and activities, and an overview of their organization or their relationship to others at the site. If possible, get a brief tour of the site.

- *30 minutes:* Discuss key topic areas relevant to your product domain in depth. We recommend that you not simply run through interview questions here. Instead, have a few topic introduction statements ready (probes) and then let the participant tell you about their experiences, thoughts, and opinions in these areas. Ask your participants to show you what and how they do something they mention. Have them recreate the last time they did that thing. Be sure to observe their behaviors carefully. Their actions may not support what they verbally express.

- *30 minutes (or perhaps just the last 15) should be reserved for getting closure:* Take care of any logistics (e.g., participant gratuities, exchange of additional contact information, and orientation for next steps) and be sure to thank your participants.

We recommend that everyone on your persona core and extended team participate in the data collection effort (e.g., each person goes out on at least two field study visits) so that everyone has firsthand experience with the data. Direct experience with users will go a long way toward helping your team once the creation process begins. Be very clear on each visitor's role before you go. It works well to have one person lead the visit and be the primary liaison with participants. A second team member can take notes. The third team member can be in charge of collecting artifacts if the participants and management have given you permission to do so. During the visit, make sure to refer back to your script frequently. It is easy to get off track and miss important topic areas. Your script should have clear priorities so that you can manage unexpected events during the visit and still walk away with helpful information.

Conduct the visit

The techniques we describe can be arrayed across a continuum that goes from observational (largely unobtrusive and unstructured) to very interactive (structured, interactive, and participatory). Qualitative research can be conducted in person and at users' places of work or residences (their environment), over the phone or Internet, and either individually or in groups. Common qualitative research methods include site visits, one-on-one interviews or surveys, and focus groups. We focus our discussion on site visits, but many of the details and specific techniques (provided as sidebars, such as on Reality Mapping) can be applied to interviews and focus groups as well. The material following provides five techniques (as contributed sidebars) that can enhance your qualitative research toward persona creation.

Day-in-the-life, image collages, and idea maps engage participants in a way that reveals personal values, goals, fears, motivations, and other emotion-laden information. Such data is valuable when deriving the aspects of personas that make them realistic and able to provoke empathy toward design. (For a brief description of empathic focus, see the sidebar by Don Norman later in this chapter.) Reality Mapping is a useful interviewing technique that is highly interactive and compellingly overt. (Note that Reality Mapping is briefly discussed as a sidebar here and then further covered in Chapter 10).

Bright Idea

"DAY-IN-THE-LIFE" EXERCISES

—Liz Sanders, SonicRim

I developed the day-in-the-life toolkit to help uncover information from users that is at the core of the persona-typical events in everyday life. It is a good tool to help people immerse themselves in thinking about their current experiences. This toolkit is best used at the beginning of an interview, focus group, or observation session, not long after introductions. This can be an important first step in getting the users to later imagine their future experiences.

What type of information/insight is this toolkit best at uncovering?

The simplicity of this toolkit enables people to think at a high level and to see their day as one continuous experience. They are quick to express the major landmarks of their day. The structure of the toolkit keeps people focused on the big picture. If directly asked, most participants will have a difficult time telling you about their day-to-day life, as it is not something they usually think about in such specifics. When you ask people to describe their typical day (e.g., see Figure 3.6) without the benefit of such a toolkit, you generally will get longwinded explanations that tend to ramble and may miss significant landmarks.

FIGURE 3.6: *Evening in a day-of-the-life of a participant from Thailand.*

How do you use this toolkit?

The day-in-the-life exercise is best done as an individual exercise. Everyone's day is different. When the same toolkit is given to a group of people, the results can be summarized, revealing a composite day-in-the-life of a target group of people. But the exercise can also be done collaboratively if you are interested in a team perspective. The day-in-the-life toolkit consists of (see Figure 3.7):

- A shape drawn on a large poster board. The shape directs the flow of the time line (i.e., either linear or circular) and represents their day.

FIGURE 3.7: *A typical day-in-the-life toolkit.*

(Bright idea, continued)

- Picture stickers, word stickers, and simple colorful shapes that can be used to represent daily events such as waking up, showering, eating, driving, meeting, talking, cooking, reading, watching TV, resting, exercising, sleeping, and so on.

Participants are each given a toolkit and instructions such as the following.

> Think about the things you do and the places you go in a typical day. [Specify whether they are to think about a weekday, weekend day, or both.] This line represents your typical day from beginning to end. You might want to put a mark on the time line to show when you wake up. Now take a look at all the stickers and shapes we have given you. Take any of the stickers or shapes that make sense to you and place them along this time line to describe your typical day. You don't have to use all of the stickers—only those that make sense to you. Also, here are some markers you can use to add anything to your typical day you cannot represent using the shapes and stickers we have given you.

We ensure them that they cannot go wrong in doing this exercise as long as their time line makes sense to them. They are the only ones who can describe their typical day. When finished with the exercise, we have the participants explain their time lines (i.e., what they mean as well as what they learned about their day from doing the exercise). At this point they are also free to elaborate on their daily activities.

Bright Idea

IMAGE COLLAGES

—Liz Sanders, SonicRim

The image collage toolkit is ideal for uncovering the emotional side of people. It is a very personal exercise that can be used to reveal a person's feelings about his/her past and future. This toolkit is best used later in an interview, focus group, or observation session, after the participant has had a chance to warm up to the idea of expressing his/her thoughts through a more concrete toolkit such as the day-in-the-life.

In addition to being useful for persona creation, the image collage toolkit is useful for other aspects of the design development process. In the early stages of the design development process, creating image collages can be used to explore people's thoughts and feelings about experience domains. Later in the process, creating image collages can be used to explore how people feel about specific products, prototypes, or events—particularly those you are developing.

What type of information/insight is this toolkit best at uncovering?

Because of its use of photographic images, the image collage toolkit tends to evoke personal and emotional content such as people's memories of the past and their dreams for the future. Image collage can be used to gain insight into specific experiences (e.g., my most recent hospital stay) as well as very broad experiences (e.g., my thoughts and feelings about home past, present, and future). For example, see Figure 3.8.

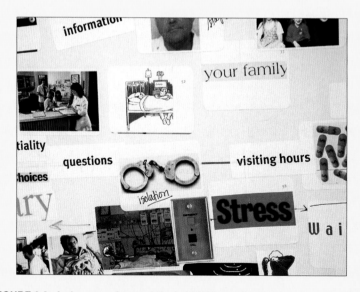

FIGURE 3.8: *A close-up of part of the hospital experience for a current patient.*

(Bright idea, continued)

How do you use this toolkit?

The image collage exercise, because of its personal nature, is most effective when done individually. It is best accomplished in a face-to-face session, but it can also be done in a self-guided manner if the instructions are clear. For example, we may send a workbook to the participant with an image collage toolkit that includes instructions for use. Image collage can also be done in a group setting, with each participant making his/her own collage. In fact, image collage can also be done collaboratively by a group of people. In group collage activities, the toolkit components need to be much larger than the components used in individual sessions.

An important part of the image collage exercise occurs when the participant tells the story of the collage they have made. In one-on-one sessions, people often tell their story throughout the entire collage-making activity. They "stick and talk." In group sessions, people tell their stories after they have all completed their collages. In telling their stories to the group, people disclose a lot about themselves to the others. We find that this disclosure facilitates later collaboration between those people. The image collage toolkit consists of:

- Large poster board
- Set of picture stickers and word and/or phrase stickers
- Colored markers, glue, and scissors.

The poster board is often blank, leaving it up to the participant to use the space in a way that is most meaningful to them. Sometimes constraints are placed on the collage-making activity and are represented on the poster board. For example, a poster board with a circle drawn on it might be used for a collage in which the inside of the circle represents "I like it" and the outside of the circle represents "I don't like it." The set of picture, word, and phrase stickers are chosen specifically for the experience that is being explored through collage. The set must be broad enough so as not to preclude any relevant ideas from being expressed. It is important to have a variety of images and words: positive and negative, abstract and concrete, and so on. For example, see Figure 3.9.

(Bright idea, continued)

FIGURE 3.9: *An image collage toolkit for exploring the hospital experience.*

Participants are each given a collage toolkit and instructions such as the following:

> You have shared your thoughts and feelings about hospital experiences. Now you will have the
> opportunity to express your thoughts and feelings about your most recent hospital experience in
> a new way. You will be making a collage about the highs and lows of your most recent hospital
> experience. We have many pictures and words for you to use in making your collage. If you do
> not see a sticker that represents something that is important in your experience, feel free to take
> a marker and add it. The positive components of your hospital experience go above the line.
> The negative components go below the line.

We assure the participants that they cannot go wrong in this activity as long as their collage makes
sense to them. The timing of the collage-making activity is critical. They need to have enough time
to collect their thoughts but not so much time that they start to edit out any ideas that have occurred
spontaneously. When finished with the exercise, we ask the participant to present his/her collage.
We might also ask them to tell us about any other thoughts they had while creating the collage.

Bright Idea

IDEA MAPS

—Liz Sanders, SonicRim

The idea mapping toolkit is ideal for exploring people's ideas for new products and/or services. It can be used in constructing your persona's expectations and aspirations for the future. Idea mapping is usually employed near the end of research sessions, after participants have been given the opportunity to think about their dreams for the future (perhaps using an image collage toolkit). The information that gets generated will help your personas be useful in the fuzzy front end of the new product development process, when a human-centered (versus a technology-centered) approach is desired.

What type of information/insight is this toolkit best at uncovering?

The idea mapping toolkit allows participants to create and express new ideas, such as that shown in Figure 3.10. It works best when they have been thoroughly immersed in thinking about both their ideal experiences and their current ones [Sanders and William 2001]. Idea mapping is also useful for obtaining insight into what is missing from people's current experiences.

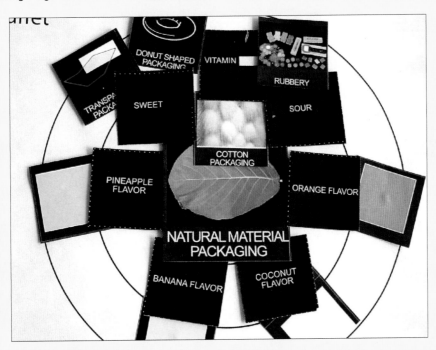

FIGURE 3.10: *An idea mapped concept for a new snack food.*

(Bright idea, continued)

How do you use this toolkit?

This toolkit is typically used in a one-on-one manner. Participants will often create very different idea maps, but outstanding themes will inevitably present themselves when observing and analyzing the group as a whole. Collaboration in idea mapping can also work with pairs of people who know each other well, such as spouses, roommates, siblings, and other family members. The conversations that take place between people in the idea mapping process are extremely valuable glimpses into the needs and dreams of the personas. Audio recording of these conversations is recommended.

The idea mapping toolkit consists of:

- Poster board
- Set of abstract and colorful shapes, borders, symbols, pictures, and words
- Colored markers, glue, and scissors.

The poster board often presents the participants with a way of prioritizing the various components that make up their idea. For example, a bull's-eye might be used to get the participants to think about which components are central to their idea and which are more on the periphery. Figure 3.11 shows an example of an idea mapping toolkit.

FIGURE 3.11: *An idea mapping toolkit for exploring new snack food ideas.*

(Bright idea, continued)

Participants are each given a toolkit, and instructions such as the following:

> Here is a set of images and words and a sheet of paper on which you will create your ideal snack. You will notice that there are items to represent different parts of a snack, including flavors, colors, packaging materials, textures, and nutrients. You can make any type of snack you want by selecting from this assortment of items. You will notice that each item comes in three sizes: small, medium, and large. The most important components of your snack would be large items that go inside the bull's-eye, and the less important components can be smaller items in the outer circles. If you do not see a sticker that represents something important to your ideal snack, feel free to take a marker and write it on. It is not anyone else's snack, so go ahead and put anything you think sounds good in your snack.

When finished with the exercise, each participant explains his/her idea mapping. When people do this in a group setting, you can follow it up with a group brainstorming session that takes off on the best ideas.

Note: The Snack Buffet is an idea generation toolkit created by a graduate student team at The Ohio State University's Department of Industrial, Interior and Visual Communication Design in the Fall Quarter of 2004. It was one of several research tools they used in an exploratory project called A Study of Snack Perception and Behavior [Chung et al. 2004].

Bright Idea

REALITY MAPPING

Reality Maps are flowcharts you can create using sticky notes and a large sheet of paper. They are easy and fun to create. The Reality Mapping method will help you structure interviews with users or subject matter experts to capture as much information from them as possible. Reality Maps are especially helpful if you don't have a lot of time or ability to directly observe people in their own environments.

What type of information/insight is this toolkit best at uncovering?

Reality Maps help you collect information about goals, specific tasks, particular responsibilities, and (perhaps most importantly) the ways people think about the task domain. Your product will probably have to *work within* and *change* the current context of tasks and goals. Maps will help you understand both the cognitive and physical landscapes of activities into which you will be introducing your product. Later, during the *adulthood* phase, you can create Design Maps for designing and exploring the new or "revised" experiences your product will support.

How do you use this toolkit?

When you are collecting data for your persona effort, you can create Reality Maps:

- In conversation with actual users of an existing product
- In conversation with people who perform tasks or have goals similar to those your product will enable or support
- With your core team after observing people completing tasks in their own environments
- In conversation with subject matter experts or other second-hand data sources.

Once you have created a Reality Map, you can iterate and validate it by talking to additional people (users or subject matter experts) and/or by comparing the experience it describes with observed experiences. The Reality Map toolkit consists of:

- Four colors of sticky notes
- A large sheet of butcher paper or paper on an easel
- Markers for writing large text

(Bright idea, continued)

As shown in Figure 3.12, Maps have four basic building blocks: steps (blue) with comments (green), questions (yellow), and design ideas (pink). Steps should be arrayed horizontally, with related comments, questions, and design ideas arranged under the steps they reference. You can read across the row of steps to get a sense of the process from end to end, or you can focus on a subset of the steps and read down the columns to understand related questions and ideas.

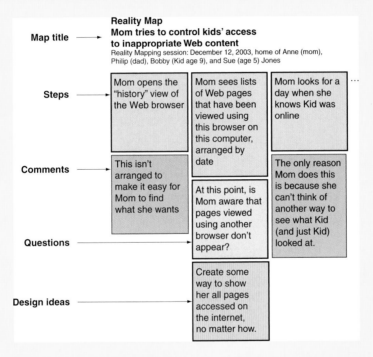

FIGURE 3.12: *A small portion of a Reality Map.*

For a detailed discussion of (and instructions for using) Reality and Design Maps, see Chapter 10.

Create artifacts to communicate the data

Shortly after your first visit, and as you conduct the remaining visits, you will want to start organizing and processing the data you collect. Conduct post-visit debriefing sessions with your extended persona team, which might include some of your stakeholders. These can be short (30- to 60-minute) meetings in which the site visit team shares key insights and anecdotes with the broader team. Put the most important findings on easel paper or some other medium that has permanence and visibility to establish a common understanding and memory.

If you utilized one of the collection techniques described in the previous sidebars, place the resulting artifacts from those activities in a place where everyone can easily access them. Consider reserving a specific meeting room, design/collaborative space, or work area to serve as the data headquarters for the visits. If you cannot locate this type of space, create artifacts that are easy to transport and display (for example, use poster board or foam-core to create sturdy posters). We also highly recommend that you create a standard profile document so that you can collect and organize the information from each site in an orderly, useful way.

As a more detailed communication device for your core team, consider creating "real people" posters or wall displays to encourage sharing of knowledge gained from the visits. Print copies of interesting photos and post them along with other artifacts on the walls. Write up short scenarios that walk through key aspects of their lives. Include personal interests and hobbies. You might also consider creating Reality Maps (see "Bright Idea: Reality Mapping" previously) for each participant after the visit, if that was not part of your site visit script.

Note that these "real people" materials should *not* be shared broadly with your larger organization at this point. Do not post them in high traffic areas or public spaces such as hallways, lobbies, or lounges. If you show them to people outside your persona team, these materials may confuse the persona effort. Your goal is to focus everyone on the personas you have yet to create, not on the data you have collected. Collect all of the information from the site visits in one location for easy access. You will be using this information and the displays to assist your persona core team in the *conception and gestation* phase.

Analyze the data

After you have completed all of the site visits (or once a significant number of them are complete), you will want to analyze the data to find common themes across the participants. We make a distinction at this point between data "analysis" and data "processing." The former is what you must do with raw data (drawing themes from a series of observations, summarizing the responses to interview questions across participants, doing frequency counts, calculating averages, and so on) to get meaningful answers (i.e., results) from the research. The latter is what you do with the results of such analyses, and that activity will happen during the *conception and gestation* phase. You generated transcripts and notes from each of the sites you visited. You should now take the next step and analyze all of that data before starting the data processing step associated with the *conception and gestation* phase.

As part of their contextual design methodology, Beyer and Holtzblatt [1998] describe rich processes for capturing and interpreting information about the target users of a product. More recently, Holtzblatt, Wendell, and Wood have published *Rapid Contextual Design: A How-to Guide to Key Techniques for User-Centered Design* [Holtzblatt et al. 2004], which provides a great deal of practical advice for integrating contextual design into the product development process. As you collect and analyze data about your users toward creating your personas, we recommend that you consult these books and consider creating one or more of the models the authors use to capture the tasks and behaviors of users:

- *Flow model:* Captures roles and responsibilities
- *Sequence model:* Captures tasks
- *Cultural model:* Captures values
- *Affinity diagram:* Captures issues (similar to the technique described in Chapter 4).

Contextual data is a natural raw material for deep, rich personas that reliably reflect the archetype characters that make up the market being supported. By collecting enough data to characterize the market, not just two or three interviews, your persona characterization will be a more complete representation of the people and issues you are trying to design for.

You can leave your site visit data as is and simply include the individual site reports as separate data sources to use during persona creation. The value of doing an analysis of your field research now is that it allows you to discover themes in your field data independently of and without influence from your other data sources. You might discover questions you would like to ask at subsequent interviews. Doing the analysis separately is more time consuming, however. Both ways can work, so you will simply need to choose the approach that best fits your schedule and resources.

COLLECT DATA THROUGH SECONDARY SOURCES

If you are not able to locate or directly conduct rigorous research about your users, and perhaps even if you can, there are additional sources of useful information you can collect and use for persona creation. For example, your own sales, product, and customer support teams have a wealth of information to share about your customers in anecdotes and case studies. Anyone on your team who has direct, frequent contact with users of your products is a likely source of data. We refer to such sources of information as secondary sources. Many times, such information has not been formally captured in any document or artifact. You will need to interview or survey these people to harvest this data. Consider interviewing the following in your company:

- Customer service and product support specialists
- Sales support and sales engineers
- Account managers
- Documentation specialists
- Training professionals.

Story from the field

IT'S NOT ALWAYS POSSIBLE TO OBSERVE YOUR TARGET USERS DIRECTLY

—George Olsen, Principal, Interaction by Design

Once I was building an extranet for the board of directors of a large financial services company. Because the board members were generally CEOs of other Fortune 500 companies, there was no way the design team could get time to interview them. Fortunately, we were able to work with the board's support staff, who worked closely with the board members, and consequently were able to tell us a good deal about the needs, goals, and computer skills of the board members.

It is important to make it as clear as possible (in the documents you create to reflect the information you gather) that this source was one step removed from the actual users who use a product or process to get something done. When you are gathering data from these representatives, keep an ear open for biases and stereotypes the representatives may have generated.

Collect assumptions as a secondary data source

It may be the case that no one in your organization has direct contact with users (or proposed users) of your product that you can collect secondary data from. In this case, you may want to loosen your definition of "data" a bit and consider assumptions—perhaps better named "educated guesses"—about your target users as a source of information for persona creation.

YOUR SALESPEOPLE KNOW A LOT ABOUT YOUR CUSTOMERS

—George Olsen, Principal, Interaction by Design

Salespeople hear about customers' needs and goals all day, so they can be a good source of information. This is particularly true if they use consultative selling techniques, which emphasize first understanding customers' needs and then selling on benefits delivered rather than on product features. (Neil Rackham's *SPIN Selling* [Rackham 1988] is a good overview of this style of selling.) Learning to speak the language of sales (such as referring to "benefits") can be useful in working with salespeople, including making the point that your role is to make the product so desirable that users want to purchase it again.

But handle salespeople's input with extreme caution. First, be sure they talk to people who actually use the product, not just the people who sign the checks, which can happen with enterprise products. Second, remember that their interest is getting the customer to purchase the product, whereas yours is what the customer does with the product after the sale. Even well-intentioned salespeople simply have different priorities. Third, most salespeople tend to sell features rather than benefits. So, you often end up with lengthy wish lists. However, you can use these as a way of working back up to the level of needs by asking what need a particular feature would address, and then move on to questions about how widespread the need is. It is wise to cross-check these needs with multiple salespeople, just to make sure it is truly something desired by customers and not just one particular account.

Assumptions are at least as powerful and influential as data, and they must be handled with care. Moreover, they are omnipresent and readily available to you. Everyone in your organization has assumptions about the target users of your next product.

Never discount the power of assumptions that already exist in your organization. There are probably some assumptions that are so strong they seem woven into the very fabric of your organization. You can collect and evaluate these assumptions just like you collect and evaluate data. Part of the value here is that through assumption-based personas you can make these implicit (hidden) assumptions very explicit and visible to your organization.

What are assumption personas and why use them?

Assumption personas are persona sketches that you and your core team can create to articulate your organization's existing assumptions about the user population. As an optional step in a more rigorous data-driven approach, we actually recommend creating assumption personas before diving into your data analysis. This might be done as part of the *family planning* phase, *especially* if this is your first foray into the world of personas.

We recommend that you create assumption personas whether or not you plan to collect firsthand data about your target users. If you cannot perform your own user research, you and your team will get many of the persona-related benefits to your process and product. If you are planning on collecting data directly from users, creating assumption personas first can:

- Help stakeholders understand the need for the persona effort
- Streamline your product-related communication
- Help you target your field research to validate (or contradict) current impressions of who users are
- Provide some practice with persona *conception and gestation* methods before you need to create your real personas.

Assumptions exist. Assumption personas merely articulate them

The truth is that everyone on your team (from marketing, to design, to development) has assumptions about users, and these assumptions do exert influence over the design of the product. These assumptions could be based on anything from hard data to personal biases. If you articulate the assumptions—draw them out into the light, where they can be examined and evaluated—you gain more control over them and the ways they impact the product. At the very least, your persona effort will make all of your organization's assumptions about target users very explicit—a perhaps painful but nonetheless valuable outcome.

Assumptions are usually formed after data has been internalized, combined, and interpreted. Assumptions almost always reflect some misinterpreted, poorly recalled, and improperly combined aspects of original data, but they do contain some data and they do reflect the ways your company has digested and understands information about your users and your business. It is likely that some elements of your company's strategy with respect to your competition, the changing market, and your evolving technology exist only in the minds of stakeholders. Eliciting assumptions helps you understand some valid and important information affecting the design and development of your product.

Assumption personas are easy to create and help people understand why personas are valuable

Assumption personas are much easier to create than data-driven personas. In a short time, you and your core team can collect, analyze, and categorize many of your organization's assumptions and create assumption persona sketches. Because these sketches relate directly to your product and will contain information that is familiar, they will help everyone in your organization see the value of personas to the design and development effort. The exercise can also help your persona core team practice the techniques you will use during "real" persona creation. We describe a relatively rigorous process for creating assumption personas, but you can also create ad hoc assumption personas at the beginning of any meeting simply by asking the participants to describe the users of the product and to name those assumptions. Ad hoc assumption personas are excellent tools for clarifying and focusing communication in meetings. (See also "Story from the field: Ad Hoc Personas and Empathetic Focus," following.)

Assumption personas can help make it clear to your managers that different assumptions exist, and that therefore a common definition of the target audience needs to be created and communicated. At the very least, making assumptions explicit will help ensure that everyone's assumptions *match*, which is no small feat! Unclear communication and mismatched assumptions can be very damaging to a product. It is actually *riskier* to allow these factors to impact your product than it is to create "bad" personas by guessing and making assumptions. Once everyone in the organization sees their assumptions collected, organized, and expressed as personas, they usually find it easier to discuss the assumptions coherently and to agree on changes as a group—or to agree that allowing extra time for data collection is a good idea.

Assumption personas can prompt data collection

Assumption personas can be the eye-opening catalyst that gets your team interested in some real user research. When your assumptions are exposed, so are gaps in your knowledge of your users. Assumption personas can lead your organization toward more rigorous UCD techniques. For a nice example of how assumption personas can trigger interesting methods for user data collection, see "Story from the field: Personas at Zylom.com" in Chapter 4.

Assumption personas, communicated and used properly, are simply not that risky

As long as you make it painfully clear that your assumption personas are based on assumptions and not on data, there is not a lot of risk in communicating and discussing them (unless your corporate culture treats some assumptions as sacred or taboo, in which case creating assumption personas at all might not be a good idea). The risk of assumption-based personas comes when the team *forgets or ignores* that the information in the personas is based merely on assumptions and treats it like data.

If you are on a tight schedule or budget—or have some other indication that full, data-driven personas are not appropriate for your needs—assumption-based personas can be used with discretion as a tool for design and development activities. This can be one way of deriving some of the benefits of personas when you simply cannot spend time or resources on creating real personas. Assumption personas align the organization's thinking around a set of common referents, which makes them valuable. If you end up using assumption personas and never move on to data-driven personas, you can still reap many of the benefits of personas. However, the entire organization must understand and agree that assumption personas are there primarily to improve communication.

When are assumption personas a bad idea?

If you believe that your organization harbors long-held "sacred cow" assumptions that people will be unable or unwilling to bring forth in a meeting, proceed with extreme caution. When you explore assumptions, you run the risk of exposing bad decisions that were made in the past and other "dirty corporate secrets" some of your colleagues may not want illuminated. If you suspect or discover this is the case, create personas only from primary data sources. Assumption personas are good for exposing, communicating, and aligning assumptions, but they are not effective tools for challenging highly political assumptions. If you want to challenge assumptions, do it with data.

Collecting assumptions to create assumption personas

Creating assumption personas is very much like creating data-driven personas, but the process is less rigorous, takes less time, and involves different people. To create assumption personas that really have impact, we recommend that you identify influential stakeholders in your organization and on your product team and identify and collect their assumptions about your target users. If this is not possible, simply gather a variety of people from your product team—ideally from different disciplines.

Once you have collected stakeholders' assumptions, you can create assumption personas with or without their direct participation. If you choose to create the assumption personas independently of stakeholders, you and your core team can simply treat the gathered assumptions like "data factoids" and use several of the techniques discussed in Chapter 4 to create the assumption personas. Once you have created the assumption personas, you should review them with stakeholders before moving forward with using them.

How long does it take to create assumption personas?

If your organization is small, you will probably be able to identify existing assumptions quite quickly, perhaps in one or two short brainstorming meetings. If you have a large organization, it could take quite a long time to schedule interviews with all of the key stakeholders, to review strategy documents, and so on. In this case, the time it takes is worthwhile because you will probably find wildly disparate assumptions that are affecting both the development cycle and your finished products in negative ways.

Step 1: Identify and collect existing assumptions

The first step is to collect the assumptions about target users, their work, and environments that exist in your organization. It is certainly possible to collect assumptions and create assumption personas in the same meeting, but we recommend that you treat collection as a step in its own right (especially if there are many influential people in your organization). There are several approaches to collecting assumptions that you can mix and match as necessary.

Meet with stakeholders and leaders

This is probably the most efficient way of collecting assumptions about your end users. Ask stakeholders to describe, in as much detail as they can, the target end users of your product. If you get answers such as, "My mother should be able to use it," ask for more detail. Try to capture exactly what that person thinks of when they think of "my mother." Have that person list specific characteristics (e.g., over 50, just purchased her first PC, and so on).

You can meet with stakeholders one-on-one or in groups. However, if you meet in groups, be prepared for debates. Remind everyone that the goal of the meeting is not to come to a consensus but to bring all assumptions out on the table. Try to forestall debates and encourage everyone to list the assumptions.

Schedule a two-hour individual brainstorming session with the product team

Getting the assumptions of the stakeholders and leaders out on the table is important, but you also need to hear from the troops. What do various members of the development team assume about the end users? What about product managers and others? Sit everyone down and ask them to record their assumptions on sticky notes. Instruct them to write one type of user on each sticky note. You'll find they can imagine many target users. When they finish, you can conduct an affinity exercise to group and identify patterns of assumptions.

Send out an e-mail questionnaire

As an alternative to a direct, in-person meeting, you can create a short questionnaire asking members of your organization to send you their assumptions about your target users. Ask them to describe, in as much detail as possible, how they envision the various people who use or will use your product. Be prepared to follow up on the questionnaire toward obtaining more details as necessary. Also keep in mind that e-mail is fairly easy to ignore, and that you might not get many responses. Your questionnaire might include questions such as the following:

- Can you describe one or two typical users of our product?
- Can you name and describe a person you know who is most similar to the types of people using our product?
- At what times of day do our users use our product?
- Where do people use our product?
- Do our users use our product because they like to or because they have to?
- Are we trying to attract different types of users with our new product? Who are they?
- What (besides using our products) do our users like to do?
- Are the people who pay for our products the same people that use the products on a daily basis?

Review existing product vision, strategy, and design documents

If for some reason you cannot gather assumptions directly from your team, you might be able to find a wealth of assumptions about target users in some of your team's planning documents. Find a copy of the company's business plan, product strategy documents, design and vision documents from existing versions of the product, and marketing strategy documents. Look for any document that records strategic decisions made by your company. These decisions often hinge on expressed or implied assumptions about the target users of the product. Write down all references to users or customers and capture the exact wording as well as the implied characteristics you find. If you plan to share this analysis with anyone, be careful to be tactful and work to avoid offending any of the original authors of the documents you are dissecting.

Step 2: Create assumption personas

Once you have collected assumptions from your team, you and your core team can either directly sketch out some personas that reflect what you have learned or use the same methods you use to create data-driven personas (affinity diagramming) by treating the assumptions as "factoids." To do the latter, simply follow the 6-step process detailed in Chapter 4. If you choose the former (directly creating sketches), we recommend that you then follow up with steps 4, 5, and 6 from Chapter 4 to evaluate, enrich, and validate your creations as is possible and appropriate.

Story from the field

AD HOC PERSONAS AND EMPATHETIC FOCUS

—Donald A. Norman, Nielsen Norman Group

Personas as a Communication Tool

Design is in many ways an act of communication, but to communicate effectively the designer must have a clear, cohesive, and understandable image of the product being designed and the user of the product must be able to understand that communication. By emphasizing the several types of unique individuals who will be using the product, personas aid the designer in maintaining focus—concentrating on design aspects individual personas require and eliminating from the design things they will find superfluous. Personas are tools for focus and aids to communication, and for this they only need to be realistic, not real, not necessarily even accurate (as long as they are appropriate characterizations of the user base). Although it is often fun to read the detailed descriptions of personas and to pry into their private and social lives, I have never understood how these personal details actually aid in the design process itself. They seem completely superfluous.

Thus, a major virtue of personas is the establishment of empathy and understanding of the individuals who use the product. It is important that each persona seem real, allowing the designer to ask, "How would Mary respond to this?" or Peter, or Bashinka?

Personas also play an important communicative role within the design community and within the company producing the product. When one discusses the product in terms of its impact on the individual personas, the language of the discussion is automatically based on that of the people who use it and the benefits (or difficulties) that would accrue to them. This is in contrast to the technical language so often applied when talking about the features and attributes of the product. Personas make it easier to be human centered. As others have noted, personas provide a common language regarding experience so that designers, engineers, and marketing people can unambiguously communicate when they talk about the product. The same tool is valuable when the product is being designed by different groups within the company—and this is always the case with any large, complex product. The use of personas helps standardize the approach of each group, so there is continuity of level and function in the different parts of the product.

Empathetic Focus

Another purpose of the persona, I believe, is to add empathetic focus to the design. By focus I mean that the design must be clear and coherent. It is not a collection of features added willy-nilly throughout the life span of the product, even if each feature by itself makes sense. Rather, it is having a clear image of what the product is meant to be—and what it is not meant to be—and rejecting features that do not fit. By empathy, I mean an understanding of and identification with the user population, the better to ensure they will be able to take advantage of the product and to use it readily and easily—not with frustration but with pleasure.

Using Ad Hoc Personas

As a consultant to companies, I often find myself having to make my points quickly—quite often in only a few hours. This short duration makes impossible any serious attempt at gathering data or using real observations. Instead, I have found that people can often mine their own extensive experiences to create effective personas that bring home design points strongly and effectively.

In one case, for a major software company, one of their major customer bases was American college students. We quickly identified several classes (called cases) of students:

- *Case 1:* A student attending a two-year community college while holding a full-time job
- *Case 2:* A student in a four-year institution who wanted to have a successful business career
- *Case 3:* A student who was only in school for lack of anything else to do and who had few desires other than to have a good time.

We quickly invented one relevant persona per case: a hard-working, single mother (case 1), a serious full-time student with no outside experience or responsibilities (case 2), and a lackadaisical, laid-back goof-off (case 3). Unlike traditional persona studies, these were not based on data, but each was described in sufficient detail (including names) so that the group all agreed they felt like people they knew.

I have found that an excellent way of using a persona is to have someone role-play the part. In this way, only one person has to develop an in-depth knowledge of the persona, and everyone else uses the role-player as an expert informant in activities such as participatory design.

In this case, I divided the attendees at my workshop into three groups to do a design exercise, with the person role-playing the relevant persona as expert informant. The result was wonderful to behold.

The teams all produced highly user-centered designs based on the products of their respective companies. The designs were all very different in type and spirit from the products of their company, even though some of the designers of those products were in the workshop. The differences were striking.

In regard to case 3, the student kept saying, "I don't care," when asked about choices, while simultaneously making it clear that he wanted a system that required no effort or thought on his part and that gave him his preferred outcome (receiving a degree, but with minimal impairment to his preferred lifestyle). In regard to cases 1 and 2, students were more involved, but because of their different requirements imposed different demands on the software. Everyone agreed that this simple exercise had altered their perspective on what a product ought to do and how they should approach design.

Another consulting job was for a major publisher of city-information products. This group of attendees consisted of the executive team for the company, and although none of them actually designed products the product groups were all under their control. For this workshop, I had the group invent two couples. One couple was young, newly married, and about to have their first child. They had only a small apartment and did not have much money. Their task was to use the city guide to find a crib for the expected child. The other couple was older, retired, and with significant discretionary income. All of their children were away from home, living independently. My original intention was to have this older couple book a travel adventure, but because we were running out of time I switched the exercise. I announced that the older couple were the parents of the expectant mother, and they wanted to purchase a crib for their new grandchild.

The new exercise was extremely rewarding because it demonstrated how the two couples approached the task very differently, with different emphases, different search characteristics, and very different values. Having the workshop attendees work on the same problem was serendipitous, for it revealed the deficiencies in the existing city guide. Interestingly enough, after the conclusion of the exercise several of the executives admitted that their own behavior mimicked that of the older couple, including the observation that they seldom turned to their own city guide as a first step. This sensitized them to the fact that their own behavior with their company's product was a relevant datum. "Realize that others might behave the same way you do," I admonished them. "Take your own behavior seriously."

The Final Assessment

These two different examples of personas are very different from the traditional usage of the concept. They were created quickly, did not use real data, and were employed without much background information and attention to detail. But even so, they serve as wonderful tools for building understanding and empathy into the design process in a way that would be impossible with any other method.

Do personas have to be accurate? Do they require a large body of research? Not always, I conclude. Personas must indeed reflect the target group for the design team, but for some purposes that is sufficient.

A persona allows designers to bring their own life-long experience to bear on the problem, and because each persona is a realistic individual person the designers can focus on features, behaviors, and expectations appropriate for this individual. This allows the designer to screen off from consideration all those other wonderful ideas they may have. If the other ideas are as useful and valuable as they might seem, the designer's challenge is to either create a scenario for the existing persona in which these attributes make sense or to invent a new persona for whom the same applies. The designer then needs to justify inclusion of this new persona by making the business-case argument that the new persona does indeed represent an important target population for the product.

TRACK AND MANAGE DATA SOURCES AS YOU COLLECT THEM

As you collect data from primary (both internal and external) and secondary sources, it is a good idea to keep a master list of all data sources and a short description of the content of each source. At the very least, for each source, list:

- Name of source
- Date the data was collected and/or analyzed
- Where you found the source
- Types of data the source contains
    - Qualitative data, quantitative data, or both?
    - Demographic, psychographic, behavioral, or some other type of data?

If you are interested in a richer, more helpful tracking system—which can be particularly useful for managing large sets of data—create a "data-collection-by-topic" spreadsheet.

G4K	G4K market segmentation	Internal market research	Sources purchased from agency	Sources found via Web searches	More data needed
Kids online					
How many kids are online?	✓				
What are the demographics of kids online?				✓Search terms: * Kids online * Schools online	
How do kids get online? Do they have their own accounts?				✓	Need more
What do kids like to do online?		✓	✓	✓	
Kids and entertainment					
What do kids do for fun?				✓	Need more
How much time do kids have for fun (vs. school?)			✓	✓	
The family and the computer					
Where is the computer in the house?			✓	✓	
How many computers are in the house?			We should buy this!	✓	
How many are using it?				✓	
Parents and their concerns					
What are parents concerns re: the Internet and their kids?					Can't find enough recent stuff!
How do parents control access to the Internet?			✓	✓	
What benefits do parents perceive re: the Internet for their kids?				✓	Need more

FIGURE 3.13: *G4K's data-collection-by-topic spreadsheet. The G4K team used this spreadsheet to keep track of whether they had data to answer persona-related questions. Check marks indicate that a type of data was found in a particular set of sources.*

Create a data-collection-by-topic spreadsheet

To create a data-collection-by-topic spreadsheet, identify the types of information you will need for creating useful personas. This list does not have to be exhaustive. You should be able to create the list within a few minutes. List your data sources as column headers. As you find data sources that help answer each question, check the corresponding column in the spreadsheet. If you like, you can enrich your data-collection-by-topic spreadsheet by listing the names or numbers of sources that meet each data need and/or include a list of keywords or search terms that helped you find appropriate data sources. A sample spreadsheet is shown in Figure 3.13.

When you include all of the existing data sources you have collected, the spreadsheet will clearly show where you are missing data. It will also show which data sources tended to answer which types of question. This should help you create a data collection plan to fill in the gaps. As such, it is useful to start this list early in your data collection efforts. It will help guide your activities during this part of the *family planning* lifecycle phase.

Create a data source index

If you are finding a lot of data sources, you should make an effort to keep them organized and easy to reference. This will help you prepare for your *conception and gestation* activities. A data-collection-by-topic spreadsheet will help you track your progress as you research particular topics. However, we also recommend that you create a data source index to track the data documents themselves.

It is a good idea to assign a unique number to each data source. For electronic versions of your data sources, prepend the document title with the number (e.g., *01_g4k_market_segmentation.doc*) and write the source number on any hard copies of the data source. Consider creating an index page that lists and links to all of your data sources. An example of an index is shown in Figure 3.14.

Personas Data Source Index					
Category	**Description**	**Date**	**Author**	**Source #**	**Incorp. into Personas?**
Kids Online	G4K Market Segmentation	oct 2003	Market research	01	✓
	Wired elementary schools in the Boston area	aug 2003	Persona team	02	✓
	Agency Report: Kids online 2002	jan 2002	Agency	03	✓
	"Kids Count" http://www.aecf.org/kidscount/	2003	Annie E. Casey Foundation	04	✓
	CLIKS online data http://www.aecf.org/cgi-bin/cliks.cgi	jun 2003	Persona team	05	TBD
	Analysphere kids online: privacy and content regulation http://www.analysphere.com/23Apr01/kidz.htm	apr 2001	Analysphere	06	✓
Kids and entertainment	kids entertainment.com	2003	Kid's Entertainment Industry	07	✓

FIGURE 3.14: *Create a data source index. Note that this example includes the category for the data, a link to the primary source, the date of creation and author, source number, and a final column for whether and when the source was used in the creation of the personas. You will use the final column during the conception and gestation phase to keep track of which data sources have been mined for their persona-related information.*

SUMMARY

During the persona *family planning* phase of the lifecycle, you have assembled a core team, analyzed your own organization, created an action plan, and collected data. Even if you have created personas many times before, you should always schedule time for the *family planning* phase.

The *family planning* phase is the time for critical thinking and analysis about your organization and your project. You need to take a careful look at your resources and your organization's needs to determine your level of investment in the persona effort. No matter what your level of investment will be, you must plan to not only create personas but to maintain them throughout their lifecycle. Taking the time to think about this now will enable you to make good choices about the structure of your persona core team, the scope of your persona effort, and the processes most likely to ensure the success of the personas.

Once you have your persona core team in place, you are ready to start identifying and collecting data sources. The relationship between data and personas continues to be an interesting and rich topic among UCD professionals. As we discussed in Chapter 1, we believe that the most effective way to create personas is to start with rich and varied primary data sources. Although secondary data (including assumptions) have their place in the persona lifecycle, primary data helps make your personas a valid and appropriate target for design and adds credibility to the persona effort among the members of the product team.

We believe that personas should be based on data. Even the *perception* that the personas are not based on data can damage their credibility and utility. Existing internal and external data sources surround you. All you have to do is identify and collect them. Once you do this, you can take a look at the information they offer and plan to collect additional data accordingly, to "fill in the gaps." It is important to have both quantitative and qualitative data to build personas from. Observational field studies can provide rich qualitative data to enhance other data and information you may have about your target users.

Whether or not you have access to data, we recommend that you create assumption personas as a starting point to help you identify and analyze existing assumptions that are part of your corporate culture. Assumption personas will, at the very least, bring assumptions to light, and assumptions you are aware of are much less dangerous than hidden assumptions. If for some reason you cannot create data-driven personas, you can use assumption personas as your design targets. If you do plan to use assumption personas as design targets, note that most of the suggestions found in Chapter 4 will work as well when based on assumptions as they do when based on data.

Once your data is collected, you will be ready to move on to the persona *conception and gestation* phase, when you will analyze your data and undertake the exciting task of developing useful personas. Chapter 4 offers recommendations that will help your team create rich personas no matter how much data you have collected or how much time you have.

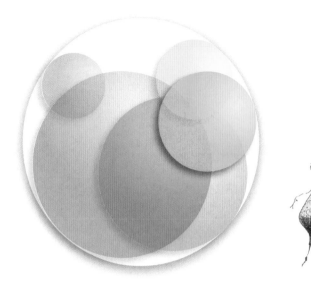

PERSONA CONCEPTION AND GESTATION

SETTING THE SCENE: WHAT'S GOING ON IN YOUR ORGANIZATION NOW?

The best time to start the persona *conception and gestation* phase is when your last product is fully out the door and your product team is poised to begin a new development effort. There's no solid direction for the new product yet, so competing visions, misinformation, rumors, and team-wide anxiety may exist. False starts are likely to occur as the product strategy and vision settle into place. Anyone involved in the early stages of planning would clearly benefit from the data you have amassed about users, customers, and the broader market. Typical activities during this phase of product development include:

- The executive staff wants to provide high-level direction, a vision, for the entire team. They will be interested in market trends, emerging technologies, and the competitive landscape. They are eager to get the ball rolling.

- Product and project managers are trying to figure out what to build into the next product, working with lists of cut features from the last cycle or investigating what customers are saying about their current products.

- The development team at large is still supporting the previous release—fixing bugs, training support engineers, or cleaning up unfinished code for a point release. But they are eager to be done with the old stuff. Some may be exploring new technologies or working on pet projects.

- Like the development team, the QA team is recovering from the previous effort.

- Usability specialists, technical writers, and information, interaction, and UI designers are likely to be working with the product and project managers, brainstorming features and new ideas.

- The marketing team is still fully engaged with the release of the last product.

WHAT IS *CONCEPTION AND GESTATION* FOR PERSONAS?

Conception and gestation is the phase of the persona lifecycle in which you actually create your personas. It is the phase in which you use data to create engaging representations of individual users that your team can use for planning, design, and development. During this phase you will face the tricky question of how many personas to create and how to prioritize them. You will process the data and/or assumptions you have collected (by prioritizing, filtering, and organizing) to discover information about your users. Using this information, you and your core team will create bulleted persona "skeletons" that key stakeholders can prioritize according to business goals. You will develop your prioritized skeletons into complete personas that are then ready to be introduced to your organization in the *birth and maturation* phase.

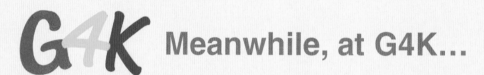

Meanwhile, at G4K...

During the *family planning* phase, the G4K persona core team was able to get a good sense of how personas could be used to enhance the portal project team's specific design and development process. They are now eager to create personas.

They collected a lot of existing data (much of which was free) and uncovered many assumptions about users from the project team and executives. They executed some very enlightening field research and now have a slew of interesting flowcharts, graphs, photos, quotes, and observation notes. They feel like they have explored as much as they can about the ways their future customers will potentially use their product. However, they also feel a bit overwhelmed at the prospect of combing through all of the data sources they have amassed. They know they must plow ahead to start the work involved in the *conception and gestation* phase of the persona lifecycle: evaluating and organizing data, creating and prioritizing persona skeletons, and enriching those terse abstractions to create complete persona foundation documents.

The six-step conception and gestation process

Persona creation is largely a serial and straightforward process in which you summarize, cluster, analyze the data to discover themes (see Figure 4.2). You use these themes to generate rough persona "skeletons." You then cull and prioritize the skeletons to focus only the most important, most appropriate, targets. Finally, you enrich skeletons into full personas by making the details concrete and adding personality and a story line. (For

- Discuss categories of users
- Process data
- Identify & create skeletons
- Evaluate & prioritize skeletons
- Develop skeletons into personas
- Validate the personas

FIGURE 4.1: *The six-step persona creation process.*

comparison, see the creation methods of Baxley in *Making the Web Work* [Baxley 2003], Cooper and Reimann in *About Face 2.0* [Cooper and Reimann 2003], Kuniavksy in *Observing the User Experience* [Kuniavsky 2003], and Wodtke in *Information Architecture* [Wodtke 2002].)

As shown in Figures 4.1 and 4.2, we recommend a six-step persona conception and gestation process that includes the following activities.

- Conception

   Step 1: *Identify important categories of users.* If you can, identify categories of users that are important to your business and product domain. Identifying these categories now (even if they are based solely on assumptions) will help you structure your data processing and build a bridge between the ways people think of users today and the data-driven personas you will create.

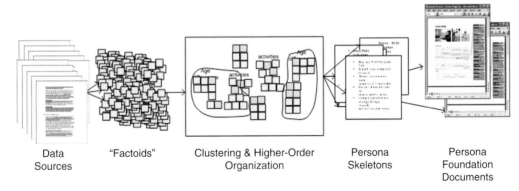

| Data Sources | "Factoids" | Clustering & Higher-Order Organization | Persona Skeletons | Persona Foundation Documents |

FIGURE 4.2: *This diagram illustrates the activities described in steps 2 through 5 of our conception and gestation process. The conception and gestation phase starts with raw data reports, which you will analyze and filter into factoids and organize into "information" to form categories of users. From these categories, you can create terse "skeletons," which you can then evaluate and prioritize. You can develop the prioritized skeletons into rich representations of target users; that is, into personas.*

Step 2: *Process the data.* Process your raw data to extract information relevant to your user and product domains and then identify themes and relationships. We suggest that you do this by conducting a collaborative "data assimilation" activity.

Step 3: *Identify and create skeletons.* Evaluate your processed data to verify the categories of users and to identify subcategories of users. Create skeletons, which are very brief (typically bulleted) lists of distinguishing data points for each subcategory identified.

● Gestation

Step 4: *Prioritize the skeletons.* Once you have a set of skeletons, it is time to get feedback from all stakeholders. You will evaluate the importance of each skeleton to your business and product strategy and prioritize the skeletons accordingly. Your goal is to identify a subset of skeletons to develop into personas.

Step 5: *Develop selected skeletons into personas.* Enrich the selected skeletons to create personas by adding data, concrete and individualized details, and some storytelling elements to give them personality and context.

Step 6: *Validate your personas.* Once you have added details, it is important to double-check to make sure your final personas still reflect your data.

We know that many of you have short windows of opportunity in which to create personas that will be available and useful throughout product design. Many of you are also probably wondering how many personas you will need to create for your product. We address these important questions before describing the six-step conception and gestation process in detail.

How long does conception and gestation take?

The amount of time you spend on *conception and gestation* activities will depend on your project schedule, the amount of data you have, and your goals for the persona effort. You can create useful assumption-based personas in less than a day, or you could take months to fully analyze mountains of data and create personas that link every detail back to a data source. In most cases, you and your team will compromise between these extremes and create useful data-driven personas in about one to two weeks.

To help determine (or justify) the amount of time you will spend creating personas, consider the length of time you will be using them. On some occasions, we have seen persona sets stay useful for several years. For example, personas for long-term projects at Microsoft have been used for five or more years. Personas for service of this length might be built, for example, to describe call-center employees or office personnel whose job functions and goals don't change significantly from year to year. Personas can prove to be useful through several product versions or release cycles. In cases such as these, your time up front should be considered a long-term investment.

In many cases, product lifecycles are much shorter (some Web sites are updated once every month or so) and taking months to create personas is simply not possible. It is also possible that your product lifecycle is long but is already underway and you feel you have to quickly "catch up" and create the personas very quickly for them to be used. In these situations, it is helpful to plan for all six of the conception and gestation steps but to (sometimes radically) shorten the time allotted for each.

Your efforts toward personas are a direct trade-off with other UCD activities or with more direct product development work. You will need to balance the time you spend on your personas with the demands of other UCD activities that are planned. As you plan these trade-offs, remember that the *conception and gestation* steps will help you fully understand your user data, which is helpful regardless of which UCD methods you choose.

Because most of us work in schedule-driven organizations, we have to work backward from a planned design-complete date to build our persona schedules. As you work on your schedule, try to plan time for the entire core team to get together often during the data analysis part of the project. It is important to build and keep momentum so that you can find and act on information that emerges from your data. In addition, schedule your persona evaluation meetings with stakeholders as early as possible. Make sure stakeholders are aware that you are going to need their attention to help with assessing appropriateness and priority across your developing target personas.

If you only have a week or two: low-budget approaches

Personas don't necessarily need to be highly detailed to be effective. Even personas created in just a few hours can be useful. If you only have a week or two (or perhaps only a few days) to create your personas, you have a couple of options, discussed in the following sections.

Create assumption personas

Assumption personas communicate and align the assumptions that already exist in your company. Chapter 3 included suggestions on collecting these assumptions. During the *conception and gestation* phase, you can assimilate the assumptions using the same techniques we recommend for assimilating data. If you decide to create and use assumption personas, an overview of your process during *conception and gestation* work might look as follows (note that we include detailed instructions for each of these processes in the analogous section for data-driven personas, below).

- *Step 1 (2 to 4 hours):* Assimilate assumptions (assumptions you have already collected or collect and assimilate at the same time). In a meeting with the persona core team and product stakeholders, identify important categories and subcategories of users.

- *Step 2 (1 to 2 hours):* Create skeleton personas with your core team. Create a skeleton persona for each category and subcategory of user. (See Figure 4.11 for an example of a skeleton.)

- *Step 3 (2 to 4 hours):* Have your stakeholders review the skeletons that emerged from your assumption exercise. Continue to develop those that are important. Add concrete details and personal facts to make them resemble real people.

You can introduce and use your assumption personas using the same methods we suggest for data-driven personas in the remaining chapters of this book.

Create quick data-driven personas

If you have had time to collect data, but need to create and introduce personas on a tight schedule, you should spend as much time as possible understanding and assimilating your data to create meaningful and relevant skeletons (there is always time to add more detail after the personas are introduced). If you decide to create quick, data-driven personas, your process during the *conception and gestation* phase might run as follows.

- *Step 1 (1/2 to 1 hour):* Meet with your core team and product stakeholders to identify categories of users that are important to your business and product domain.

- *Step 2 (2 to 4 hours):* Process the data. The core team should thoroughly read the data sources, identify important factoids, and complete an affinity exercise to cluster the factoids around the categories of users.

- *Step 3 (2 to 4 hours):* Identify and create skeletons (either in a meeting with your core team or independently). Evaluate your processed data to verify the categories of users and to identify subcategories of users. Create skeletons from the key data points for each subcategory you have identified.

- *Step 4 (2 to 4 hours):* With your core team and product stakeholders, prioritize the skeleton personas. Add concrete details and personal facts to enrich and personalize the skeletons. If you need to speed up the conception and gestation process, spend your time making sure that the skeletons you create the sketches from reflect the assimilated data and your conclusions about the resulting categories.

If you do need to create your personas quickly, be aware that the stakeholder review and prioritization can be an unpredictable and time-consuming process. To get these done quickly, you will have to be well organized and very proactive. For example, you will need to provide clear goals, explicit instructions, and time lines to your stakeholders.

If you have several weeks or more: getting the most out of your data

If you have a lot of data, or if you can only eke a few hours out of every week to work on personas, allot more calendar time for conception and gestation. If you find it difficult to convince your manager to dedicate resources to persona creation, consult Chapter 7 for some ideas on how to communicate the return on investment for a persona effort. Identify a few particularly important data sources and explain how your persona effort will help the development team fully understand and benefit from the information the personas contain.

The majority of your time during the *conception and gestation* phase will be taken up with understanding and organizing your data sources. The remaining steps (creating and prioritizing the skeletons, building and enriching final personas, and validating the personas you created) don't have to take a long time, but they do require core team collaboration.

Story from the field

A QUICK BUT EFFECTIVE PERSONA-BUILDING PROCESS

—Colin Hynes, Director of Usability, Staples.com

When I was ready to create personas, I began by blocking off my calendar for two days. Then I wrote out one defining sentence on each persona. For example, "Comes to the Web site to research so she can buy in our store." While writing the descriptions, I recalled vividly the experiences I had while visiting offices during our extensive contextual inquiry studies and when listening to customer phone calls through customer service representatives. I used this information to build the persona descriptions, which were then reviewed with members of the Usability team.

As a team we filled in color about the personas' motivations, goals, up-sell potential, defining quote, onsite conversion potential, and other key factors that created the whole of each persona. We started with nine personas and then cut it back to six when there seemed to be too much overlap. Even though the process wasn't as rigorous as some, it was incredibly useful to "get the personas down on paper" so that I would have something for stakeholders to react to.

How many personas should you create?

We have found that roughly three to five personas is a good number to target. However, we believe that although you may choose to communicate just a few personas to the development team, your businesses' goals and your data should drive the number of personas you create. During the *conception and gestation* phase, your goal is to create a set of personas that are:

- Relevant to your product and your business goals
- Based on data and/or clearly identified assumptions
- Engaging, enlightening, and even inspiring to your organization.

Note that your goal is *not* to describe every possible user or user type, *nor* to detail every aspect of your target users' lives. Your personas will aid decision making by both narrowing the field of possible targets and highlighting user data that is important and highly related to the product you are creating. This chapter will help you analyze your data sources, decide how many personas to create, and determine what (and how much) information to include in each persona and which personas to prioritize.

The argument for a single primary persona

In their book *About Face 2.0*, Alan Cooper and Robert Reimann [2003] include an axiom that states, "Design each interface for a single, primary persona." Cooper argues that you must prioritize your personas to determine which single persona should be the primary design target for any given interface. We have noticed that many people assume that this means there should only be one primary persona for the entire product. We believe this is a misinterpretation of Cooper's axiom. Yes, there should be one primary persona per interface, but many products have several interfaces (e.g., the interface you use when you read e-mail is quite different from the interface used by the administrator who maintains the e-mail server, but both interfaces are part of the same product). There are also secondary personas— perhaps those that use the product less often or use a particular interface as a peripheral aspect of their job.

Cooper recommends that we start by creating a "cast of characters." We should then identify primary (preferably one) and secondary (probably several) personas within that cast. By definition, each primary persona will require a unique interface (because to be primary the persona must be satisfied, and it cannot be satisfied by any other persona's interface [Cooper 2003, p. 137]). If you must create more than three primary personas (and therefore three interfaces), Cooper argues that the scope of the project is probably too broad.

Cooper's insistence on clearly identified primary personas is the cornerstone of his approach, for good reason. One of the benefits of personas is that they focus and clarify communication around the qualities and needs of target users. Of course, personas are only clarifying if they are actually used by the product team. If people don't remember who the personas are and don't use them in their everyday communication, the focus and clarity will be lost. Thus, your personas need to be visibly representative of the customer base and unfalteringly credible to your product team.

Strictly limiting the number of personas also forces stakeholders to make difficult and important decisions very early in the design process. Your work will be a forcing factor for clarifying business goals as early as possible, and the earlier you understand clear business goals the easier it is to build a product to suit those goals.

Creating the one person to design for: great in theory; complicated in practice

In many cases, you, your core team, the product team, and/or business stakeholders will not accept a single primary persona. This might be because focusing so specifically may simply not *feel* right. It is difficult to convince an executive team that all design efforts should target a single person because the thought of building a product that "will only appeal to one person" is sometimes too difficult to combat. Top-down buy-in for your persona effort is important. If people (especially stakeholders) are uncomfortable with your cast of personas, they will not support or use them.

Even if you do have a go-ahead from the executive team to create one primary persona per product interface, you may not know how many unique interfaces (and therefore how many primary personas) you should create. Many find themselves facing a chicken-and-egg dilemma: should you decide how many unique interfaces your product needs and then create personas or should you create the personas first and then create user interfaces accordingly?

In addition, if it is so important to create a single primary persona for each unique interface (or for the entire product), why create secondary personas at all? And if you do create secondary personas, how should you use them to enhance but not interfere with the design process?

Because each project, product, and team is different, there is no "right" number of personas to create. However, saying "it depends on your project" is certainly not very helpful. The type of product you are building, the nature of your target audience, the information you discover in your data, and the particulars of your business goals should help you answer the following questions.

● How many personas do I need?
● Which personas do I need?
● Which personas should be primary or secondary?
● How do I use secondary personas without designing "for everyone"?

We believe that the best way to answer these questions is to analyze user goals, user roles, and user segments to identify important categories and subcategories of users of your product. For each category and subcategory, you will create at least one skeleton persona.

You can prioritize your skeletons according to business and product objectives. Finally, you will enrich your prioritized skeletons to create personas.

Your final personas will each include details about that persona's goals, role or roles, and segment. Because of this, we believe you can define categories of users according to whichever makes the most sense for your business and your product. Rönkkö et al. [2004] describe the process as follows.

> [Our] personas were not conventional creations in the original sense of persona. Personas are defined by their goals, at the same time as the goals are defined by their personas. Hence, personas and goals are discovered at the same time in the initial investigation of the problem domain. The three personas developed were not derived from a strict process of identifying groups which share the same goal; instead the process combined finding similar goals, trends, age groups, sex, professions and interests and relating these in a creative way to possible usages of mobile smart artifacts [Rönkkö et al. 2004, P. 115].

In step 1 of material to follow we describe how to identify your categories of users (if possible, before you process your data). In step 3 we tell you how to use your processed data to identify subcategories of users, prioritize the categories and subcategories, and prepare to create at least one persona for each.

When should I determine how many personas to create?

We believe you should identify *categories of users* as early as possible. If you know that stakeholders in your company are already attached to thinking about your target users in a particular way, use this information to define the categories of users *before* you begin your data assimilation. After you have completed your data assimilation exercise, you will be able to validate the categories, identify subcategories, and make final decisions on how many (and which) personas to create. The final decision occurs in step 4 of our process.

DEVELOPING PERSONAS AND ORGANIZATIONAL ARCHETYPES

—Tammy Snow, Robin Martin Emerson, Leslie Scott, Trinh Vo Yetzer,
and **Dawn Baron,** Windows Server, Microsoft Corporation

This case study describes our approach to developing personas to meet the needs of the Windows Server product and development team. In two years of work we have modified the persona process by first describing a set of fictional businesses and then describing the IT Pro personas associated with each business. As a result of this process, we have developed over 30 personas spread across four fictional companies representing small, medium, and large organizations. We don't propose that what we describe is the best or most appropriate use of personas but rather provide a description of why we chose this particular approach and how it has affected our product team and the work they are doing. The primary goal of persona development was to help our product team identify and understand its target audience.

Brief Overview of the Windows Server Product and Development Team

Microsoft Windows Server is the operating system that enables organizations to build and operate their IT infrastructure. The Server operating system has evolved from Windows NT to Windows 2000 Server with Active Directory, to the current version, Windows Server 2003. The product team is now working on the next version of Windows Server code named "Longhorn." There are over 12 different development teams and over 3,000 people working on Windows Server. Most of the teams work on specific server functionality that is used and managed by unique individuals in the IT organization. That being the case, we have a significant challenge in helping each of these teams identify and design for its target users. This case study describes an approach we chose to take in helping our product teams understand their customers.

The Problem

Historically, the Windows Server product team has relied on market research data and intuition in understanding who their customers are and what they need. Over the past few years it has become increasingly clear to the leadership for Windows Server that to better meet our customers' needs we need to understand who they really are. Because personas had been developed by other teams at Microsoft (including Windows Client and Office), and because those personas were gaining exposure and credibility, it became apparent that there needed to be personas developed for Windows Server.

Early in development we determined that we could not take a traditional approach to developing server personas. The problem was twofold: (1) servers are about providing IT infrastructure for companies and organizations rather than for individuals, and (2) often IT tasks are done by multiple individuals at different times across multiple computers (servers and desktops). In addition, we had reason to believe that IT organizations and IT pros differed in establishments of different sizes.

(Story from the field, continued)

The Solution

As a solution we decided that we would start by developing models to describe fictional companies that use our server technology. We called these models *archetypes*, for short, though they are really organizational archetypes. We would then define personas within each archetype and describe the work practice and work flow involved in deploying and managing server technologies. In addition, we would define the overall IT organization, IT budgets, the IT purchase decision model, and any relevant information related to purchasing and using Microsoft Server products. We determined that by taking this approach we could provide rich context about IT organizations and how server tasks are often completed by a number of server administrators working together.

The first step in the process of developing archetypes was determining what we would base our model companies on. We knew from the outset that there were often discussions among the product team about how organizations of various sizes purchased, deployed, and managed our solutions, so we decided to use organization size as the key determinant for the archetypes we would develop. We believed that the context of organization size would be a key to helping us understand what different IT organizations look like and how this influences work practice—what administrators do and how they do it.

We developed archetypes to represent four distinct business sizes defined by number of PCs and number of servers. Our work focused on one small business archetype, two medium business archetypes, and one large business. Because the medium business is one we felt we knew least about, we determined a need to look at medium-size organizations at both the small and large end of this category. The table shown in Figure 4.3 outlines key characteristics for each of our archetypes.

Archetype	Range of Servers	Range of PCs	Avg. # of IT pros.
Small orgs.	1–3	1–24	0.6
Core Medium orgs.	4–15	24–249	3
Upper Medium orgs.	16–99	250–499	8
Large orgs.	100+	500+	56

FIGURE 4.3: *Key characteristics of our windows server organizational archetypes.*

Developing the Archetypes and Personas

We started our work by reviewing all existing usability and Microsoft-sponsored market research data related to each size of organization we were targeting. We analyzed these data sets looking for trends toward generalizing and developing a data-informed framework describing each of the four sizes of organization. Each archetype described a representative company, including size, type of business, number of office locations, and so on. In addition, we included any information we had about needs, pains, and issues related to our technology. It is important to note that we reviewed data from many types of organizations because we were not interested in creating vertically specific archetypes.

Once we had reviewed existing data we started conducting original research to validate what we had learned from our initial analysis and to fill in gaps not covered by existing data. Our research was qualitative in nature and involved interviews with over 100 IT professionals. Information from these interviews was analyzed, again looking for trends that could be generalized. These generalized findings were then added to the archetypes and used to develop our first set of personas for each archetype.

The Outcome

Once we had completed the first version of our archetypes and personas, we had 32 unique IT-related personas. The large-organization archetype incorporated 23 total personas, including personas specific to Microsoft Windows Server and related products, to UNIX administration, and to mainframe systems. The small-organization archetype had a single IT-related persona, and the medium-size archetypes had two (for core medium organizations) and seven (for upper medium organizations) personas.

As initially suspected, we found some clear distinctions in the way IT pros organize themselves and perform their jobs based on company size. In large organizations, there is a high degree of specialization for IT pros (i.e., an individual is responsible for working on a specific type of technology, such as messaging or databases). In addition, large IT organizations tend to have well-defined processes for purchasing, deploying, and managing technology. As organizations become smaller, the level of technology-specific generalization goes down and you see a minimal process for purchasing, deploying, and managing technology.

Dealing with Many Personas

One of the more frequent questions we hear from people is, "How do you deal with 32 unique personas?" Clearly we can't expect people to know about and remember all 32 personas! Fortunately, no one team in the Windows Server division would ever deal with more than four or five personas in developing their features. The challenge is working with the various teams to help them identify their target personas and then make use of those personas in defining, designing, and developing their features.

[For further details on how Snow and her colleagues helped their product team use these personas and organizational archetypes, see the sidebar in Chapter 5 titled "Story from the field: Dealing with Many Personas."]

Step 1: Identify important categories of users

- ● **Discuss categories of users**
- ○ Process data
- ○ Identify & create skeletons
- ○ Evaluate & prioritize skeletons
- ○ Develop skeletons into personas
- ○ Validate the personas

During family planning, you probably found that your company and your product team already think about your users as being in several categories. Before you begin processing the data you have collected, it is important to articulate these findings.

Categories of users are usually defined as sets of characteristics that groups of users share. The sets of characteristics you found are probably highly related to the business goals of your product. Identifying these categories now (even if they are based solely on assumptions) will help you structure your data processing and build a bridge between the ways your organization thinks about users today and the data-driven personas you will create.

If you found that your company or team does not currently think or talk about users at all, we believe you should try to define major categories of users before you begin processing your data. If you conducted your own user research as part of the *family planning* phase, you likely already defined user categories as you recruited participants.

You can articulate or define large categories of users by describing common user roles, user goals, or user segments that are important to your business and product. Note that identifying important categories of users does *not* mean identifying every possible way of grouping your users. In our experience, major categories of users tend to stand out (see the following G4K case study).

Even if they don't reveal themselves easily, we recommend that you simply put forth a proposed set of user categories as high-level conceptual targets. Either way, your data will establish the appropriateness of these categories during the analysis process.

Why should I try to identify categories of users *before* I look at the data?

There are two reasons to identify categories of users before you look at the data. The primary reason is to ensure that your data assimilation exercise produces results that are relatively easy to create personas from. The second is to establish a clear connection to the existing language used to describe users.

The data assimilation process is typically a bottom-up deductive process in which you find important relationships between and among the data sources. Using high-level categories to provide structure to assimilation adds a layer of top-down inductive analysis. The use of categories ensures that you will be able to express the information you find in the clusters of data as personas. Without categories, your clustered data will yield interesting information but you might have a difficult time using this information to form personas.

When you are ready to communicate and use your personas, you will find it much easier to do so if you can describe them in language that is already familiar—even in the case where your data suggests that the initial categories should be replaced by different ones. In the next three sections we describe three differences between target users that can be used to discover and define the categories important to your business and product: differences in user roles, user goals, and user segments. Each of these is accompanied by an example scenario. All of the scenarios describe the same company (a bank) and project (an online banking system). In the example scenarios, we show you how differences in roles, goals, or segments can be used to create high-level categories of users depending on business objectives and the existing corporate environment.

In our banking examples, no matter which personas the team ends up creating, all of them should be traceable back to the categories of users. When people ask, "Why did you create these particular personas?" (and this question will come up) the answer will be something similar to the following: "We created at least one persona for each major category of user. We create these categories for one of the following reasons:

● Stakeholders identified *user roles* our product had to support to be successful.

● Stakeholders identified *user goals* we had to satisfy to have a successful product.

● Stakeholders identified *user segments* we had to satisfy to have a successful product."

Story from the field

MOLDING MAJOR CUSTOMER SEGMENTS OVER TIME

—Noel Holmes, Director of Customer Experience, Travelocity

Our personas were conceived by identifying major customer segments from demographic/psychographic data based on members' zip codes. In the early formative months, we molded the personas based on interviews, surveys, and focus groups populated from the key segments identified. We also included our own user-centric expertise and sprinkled their personalities generously with creativity. The personas we created were immediately put to use. We were on the verge of launching an online tour of a new product featuring characters representing two different user types. We changed the names of both characters and aged them slightly to better match their respective personas.

No matter how you initially categorize your users, all of your completed personas will include information related to that persona's role, goals, and segment. In other words, it is completely acceptable to create categories of users based on existing assumptions if you think that will help people understand and accept the personas you end up creating. Your data will validate and enrich the categories or will provide solid information to show that the existing categories are inappropriate. It will also allow you to define important subcategories of users that should also be expressed in personas.

Thinking about user roles, user goals, and user segments

The sections that follow explore processes for thinking about user roles, goals, and segments.

User roles

When you describe a person according to sets of tasks, job descriptions, responsibilities, or other external factors related to his or her interaction with your product, you are describing the user in terms of his or her *role*. For the purpose of software development, a user role is often defined with regard to the relationship between the user and a system (see also Chapter 8). Specific roles don't necessarily map to specific users. Individual users might find themselves in any of these roles at different times. Roles are generally related to business, work, and productivity. In fact, sometimes they are directly related to job type, position, or responsibilities. However, they may also be related to an activity that defines a person as a type of consumer (e.g., the "shopper," the "browser," the "agent" or the "assistant"). For example:

Scenario 1: Create categories based on user roles. Your bank is large and offers many services for many different tiers of customers. Everyone at the company knows that the bank's Web site is going to continue to evolve over the next few years and will eventually support the specific needs of many types of customers. However, for now you have to figure out what features you need to build *first*. That is, which will give the bank the most bang for the buck as they try to attract more customers and reduce their current customer support costs. You decide to create your categories of users based on various user *roles*. In this scenario, it would be appropriate to describe the following role-based categories of users.

○ The new account shoppers

○ The existing account holders

○ The borrowers

○ The investors

Story from the field

MAPPING PERSONAS TO ROLES

—Len Conte, BMC Software, Inc.

Usually our personas map to roles that users perform within the system. Although we typically have at least one persona per role, we also create multiple personas per role based on the size of the enterprise the persona is supporting. For example, in a recent application we created three personas for "capacity planners." One persona supports a large company, one supports a medium-scale company, and one supports a small mom-and-pop company.

User goals

When you describe a user in terms of what he or she is trying to achieve—in his or her own terms—you are describing the user's *goals*. Individuals have general goals that apply to many things they do in their lives, including the way they approach products. People also have specific goals that relate to tasks. Goals have a timelessness that roles do not. Whether or not you use goals as your primary differentiator, communicating your personas' goals will be critical during the *birth and maturation* and *adulthood* phases. For example:

Scenario 2: Create categories based on user goals. Your group has been assigned to create an online banking experience to help the bank catch up with its main competitor. You also need to satisfy some of the customer requests that have been coming in for online access to account information and management tools. Your bank has been working hard to build a reputation as a trustworthy, solid financial institution and you know that the online banking application needs to reflect this reputation. Your research shows that many people are dissatisfied with current online banking options because they are not sure the Internet is completely safe and reliable. You decide to create your categories of users based on different user *goals*. In this scenario, it would be appropriate to describe the following goal-based categories of users.

- ○ Users who "want my financial life to be simpler"
- ○ Users who "want my money to work for me"
- ○ Users who "want to feel like my money gets as much attention as a millionaire's money"
- ○ Users who "want to feel safe when I'm banking online."

User segments

When you describe a user in terms of characteristics he or she shares with many other users, you are describing the user in terms of a segment. Segments are defined according to shared demographics, psychographics, attitudes, and/or behaviors. In marketing, segments are often used to create targeted messaging and advertising to increase product sales. Marketing teams, product planners, and/or business development groups often define their objectives in terms of segments they have built to reflect the existing market and opportunities for innovation and new sales.

Segments can be rigorously defined through quantitative analysis of data, but they can also evolve through casual references to groups of users or customers (which, by the way, are sometimes referred to as "user classes"). Because segments are often used as shorthand when business stakeholders are talking about users and customers, they exist (are embedded) in the culture and lingo of many companies regardless of how rigorously they are defined. If segments already exist in your company's vocabulary, they will influence your persona project. For example:

> ***Scenario 3: Create categories based on user segments.*** The bank executives have been walking around for weeks talking about critically underserved markets for your bank's service, and their desire to fulfill some of these unmet needs through the new online banking services. The executive team asked the marketing team to identify segments of consumers who would be likely to sign up for a new online banking service. The marketing team did some research and identified three main segments, which they described as *enthusiasts*, *ostriches*, and *neophytes*. You know that if your personas don't fit within these segments your executive staff will reject them. You decide to use the *segments* (as they are currently defined by market research) to describe the following categories of users.

Handy Detail

SEGMENTS CAN BE CONCEPTUALLY SIMPLE.

Some companies describe market segments in fairly simple terms (e.g., "current customers," "potential customers" (no one's customers), and "customers of our competitor"). Figure 4.4 shows an example of one way Hewlett-Packard publicly describes its user base. In the right hand column of their home page, they present the following five major customer groups.

- Home and home office
- Small and medium business
- Large enterprise business
- Government and education
- Partners and developers

Categories such as these tend to be strategic business divisions, and though they might have strict definitions (e.g., small business = companies with 10 or fewer employees) they are conceptually simple. They are likely not quantitatively derived segments based on customer/market research and their definition might not include anything specific to users and/or consumers. Either way, if such segments have a long tradition of use in your organization they may be an appropriate and politically acceptable starting point for creating personas. You will be doing your organization a huge favor by putting quantitative and qualitative data, along with engaging and memorable stories, behind the existing terms.

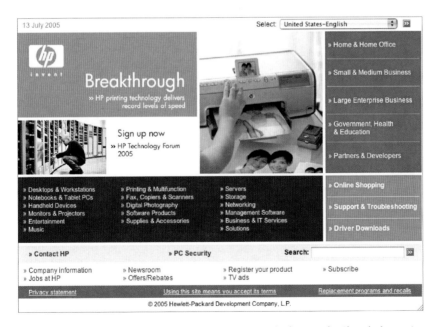

FIGURE 4.4: *HP.com has five customer groups presented as navigational elements on the right-hand side of their main home page. These might serve as the starting point for five or more personas.*

○ *Financial enthusiasts:* 35 to 65 years old, urban or suburban, professional, college educated, yearly household income of $50K–$250K, make decisions related to finances and review all account balances and activity at least once a month, aware and wary of Internet security issues, and careful researcher and informed consumer of financial services

○ *Financial ostriches:* 25 to 40 years old, urban or suburban, professional, college educated, have children, yearly household income of $35K–$90K, busy with life and work, seldom balances checkbook, seldom reviews financial decisions, have several accounts at various financial institutions (including IRAs from old jobs), not entirely sure what they have at any given time, and feel overwhelmed whenever they think of organizing finances

○ *Financial neophytes:* 18 to 25 years old, some college, yearly household income of $10K–$60K (with potential for considerable income growth), newly financially independent, tend to be interested and motivated but nervous, very aware of current financial status, tend to have debt and credit concerns, and think of money in terms of "what I can afford today."

Hold a meeting to determine categories of users

If these categories of users are not clear from your work in the *family planning* phase, hold a meeting with your stakeholders to make this notion explicit. Plan to meet for about an hour to discuss preexisting categories of users used in your company, as well as roles, goals, and segments to determine the best strategic target groups for your product. The following is a recommended agenda for the user categories meeting.

1. Describe the goals, rules, and outcome of the meeting.
2. Discuss preexisting language for customers and users at your company.
3. Discuss the concept of roles, goals, and segments.
4. Brainstorm on your company's most appropriate categorization scheme or consider generating assumption personas (introduced in Chapter 3 and further discussed in material to follow).
5. Generate the proposed high-level groups or categories of users.
6. Get consensus on the high-level target groups before closing (you will want roughly three to five groups).

As an example of what might result from such a meeting, consider the following story from G4K.

Story from the field

THREE TYPES OF PERSONAS AT RAZORFISH

—Karen McGrane, Vice President, User Experience, Avenue A | Razorfish

I find that the type of persona we create varies based on the type of project and the way the persona will inform our design decisions. Although the underlying goal for using personas remains the same, the specifics of the execution—what details we include and how they are presented—vary based on the type of persona we are developing. I realized that the personas can be categorized roughly into three types, discussed in the sections that follow.

Type 1: Job Role

We would use Job Role personas largely for Business to Business (B2B) or Intranet projects, where a user's interaction with the site would be primarily defined by their relationship to the company. For example, we might use "Sales Manager" and "Sales Consultant" as personas, and identify the work situations and tasks specific to each. Job roles are perhaps the most straightforward personas to define, because they often map to familiar segments for the client and because it is easier to conduct user research with a "captive audience" of employees or business partners. However, one of the challenges in creating personas based on job roles is that clients may expect to see personas for every possible job title. Clients are sometimes resistant to coalescing different job titles into a single persona, even if all of those job titles have similar needs and perform similar tasks.

Job Role personas are usually illustrated with a name, a photo, and relevant details about the persona's work experience, computer experience and access, and attitudes toward the task. Task analysis and scenarios are usually important for these personas, particularly if the system we are designing is replacing a task previously completed offline. Demographic details such as age, race, gender, household income, and location are typically not relevant.

Type 2: Brand Preference

Brand Preference personas would be created for consumer marketing or brand strategy projects. These personas are not used to clarify the tasks someone would perform on a Web site. They are used to define the characteristics that would lead someone to prefer one brand over another. For example, imagine creating two different personas: one to illustrate a typical Target customer and one to depict a typical Wal-Mart customer. It is easy to picture the difference between these two personas, just based on what you know about each company's messaging. Brand Preference personas are often used to describe the "ideal customer" across all touch points. We are seeing them used in a variety of consumer marketing projects, as companies use them to filter and make sense of the massive amounts of data they have about their customers.

Brand Preference personas are also typically illustrated with a name and a photo, but in this case demographic segmentation details such as age, gender, and household income are extremely relevant. Psychographic information—such as magazines subscribed to, automobile types owned, or preferences for other consumer products—can be used to round out the picture of the customer, but it is important that these tie back to real data. In many cases task information isn't relevant for these personas. We are interested in who the customer is, but not necessarily in what they do.

Type 3: Task Mind-set

These personas attempt to capture the goals and mind-sets that people bring to a particular task. These personas are for the most part relevant to consumer-facing transactional projects such as travel or retail shopping. Unlike personas for B to B or employee portal projects, wherein the user's relationship to the company is fairly stable, personas for consumer-facing commerce projects have fluid customer relationships and mind-sets. What is unique about these types of personas is that an individual person can "wear" many mind-sets, and the mind-set that person brings to the task can change over time. The same person may shop differently based on whether he is planning a family vacation or scheduling a business trip, and his mind-set may change from when he is conducting exploratory research to when he actually books the trip. A cosmetics shopper may approach browsing for a new perfume very differently than she handles purchasing a new tube of the same mascara she has used for years.

Because people's task mind-sets can change over time, we find it is less effective to illustrate Task Mind-set personas with a name and a photo. We generally place the emphasis on a descriptive label such as "Surgical Shopper" or "Insider Traveler." We don't want to give the inaccurate impression that "Sarah" is always a surgical shopper. Similarly, presenting any demographic information can be distracting and irrelevant. Task analysis and scenarios often highlight how different mind-sets change the user's perspective on the same task, or how the sequence of activities that lead up to successful completion of the task varies because of the different attitudes and goals the user brings to the task.

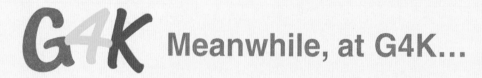

Meanwhile, at G4K...

G4K DISCUSSES USER CATEGORIES

Let's take a look at how G4K thinks about user categories and their relation to user roles, goals, and segments. Historically, G4K has focused on four categories of users: children in four main age/grade groups.

(Meanwhile, at G4K..., continued)

When discussing children, they also make a big distinction between boys and girls (doubling the number of distinct user categories to eight). Thus, they have the following eight categories of users:

- Preschool and kindergarten (girls, boys)
- Grades 1 and 2 (girls, boys)
- Grades 3 through 5 (girls, boys)
- Grades 6 through 9 (girls, boys)

Obviously, they consider children their "users." Children are the people that directly use their software products. However, children don't have the direct power to purchase G4K products. Thus, G4K also considers the following five types of "customers" in their business model:

- Parents
- Educators (teachers, specialists, and educational administrators)
- Librarians (or library administrators)
- Retailers and partners (typically business managers or product specialists at toy store outlets)
- Industry analysts, investors, and other influencers (individuals, investment capitalists, agencies, and institutions G4K needs to stay on top of)

As mentioned previously, their current Web site (*www.G4kids.com*) was created to communicate the corporate image and vision, promote the mass sale of products, and more generally serve the needs of their "customers." It was not thought of as a destination site for their "users."

In the meeting to discuss categories of users for the creation of their destination site (*www.G4kids.com*), the stakeholders agreed that "users" would take focus (all eight categories) along with parents and teachers. The latter three "customers" would still be served, but only through their existing corporate Web site.

This was an important and freeing decision for the persona core team. However, this wasn't good enough. The persona core team needed to push back a little bit on the stakeholders. They didn't think they could easily distinguish and target all 10 categories at once (eight classes of children plus parents and teachers). So, they asked the stakeholders to brainstorm a bit regarding other ways of conceptualizing segments, roles, and goals. They explored a few interesting dimensions of their users along the way. The groups listed in the following sections were discussed in detail.

Possible Categories of Users by Role

- The child as a game player
- The child as a learner/student
- The parent as guardian/monitor/investigator
- The parent as purchaser/enabler
- The teacher as direct educator/assistant/learning partner
- The teacher/administrator as curriculum advisor/creator

(Meanwhile, at G4K…, continued)

Possible Subcategories of Users by Goal
- Kids
  - Have fun/be entertained
  - Feel independent
  - Get better at a game than another kid
  - Excel at school (please my parents and teacher)
  - Make and maintain friends
- Parents
  - Make good choices for my kids
  - Not have to worry about my kid on the Internet
  - Make sure my kids don't screw up my computer
  - Ensure kids are being productive with their time
  - Build my kids' self-esteem
- Educators
  - Be on the cutting edge, and not fall behind
  - Get new ideas and find content that is relevant and interesting
  - Please the parents by what I provide the kids
  - Stay within budget
  - Look and be professional

Possible Subcategories of Users by Segment
- Kids
  - Age: young children/kids vs. school-age children vs. teens
  - Users vs. nonusers of our existing software products/games
  - Homes with computer/Internet access vs. only access is at school/library
  - Girls vs. boys
  - Sitters (indoor playing, TV, PC, gaming) vs. physically active kids (sports minded, outdoors)
- Parents
  - Computer savvy/not
  - Highly involved/not as involved
  - Age/generation (Generation X parents, baby boomers)
  - Moms vs. dads vs. grandparents vs. guardians
  - Educational background
- Educators
  - Years of experience
  - Access to technology
  - Fear or embracement of technology/computers
  - Education level
  - Grade/subject they teach

(Meanwhile, at G4K..., continued)

In the end, the stakeholders felt that a good starting point for personas would be a simplified combination of user roles and segments. Everything they discussed felt important to them, but the only categories they knew they wanted to capture from the start were children, parents, and educators. So, they decided to keep it simple and let the data confirm the categories and determine whether additional subcategories would be needed.

Bright Idea

ASSIMILATE ASSUMPTIONS TO DEFINE CATEGORIES OF USERS

As we discussed in regard to *family planning*, it is sometimes necessary, and almost always valuable, to create assumption personas. You can do this to identify assumptions about categories of users if they have not been made explicit. Whereas we describe the assimilation process in detail in the next section (for processing your data), the following are a few ideas specific to assimilating assumptions. The following is a recommended meeting agenda for assimilating assumptions.

1. *Describe the goal and intended outcome of the assumption exercise.* It is especially important to be clear about your goals when creating assumption personas (e.g., "Our goal is to create a temporary set of target personas that will be used for initial planning discussions but validated later with research"; "The outcome of this meeting will be that each of the stakeholders has a clear and agreed-upon vision of our most strategic customer targets"). Make sure that everyone involved knows why you are doing this exercise and why you believe it is worthwhile.
2. *Solicit assumptions and record them on sticky notes.* Ask everyone to write their assumptions about users' roles, goals, and/or segments on sticky notes. Sticky notes might say things like "4th grade boy who hates homework but loves computers," "involved mom who isn't tech-savvy and worries about her kid online," "good student looking for information about an assignment," and "social pre-teen who wants to chat with friends." What are their important characteristics: physical attributes, skills, behaviors, activities, goals, needs, preferences, and opinions? Ask everyone to record each idea on its own sticky note.
3. *Assimilate the sticky notes.* See step 2 in the next section of this chapter for detailed instructions for assimilation.
4. *Create higher-order categories of users and persona sketches.* Identify the major categories or classes of users the groups of assumptions relate to. Then sketch out individual profiles for each category, providing specific and concrete values for important characteristics to the extent possible (e.g., pre-teen should be specified as "in 5th grade," 8-11 years old, or even exactly 9 years old).

Story from the field

THE BENEFITS OF CREATING ASSUMPTION PERSONAS

—Laura Grange, Program Manager, and **Rahul Singh,** Software Developer, Amazon.com

At Amazon.com, we decided to create a quick set of assumption personas as the first step before creating data-driven personas—in this case, for a particular product being built for the software developer community. The product manager sent out an invitation to the entire team, inviting them to participate in the brainstorming session. She got a reply from her boss asking why we were creating personas in a brainstorming session. He thought, quite rightly, that "You don't brainstorm personas. You put them together through customer information, analysis, and feedback."

The product manager replied, "This is a valid point. We're using assumption personas as a method of jump-starting persona development. The team gets together to get all assumptions about the target user population out on the table. We create assumption personas out of these, which we can do quickly—in one or two two-hour meetings.

We then use these assumption personas as the basis for evaluating the research and data we have, so the persona data effort becomes centered on validating the (usually) fairly accurate assumptions. Why do it this way? For several reasons:

- The assumptions about the target user population typically reflect significant contribution from teams that have been working on products for a while. Creating assumption personas capitalizes on this rich but unarticulated information and quickly aligns all of the assumptions. This alignment is valuable even if the persona effort goes no further. There is value in creating the assumption personas simply for the benefits derived from aligning the team's assumptions.
- Using data to validate assumption personas is a lot easier and quicker than creating personas from scratch (from data).
- If you create personas from scratch without surfacing the assumptions first, you end up with personas that are more difficult for the team to use. Building assumption personas helps build buy-in."

This quick explanation was enough to give the manager confidence that the exercise was worth the limited amount of time it would take. It was great to hear that he already knew about personas and their relationship to data! After the first assumption persona session, we got the following e-mail message from one of the developers on the project, who was dubious at the start of the meeting but soon became an active and enthusiastic participant.

"I was one of the people in the persona brainstorm and I just wanted to say that it was really quite a good exercise IMHO (in my humble opinion). I went into it thinking it was going to be a waste of time, but it wasn't. In fact, parts of it were quite scary and a bit too close to home."

This quote is especially interesting because I was working with developers to create assumption personas who were also developers! It was easy for the development staff to assume they knew the users because the users in this case share the same job description as the development staff. During our first two-hour session we identified several assumption personas that we were able to discuss and invite stakeholders to prioritize.

○ Discuss categories of users
◉ **Process data**
○ Identify & create skeletons
○ Evaluate & prioritize skeletons
○ Develop skeletons into personas
○ Validate the personas

Step 2: Process the data

During the *family planning* phase, you collected and reviewed many data sources, including research reports containing summaries, highlights, and significant details extracted from raw data of some sort. Your next task is to process these research findings, pulling out the bits and pieces that are relevant to your team and product domain. Once you have isolated these relevant factoids, you and your core team will process them (through an assimilation exercise) using the user categories you agreed upon in step 1.

Data processing methods

There are many ways you can go about processing your data to create personas, and we strongly recommend a specific approach: affinity diagramming (which we and others often refer to as "assimilation"). We use the assimilation method because it is quick, easily under-stood, and overtly collaborative. It also works across a variety of data types and formats.

As an alternative, you might consider doing quantitative analysis (such as factor analysis, cluster analysis, or some other multivariate statistical procedure) or qualitative analysis (with a tool such as Atlas.ti, HyperQual2, HyperRESEARCH, NUDIST, or Xsight, a trimmed-down version of NUDIST). These tools are quite useful for extracting the underlying themes from any type of data, as you possibly did with raw data during the *family planning* phase. For example, Rashmi Sinha [2003] describes a persona creation process using principal components analysis to identify the critical underlying dimensions. Her analysis uncovered independent clusters of needs (very similar to goals), which were then used in combination with other information as the basis for creating distinct personas. Such an approach is simi-lar to cluster analysis and other statistical techniques typically used in the creation of quanti-tative market segments. Although we believe that analyses such as these can be a great starting point, we recommend that you also conduct a data assimilation exercise as the primary method of persona creation, particularly when combining data from a variety of sources.

Story from the field

IT DEPENDS ON WHAT YOU MEAN BY "REPRESENT."

—Diane Lye, Ph.D., Senior Manager, Data Mining, Amazon.com

You can use personas to "stand in" for and humanize mountains of data—to make important aspects of the data usable and accessible to product designers and developers. But you have to be very careful not to assume that finished personas are fully representative of the richness and specific details of the data from which they are built.

For product designers and developers, personas represent the data perfectly well for their purpose: to help a team make good decisions about the design of a product. But for data analysts, and for the work that statisticians and data miners are often asked to do, personas may not represent data in the same way.

Statisticians Care About *Representativeness*

Statisticians describe our discipline as a set of techniques for summarizing information. The purpose of summarizing is to be able to draw inferences and make predictions. Sometimes we summarize patterns (e.g., 60% of people who attend baseball games purchase peanuts), and sometimes we summarize relationships (e.g., the probability of a baseball fan buying a beer increases when he or she buys peanuts). We summarize in order to be able to make inferences and predictions. For example, if I sent you a list of the purchases of all fans at a game in Yankee Stadium it would be virtually impossible for you to make predictions about which items the fans have a high probability of buying together. However, if I use statistical techniques to summarize the data it would be fairly easy for you to spot that fans who buy peanuts also buy beer, and therefore to make predictions like, "If you can get them to buy peanuts you're more likely to sell them a beer."

When summarizing data to draw inferences and make predictions, statisticians care about having representative data and about accuracy. For statisticians, saying that data is *representative* means something very special. It means that you can generalize your conclusions to the entire population and make highly accurate predictions. It also means that you can measure your predictions. If my data is representative, I can build a statistical model that accurately predicts how many, and which, customers buy peanuts and beer at baseball games. In addition, I can measure the accuracy of the prediction by seeing how often I was right. Personas can be specific, but they can't be *representative* in the same way statistical models can.

How Do Personas "Represent" Data?

Personas are another way of summarizing data, but the two methods (use of statistics and use of persona data) do different things and have different goals and uses. Statistics are helpful for making predictions but not particularly helpful for making design decisions. Personas can put a "human face" on statistical patterns, which is very helpful for making design decisions but not for making the types of predictions you can make with statistical models. For example, a persona who "always buys peanuts at baseball games" may be based on data showing that 60% of fans buy peanuts. I can use this characteristic to help me design a new stadium arm rest with a snack holder, or a new type of stadium trash receptacle. However, I shouldn't use my persona's behavior to predict the behavior of all baseball fans. In other words, I can't use my 100% peanut-loving persona to infer that 100% of baseball fans buy peanuts.

Why Does This Distinction Matter?

In short, personas are not a substitute for data when data is what you need to get the job done, and data is not a substitute for personas when you need to design. You cannot design a chair for an "average" person, especially if the chair will be used by children in kindergarten. On the same note, you cannot use a persona when you are trying to predict which people will respond to a 30% discount on chairs. You need the right tool for the job, and the jobs are different. In the best of all worlds, you will have great quantitative data and great personas.

If you are working with a statistician or data mining professional, it is a good idea to have a conversation about what, exactly, you each mean when you say that your personas are there to represent data. In addition, when you decide how to apply your personas to various business questions you should consider whether they represent the data *sufficiently* in each particular instance. If you are working on a design (e.g., of a new snack holder), a persona can represent your data perfectly well. If you are trying to target an audience, or make broad inferences or predictions that apply to an entire population, remember that personas cannot be truly *representative*. In these cases, stick to statistics.

Story from the field

RAPID USER MENTAL MODELING (RUMM)

—Rashmi Sinha, Founder and principal, Uzanto Consulting

User-centered information architecture (IA) requires understanding of how users tacitly group, sort, and label tasks and content. Although personas have gained popularity, it remains difficult for information architects to incorporate them into their design process. For information-rich domains, personas need to incorporate input about the ways in which people think about the domain, and their information needs and mental models. The cast of personas chosen should reflect the types of information needs.

In the course of our work, we have developed RUMM. This is a three-stage persona-creation and mental modeling tool set for interaction designers. The RUMM process begins with open-ended exploration (stage 1: Explore); progresses toward a more detailed understanding of user needs,

(Story from the field, continued)

mental models, and personas (stage 2: Understand); and ends with a verification and test of preliminary information architecture (stage 3: Verify and Refine). RUMM produces reliable and repeatable results by basing personas and mental models on data.

RUMM also offers a specific series of steps for using personas to drive IA design. In addition, both mental modeling and personas can draw from the same set of user research, reducing time and effort and reducing the risk that personas and mental modeling will drive the design in different directions.

In this case study, we describe how we used the RUMM methodology to redesign the IA for a complex Web site with a varied user base. The site was an online travel site that offered the ability to make reservations (air, hotel, car rental, cruises) and contained a great deal of online content (about visas, day trips, sight-seeing, and so on). In that the site had such varied content, organizing the content was a major challenge. The company had recently forged a partnership with a travel content provider and wanted to add a lot of new information to the site. The old IA could not accommodate this new content.

RUMM Stage 1: Explore the Information Domain

Our first step was to understand the scope and boundaries of the domain in users' minds. We used a free-listing exercise (targeting both current and prospective users) and asked participants to list all of the types of information they might look for when planning for a trip (e.g., passport requirements, weather, accommodations, car rental, food, tourist spots). They were also asked to list the factors they consider while planning a trip (e.g., price, travel time, taxes, penalty for late changes, and so on) The exercise was conducted (via an online survey) with various types of users, including business and leisure travelers of various ages.

As you can imagine, we got a wide and varied assortment of responses, so we sifted through that data to get the most frequently mentioned types of content (for example, cancellation policies).

We also met with executives at the company and got them to identify which pieces of content they felt were critical to the business success of the company. Combining these two lists, we were able to arrive at a list of content topics that although not exhaustive represented the most critical content on the site.

RUMM Stage 2: Understand Users' Needs and Mental Models

In the second stage, we took the list of critical content that had been generated in stage 1 and asked 55 respondents to rate the subjective importance of types of travel content and factors they considered while purchasing airline tickets.

Through statistical analysis (principal components analysis), we were able to identify clusters of users. One group of users had an extremely narrow focus of interest: they were only interested in one destination, they were not overtly interested in price-comparison features, and they were not interested in destination details (e.g., sight-seeing information, day trips, or restaurant ratings).

(Story from the field, continued)

Another group of users found much of the travel-related content to be of interest (e.g., tourist information, restaurant information, accommodations, and passport and currency information). They were also interested in price/destination comparison, and were much more interested in destination details. We used this information (in conjunction with other qualitative information) to craft a primary and a secondary persona for the site.

Primary Persona: Irene the Comparison Shopper

Irene (62) used to work as a secretary at Greenfield Community College. Bill, her husband of 30 years, just retired from his job running a small pet store. They had always wanted to travel after their retirement, and saved carefully so that they would be able to afford to do so. The first year after retirement, they joined a group tour of the Italian countryside. This left them wanting more. This year, they want to go to Italy again (but this time on their own). Last year's trip cost too much and they want to keep costs down.

Their son has been telling them about the cheap fares one can get on the Internet if one looks hard. Irene has been spending a lot of time looking on travel sites, trying to find tickets to fly to Rome and hotels to stay in once they get there. They want to visit some vineyards and go to the Vatican for a day.

Irene is an amateur painter and is interested in visiting sites associated with art. She is also fond of Italian food, but not all the time. She likes to stay in tourist areas so that she can easily get American food when she wants.

When she searches travel sites, she looks for cheap fares. She is flexible about dates. While looking for airline tickets, she also looks for hotels. In planning her itinerary, she looks for travel information about the various cities she is thinking of visiting. She does not mind if it ends up taking a little time to find what she wants, but she gets very frustrated when the system does not give her all of the information she is looking for. For example, she likes to know exactly how much time the flight will take, how much the tax will be, and what the fee will be for changing or canceling a ticket. She does not like to click on numerous links to obtain each piece of information.

Secondary Persona: Mark "All Business, All the Time"

Mark (36) is a sales professional for SOP, an enterprise software firm headquartered in the Bay Area. He travels a lot for work. He is married and has two kids. His wife works at the same firm (in the marketing department). They live comfortably, but much of their income is spent on the mortgage for their suburban house and on child care.

Due to recent cutbacks, for the first time in his career Mark is responsible for making his own travel arrangements. He finds this very frustrating and wants to spend the least amount of time possible on the task (after he books the ticket, he can go home for the day). He prefers staying at hotels near the airport, renting a car, and driving to where he needs to. He does not care about price information because he is not spending his own money. However, he favors one particular airline so that his travel miles don't get spread between multiple accounts. He has so many travel miles that he is often able to upgrade his seat or room, and still has plenty of miles left over for his personal travel.

He does not like the recent airline strategy of not offering meals any longer, though he generally ends up purchasing a meal. He likes to sit near the exit rows so that he gets more space. He wants to book a hotel, car, and plane ticket with no cancellation penalties because his plans often change.

In addition, he likes a travel agency to have good phone support because he often needs to make changes when he is away from his computer. He would really like the ability to enter a detailed profile with all of his preferences so that he could find suitable tickets faster.

The next step was to understand user mental models. We had run an online card-sorting exercise at the same time as the online survey. Users were given the list of items we developed in stage 1, and were asked to put them into categories and provide a label for each category. We then used cluster analysis to create hierarchical models representing how users think about the domain of online travel information. We generated a generic hierarchical model from the entire population, and models from the two subpopulations we had identified (business and leisure travelers).

To craft an initial cut of the IA, we took the hierarchical model from the population from which the primary persona (Irene) was derived. We then verified that the limited content the secondary persona (Mark) would be interested in had entry points that made sense from the perspective of his hierarchical model.

RUMM Stage 3: Verify Preliminary Information Architecture
In stage 3, we tested our proposed IA on a larger population (120 respondents) of the site through an (online) closed card-sort study. We made sure that our survey included participants from a variety of backgrounds, including business travelers and leisure travelers.

The closed card-sorting study was used to examine the suitability of the hybrid IA we designed in stage 2. Any items that were frequently placed in different categories, or were placed in the "other" category by a large number of users, were revisited in the design. In this way, the closed card sort served as an early usability test for the IA.

Summary
Over the three stages of the RUMM process, we gained an understanding of (1) the scope of current and planned content/functionality, (2) the hierarchical structure of user mental models for the content/functionality, and (3) which content matters to which users. We used this information to craft personas, and used those personas to design an IA that served as a basis for the successful site redesign.

Collaborative assimilation has side benefits

Because the entire core team is involved in the assimilation exercise, everyone has an opportunity to see the factoids from all data sources. By the time the assimilation exercise is complete, everyone on the core team will have been exposed to the data and to the inherent patterns, themes, and relationships in the data. This shared understanding is priceless. As a side benefit, through your assimilation exercise you create a core team that is fully cognizant of a huge amount of data from a wide variety of sources. Armed with your clustered and labeled data, you and your team are perfectly prepared for the next step: identifying and creating skeletons.

Assimilation works well, but it does have a few drawbacks

Assimilation does have a couple of drawbacks you should be aware of before you begin.

- During an assimilation exercise, you and your team will group factoids that have been extracted from their original contexts. Factoids that are unrelated when you read them in context may seem related (and end up grouped) after they have been extracted from their sources and copied onto sticky notes. This opens the possibility for misrepresenting the original data in your final personas.

- Identifying relationships between factoids is a subjective exercise. Two different teams might group factoids in different ways and end up with different conclusions.

Because affinity diagramming does open the door to misrepresentations of your data, we encourage you to schedule enough time to validate your personas after you have created them. However, it is also important to remember that personas can never fully express or represent the data in the same way it is expressed in the original sources, and that this is not the point of the personas. Rather, personas will help you communicate the essential and helpful information the data contains. The danger that some aspects of the personas *may* misrepresent some aspects of the data is outweighed by the guarantee that the personas *will* convey important and data-driven information to your product team.

Plan your assimilation meeting

An assimilation meeting typically lasts two to four hours. It should include all members of your persona core team. These meetings work best in medium to large rooms that have plenty of wall space (or floor space). Before the meeting, make sure you have plenty of sticky notes, markers, tape, and large sheets of paper on hand.

If you have a relatively small to medium amount of data, you should be able to assimilate all of it in a single meeting. If you have a large amount of data, consider distributing the data

<aside>

Handy Detail

WHAT TO DO IF YOU ARE DROWNING IN DATA

If you have collected a lot of data during the *family planning* phase, you might find it difficult to get started with your data analysis. Staring at a huge stack of printouts can be incredibly intimidating. If you are having a difficult time getting started, try sorting your printouts into three stacks: very relevant (to your product domain and intended users), moderately relevant, and not very relevant. Conduct an assimilation exercise with only the very relevant documents and see what types of clusters you get. After you run your first assimilation exercise—even if it is just with a subset of the data resources collected—you will find that it is easier and much quicker to identify interesting factoids in future exercises. If you are then still dissatisfied with the depth of insights revealed initially, and have the time, you can continue assimilating with less relevant data.

</aside>

NUMBER YOUR DATA SOURCES

During your meeting, you will be asking everyone to find important points, or individual factoids, in the data sources and transfer these individually to sticky notes. It is a good idea to number every data source before the meeting, record the number on the data source itself (write the number on the first page of the document), and record the data source titles and their assigned numbers in a data index (see Chapter 3, Figure 3.14, for an example of a data source index). Then, as people identify factoids and transfer each to a sticky note they should record the source number to make it easy to track the factoids back to their original sources later.

sources and request that your colleagues identify relevant factoids before the meeting. Alternatively, simply schedule multiple meetings that focus independently on each identified user category. If you do the latter, make sure to have a final meeting in which the assimilation results for all user categories are reviewed together. Generally, the agenda for an assimilation meeting should be as follows:

1. Describe the rules, goal, and outcome of the meeting.
2. Identify key data points (factoids) in the data sources.
3. Transfer key data points (factoids) to sticky notes.
4. Post user category labels in various locations in the room.
5. Assimilate the key factoids.
6. Label groups (and do some higher-order organization).

Describe the goal and outcome of the meeting

Your goals for this meeting are fairly simple.

● Filter and prioritize the data down to the most important and relevant bits of information, or factoids, for your specific product and team.

● Organize these factoids into meaningful, related groups, paying attention to the user categories you identified in step 1.

These groups of factoids will serve as the core content and structure for creating personas, but note that when this meeting is over you will not have personas in hand.

Identify key data points (factoids) in the data sources

The first step in processing the data is to review and filter the information in each of the research reports. You do this because not every data point in a given study/report is relevant to the definition of your target audience or to the design of your product. Whether it is done before or during the meeting, ask your core team members to highlight findings they think are key in understanding your target audience or that are highly insightful toward defining aspects of your product. In other words, you want them to look for findings that are relevant to your market, industry, or domain. Highlight any facts that seem important to your product's audience or to the product itself. The case study following shows examples of highlighting in two different data documents: a qualitative site visit report and a quantitative market research report.

Determining what pieces of information are important may seem daunting at first. Don't fret too much over this until you have tried it. When in doubt, be inclusive. It is better to start with too many factoids than too few. You might be tempted to develop criteria ahead of time (e.g., criteria for factoids that are irrelevant, too detailed, too broad, or otherwise not very helpful). We recommend that you do not. In our experience, such criteria are not easy to come by and are difficult to apply. Attempting to generate them consumes valuable time that could be used more directly with the data. In fact, because your core team consists of key individuals across your organization and from different disciplines, each person will have different insights and perspectives on what is important. This is good. You will find that agreement on the importance of any individual piece of data actually happens through the assimilation process.

In the end, even your full personas will *not* include or reference all of the data you find and cluster. If you find yourself drowning in data or your team stuck in "analysis paralysis," just force yourself to move on to the next step and trust that the process will still work. Be willing to try things out, and plan to use your time on iteration (not initial perfection).

Transfer factoids to sticky notes

After everyone has had a chance to comb through their assigned research documents, it is time to go back through the items they highlighted, reevaluate their importance, and then transfer them to another medium to enable assimilation. Each important factoid should be copied or cut out of the original document. We prefer to do the factoid assimilation using sticky notes (as shown in the following case study), though larger sheets of paper (e.g., 8-½ × 11 or easel sheets) can be useful for readability and easier collaboration. It may be more practical to simply physically cut the data points out of the research document with scissors and then glue/paste them onto 3 × 5 index cards. (You could also use printable sticky notes or 3 × 5 cards and have someone type them in and print them during the meeting.) Either way, remember to note the source and page number on each factoid.

THE G4K CORE TEAM IDENTIFIES FACTOIDS AND TRANSFERS THEM TO STICKY NOTES

As discussed in Chapter 3, the G4K persona core team had amassed over 25 relevant research studies and had conducted a series of observational site visits with families that use their products and the Internet. Because they had so many data documents, the team decided to do the data filtering process prior to their assimilation meeting. To ease the load, they distributed the documents across the five core team members (five or six documents per person). They then agreed on a general rule that no document would get more than about 30 minutes of a person's time. In total, the data filtering took roughly three hours of each team member's time. During the process, each person independently scanned through his or her assigned reports and marked findings that seemed critical

(Meanwhile, at G4K..., continued)

to their audience and overall project. Figure 4.5 shows the resulting highlighting in one such document—one of the market research reports (found on the Web for free) relevant to their domain.

While 38 percent of White non-Hispanic children and 35 percent of Asian and Pacific Islander children used the Internet at home, just 15 percent of Black children and 13 percent of Hispanic children did.[5]

More school-age children use computers at school than have access to them at home.

School is a major influence on children's access to computers. Among children of school age (6 to 17 years), 2 in 3 had access to a computer at home in 2000. However, 4 in 5 actually used a computer at school.

More than half of school-age children had access to computers both in school and at home (57 percent). However, many children had access in only one location or the other. Of them, far more had access in school than had access at home. Twenty-three percent of school-age children had access to a computer only at school, compared with just 10 percent who had access only at home. Adding all three groups together, 9 in 10 school-age children had access to a computer somewhere, leaving just 10 percent of children who had no access to a computer in any locale (Figure 2).

Schools level the playing field by giving computer access to children who have none at home.

For children 6 to 17 years old, computer use at school was more nearly equal across different income, race, or ethnic groups than computer access at home (Figure 3).

School-age children in family households with incomes of $75,000 or more had the highest rates of home

[5]The proportions of home Internet users among Asian and Pacific Islander and White non-Hispanic children were not significantly different. The proportions of home Internet users among Black and Hispanic children were also not significantly different.

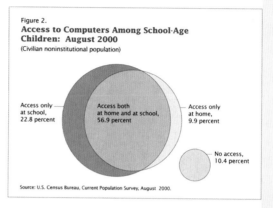

Figure 2.
Access to Computers Among School-Age Children: August 2000
(Civilian noninstitutional population)

Access only at school, 22.8 percent

Access both at home and at school, 56.9 percent

Access only at home, 9.9 percent

No access, 10.4 percent

Source: U.S. Census Bureau, Current Population Survey, August 2000.

computer access, at 94 percent, compared with those with incomes below $25,000, at 35 percent (a difference of about 60 percentage points). But at school, while 87 percent of those with the highest incomes used a computer, 72 percent of those with the lowest incomes did so, a difference of only 15 percentage points.

Figure 3 illustrates a similar equalizing effect observed among children of different racial or ethnic groups. At home, access varied from high to low by 41 percentage points. However, at school the range was much smaller, just 14 percentage points.

The net result of the effect schools have in giving computer access across income, racial, and ethnic groups is a leveling of the computer access that children of different groups have compared to what they would have had if home were the only place available for them to use computers. The absolute percentage-point gap in total computer access between children from family households with the highest and lowest incomes was only about one-third as large as the gap in

home access between these two groups. Similarly, the overall computer access gap between White non-Hispanic school-age children and Black or Hispanic school-age children was just over one-third the size of the gap between these groups in home computer access.[6]

ADULT ACCESS TO COMPUTERS AND THE INTERNET

More adults have computers and use the Internet at home than ever before.

More than half of all adults 18 years old and over, 55 percent, lived in a household with at least one computer in 2000, compared with only 46 percent in 1998. Thirty-seven percent of all adults used the Internet at home, compared with just 23 percent in 1998 (Table C).

The oldest adults had the lowest rates of home Internet use. Only 13 percent of those 65 years old or over used the Internet at home.

[6]The proportions of overall computer access among Black and Hispanic school-age children were not significantly different.

U.S. Census Bureau

5

FIGURE 4.5: *Data highlighting in a quantitative market research report. (Adapted from U.S. Census Bureau, 2001.)*

(Meanwhile, at G4K..., continued)

As a second step, they met as a group for an hour to transfer the resulting highlighted information onto sticky notes. They did this together in case there were questions about the inclusion of specific facts, and what surrounding details might need to be captured. Figure 4.6 shows an example of some of the facts that were pulled from one of the field study reports (qualitative findings). Across the many research documents, they amassed over 500 sticky notes containing important findings, or factoids (about 15 or so factoids per research article). They were now ready to do the assimilation exercise.

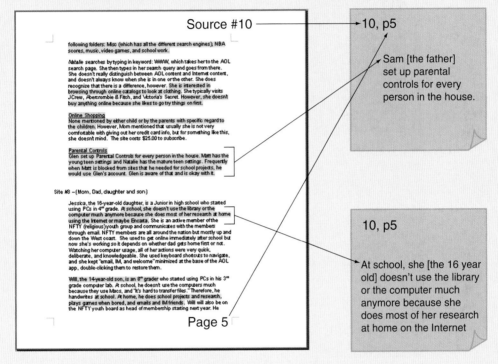

FIGURE 4.6: *An example of two factoids identified in a qualitative research document (field study report) and transferred to sticky notes.*

Post user category labels around the room

Before starting your assimilation exercise, it is important to "seed" the room with the user category labels you identified in step 1. If your categories are based on quantitatively derived segments, include the major defining characteristics of the segments as well. These labels will serve to direct your initial placement and high-level organization of the factoids. We recommend that you do this with larger sheets of paper instead of sticky notes to ensure

FIGURE 4.7: *Seed the walls with your user category labels. (Photograph courtesy of Jonathan Hayes.)*

that they are salient and visible (see Figure 4.7). Be sure to leave room between and underneath each label for the multitude of sticky note factoids that will be placed in relation to them. Your assimilation and prioritization activities, detailed in the following, will revolve around these predefined categories, so make sure everyone in the room is intimately familiar with them.

Assimilate the factoids

Now the interaction (and fun) begins. To do the assimilation, everyone will get up (at the same time) and place their factoids around the room, positioning related factoids near each other to form groups or clusters. Ask everyone to review their factoids and start putting them on the wall or floor in relation to other people's factoids (and in relation to the predefined categories).

For example, if one person has a factoid about children's Internet use behaviors after school, and another has a factoid about children's daily entertainment activities in the home, these two factoids might be placed near each other. As everyone adds their factoids, similar or related factoids will cluster, and factoids that are not related will end up far apart. Figure 4.8 shows an assimilation exercise in progress.

During your assimilation exercise, you might find "factoid islands" of sticky notes that turn out to be difficult to cluster. If you find factoids that cause extended arguments or that you

FIGURE 4.8: *An assimilation exercise in progress. In this case, the factoids are written on larger sheets of paper to facilitate collaboration. (Photograph courtesy of Jonathan Hayes.)*

feel you have to force into a cluster, put them aside and return to them later. You won't use every factoid you have created and clustered in your finished personas.

You might also find that a single factoid fits well in more than one location. Make copies of the factoid and put it everywhere it belongs. As the assimilation progresses, you will find that your opinions on how to cluster factoids evolves. Your team will probably want to redistribute factoids and even move entire clusters as the exercise progresses, and you should encourage them to do so until they feel that the clusters make sense.

Look for "puddles" of sticky notes: If you see more than 5 to 10 sticky notes clustered closely together (in a "puddle"), try to find additional distinctions between the factoids on those sticky notes. Instead of a single large cluster, try to create several smaller clusters that reflect these distinctions.

Label the clusters of factoids

As the clusters of factoids (and/or assumptions] become stable, begin labeling the clusters with sticky notes. Be sure to use a different color for the labels (see Figure 4.9). Remember that assimilation is given structure by the categories you initially identified, but at its core the resulting clusters are determined by the data (i.e., it is a bottom-up process). Not all of your clustered factoids have to fit cleanly

Handy Detail

YOU CAN INCLUDE COLLECTED ASSUMPTIONS IN YOUR ASSIMILATION EXERCISE

If you collected assumptions during family planning (or to help you identify categories of users), you can assimilate these along with the factoids. Assign one sticky-note color to indicate assumptions so that you don't confuse them with factoids. Assimilating assumptions along with your factoids allows you to easily see which assumptions are supported by data (those that end up clustered with factoids) and which are not (those that end up alone or in small clusters with other assumptions).

Assimilating assumptions in with your factoids can produce some very interesting results. For example, you can create your categories, assimilate your assumptions (perhaps using yellow sticky notes), and then assimilate your factoids (using blue sticky notes). After your assimilation is complete and you have labeled all of your clusters of factoids (see material following), you will probably find that some clusters include only blue stickies (factoids) or only yellow stickies (assumptions). This is helpful information. If a cluster includes only factoids, it could mean:

- Your organization doesn't have any assumptions about this topic
- Your organization does have assumptions about the topic but you have not surfaced these assumptions yet.

To find out, you can ask your stakeholders to tell you their assumptions about the topic in question. If a cluster includes only assumptions, it could mean:

- The data does not support the assumptions
- You did not find and use the data related to these assumptions in your exercise.

If you find a cluster with only assumptions, look for more data to either support or specifically contradict the assumptions. You know that the assumptions exist and therefore could exert influence on the design of your product. It is worth looking for data now.

into your defined categories. When you label your clusters, you will identify supporting data related to your categories, distinctions in categories (subcategories), and new information about your targeted users.

Data tends to cluster in expected and unexpected ways

The data you have assimilated had many different authors with many different purposes. It is not possible to determine before you assimilate it what truly insightful and compelling relationships in information you will find. Factoids will not all naturally cluster in ways that seem immediately relevant to your persona effort. This information may not map neatly to user types or goals, but it may contain domain-related insights that prove invaluable to

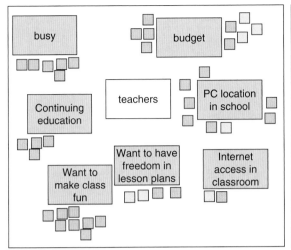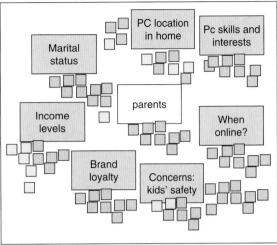

FIGURE 4.9: *Categories of users (white), cluster labels (pink), factoids (blue), and assumptions (yellow) after an assimilation exercise. In this illustration, we show the labels (pink) much larger than the sticky note clusters. This is simply so that you can read the cluster labels. We recommend that you use sticky notes to label the clusters of factoids (in this example, blue stickies) and assumptions (in this example, yellow stickies) you find during your assimilation exercise because this facilitates moving and changing the labels as needed.*

your effort. If you find "odd" clusters developing, don't try to force them to fit. Examine them for insights into your user base. (See "Case Study: G4K Assimilates Its Factoids," following.) You may want to follow up any perplexing questions with additional user research.

Know when to stop

Continue the assimilation and labeling exercise until:

- Everyone has placed their set of factoids on the floor or wall in relation to other factoids
- The groups or clusters have started to settle.

Note that you may have to just force yourself to stop, as the organization of factoids, labeling, and reorganization can go on for a long time. One way to force the issue is simply to stop once every group has a label (even if you don't have agreement on the current organization and labeling).

○ Discuss categories of users
○ Process data
● **Identify & create skeletons**
○ Evaluate & prioritize skeletons
○ Develop skeletons into personas
○ Validate the personas

Step 3: Identify subcategories of users and create skeletons

During step 3, you will evaluate your assimilated data to confirm the original categories of users you

G4K Meanwhile, at G4K...

THE G4K CORE TEAM ASSIMILATES FACTOIDS

Earlier, the G4K team decided that a simple set of categories (children, parents, and educators) was an appropriate starting point for the assimilation exercise. These three category labels were placed in large print on the meeting room walls. They each gathered their sticky note factoids and started the process. Everyone began posting sticky notes on the wall under one of the three major category labels. For each sticky note, that person would look at the posted sticky notes and decide if their note was related or unrelated to those notes. If related, they would post their sticky note in or near the other notes. If unrelated, they posted their note separately to possibly form the beginning of a new group of notes.

Clustering

During the assimilation exercise, they began noticing that many factoids were very specific about behaviors and interests related to specific ages, which was not a surprise to them. So, they put up some additional labels to mark the age groups that were emerging. "Tweens" was one of these emerging groups (ages 9 to 12). They found the word *tween* occurring over and over again in factoids related to this age range. They also began putting labels on the smaller clusters of notes that were forming, as shown in Figure 4.10.

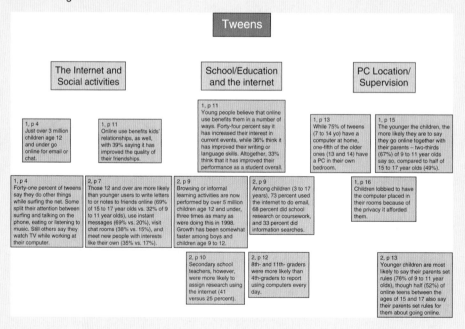

FIGURE 4.10: *Some example clusters of factoids for the Tweens group (ages 9 to 12).*

As the majority of the factoids got placed, the team found many meaningful clusters and subclusters. There was a big division around gender for the older children (those from 9 to 12 years old), as well as for parents (moms versus dads), but not for younger children. As they expected, their original main categories of users remained stable throughout the exercise. But some of the groupings of factoids got moved around, relabeled, or even distributed as the group gathered insights through the process.

Whenever a cluster got too large (that is, it contained more than 10 sticky notes), someone on the team would attempt to split it up into subclusters. For example, initially a large cluster of factoids about the general activities of teens had formed, but then the team found many ways to divide these into meaningful clusters. "Teen activities" became "teens and school," "teens and social activities," "teens and the Internet," "teens and gaming," and so on.

The G4K Team Found Unexpected Clusters

The core team found several clusters that did not specifically relate to any of their preconceived notions of users and their characteristics. For example, they found an interesting cluster of factoids that included information on the placement of the family computer in the home and the behavior of various family members to the computer. They even found some clusters consisting of government guidelines and laws, including laws related to targeting minors and collecting any type of information from them via the Internet.

started with and to identify interesting subcategories of users. You should plan to create one skeleton persona per unique category or subcategory. This will ensure that you have a set of skeletons that reflect and cover the data you have collected. Once you have created your skeletons, you (and your stakeholders) can prioritize them. Using this process, you may create a relatively large set of skeleton personas, but this does not mean that you will communicate all of these possible target personas outside your core team during the *birth and maturation* and *adulthood* phases of your project.

Identify subcategories of users

When you created your categories of users in step 1, you thought about the differences in user roles, user goals, and user segments between groups of your target users. To identify subcategories of users, you will now think about these differences *within* each of your categories based on key findings across the clusters. For example, if you created categories of users defined primarily by differences between user roles, you can now examine each of those categories for important differences in user goals and user segments. You may also find that there are specific subroles that form subcategories. You should create a subcategory to describe any product-significant differences you find within your categories that seem important and are clearly indicated in the assimilated data.

Clusters identify groups of facts; subcategories identify groups of people

Look at the data clustered under each of your user categories. As a team, evaluate and discuss the possibility that each category should be divided into two or more subcategories. Consider roles, goals, and segments in this assessment. As you identify subcategories, you can write them on a whiteboard. You might also find it helpful to transfer the subcategory names onto sticky notes and place them appropriately in your assimilated data. In doing this exercise, you are simply exploring the possible groups of users that have emerged from your data.

When does a difference merit a subcategory?

The most difficult part of this process is determining whether a difference is *meaningful and useful*. Step back and see if subcategories are "bubbling up" out of your assimilated data.

Your goal is to express what Bob Barlow-Busch (in his contributed chapter "Personas and Marketing") calls "the differences that make a difference" between the types of people described in your data sources. As your core team discusses the results of your assimilation, consider the following questions in determining which merit the creation of subcategories.

- *Does this subcategory represent a group of users important to the design of our product?* Does this subcategory likely require different features from other subcategories and different ways of interacting with our product?

- *Does this subcategory represent a group of users important to our business?* Does this subcategory produce revenue, bring mind share, or influence other people regarding your product?

- *Is this subcategory clearly unique compared to the other subcategories?* Is the subcategory different enough to warrant a separate and distinct persona?

What if we end up creating a lot of categories and subcategories?

As long as you feel you can distinguish the categories and subcategories you discover in the data, it is fine (and often a good idea) to create subcategories. Create as many categories and subcategories as it takes to capture your data. You will not necessarily create personas for all of them. The product design and development team will likely not be able to embrace more

Story from the field

IDENTIFYING YOUR MOST DEMANDING USERS

—George Olsen, Principal, Interaction by Design

Personas are commonly built around the "neediest" users. That is, if you can solve a design problem for them you will likely solve it for all of your other users as well. But it can also be useful to look at your most demanding users—those most vocal. Although this runs the risk of tilting toward power users, it is not uncommon for consumer-facing products to have a minority of customers account for a majority of profits. It therefore makes sense to highlight their needs. (It might also be the case that noncustomers, who the company hopes to attract, want more out of the product than it currently delivers.) But the principle is the same as designing for the neediest users: see if by satisfying a design problem for the most demanding users you can satisfy a much larger group of users. Thus, this can be valuable complementary approach, but just use it with care.

than about five to seven personas effectively. In the next section, we describe how to prioritize your categories and subcategories of users generated after first turning them into skeleton profiles.

Create skeletons

Once you have identified and agreed upon the categories and subcategories of users, you are ready to create *skeletons*. Skeletons are very brief, typically bulleted, lists of distinguishing data ranges for each subcategory of user. Skeletons help your core team transition from thinking about categories of users to focusing on specific details. They also allow your team to present the key findings of the assimilation exercise to stakeholders.

Create one skeleton for each of the subcategories you identified. On each skeleton, list the cluster labels that relate to that subcategory. These cluster labels will become headings in your skeleton. Because you will be comparing and prioritizing skeletons against each other, it is important that each contains at least somewhat comparable information. Consider including common characteristics or headings across all of your skeletons. If you do this, you may find that you are missing information for some skeletons. In these cases, either leave that information blank, perhaps marking it as "need data," or make an informed estimation

Skeleton	Sketch
Boy, age 10–13 **Computer use at school** • Has access to a shared computer in his classroom or a computer 'lab' shared by the whole school • Has at least one computer-related assignment a week • Finds computer use at school 'boring' **Internet use at home** • Shares a home computer with family • Uses internet to play games and (sometimes) do school work **Interests/Activities** • Likes to talk about games with friends • Likes video games more than computer games • Participates in multiple organized sports	**Danny** Danny is 12 and he just started 6th grade, which is very cool. He has computer lab once a week and he likes it alot. He usually spends recess in the computer lab looking for info about the Lakers and for new games to try. He thinks he's a computer pro; his mom's been coming to him for help with silly stuff for years now.

FIGURE 4.11: *A skeleton versus a sketch persona. Note that the skeleton includes headings derived from cluster labels (from the assimilation exercise) and data points. For now, avoid any narrative details that might distract stakeholders as they try to prioritize the skeletons.*

about what it might be. If you do the latter, be sure to indicate that it is an assumption to be followed up on.

Under each heading, create a bulleted summary of the information you found in the data. You are not exhaustively including every aspect of the associated factoids. Try to identify the key points that capture the essence of the subcategory. Do not give the skeletons names or other personal details that make them feel like people (which may relate to, but are not specific to the data). As shown in Figure 4.11, skeletons are not sketch personas; they are selected facts that define and distinguish your subcategories of users.

How many skeletons should I create?

We recommend that you create skeletons only for subcategories of users you believe are interesting or important to your product. If you create a large number of skeletons, you can use the prioritization exercise following to narrow in on the few you will evolve into personas. However, it is much easier for stakeholders to prioritize fewer skeletons. Use the criteria listed previously under "When does a difference merit a subcategory?" to discuss each skeleton as you create it and to combine, augment, or discard skeletons.

Handy Detail

THINK ABOUT YOUR USERS

Earlier in this book, we reminded you to think about the users of your own work products.

Skeletons are a perfect example of the importance of this. Skeletons are documents you use to communicate with your business stakeholders. You will ask these stakeholders to prioritize the skeletons in accordance with business objectives. This is precisely why you do not want to include fictional details (such as a name, favorite color, or favorite activity). Any information in the skeleton document that is not obviously derived directly from data will distract the stakeholders and invite debate on details—and this is not the appropriate time for that debate.

Handy Detail

WHAT IF YOU FIND "SCARY" INFORMATION IN THE DATA?

What if you have some data that makes you create a persona that inherently will not like your product? For example, maybe you are building a product for television and the data says that people in a key set of target users are too busy to watch TV. What do you do? If you run into this type of problem, you can

- Escalate the data you have found to the stakeholders, so that they can reevaluate the strategy for the product. If they push back, show them the data that led to your conclusions.
- Reevaluate your data sources to consider whether they are really in line with the existing strategy with respect to target users.
- Build this information, and the related design challenges, into the personas you create. Given that your targets don't like to watch TV currently, and that you cannot change the delivery medium, how do you get these people to change their behavior and turn on the TV to access your product? How do you build a specific product that will appeal to them, given their needs and goals?

G4K   Meanwhile, at G4K...

THE G4K CORE TEAM IDENTIFIES SUBCATEGORIES OF USERS AND CREATES SKELETONS

During the assimilation exercise, the G4K core team discovered many clusters of factoids related to each of the initial three main categories. Before they began the assimilation exercise, the G4K team knew that kids tend to behave very differently depending on their ages (after all, G4K is a game software company, with a lot of experience with kids). Their assimilated data corroborated this basic notion. What they did not know up front was how kids behave *online*, and which age groups were the best targets for the Internet portal project. They also did not know that "tweens" (often defined as kids between the ages of 9 and 12) would factor so much in the data. G4K never used the term *tween*, and this was a new concept for the organization.

The team also discovered clusters of information about gender differences in kids of different ages. Generally, they found that boys and girls differ in terms of activities and interests (e.g., girls are more active in social activities) but do not differ in their overall amount of PC/Internet use. Interestingly, differences in gender were much stronger as kids got older.

The G4K team expected to find differences between kids at school and kids at home or in their leisure time. Although they did find factoids on these topics, the factoids did not cluster in a way that suggested that kids have different goals or roles at school and home when it comes to online activities. The sections that follow describe subcategories that were most meaningful and unique.

Kids

The G4K team created a list of the meaningful subcategories they found in the assimilated data for kids, with loads of interesting clusters of findings for each. The resulting groups were not surprising to the team. After evaluating these possible groups and the data in the clusters (particularly related to gender differences), they decided that six subcategories would be enough to represent the general category.

- Boys and girls 3 to 5 years old (no relevant gender differences)
- Boys and girls 6 to 8 years old (no relevant gender differences)
- Boys 9 to 12 years old (tweens)
- Girls 9 to 12 years old (tweens)
- Boys 13 to 15 years old (young teens)
- Girls 13 to 15 years old (young teens)

Parents

In the clusters of data describing parents, the G4K team was quite surprised to find that there were several distinct clusters of data related specifically to moms (in addition to the clusters related to parents)—specifically, data about mothers and their attitudes regarding kids and online activities.

(Meanwhile, at G4K..., continued)

In fact, much of the data indicated that female adults (moms) were a stronger target for considering G4K design issues than adult males (dads). Other factors—such as the number of children in the household—seemed to play only a small role in determining activities, interests, and other factors related to the G4K domain. However, single versus multiple adult households did show some interesting differences. Ultimately, the G4K team decided on one subcategory of parents that was important and unique.

- Parents (usually moms) who take a very active role in their children's use of computers and the Internet

Educators

Regarding the domain of teachers, they found that computer access was a fairly common thing in most schools. However, newly hired (recently trained) teachers showed a greater affinity for the use of technology in the classroom. They were more comfortable with computers and thought that providing children with related experiences was important. They found that some teachers avoid technology in the classroom (for a variety of reasons) and that although almost all schools have PC and Internet access not all have such capabilities directly in the classroom. Thus, there were several possible subcategories of teachers.

- Newly hired teachers with in-classroom PC/Internet facilities, and an interest in promoting/ exploring new technologies for education
- Established teachers who had a desire to control or expand their curriculum, but were less versed in technology
- School librarians or educational specialists that run a centralized computer facility for the entire school

From these 10 subcategories of users, the persona team assembled 10 skeletons, defining their core attributes using the associated clusters of factoids.

○ Discuss categories of users
○ Process data
○ Identify & create skeletons
● **Evaluate & prioritize skeletons**
○ Develop skeletons into personas
○ Validate the personas

PERSONA GESTATION: STEPS 4, 5, AND 6

Once you have a set of skeletons, it is time to get feedback from your stakeholders. You will evaluate the importance of each skeleton to your business and product strategy and prioritize the skeletons accordingly. During gestation, you will identify a subset of skeletons to develop into personas.

Step 4: Prioritize the skeletons

It is time to prioritize your skeletons. To do this, schedule a meeting with members of your persona core team who understand the data you have collected and stakeholders empowered to make decisions about the strategic focus of the company. If stakeholders are not aware of the data and general process that led to these skeletons, present that information before introducing the skeletons to them. It is important to carefully plan and manage your prioritization meeting. Before you get started, remind everyone of the goals of the meeting and the impact their decisions will have on the project.

- *These skeletons were derived from data,* and should map fairly clearly to the user types (categories and subcategories) you already reviewed together.

- *Prioritization should focus on immediate goals or low-hanging fruit.* Remind the team that the goal is to reduce the possible set of targets to just those that are critical *to your current product cycle.* Remember that you can prioritize the skeletons differently for subsequent versions of this product or for derivative or sibling products.

- *Prioritizing does not mean abandoning the interests of the lower-priority skeletons.* It simply means deciding that in the case of feature or functionality debates the interests of the persona derived from the most important category or subcategory of users should be considered before anyone else's. If the stakeholders insist that all of the skeletons are critical, ask them to consider which would be *most useful* to the development staff. For example, have them do a Q-sort in which they can place a particular number of items in each of three priorities (high, medium, and low) and then have them sort with each category for one more gradation. You can always provide a slightly different set of personas to those teams who might benefit most from them (e.g., provide to your marketing team the set of personas closest to purchase decisions).

- *Prioritizing should be relatively easy if the business and strategic goals for the product are clear.* If prioritizing is difficult, it may mean that the stakeholders have some more work to do on their own. The skeletons and the detailed category and subcategory distinctions may be able to help them in this work.

It is important to reach consensus on the importance of the various skeletons, but it is not often easy to do so. When you ask your stakeholders to rank the skeletons you identified, they will probably respond in one of the following ways:

- "These three [or some subset] are the ones we really need to target."
- "They are all great."
- "They are all great, but we need to add X, Y, and Z customers to this list," or "You are omitting many of our major customer groups."
- "None of these are good."
- "I can't tell you which ones are the right ones."
- "Wow, we need to do some (more) customer research," or "We really need to know X about our users."

Although getting the first answer is the best, all of these answers are actually okay.

They provide useful, actionable information. Of course, you could get a completely different response from each stakeholder. If that happens, know that it is useful information and take note of it (in Chapter 7 we provide suggestions for expressing the value of the persona effort, and providing "proof" that key stakeholders had very different ideas about the target users before the personas were completed can be helpful).

Some of your stakeholders' answers may point to problems in your organization—problems in business strategy or lack of real knowledge about your customers. If this is your first time doing personas, we can pretty much guarantee that there will be difficulty and indecision. You are asking difficult questions that your stakeholders may not have been asked before, or probably have not been asked this early in the product cycle.

Structure the discussion

It is helpful to provide some structure to the prioritization exercise. The first step is simply to have them rank order the skeletons by perceived importance. There will likely be some disagreement as they sort the list. That is okay at this point. Once you have a rough order in place, we suggest assigning each skeleton one or more values that can more closely be tied to data.

- *Frequency of use:* How often would each skeleton use your product? Daily users would likely be more important regarding design decisions than those that only use your product once a month.

- *Size of market:* Roughly how many people does each skeleton represent? Larger markets are usually more important than smaller ones. Do you plan to aim your new product at a new market? In that case, you might consider the importance of a small market with growth potential.

- *Historic or potential revenue:* How much purchasing power does each skeleton encompass? If this is a new product, you may have to estimate this amount (e.g., through trade journals, market trends, market research, and understanding spending behaviors in related markets). In many cases, users might not directly make the purchase. Someone else buys such products for them. Still, they may influence those purchase decisions.

- *Strategic importance:* Decide who is your most strategically important audience. Is it those who make the most support calls, those who rely on your product for critical activities, those who use your competitor's product, or those who don't use yours or anyone's product yet? Are you trying to expand or grow your market? If that is your primary goal, do your skeletons include nonusers, technology pioneers, or trend setters? Which target audiences will help your team innovate or stretch?

You might derive other attributes that are more directly related to your line of business. Either way, you can use just one of these attributes or some combination of them to more accurately prioritize the skeletons. If time is critical for your stakeholders (which is usually the case), consider generating the values for these attributes yourself, and even doing the prioritization, prior to the meeting. To help your leadership team through the review process and toward a conclusion, remind the stakeholders that validation work can and will happen later in the process, to ensure that the current decisions and resulting personas are on track.

Bright Idea

IF YOU ARE STUCK, CREATE ANTI-PERSONAS

Consider preparing skeletons of clear *nontargets* for your stakeholder review meeting. These are audiences that no one would refute as being outside your product's audience. Cooper refers to these as negative personas in *The Inmates are Running the Asylum* (Cooper, 1999, p. 136). These are usually quite obvious once described, but it is helpful to make it clear that your product is not for everyone in the known universe. For example, if you are developing an e-commerce Web site your target audience probably shouldn't include people who are non-PC users, people without Internet connectivity, or (more ridiculously) infants and toddlers.

This is particularly useful if your team members see themselves as the target audience. It is also useful if there is a well-known audience or well-liked audience that is not a good business target. For example, anti-personas might include:

- Extreme novices ("my mom can't use this")
- The seasoned expert or guru ("macros and short cut keys are critical!")
- The domain enthusiast (an obvious audience that might actually be very small in size and thus not a good target for the business).

Story from the field

IN THE END, THE CHOICE OF TARGETS IS A MANAGEMENT DECISION

—Matthew Lee, Usability Engineer, InfoSpace, Inc.

At a financial services company I worked for, management did not agree that one person could be an identifier for an entire segment (over 1 million people). The segment in question included a huge portion of the population (lower-income people who rent their homes). This segment included many types of people, from single mothers with kids, to older retired people living on Social Security, to people living paycheck to paycheck. Management didn't believe that one person could represent all of these people in a meaningful manner, and insisted we create three personas to represent the segment.

G4K Meanwhile, at G4K...

THE G4K STAKEHOLDERS PRIORITIZE SKELETONS

Now that the G4K core team had 10 skeletons resulting from the assimilation exercise (six kids, one parent, and three educators), they needed to get input from their stakeholders. The core team arranged a one-hour meeting with the stakeholders.

During the meeting, they first reviewed the initial subcategories and resulting skeletons for each major category separately. For kids, the stakeholders were not quite convinced that gender could be collapsed for the younger age groups. So, the core team provided the clustered factoids and some of the original data reports to help them understand the reasoning.

The stakeholders were surprised to hear that the team discovered only one important and unique group of parents (moms that take a very active role in their children's use of computers and the Internet). However the stakeholders understood that it would not be worthwhile to target groups of parents unlikely to visit the site. The core team suggested that one parent target could be used to explore multiple reasons for visiting the site (e.g., surfing together with a child, buying a present for a child, snooping around using the browser history to view sites a child had visited recently, and so on). The stakeholders agreed this would be adequate.

The stakeholders believed that all of the educator skeletons were good targets. But the core team pressed them to identify which of the three educators would be most fruitful to focus on. After some deliberation, the stakeholders came to believe that focusing on one would cover the needs of the others. They felt that the first segment (newly hired teachers with an affinity for technology) would be the most appropriate.

Once they moved past these initial issues, the core team asked the stakeholders to prioritize the skeletons by discussing aspects of frequency of use, size of market, potential revenue, and strategic importance. Considering these factors, they devised a loose prioritization scheme by collectively assigning percentages to subcategories such that they equaled 100%. The results were as follows:

- Kids (75% focus total)
  - *Segment: Boys and girls 3 to 5 years old.* **5%** (key targets for G4K's early educational products, but not able to use the Internet alone)
  - *Segment: Girls 6 to 8 years old as a growth market.* **25%** (interested in creativity and education, an important strategic target, G4K has game products that are popular with younger girls, but no offerings that are strong in this category, somewhat less influential than older users)

(Meanwhile, at G4K..., continued)

- *Segment: Boys 9 to 12 years old (tweens).* **30%** (current users of G4K shrink-wrap games and the Internet, focused on entertainment, the most frequent visitors and likely to influence purchase decisions of parents)
- *Segment: Boys 13 to 15 years old (early teens).* **15%** (composed of more hard-core gamers, tough audience to keep pleased, but important for branding and market influence)
- Parents (15% focus total)
  - *Segment: Parents (usually moms) that take a very active role in their children's use of computers and the Internet.* (involved parents, especially moms, are more likely to be aware of the G4K brand and tend to participate in online activities with their kids)
- Teachers (10% focus total)
  - *Segment: Newly hired teachers with in-classroom PC/Internet facilities, and an interest in promoting/exploring new technologies for education.* (this segment is interested and capable of exploring online content and activities, but they may not be aware of the G4K brand)

The most surprising result of this prioritization exercise for the persona core team was that the stakeholders realized that two of the skeletons were not critical for initial success. They agreed that, for this first version of the portal site, it made the most sense to focus on audiences already familiar with the G4K brand and those with a propensity for gaming. As a result, two of the six kid skeletons were put on the sidelines and would only be considered at a later date.

Bright Idea

GOT A LOT OF POSSIBLE USERS? PLOT THEM BY CRITICAL DIMENSIONS

—Len Conte, BMC Software

Are you creating a product that will have many users? Not sure how to approach creating personas that will be useful? We suggest plotting large groups of users according to the critical dimensions of technical and domain expertise and looking for clusters of users (see Figure 4.12). For example, for an online media player you could collect a large group of assumption personas or sketch personas and cluster them according to their domain knowledge (how much expertise do they have with respect to media?) and technical expertise (how facile are they with computers and the Internet?).

Wherever you find a group of dots, that's where you need a persona. This can be a great tool for a reality check on assumptions. Perhaps one or more of the executives assumes that the target market is largely in the top right quadrant (perhaps highly technical music enthusiasts) but your data shows that most potential users of your product cluster in other quadrants.

(Bright idea, continued)

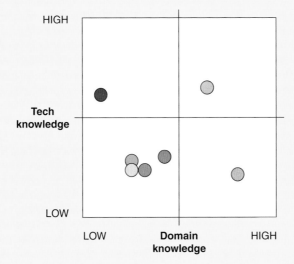

FIGURE 4.12: *A plot of technical expertise and domain knowledge. Each colored dot represents a large group of current or target users. You'll need at least one persona wherever you see a cluster of dots.*

Finally, you will want to ask your stakeholders if there are any missing skeletons (i.e., categories or subcategories of users) that are truly important to your company. If the answer is yes, have the stakeholders create those skeletons based on their collective knowledge and assumptions. You should include those additional "assumption skeletons" in the prioritization process.

Identify primary and secondary targets

It is important that you identify the primary and secondary user targets for your product and eliminate any skeletons that are not critical to the success of the current development cycle. In the next steps, you will create personas based on the prioritization decisions you make here with your skeletons. If there are too many primary targets for your product, the personas will lose some of their strength and utility. Therefore, even if the differences in priority are small you must clearly define which skeletons are going to be focused on and which will not (for now). Select the top three to five skeletons by priority values to be enriched into complete personas.

Why insist on what could result in some difficult discussions or even arguments? Because the alternative is to invite difficult discussions and arguments later in the development process. Personas must be able to end arguments. To do this, they must narrow the design space to something that is manageable.

Story from the field

SOME USERS ARE MORE VALUABLE THAN OTHERS

—George Olsen, Principal, Interaction by Design

Acknowledge that some users are more valuable than others when it comes to the business. Although personas should be based around user needs, it is also useful to evaluate them in light of their value to the business. Most business do make 80% of their profits from 20% of their customers, so it is good to see if these customers have important behavioral/attitudinal differences. In addition, are there differences between the business' core customers and customers they are trying to attract?

Likewise, it is important to ensure your highest priority persona is not someone who actually costs the business money to serve. Although heretical to UCD, in the business world it is sensible to discourage money-losing customers from doing business with you. But building a persona around these costly customers may enable you to discover ways to make them more profitable, either by discovering a benefit that they are willing to pay more for or by creating ways for these customers to be more self-sufficient (and therefore less costly to service).

Handy Detail

CUSTOMER SEGMENT VALUE CREATION SCORECARDS CAN HELP YOU MEASURE THE RELATIVE VALUE OF DIFFERENT GROUPS OF YOUR CUSTOMERS

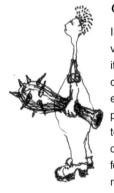

In their book *Angel Customers and Demon Customers,* Selden and Colvin [2003] build a convincing argument for completely reorganizing your company's efforts to satisfy your most profitable customers. Although initiating a corporate reorganization may be a bit beyond the scope of your persona effort, some of Selden and Colvin's tools could generate important insights—especially if you are trying to quantify the financial value of each customer segment and/or persona. Selden and Colvin describe "The Customer Segment Value Creation Scorecard" as a tool to analyze the profits and expenses related to each customer segment. This scorecard can show you which of your segments are currently the most profitable and which are underperforming—and potentially dragging down the overall value of your company. Selden and Colvin relate the following:

(Handy Detail, continued)

When a company views itself as a portfolio of customer segments and completes its Customer Segment Value Creation Scorecard, the realization that some segments are more valuable than others, based on short-term economic profitability and future profitable growth opportunities, suddenly becomes blindingly obvious.... We see immediately that *we can't treat these segments the same*. It's imperative that we keep and grow the most valuable segments, so we need to meet their needs better than average; the least valuable segments, which may actually be destroying shareowner value, must be treated different, in a way that gets them generating positive economic profit... [2003, p. 84].

Selden and Cohen's instructions are much more detailed than we have room for in this sidebar. If you are interested in calculating the value of your customer segments, we recommend that you obtain their book. If you do, and you complete the scorecard for your company, you can create your categories of users based on your customer value segments. If you prioritize and select your skeletons in relation to your most profitable customers—and include details related to which behaviors make these customers so profitable—your resulting personas will help you create designs that continue to satisfy and attract highly profitable customers. You might also create personas to represent your "demon" customers. You can use these personas to understand and address the issues and interactions that make these customers so costly to your business. You can read more about tying personas to customer segment profitability in Colin Hynes' "Story from the field: Putting Real Values on Your Personas" later in this chapter.

Bright Idea

OUT OF TIME? YOU CAN STOP RIGHT HERE

If this is your first persona effort, if you have very little time, or if there is any other reason you feel intense pressure to stop creating the personas and start using them, you can choose to use your skeletons without enriching them to the point of being well-rounded and complete personas. If you decide to do this, consider giving them a few concrete personal details to bring them to life (a name, a tag line, a photo). Skim step 5 in the following and consider whether or not you should add a little bit of narrative to give each skeleton a brief storyline so that they are more distinct and memorable. In doing so, you are creating persona *sketches* from your skeletons.

These sketches can seem like real people to your team, but they will also feel somewhat fictitious. So, be sure to add reference information (e.g., the sources from which you extracted the

(Bright Idea, continued)

information in the sketches) so that everyone is aware that the sketches were derived from data. Then continue on to Chapter 5 and decide how you want to introduce your sketch personas into your organization. Keep in mind that you can always come back to these bare-bones sketches and add more details over time.

Handy Detail

ARTICULATE THE ROLE OF THE NONPRIMARY (OR SECONDARY) PERSONAS

Whether or not you decide to enrich the skeletons of your nonprimary categories and subcategories into full personas, you should make some solid decisions about how you might use them. These less important targets can serve, among other ways, as tie-breakers, brainstorming tools, or heuristics. Alternatively, there may be some critical scenarios with nonprimary personas. For example, one persona may be an IT manager who has to install the software.

You and your team can evaluate the design as it progresses from the points of view of the nonprimary personas you build from these categories and subcategories. This will give you a perspective that is illuminating and still grounded in data. If you are clear on the role of the nonprimary personas, and communicate the fact that they will not be discarded despite not being selected, you will free your team and stakeholders to make the difficult decisions that will result in a streamlined set of primary personas.

○ Discuss categories of users
○ Process data
○ Identify & create skeletons
○ Evaluate & prioritize skeletons
● **Develop skeletons into personas**
○ Validate the personas

Step 5: Develop selected skeletons into personas

You now have a reduced set of basic skeletons your stakeholders helped select. Your task at this point is to enrich these skeletons to become personas by adding data as well as concrete and individualized details to give them personality and context. You will also include some storytelling elements and photos to make the personas come to life.

As you build on your skeletons, all of the details of your personas will be encapsulated in a *foundation document*. Depending on the available time and the needs of your product you might create full personas for just the small set of primary personas you defined, or you can create full personas for a larger set of primary and secondary personas. We have found that it is time- and resource effective to first fully develop the high-priority primary skeletons and then to enrich, but not exhaustively complete, the nonprimary skeletons into sketch personas.

What is a persona foundation document?

We use the term *foundation document* to describe whatever you use as a storehouse for all of your information, descriptions, and data related to a single persona. The foundation document contains the information that will motivate and justify design decisions and generate scenarios that will appear in feature specs, vision documents, storyboards, and so forth.

Foundation documents contain the complete definition of a given persona, but they do not have to be long or difficult to create. Depending on your goals and the needs of your team, your foundation document could range from a single page to a long document. Creating a foundation document for each persona will provide you and your team with a single resource you can harvest as necessary as you create your persona communication materials. At the very least, complete personas must include *core information essential to defining the persona*: the goals, roles, behaviors, segment, environment, and typical activities that make the persona solid, rich, and unique (and, more importantly, relevant to the design of your product). If you have time, your completed foundation documents should contain:

- Abundant links to factoids
- Copious footnotes or comments on specific data
- Links to the original research reports that support and explain the personas' characteristics
- Indications of which supporting characteristics are from data and which characteristics are fictitious or based on assumptions.

As your foundation document grows, it is helpful to add headings and a table of contents. Consider creating your foundation documents as an HTML page for each persona. This will allow you to add links and keep your materials organized while providing access to your various core team members and stakeholders during its development. We provide an example of a more detailed and complete foundation document in Appendix A (see the completed G4K persona, Tanner Thompson).

The more details you include now the easier you will find the *birth and maturation* and *adulthood* lifecycle phases. Complete multi-page foundation documents can contain a tremendous amount of information and take considerable effort to create. It is up to you and your team to decide how rich your foundation documents need to be, and how you will collaborate on or divide the work required to create them.

| Persona Name: | Persona Name: |
| Photograph Goes Here | Photograph Goes Here |

```
┌─────────────────────────────────────┐  ┌─────────────────────────────────────┐
│  ┌──────────┐  Persona Name:         │  │  ┌──────────┐  Persona Name:         │
│  │Photograph│                        │  │  │Photograph│  User Class or Segment  │
│  │Goes      │  Job/Role Description:  │  │  │Goes      │  (including market size, │
│  │Here      │                        │  │  │Here      │  importance):           │
│  └──────────┘                        │  │  └──────────┘                        │
│                                      │  │  Job, Role, Activities:              │
│  Short Narrative (description of the │  │                                      │
│  persona acting out his or her       │  │  Goals:                              │
│  primary scenario(s)):               │  │                                      │
│                                      │  │  Abilities, Skills, Knowledge:       │
│                                      │  │                                      │
│                                      │  │  Personal Details:                   │
│                                      │  │                                      │
│  Data Sources and/or Sources of      │  │  Data Sources and/or Sources of      │
│  Assumptions:                        │  │  Assumptions:                        │
└─────────────────────────────────────┘  └─────────────────────────────────────┘
```

FIGURE 4.13: *One-page (left) and resume-style (right) foundation document templates. These are the shortest possible foundation documents, and in most cases (unless you are extremely time and resource constrained) your foundation documents will include considerably more detail. Note that it is a good idea to develop your own template before you dive into creating your foundation documents. The templates help organize your work as you add and look for data to include in the document.*

If you are extremely time and resource constrained, you can start with brief one-page description or resume-style foundation documents. Then, as you find the time you can always come back and add to the information in these short foundation documents. Figure 4.13 shows one-page and resume-style outlines for these brief foundation documents. Appendix B provides several example foundation documents (from real products) that range in size and detail from bulleted text to short narrative to richly detailed persona descriptions.

Story from the field

LET YOUR TEMPLATES BE YOUR GUIDE

—Bob Murata, Design Manager, Adobe

At Adobe, UI designers go off and create the first draft of the persona, pulling together the pieces o information they found through their research and pouring it into the template. Choices are made in regard to what pain points should be emphasized and what is the best representative information fo any given persona. The template drives the minimum amount and type of information that should be included.

Story from the field

PERSONAS ON A SHOE STRING—CREATING RICH PERSONAS QUICKLY AND COST EFFECTIVELY

—Tom Pease, Microsoft Corporation

Personas can be rich as you want to make them, or as rich as your pocketbook will allow. Can you create a set of meaningful personas if you are short on money and time? In my experience, the answer is yes.

The Story of InfoPath

InfoPath is a new Microsoft Office application in development for creating intelligent business forms (e.g., dynamic and interactive order forms, requisitions, and invoices). It has two fairly distinct pieces: a design interface for creating the form and the underlying data structure and an editor interface for filling out the forms. It also contains a set of standard business forms that can be used as is or customized.

The goal of the product is allow nondevelopers to create their own business forms while allowing developers to connect complex forms to existing business applications. The editing experience (filling out the form) was designed to be "Office-like." In other words, InfoPath documents should be as flexible and easy to create and edit as documents in Microsoft Word.

The Need for Personas Surfaces

From the start of the project, the product team had been talking about building a product for nondevelopers; in our team's terms, the "low-end developer" or LED. The problem was that everyone had a different definition of this low-end developer. Depending on who you talked to, the answers ranged from "anyone who doesn't know C++" to "anyone who uses formulas in Excel." This range of definitions made it difficult to understand the users' tasks, abilities, and knowledge. Halfway through the product development cycle things were getting difficult. Development time was limited, and there was a laundry list of features as well as some significant usability issues. The team needed a clear understanding of the user.

Program management asked the user research team, which basically consisted of me, to develop a set of personas to help the team define the tasks, skills, and knowledge of the user types the team had been discussing. The team needed a set of personas that would help them prioritize the usability issues and the product features. There wasn't time to do market research or large-scale data validation. The team had a little more than a month to complete the personas.

What Can We Do, Given the Schedule?

When we started on our personas, their use was already well established in other divisions of the company. Many of these other persona efforts involved extensive data collection and analysis, yet for this project we couldn't afford to spend that much time and effort. We found that we were not the first to find ourselves developing personas late in the game. A few other teams faced with this short cycle dilemma had simply fabricated their personas. Even though we didn't have the time or budget for the extensive research, we didn't want our personas to be totally fabricated either. So, we felt it key to define up front the questions we wanted our personas to answer.

Understanding the Needs and Goals of Our Personas

I began working with two lead program managers on the team to agree on the specific questions we wanted our personas to answer. We knew we couldn't answer all 15 questions we had generated, so we prioritized them with a broader group of program managers (which helped get the team involved and bought in to the process). The following are a few of the key questions we had for InfoPath:

- Should the UI be modeled on existing XML editors or on database tools such as Access?
- Although the editor had to support occasional use, how important was efficiency?
- How were the forms built using the product going to be deployed? Were they going to live just on one machine, a network share, or be sent around in e-mail?

We then turned those product-oriented questions into more generic questions about our users:

- What knowledge and skills do typical developers possess?
- Are there different usage patterns for editor users?
- What tools and applications did our users already know how to use?
- What solutions were they going to build and who would be using them?

Thinking About Target Categories of Users

Obviously, because InfoPath had two very distinct pieces of functionality (the design and editing interfaces), we likely had two distinct sets of users. We needed personas for both. Initially, we thought we had about four personas. For the design interface, we had the LED and the professional developer. For the editor interface, we had the occasional form user and the data entry specialist. We decided to brainstorm a more exhaustive list. We generated eight, but as we sketched them out there was a lot of overlap among them and we quickly narrowed them down to six personas.

Treasure Hunt: What Did We Know About Our Users?

Given that we didn't have time for any new research, we had to base our personas on the data that already existed. Although we didn't have a market segmentation describing the users, we did have a good amount of related customer data that had been collected since the project started. There were a series of focus groups, a few site visits, and three or four usability studies. Of course, these were not executed with the goal of informing personas, but we knew there was plenty of information we could harvest.

We started by reviewing the usability data. This may seem a little strange, given that there were only a handful of usability studies and (generally speaking) focus groups and site visits are considered better for providing information toward personas.

From a pragmatic standpoint, the participants in the usability studies were fresh in my mind and the information from the older and less memorable focus groups and site visits wasn't well organized. I would have had to dig through large amounts of raw data to find what I was looking for. I decided I would review those findings after I went through the usability data.

Another reason I started with the usability data was that it wasn't just performance data. Because we knew we didn't know much about our users, we did a mini interview at the beginning of each usability session aimed at understanding characteristics and attributes of our users. Interviewing usability participants was a very efficient way of getting critical information.

For Some User Categories, We Didn't Have Any Data

The biggest challenge we faced was the developer persona. The only developers we had talked to were a few employees outside our team, who were using XML. I had little confidence in this data. Given all of the previous talk about not fabricating personas, our developer persona was going to be for the most part fabricated. There were several reasons I was comfortable with this approach for this persona:

- We knew developers were not our target users. There were already a number of high-end XML tools available on the market and we weren't competing directly with them.
- The team's idea of this user was probably the most accurate. We had a number of people on the team who had come out of the XML community. They had done XML development outside Microsoft, which constituted examples of real products built by possible customers. In addition, these team members were well connected with people in other companies doing XML development.
- We knew that many of our beta customers would be large IT departments looking to have their developers build customer solutions. We were going to hear from them what InfoPath needed to do from a developer perspective.

I couldn't have done this with the other personas because from my early investigation I knew the team had very diverse opinions of what those users actually did, and no one on the team really did the same type of work as those personas.

What Did We Include in Our Personas?

While I was working with program management on identifying issues and developing the questions, I was also reviewing other sets of personas I had collected to get a feel for the type of information they contained and how they were organized. I found literally dozens of attributes that would be useful–everything from the size of the company for which each person worked to their education and career goals. Although I had my thoughts on what we should and shouldn't include, I brought that list to the team so that we could prioritize it together. That drove us to focus on a few key pieces of information:

- Job title and responsibilities
- Key usage scenarios

- Skills and knowledge related to the product
- Common tools used.

The first three attributes were common across all personas I reviewed. The "Common Tools Used" section was the only area for which we really diverged from the mainstream. This was completely product-specific. Many of the team members had been working with XML for some time, so they thought our product should work like other XML editors. Others thought that because it was essentially working with data we should model it on MS Access. It was important to settle the issue because the basis of a UI metaphor depended on the tools these people already knew how to use.

What Did We Leave Out?

We knew we wanted information that had a clear link to the product. We also knew we didn't have a lot of time, so we couldn't include information that was going to be expensive or time-consuming to collect. The following are a few pieces of information we decided to leave out of our InfoPath personas:

- *Lifestyle information:* The type of car they drive, age, interests. We knew this information could be useful for developing a visual design approach or other aspects of the product, but it wasn't going to help answer our questions about skills, tools, and knowledge.
- *A "day in the life" scenario:* A time line representing a typical day for the persona can be very useful in helping understand the broader environment of the persona. In our case, this information would have helped us understand the context in which the product is used, but it wasn't clear how it related to our key questions. In addition, we didn't have any data that would allow us to accurately represent a day in the life of the LED.

Building the Framework

At this point, we had a good handle on the questions we wanted to answer and a rough classification of our personas. In the interest of time, I went looking for those users who seemed to match our notions of each category. For example, for the LED I looked for participants who had worked with database tools, people who had done Excel formulas, and so on. I reviewed the usability notes to see how well they were able to complete the basic tasks.

As I looked through the notes, I began to create bulleted lists of traits: they were self-taught, they had a job outside developing solutions, and the solutions they built were for personal use or a small group or department. I also looked for the possibility of new personas.

I spent about two days developing a draft set of skeleton personas, reviewing the descriptions and creating consistent areas across each of the personas (see Figure 4.14). In the case where I didn't have strong data, I made my best guess at their attributes based on the information I had. At the end of that process, there were six skeleton personas (three designers and three editors).

(Story from the field, continued)

Skeleton: the "occasional" user

Could be a project manager, senior planner, analyst, or department manager. Uses XDocs because that's what the company has adopted.

How does this person use XDocs?
• Uses forms created by other, more technical people.
• Regularly uses some forms, but uses most forms infrequently.

What's important to the occasional user?
• The easier XDocs is the better.

• Pre-populating fields in the form keeps them from having to look up information.
• Wants easy ways to get the needed information to quickly fill out forms.
• Wants to be able to work offline, because they are sometimes mobile.
• Expects the process for opening, saving and submitting forms to be simple.

FIGURE 4.14: *Example of an initial skeleton: the "occasional" user.*

Narrowing Down the Options

After I developed this draft set of skeletons, I reviewed them with the same group of program managers I had worked with earlier. The intent of that review was to ensure we were capturing the right content and that the personas were believable, as well as to help the team understand where the information came from. As we worked through the description of each persona, it became clear that we had some overlap between two personas.

We really wanted to keep the number of personas down. We reasoned that the fewer we had the more distinct they would be and the easier for the team to understand the differences among the personas and to learn the entire set of them. We had one persona that actually used the design interface and the editor interface. At first I thought this was a very important trait. It was a user we hadn't thought about. As we went through the review, we saw that her role in regard to the design interface was distinct but her role as to the editor interface was very close to other personas. Therefore, we decided to make that a design-focused persona.

This left us with five personas: three for the design interface and two for the editor interface. At this point I had buy-in from my project managers. Now that the personas were taking shape, we had to determine the proper level of detail and how we should organize and present the information.

Filling In the Blanks

As I narrowed in on the personas from the usability study, I found a lot of missing information. I knew a little bit about their jobs, but maybe not their tools—or I saw one user who had experience or knowledge others didn't. It was at this time I did a quick review of the phone-interviews focus group and site visit data to validate what I heard in the usability study (as well as to fill in any blanks). From this information, each of the attributes listed in the skeleton personas became a more detailed sentence or paragraph.

The Review Process

After adding the information from these other sources, I sent the personas back for review and iteration with the lead program managers. Once it felt really solid, we presented it to the managers of the product team. This group included the development manager, the manager of program management, the director, and the test manager.

In the end, this review was the most important activity of the process—particularly for the one persona that was based on little data. When the key attributes and assumptions were written out clearly, management was able to articulate how they thought about these people. We had a very interactive meeting and several long e-mail threads about the characteristics (as well as our business objectives and product vision). Did low-end developers write script or not? Does the occasional user read help? Throughout this process I was regularly being asked these emerging questions.

I kept going back to the data to ensure I was giving informed decisions. It was at this stage I really began to pull in the other data I had collected. For example, when the question became specific, such as "did any of the LEDs know XML or write script", I reviewed all data looking for this specific information. Combing through the data when I had specific questions in mind was far easier than trying to comb through it hoping to find patterns. I was also careful not to overstate my conclusions. The team listened.

After we had agreed with management on the bulleted points for those personas, we presented the personas to all of the leads. At this point, the personas were in the form of short sketches (which included a photo, a few usage scenarios, and several key attributes; see Figure 4.15). We attended staff meetings in which the manager of the group had already bought into the process. That gave the leads a chance to ask questions, add their input, and talk about why we had what we did. Given that their manager had already been involved in the process, they helped their team understand how we reached the conclusion we did. I always took one of the lead program managers from the original team into those meetings. They acted as another voice, helping to explain the process and the personas from a slightly different perspective.

Keeping to a Core Set: Personas are about norms, not about exceptions.

During those reviews, the team asked about the "gaps" in the personas. What if we have a *low-end developer* that understands XML? What if we had a user that filled out our sample PO form 50 times a day? The tendency for the team to want to create a different user for each scenario they come up with doesn't go away just because you have a set of personas. We had to show the team that the personas covered most of the stories and that adding more is at a point of diminishing returns. It was important to run through this exercise to make sure we did have the right number of personas as well as a set that was distinct and easy for the team to talk about.

- We asked questions such as how likely it was it that users would have this set of skills. All we could say was that of the X people we saw in all of these situations we either never saw them or rarely saw them.

(Story from the field, continued)

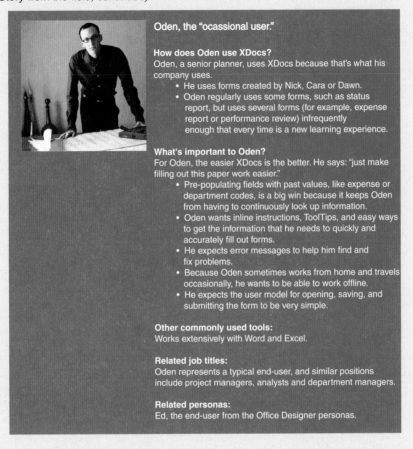

Oden, the "ocassional user."

How does Oden use XDocs?
Oden, a senior planner, uses XDocs because that's what his company uses.
- He uses forms created by Nick, Cara or Dawn.
- Oden regularly uses some forms, such as status report, but uses several forms (for example, expense report or performance review) infrequently enough that every time is a new learning experience.

What's important to Oden?
For Oden, the easier XDocs is the better. He says: "just make filling out this paper work easier."
- Pre-populating fields with past values, like expense or department codes, is a big win because it keeps Oden from having to continuously look up information.
- Oden wants inline instructions, ToolTips, and easy ways to get the information that he needs to quickly and accurately fill out forms.
- He expects error messages to help him find and fix problems.
- Because Oden sometimes works from home and travels occasionally, he wants to be able to work offline.
- He expects the user model for opening, saving, and submitting the form to be very simple.

Other commonly used tools:
Works extensively with Word and Excel.

Related job titles:
Oden represents a typical end-user, and similar positions include project managers, analysts and department managers.

Related personas:
Ed, the end-user from the Office Designer personas.

FIGURE 4.15: *Completed sketch of Oden, the "occasional user."*

- If these users do exist, are they really doing significantly different things with the product? Do they have very different goals? Are they performing different tasks?

The Finishing Touches

Now that we had reviewed the personas with most of the team, I went back and did one last pass on the bulleted points. Some of the explanations were quite long and we knew we couldn't have paragraphs of text to explain each point. I asked our user assistance group to review them. Their edits made the descriptions clear and crisp. It also served as a beta test. After all, the user assistance group would be using the personas. If they didn't understand them, it was unlikely anyone else on the team would.

[For a continuation of this case study in regard to the *birth and maturation* phase, see "Story from the field: Moving from Bulleted Sketches to Rich Illustrations" in Chapter 5.]

Choose persona characteristics to include in the foundation document

Your assimilated data as well as your product- and team needs will dictate what content to include in your foundation documents. When you created your skeletons, you were purposely selective in what information you included. Now you need to be more exhaustive. This means that you need to include all headings and information appropriate and useful to understanding your audience and developing your product. Different types of information will be relevant for different people on your team, and will have different uses toward product development.

Your skeletons will serve as the starting point for the foundation documents. Each skeleton has a bulleted list of characteristics. Your next step is to add important content headings based on three things:

- The labels for the clusters that came out of the assimilation exercise
- Topics relevant to your product domain or business (e.g., if you are creating an Internet product you probably need a section on Internet activities, equipment, and/or Internet connection environments)
- Some common headings in persona documents that help create a persona that is well rounded, realistic, useful, and complete.

Regarding the second and third of the previous items, consider the following list of persona characteristics that you can use as a content "menu" and template for your foundation documents. When you are deciding which characteristics to include in your foundation documents, think about the types of information that will be most helpful to your core team and to the development team. We recommend that you include at least rudimentary information in each of the following categories of persona characteristics:

- Identifying details
  - ○ Name, title, or short description
  - ○ Age, gender
  - ○ Identifying tag line
  - ○ Quote (highlighting something essential to that persona, preferably related to the product)
  - ○ Photograph or brief physical description

- Role(s) and tasks
  - ○ Specific company or industry
  - ○ Job title or role

- ○ Typical activities
- ○ Important atypical activities
- ○ Challenge areas or breakdowns, pain points
- ○ Responsibilities
- ○ Interactions with other personas, systems, products

- ● Goals
  - ○ Short term, long term
  - ○ Motivations
  - ○ Work-related goals
  - ○ Product-related goals
  - ○ General (life) goals, aspirations
  - ○ Stated and unstated desires for the product

- ● Segment
  - ○ Market size and influence
  - ○ International considerations
  - ○ Accessibility considerations
  - ○ General and domain-relevant demographics
    - ■ Income and purchasing power
    - ■ Region or city, state, country
    - ■ Education level
    - ■ Marital status
    - ■ Cultural information

- ● Skills and knowledge
  - ○ General computer and/or Internet use
  - ○ Frequently used products, product knowledge
  - ○ Years of experience
  - ○ Domain knowledge
  - ○ Training
  - ○ Special skills
  - ○ Competitor awareness

- Context/environment
  - Equipment (Net connection, browser brand and version, operating system)
  - "A day in the life" description
    - Work styles
    - Time line of a typical day
  - Specific usage location(s)
  - General work, household and leisure activities
  - Relationships to other personas

- Psychographics and personal details
  - Personality traits
  - Values and attitudes (political opinions, religion)
  - Fears and obstacles, pet peeves
  - Personal artifacts (car, gadgets)

This list was partially adapted from Mike Kuniavsky's list of attributes in *Observing the User Experience* [Kuniavsky 2003, pp. 136–143] where he provides detailed descriptions of these and other possible persona attributes.

Story from the field

GETTING THE RIGHT GOALS

—Kim Goodwin, VP Design, Cooper

It takes practice to create accurate, compelling personas that are useful as design tools. In all the years I've been teaching people how to do so, I've consistently seen them struggle with a handful of issues. The most obvious problems occur when people don't stick to their data (or worse, don't have good data to begin with). One of the trickier problems people often don't expect is getting the right set of goals.

Each persona should have a few goals that shed light on his or her priorities. There's not a magic number of goals any more than there's a magic number of personas; it depends on what you see in the data. However, three or four is a typical number; I've never met a persona who didn't have more than one goal, and I've never seen a persona with half a dozen goals that were all goals and not tasks.

The most challenging part for most people is getting the goals at the right level. If they're too high-level or ambitious, they won't seem relevant to the product at hand. If they're too low-level, though, they won't challenge you to think beyond basic screen layout. There are two types of goals that will help you focus at the right level.

Life goals, which are generally long-term and not something your product can really influence, are only occasionally useful in design. For example, "Retire by age 45" would be of little use if you were designing a word processor, mobile phone, or PDA, but it may offer valuable insight when you're designing a financial planning tool. When you think you've found a goal for your persona, ask yourself whether the product can help them accomplish it. If not, your goals are too high-level.

You may wonder whether there's any harm in including life goals anyway. While it may not be obvious at first, life goals that don't add value will only clutter up your persona description and de-emphasize the more important goals. If you're designing network management software, who cares if your system administrator persona really wants to write a rock opera? It's much more important for people to understand his goal of always knowing what's going on. People may just laugh about the rock opera thing and not take the rest of the persona seriously.

That said, in a few instances I've really needed to convey that the persona just doesn't care. This isn't something I've had to do often, but when a product team believes their product is the center of the persona's universe, it can be useful to have a persona essentially say they'd rather be somewhere else. This helps set everyone's expectation that this persona is willing to exert zero effort to learn or use the tool.

Most of your persona goals should be **end goals** that focus on what the persona could get out of using your well-designed product or service. In the case of a financial planning tool, retiring at age 45 is an end goal as well as a life goal, because it's something the product could help accomplish.

The trick with end goals is to avoid getting too low-level. To see whether your end goal is really a goal and not just a task, ask yourself whether it's in service of something else. For example, if you interviewed me for a digital photo organizer product, you'd see that I spend a lot of time organizing my photos and assigning keywords to them, even though it drives me crazy to spend that much time. If you took that at face value and assumed that "easily organize photos" was my goal, you'd be missing the point. Instead, ask yourself why I spend all that annoying time, and you'll see that I do it because it's the only way I can find specific photos later. Every time you think you have a good goal, ask yourself, "Why does our persona want that?" If you have an easy answer, it's probably not a goal; if your answer is "Because she just *does*," you've probably found a genuine goal.

You can also ask yourself *whether* the product can help people progress toward the goal, or whether it will accomplish it entirely. In most cases, good end goals are things the product won't entirely accomplish. For example, if a manager wants to be more proactive and spend less time dealing with emergencies, a better forecasting tool can help, but won't eliminate emergencies entirely.

Experience goals are another type you may find useful for certain projects, though less frequently than end goals. They describe how the persona wants to feel when using a product; having fun and not feeling stupid are experience goals. Not every persona needs an experience goal; we usually assume that no one really wants to feel dumb. However, if you have a persona with an exceptional level of anxiety about technology, calling that out is a good idea.

Experience goals have limited usefulness for most interaction design problems, but they tend to be very helpful for branded visual design. If you're not just using the standard look of an operating system and you need to make choices about color, typography, and style, an experience goal can help guide those choices. For example, someone doing online banking wants to feel very safe about the transaction, so a lot of navy blue and a professional-looking typeface would be appropriate, but lime green, orange, and Comic Sans would not.

Once you have the right goals, it can be helpful to articulate them in the way your personas would say them. For example, if you're describing an avid shopper's goals, which works better: buy the right thing, or find the perfect gift? The latter conveys a sense that shopping is a quest, and that there's a sense of accomplishment involved in it.

The persona's goals are, in some ways, the most fundamental part of the whole description, because they help us understand what motivates people and how they will react in a certain situation. If you watch Mr. Data, the android on Star Trek, which gives us more insight into his behavior: what his duties on the Enterprise are, or the fact that he not-so-secretly wishes he were human? Our understanding of goals is what helps us create future scenarios for successful products, since we have to understand our users' goals before we can design products that help accomplish them.

To further help you think about what information you might want to include in your personas, we have included a brief content analysis from several personas we have collected over the last few years (see Figure 4.16). These personas were created for a variety of products in several different industries (though all are for either software or Web site products or services). Our goal here is to show you what others have typically included, and perhaps to inspire you to include certain information you had not considered previously.

Frequency of persona characteristics across 31 sample personas

Basic Details		Job/Work Information	
Name	90%	Typical Activities	92%
Photograph/Illustration	71%	Job Title	84%
Tag Line ("essence" title)	39%	Goals	81%
User Classification/Segment	32%	Job Description/Responsibilities	74%
		Company/Industry	65%
Personal Information		Challenge Areas/Breakdowns	61%
Age	84%	Interaction with Colleagues	61%
Fears/Obstacles	75%	Work Style	58%
Motivations/Aspirations/Goals	67%	Typical Workday/Timeline of Day	58%
City/State/Country	61%	Core Competencies/Skills	55%
Marital/Family Status	55%	Professional Motivation	52%
Hobbies/Leisure/Social Life	55%	Quote(s) about work	45%
Educational Background	45%	Previous Work History/Experience	32%
Description of Environment/Home	42%	Workplace Description/Artifacts	29%
Other Personal? Responses: books, Current state of mind for disability claimants, knowledge of SSA programs, context of use, i.e., working at home, in short sessions, using library or neighbors, computer, daily life style, symptoms, disabling condition, description of family, gender, relationships with others and their descriptions (e.g., brother)	42%	Opinion of Company	19%
		Workspace Photo/Sketch	10%
		Salary	3%
Personality Traits	32%	Other work related? Responses: Geographic area, traffic and workload in field office, type of clientele they service, whether they are a specialist or a generalist	
Car/Significant Personal Artifacts	23%		
Email Address	13%	**Technology Access and Usage**	
Social/Political Opinions	10%	Computer/Internet Use	58%
Physical Description of person	10%	Applications/Languages Used	58%
		Technology Opinions/Attitudes	68%
Other		Hardware Spec/Equipment & Technologies Used	45%
Relationship to your product/Attitudes and Opinions towards your product	83%	ISP/Connection Speed	83%
Market Size, Spending/Buying & Influence (indicator of the importance/priority of your persona)	50%	Other Technology Related? Responses: Tools used in their job, domain expertise, time of day using internet, competitive products used and why, types of gadgets used and why/how	50%
Scenario(s)/Walk-throughs with your product or features of your product	45%		
International Considerations	33%		
Supporting Research/References	29%		
Accessibility/Disability Considerations	25%		
Other? Responses: Type of persona. We identify who's primary, secondary, and anti, how designing for one persona can influence/serve other audiences.	17%		

FIGURE 4.16: *Frequency of persona characteristics across 31 sample personas used in a variety of companies to design a wide range of products.*

Story from the field

ADDRESSING ACCESSIBILITY ISSUES

—George Olsen, Principal, Interaction by Design

Rather than having separate personas to represent users with disabilities, I find it more useful to incorporate accessibility issues into personas as long as it doesn't distract from the persona's main purpose. This can be as simple as having personas who occasionally forget their glasses (resulting in low-vision issues) or who have color-blindness. It is true that doing this will overrepresent users who actually have these issues, but personas are a design tool, so I bend reality when needed to highlight an important design issue.

Figure 4.16 shows the frequency of basic characteristics across many personas. There are 31 personas included in this analysis, each representing a different company and product. We have organized the characteristics by high-level category: Basic Details, Personal Information, Job/Work Information, Technology Access and Usage, and Other. Within these groups, we have ordered the characteristics by frequency of occurrence among the 31 sample personas.

Persona Skeleton:
Boy, age 10–13

Computer use at school

- Has access to a shared computer in his classroom or a computer 'lab' shared by the whole school
  - o Factoid
  - o Factoid
  - o Factoid
- Has at least one computer-related assignment a week
  - o Factoid
  - o Factoid
- Finds computer use at school 'boring'
  - o Factoid
  - o ...

FIGURE 4.17: *Transfer factoids verbatim into your skeleton document. This document will evolve to become your persona foundation document, which will be the repository for all information on each persona.*

Use the information in Figure 4.16 as a guide. Your product needs will likely dictate that you use only a subset of these characteristics, or some that are not included here.

Start a foundation document (transfer factoids into your skeletons)

Your skeleton documents are a template you can use to create a foundation document for each persona. Each skeleton should now have a similar set of headings. For each of those headings, transfer the appropriate factoids into the related sections (as shown in Figure 4.17). It is likely that some sections will have a lot of factoids in them and others will be nearly empty.

Get specific about each core characteristic

Once you have copied your factoids into your skeleton documents, evolving the skeleton into a more precise persona can be relatively easy. You will create a concrete fact, phrase, sentence, or paragraph to replace each factoid or set of factoids in the skeleton. To this point, you have likely been dealing largely with ranges of values (e.g., age = 25 to 35, parent, works full time) instead of specific values. You purposely stayed at this abstract level when considering the few attributes of your skeletons in order to stay as close as possible to the actual data during the evaluation process. Now it is time to turn most of the characteristics in your skeleton personas into very specific and more concrete values. For example:

● Works full time *becomes* a specific job, such as bank teller, department store manager, or high school teacher.

● Parent *becomes* mother or father.

● 70% female *becomes* Laura, Dianne, Irene, and so on.

● Lives in a major metropolitan city *becomes* Chicago, Los Angeles, or Houston.

More specifically, from your skeleton (see Figure 4.18, left) transform your headings and factoids into specific, concrete details in your foundation document (Figure 4.18, right).

As you replace factoids with specific details to enrich your persona, copy the factoid or set of factoids into a comment or a footnote in your foundation document. A lofty but worthy goal is to have every statement in your foundation document supported by user data. You likely will not achieve this, but the attempt helps you to think critically about your details, and highlights places where you might want to do further research. (In fact, when such research questions come up it is a good idea to make a note of them directly in the foundation document.) By the time you finish creating a description for each persona, you will have also created a very rich document that is full of direct references to data (as illustrated in Figure 4.19).

Parent (skeleton)	Irene Pasquez, the involved parent (1) (foundation document)
Demographics: • People who make enough money to have two computers in their home tend to live in major metropolitan areas (source 3, p 1) • etc. Work: • 85% of parents surveyed work full time in white-collar professions (source 5, p 2) • etc. Goals, fears, aspirations of parents: • Mothers are more concerned with their child's behavior online than fathers (source 2, p 10) • etc.	Overview: Irene lives in a suburb of Houston (2) with Emanuel, her husband, and her one child: Preston, who just turned 5. Even though Irene works full-time as a manager in a local branch of Bank of America (3), she is heavily involved with Preston's daily activities and has the opportunity to see him during the working day because... etc. -- Data references 1. Mothers are more concerned with their child's behavior online than fathers (source 2, p 10) 2. People who make enough money to have two computers in their home tend to live in major metropolitan areas (source 3, p 1) 3. 85% of parents surveyed work full time in white-collar professions (source 5, p 2)

FIGURE 4.18: *An example skeleton (left) being transformed into a foundation document (right).*

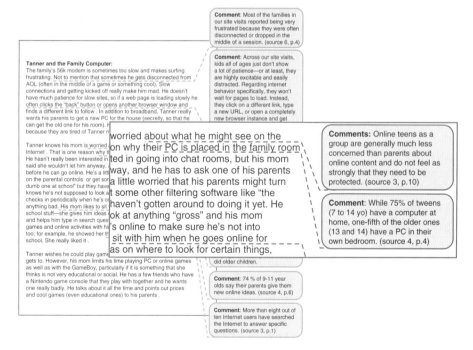

FIGURE 4.19: *An example of statements in a foundation document supported by factoids using the "insert/comment" feature in MS Word.*

THERE ARE MANY WAYS OF INCLUDING REFERENCES IN YOUR FOUNDATION DOCUMENTS

Many word processing programs and HTML editors allow you to add annotations, references, or even pop-up comments to your text. For example, in Microsoft Word you can use the Comment feature to do this linking and annotation. To do so, highlight a word or phrase, select Insert/Comment, and type or paste your factoid into the comment field. This makes your links not just explicit but very salient to the reader (see Figure 4.19). If you are creating HTML foundation documents, you can create hyperlinks directly to electronic versions of data or pop-up windows containing direct quotes or summarized data from your original sources.

If you use MS Word to add comments in support of specific details, consider checking the options/security "hide personal info" so that the reader of the document will not see who inserted the comment:

- Select Tools > Options…

- In the Options dialog box, select the User Information tab

- Check the box to Remove Personal Information from file properties on save.

This is a particularly good idea when multiple people are creating the foundation document. When you find yourself referencing a factoid from a data source, don't forget to include the bibliographic information for that source in the "References" area at the end of the document.

Moving toward precision means moving away from accuracy

In many cases, the accuracy of your data lies in its ranges (not just central tendencies but descriptors of variance, percentages, and skew). By selecting precise descriptors you are going to lose some of that accuracy. For example, if a category includes males and females you cannot create a single individual who 'represents' the entire category. Rather than trying to represent every nuance of the entire category, try to pick values that are reasonable, believable, and meaningful.

As you choose specific details to include in your personas, you are zooming in on a particular person. That is, you are transitioning from rough descriptions of categories and subcategories of users to precise values and detailed depictions of a particular persona. As you build these detailed depictions, you will be making educated guesses and adding fictional elements, some of which will be directly related to the data you have collected and some of which will not. (It is a good idea to document these assumptions and to consider them possible research questions that may need answering during the validation of your personas.)

Think of your data, and your categories and subcategories of users, as describing *neighborhoods* of related users of your product. As you create your personas, you are describing a specific "resident" of each neighborhood. As in real life, each resident *inhabits* his or her neighborhood, but no one resident can *represent* all qualities of all people in the neighborhood.

No one who reads a persona description can understand all the intricacies of the data behind that persona. However, as design targets personas can *stand in* for all data in your communications. Think of a town meeting. Each neighborhood might send a single representative who *stands in* for everyone else in the neighborhood, even though that one person cannot accurately communicate the particular demographics, attitudes, needs, and desires of every one of his or her neighbors. Instead, the representative communicates the *essence* of all of his or her neighbors' needs. Your personas will represent your data in the same way that a single neighbor can represent an entire neighborhood. (For additional discussion of this, see "Handy Detail: It Depends on What You Mean by 'Represent,'" by Diane Lye, earlier in this chapter.)

When in doubt, choose details that are precise and memorable

As you select specific characteristics for your personas, try to choose values that are clearly within the range and essence of the data and findings from which they came. You may choose to select values in the middle of the ranges described in your data, but you don't have to. Try to choose values that are reasonable, believable, and meaningful. As a rule, try to choose values that have face validity while not adding any extra "baggage." Your goal is to create personas who feel real and relevant, while being memorable and even interesting. If selecting an off-center value helps you make a more memorable persona, we would argue that it is good to do so.

Incorporate narrative and storytelling elements

Enriching your terse skeletons into personas that are realistic and engaging requires some storytelling. To do this well, remember that you are trying to "tell the story" of the data in your foundation documents with narrative. What do your personas sound like and act like? What can they do or not do? Turn your factoids and specific details into a running story; that is, a sequence of actions and events with interaction and even a plot. Demonstrate their interactions with people, objects, and systems. Narratives in persona documents are typically written in third person, active voice. The following is an example of a descriptive overview for G4K's persona Tanner written as a narrative.

Tanner is nine years old and is a fourth-grade student at Montgomery Elementary School, a public school. He lives with his mother and father (Laura and Shane Thompson) in a suburb of Chicago, Illinois. Tanner has been using computers at school since kindergarten and has had a family computer at home for two years. He has been using the Internet in his school's computer lab for some time, but only recently got Internet access at his house (six months ago through his family's AOL account). Even though Tanner loves to be physically active (riding his skateboard and bike, playing in the yard and nearby creek, participating in organized sports, and so on), Tanner thinks computers are really really fun and prefers the PC to the TV. He uses the PC mostly to play games and to surf the Web for "stuff" but occasionally does research for school projects. His favorite computer game of the moment is The Sims 2. His uncle gave it to him for his birthday (his mom and dad usually just buy him educational games). He also really likes Roller Coaster Tycoon 3. Since his dad likes computer sports games like NBA Live 2005, Tanner sometimes plays those with him. Tanner has a GameBoy Color and saves up his allowance to buy new games for it, but his parents say he can only play GameBoy for half an hour each day (they tell him "it will rot his brain").

Writing these stories can be difficult at first. This part of persona creation does take creativity and inspiration. If you have skilled writers on your persona core team, you should likely enlist them to do this part. Start writing your stories by simply expanding the bulleted factoids with context, adding situations, other characters, objects, actions, and events. If you feel blocked or awkward in writing narrative, look through the raw notes and observations from your field research and other qualitative data; that is, use anecdotes and incidents from those real people to enrich your personas. (For more ideas and a deep discussion of personas and storytelling, see Chapter 9 by Whitney Quesenbery.)

Derive specific details and stories from real observations

You will notice that we are now moving from the realm of hard, accurate data, observations, and facts to more subjective, "best guess" information and particulars (i.e., toward fiction). In other words, you are starting to include details that are not solidly derived from data. This step is generally uncomfortable, but it can be fun too. Like you had to do when you were determining what types of information (including the categories and headings) would go into your foundation document, you now have to make decisions about specific details that are based on the data, the needs of your team and product, and your knowledge of the world. Your personas need backgrounds and context to be real. Consider using specific, observed information from your site visits or other research as the exact values or characteristics of your profiles. Doing so can ease the burden of being creative, stop disagreements among your persona creation team, and add an aspect of credibility or authenticity to your resulting personas.

Bright Idea

COMBINE VALIDATION AND DATA COLLECTION TO HELP FINISH YOUR CREATION PROCESS

If you did not have time to collect qualitative and quantitative data before you started creating the personas, or find that you need additional information to create good narratives for your personas, you can stop your persona creation efforts now and embark on your validation exercise before continuing (discussed in material following). As you do the footwork necessary to validate your developing personas, you can collect the "missing" qualitative information that will allow you to add narratives to your personas based on observations rather than assumptions.

You can use stereotypes, but use them with care

You may be tempted to use stereotypes and common knowledge or cultural lore in your personas. If you do, do so carefully. For example, consider the following transition from abstract profile to specific details to stereotype/cultural phenomenon.

> Yvonne Chandler lives in suburban Chicago with her husband, William, and their two kids, Colbi (age 7) and Austin (age 13). Yvonne works part-time now that the kids are in school, but she always arranges her work schedule to accommodate a fairly complex system of carpools and after-school activities (she has become a "soccer mom"). She feels tremendously busy but wants to make sure that her kids have a lot of opportunities and learning experiences. She also feels pressure to "keep up with the Joneses" in many aspects of her life, from the activities she involves her kids in to the entertaining she does at home. Before she had kids, Yvonne was known as the neighborhood "Martha Stewart" because of the dinner parties she would host. She would like to entertain more but right now she is just too busy with her kids.

If you are creating a persona of a user who happens to be a suburban mother, you may find yourself tempted to add details based on your own perceptions of a "typical soccer mom" or a "Martha Stewart type." In both cases, utilizing a stereotype or strong cultural icon can be dangerous. The "soccer mom" stereotype is very evocative, but perhaps in ways that work counter to the persona effort. For example, maybe there is someone in your organization who has a similar set of responsibilities, and recognizes herself in the persona, but is put off by the reference to "soccer mom" because she does not want to think of *herself* that way. Perhaps there are others in the organization who are scornful of "soccer moms" and the stereotypical suburban lifestyle. This distaste can get in the way when you ask your colleagues to use the personas in their everyday work. Similarly, Martha Stewart generally evokes a fairly strong image, at least for a North American audience—one that is either positive or fairly strongly negative.

Persona use brings sociopolitical issues to the surface. Each persona has a gender, age, race, ethnicity, family or cohabitation arrangement, socioeconomic background, and work and/or home environment (even if you don't include all of these directly in the persona description, the photos you use will imply decisions on these details). This provides an effective avenue for recognizing and perhaps changing your team's assumptions about users. In his chapter "Why Personas Work" later in this book, Jonathan Grudin argues that stereotypes are very powerful influences that must be handled with caution because they can create a one-dimensional character—one that is not likely to be as rich and complex as most people naturally are. Futhermore, Lene Nielsen (2003b) argues that stereotypes are naturally formed by our teammates and can be difficult to work with in a design process. To overcome a stereotype, "It is necessary to get access to the users' feelings and knowledge as more than one dimension of the character is needed to raise sympathy" [Nielsen, 2003b, p. 4].

Beware any details that can evoke strong emotional responses

Note that there are other types of information that can evoke strong responses. For example, if we say that Philip is a concerned dad who is recently divorced and battling for custody of his children, does this information get in the way of the more salient info about how he relates to his child as an online consumer? The information may be memorable and even be reflective of the data, but does it help your persona be effective as a design target?

So, be careful when evoking stereotypes or any information that could elicit a strong personal response. When in doubt, choose to include details that help others see your persona as a real person, with particular goals, needs, and interests that are understandable. Allow realism to win out over political correctness. Avoid casting strongly against expectations if it will undermine credibility. Break the mold if it helps get people on board with your effort. Alan Cooper [1999, p. 128] addresses this issue by stating, "All things being equal, I will use people of different races, genders, nationalities, and colors."

Story from the field

THE VILLAIN IN US

—Christina Wodtke, author of *Information Architecture: Blueprints for the Web*

When a group gets together to create personas, a funny phenomenon almost always occurs. They make a bad guy. It will start innocently enough, with a set of characteristics: a male in his thirties making six figures on the east coast. Then, as your team develops him into a persona—let's call him "Fred"—he only wears gray, has a gray BMW, and is a young securities trader who works 90+-hour weeks. Then he's suddenly a jerk who doesn't have a girlfriend because he's too selfish, and he underpays his secretary and doesn't recycle. What happened?

Perhaps it is because we know people like this. Perhaps it is our human need to create villains. They are fascinating creatures, from the wicked queen in Snow White to James Spader's amoral lawyer on *The Practice*. But the problem is that personas are not protagonists and antagonists; they are design targets. You have to feel for them, or you won't be trying your best to make an interface that makes cconsumers happy: "Yeah, that jerk, he makes twice what I do. He can figure out the navigation himself."

The solution, interestingly enough, also comes from narrative: redemption. Except that in narrative you usually wait until the end of the story to redeem your villain (if indeed you plan to do that rather than, say, drop him off a cliff). With personas, you have to redeem your villain with a bit of editing and a bit of back story before you begin your scenarios. In this example we simply need to remove the fact that Fred underpays his secretary (it's probably the company's fault anyhow). Now we need to get into the facelift.

"He only wears gray." This could be seen in a number of ways. Let's make him colorblind. Now he's afraid to wear color for fear of being unable to match his clothes. Fred knows that if he goes into work wearing green and orange he will be mocked by his co-workers and his boss won't take him seriously. With this change, we have both made him more humane *and* given him a useful trait for our design work. When a designer makes an interface choice, he will remember that it needs to be high contrast with redundant channels of information for Fred, who is afraid of looking stupid at work. The designer cares, because we have all been afraid of looking stupid at work.

Now we can continue. Fred is a first-generation Chinese-American, and is saving to purchase a house for his parents. He works long hours for that. He has a gray BMW, but it's a 202 and he works on it on weekends for fun. He is a 202 enthusiast, and finds it easier to talk to other car geeks than to girls. But nothing would make him happier than a girlfriend, and his parents have started to bug him about it. Obviously, if this were a car site or a dating site, one aspect or another of the back story could be played up. But we now not only feel for him but understand what motivates him.

The villain is cool, seductive, and powerful—but he's not useful. Some may argue, "Some of our users are like that," but can you really do your best work designing to make a jerk happy? Redeem your personas, and redeem your design.

Don't overdo it

Be sure to keep your stories to an appropriate length. You are not writing a novel. You will want to create interest and provide some background and context for your teammates, but keep your stories in check and don't include detail that is superfluous and highly irrelevant.

Some of the details you create will naturally be relevant to the design and development of your product, and others will seem completely irrelevant. That your persona "lives in Chicago" or "has been married for 10 years" may not inform any design decision. However, seemingly irrelevant details do have their place. Their purpose is to help make the personas into people—to make them believable and memorable. Think of this "irrelevant" content as you would salt and pepper or other spices used in cooking. You are adding flavor to your meal, but too much will ruin the taste. In regard to level of relevant and irrelevant detail, consider the following three examples written in narrative style:

- Too little detail

  Tanner arrives home from school at 3:15 and calls his mom to let her know that he's there. He plays a computer game and watches TV until his mom arrives home.

- Just the right amount of detail

  Tanner rides the bus home after school and arrives home at 3:15. Laura, his mom, is still at work, and per her requested routine Tanner gives her a phone call to let her know that he made it safely home. Tanner throws his backpack on the floor in the entryway and immediately heads to the family room. He turns on both the TV and the family PC. Within minutes, he is watching his favorite after-school shows and IMing two of his friends and playing an Internet game on his (currently) favorite site. He knows that he only has 45 minutes of "free" time before his mom arrives home.

- Too much detail

  Tanner rides the bus home after school and arrives home at 3:15. He likes his bus driver because he reminds him of the bus driver on the cartoon show The Simpsons. Laura, his Mom, is still at work. Having a part-time job, she works until 4:00 p.m. three days a week. She worries about Tanner being home alone after school—particularly regarding his trip home. She worries less once he is there, and so per her requested routine Tanner gives her a phone call to let her know that he made it safely home. Tanner throws his backpack on the floor in the entryway, spilling some of its content on the floor, and immediately heads to the family room. He turns on both the TV (a nice but old 34-inch Sony Trinitron) and the family PC. Within minutes, he is watching his favorite after-school shows and IMing two of his friends and playing a flash-based Internet game on his (currently) favorite site. He makes the most of this play time, because he knows that he only has 45 minutes of "free" time before his mom arrives home. Laura arrives home a little late due to traffic, and gets a little irritated by the mess Tanner created in the entryway. She snaps at Tanner to get started on his homework.

Story from the field

CHOOSING THE RIGHT LANGUAGE AND INFORMATION FOR YOUR AUDIENCE

—Lori Landesman, The MathWorks

One of the biggest hurdles I have had to overcome to use personas successfully at The MathWorks is understanding the language my developers and the audience use, because I'm not an engineer or mathematician. I can't represent our users authentically unless I have the development engineers involved in the process with me, helping to refine the vocabulary and add realistic elements to the scenarios. Although this prolongs the process and requires me to involve more people, it gets the development team bought in from the beginning and gives them more of a stake in the process and in the success of the resulting product. The following is an example of the types of personas we produce when we work together.

> *Chuck S., researcher/scientist at Monterey Bay Aquarium:* I know that dolphins that travel in large schools are more at risk because tuna fishermen look for large schools of dolphins when casting their nets. They know that beneath a large school of dolphins there's likely to be a large school of tuna. Because of that, I'd like to determine what percentage of dolphins is at risk. I have data showing how many groups of different-size schools I've observed. I'd like to fit a distribution to that data, and then determine what percentage of dolphins travel in schools containing over 1,000 dolphins. I don't have any theoretical grounds on which to choose a particular distribution, so I want to try a few (gamma, Weibull, and lognormal, say) and see whether one of them fits the data better than the others, and whether my conclusions about the percentage of dolphins at risk would be different for the different fits.

Of course, part of your goal here is to make the persona memorable and engaging. It is possible that the detail that will make the personas stick in your organization will be something "irrelevant" with respect to the product. Try to find out what resonates for folks, what they all agree on, and what they love to debate and talk about. In one company, it was the persona's car that really made the persona seem real, tangible. Others have relied heavily on the tag line or user class. In the end, the most memorable part of any persona tends to be the name and the picture—and these are so useful in streamlining communication that it is worth adding any details that will secure the basics in the minds of your teammates.

Finally, it is important to note that not every section of your persona foundation document needs to be written as a story. Some sections are best left as bulleted lists, tables, or other summary formats. In our experience, narratives are especially useful in foundation documents for providing an overview, describing a "day in the life," and facilitating key usage scenarios including motivations, fears, and aspirations of the persona. Sections regarding goals, knowledge, skills, and equipment or environment might be best written as bulleted lists.

Handy Detail

DETERMINE WHERE PERSONAS STOP AND SCENARIOS BEGIN

A foundation document as we define it is a rich and detailed description of an individual, which may include stories about how he or she approaches work, gets things done, and interacts with colleagues and products (possibly yours). The stories you include in the personas should be there to help people deeply understand who that persona is. But this doesn't mean that your foundation document will contain all possible stories for that persona.

In Chapter 6 we discuss how additional stories, specific scenarios, Design Maps, and use cases can be created and used outside the foundation to help your team explore and define solutions to be built into your product. Scenarios, Design Maps, and use cases are typically much more specific and focused than the stories in foundation documents. They are stories designed to specifically describe a particular person interacting with a particular part of a product in a particular situation. Your personas will become the "particular people" (or "actors") in these additional stories.

Personas are generative in nature. That is, they can drive the creation of an almost endless set of possible scenarios. When defined appropriately, your personas serve as the motivational factor and grounding requirements for future scenarios—detailed scenarios in specific domains.

Know when to stop

Once you start enriching your skeleton personas into full foundation documents, you might find it difficult to stop. You and your team will discover new data sources and will want to incorporate new information into the sketches. That is fine, but it should not get in the way of sharing and "birthing" the personas into your organization. At some point, you and your core team will have to decide that you have enough information in each persona and are ready to move on to the next phase. Remember that it is likely that no one outside your core team will ever read the entire foundation document. The document need only be complete enough to support your *birth and maturation* and *adulthood* activities to the extent that you are "ready." This does not mean that you cannot keep adding information. In Chapter 5 we recommend that you assign an owner to each persona. The owner can be responsible for keeping the persona up to date and integrating new data and information as appropriate.

Illustrate your personas

Each persona needs a face, a photo or set of photos, to make them real. We believe photos or illustrations are critical. They help your team believe in the personas and understand that each persona describes a single person. The choice of what specific photos to use is difficult. These illustrations of your personas are extremely influential, and can significantly affect how your personas are perceived.

A photo is more than just a face. The model's clothing, expression, activity, and general appearance—along with the setting and background—will communicate or dictate some of the characteristics of your persona. You can either take advantage of this fact or continually fight it. The sections that follow offer some suggestions to help you with this.

Don't use stock photos

Stock photos can look too professional and slick, as the people in them tend to look like professional models (see Figure 4.20). With stock photos, you do not have control of the model's context, activity, or expression. There are also usually only one or two photos for a given model. As you'll see in the next chapter (Birth and Maturation) it is useful to have a

FIGURE 4.20: *Stock photos can look too professional. The people look like models.*

variety of shots of the same model. In addition, we have experienced situations in which a stock photo that was used for one team's persona was coincidentally used for a different persona for a different team in the same company. We have also seen stock photos for personas show up in magazines and on billboards. "Hey, isn't that our 'Dianna'?"

Instead of using stock photos, locate people who look the part and hold your own photo shoot. Photos of friends-of-friends will look approachable and real (see Figure 4.21). Using local, known people for your models means that you will likely be able to get additional photos at a later point if the need arises. If you choose to take your own photographs (which

we highly recommend), you should start looking for models the moment you decide on the primary personas. The time-consuming part of this step is finding just the right faces. Each photo session takes about an hour.

If you can't locate your own models or do your own photo shoot for some reason, there are other options. We recommend Web sites such as *stock.xchng* (*www.sxc.hu*), which share photos by amateur photographers. If you find a photo you like, you can use it for free and can potentially contact the photographer to request more photos of the same subject. If all else fails, you can find good photos of people from pay-per-use online sources. Three good ones available at the time of this writing are *www.gettyone.com*,

FIGURE 4.21: *Photos of local people can look more real, more approachable.*

Handle Detail

HOLD YOUR OWN PHOTO SHOOT

To do a photo shoot, start with stock photos that have the basic look you want. Then, ask your teammates and friends if they know anyone that resembles the models in the stock photos. Once you locate a few candidates, have them send a photo of themselves and have your core team evaluate which local model would work best. Then schedule 30 minutes to an hour with each model to do a quick photo shoot (preferably with a digital camera).

You will want your team to see different aspects of your personas. During your photo shoot, make sure you have the model pose in a variety of places—with different expressions and doing different things (talking on the phone, drinking a beverage, working at their desk, getting out of their car, and so on). Choose settings and activities that are core to each persona. Bring your own appropriate props to help make the right statement. Have the model bring a few changes of clothing. You can likely take 100 or more shots in an hour-long photo shoot. If possible, use a digital camera so that you get immediate review of your work. You will need about 5 to 10 good shots when you are done.

Consider paying your models with gift certificates, or perhaps free products or services from your company. Finally, be sure to use an image release form with these models. You can find an example of such a form at the end of this book (see Appendix C). This short form grants limited use of the images for internal, product development purposes. We recommend that you consult your company's legal representative before using this or any other legal form.

---

www.istockphoto.com, and *www.wonderfile.com*. There are also free images available from the Microsoft Design Gallery at *http://dgl.microsoft.com* and photos available at *www.flicker.com/ creativecommons* have varying permissions for reuse associated with them.

Note that it is critical that you review the details of the agreement on how these photos can be used. Ignoring the terms can get you into trouble. For example, there are collections of clip art (with photos) that say you cannot use more than 100 copies for a particular activity and/or that the use must be for educational purposes (such as passing out slides at a conference). These are normal conditions of the "fair use" clause under copyright law. It might be worth making a copy of the license for your records from whatever sources you use.

Illustrations can be an interesting alternative to photos

Consider having an artist generate sketches to represent your personas. Although sketches feel less "real" and may detract from credibility, they do have their place. For example, sketches can keep your personas from being interpreted too literally. Further, you have a lot of control over what the sketches look like, what the personas are doing in the sketches, and so on. For more on this topic, see the following Story from the field.

Story from the field

—Rósa Guðjónsdóttir, Usability Consultant, Pink Puffin, Sweden, *www.pinkpuffin.com*

Since I started to work with personas I have always used sketches to visualize the personas I create in the projects I work on. I firmly believe that sketches are the best way to visualize personas. A sketch is unique, just like the persona.

I have discovered in my projects that it is important to emphasize that personas are fictitious. Therefore, I believe that the visualization of the persona should also be just like the persona—fake, as it were. If you have sketches, the project group focuses on the persona, not the person "acting" the persona (in a photo, for example). Figures 4.22 and 4.23 show examples of persona sketches from various projects.

Using sketches was particularly important when we were working on a project for an African client and our target groups were Africans living within and outside Sub-Saharan Africa. We obviously could not have created a believable and authentic environment for the photo shoot. We instead got inspiration from books, magazines, newspapers, and TV programs from several African countries. Our project group had no problems accepting the personas and quickly got a feel for who the portal's target audience was and how to use the personas in the project.

Another advantage of using sketches when visualizing personas is, I believe, that it is easier to remember a sketch than a photo. It is also easier to emphasize elements that are important to the persona character without losing the credibility of the scenario situation. Sketches also increase the credibility of the personas because there is no one acting out the persona.

FIGURE 4.22: *Patrik was created for an intranet project for a political party in Stockholm. (Photograph courtesy of Cecilia Karlsson.)*

(Story from the field, continued)

FIGURE 4.23: *Claire was created as a portal design project for an African client. (Photograph courtesy of Olle Torgny.)*

Sketches also allow you to adapt the "feel" of the sketches to the type of project group you are working with. A very humorous and fun-loving project group appreciates more comical sketches, whereas for another group it might be important to use a more serious style.

Bright Idea

COLLECT PHOTOS FROM MAGAZINES

—Whitney Quesenbery, Whitney Interactive Design, LLC

The photos of people in stock photography books often look too perfect to represent the personas I work with. Instead, I have a box of pictures I cut out of magazines. Family, health, cooking, and fitness publications often have good pictures of many diverse people: old and young and many ethnic backgrounds. They also use a wide variety of settings, including homes, neighborhoods, the outdoors, and work places. This is an easy way of collecting a lot of photographs to use for inspiration in giving your personas a face.

Note: Of course, these pictures cannot be reproduced (by *any* physical means) or disseminated (by *any* means, including passing around a folder). Any other use than private reference is illegal.

Audition the photos and/or illustrations

Hold auditions for proposed photos (or illustrations or models). Let a variety of teammates have a say in what photos or specific models are used for your personas. Doing so will obtain buy-in and should result in more broadly acceptable images. Generally, the selected models should be attractive; not supermodels, but people that have a look that is likeable, approachable, trustworthy, nice, and engaging. In addition, the facial expressions in the photos should be pleasant. These images will likely be around for a long time—perhaps several development cycles. Choose images that are easy to look at and that inspire your team to build great products.

Name your personas

The names you give to your personas are important, perhaps on par with the importance of the illustration. In many cases, the persona's name is the one detail that everyone will know and remember. Choose names carefully. There are several simple rules of thumb for selecting persona names:

- Don't use the name of anyone on your team or in your organization
- Avoid using the names of famous people (such as Cher or Britney)
- Avoid using names that have any negative connotation
- Do use names that are unique and distinctive
- Consider building a mnemoni device into the persona names to help people remember them. For example, if you create personas for segments that are already named *enthusiasts, ostriches,* and *neophytes,* why not select names that share the first letter of each segment? For example, the enthusiast could be named Eddie, the ostrich Omar, and the neophyte Nanette.

Story from the field

APPROPRIATE NAMES ARE CRITICAL

—Ken Seiff, Founder of Bluefly.com and CEO, Glowcast Ventures

Although it seems like a silly thing, I strongly believe that naming personas correctly is critical. There is a real balance that needs to be achieved to most effectively work the "magic" of personas. In the best of all worlds, the name must be personal enough that it clearly reflects a real user and descriptive enough that everyone in the company can attach the name to the persona's goals and behavior. We tend to favor names such as Sally Searcher and Donna Discount. They are not pretty but they do the job most effectively. Half the battle with personas is getting the names entrenched in everyone's lexicon so that the word *user* is eliminated from discussions. When that happens, you begin to develop a personal relationship with your customer.

If you need help in coming up with interesting and memorable names, you might look up one of the many baby name Web sites (there are many to choose from). If your personas are different ages, you can also look up popular names for the years each was born.

Consider getting your larger organization involved in the naming process. This serves the purpose of both getting good, agreeable names and getting your organization engaged early with your personas (see "Buzz Generators" in Chapter 5). If you decide to do this, we recommend that you select a set of names for each persona and allow everyone to vote during the *birth* activities.

Create name + tag line combinations

Generally, we recommend creating a name and tag line together, usually something alliterative. For example, you might have "Toby the Typical Teenager," "Abe the Active Administrator," or "Connie the Conscientious Consumer." Tag lines make personas easier to remember and to differentiate. Along the same line, you might consider using a simple quote or job title to bring meaning to the name. You want to highlight a key differentiator/characteristic for each persona. However, be careful not to choose something potentially offensive (e.g., "filing goddess" or "obsessive organizer"). As a check, consider if it would it bug you to be have these lines added to the end of your name.

G4K Meanwhile, at G4K...

G4K'S PERSONAS ARE COMPLETE

G4K's persona core team created six personas to help with the development of their children's portal site. Figures 4.24 through 4.29 show and explain who these personas are.

FIGURE 4.24: *Tanner Thompson (the tenacious tinkerer) is an intense nine-year-old boy who loves computers, games, and gadgets of all types. He is an entertainment enthusiast and active gamer. Generally speaking, he just loves to play. Tanner is familiar with G4K game titles and is a likely frequent visitor to the G4K site—seeking out new ways to entertain himself. Tanner has significant influence over his parent's spending on family fun.*

FIGURE 4.25: *Colbi Chandler (the creative child) is a charming seven-year-old elementary school girl who loves to do anything imaginative, crafty, or fun. She enjoys reading and writing and has always loved school. Colbi will be an occasional visitor to the G4K site, lured there because of the creative content and because her friends go there. Colbi is the little sister of Austin.*

FIGURE 4.26: *Austin Chandler (the active competitor) is an athletic 13-year-old boy who is interested in anything competitive or challenging. Austin loves to play sports of all types and is a disciplined achiever. Austin plays video and PC games for the sense of competition and the thrill of victory. Austin will likely come to the G4K site seeking out new games, hints, and tips, as well as worthy opponents.*

FIGURE 4.27: *Preston Pasquez (a precocious preschooler) is a bright-eyed and inquisitive three-year-old boy who is intrigued by anything new. He loves his parents' PC, but his mother, Irene, won't allow Preston to play on the PC by himself, especially when it is connected to the Internet. Irene will always be present to help Preston visit the G4K site.*

FIGURE 4.28: *Irene Pasquez (the involved parent) is mother of Preston, and is (to sum her up in one word) engaged. Irene is vigilant and involved with Preston to the highest degree. She loves to spend time directly interacting with and fully focused on Preston. She believes that the PC is a vital tool to help educate her children and stimulate mental development. Irene actively seeks out good experiences on the PC for Preston. She will visit the G4K site on occasion, but as a partner with ever-present Preston. She is not currently aware of specific G4K products.*

FIGURE 4.29: *Elaine Evans (the enlightened elementary school teacher) is a young and relatively new elementary school teacher who loves what she does and takes it very seriously. Elaine has interest and direct training in promoting technology as an educational tool for children. She sees the PC as a vital tool for today's youth and tomorrow's leaders. Elaine is vaguely aware of the G4K brand, but doesn't have any direct experience with G4K products.*

(Meanwhile, at G4K..., continued)

Tanner, Colbi, and Austin are the primary personas for this endeavor. Preston and Irene are secondary targets and will generally be considered in combination, as Preston is not allowed or able to use the PC and Internet alone. Elaine, the enlightened educator, is also a secondary target. A complete example foundation document (see Figure 4.30) for Tanner is provided in Appendix A.

FIGURE 4.30: *Tanner document.*

(Images courtesy of CanStockPhoto.)

○ Discuss categories of users
○ Process data
○ Identify & create skeletons
○ Evaluate & prioritize skeletons
○ Develop skeletons into personas
● **Validate the personas**

Step 6: *Validate your Personas*

You have just spent a lot of time crafting a persona to stand in for the users you researched. Your personas should now be looking and sounding great—full of solid information and complete with illustrative photos and meaningful names. Your stakeholders have reviewed them and you now seem to have the right set of target customers in your focus. But how can you be sure your personas embody the data you worked so hard to collect?

Your personas were likely created from a variety of data sources (primary and secondary sources; some older, some newer, some quantitative, some qualitative) all stitched together by educated guesses, assumptions, and business strategy. You have pieced together data points that may or may not actually fit together—some of which may not be directly comparable or inherently compatible.

Your goal during validation is to ensure that you did not stray too far away from your data when you made their characteristics specific and concrete and added elements of storytelling. Although it is true that personas cannot and do not need to be completely accurate, you do want to ensure that they reflect the essential information about your target users that you found in your data. If you built assumption personas, you want to ensure that the personas you created really do capture the assumptions in your organization. We discuss five approaches to validating your resulting personas (presented in order of increasing cost and rigor).

- Review your personas against the original data sources.
- Have experts (those closest to your users) review your personas.
- Have representative users of each persona review "their" persona.
- Conduct "reality check" site visits.
- Conduct large sample surveys or interviews.

These five approaches are not mutually exclusive, nor are they the only means of validating your personas.

Story from the field

PERSONAS AT ZYLOM.COM

Erik Goossens and **J. Vanzandbeek,** Zylom.com

At Zylom.com, we make interactive word and puzzle games. Our target audience is mostly women, age 30 and over, who typically like to play games at home when they 'have a little break during the day.' We saw a presentation on personas at Shop.org and decided we wanted to try using them. Our goal was to redesign our corporate Web site from an information source for our advertising business to a try-and-buy storefront for our games. We wanted to get started right away, so we came back to the office and created assumption personas. To do this, we created a core team of five people, which included colleagues from management, market research, games development, and process experts. The core team brainstormed to capture our existing assumptions about our users on a whiteboard; these assumptions were based on our experience in this business and some market research data from a survey done to profile our audience for our advertisers (completed last year). We initially created three assumption personas to represent older women, younger women, and men: Maria, age 51, Sophie, age 31, and Michael, age 29.

Our resulting personas felt right to us, but we wanted make sure we were on target. To validate our assumptions, we bought a survey tool and created questionnaires for various groups of users. We put together a representative sample of users to survey, based on our analysis of 'typical' usage patterns we found in our data. After we collected and cross-tabbed the data from the surveys, we cross-referenced our findings with other data sources, such as transactional data from our site, user characteristics collected during registration, time spent on the site, etc.

We concluded that all of our data made sense and was presenting us with a very clear picture of our actual users and how they were similar to (and different from) our assumptions. For example, through our data, we realized that women approach and use online games differently depending on their ages, so we revised our definitions of Maria and Sophie to comply with these findings. We also found that men comprised only 15% of our market. After this realization, we decided to focus or redesign efforts on Maria (our most profitable target) and Sophie, using Michael as a secondary target when appropriate.

Once we had our personas firmly in place, we:
- Defined Maria's and Sophie's goals for the site
- Created mockups of the site
- Brought in "Marias" and "Sophies" so we could watch (and videotape) them using the functional mockups
- Iterated the mockups
- Built and deployed the site.

From start to finish, this entire process took three weeks, and the new site was up and running less than 4 months after the presentation on personas that we had attended.

[For a continuation of this case study in the Adulthood phase, see the "Story from the field: Persona Fridays" in Chapter 6.]

Check back in with your data

Now that you have enhanced your personas with details and narrative, schedule a short meeting with your persona core team. Ask everyone to skim back over the data sources from which the key factoids were derived. If you have transcripts or profiles from qualitative research, we suggest that you focus your review on these. As you skim the original data, ask each core team member to identify any ways in which the completed personas seem to contradict the data sources and decide together whether these contradictions are acceptable. Make appropriate revisions to your personas to ensure they are as representative of the data as possible.

Have subject-matter experts review your personas

Consider taking your personas to people who know your target audience. Look for domain experts that have direct contact with your users (or proposed users) and who were not involved in the creation of your personas. These may be sales personnel, product support engineers, trainers or educators, or people who have directly conducted research with your audience (focus group moderators, usability engineers, ethnographers, and so on). If you built your personas to help redesign an existing product, you might have access to people in your company who are very close to your existing user base and can help you validate your personas. For example, you can show your personas to members of the sales and support teams, who should be able to tell you if your personas remind them of the customers they talk to every day. The marketing team can also help you validate your personas, though you should bear in mind that the marketing team's targets may be the purchasers of the product, not the users of the product.

Ask these experts to read the foundation documents and point out things that don't match their experience with these users. Again, make revisions as appropriate to the personas so that they best fit the original data and your experts' observations.

Show your personas to real users

Another simple but slightly more demanding way to validate your personas is to show them to the actual people they are designed to represent. For example, if you created a bank teller persona, show your persona to several bank tellers. Tell the real bank tellers that your goal was to create a profile of a typical bank teller and you would like to know if your persona "looks right" as such (see the following Story from the Field). You want to know what aspects of the persona resonate with real people that fall into that category of users.

In our experience, you only need to do this with a handful of people per persona. You will likely find that comments start to significantly overlap after the first three or four reviews. You might consider doing minor revisions after each review so that the next real person sees only the most "true" persona. As you do these reviews and revisions, make sure you are not violating your original data. If there are major conflicts, choose the characteristic you trust the most and note the need to do further research if the discrepancy falls in an area important to your product domain.

Story from the field

SHARING THE PERSONA WITH THE PERSONAE

—Debby Catton, Technical Writing Consultant, and **Jennifer Dunne,** Technical Writer, Sun Life Financial

Gaining approval to create personas wasn't an easy task. We were either too busy or people just didn't see the value. Finally, after two years of persistence, our assistant vice president (AVP) gave us permission to proceed. Because we had a number of different personas to create and were new to the process of creating a persona, we decided to first create the persona on our smallest but perhaps most significant user type—our financial center trainers.

We were somewhat shy during our first interviews with the trainer, but soon every interview was a completely successful and passionate experience! As the time drew near to present our persona to our AVP group, a twinge of doubt crept in. What if they didn't see the value in our work? What if they told us we couldn't proceed with the other personas?

We decided that if we presented the completed persona to the trainers we interviewed and got their opinion on how this work would benefit them, our leaders couldn't dispute the effectiveness of this tool. And we were right. The trainers loved the concept and provided the following statements.

- "Wow! You have done an excellent job at capturing our persona in my opinion. I like the perspective you took and how you personalized it. Good write-up. Hoping that the powers that be are able to get a better grasp of the role and how it works out here in the financial center."
- "It is a good generalization of the role as I am sure that each of us trainers has a broad and varied role. No two are exactly the same."
- "I like Sandra! Sounds like you have captured us — mood, job, etc. Great job. Now I hope that others who influence and affect our position and the tasks we undertake have a real good read and get to know Sandra intimately."

Having the blessing and acceptance of our personas made a huge impact at our presentation to our leaders, as we received unconditional approval to proceed with the rest. We know what a great communication and decision-making tool a persona can be. As the creators of personas, we have found that the process is an invaluable exercise in truly understanding our audience.

Conduct "reality check" site visits

A more involved way of approaching persona validation (if you have the time and budget) is to visit people who are very similar to your personas and attempt to ascertain if your personas match your observations. The goal here is to visit users who match the personas on high-level characteristics to see how well they match on low-level characteristics. This goal is the same as with the previous validation technique, but here you are relying on your ability to see how real users actually are and how they behave, not just what they think about themselves and their reflection on their actions. We call these "reality check" site visits. To do this, you will take the steps described in the following sections.

Create persona profile screeners

Work backward from your rich persona to a set of characteristics that are essential to that persona. The sketches you started from are likely to be useful here. From this set of characteristics, you will develop questions that can be used to evaluate whether or not any candidate participant is a good representative of one of your personas. For more information on doing screeners (including an example), see the section "Use personas as a recruiting profile for usability testing and market research" in Chapter 6.

Recruit representative people and visit them

Using your new persona screeners, locate several people who are good representatives of each persona. Three to five people per persona should be adequate. Visit those people and conduct a brief observational study and interview in an attempt to determine how well the low-level and peripheral characteristics of your personas match these people. Alternatively, hold focus group sessions with groups of representatives of each persona. Use the outline of the foundation document as a rough script for your discussion sessions. In either of these cases, and in addition to your direct observations, you can also show them personas and get their feedback as you would using the previous validation technique. With these observations and feedback, revise and refine your personas, being careful not to violate the original research findings that made up your personas. You will likely find that you are simply tweaking bits and pieces of the design-irrelevant details or fictional components of your personas in order to fit your validation findings.

Conduct large sample surveys or interviews

If you have even more time and resources, you can consider doing a more sophisticated validation effort. Using surveys, you can determine how pervasive your personas are in addition to the existence and coexistence of their attributes. To conduct this research, you will need to identify individual characteristics per persona and translate them into a form that real users can respond to as part of a questionnaire or survey. For example, you might generate a series of statements that respondents can rate (examples A and B following) or check as appropriate (example C).

- Example A
  Rate the following "After-school activity" statements regarding your own behaviors:

    a) I usually watch television after school. (strongly agree, agree, disagree, strongly disagree)

    b) I usually play computer video games after school. (strongly agree, agree, disagree, strongly disagree)

    c) I usually play outside at home after school. (strongly agree, agree, disagree, strongly disagree)

    d) I usually talk on the phone with friends after school. (strongly agree, agree, disagree, strongly disagree)

- Example B
  Indicate the frequency with which you engage in the following activities after school:

    a) Watching television (frequently, sometimes, never)

    b) Playing computer video games (frequently, sometimes, never)

c) Playing outside at home (frequently, sometimes, never)

d) Talking on the phone with friends (frequently, sometimes, never)

- Example C
  Indicate which of the following activities you engage in regularly after school (check all that apply).

    a) Watch television

    b) Play computer video games

    c) Play outside

    d) Talk on the phone with friends

Analysis of such data can take many forms and can be quite complicated. This can be similar to segmentation or cluster analysis, which you might have started your persona effort from, only now you have target profiles to evaluate the responses against. Your goal is to understand how the characteristics of a broad sample of users relate to the known (or proposed) characteristics of your personas. The details of doing such an analysis are beyond the scope of this book. We recommend that you do not undertake such a validation effort without the involvement of a trained statistician or researcher. Keep in mind, however, that this approach can be greatly simplified by focusing on only a few of the key attributes of your personas. The analysis for this simplified approach can be as basic as comparing a few descriptive statistics (e.g., averages or a series of frequency counts) or doing a correlation analysis. For an example of this, see the following sidebar by Colin Hynes regarding putting real values on your personas.

Story from the field

PUTTING REAL VALUES ON YOUR PERSONAS

—Colin Hynes, Director of Usability, Staples.com

After a lot of effort went into creating meaningful and valid personas for our development team, and when our final personas were presented to the senior executives, our VP of Marketing commented, "I wish we knew how much each of these personas was worth in bottom-line dollars." This kicked off our "persona valuation project."

The main thrust of the persona valuation project was a joint effort between the Usability and Marketing teams. After several meetings between the two groups, we decided that data would be gathered through a survey with one simple question tied to the defining quote of each persona. This, of course, put much pressure on the defining quotes to fully encapsulate the essence of the persona. Our hope was that a user would read one of the quotes and immediately see himself in the statement.

(Story from the field, continued)

Then we decided on the criteria for distributing the survey, which was simplified: people who had purchased from Staples (any channel) in the last six months, had visited *Staples.com* in the last six months, and who had an e-mail address. We also decided to offer an incentive ($10 off) to participants, even though the survey was only going to be two questions. One requirement was that we had to be able to link responses to other info in the database for calculation of "value" regarding each respondent (see Figure 4.31).

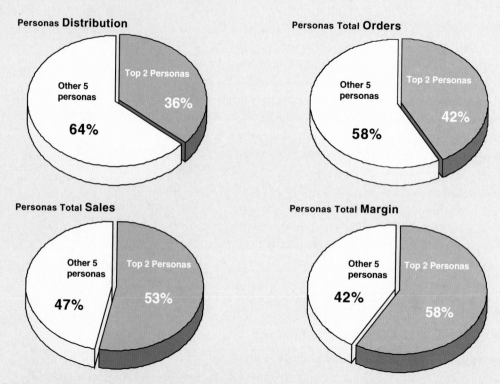

FIGURE 4.31: *Staples was able to attribute spending per persona by matching survey respondents to purchases in their transaction database. As they looked at the data across different purchase metrics, a clear picture of the most valuable personas emerged.*

The invitation started with a subject line explaining, "Get $10 off your next purchase by filling out a quick survey." We sent the link out to 15,000 customers from our database. On the survey page, each respondent was presented with the seven defining quotes and an "Other" option for those who did not feel they bucketed neatly into any of the persona statements. After scrubbing the data, we ended up with 1,048 valid responses.

(Story from the field, continued)

Upon our initial high-level analysis of the data we were somewhat disappointed that respondents were fairly evenly distributed across the seven personas. There were some slightly heavier buckets, but all personas garnered between 10 and 20% of the overall distribution. The Usability hypotheses that two particular personas would dominate the distribution was not supported. We feared that without one or two clear-cut "winners" we would be left trying to serve all personas. Our ultimate concern was that this would manifest itself in a Web site design that tried to be everything to everyone, instead of having focus.

One highly encouraging data point was that only eight of the more than 1,000 respondents bucketed themselves as "Other." This made us feel confident we had nailed the original persona descriptions.

Although the distribution did not give us the clarity we were hoping for, when we matched the responses against 12-month sales figures the picture became crystal clear. We calculated the percentage of orders, sales, and margin generated for each persona. The figures were an aggregate of all purchases made through any channel. Strikingly, the data showed that two personas that made up a combined 36% of the distribution also made up 42% of the orders, 53% of sales, and 58% of the margin (see Figure 4.31). Further, if we were to map the personas out in a Venn diagram to illustrate overlap in goals these two personas would have the greatest overlap. Note: We tried to have as little overlap as possible overall in the personas. If we deemed that there was a significant overlap between personas we combined the personas in the creation process.

It is difficult to overestimate the impact this data had on the future design direction of *Staples.com*. To ensure accuracy, we reanalyzed the data and obtained the same results. At that point we knew we had lightning in a bottle. With the inclusive nature of the study and the airtight research design, the results were difficult to dispute.

Validation is an opportunity for data gathering

You may have created your personas based almost completely on existing data sources. If this is the case, you are probably missing some of the qualitative information that can inform the narrative surrounding your persona. If you utilized only qualitative information, you might need to understand aspects of your personas related to market size, spending, or other quantitative or domain-specific information. You can organize your validation efforts to serve two purposes: validate the persona details you have developed from your data sources and collect the additional information that will help complete the personas.

As you finished your assimilation exercises and moved on to create skeletons and full personas, you probably noticed some categories of information missing. For example, you may have collected tremendous amounts of data related to a teenager's schoolwork and entertainment interests, but may find yourself with virtually no information about typical family activities and concerns. When you create the narrative for your teen persona, you can:

- Fill in this information based on assumptions
- Return to your clusters, or even your original data sources, to see if there was relevant information you simply didn't use
- Take the opportunity to look for more details as you conduct your validation activities.

Before you recruit people to survey or observe toward refining your personas, create a list of the types of information you still need, and use this additional data to inform targeted content areas or to create the narratives and storyline. It is perfectly reasonable to create the data-driven persona details and wait to build additional narrative until you have completed most of your validation activities.

Completed personas do not mark the end of user research

At the point you finish the creation of your personas, you may be tempted to think that you do not need to further understand (do research) or involve real users in the development of your product. From our perspective, this couldn't be further from the truth. We believe personas are a great starting point for understanding and incorporating user information in the development cycle.

As you will find in Chapter 6, personas can (among other things) be used to create excellent recruiting profiles for further testing and insight. User testing, focus groups, beta testing, and other methods of involving real users in the process should continue as possible throughout the entire development cycle. Personas can serve not only as recruiting targets for these activities but as a communication device and a repository for new findings. You may find that you need to update your completed personas every six months to a year as your target audience changes, though you must be thoughtful about how you approach this (for more discussion of this, see Chapter 7). In other words, even though other activities now take focus the validation of your personas should continue throughout the persona lifecycle.

Story from the field

ADAPTING PERSONAS TO INTERNATIONAL MARKETS

—Mina Gharb-Hamil, Sandra da Costa Neto, and **Armando Pita,**

Window International, Microsoft Corporation

Many times, personas are created almost completely from information collected within the country that the development team exists in. Adding international information to personas can help ensure that products will delight customers worldwide. This case study shows how the Windows International Program Managers team (henceforth referred to as WI PMs) helped the USA-based Windows product development team adapt their target personas as they worked to design and develop a product to suit the global marketplace.

Why Consider Internationalization of Your Personas?

Anthropological, social, economic, cultural, and political uniqueness require a different approach for global markets. Figure 4.32 presents an example of how PC activities vary among regions of the world. Note that the top activity in the United States, word processing, is not even present on the Latin American list. Consequently, the more attention we pay to these differences when designing products the more appealing the product will be for customers worldwide.

Comparison of PC activities			
United States		Latin America	
Word processing	66%	Games	49%
Games	53%	School work	49%
Household records	46%	Graphic art and design	31%
Learning devices for children	30%	Household records	21%
School work	28%	Office work at home	21%

FIGURE 4.32: *Statistics showing the differences in PC activities between the United States and Latin America.*

By not understanding how international customers use products, we are missing business opportunities. Look at mobile phones, for example—how can we satisfy our users if we don't consider how our international customers use their mobile phones? In some international markets, almost 100% of households have a cell phone versus 71% in the United States. Further, pagers were completely discontinued (for several years now) when the second layer of mobile phones started conquering the marketplace (about 1997/1998), whereas in the United States they are still a common means of communication. In international markets,

(Story from the field, continued)

the percentage of mobile phones with Internet access is almost three times higher than in the United States: 16% versus 6%.

For the WI PMs team, the need to adapt personas came from the fact that they were involved in the process of giving feedback to feature specifications for a new product. To test the scenarios against several international market segments, there were two options.

- Create new personas to represent different international markets, probably divided by region. This process would have generated a great variation of new personas from scratch, which would vary a lot depending on the world region with which they were associated. This would have consumed too much time, not to mention that the scenario evaluation would be very complex and the product development team would not have had the proper means of producing a better user profile adaptation for each world region involved.
- Leverage the personas that already existed. To do this it would have been necessary to adapt each persona's individual characteristics and habits to each country, consolidating it by ethnographic regions afterward. (An ethnographic region consists of all countries that share similar ethnic and linguistic origins. For example, Latin Languages countries covered by the WI PM team are all countries in Latin America, as well as French Canada, Portugal, Spain, Italy, and France. Eastern Europe countries are Russia, Hungary, the Czech Republic, Poland, and so on.)

The Adaptation Process

WI PMs are based in Microsoft's international subsidiaries and are responsible for providing accurate and relevant information on local user needs, market requirements, and competitive situations. As natives of the countries they work in, they have the background to understand cultural, social, and political issues.

WI PMs collected the data from a variety of sources, including local market research; corporate customer visits; analysis of how their local friends, family, and colleagues interacted with their computers; and other local country data sources such as the subsidiaries' market intelligence reports and local associations. The process for integrating this data was as follows.

1. We studied the existing personas in order to have an in-depth knowledge of each. All related material was provided by the personas team, with which the WI PMs worked in very close cooperation.
2. We then selected the U.S. personas that represented the user scenarios they wanted to address, which meant all of those that were already common to international markets in accordance with known research data. Furthermore, special focus was given to the personas representing the Consumer and Enterprise segments.
3. Next, the U.S. personas were compared with the international market data in order to interpret activities and attributes for each international persona.
4. We then sketched the basic characteristics for each internationally adapted persona (which varied according to country) and compiled the resulting data for each region.

(Story from the field, continued)

5. The activities and attributes identified as important to each of the international countries' markets were used to assign a similarity rating. Ratings were assigned as follows: 5 = same as the United States, 4 = mainly similar to the United States, 3 = neutral, 2 = largely different, 1 = completely different. For example, the similarity rating for the EMEA Teenager persona for Online Shopping would be low because in most of the countries in that region it would be illegal for him to shop on the Internet, as a consequence of citizen protection laws being much more strict in Europe than in the United States.

6. We then documented the similarity ratings, all of the market data the ratings were based on, and references to the analysis of each country—highlighting all potential opportunities and risks so that everyone on the team could access the information according to their respective regional groups.

7. The resulting feedback was posted for each persona on the Windows International Program Managers Web site and incorporated in the Personas Foundation documents in the "International Considerations" section.

At the end of this process, for each U.S. persona it was possible to identify a corresponding persona for each ethnographic region. One such persona was the EMEA Teenager, for whom there was a special "Overview" section (describing his main characteristics, habits, and daily activities) and a "Differences from the U.S. Persona Macro Analysis" section (containing all items rated largely or completely different from those of the U.S. persona).

Benefits of Using the Adapted Personas

When the development team uses our internationally adapted personas, they can detect which features are important to our international customers. For example, by understanding how the EMEA Teenager uses his mobile phone the product team would recognize that a communication feature that allows him to send and receive messages between his mobile phone and some Windows components would be very welcome. Or why not go even further and allow him to give instructions to his printer, fax, or any other hardware device via SMS (Short Message Service) through his computer?

The personas can also help teams adapt existing features for upcoming versions of a product. For example, what type of privacy considerations are people around the world expecting from Microsoft? Let's assume that in order to register a new product the customer will be asked to send personal information. In the United States, we expect this inquiry and will probably send the requested information. But if we analyze the social behavior of EMEA knowledge worker personas, we find that they are very concerned about privacy and would be upset with Microsoft for asking for their personal information. Conversely, the Latin American knowledge worker personas would gladly provide this information and would even develop a better perception of Microsoft if this data were used to foster a relationship with them.

(Story from the field, continued)

Conclusions

With this information available to them, product teams should be thinking about how to offer software registration that will address the comfort levels in their various international markets. Writing software adapted to the international markets will surely increase worldwide customer satisfaction toward our products, as users will feel identified with them. This translates into a significant added value. Internationalizing our personas helped to fill this previously existing gap into the most variable user profiles.

HOW TO KNOW YOU ARE READY FOR *BIRTH AND MATURATION*

You should now have a set of rich, meaningful personas that have been validated against real users. Still, you may be tempted to keep refining your personas until they seem perfect. You may feel hesitant about putting them "out there" for people to see and use. How do you know when you are ready to begin introducing them to your broader team? There are signs that will indicate you are ready. You will notice that the amount of tweaking and reexamination slows down or stops. You may still have some open questions, but you shouldn't have any blank sections in your foundation document that are truly critical to your product domain. The personas will just *feel* right to you and your core team. In addition, your stakeholders should have signed off on your work. They now agree that no critical audience is missing and that the personas are robust, credible, and in line with your business objectives.

If your creation process took several weeks to several months, it may be that your product planning and design is now underway—or worse, that coding has begun. If so, it is likely that your broader team is becoming eager to obtain information about your target audience. They may be asking for you to deliver your personas ASAP. All of these things tell you that you are ready to deliver—that the *birth and maturation* phase should start. *Birth and maturation* is the phase in which you not only introduce your personas to the team but begin a persona communication campaign. At this time you introduce the persona method and other UCD techniques, many of which will directly employ your personas (possibly changing the team's design and development process forever).

SUMMARY

The *conception and gestation* phase of the persona lifecycle involves a great deal of activity, teamwork, and decision making. You have become an alchemist, combining data, assumptions, and your understanding of what will and will not work in your company to create a rich set of design targets. You have translated raw data into information, and that information into prioritized categories and subcategories of users. You have created a set of personas that combines fact and fiction to reflect your business priorities and convey the essential information about your target users you found in the data. As much as possible, you have with explicit links to the original data supported every important characteristic and statement found in your foundation documents. Last, you have done validation work before finalizing your personas.

As we have stated several times previously, we believe very strongly that personas should be based on data. Even the *perception* that the personas are not based on data can damage their credibility and utility. However, it is practically unavoidable that some elements of personas are generated from educated guesses or are simply made up. Your job in the *conception and gestation* phase is to make informed decisions about how much fiction and storytelling is needed to make your personas feel real and be truly engaging. Creating personas involves straightforward fact gathering, but there is also an art to it. Be inventive, but also be practical and stay as close to your data as possible. Even assumption-based personas can be highly valuable if they are agreed-upon and visible targets.

Once your personas are complete, substantive, and stable, you have only just begun. You are now ready to begin the education process. Communicating your personas will take time and effort. You will have to be strategic, persistent, and patient. Once your personas are out there, they will need to actively participate in the design and development process (the *adulthood* phase of personas). Your personas are ready to be born. Labor can be painful.

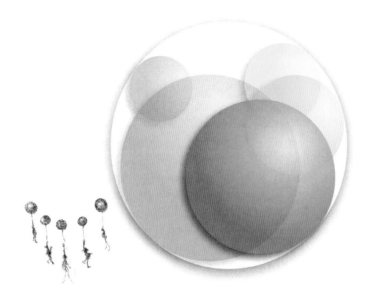

5

PERSONA BIRTH AND MATURATION

Giving people the wrong information at the wrong time is like trying to teach a pig to sing. It wastes your time and it annoys the pig.

— adapted from Paul Dickson

SETTING THE SCENE—WHAT'S GOING ON IN YOUR ORGANIZATION NOW?

You have likely been planning and creating personas for a little while now. Unless you started your persona work well before this new product cycle began, the rest of your organization has not been sitting still, waiting for the fruits of your efforts to enlighten them. Instead, they are well on their way to defining a product, perhaps even starting to build it already. You may have been regularly asked if you are done yet: "We need those target user definitions yesterday!"

Overall, by this time, the product team is beginning to settle into their work. People are more confident in what they are tasked to do and they are beginning to do it. As such, each team member is getting focused on his or her own responsibilities.

- The executive staff is has provided at least a draft of the high-level direction and vision for the product. By including members of the executive staff in reviews of the provisional target users in the last lifecycle phase (*conception and gestation*), you helped them get clarity on their own thinking related to target audience. They are now in the process of defining the product schedule more accurately.

- The product and project managers are busy defining requirements, determining functionality (feature lists), investigating possible implementation issues, and creating schedules. They have solid ideas about what they are going to build, even though the target audience has not been defined clearly for them.

- The development team is finally starting to focus on this new product or version. Most of the issues from the last release are solved or deferred.

- The QA team is also now fully preparing for this upcoming effort. They are redeploying their resources, retooling, and finishing a few one-off projects that were possible after the last release cycle.

- Usability specialists, technical writers, and UI designers have been very active during this phase, doing either forward-looking user research (field work, focus groups, surveys, and so on) or exploratory design projects.

- The marketing team is now engaged in forward-looking market research, as they have also finally engaged with the work toward a new product or "next version."

At this point, many people in your organization would greatly benefit from having a clear definition of the target audience. It is probably the case that only key individuals and your stakeholders have seen the gory details of what you are up to.

If the *conception and gestation* phase went well, you now have a set of personas in hand and you are more than ready to unveil them to your product team. You have answered some

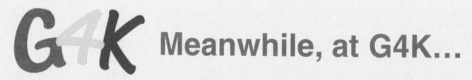

Meanwhile, at G4K...

THE G4K CORE TEAM IS ANXIOUS TO INTRODUCE THEIR PERSONAS

During the *conception and gestation* phase, the G4K persona core team analyzed their data, created several skeletons, and enriched those selected by their stakeholders into full personas. They are eager to show off the fruits of their labor to rest of the team. They want to make sure that their personas—Tanner (the tenacious tweener), Colbi (the creative child), Austin (the active competitor), Preston (the precocious preschooler), Irene (the involved parent), and Elaine (the enlightened teacher)—aren't ignored once development ensues.

tough questions about the persona method from your stakeholders and have done some enlightening reality check site visits, which confirmed that you are on target with your personas. You are ready to start the process of introducing your personas to the product team.

WHAT IS *BIRTH AND MATURATION* FOR PERSONAS?

Birth and maturation is perhaps one of the trickiest phases of the persona lifecycle. It marks the transition from persona creation to persona use. During the *birth and maturation* phase, information about your complete personas is sent off into your organization to interact with other people. Your personas are fully formed but will now begin to develop in the minds of your product team. Although introducing personas to your organization may seem straight-forward, it usually isn't.

The most important thing to remember during *birth and maturation* is that personas are effective only if you can make them come alive for your colleagues. You just spent a lot of time creating rich, detailed foundation documents with a fully bought-in persona core team, and now you and your core team must understand that almost no one else in your organization will ever read the foundation documents from end to end (and at most they will read them only once). So, you will need to progressively (and strategically) disclose information about each persona in small, highly digestible chunks. You will educate your colleagues on the very specific ways they can (and should) use the persona information in their day-to-day work. The *birth and maturation* phase of the persona lifecycle consists of three distinct activities.

- *Step 1: Enrich your communication strategy (prepare for birth and beyond).* During *family planning*, you created a communication strategy to help you communi-cate the basic value of personas to a possibly less-than-interested audience (see Chapter 3). During step 1 of *birth and maturation*, you must transition from a relatively heads-down period of hard work and creativity, with a core team that is already convinced of the usefulness of personas, to a period of heads-up, active evangelism.

- *Step 2: Introduce the persona method and your personas (birth)*. During *birth*, you and your core team will put your communication strategy to work as you embark on a communication campaign. You will introduce the persona method, your reasons for creating the personas, and basic information about the personas you have created and how you expect them to be used.

- *Step 3: Progressively educate and maintain focus on your personas (maturation)*. During *maturation*, you will progressively disclose persona details, persona uses, and persona benefits. Your personas really come to life during this phase. During maturation, your job is to help your colleagues as they prepare to incorporate the personas into their design and development processes.

We recommend that you read about all three steps before you complete your own communication strategy. During steps 2 and 3, you and your team will create and distribute persona artifacts. For easy reference and comparison, we have included information about all artifacts in support of *birth and maturation* activities (including G4K's communication strategy) later in this chapter.

STEP 1: PREPARE FOR BIRTH AND BEYOND

The key to success during the *birth and maturation* phase is a willingness on your part to step back, look around, and remember that people outside your core team are going to need a lot of help with the personas you have created. Your colleagues need to understand what personas are, why you are asking them to use personas, and how to integrate personas into their already packed work schedules. In an organization with existing user-centered processes, your strategy may be quick and fairly straightforward. In an organization new to the idea of UCD, your tasks during the *birth and maturation* phase may be more onerous.

It is time to revisit the action plan you created during the *family planning* phase (see Chapter 3) and enrich your communication strategy with specific plans you will put into action in a persona "communication campaign." Your communication strategy should address who, what, when, and how: who you need to communicate the personas to, what information each audience will need, when you will present each type of information, and how you will convey the information. To build an effective communication strategy, you and your core team should think not only back to the work you did during family planning but ahead to your plans for *birth, maturation, adulthood*, and beyond.

When you are ready to create your enriched communication strategy, first refer back to the information you uncovered from organizational introspection and the resulting action plan you derived from it during *family planning* (see Chapter 3, "Creating an action plan").

During *family planning*, you did organizational introspection and used the resulting insights to create for your team an action plan that included:

- Definition of the scope of the project and the associated goals for the persona core team
- Description of a communication strategy
- Listing of milestones and deliverables.

When you created a communication strategy to include in your action plan, you prepared yourself and your team to answer the following questions:

- What is the persona method, and why does it work?
- Who are your personas?
- How were your personas built, and why did you build them that way?
- How should your personas be used during the design and development of your product?

Although the communication strategy in your action plan should cover the entire lifecycle, most of your critical persona communication work will be done during the *birth and maturation* phase.

Enrich your communication strategy

In the beginning of your persona project, you were very selective about who you involved and how you invited their involvement. Now, as you embark on your communication campaign, you are essentially planning how to leverage the original buy-in you created. Think of your communication campaign as the work you do to create a set of ever-widening concentric circles of buy-in. The more top-down (or, in the concentric-circle metaphor, the more center-out) involvement you get the better. The more your stakeholders treat the persona information as familiar and useful the more likely it is that the rest of your organization will as well. Attempt to align your goals with corporate/business goals so that stakeholders see something familiar or something they can relate to.

Your communication strategy is your plan for your communication campaign. Your complete communication strategy should not only describe all of the activities and materials you will need to achieve your communication campaign goals but relate the timing of those events and content. In your communication strategy, include a specific schedule of the activities, presentations, and distribution of materials you will use to achieve your goals. Your plan should be fully dependent on the schedule of milestones in your product development cycle (refer back to the "Identify milestones and deliverables" section of Chapter 3). Your communication strategy should include the following.

Goals for the communication campaign:

○ Support the action plan created during *family planning.*

○ Introduce the persona method, help colleagues understand the reason we are using personas for this project, and provide the right amount of background on how we created the personas we are about to introduce.

○ Bring the personas to life in the minds of all colleagues who influence the design and development of the product (or whichever subset of these people you decide to focus on).

○ Progressively disclose the right information to the right people at the right time to ensure that the user data embedded in the personas is understood and absorbed.

○ Ensure that the personas are used during the decision-making process in whatever ways you and your core team determine (see Chapter 6).

Communication strategy (who, what, when, and how):

○ *Identify who:* Who are the audiences for your personas? Are there different audiences with different needs?

○ For each audience, identify

▪ *What:* What specific information about the personas do these individuals need? Identify the subsets of the persona-related information you believe will be most helpful to each audience.

▪ *When:* When should you introduce the various types of information to this audience? After you have introduced the persona basics, when is the best time to introduce *new* or *enriched* information about the personas into your development cycle?

▪ *How:* How should you and your core team communicate various aspects of the personas and the ways they can be used? What are the best ways to deliver persona-related information so that it will actually be "consumed"?

In this section, we discuss the work you will do to prepare your core team and stakeholders for the birth of your personas. In step 2, we include suggestions for introducing the persona method and the personas into your organization. In step 3, we provide recommendations for progressively disclosing information about your personas to bring them to life in your organization.

Creating your communication strategy and realizing the strategy in a communication campaign don't have to take a long time. Your plan can be as short as a few notes on which topics you need to address, or as long as a detailed set of presentations you will deliver to various audiences. You can choose to cover all four of the important topics listed previously in a single meeting if that is appropriate for your situation.

Bright Idea

SET A GOAL TO ELIMINATE THE WORD "USER" FROM YOUR ORGANIZATION

It is fine to say that the goal of the persona campaign is to ensure that everyone in your organization knows your target users and customers—but that is a fairly abstract goal. One could argue that all UCD professionals have been working toward this basic goal in all of our activities for years. We believe a far more measurable and actionable goal for your persona communication campaign is to eliminate the word *user* from all communication and planning artifacts related to your product and replace it with the persona names.

Simply replacing all instances of the word *user* with persona names may seem too simplistic to express your ongoing and larger goals. However, the simplicity of this goal is deceptive. Banishing the word *user* in favor of persona names in all communication artifacts—from hallway conversations to design wireframes, storyboards, strategy documents, full technical specification documents, and so on—is more easily said than done.

We think this goal is handy because it is simple to understand and inherently measurable. It is not difficult to identify all communication artifacts related to any product, and it is not difficult to assess whether the word *user* appears in these artifacts (with the exception, perhaps, of measuring whether the word *user* continues to appear in casual and undocumented conversations regarding the product). However, to achieve this goal you must convince each of the owners of each of the communication media—right down to the people having casual conversations in the hallways—that banishing the word *user* is a good idea, that the alternatives are easy enough to use and will not get in the way of "real work," and that the incorporation of these alternatives (especially persona names) increases the value of communication artifacts.

As a simple measure of ROI, count the before-and-after references to "user." That is, keep a record of how many references to the word user (and any similar words, such as *actor* in UML documents, *customer*, or any synonym your company uses) you find in the documentation for the last project. When you are finished with your current project, you will be able to show that you have eliminated user in favor of much more specific terms (e.g., the persona names), and you will be able to point to ways in which the product documents are clearer and more helpful. For example, when persona names are referenced in use cases, there is no confusion about which '*user*' the use case refers to. In addition, you can point out that the use of persona names in documents helps keep everyone on the product team focused on the personas and the particular needs and goals of each, rather than on an inspecific '*user.*' This can help you prove the ROI of the persona effort in terms of improvements to your company's internal processes (for example, you can describe ways the addition of a specific user-related lexicon allowed the team to create documents that required fewer revisions; see Chapter 7 for more details.)

Clearly, no one can get every artifact owner in an organization to replace the word *user* after a single presentation on personas. That is why you need a strategy for your communication campaign. You need to set your sights on measurable goals and create presentation and persona materials to help you achieve them.

Bright Idea

DON'T SURPRISE STAKEHOLDERS IN PUBLIC

—Sarah Bloomer,
The MathWorks

Don't surprise stakeholders in public. If you present to a group of stakeholders, make sure those who might be key or most directly impacted by your proposals have heard and responded beforehand. I have found that doing this groundwork leads to a better result and avoids potentially alienating a key champion.

Keep stakeholders "in the know"

Clarifying your own goals is important. Making sure that your goals jive with the current business or product goals is critical. As you develop your communication strategy, remember to involve (or at least inform) the key stakeholders who can help to make or break your communication campaign. During the *family planning* and *conception and gestation* phases, you identified (and in many cases involved) key stakeholders in your persona project.

Make sure these stakeholders are aware of your plans and understand that you are about to stir things up a bit by introducing this new persona method to additional teams. Consider enlisting the help of a more senior team member who understands the organization, culture, and players. During your meetings with stakeholders, remember to ask them about their thoughts, plans, and any important changes that could affect the persona effort. Stakeholders need to keep their fingers on the pulse of the organization. It is a good idea to keep your fingers on the pulse of the stakeholders.

The best way to ensure top-down involvement is to make sure that key stakeholders are well aware of your goals and how you plan to pursue those goals. Although stakeholders may like the idea of personas in the abstract, they may be dismayed to hear that you want to change, for example, the way product design documents are written. Make sure stakeholders are aware of what you are trying to do, why you are trying to do it, and what measurable goals you have set and the plans you have to see those goals to fruition. Create a draft communication plan—complete with goals, possible measures of ROI, etc.—and obtain feedback from stakeholders. You will be surprised how many political landmines stakeholders can help you avoid with their view of the big picture and an understanding of the pressures being exerted on the various teams you will be talking to.

Evaluate your audiences and determine <u>who</u> needs <u>what</u> information

During family planning, you analyzed the audiences for your personas: the individuals and groups that comprise your organization. You identified obstacles to your persona effort, including people you thought would resist the personas, the inertia of various work habits and processes, and other environmental factors. Now it is time to take a close look at the findings of your analysis and to get creative. It is time to enhance your communication strategy to account for all of the obstacles you have identified and your best guesses about what types of information different people in your organization will respond to. First, evaluate how many different audiences and needs really exist in your organization.

- What are the major divisions, roles, and disciplines on your product team?

- Do these people and groups already understand anything at all about users and UCD? What are their work goals and challenges?

- Which parts of the product development process do they have ownership over?
- What types of information about the personas would help them in their job?
- When do you think they will have time and mental energy to devote to learning about personas?

You will probably find that the answers to these questions can vary quite radically from group to group and role to role, and that it makes sense to create slightly different strategies for communicating the personas to different sets of colleagues. You will probably deliver some of your education on a broad level—to everyone at once—but you might want to follow up with smaller meetings involving people with shared interests.

For example, the agenda for the product managers may be quite different from the agenda for the developers. Product managers will understand the value of the personas quite quickly, but will be interested in how much buy-in you have on the persona process throughout the organization. Developers are more likely to ask a lot of questions about how and why you created the personas and how they relate to data, how you expect them to use the personas, and the dangers of designing for the "wrong" persona. Create a schedule for the delivery of persona-related information appropriate to the various teams and key team members in your organization.

Handy Detail

WHO IS THE PRIMARY AUDIENCE FOR PERSONAS?

We asked 25 experienced persona practitioners, a mix of user experience consultants and in-house specialists, who they thought the primary audience was for their persona efforts. The resulting list of audiences in order of priority was:

1. Designers
2. Program/product managers
3. Developers/engineers
4. Executives, business strategists, and "clients"
5. Marketing.

Many of these practitioners noted that these audiences were important at different times in the development cycle (executives early on for funding and go-ahead approval, product managers throughout, developers starting in the middle onward, and marketing later). Of course, there are plenty of other audiences for your efforts and we strongly believe you should strategically seek

(Handy detail, continued)

those out (e.g., QA testing, user assistance/documentation, market research, product planning, product support, and so on). The following are quotes from practitioners on this subject:

> *In our experience, developers tend to use the names for communication purposes. Other users—such as QA, usability, and tech writers—seem to use more of the persona characteristics in writing tests, user guides, and creating application user interfaces.*
>
> —Holly Jamesen Carr, *GreenShape LLC*, formerly Usability Specialist, *Attenex Corporation*

> *The developers refer to the persona most, so it is mostly geared to them. I included QA and documentation because they might refer to it.*
>
> —Lori Landesman, *The MathWorks*

> *Aside from the usual things people need from personas, here are some differences I've observed:*
> * *Marketing folks are more interested in purchase motivators and the context in which the decision to buy is made*
> * *Executives use the personas in road shows as evidence 'that our organization actually knows how to walk the walk of being customer centered.'*
> * *QA looks for the core tasks that people perform, so that they can build robust test cases early in the project.*
> * *Usability specialists use them to create task descriptions and scenarios and to determine criteria for recruiting test participants.*
> * *Project managers look for clues to help them prioritize work, and to ideally remove work entirely from the project schedule.*
>
> —Bob Barlow-Busch, *Quarry*

> *From what we've seen so far, the executives don't tend to read the profiles, they just want to know that they are there. Marketing tends to focus on the demographic and buying pattern related information. However, in general everyone is focusing on the overall picture of the user so tailoring the persona to the different audiences is currently less of a concern.*
>
> —Bob Murata, *Adobe*

As you can imagine, each audience will have its own needs and interests related to the personas. Product planners and marketing are interested in purchasing behavior, desired features, and influence. Designers are interested in effect, style, brands, and preferences. Usability and market research need participant screeners (high-level must-have characteristics) for recruiting in studies, interviews, and focus groups. Executives want the market characteristics, revenue projections, and demographic data related to these personas as customer segments. Moreover, and as you will see in the next chapter, each will need to have specific ways of using your personas spelled out for them.

CREATE PERSONAS TO REPRESENT YOUR INTERNAL COMMUNICATION TARGETS

As you build your communication plan, you are spending a lot of time gathering and assessing data and assumptions. Sound familiar? You have just been through the *conception and gestation* phase to build the personas that represent the users of your product. You might want to take an hour or two to create quick personas to represent your organizational colleagues. These quick personas can include job descriptions, current pressures, work habits, and so on. These can help your core team build a user-centered communication plan. Don't go overboard here. Your goal is not to create a fantastic set of personas to represent your co-workers. Don't get too detailed or personal, and think twice before you share these internal personas with anyone other than your core team. You don't want your colleagues' reactions to how they themselves were represented to taint their impressions of the real personas.

Birth can be a "private" event if necessary

If the answers to the questions in the previous section lead you to believe that no one in your organization is going to be receptive to any persona-related information and that nothing you can do will change this, you may decide not to publicly announce your personas. There are many reasons to keep personas visible to only select people, even if you have spent a great deal of time creating and perfecting them and are antsy to put them to work. The fact that you have put so much effort into your personas is a great reason to be cautious before sharing them with others.

In Chapter 3, we talked about the importance of the first impression the personas make. If you are sure your organization as a whole will simply not welcome the personas into your development processes no matter what you do, you do have other options. It could be that in the time it took to create the personas your development team raced ahead and it feels too late to use the personas for the current project. Perhaps a very vocal co-worker is actively advocating a different new development process. There are always obstacles to introducing personas as a new method, and you shouldn't balk at the challenges these obstacles produce. However, remember that your goal during *birth* is to introduce the personas in order for them to help your colleagues in their work. If you really believe that the obstacles you face in introducing the personas to your organization are currently insurmountable, consider alternatives so that the personas can live to emerge another day.

Planning for limited exposure is an alternative when the timing for launching personas to everyone just *feels* wrong. Launching your personas to select individuals, people who will be able to use them right now to make important decisions, will help you argue the benefits of personas to a larger group later.

Story from the field

GIVING BIRTH QUIETLY

—Noel Holmes, Director, Customer Experience, Travelocity.com

To firmly establish the personas as part of the extended family, we found it very helpful to make the persona creation a group effort that included members from research, business, user interface, and design. However, our personas have had a very quiet delivery. There were no birth announcements or baby pictures (cardboard cutouts or postings on the intranet). We have been introducing them to one product team at a time in an effort to get the teams to take ownership. We keep our personas alive by asking various teams and individuals to contribute on a continuing basis to their care and feeding.

Story from the field

PERSONAS EFFORTS DON'T ALWAYS NEED A LOT OF HOOPLA

—Sarah Bloomer, The MathWorks

I was a director of the consulting company The Hiser Group for many years and since about 1991 personas have been key to our success (though we call them "user profiles"). Unless we could describe the target users, we weren't sure we understood them. We wrote "activity scenarios" to place these users into a context of use. We didn't do a formal launch or marketing of personas, but the design team would discuss them by name during design sessions. We also involved a "champion" (or "shadow") from our client company, who worked side by side with us so that they took ownership of the user profiles and "owned" them when we left the project. We never had to convince our clients of the usefulness of personas. Rather, they were a way to validate that we understood the problem and design issues. Moreover, they served as a fundamental communication device that gave us a common language: "Mark, the novice customer service rep, would benefit from that level of just-in-time help, whereas Marge, the expert, needs to be able to turn it off."

Story from the field

YOUR TEAM WILL NEED SPECIFIC TRAINING TO USE PERSONAS

—Matthew Lee, Usability Engineer, InfoSpace, Inc.

Product management and development need training and presentations to understand why they should use personas. At a financial services company I worked for, we found great interest from marketing (who desired better tools to focus their marketing efforts), but product development did not have that same desire. They needed to be shown how the data could be useful in order to help them create products that best fit the needs of their consumers. Only now, six months after initially presenting the personas and their value, is there traction and desire for understanding and using the personas among the development staff.

Be realistic about your timing

While you were working on the first two persona lifecycle phases, a lot may have changed. The overall vision might have evolved, tactical plans may have solidified, and coding may have already started. Now that you are ready to introduce the personas, is your organization really ready for them? Where exactly are you in your development cycle? If you find that the development cycle is already pretty far along before you start communicating anything, don't create a long and complicated communication strategy. Instead, create a "just-in-time" education approach. Instead of planning to carefully introduce each group to the personas in the order they will use them, approach the specific owners of the *next* document or artifact in the product development cycle. For example, if the product vision or technical specification documents have already been written, talk to the designers and try to convince them to incorporate the personas' names into wireframes, storyboards, and visual prototypes.

More generally, you don't want to lose your window of opportunity to contribute the personas at a time when they will be useful and used in the overall development process. If you take too long in creating them, the rest of the team will be so far ahead that your work will not be useful or used. You have to stay very much in tune with where the rest of the project is and with all that is happening politically. You may even need to introduce your skeletons (or brief sketches based on them) before enriching them into full personas.

(Story from the field, continued)

The fact that it was designed for a very specific customer that did not represent the typical customer shop was not considered. The facts that the team that built it had to spend weeks holding the hands of the customer's staff to get it going there and that the company could certainly not afford to do that for all of its customers were not considered. We were shut down. The interim product went forward as *the* product, with no usability activities at all. Of course, it was eventually abandoned because it could not be used without extensive training by all small customers—but that is typical of many software projects.

The Moral: It does no good to spend a great deal of time "doing it right" if the developers are not going to wait and are going to plunge ahead without you—and if the executives don't understand the difference.

Story from the field

EXTREME PROGRAMMING ALMOST KILLED OUR PERSONAS

—Holly Jameson, GreenShape LLC, formerly Usability Specialist, Netpodium, Inc.

Our greatest failure with personas at Netpodium occurred when persona creation and user scenario mapping virtually vanished from our software development process. This happened because from the executive staff on down the focus was on trying extreme programming. No value was placed on personas or task analysis, and when we suggested that these tools could complement extreme programming the push-back that we got was that "it would take too much time." We created a set of personas anyway, and had the opportunity to make them useful about halfway through the development cycle. When the programming process settled into a hybrid process and the coders needed questions answered regarding the user interface, we were ready for them.

Prepare the core persona team for their new roles in birth and beyond

When you have a plan, you and your core team need to switch gears from analysis to action. You need to transition from "creation mode" to "communication mode." It is understandable that some teams never make the transition from persona planning and creation to active and ongoing communication. Core team members used to the heads-down, highly collaborative, core-team-only, detailed conception and gestation work don't turn into heads-up progressive disclosers without some thought and direction. Even teams who do manage the transition are often unprepared for the ongoing responsibilities related to supporting and promoting personas.

Persona core team members transition into "persona wranglers"

Until now, your team's ownership of the persona process and the personas has been complete and insular. As the persona creators, you and your core team made all decisions (with some input or approval from your stakeholders)—from what data to use to how many personas to create to how to structure the foundation documents. For personas to flourish in your organization, you must allow your other colleagues to take some ownership of the personas and the processes surrounding their use. As you launch into *birth and maturation* activities, you also have to be prepared to share ownership of the personas and take on the role of "persona wrangler."

We use the term *wrangler* here purposefully. Like the InfoWranglers that Saul Carliner describes in his 1998 article [Carliner 1998], persona wranglers must "act as messengers in the communication process…. The work of the InfoWrangler solves a business problem; it does not merely document the system…." In his discussion of sharing user profiles, Kuniavsky also recommends creating the role of wrangler:

> Although you can share a lot of information, there is always going to be more information than everyone can remember. A profile wrangler (or profile keeper) position can be useful for centralizing the information. The wrangler is present during the profile creation process and is responsible for keeping profiles updated. He or she also serves as a resource for interpreting profiles to the development team ("What would Jeff think about a Palm Pilot download option?") [Kuniavsky 2003, p. 153].

As persona wranglers, your core team will be responsible for maintaining the integrity of the personas (and their underlying data) without standing in the way of their acceptance and use by your colleagues. You will need to ensure that your personas are known, accepted, and utilized. It is not an easy task.

Assign a wrangler for each persona

Assign ownership (really, "wranglership") of each persona to a single team member. If you don't have enough core team members to assign every persona to a different individual, you can assign more than one persona to each team member, or you can consider enlisting people outside the persona core team. The fewer personas each team member has to

wrangle the better. Each wrangler should become the absolute expert and identified go-to person for the persona they own. The team member should assume responsibility for fully knowing and maintaining the foundation document for his or her assigned persona. This is not to say that each wrangler will make all decisions related to updates and revisions, but he or she will be the person to bring the need for a correction or update to the attention of the core team, and will make the eventual alteration to the official version of the foundation document.

Why assign a wrangler for each persona? Why not let the core team as a group maintain all personas? Because the transition into *birth* requires that you, the overall persona champion/owner, shift your attention from the details of each persona to the grand challenges of communication and facilitation with your colleagues. It will become more and more difficult to keep track of all details incorporated into all personas. Assigning individual wranglers ensures that each persona will have at least one team member who maintains a deep understanding of that persona's details and data. This frees you to take care of broader issues. The wrangler's job is to:

- Field questions regarding the persona from the organization
- Track down the answers to these questions (in collaboration with the core team)
- Communicate the answers as needed
- Revise foundation documents or other materials as applicable.

For example, if someone asks, "Does Laura have a wireless network? I didn't see the answer to that in the materials," Laura's wrangler should be ready to reply: "Good question! Let me find some data on that" (and follow up). Note that not all questions and issues with your personas need to be immediately addressed. So that such issues do not become overwhelming, you might want to have a weekly or monthly meeting to collectively prioritize and discuss such issues.

Agree on which persona characteristics must be protected

Although you must maintain the integrity of the data, you must also invite your colleagues to "adopt" the personas as resources. Your carefully crafted personas may change a bit during the *birth and maturation* process and throughout *adulthood*. In fact, one of the powerful aspects of personas is that they are generative and extendable (a notion we introduced in Chapter 4, "Handy Detail: Determining Where Personas Stop and Scenarios Begin," and further elaborate upon in Chapter 6, where we discuss the use of personas in scenarios, Maps, and storyboards). Your personas will be put into new contexts, complete new tasks, and accomplish their goals in new ways as they are applied to the design of your product. Your team members will push the boundaries of your personas to fit the needs of the domain they are working in and to answer the questions that arise about their specific areas.

This extension is good—and dangerous. You must be ready to decide which changes and extensions are acceptable and which are not. There is a fine balance here. You have to protect the data, but you also have to be willing to accept some changes. Without assigned wranglers, foundation documents can easily become dated and lose some of their utility as reference materials. As your team focuses on communication, education, and the creation of new persona artifacts, you will all have less and less time to concentrate as a group on the foundation documents. Because each wrangler is fully responsible for maintaining and revising the foundation document as new data surfaces, you will not have to worry about important details falling through the cracks.

STEP 2: BIRTH

Birth is the introduction of your personas to the product team, which you will achieve by launching a communication campaign based on your communication strategy. *Birth* should include an organized and ongoing series of educational, political, and tactical activities that help your colleagues understand what you have been doing, what the personas are and how they enable UCD, how they fit into your existing processes, and how you will continue to support the use of personas as the product development efforts gear up and proceed. You must fully convince colleagues who may never have heard of personas or their benefits, and you must do so relatively quickly. Problems during the *birth and maturation* phase can lead to lack of acceptance and to personas that die on the vine. Worse, a single failed persona effort can sour your organization and therefore make your job a lot more difficult in future persona efforts and even in regard to other UCD techniques.

Handy Detail

REMEMBER THAT UCD PROFESSIONALS ARE TERRITORIAL!

During one of the persona workshops, we had an interesting discussion about the territoriality of UCD professionals. We all agreed—about ourselves!—that we often have difficulty letting go and allowing others to influence our pet projects, and that this could get in the way of persona birth and maturation. This could be because we've had to spend so much time arguing for and defending the value of what we do and ensuring that our opinions are valued for the experience and data behind them. If you think you and your core team are feeling territorial, it might be worth having a frank conversation with the broader product team. Figure out what aspects of the personas you should be territorial about (e.g., the information you have derived directly from the data) and which details you are willing to let go of. Discuss the larger goals of the persona project, which should include improving communication among the various teams in your organization.

Introduce user-centered design, the persona method, and your persona project

You will need to communicate three related-yet-distinct topics before finally introducing your specific personas:

- The benefits and methods of user-centered product design (UCD evangelism)
- Basic information about the persona method (persona method evangelism)
- How the persona method will fit into and enhance your existing processes (the persona method in context).

These can be covered together in a single kickoff meeting to your entire product team or in separate meetings over time. Your communication challenges with each of these topics will depend on several factors, including:

- Your specific goals
- The differences in your audiences' current level of knowledge and interest
- The timing of the communication relative to the progress of your product development cycle.

Similarly, the types of materials and communication strategies that will work best for you will vary. In the following sections we include a variety of suggestions for you to choose from.

Communicate the benefits of user-centered product design

Birth can be a golden opportunity to educate your colleagues on the benefits and methods of UCD. Consider spending some time describing and discussing your organization's current commitment to and understanding of UCD. Is your organization already committed to UCD? If so, your personas will be just one of many user-centered methodologies in your development process. Does your organization talk about being user or customer centered but lack concrete processes to back this up? Or is the entire concept of user-centered product design relatively new for your organization?

We recommended in Chapter 3 that you surface assumptions about target users of your products. Now take time to understand how much your colleagues really know (and don't know) about creating user-centered products. Talk to colleagues and find out exactly how much each group knows and does not know about the UCD process. The results of this investigation might surprise you. It is an unusual company or product development group that does not call itself "dedicated to our users/customers" or "user/customer focused"—but it is also an unusual company that truly walks the walk with embedded and supported UCD processes. If you conducted a UCD questionnaire, as described in Chapter 3, the results of that survey can be used here.

If there are already other user-centered methods incorporated into your development process—such as field research, contextual inquiry, user testing, surveys, and focus groups (see the Usability.Net site at *www.usabilitynet.org/tools/methods.htm* for a complete list)—your challenge will be to help people understand how personas will enhance and in some cases alter the existing processes. It is your job to evaluate when and how (within the overall development process) current UCD methods are employed and to propose changes to integrate the personas. (See Chapter 6 for examples of how personas can be used in conjunction with other UCD methods.)

If your organization talks about being user centered but doesn't currently have any user-centered methods integrated into the development process, or if the entire concept of user-centered product design is relatively new to your organization, you have a bigger challenge. In these cases, you may want to educate your organization on practical UCD and why you think UCD methods will make good business sense for your company. There are several books on the market that make a strong case for UCD. For example, see the books by Donoghue [2002], Garrett [2002], Hackos and Redish [1998], Kuniavsky [2003], Mayhew [1999], Preece et al. [2002], and Vredenburg et al. [2001] in the References at the back of the book. Although you and your core team might want to read these books cover to cover, remember that the rest of your colleagues will only have time and patience to read summaries or listen to a short presentation.

It is also possible that broaching the subject of UCD is too much for your organization at this point. The success of your persona effort does not necessarily depend on broad UCD commitment from your organization. This is a topic you may want to start pursuing either very early on (e.g., during *family planning*) or even after the current development cycle is complete (i.e., after your personas have provided some utility and user focus for your team). Again, an understanding of your organizational culture and the potential acceptance of UCD should influence your decisions here—whether UCD is overt or covert (usability/UCD "by stealth"), whether a champion needs to participate, or whether it needs to be labeled something different (such as "continuous improvement" or "market-driven design") to meet with better acceptance.

Communicate the benefits of using personas

During family planning, when you created a communication strategy to include in your action plan, you prepared yourself and your team to answer the following questions:

- What is the persona method, and why does it work?
- Who are your personas?
- How were your personas built, and why did you build them that way?
- How should your personas be used during the design and development of your product?

Why take the time to evangelize the persona method in general? Why not dive in and talk about the ways personas can be used in your organization and for your products? One reason for evangelizing is that the persona method is still quite young

EVERYONE ELSE IS TERRITORIAL TOO!

UCD professionals are certainly not the only territorial people in your organization. Even though you have been strategic in thinking about who is likely to be resistant to the persona effort, you are still going to come across people who are resistant to the idea of anyone or anything having the power to trump their opinions when it comes to decision making. Personas do tend to change the corporate culture, and this is a big deal. As a persona specialist, you also have to become a change manager. Approach people by focusing on the benefits of personas with respect to colleagues' jobs and responsibilities. For example, consider focusing on the ways personas can help get some of the less interesting work off people's plates. For example, remind developers that personas are worth trying even if all they do is make meetings more productive and product requirements clearer. Be patient and let the use and acceptance of personas evolve. Don't expect too much too soon. Be aware that change management is a large and complex topic, and that trying to encourage and manage change can be quite difficult unless you have a certain amount of power and influence in your organization. If you are interested in learning more about methods and tools for change management, see Davidson [2001], Hiatt and Creasey [2003], Mouriere and Smith [2001], and Senge [1999].

and even controversial in some circles. There are some (very predictable) questions your colleagues will have. It is not easy to tackle these general questions and the specifics of how you would like to see personas used in your organization at the same time.

Return to the work you did during family planning to predict the particular benefits personas would bring to your organization. Also revisit the "Persona Rude Q&A" list of questions (see Chapter 3). As you review these questions, think about which of these questions you should "head off at the pass" by addressing them in your persona kickoff meeting. It is likely that questions you and your core team discussed and debated during your conception and gestation work will be the same questions you are faced with as you introduce the persona method to the rest of your organization.

Communicate the specifics of your persona effort

After you have educated your organization on the principles of UCD and have introduced the persona method, you will want to talk more specifically about how you see personas fitting into your organization's processes. Your colleagues will want to know how you developed the personas for your organization, and they will want to know what process changes you expect them to make to accommodate the personas.

How your personas came into being

Before your introduce the personas and encourage people to use them, you should "open up the books" and tell people about your persona effort thus far. Let them know the following things:

● Who is on the persona core team, and why you invited these particular people to participate as members (as opposed to other individuals or a large group).

- The process you used to identify data sources, gather data, and analyze data (or the process you used to identify and evaluate assumptions), and what those data sources are. Offer to share the data.

- How you validated, or plan to validate, the personas.

- How you plan to measure the internal ROI of the persona process (and impact on the costs of development).

In other words, help everyone understand where the personas came from before you introduce the personas themselves. This will help preempt questions related to the credibility of your work or process and the validity of your resulting personas.

How your personas will fit in to your existing development cycle

If you are trying to create a more user-centered organization, you probably have a lot of ideas related to improving the product development cycle. You probably wish that UCD professionals were involved earlier, that visits to customers were funded, that usability testing was accepted and scheduled early enough to make a real difference, and so on. Although many of these methods are linked, and successfully introducing one may increase the likelihood of introducing more, it is helpful to maintain focus and to not try to change too much all at once. Even if you think the current development process is riddled with problems you should still try to communicate the value of personas in the context of the development process as is. If you try to make too many changes at once, you will run the risk of alienating the very people critical to the success of the persona effort.

Simply introducing personas can—and should—have fairly significant effects on your development process, and you should take the time to envision all of its potential effects. (See Chapter 6 for an array of examples showing how personas can be directly used in design and development.) Once you have the big picture and a list of all possible changes the persona effort could engender, you need to take a close look at the list and decide which changes could have the most significant effect on the quality of the product.

The everyday benefits of personas

If you can prove that personas will make their lives easier, your colleagues will be much more likely to accept the personas into their everyday work. By citing examples of the daily benefits of personas your colleagues can easily identify with, you can start to prove that personas make things easier even before you introduce them.

- *It will become easier to communicate.* At the simplest level, the persona names will replace the word *user*. When we talk about the features and functions of our product, we will be able to use the persona names to communicate unambiguously about who we are building things for.

- *Decisions will be based on data, not opinions.* How many times have you been in meetings in which someone has said, "The user is never going to want this," or "Let's put our user hat on now?" Let's face it: when we argue about what "the user" wants we end up making decisions based on who in the room is loudest, the best arguer, the most powerful, or the most annoying. Personas will help us stop this pattern. Instead, we will be able to refer back to the data that is the source of the personas.

- *Data will be a lot easier to use.* Personas are memorable "digests" of data, and they help us remember to access relevant data at the right times. As we continue to gather new data and revisit old data sources, the personas will serve as the equalizers and homogenizers of disparate data sources. Old and new data will stay accessible and relevant as facets of the persona descriptions.

- *You will find new sources of inspiration.* Personas are deep and detailed descriptions of your target users. Just like real people, they have habits and personalities and you can get to know them well. Innovation can come from the combination of your technical knowledge and your observations related to unmet needs of real people.

- *You will find better ways of working with the Quality Assurance department to deliver a great product.* QA can write test cases based on the personas and the experiences the product is designed to support. Keeping test cases connected to personas guarantees that the QA staff focuses on the complete user experience of the product in addition to the technical underpinnings.

Introduce your personas

Once your product team is properly prepared, you will be ready to introduce the actual personas you have worked so hard to create. As you introduce the actual personas to your colleagues, you should embrace the notion of "progressive disclosure." The trick is to give everyone just the right amount of information to ignite their imaginations, enable them to continue doing their work (perhaps more easily than they did it before), and inspire them to come back for more information when they are ready for it. With that in mind, the real work of educating your teammates about the details of your personas really happens during step 3 (*maturation*) and runs through the end of persona *adulthood*.

In Chapter 3, we recommended that you create detailed foundation documents for all of your main personas. These foundation documents capture all information you have about your personas, including links to the data sources from which that information arose. Completed foundation documents are likely to be rich and complex, and as such do not make for light reading. You probably cannot expect everyone on your product team to read and remember every detail in these documents. You will have to prioritize and target the information you want your broad team to really know about your personas. Your personas live in the minds of your product team, not in some document or communication artifact. You will have to be strategic about how you make that happen effectively and efficiently.

The material following in this chapter lists and describes three categories of persona artifacts you and your core team can create (buzz generators, comparison facilitators, and enrichers). For *birth*, select a subset of these artifacts—primarily buzz generators and perhaps one

or two comparison facilitators—according to the communication strategy you have created. For example:

- If your organization is not very user-centered and people are potentially going to be resistant to the persona effort, create several buzz generators that introduce your personas and express the value of personas in general, perhaps including quotes taken from the sidebars in Chapter 7 of this book (which express the ROI others have derived from their persona effort). After these have been posted for a while, create some introduction posters that include important data points on them. Build a presentation that conveys how much data was used to create the personas, perhaps by including a slide that shows the long list of data sources you and your core team used. More generally, be sure to make the link between the personas and the data as clear as possible. The fact that you have used data as the foundation for the personas will speak volumes and will defuse most push-back related to the validity of the personas. Consider making a fact sheet to hand out with critical factoids about your target audience. Finally, make sure that copies of the original research reports are available to anyone who is interested.

- If your organization is likely to "get" personas quickly and be eager to learn more, start with more modest introduction posters and perhaps a few basic comparison facilitators. A little while after you introduce the personas, plan to use enrichers to communicate additional details centered on data points.

However you decide to introduce your personas, focus on the key attributes that define them and make sure to highlight the main differences among them. Plan to explain why these particular personas were chosen, reviewing the highlights of your evaluation and prioritization work in the *conception and gestation* phase. Consider discussing a few of the user categories, skeletons, or sketch personas that didn't make the cut (and explain why).

Story from the field

DEALING WITH MANY PERSONAS

—Tammy Snow, Robin Martin Emerson, Leslie Scott, Trinh Vo Yetzer, and
Dawn Baron, Windows Server, Microsoft Corporation

[In Chapter 4 (see "Story from the field: Developing Personas and Organizational Archetypes"), the Windows Server persona team described their approach to creating personas, which included organizational archetypes and a large number of unique personas. Here they discuss their approach to deploying these personas.]

Our approach to personas involved the creation of 32 unique personas subsumed under four organizational archetypes (i.e., four data-derived representations of companies). Such a large number of personas is obviously untenable by anyone on the product team. Fortunately, no one on our team is

(Story from the field, continued)

expected to deal with more than three or four personas in developing their features. We directly work with the various teams across our division to help them identify their target personas and then make use of those personas in defining, designing, and developing product features.

Choosing the Target Archetype

The first step is helping teams target the archetype their solution is most likely to benefit. We help teams do this by evaluating what their solution purports to provide against what the archetype is likely to need. For example, we have a team developing a solution designed to enable rapid deployment of the Windows Server operating system (see Figure 5.1) onto servers across large-scale installations. We therefore logically determined that their target archetype would be the large organization.

FIGURE 5.1: *Examples of posters used to evangelize Windows Server archetypes.*

Another example involves working with the team responsible for providing desktop software deployment services within the operating system via a service called Desktop Management Services (DMS). In this case, we know that we provide a value-added product called Software Management Services (SMS), which can be purchased as a separate product. We analyzed market research data about deployments of SMS in the various sizes of organization and determined that deployments are highest in large organizations, followed by upper medium (whereas core medium and small organizations rarely deploy SMS). Given this information, we targeted the core medium organization as the archetype for this feature team.

Choosing the Target Personas

The next step is to work with the team to choose their target personas. If we have data that describes how a feature or solution is used in IT organizations, we can pull from that to determine the target personas. If data does not exist, we work with the team to develop a hypothesis about their target personas and then conduct research to validate the personas. In the example of the deployment solution previously cited, we would target four of the large organization personas to design for. In the example of the desktop software deployment services, we looked at the two personas in the medium organization archetype and determined which of the two was most likely to perform software deployment to desktops. That persona became the target.

Ensuring That the Chosen Personas Are Relevant

In many cases, our personas may lack the level of detail needed by each feature team in defining, designing, and developing product features. This is due to the fact that we wanted to provide broad, general descriptions of our personas to enable usage by multiple teams. To accommodate each feature team, we provide research support or consultation to help them detail the personas appropriately. We have also developed a process for extending our core personas. This process involves allowing each team to use the core definition of the personas as they currently exist and then add feature-specific information based on their research. In cases for which we are unable to conduct the research for teams, we provide them with consultation services that include a discussion guide for their interviews with customers and interview training. Once they have completed their research, we provide guidance on data analysis and review their final written persona extension. When this is approved, we add the extended information as links from the core persona.

What if birth makes you realize something is wrong with the personas?

As you introduce your personas to the product team, the questions will start flying. For many of them, you will have solid answers. Others will be worth noting and will lead you to further research as you realize you need data to fill in some key characteristic. Still others will leave you dumbfounded, perhaps pointing out some flaw in your collective thinking. Hopefully you found most of the major issues as you reviewed the personas with your core team and stakeholders during *conception and gestation*, or perhaps during your reality check site visits. If there are now new small changes that need to be made, just make them. However, be sure you are thoughtful and careful about it. Reconvene the core team and discuss the changes before you make a final decision. If a major change does have to be made, our experience is that if you do it early in the process it won't be as much of a step backward as it might seem. Don't wait. It is good to just bite the bullet, make the necessary revision, and move on. Also, remember to plan for reintroduction of the personas after any major changes are made.

Don't assume that you can simply revise your communication artifacts with new information after a major change without announcing that the revisions have taken place.

In some cases, the changes required might be too large to integrate into the existing personas. Remember to respect the "personhood" of the personas. If you discover that you have created the "wrong" persona, it is a good idea to shelve the old persona completely—particularly the personal details that make him or her seem real—and create a new one based on existing and new information.

What if birth just doesn't work?

There is a slight but very real possibility that your personas and the persona method will be rejected by your broader product team. It may not happen overtly, but then again it may. Either way, you will need to adjust your plans, refocus your management's expectations, and mitigate your losses to maximize your existing investments. At the very least, you can use the personas in a small circle of colleagues—the smallest being just you and the core persona team. Our own experience with personas has led us to believe that our personas have been valuable toward our own job responsibilities, and that alone has been worth the effort.

Story from the field

WHEN PERSONAS WERE NOT FULLY EFFECTIVE—THE MASTERY,
APPROPRIATION, AND AUTHORITY OF A DESIGN TOOL

—Mattias Arvola, Interaction Design Researcher, Linköping University, Sweden

At a company we will call Q, a set of personas was created and attempts were made to use it as a design tool, but we found that the personas were not fully and effectively utilized. In this case study, we briefly describe what happened and provide some reasons for this outcome. (For additional information related to this case study, see Blomquist and Arvola [2002]).

A behavioral scientist who worked at Q developed the two primary personas, which were based on interviews and observations with potential users of the portal. The design team used the personas to create scenarios describing general work tasks and situations of use. At design and project meetings, the scenarios were discussed and quite often they were shared through links in e-mail. As design specifications were completed, screen dumps were put up on the wall together with scenarios that described the ways each screen would be used.

Scenarios, early sketches, and design suggestions were combined in storyboards. Questions or design problems that arose were documented on sticky notes that were placed on the storyboards. The interaction designers produced sketches and paper prototypes for visualizing "look and feel" and interaction. These sketches and prototypes were used to communicate design ideas to the development staff. The goal was to have a tight dialogue so that everybody knew what was going on in the project and that no time would be spent on designing or implementing sub-optimal solutions.

Whereas some aspects of the persona effort worked well, others did not. A number of conflicts and problems appeared in relation to the use of personas, which led to breakdowns in the design activity. Within the user experience team the use of personas worked quite well, but the personas were not used by the cross-disciplinary project team. We concluded that there were four reasons for the failure of the personas:

- Only the interaction designers had know-how in goal-directed design.
- The interaction designers did not have authority to advocate the use of personas.
- Other, more familiar, design techniques such as use scenarios and user participation were used instead of personas for expressing who the user was.
- The interaction designers themselves did not trust the primary persona. They had not participated in the creation of the persona and did not trust that the persona was grounded in data.

In his 1998 book *Mind As Mediated Action*, James Wertsch offered several reasons for the failure of tools, and we believe that his arguments can shed some light on the partial failure of personas as a design tool at Q. The notion of personas as a design tool raises a number of issues related to tools in general. A tool is something that enables us to perform an action. It mediates our engagement in the world. Personas mediate our expression of who the user is. Personas highlight some features of users and conceal other features. A tool is also situated within several communities of practice [Wenger, 1998]. The use of personas is situated within a practice of interaction design as well as within a practice of systems development.

Wertsch [1988] argues that mastering a tool is not sufficient for guaranteeing the use of the tool. One must also *appropriate* the tool. The processes of mastering and appropriating a tool are highly intertwined, but they need not be. For example, if I am quite proficient at using a particular word processor I have *mastered* it, but if I don't feel at home with it I have not made it part of my identity. I haven't *appropriated* it.

Similarly, for me, this is the case with many of the 'languages' used to create formal notations for UCD. For example, UML prevents me from expressing myself the way I want to and it therefore remains alien to me. The uptake of a tool is always characterized by some form of resistance, where the tool needs to be molded so that it fits with the individual who is using it. On the other hand, the individual needs to change his or her stance in relation to the tool. Making personas work in practice is a process of mastery as well as appropriation, but we also observed that there were issues of authority.

A tool is inherently an instrument of power, and this is just as true for personas as for any other tool. By declaring that all projects should follow a goal-oriented process and use personas, management can demand that we learn to master it as well as make it our own. This has inherent resistance, which must be acknowledged and respected if people are not to be alienated. When management uses its authoritative voice to introduce a method or a design tool, two types of appropriation are available: total affirmation or total rejection. There is no invitation to take part in the give-and-take of dialogue, which means that you cannot agree with one piece, partially accept another, and entirely reject a third.

This was the case in the project at Q. The old-timers in the Q User Experience (UE) team had completely appropriated and affirmed personas, whereas the newcomers struggled with the resistance of mastering and appropriating them as part of their process of becoming full participants in the UE team. The cross-disciplinary project team thought that the idea of personas was good, but personas are not a familiar tool of their trade. They didn't appropriate the personas. In addition, they lacked motivation to do so because they did not seek to become full participants in the community of the UE team. It became very difficult for the not-so-experienced interaction designers to engage in dialogue where the project team could take up personas part by part, in that they themselves were just getting to know the tool. Had management entered with an authoritative voice they would have risked splitting the team into those for and those against personas.

The key factors behind the lack of uptake in the project team at Q were the processes of mastery and appropriation together with the inherent authority associated with the use of any tool. This is where one must strike a balance and work toward what Schön [1983, 1987] has called a reflective practice, which refers to being open to learning. For successful uptake of personas in systems development, such a reflective practice is necessary not only in regard to UE team practices but related practices such as programming and marketing.

If you get an extremely negative response at your kickoff, talk to a few trusted colleagues on the product team and ask why it didn't work. They should be able to tell you. From our collective experience, it is probably due to one or more of the following:

- The team didn't really understand exactly what personas were for, how they would be beneficial, or how they were created from and related to data (i.e., the personas themselves didn't seem "rigorous" or right).

- The timing was wrong. If they were under too much pressure to "get real work done" they were likely not open to any new method that would impact their familiar process, especially one that can feel as loose and "made up" as personas can (if they are not communicated well).

- Individuals were not clear on exactly how personas would help in their specific jobs. A gut reaction is that "these things are for marketing people, designers, or usability people—not for me."

Knowing the specifics of their reactions can help you to fix the problem. Remember that you can always just scope the effort down to specific uses and roles. Seek out those individuals who do find the personas interesting and potentially useful and help them to make real use of the personas in their work. We have seen situations in which, after introducing personas and failing to get engagement, product team members became more aware of the differences among users. Ultimately, through repeated exposure, they began to meet or see customers similar to the personas they were first introduced to. That experience made it more real for them and the personas began to have a sense of credibility they didn't have initially.

Story from the field

IF BIRTH FAILS WITH ONE GROUP, DON'T GIVE UP

—Lori Landesman, The MathWorks

I've known some groups not to use personas because they just weren't familiar with the technique, not because they didn't like the idea or had negative experiences. That said, one of my colleagues tried putting together some personas for her development team and was frustrated by the experience because her developers didn't make good use of them. To her surprise, the marketing organization commandeered her personas, making good use of them. That hadn't been her intention but it still worked out advantageously.

Finally, as you transition from *birth* to *maturation* activities consider some of the best practices and lessons learned from the E-business server team in the following story, continued from Chapter 2 ("Story from the field: Personas for E-business Server Products: A Case Study").

Story from the field

PERSONAS FOR E-BUSINESS SERVER PRODUCTS: LESSONS LEARNED AND BEST PRACTICES (Continued from Chapter 2)

—Nancy Lincoln, Melroy D'Souza, Tonya Peck, Kaivalya Hanswadkar, and **Arnie Lund,** Windows Server System, Microsoft Corporation

The E-business server persona team provided some lessons learned and best practices that are particularly helpful to consider as you move into your *birth and maturation* activities. (The full "Story from the field" was presented in Chapter 2.)

Lessons Learned

- We relied only on informal documentation of our process (status reports, newsletters, and brown bag presentations). In hindsight, we wish we had been more systematic about creating process artifacts that could be leveraged by us and others in future design and development cycles. We strongly recommend that you document your process, even the minor details, as you proceed so that other teams in your company can learn about using personas.
- Assume that your personas will evolve. They can live and change with your customers, product targeting, and market conditions. Therefore, they should be regularly updated and substantiated with continuing user research. We do conduct ongoing research, but the rigors of product delivery deadlines can make it a challenge to regularly update persona versions once product development is underway.
- Tracking the success of your persona efforts can be difficult. We found that you need to be deliberate and forward thinking about it in order to prove their success. It is useful to know how many people in the product delivery chain (managers, developers, marketers, and so on) know about them and use them, and how many don't. But that may not be enough to promote continued use of the technique.
- In the complex corporate server space, end-to-end usage scenarios might touch more than one product in the product suite. Going forward, by developing cross-product personas, we hope to gain an even richer overall understanding of our customers; highlight any persona, feature, or functional overlaps; and rationalize personas in or out of future product design and development.

Best Practices

- Make the process fun. We used internal contests, surveys, brown bag lunches, posters, and life-size mockups of personas to generate interest and excitement about our users.
- Cross-group collaboration and buy-in is essential for accuracy and adoption. We courted key stakeholders and early adopters on the wider product team, and then leveraged their support to garner the resources, attendance at review sessions, and wider endorsement needed to seed the product cycle with persona-based thinking.
- Develop your "elevator pitch" to educate the product team on the use of personas throughout the product development phases. With such a large product team to influence, we focused on a set of success stories that could illustrate, using real examples, the value personas brought to

various subteams at different points in the product cycle. We used these stories to attract additional support and to educate new product team members as people rolled on and off the team.

- Evaluate the personas of complementary product teams to see if they apply to your product and domain area, but keep in mind that blindly reusing another team's personas without researching the backing data and domain can be a mistake.
- Plan your persona campaign early and ensure that you have sufficient budget for the materials and collateral needed to communicate with the product team.
- Be open to new ways of using personas—especially if these ideas come from the product team.
- Communicate your persona findings across the company, especially to related product teams, so that the company can leverage and/or repurpose relevant persona material.

STEP 3: MATURATION

Birth is an event. *Maturation* is an ongoing process. It is what should happen after the personas are introduced. It is the process of the personas being adopted into the culture and vocabulary of your organization. As your colleagues come to understand what personas are, why they are valuable, and the particulars of the personas you have built, they will move past the need for basic education. Your colleagues will need time to digest the new information about the persona process you have introduced. Once they fully understand the purpose of personas, they will be ready for more details about the personas you have created.

Progressively educate and maintain focus on your personas

Remember that personas live in the minds of your teammates. This doesn't happen overnight. It is an ongoing process that carries through from birth to the end of adulthood and perhaps beyond. You will facilitate this process by creating a series of communication artifacts and engaging in communication activities—the variety of which is described in material to follow.

As we said earlier in this chapter, *maturation* should be built on the notion of progressive disclosure of information and consideration of keeping the personas fresh, updated, and interesting. Depending on duration and current progress in your development cycle, you will need to spread your communication activities out appropriately.

Send your personas out into the world, but maintain ownership

Whatever artifacts and activities you choose to pursue, you and your core team should focus on maintaining your roles as persona wranglers. Remember that *maturation* continues through to the end of the next phase, *adulthood*. So, continue meeting with your core team regularly to discuss how *maturation* is progressing and to reevaluate the artifacts you are using to progressively disclose persona details.

Although it is important to keep a close eye on your personas as they are adopted and used by your colleagues, it is also important to stay open to suggestions and be willing to make some changes if necessary. It is possible that small changes in the persona descriptions, or in the way you present the personas, could make a big difference in your colleagues' willingness to use them. You already identified influential people in the organization during *family planning*. Ask these people for candid feedback on the progress of your communication campaign as it is undertaken. If you discover that changes would help, reconvene the core team, discuss the changes, and create a plan to reintroduce the "new and improved" personas.

Work to build credibility

In many organizations, you are likely to get push-back related to the validity and reliability of your personas, where the personas came from, their accuracy, and their value. As you create the variety of communication artifacts appropriate for your team, product, and process, you will want to incorporate information that builds up the credibility of your personas. Credibility is created by building trust and demonstrating expertise and rigor. Your product team might be wondering if the creation process was rigorous, if the personas were based on research, if the management team has bought into them, and if other companies have used them successfully.

As we discussed in Chapter 4, foundation documents should contain explicit links to the underlying data from which personas were derived. This is recommended for exactly the same reason here: to build credibility (though it also enables and encourages your teammates to explore the data directly). Your communication artifacts probably should not contain the specific supporting data on the personas—at least not in large quantities (the artifacts would lose their ability to communicate effectively). However, they should point people to the foundation documents or provide references to relevant studies or reports.

Conduct persona-based user research

Now that you have introduced the personas and are helping your colleagues learn more about them, you and your core team can plan your next steps for the personas. If you have time,

it is a good idea to conduct ongoing user research (as possible) to continuously enrich your understanding of the personas.

In Chapter 6 we describe how your personas can be used as recruiting targets for usability testing, field studies, and market research. As you continue to research your target users, and bring them in to test mockups and prototypes, you are gathering more and more data relevant to the personas. A very strong credibility builder is to report your research findings in relation to your personas ("The 'Lauras' we tested had difficulty using the Sign-up Wizard, whereas the 'Tanners' whizzed right through it"). An even stronger communication device is to invite your teammates to examine these studies as they are in progress. Alternatively, you can consider using video to really engage your team. For example, showing a variety of short clips from your site visits or user tests can go a long way toward communicating that you observed real users who are represented by your personas. Seeing a few "Tanners" in the lab or "Lauras" in a focus group can be a dramatic, eye-opening, and highly enriching experience. We have had teammates come to our studies and walk away saying, "That was such a 'Laura'." These teammates now know Laura on a direct and personal level.

(Story from the field, continued)

Over the next six months the visit leaders took people from their product team (usually in groups of three) to visit their knowledge worker at that person's workplace for roughly a two-hour visit. We provided the visit leaders with a small amount of training beforehand and a brief site visit guide to follow. The visit itself had no real agenda for data collection. It was all about just having direct contact with our users, whom our personas represented, in a broad way across our rather large product team.

By the end of the program, 208 people from our team had spent over 550 hours listening to knowledge workers as part of the program. Ninety-six percent of attendees felt they gained critical customer insight from the visit. One of them described the experience as follows: "As an exercise, it is very useful because it keeps people real—it keeps you grounded in what people are actually doing. The more reality we can inject into the work we do the more our work is going to resonate with our customers." Having our teammates experience real examples of our personas helped build credibility and direct personal understanding of our users.

Focus on more than getting the personas known; focus on getting them used

As the *maturation* process ensues, your product team (and perhaps your entire organization) will become familiar with the names, images, and more critical details of your personas. Hopefully, they have begun to discuss and understand the meaningful characteristics of your personas. In fact, a bit of "persona mania" is not uncommon. Your next task is to get your personas actually integrated into your team's design and development activities. If your team's immediate response wasn't to inquire about how they should actually use the personas in their jobs, you can trust that they will be asking about that within a short period.

Persona *adulthood* is all about getting explicit use and utility from your personas. Every job role on the team can incorporate some level of user focus into development activities. Your job is to find those appropriate uses of the personas and push them into action. As we said earlier, persona *maturation* (i.e., the communication campaign) continues all the way through *adulthood*. In fact, successful *adulthood* depends on a relentless maturation of your product team's awareness and understanding of (and intense focus on) your personas—and more importantly on your target users.

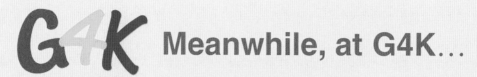

Meanwhile, at G4K...

THE G4K CORE TEAM'S COMMUNICATION STRATEGY

During family planning, the G4K core team created an action plan. Now that they are ready to introduce the personas to the rest of the G4K kids' Web portal team, they know they need a more specific communication strategy. While the core team has been working on the personas, others on the portal team have been working hard to identify requirements. The G4K team knows they can't ask the

Who	What	When	How
Stakeholders who have advised us on our persona effort to date	Method evangelism: about the persona method and our personas	Tomorrow or as soon as we can get on their calendars before we begin presenting to the other audiences listed in this document.	Meeting to describe our work to date, create 5 slides on UCD, personas in general, and how and why we create personas. Any more than this won't be effective. Prepare our proposed schedule for of persona information and how it will be used (perhaps a version of strategy document?)
All	Introduce the persona method and put it in context for this project	As soon as possible	Pizza-party Kickoff meeting–use the intro slides from stakeholder meeting, they worked well. Buzz Generators: create intro posters someone to post intro posters all over halls while we do kickoff meeting
Product managers	Info about each persona's roles and goals	As soon as possible	Ask product managers and other product designers what info they need to feel comfortable including persona names and roles in all requirements and specific documents
Developers	Basics about this set of personas (introduce them to the people)	After requirements docs are complete and have been presented to development staff	Create comparison facilitators and enrichers. Focus on the aspects of the personas that are clearly tied to data about large groups of people (characteristics of Abby as "a mom," elements of Tanner that are familiar with our shrink-wrapped products). Clear information about how these personas will have different expectations for the portal than they do for shrink wrapped games. Enrichers on the persona method: include some specific examples of how we'll use the personas (persona weighted feature matrix, replacement of 'actor' in scenarios for the Web site)
User testers, QA team, user support team	Core team assumes that these audiences can use same info as developers for the time being. Later they might need additional information.		

FIGURE 5.2: *A section of the G4K core team's communication strategy.*

(Meanwhile, at G4K..., continued)

rest of the product team to redo any of the work that has been done without the aid of personas. Instead, they have decided to create a strategy to make the most of the personas for the rest of the product development process. To them, this means embarking on a communication campaign to very quickly express the value of the personas in time for the persona names to be included in the final versions of requirements and specification documents. The core team also hopes the personas will help once development gets underway. They know that there will have to be some serious feature triage if the portal is to be launched in time. The G4K core team identified several goals for their communication campaign:

- Support the action plan we created during *family planning*
- Bring the personas to life in the minds of all colleagues who influence the design and development of our G4K kids' Web site as fast as possible (no one is going to stop what they are doing to help with this)
- Progressively disclose the right information to the right people at the right time to ensure that the user data embedded in the personas is understood and absorbed. We have limited resources, so we need to try to be efficient in introducing the personas to the various teams we hope will use them
- Make sure everyone who is introduced to the personas knows how we hope they will use the personas in their everyday jobs. This means we have to be very specific about the changes to our usual design and development processes and documents.

Figure 5.2 shows a portion of a G4K communication strategy (who, what, when, and how) document.

PERSONA ARTIFACTS (THE WHAT AND HOW OF COMMUNICATING YOUR PERSONAS)

You should now have a good top-level understanding of the three basic steps involved in the *birth and maturation* phase. In the following sections, we provide many examples of artifacts you and your core team can use to make *birth and maturation* happen.

Once you have created your persona foundation documents, which include all links between the data and the persona details, you can pick and choose which additional materials and artifacts you want to create. There are many different ways to communicate your personas to your team, including different types of documents, posters, handouts, activities, and other materials. However, keep in mind that these materials don't have to be fancy, expensive, or time consuming to create in order to be useful.

The persona artifact design process: things to consider whatever materials or format you use

Remember that the artifacts and materials you create to communicate information about personas are very important. They are the user interface for your personas and the data behind them. Well-thought-out and well-designed persona materials can add credibility to your entire persona effort and help enormously with your persona communication campaign. Note that it doesn't take a lot of these artifacts to have an effective communication campaign. We present numerous examples in material following to help illustrate the possibilities. Be very strategic and frugal in your choices. In approaching the creation of any persona artifacts thoughtfully, consider the following:

Agree on the specific goal of the artifact. Why are you creating this specific artifact? The goal will probably be related to one of the three categories of artifacts (buzz generators, comparison facilitators, and enrichers) described in the following.

Agree on the audience, timing, and distribution method for the artifact. Your persona artifacts should eventually be everywhere around your office (on doors, in hallways, coffee rooms, meeting rooms, stakeholders/leaders' offices, and so on), but they should appear progressively. For every artifact, consider who is going to see it, when (in the development cycle) they are going to see it, and how the environment will affect their ability to digest the information. For example, you might decide to create different buzz generator posters (see material following for a description) for the developer's hallway versus the marketer's hallway. If you work in a place that doesn't allow posters and such to be displayed around the building, create artifacts that can be handed out to individuals, carried around, or placed on desktops.

Agree on the information elements that should (and should not) be included on the artifact. By the time you are ready to create persona artifacts, you will have quite a bit of information about each persona at your disposal. The information you have will all seem highly relevant and deeply interrelated, and it can therefore be difficult to comb out small snippets to include on individual artifacts. Remember that the easiest way to create a useless persona artifact is to overload it with information. For example, you might decide to create "wanted" posters to create buzz and to convey the name, role, and picture for each of your primary personas. It will be tempting to include a quote and maybe a few bulleted details with additional information. However, remember your priorities. If you really do want to build buzz and interest, consider limiting the poster to just a photo, a name, and a role. When in doubt, always opt for less information and leave your audience craving more.

Agree on the relative priorities of the information elements on the artifact. Once you decide which information elements should be included on an artifact, prioritize these elements according to how important it is that the element is read and understood. For example, on the "wanted" posters the photo and name should probably be very large and eye-catching. In contrast, a comparison poster you distribute a few weeks or months later should include names and roles, but these are probably not as important as comparative information about each persona's goals, abilities, desires, and so on.

Don't use up your entire budget on birth and maturation. If you have limited resources (e.g., very little money to use on persona artifacts), think carefully about the artifacts you will need now and try to predict what you will need later. Don't use your entire budget on artifacts distributed early. Remember that you still face the challenge of keeping the personas alive and useful throughout the *adulthood* phase.

Select the best communication tool for the job: three categories of persona artifacts

We have separated the persona communication materials into three basic categories that describe the goals the materials support: buzz generators, comparison facilitators, and enrichers. Within these categories, we describe which types of materials tend to work best early in your communication campaign (closer to *birth*) and which work best later, when the personas are fairly well known and you are working to keep them alive in the product development process. You will probably create one or more artifacts from each of these categories. Throughout this section is a discussion of printed posters to be hung on walls around your building and offices. Posters can be easy and inexpensive to generate. But don't let our inclination toward posters distract you or lead you to create artifacts that are inappropriate for your corporate culture. Keep in mind that there is no "right" way to communicate your personas, and that it is important to continue to stay alert to the needs and difficulties arising in your organization.

Buzz generators

Buzz generator artifacts are materials that get people talking and interested. Although they may include some small amount of practical information, their purpose is *not* to convey detailed information about what personas are or how your personas should be used. Rather, their purpose is to generate excitement and interest in the *idea* of personas. They should be eye-catching and encourage people to think that something new, fresh, and exciting is happening in the product design process. They should leave people wanting more information and asking questions. Buzz generators foster a sense of anticipation and a bit of mystery. You can enhance this by posting new buzz generators only after everyone has gone home, so that your team is greeted first thing in the morning with new posters and questions that seem to have appeared magically overnight (or over the weekend).

Early buzz generators

There are many buzz generators that work best early in the development process. These tend to be artifacts that let people know that "the personas are coming" and that things are going to change. They *can* capitalize on and enhance the ramp-up of excitement and

energy that marks the start of work on a new product. As posters or other physical artifacts, buzz generators should be visually interesting, bright, easy to read, and very light on information. As such, they tend to be at home almost anywhere in office spaces.

"Do you know who our users are?" posters

Before you introduce the idea of using personas to stand in for users, why not get people thinking about how much they do (or, for the most part, don't) know about your user population? "Do you know who our users are?" posters don't mention personas and don't include any data. Instead, they should plant interesting questions in the minds of your colleagues. These posters can be very inexpensive and easy to create. Remember the "Got Milk?" advertising campaign that featured large billboards with just those words? Your "Do you know who our users are?" posters can be similar. You can print single questions in a large font size on tabloid-sized paper and post them all over your offices. Think of questions that will "stick" and will inspire some curiosity and discussion. Figure 5.3 shows an example of this.

You will want to follow up with answers to these questions once your personas are introduced. If you executed a team- or company-wide UCD survey (as discussed and recommended in Chapter 3), now might be the time to use some of those findings. Consider posting a chart or two that illustrate how well your team knows or focuses on users. You might even put together a brown bag presentation to address this topic and present the results of your survey.

"The personas are coming" posters

"The personas are coming" posters (see Figure 5.4) generate buzz around the idea of using personas as design targets. They are useful if your company has never used personas before (to get people wondering what personas are and what it means that "they're coming") and if you are introducing a new set of personas to colleagues who already have experience using personas ("Oh! We're getting new ones! I wonder who they are this time?"). These posters can also be very easy and inexpensive to create: simply take the persona photos you have and create back silhouettes of the faces. Print these (black and white is fine) on large sheets of paper with a simple statement that lets people know that more information is on its way.

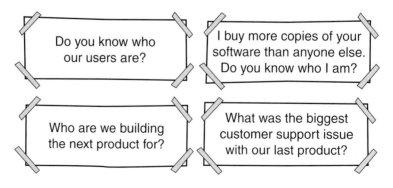

FIGURE 5.3: "Do you know who our users are?" early buzz generators.

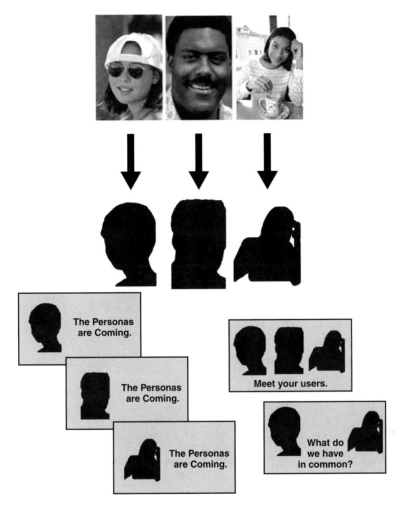

FIGURE 5.4: *"The personas are coming" early buzz generators.*

"SELF-SATISFIED SAM" GAINS ACCEPTANCE

—Domenick J. Dellino, Ph.D., Director of User Experience Research, Washington Mutual Bank

Creating personas is one challenge, but getting them adopted by your team is quite another. Here's what worked for me. While on the Microsoft CarPoint.com team in 1999, I was faced with the challenge of creating personas from market segmentation data, but my principal concern was that all the hard work would we embraced by my team. So, "How do I engage the team?" became the question.

(Story from the field, continued)

We all know that there is nothing like participation to facilitate adoption, so I had to come up with a plan that would get people to participate in the process and to be invested in reading the personas. One thing we all had in common—from technical writer to development lead—was an interest in cars. So, it seemed reasonable to engage the team by asking them to vote for the photo and the car driven by each persona.

Time and resource constraints being what they were, I created five personas and posted the textual materials in large, easy-to-read type on five tabloid sheets. I placed the sheets on bulletin boards just outside the developers' offices. Each persona contained a persona name (e.g., "Self-satisfied Sam" and "Manager Mary"), a brief biography, related demographics, and relevant car-shopping preferences.

I left a 5-inch by 7-inch space in the layout for the photograph and a 4-inch by 6-inch space for the type of car they would drive. Next to each tabloid sheet were two separate legal-size sheets—one with six potential photographs of the persona and another with six possible cars the person might drive. Brightly colored sticky notes, prefaced with an e-mail to the team, encouraged everyone to vote for their preference by placing a tally next to their favorites for each persona. (I used tallies, but you might consider signatures to discourage multiple votes per person.) I'd allow two or three days to catch everyone's attention.

The team got engaged and watched closely as front-runners began to emerge. When the voting was complete, I reassembled the tabloid sheets with the winning photos and "rides" in place. The rest is history. Even if no one ever read the persona's characteristics again, having to read about "Self-satisfied Sam" to choose a photo and a car for him got his persona into the team's lexicon.

Introduction posters

Introduction posters are very popular among persona practitioners. They are usually the first public artifacts that include the names, roles, and photographs of your primary personas. Unlike "Do you know who our users are?" and "The personas are coming" posters, introduction posters often stay on the walls throughout the project. They are worth spending some money and time on. Introduction posters work well when hung in public places with a lot of foot traffic, such as hallways and lobbies.

These posters, examples of which are shown in Figure 5.5, should definitely include the persona's name and a photograph. They might also include quotes that express the persona's interests or point of view, the market share related to the persona, photographs of the persona's environment, and so on. Introduction posters should not require more than ten seconds of directed attention to comprehend. It is a good idea to include directions on how to obtain more information—either the name and contact information for that persona's wrangler or perhaps a link to your persona Web site.

FIGURE 5.5: *Two very simple persona introduction posters for Tanner. Note that these posters intentionally communicate little more than the name of the persona and a few characteristics. Although they do contain a few tidbits of key information, they are designed to be taken in within a few seconds. The goal is to help the team learn the names and faces first, before providing more detailed information. Illustration created by Craig Hally.*

Later buzz generators

Buzz generators are a great way to revive interest and encourage people to refocus their attention on the personas. Like early buzz generators, they should be light on information but packed with as much of a punch as possible. If you have additional photographs of your personas you have not shared with the team, use them in your buzz generators. You might even consider getting your persona models to come back so that you can take photos of them interacting with product mock-ups or prototypes as they are developed, subsequently using these new photos in the artifacts you produce.

As the development process progresses, people on the development teams will become overwhelmed with their daily responsibilities and will be less and less open to new ideas and methods. Respect this, and make later buzz generators fun and, if possible, a relief from the everyday grind. Remember that once the development process starts in earnest documents will be flying everywhere. Stacks of them will have appeared on people's desks, whiteboards will be full of words and diagrams, and there will be project scheduling charts on the walls. Don't add to the paper nightmare, or especially to the reading-related workload. Later buzz generators work best if they are intrinsically interesting and in a format different from other product-related information sources. Toward this end, use new photographs of your personas, fresh information, and attractive artifacts. Consider a range of media and formats, such as video, physical objects (custom key chains, laminated place mats, mouse pads, coffee mugs, stickers, magnets, and so on), and e-mail (newsletters, updates, "persona fact of the week").

Product development teams love to be fed. Morning doughnuts, lunchtime pizza, and fridges full of free soft drinks are used almost universally as morale and energy boosters. If you want some more attention focused on your personas, why not make your product development team encounter some useful information on their way to free food? Lay out boxes of doughnuts and put persona information on the inside of the box lid. Print and cut out small circles with photos and information snippets and place them *on* the doughnuts. Have a pizza party and have napkins printed with the persona names. If you decide to offer food and want to present information verbally, you can certainly do this. However, remember that there is nothing more annoying than being offered something for free (such as pizza) and then finding you really do have to pay for it (by listening to a long, boring presentation). Whatever information you decide to impart to your invited snackers, keep it short and sweet. Leave them looking forward to the next invitation they get from the persona team.

Trinkets and gizmos (if you have a budget)

If you have a budget and need to generate some buzz, consider outsourcing the production of a custom "persona collectible." Trinkets and gizmos create desire ("Hey! Where'd you get that? I want one!"). If they take up residence on people's desks, gizmos can successfully transmit information for a long time. There are hundreds of companies that specialize in creating the customized "trash and trinkets" we have all picked up at trade shows and conferences. You can get virtually anything printed on anything, if you have the budget. Most custom printing companies have very large catalogs and offer custom-printed items at a wide variety of price points, so even if you only need a few items you will probably find something that will fit your budget. The following are examples of professionally printed trinkets and gizmos.

- *Coffee cups, beer glasses, squeeze toys, tumblers, yo-yos, magnet sets:* You can't print much on any of these types of trinkets (see Figure 5.6), but you can certainly include the names and roles of the personas, which can help to embed the personas more deeply into the corporate culture and conversation. Consider including a drawing or cartoon of the personas instead of a photograph. Illustrations tend to print and look better on the finished product (for more information on persona illustrations, see "Story from the field: Using Illustrations Instead of Photos" in Chapter 4). Also, illustrations can be printed in one color. The more colors you include in the printing process the more expensive the trinkets will be.

- *Persona T-shirts:* Logoed or customized clothing is almost always a hot item. You could create a design per persona or a single shirt that advertises some aspect of all of them. You might give them out as prizes (e.g., teammates who go out on site visits or participate in some other UCD activity get an "I really know my user" T-shirt). You will need to keep the information to a minimum on these items. They are more about engagement and awareness than education.

- *Mouse pads:* Due to their size, mouse pads can include more information than the previously discussed trinkets. You might want to have one printed that includes the photos, names, and roles of all of your primary personas, and the address of your personas Web site (which is a good item to include on all persona-related materials).

Trinkets and gizmos (if money is scarce)

Even if you don't have much money (or just want to be resourceful), you can still create effective persona trinkets. These artifacts just require creativity and time to produce. The following are examples of inexpensive, hand-made trinkets and information sources.

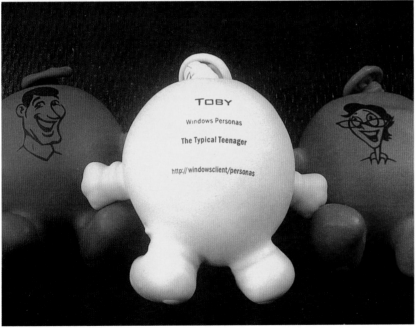

FIGURE 5.6: *Persona beer glasses and squeeze toys.*

BRING YOUR PERSONA MODELS TO YOUR KICKOFF EVENT

As part of your kickoff, if your persona "models" are local people consider inviting them to participate as a living persona. Basically, you are asking them to serve as actors for your event. You will need to prep them with the persona foundation materials and script a small role for them as part of your meeting. In their paper "Focus Troupe: Using Drama to Create Common Context for New Product Concept End-user Evaluations," Salvador and Howells [1998] describe how the acting out of dramatic vignettes can be a powerful and effective tool for user research. They report that the Focus Troupe method can establish a common, shared, and surrogate contextual experience for the audience. Extending this notion with personas toward the education and engagement of your own product team could be a valuable exercise during the *birth and maturation* phase. (For more information on theater techniques, see Sato and Salvador [1999].)

- *Laminated summary sheets:* Instead of investing in a professionally produced mouse pad, you can create and print place mats that include summary information about your personas. It is relatively inexpensive to print these mats in color and have them laminated at your local print shop. The fact that these mats are in color and laminated will make them seem less disposable to the product development teams, and they will be more likely to take up permanent residence on desks, bulletin boards, and walls than nonlaminated printouts.

- *Custom candy wrappers:* It is not difficult to find, or even create, a custom candy wrapper template. To create your own template, carefully remove a wrapper from a chocolate bar. Measure the entire wrapper and the areas that appear on the front and back of the candy bar. Use whatever software you are comfortable with to create a template using the measurements of the bar. Include a photo and a small amount of interesting or important information about the persona. For example, the "Tanner Bar" might include information on the type of homework Tanner does. Print the wrappers on a color printer using glossy paper. Cut out the wrappers and glue them *over* the existing candy wrappers (to avoid any unlikely, but possible, liability issues). Create a series of candy bars with the primary personas and encourage people to "collect them all." You can even use different types of chocolate bars for the various personas. Leave the candy bars on people's desks after everyone has left the office.

Bring the personas to life (or life-size!)

As the product development process continues, you might find that people are so busy that trinkets won't be enough to get their attention and refocus them on the personas. In this case, consider more drastic buzz-generating activities that really bring the personas to life for the development staff. Consider bringing in live actors and stage some role-playing activities in which the actors (who could be talented friends of yours) play the personas. The kickoff meeting might be one good time to do this, but also consider bringing in persona actors for spec or mock-up reviews. Prepare the persona actors so that they feel comfortable walking through whatever design materials exist from the perspective of the persona they represent.

Comparison facilitators

Comparison facilitators are artifacts that help people understand important differences among personas. Comparison facilitators are especially useful for anyone working on or making decisions related to more than one interface. Product managers, documentation specialists, trainers, and user interface designers and developers are great target audiences for comparison facilitator artifacts. By their nature, comparison facilitators contain different details than most buzz generators and enricher artifacts (covered later in this chapter). Enrichers provide deep details, whereas comparison facilitators provide a broader context.

Story from the field

CREATING LIFE-SIZE PERSONAS

—Rósa Guðjónsdóttir, Usability Consultant, Pink Puffin, Sweden, *www.pinkpuffin.com*

While at IconMedialab in Stockholm, we created a set of nine personas representing a number of diverse target groups within and outside the African Continent, to aid in the development of a content-rich Internet portal. The personas were based on several focus group sessions that discussed the Internet and how the participants made use of it. The personas consisted of a primary goal, as well as a scenario whereby the persona fulfills the goal by using the portal. The persona also included a portrait and a scenario picture for visualization purposes.

When the personas were first introduced to the project team and the client, the portrait and scenario pictures were used. However, given the large number of personas, and the large differences in cultural settings that existed between the project team and the target groups, the task of getting the project team acquainted with the personas was unusually difficult. The personas only existed in documents, which required the project team to read the documentation, memorize it, and try to develop a unified feel for them. It became apparent that some type of mnemonic device, which was not bound to the documentation, would facilitate this process.

The solution was the creation of life-size images of the personas. The life-size images were made out of white cardboard. Pasted on their backs were their personal description, goal, and scenario (see Figure 5.7). The life-size images were then introduced to the project team, and the team members got to choose a persona to "adopt" and were to arrange them in the workplace (see Figures 5.7 and 5.8).

FIGURE 5.7: *The life-size personas coinhabited our offices with the product development team.*

(Story from the field, continued)

FIGURE 5.8: *Two of our life-size personas.*

The Results

The life-size images turned out to be an effective tool for assisting the project group in becoming more familiar with the personas. They became the center of attention in the project workplace and created an atmosphere that smoothed the process of the project team getting to know the personas. The life-size images were also a useful interface between the two groups (programmers and graphical designers) within the project team. The project team started to interact with the life-size personas, putting jewelry and scarves on them. Mbabu, a cool Rasta, was even asked out on a date.

Formal interviews with the project team as well as participant observations during the project work revealed that the life-size images helped the project team members get acquainted with the personas and become aware of their purpose and importance in the design of the portal. It was as though the personas were working with the project team, literally looking over their shoulders while they were working on the design of the portal. The life-size images (see Figure 5.9) not only increased the target group awareness for this particular project but increased general user awareness (i.e., that there were real people with real lives that would use the product the project team was designing).

FIGURE 5.9: *Rosa adds information to the back of one of the life-size personas.*

They work best when created in a form that enhances examination and reflection and are posted in places where people have time and inclination to examine details. In other words, don't post comparison facilitators in busy hallways, but do consider posting them near the microwave, coffee maker, on meeting room walls, in bathroom stalls, or anywhere you have a captive audience.

Early comparison facilitators

Early in your communication campaign you can use comparison facilitators to help everyone understand the collection of personas you have created and the roles they have with respect to your product. Comparison facilitators will help you convey information basics about more than one persona at a time.

Persona rosters

You have probably already created individual information posters for your personas, which might include the persona's photo, name, role, and perhaps even a quote. Consider creating a roster poster (see Figure 5.10) that shows this basic information for all of the personas (not just one at a time). We mentioned earlier that you could put such comparison information on a mouse pad or other artifact that has a little more space.

A persona communication constellation

A communication constellation shows the "use community" represented by your personas. Communication constellations show how your personas are linked to or interact with one another through your product. This is much like the model for roles, except that it is simpler and is created as part of the contextual design process [Beyer and Holtzblatt 1998]. To create a communication constellation (see Figure 5.11), generate an image that expresses the (highly simplified) relationships among the personas. Include all personas and the product you are creating, and draw lines between these images to show the connections and the relative "proximity" of each persona to your product. You can also include other users (roles), artifacts, systems, or products that will affect the use of your product. Communication constellations are highly useful early in the communication campaign to help people understand why you

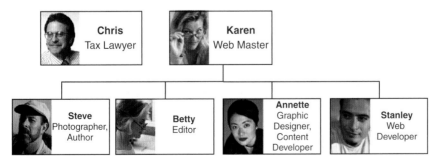

FIGURE 5.10: *Persona roster in the form of an org chart overview (http://ccmredhat.com/ user-centered/personas.html).*

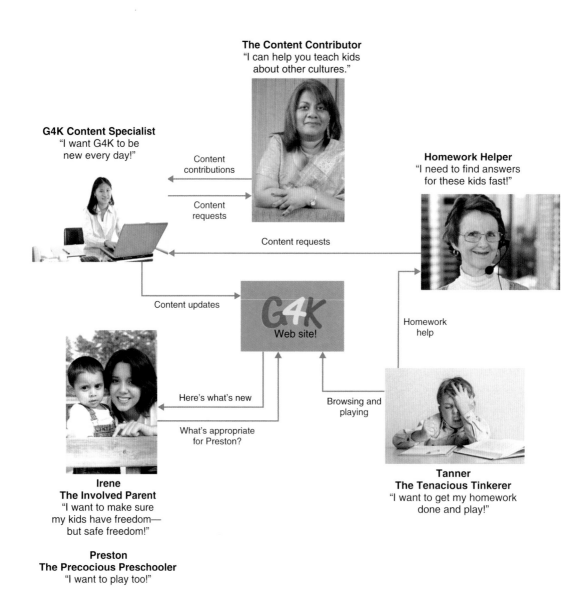

The Content Contributor
"I can help you teach kids about other cultures."

G4K Content Specialist
"I want G4K to be new every day!"

Content contributions

Content requests

Homework Helper
"I need to find answers for these kids fast!"

Content requests

Content updates

G4K Web site!

Homework help

Here's what's new

Browsing and playing

What's appropriate for Preston?

Irene
The Involved Parent
"I want to make sure my kids have freedom— but safe freedom!"

Tanner
The Tenacious Tinkerer
"I want to get my homework done and play!"

Preston
The Precocious Preschooler
"I want to play too!"

FIGURE 5.11: *A persona communication constellation. Designed to show the "use community" created by your personas, a communication constellation is light on persona details. Instead, it should show relative proximity to the product. These constellations can help your team understand who the personas are, what their roles are with respect to the product, and how they interact (or don't interact) with one another (or even other relevant systems).*

created your particular personas and the fact that the personas will have different levels of interaction with the product.

The executive summary slide

The product development team is not the only group that needs your focus! Create an executive summary slide (see Figure 5.12) in a program such as PowerPoint so that anyone (including VPs, managers, and even salespeople) who needs to speak about your target audience can include it in any slide presentation. The executive summary slide should include only very basic information about the personas—just enough so that anyone looking at it can understand who the personas are. You may also want to create a few slides that describe your basic development process, including how the personas fit into this process. It is a good idea

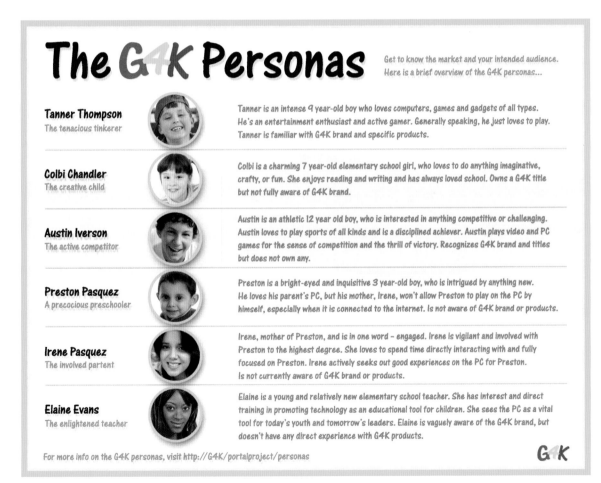

The G4K Personas

Get to know the market and your intended audience. Here is a brief overview of the G4K personas...

Tanner Thompson
The tenacious tinkerer

Tanner is an intense 9 year-old boy who loves computers, games and gadgets of all types. He's an entertainment enthusiast and active gamer. Generally speaking, he just loves to play. Tanner is familiar with G4K brand and specific products.

Colbi Chandler
The creative child

Colbi is a charming 7 year-old elementary school girl, who loves to do anything imaginative, crafty, or fun. She enjoys reading and writing and has always loved school. Owns a G4K title but not fully aware of G4K brand.

Austin Iverson
The active competitor

Austin is an athletic 12 year old boy, who is interested in anything competitive or challenging. Austin loves to play sports of all kinds and is a disciplined achiever. Austin plays video and PC games for the sense of competition and the thrill of victory. Recognizes G4K brand and titles but does not own any.

Preston Pasquez
A precocious preschooler

Preston is a bright-eyed and inquisitive 3 year-old boy, who is intrigued by anything new. He loves his parent's PC, but his mother, Irene, won't allow Preston to play on the PC by himself, especially when it is connected to the internet. Is not aware of G4K brand or products.

Irene Pasquez
The involved parent

Irene, mother of Preston, and is in one word – engaged. Irene is vigilant and involved with Preston to the highest degree. She loves to spend time directly interacting with and fully focused on Preston. Irene actively seeks out good experiences on the PC for Preston. Is not currently aware of G4K brand or products.

Elaine Evans
The enlightened teacher

Elaine is a young and relatively new elementary school teacher. She has interest and direct training in promoting technology as an educational tool for children. She sees the PC as a vital tool for today's youth and tomorrow's leaders. Elaine is vaguely aware of the G4K brand, but doesn't have any direct experience with G4K products.

For more info on the G4K personas, visit http://G4K/portalproject/personas

G4K

FIGURE 5.12: *An example of an executive summary slide for the G4K personas. Illustration created by Craig Hally.*

to have these materials on hand and readily available to distribute for inclusion in presentations. If you don't, at best you will be asked to create them at the last minute. In the worst case, you will not be asked to create them because someone else will have—and you may find that your personas and the persona effort are misrepresented.

Remember that many different people in your organization will be talking about development progress and process and should likely be referring to the intended audience for the product. Make sure you provide good, high-level materials that accurately represent your personas (and how you are using them, if you think this information will be useful).

Later comparison facilitators

As your project progresses, you will probably notice that many people in your organization start to have similar questions about the personas and their different needs related to specific parts of the product. Comparison facilitator artifacts are a great way to answer these questions. They can be designed to convey parallel information about any set of relevant personas. Showing both the details and the big picture of how the personas differ from one another (with respect to these details) can be incredibly helpful. The main difference between early and later comparison facilitators is the level of detail. As projects progress, team members tend to need much more specific information in particular domains.

Detailed comparison posters

Detailed comparison posters (see Figure 5.13) are similar to the brief persona rosters described earlier, except that they contain more information. On these posters, detailed information is provided in several domains—key domains important to your product. These posters can be created so that they are broadly interesting, highlighting key information that won't change or become less important over time. Like the enricher artifacts described in the next section, they can also be created to answer specific questions or domain issues known to be critical to your product's development (see Figure 5.14). The specific details in this comparison artifact are probably only interesting while certain decisions (related to those details) are being made. Thus, like many of the artifacts we have suggested, these posters may have a limited shelf life (though probably longer than buzz generators).

There are other artifacts you can use to facilitate comparison among the personas, including the following:

● *Persona trading cards:* If you have a lot of personas for your team to learn about and keep track of, you might consider creating trading cards (see Figure 5.15). With fewer personas, you can get the same effect by creating playing cards with persona info on the backs of the cards. These are a cross between buzz generators (because they are cool and interesting) and comparison facilitators (because they include more information than

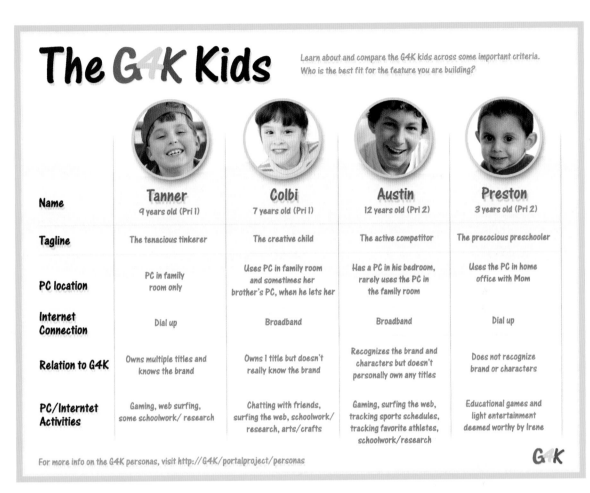

The G4K Kids

Learn about and compare the G4K kids across some important criteria. Who is the best fit for the feature you are building?

Name	Tanner 9 years old (Pri 1)	Colbi 7 years old (Pri 1)	Austin 12 years old (Pri 2)	Preston 3 years old (Pri 2)
Tagline	The tenacious tinkerer	The creative child	The active competitor	The precocious preschooler
PC location	PC in family room only	Uses PC in family room and sometimes her brother's PC, when he lets her	Has a PC in his bedroom, rarely uses the PC in the family room	Uses the PC in home office with Mom
Internet Connection	Dial up	Broadband	Broadband	Dial up
Relation to G4K	Owns multiple titles and knows the brand	Owns 1 title but doesn't really know the brand	Recognizes the brand and characters but doesn't personally own any titles	Does not recognize brand or characters
PC/Interntet Activities	Gaming, web surfing, some schoolwork/ research	Chatting with friends, surfing the web, schoolwork/ research, arts/crafts	Gaming, surfing the web, tracking sports schedules, tracking favorite athletes, schoolwork/research	Educational games and light entertainment deemed worthy by Irene

For more info on the G4K personas, visit http://G4K/portalproject/personas

G4K

FIGURE 5.13: *A detailed comparison poster showing the G4K kids. Note that this poster does not compare all of the G4K personas along every possible dimension. Rather, in this case it shows the differences among the primary personas across important characteristics for the G4K portal project. Illustration created by Craig Hally.*

most buzz generators and allow easy comparison across personas). One valuable aspect of these cards is that they can be brought along to a design meeting or other activity for which having a quick reference to your target customers is useful (see Figure 5.13).

● *Persona reference booklet:* You can very inexpensively create a little reference booklet (e.g., in a 5-inch by 7-inch ring binder) that teammates can carry with them to meetings. Like trading cards, while providing mobile access and utility for your persona information they will serve to make others aware and perhaps even promote learning and usage. With this artifact you can cram a lot of information into a small space. Even so, the information should still be well designed (but not completely exhaustive). For an example of this type of artifact in context, see the following Story from the Field.

Primary Persona   Secondary Persona

Elena Montgomery	Carl Stephens Ph.D.	Gillian Winters	Martin Schwartz	Otto Bauer
Human Resources Coordinator, Amino Pharmaceuticals	*Laboratory Manager, Amino Pharmaceuticals*	*Human Resources Manager, Lacy's Department Store*	*Dir. of Manufacturing, Sunny Electronics, USA*	*Organizational Planner, Volksmotorwerks AG*

"This form requires the manager's signature."	"Didn't we just do reviews?"	"People are our number one asset."	"Can you get me those numbers by Tuesday?"	"Let's start thinking about your succession planning."

Elena spends most of her day processing all the forms required to hire, transfer and terminate employees in the R&D division of Amino Pharmaceuticals. When something's incomplete or unclear, she takes the time to track down the answer. She's an expert on all the necessary forms and procedures.

Elena's Goals
Move up in HR
Excellence through accuracy
Be helpful
Don't fall behind

Although his main job is research, Carl also creates budgets, hires and trains employees, writes reviews and distributes bonuses. Carl wants to make sure his employees and his manager are happy, but he regards HR paperwork as a distraction from his real work.

Carl's Goals
Focus on his experiments
Keep his people happy
Keep his management happy
Grow his department

Gillian wants to help build strong teams by improving communication between managers and employees and watching for "hot spots" that require her attention. She needs context to help her quickly find and solve problems.

Gillian's Goals
People not paperwork
Partner with management to build healthy departments
Be proactive
Build relationships within the corporate-wide HR departments

Sunny Electronics has manufacturing divisions all over the world. Martin needs access to headcount and salary information to help him understand the performance of his divisions and projects and plan for the future.

Martin's Goals
On time, under budget
Understand the bottom line
Maximize productivity
Controlled growth

Otto helps VP's and Directors structure their organizations for best productivity. He wants access to HR statistics about employees so he can understand historical performance of projects and forecast future changes to the company.

Otto's Goals
Build a healthy organization
Partner with divisions and upper management
Find danger and opportunity in the workforce
Set the vision, chart the course

FIGURE 5.14: *A persona summary matrix from Cooper Interaction Design (http://advance.aiga.org/timeline/artifacts/Matrix.PDF).*

FIGURE 5.15: *Persona trading cards (see "Story from the field: Dealing with Many Personas" earlier in this chapter for more information relating to this example.)*

FIGURE 5.15 *(continued)*

Story from the field

KEY-RING FLIP CARDS

—Holly Jamesen Carr, GreenShape LLC, Formerly Usability Specialist, Attenex Corporation

We created a set of persona flip cards and distributed them to every member of the product development staff at our organization. The flip card set included six inexpensively produced cards printed front and back and attached to a simple key-ring style clip (see Figure 5.16).

To create a set of handy flip cards for your development team:

1. Print card-size versions of each persona's photo. We decided to include a uniquely colored border for each persona to make the cards easily distinguishable at a glance. Under the photo, include the persona's name and job or role. Our cards measured approximately 3 inches by 5 inches. If you use a similar format, you should be able to print at least four photos on a single sheet of paper.
2. Print card-size summaries for the back of each persona card. We chose to include three to five bulleted items describing each persona's goals and job description. You can choose the information you feel is most important to distribute. We also included a colored border to match the color surrounding the persona's photograph.

(Story from the field, continued)

3. Cut out the photos and the summaries and glue them to the front and back of card stock or index cards.
4. Finally, punch a hole in each card and string together sets of these cards, so that each set includes all of your primary personas, and distribute one set to each team member.

FIGURE 5.16: *Persona flip cards.*

My team found these flip cards very useful and fun. They brought them to meetings and sometimes ran out of the meeting to go get them to answer a specific question. They were inexpensive and did not take much time to create.

Enrichers

Enricher artifacts allow you to communicate very detailed information about your personas. Unlike buzz generators, these artifacts do not necessarily need to be fancy or eye-catching, but they do need to be very well designed and, more importantly, their content must very well thought out and highly relevant. Enrichers are any artifacts or activities that tie the personas to more information, especially data or detailed descriptions of the persona with respect to a particular information domain (such as a persona's activities, knowledge level, behaviors, biases, and so on).

Enrichers don't necessarily need to stick around. They may not need to take up residence on everyone's desks and even may not be relevant after a particular set of decisions has been made. Rather, their purpose is to enhance your team's understanding of the personas, usually with respect to a particular domain or set of questions. The information in enricher artifacts should enable the product development staff to make persona-driven (and therefore data-driven) choices for specific aspects of the product. In many cases, simply pointing the development team to particular areas of the persona Web site over time is all you need to do.

Enricher artifacts tend to contain more information than other artifacts. They are designed to enrich understanding of the personas in a deep way in some domain, probably one that hasn't been on the beaten path so far. For example, an enricher could describe every little thing about how a persona goes about printing, or what she does with books once she gets home. Many of the buzz generators described previously also have enriching elements in that they contain some detailed information in a particular domain, enhancing the understanding of your personas. For example, persona trading cards include selected persona details in addition to photographs, names, and job descriptions or roles.

Persona one-pagers

After the bare-bones persona basics have taken hold in your organization (that is, when you start to hear people talking about the personas by name), you might want to distribute persona one-pagers. These résumé-like documents are probably what most people think of when they envision "personas." Examples of one-pagers can be seen all over the Web. Similar to résumés, persona one-pagers should include only the most pertinent information (as compared to, for example, a curriculum vitae)—information you think will be of particular interest to your product team.

If you have the time and resources, you might consider creating different one-pagers for different groups in your organization, highlighting somewhat different information from your foundation documentation as appropriate. For example, the details interesting to the marketing group are probably quite different from the information that will be useful for developers. Because you have all of the persona information at your fingertips (in the persona foundation documents), you can be selective about which information elements you put together in the one-pagers in line with the audience for each. However, we highly recommend that the one-pagers be consistently formatted. In other words, if you create a set of one-pagers for the marketing team, make sure the format is the same for each persona, so that the reader can easily find the information he or she is looking for. If you create one-pagers for each persona, you can take them to a copy shop and have them bound into a reference booklet, or provide easy-to-access direct links to online versions. An example of a one-pager is shown in Figure 5.17.

Meet...

Tanner Thompson

Summary:

Tanner is an intense 9 year-old boy who loves computers, games and gadgets of all types. He's an entertainment enthusiast and active gamer. Generally speaking, he just loves to play.

Tanner is familiar with G4K game titles and is a likely frequent visitor to the G4K site – seeking out new ways to entertain himself. Tanner has significant influence over his parent's spending towards family fun.

Description:

Tanner is a 4th grade student at Montgomery Elementary School, a public school. He lives with his mother & father (Laura & Shane Thompson) in a suburb of Chicago, Illinois.

Even though Tanner loves to be physically active (riding his skateboard and bike, participating in organized sports), Tanner thinks computers are really really fun and prefers the PC to the TV.

Tanner has been using computers at school since kindergarten and has had a family computer at home for two years.

He uses the PC mostly to play games and surf the web for "stuff" but occasionally does research for school projects. His favorite computer game of the moment is The Sims 2. He also really likes Roller Coaster Tycoon 3.

for more info on Tanner, visit http://G4K/portalproject/personas

G4K

FIGURE 5.17: *A persona one-pager for G4K's Tanner persona. Illustration created by Craig Hally.*

Story from the field

MOVING FROM BULLETED SKETCHES TO RICH ILLUSTRATIONS
(*Continued from Chapter 4*)

—Tom Pease, Microsoft Corporation

[In Chapter 4, Tom Pease described his team's experiences while creating personas (see "Story from the field: Personas on a Shoe String—Creating Rich Personas Quickly and Cost Effectively"). Now he discusses how the team moved from bulleted sketches to richer descriptions as they communicated their personas.]

As a final step in creating our personas, I had asked our User Assistance group (experts in technical writing, among other things) to review the bulleted sketch descriptions (see Figure 5.18) to help make the descriptions clear and crisp.

While the text was being reviewed, I asked one of the designers to start exploring presentation concepts. Other teams had done posters of their personas, so we were pretty sure we wanted posters as well. But what should the posters look like? We did a number of variations on the personas, using various layouts and color schemes to help us answer this question.

Over the next two weeks, we reviewed and refined the visuals with the management team. As the personas were given names and had pictures associated with them, they began to come to life. People on the team became excited.

Personally, I was pretty wedded to the idea of a bulleted list format for the persona posters so that people could read the characteristics from a distance. However, Jim, a designer, really wanted to move away from bullets. He wanted the personas to be more narrative, to tell more of a story to help "humanize" the personas. He broke the personas into two sections: one that described the persona and what the persona did and one that talked about how the persona would use the product (InfoPath).

To address my concerns about drawing people in to most important characteristics of each persona, he applied a number of sophisticated visual techniques to the posters. The titles and a portion of the introduction were done in large font. Instead of just one picture of the person in the corner, he broke the picture into several pieces of differing sizes and spread them around the area, creating a very interesting graphic. The posters used rich contrasting colors. In the end, the posters were so attractive and compelling they were guaranteed to catch our teammates' attention. Once anyone stopped to look at the poster, the narrative would further draw them in. Figure 5.19 shows the final poster for Oden.

(Story from the field, continued)

Oden, the "ocassional user."

How does Oden use XDocs?
Oden, a senior planner, uses XDocs because that's what his company uses.
- He uses forms created by Nick, Cara or Dawn.
- Oden regularly uses some forms, such as Status Report, but uses several forms (for example, Expense Report or Performance Review) infrequently enough that every time is a new learning experience.

What's important to Oden?
For Oden, the easier the XDocs is the better. He says: "Just make filling out this paper work easier."
- Pre-populating fields with past values, like expense or department codes, is a big win because it keeps Oden from having to continuously look up information.
- Oden wants inline instructions, ToolTips, and easy ways to get the information that he needs to quickly and accurately fill out forms.
- He expects error messages to help him find and fix problems.
- Because Oden sometimes works from home and travels occasionally, he wants to be able to work offline.
- He expects the user model for opening, saving, and submitting the form to be very simple.

Other commonly used tools:
Works extensively with Word and Excel.

Related job titles:
Oden represents a typical end-user, and similar positions include project managers, analysts and department managers.

Related personas:
Ed, the end-user from the Office Designer personas.

FIGURE 5.18: *A bulleted sketch version of our persona Oden.*

Once we got final agreement on the posters, we printed a number of them on nice heavy stock and pasted sets across all main hallways and in all of the conference rooms. There isn't much chance of anyone escaping in this way. We actually had the personas in the rooms where people were doing design and decision work. I sat in on a number of meetings in which people would go to the wall and read "Nick does this…" Those were magic moments to me.

Note: The author would like to acknowledge the work of Jim Watkins and Shannon Banks in their persona creation effort.

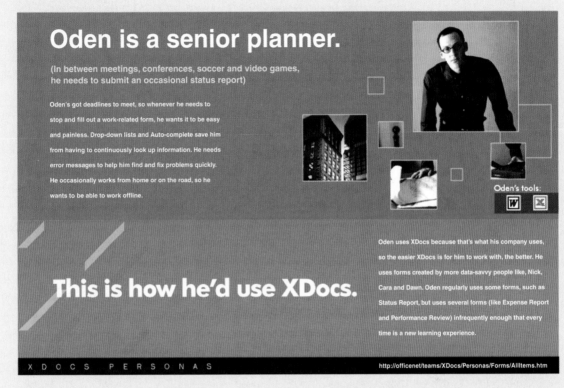

FIGURE 5.19: *The final poster for our persona Oden.*

Targeted detail posters

Targeted detail posters can be created to help you communicate specific information about your personas. These should be created in relation to hot topics or current needs of the development cycle. They can help create organizational focus, putting everyone in the same frame of mind about the same domain or topic. Figure 5.20 shows an example of a targeted detail poster done for the G4K team. Of course, the G4K team is very interested in PC and Internet use, as well as entertainment and gaming activities.

Targeted detail handouts (candy, gizmos, and so on)

Many of the buzz generator artifacts discussed earlier can also serve as enrichers, depending on the amount and type of information you include. Like the persona flip card set described previously, candy wrappers can only hold a small amount of information, but you have a lot of choices when it comes to which information you decide to include. Remember that

Tanner has already been using computers for years

Computer use begins at an early age. About three-quarters of 5-year-olds use computers, and over 90 percent of teens (ages 13-17) do so.

About 25 percent of 5-year-olds use the Internet, and this number rises to over 50 percent by age 9 and to at least 75 percent by ages 15-17. (28)

Tanner uses the PC for gaming, surfing the web and schoolwork

A majority (59 percent) of 5- through 17-year-olds use home computers to play games, and over 40 percent use computers to connect to the Internet (46 percent) and to complete school assignments (44 percent).

Tanner
the tenacious tinkerer
is a great target for G4k..

Tanner considers the PC as entertainment

The number of children age 12 and under going online for entertainment and games more than tripled between 1998 and 1999, reaching 9.2 million and surpassing homework as the most popular activity in this age bracket.

Growth has been exceptionally fast among boys age 12 and under. (1) Sixty-three percent of those surveyed prefer going online to watching television, and 55% choose online over talking on the telephone. (11)

Tanner is picky, easily distracted, and a multi-tasker

41% of tweens say they do other things while surfing the net. Some split their attention between surfing and talking on the phone, eating or listening to music. Still others say they watch TV while working at their computer. (4)

for more info on Tanner, visit http://G4K/portalproject/personas

G4K

FIGURE 5.20: *This targeted detail poster targets specific information about Tanner's PC and Internet use. Illustration created by Craig Hally.*

trinkets and other giveaways never lose their appeal. Consider using different types of artifacts to convey different types of information (e.g., a key chain for targeted information about mobility, a mouse pad for PC activities, or a coffee mug for leisure activities). However, remember that it is always a good idea to always include the basics, including the persona's photo, name, and job or role. You may also identify other information elements you want to consistently include on all persona artifacts, such as the persona's goals or a defining quote.

Story from the field

A-TIC, A-TAC, A-TTENEX

—Holly Jamesen Carr, GreenShape LLC, formerly Usability Specialist, Attenex Corporation

I decided to give edible reminders of the persona set for a new project to the Attenex engineering and QA teams. Early in the development process I created custom candy bar wrappers, which included very basic information about each persona: a photograph, name, role, and a few goals. I encouraged the team to "Collect all 6!"—one for each persona in the project—and enjoy a chocolate treat. Later, I created another candy handout: Tic-Tacs relabeled "A-tic, A-tac, A-ttenex." This time, in addition to the photo and name I included a job description and more specific information about what each persona would expect from the product interface.

Some engineers good-naturedly inquired if the Tic-Tacs were a not-so-subtle commentary on their breath, but found the visual cues a useful reminder as they worked. Today, empty Tic-Tac dispensers and persona candy bar wrappers (see Figure 5.21) are still proudly displayed in workspaces throughout the development department.

FIGURE 5.21: *Persona candy wrappers.*

Persona e-mail campaigns

Persona e-mail campaigns can be extremely valuable. They can help very naturally roll out more and more information about your personas over time. A well-crafted e-mail campaign can be fun and interesting, and can help you communicate details quickly and effectively. However, people tend to be highly sensitive to getting too much e-mail, and are very quick to label certain types of e-mail as spam. The last thing you want is to associate your persona effort with spam. As you plan a persona e-mail campaign, plan to keep e-mails as short and sweet as possible, and build in checkpoints to evaluate how your colleagues are reacting. In some cases, you may want to allow people to opt in or out of the e-mail campaign, and it is a good idea to post the e-mail messages on your persona Web site so that those who opt out or miss the e-mails still have access to the information.

- *Monthly persona newsletters:* Once a month or less, you can create a short newsletter to communicate specific information across all of your personas. For example, the following are newsletter headlines: "What Preston and Irene Do in Their Leisure Time," "Why Elaine Is Afraid to Upgrade," and "What Austin, Tanner and Colbi Think About Our Competitors." Various topics or domains will become important to your developing product over time. Focus your newsletter on those topics (e.g., setup/installation, security, internationalization, mobility, "check out" or purchase, and so on). To create a newsletter, simply write a small blurb for each of your personas regarding the topic at hand; add a few photos, data charts, or other illustrations; and include links for obtaining further information (e.g., a link to your persona Web site, links to your persona foundation documents, or direct links to supporting research reports). Alternatively, you might use your personas as an organizing scheme for reporting progress and other developments on your product. Through the eyes of your target audience, report important design decisions or feature changes that have occurred. Report the various activities or ways in which your personas have been utilized. If you have engaged in ongoing research and other UCD efforts, you might consider lumping all of your "user" information highlights into one coordinated report.

- *Weekly factoid e-mail:* You don't have to create a full newsletter to convey persona-related information via e-mail. Create a "fact of the week" (see Figure 5.22) to send out to the organization, and choose facts based on the type of information you think will be most welcome. This can be a great opportunity to reconnect with the core team. A "fact of the week" meeting is an opportunity for all of the persona wranglers to get together and talk about how the personas are, and are not, being used. The weekly fact e-mail should be very brief—short enough to read in total in the area of the viewing window (i.e., a few sentences or one paragraph). To help keep it short, be sure to include a link to further information.

- *Persona e-mail addresses:* Ask your e-mail administrator to create an internal e-mail address for each persona (or, if you get resistance to this idea, you can create an e-mail address using one of the free Internet e-mail services, such as Hotmail or Yahoo!). If possible within your organization, e-mail sent to this alias should be automatically redirected

To: G4k portal team

Cc:

Subject: Persona fact of the week – Tanner uses the web to extend his game playing activites

Bcc:

Signature: None

Evidence from different sources indicates that more and more Tanners will be going online as a preferred activity. Game playing online is similarly on the rise. . .

- The number of children age 12 and under going online for entertainment and games more than tripled between 1998 and 1999, reaching 9.2 million and surpassing homework as the most popular activity in this age bracket. Growth has been exceptionally fast among boys age 12 and under. (Source 1)

- Young People Prefer Online to Television and Telephone: The centrality of Internet use can be seen in the degree to which it has supplanted other favorite activities. Sixty-three percent of those surveyed prefer going online to watching television and 55% choose online over talking on the telephone.   (Source 11)

- The popularity of online games has risen since 1999 when only 18 percent participated. The 2003 poll revealed that more than 1/3 (37%) of frequent game players go online to play - up from 31% in 2002. (Source 9)

- Overall, boys are more interested in technology, seeking out game-playing resources, building web pages, downloading software, and even downloading music files. Teen boys largely use the Internet for game playing and game-playing advice.   (Source 18)

For more information on Tanner and our other personas, see http://G4K/personas.

Ingrid Dante | Interaction Design | G4k Portal Team

FIGURE 5.22: *An example of a "fact of the week" e-mail for G4K. This example describes Tanner's web and gaming behaviors.*

to the wrangler for the persona campaign. There are several ways you can use the persona e-mail accounts. Consider sending kudos and "thank-you" messages to team members who have done something good to benefit your end users (perhaps sent from the one persona who will benefit the most from their efforts). Doing so serves two purposes: it promotes the existence of the personas and encourages team members to be pursuing user-focused work. Advertise the existence of the accounts to your organization and invite people to send persona-related questions to the e-mail addresses. The individual persona wranglers can then research and address these questions, and reply "from" the persona.

Although sending e-mail messages from your personas may sound extreme, we have actually tried this technique. Most of our team thought it was fun and interesting. There are considerable benefits and risks of using persona e-mail aliases. If you receive many e-mails, you can collect them and evaluate them at the end of the project to help in the measurement of ROI. You can argue, and show examples, that the personas were a well-used and effective means of conveying important user data. On the downside, in some cases, e-mail from personas can seem silly and possibly annoying.

Anti-personas

One way to enrich the understanding of your personas is to show your team who they are *not* targeting by creating anti-personas (or negative personas as Alan Cooper originally defined them in *The Inmates are Running the Asylum*, p. 136). As described in Chapter 4, anti-personas are brief persona sketches that exemplify people you do *not* want to build the product for.

If many people in your organization have strong but incorrect ideas about your target audience, you *might* want to consider creating anti-persona communication materials.

This happens many times where the product team members are users of the product you are developing, or are intensely engaged in your product's domain area. For example, the G4K core team might find that the development team is very engaged in gaming. Perhaps many people on that product team are parents of young children (like our Irene persona). The people on the development team may relate to the target audience in significant ways. What they don't realize is that they may be different from the target in significant ways as well. For example, your development team is likely to be much more technical and technologically inclined than your target audience. Anti-personas help convey these differences and strengthen the notion that "you are not the typical user."

Anti-personas don't have to represent "bad" people or users with inherently negative connotations. They are simply used to surface misguided assumptions about target users that are circulating in your organization, and to clearly express that this is *not* the persona everyone should be designing for. As an example, for G4K an anti-persona might be an older teen or adult who is an "extreme gamer"—someone who takes gaming very seriously. They own multiple gaming consoles/platforms, purchase every new game that comes out, subscribe to gaming magazines, and even compete in local and online game tournaments. Perhaps many of the people that work at G4K actually fall into this category. Clearly, that type of person is not a central target for the *G4K.com* portal.

Create real people posters

Finally, you might create a few artifacts that are more about building credibility than providing useful information. For example, consider creating a poster that simply has real quotes from real users that fit a specific persona. Figure 5.23 shows one such poster with a variety of Tanner-like kids talking about themselves and computers. These posters show that the personas are made up of data about real users who have real needs.

Create a central repository for your persona artifacts

No matter how many (and which) materials you choose to create, it is a good idea to keep a centralized storehouse of all of your materials. This will help your core team keep track of which materials exist and monitor how they are being used, and it will enable people

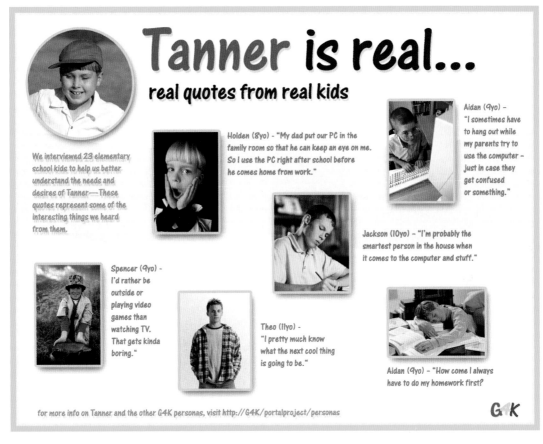

FIGURE 5.23: *A real people poster showing quotes from real kids who fit the Tanner profile. Illustration created by Craig Hally.*

throughout your organization to come to one location for all of the information they need. There are several ways to accomplish this.

First, consider simply making a specific room (e.g., a meeting room) or work area (a table in a common room) your persona headquarters. Place copies of your foundation documents, research reports, and communication artifacts in this space. Post a FAQ sheet and create a suggestion box or announcement board to encourage interaction. Keep this area organized and up-to-date.

In addition, if your company has a broadly accessible (but private) network or intranet, set up a share folder or Web site. We have found that creating an internal persona Web site enables you to really structure your content and easily focus your team's attention on important materials.

The persona Web site

If you have the resources available to do so, we think it is a good idea to create an internal Web site to serve as a central repository for all of your persona data, descriptions, and materials. Of course, you can create your persona Web site in any way you see fit. However, we suggest that your Web site be designed to progressively disclose the large amount of information your personas might contain. At the topmost level (your persona home page), you will want to provide three basic things:

● A list of the primary and secondary personas, with links to more information for each persona (Who is our target audience?)

● Links to information and tools or templates for specific uses of the personas (How do I use these personas?)

● Links to information about the persona method and your persona creation process (What are personas and why should I care?)

Ironically, the first materials that are ready to be included in your Web site are those that should reside deepest in the information hierarchy: your foundation documents and the raw data sources (or links to them). The materials you want to provide easiest access to should be those designed for buzz generation, summaries or sketches that include the most fundamental or critical qualities of your personas, and any navigational elements designed to help visitors find any deeper information they need.

Rather than simply linking the foundation documents directly from the home page, we recommend that, for each persona, you include an interstitial summary page with basic information. Include roles and goals and any primary description information that helps progressively disclose the persona definition without overloading the reader with too much detail. You might also consider including a simple comparison page that presents the most basic and key characteristics of your personas (formatted to be easily scannable) to visitors so that they can quickly understand how the personas are different. More generally, try to include easy-to-access materials that will answer most of the questions visitors will have, and "bury" potentially overwhelming details.

Your persona Web site is the one "artifact" that allows you endless depth and breadth as well as technology to help bolster your team's faith in your personas. You can use your Web site to increase awareness of seemingly peripheral information (your data and the process) as people casually browse primary information about your personas. Make sure that the relationship between your personas and their underlying data is clear. By using hover-over effects and hyperlinks, you can easily connect characteristics to data points. The original data reports can be linked from your home page or from the foundation documents that should also be available on your site. Sometimes people just want proof that you have looked at data, and don't need the details. If you created a data source index, as discussed in Chapter 3, you should make that available on your site. You may want to post links to information on the persona method itself, such as case studies, examples of use, and so on. Your persona Web site should be an ever-growing source of information about target users and your UCD activities.

IF YOU ARE A CONSULTANT

Birth and maturation can be quite difficult for the outside consultant. Your client may not be receptive to or understand the importance of broad education and ongoing persona communication. Getting funding for artifacts or billing for time related to creating them may be a difficult endeavor. Moreover, you simply won't be able to hang around throughout your client's development cycle to promote and monitor the proper use of your personas. Unless you can find an "insider" champion for the campaign, your personas may die on the vine and the likelihood of repeat business for your service may be diminished. We offer a couple of suggestions to help you along in this regard.

First, encourage participation from the client in any and all of your persona creation and communication activities. It is likely that if the client team is involved in the persona creation process you will need less of a direct evangelism effort yourself. You will want their input on appropriate artifacts. Our advice is to stay on the inexpensive side here. If you can make it happen, have client team members run the kickoff meeting and do the presenting. This will garner ownership but could possibly decrease credibility (that is, as a consultant your input is often taken as gold, as you are viewed as a guru). Be vigilant in your meetings with the client so that you can find and target an influential team member as your persona champion. Spend extra time to personally convince them of the value and need for an ongoing persona wrangler.

Second, if personas are a major part of your deliverable to a client, make sure your client has very explicit knowledge, instructions, and expectations regarding the personas. Moreover, provide them with tools to help them manage the personas and the ongoing campaign (e.g., Photoshop templates, spec templates, example documents, and communication campaign ideas). Not only will you need to convince your client regarding the need for ongoing persona communication, but you will have to convince them to spend the money on good artifacts (and not just rely on the persona documentation to do the communication). At the very least, make sure they have big posters mounted on poster board that they can invite into the meetings and actually set up on the chairs. Include a lot of data on these posters so that it is always right there and doesn't have to be hunted for. Chapter 6 explores some specific tools (e.g., the scenario spreadsheet) you can prepare and hand over to the client that will aid in persona management and persona usage.

Story from the field

KNOW WHY YOU ARE DOING PERSONAS

—Robert Barlow-Busch, Quarry Communications

We did some great research and created a solid set of personas, but they haven't really been used by the client. Why? The client was so excited by the concept of personas that they engaged us to create some without really knowing what they wanted to do with them. We tried to address this issue at the project's onset, but because the personas weren't originally driven by a clear need on a particular project they seem to have become homeless in the end despite our efforts.

Finally, make it a point to check back with your client several times throughout their development cycle and product launch after your consultancy has ended. If nothing else, you will remind them that it is important to keep referring back to their target audience after the initial design phase is complete.

In the end, it may be difficult to explain the amount of work that has been done to create personas and not give the client the feeling that you have been wasting time. It may also be difficult to convince them to invest more time and effort into their continued evangelism. Remember that what your client really wants to see is good design, not good personas. Invest your efforts where they will have the most impact and value.

SUMMARY

Birth and maturation is a period of strategic communication and determined execution of plans. It may not seem like it, but it is a time when you and your core team must re-double your dedication and effort toward the persona method. During this phase, you analyzed your internal audience (your teammates) and created communication devices tuned to their needs, styles, and environment. You educated your broader team about UCD, the persona method, your particular persona creation process, and your resulting personas. You have planned a progressive disclosure of information about your personas, starting with the creation of "buzz"—a general awareness and excitement that something interesting is coming. Hopefully this will have the result that your team will be enlightened about its users to a degree never before achieved in your company.

You will continue with various forms of knowledge enrichment, making sure that the personas are easily differentiated from one another and that your process and personas are seen as credible, important, and useful. In the end, if *birth and maturation* activities are executed appropriately your team will be primed for and even enthusiastic about incorporating your personas in their design and development activities. Your next job is to show them how that is done.

PERSONA ADULTHOOD

6

The basic outlines of the product you are building (the business plan and vision) are clear, and the time has come to write the spec (specification document or documents), get it approved and "costed," and then get down to the business of building something. Time pressure is on and decisions have to be made fast. A bad decision can result in an unusable, unuseful, or undesirable (in short, unsellable) product later. There is a sense of needing to both go faster and maintain control of the frenzied activity. Assumptions are mixing with facts, and both are complicated by politics. Everyone is afraid of being a bottleneck, and yet no one has enough information or clarity to make all of the important decisions they have to make.

Once an organization starts to build a product, everyone (or almost everyone) turns from thinking strategically to acting tactically. Everyone can see just a piece of the puzzle, and communication among internal feature teams, organizational roles, and disciplines is both critical and difficult. Often, large groups of people have to work together to make feature and implementation decisions, and no one person in the group can see beyond the one or two pieces of the puzzle that "belong" to her. Each is responsible for some of the hundreds of daily decisions that affect the customer experience, and each brings a set of (usually implicit) assumptions about the eventual users of the product to bear on each of the decisions she makes. In short, your organization is probably in a state of creative, productive, and time-pressured chaos. The stakes are

345

G4K Meanwhile, at G4K...

THE G4K CORE TEAM IS READY TO PUT THEIR PERSONAS TO USE

During birth, the G4K persona core team introduced the persona method and the G4K personas to the G4K kids' portal team and executive staff. There are some new persona posters on the walls and people around the company are beginning to talk about target users. The persona core team is eager to see the personas used toward the development of G4K's new Web site. They have several specific uses in mind already and have begun to contact team members who will be involved in those activities.

The development cycle will be short. In fact, some of the coding has already begun!

The use of personas will have to be tactical and carefully targeted. Still, the core team knows from previous development efforts that real focus on users has been difficult to achieve. Even if the personas help just a little bit, the effort will be worthwhile.

very high, the work is tricky, and there are many voices competing for air time. At this point, every team member or stakeholder is focusing on his or her own responsibilities. For example:

- The executive staff feels like they have made good decisions and are eager to see some palpable progress from their technical staff. They are clear on what they want, and they are ready to see some results.

- Product and project managers are feeling a huge amount of pressure, as they are usually those responsible for translating the product vision into an executable plan. They are responsible for the spec that will serve as the "bible" for product developers.

- The development team is researching technologies and techniques, driven by scant information about requirements but pressure to "hit the ground running" when they get clarity from above.

- The QA team is scrambling to get "in the loop" and understand what features are being designed so that they can build appropriate test plans.

- Usability specialists, technical writers, and UI designers are also struggling to stay connected and involved in decisions being made, and to influence these decisions based on their expertise. Like most of the others on the team, they want to be able to plan their work for the coming development cycle.

● The marketing team is getting information on the yet-to-be-built product from the executive staff and product and project managers. Their goal is to build a plan for advertising and launching the product when it is ready.

Within this organizational stew, you are going to try to champion the use of your now mature personas, who may be seen as unwelcome intruders into an already complex environment and a known and accepted process. They are, after all, yet another set of voices to be reckoned with. However, these are voices that are ready to aid your team in solving problems and simplifying decisions—if they are used effectively. Personas can help make the translation of data and assumptions, and the decision process itself, more *explicit*.

WHAT IS *ADULTHOOD* FOR PERSONAS?

Adulthood is the phase of the persona lifecycle when you put your personas to use. To ensure that your personas are used, you must provide your teammates with persona-related procedures, instructions, guidelines, templates, and tools they can easily weave in with their other tasks. We think *adulthood* is one of the most exciting aspects of the persona lifecycle model. Until now, there have been very few documented methods for *using* personas beyond suggestions to include the personas in design discussions.

In this chapter, we provide sections on how to "wrangle" and promote personas as they are used by your product design and development organization. We then break the chapter into sections dedicated to specific persona methods you can use to help plan, design, evaluate, and release your product. Each section provides structured activities, tools, and in most cases several case studies from other persona practitioners.

What to expect during persona adulthood

When you start promoting and using personas around your organization, you might get a bit carried away. Everyone does. Personas are charming. They are fun, creative, interesting, and new. Personas highlight interesting issues that are engaging and feel important. Such issues are probably considerably more intriguing than most others you are dealing with. However, personas also raise complex questions that may require deeper analysis and other techniques to truly understand and solve problems. Personas cannot do everything.

Keep your wits about you. Do not let yourself—or your organization—get swept up in persona mania. Remember that personas are most effective when they augment existing design processes. They cannot solve every problem in your organization or inform every design decision. Persona mania happens when all anyone in the organization can talk about are the personas, when no other UCD techniques are being employed, and when all you want to do in your own job is work on the personas and related materials. When you feel yourself slipping into persona mania (and we bet you will), come back to this page and reread some of our persona caveats.

Personas are not a panacea, and other methods do work. Personas should augment, not replace, existing design processes and UCD methods. They can help you maintain focus on your target audience and answer certain types of questions. They cannot guide every design decision. Many decisions need to be based on competitive strategy, technological constraints and feasibility, or simple economic or political reasons. There are some things personas simply cannot do. Many times, when your personas do not provide an appropriate or reasonable answer, it is an indication that some other UCD technique or market research is needed. Don't abandon the other tools in your toolbox.

On the other hand, you do not necessarily have to abandon the methods in this chapter if your personas do not quite catch on. Maybe the data-driven personas have not caught on, but you do find your organization talking about simple user classes, market segments, delineated roles, profiles of real users, or loosely defined assumption personas. If you find yourself in this situation, you can still try the tools and techniques we provide in the following sections. Of course, we believe that these techniques are all done best when using rich and rigorously defined personas, but any user representation is better than nothing.

Personas are not "golden." Although we do argue that personas should be derived from data, we do not believe it is possible to create perfect, infallible personas. Persona use requires decision making. They are a useful method and tool, but not a science. If not used appropriately, personas can be as dangerous as any other powerful tool. Powerful tools can easily lead you down the wrong path if you are not careful. (We are all familiar with the hazards of showing nonrepresentative video examples, over-cuing participants in usability tests, and "lying" with statistics or misleading graphics.) Always use common sense, gather information and requirements from many sources, and validate your decisions with real users and other data.

Personas are not your company's product. You were most likely hired to help your company create excellent products and services, not personas *per se*. Your company does not sell personas. Personas are a means to an end, not an end in themselves. Your real product is what generates revenue for your company. So, be judicious with your time and effort toward personas. If you cannot find the time to work on personas and maintain your other responsibilities, scale back the persona effort.

Personas will never be universally loved and respected. Although your personas can capture the attention and imagination of your organization, some of your teammates are going to resist them. Personas simply will not appeal to, nor will they be useful to, everyone. Even colleagues who completely buy in to the persona effort will not focus on the personas all of the time, and they are likely to forget why and how the personas can help them do their jobs. When team members do use the personas, many of them will try to twist the personas "just a little" to align them with pet technologies and features or strongly held beliefs. To add insult to injury, after the product is complete no one will be certain if your personas did anything for the team or the project. That is just the way it is. Be comforted by the fact

that many a persona practitioner has been there before you, and we have done our best throughout this book to give you practical advice for spotting and solving these problems.

Help your personas "settle in"

Your personas are like new employees in your organization: they could be embraced as invaluable resources your team can't imagine living without or they could be marginalized and deemed useless. It is your job to help these "new employees" settle in. Personas can bring fresh insights and new energy, but they will also need to be "trained" a bit to suit the work habits of the rest of the organization. In Chapter 5 we recommended that you assign a wrangler to each of your personas. Each wrangler should be responsible for keeping an eye on the use (and misuse) of the personas during *adulthood*.

Each wrangler should think of himself as the persona's boss. You have prepared your organization for their arrival, you have introduced them, and you have provided them with high-level goals or tasks. Now you have to let go enough to allow the personas to do their jobs. Just like a boss, each persona wrangler will have to check in with the personas and to a certain extent manage and even police the way they are working in the organization. In other words, you have to allow your colleagues to engage with and use the personas fairly freely, but you have to ensure that the personas are not being misused, dying on the vine, or becoming "feral."

In general, the key to keeping personas in *adulthood* present and alive throughout the churn and chaos of a long product development cycle is to assign them jobs to do that are specific to the disciplines and roles of your teammates.

Start with the basics: invite personas into your offices and into your meetings

Adult personas are ready to be put to work in a variety of ways. We provide some very specific (and structured) ways of using personas in the four main sections of this chapter. However, personas can be used more generally (in nonstructured ways) across your entire organization and throughout the entire development cycle. They can help by answering difficult questions and by focusing activities in a way that takes the guesswork out of making customer-driven decisions. Adult personas can participate in your product planning, design, and development process by:

- Being present at your meetings and representing the voice of your customer throughout the development cycle

- Providing consistency by serving as a common reference point across your organization, even in a highly chaotic, fast-moving, ever-changing environment

- Providing a way for all of the product teams to touch base using a common language and by serving as a means of assurance that everyone is staying focused on creating a good experience for the right audiences.

Personas can only be involved and helpful in these ways if they inhabit your workplace and attend your meetings. Even though they are not real people, personas can become the most powerful voices in the room. You will need to expend considerable effort on creating communication devices for your personas, many of which you can use to help your personas "move into" your workplace and conversations (see Chapter 5).

(Story from the field, continued)

These sessions have the dual intention of raising awareness of customer experience and of identifying better ways to serve our clients. For the first half of the meetings, I spend a great deal of time talking about those things that directly impact our clients: how our channels operate, what our processes are like, how our clients feel when things go wrong, and what the experience should be like. In the second half of the meetings I open it up to the audience to discuss ways of improving the customer experience. I often find meetings breaking down as attendees start to get obsessed with internal issues and finger pointing—things that have nothing to do with the client.

So, today I take "Herr Schultz" with me. Schultzy, as we affectionately call him, is a life-size poster of one of our clients. I put him right next to me at the front of the room. I also hand out a profile of Schultzy to all attendees, so that they can get to know him. And I set a simple rule: If Schultzy wouldn't care about it we don't talk about it. This technique has two benefits. First, it gets people focused on the idea that we are here to talk about the client. Second, it ensures that people talk about things that directly impact our clients, and that we don't talk about internal politics, historical reasons why things are not done, or people's pet projects. And Shultzy gets around. We lend him out (with instructions for how to "care" for him) to anyone in the business who wants to borrow him for team meetings or project work. Shultzy has been an incredibly useful partner in our endeavors.

Beyond bringing the personas into the team spaces, you can and should specifically invite your personas to meetings. During any meeting, start looking for opportunities to use the personas to help answer issues that come up. If a disagreement about features or priorities comes up during a meeting, one of the personas will likely offer a fresh perspective.

Story from the field

PERSONAS CAN HELP YOUR TEAM OUT OF RAT HOLES

—**Bob Barlow-Busch,** Practice Director of Interaction Design, Quarry Integrated Communications, Inc.

I'm a consultant, and I'm often in the difficult position of seeing personal and organizational politics get in the way of good decision making. In one meeting, I watched and listened as a large product team argued about a particular feature and whether it should go into the product. They argued about schedules and effort and their opinions about what "the users" really needed. Finally, I got up and left the room—but I came back, carrying the persona posters I had delivered the week before. Suddenly, there was a path out of the deep rat hole they had dug for themselves. They stopped talking about whether "the user" needed the feature and discussed which persona was most likely to have trouble if the feature were absent. Within a few minutes they decided that the extra effort for the feature was indeed worthwhile. I think they were just as relieved to find a way out of their opinion-entrenched argument as they were to make the decision about the feature.

Refer often to the persona details listed on the posters or other artifacts and consider recording decisions directly on them. For example, add notes to the persona posters with sticky notes if the personas help with a decision: "Frank says we don't need support for high-resolution graphics, because he never needs to print things out!" or, "Sarah reminded us that she uses a 56k modem—and she's going to leave if the page size takes too long to load." Include the date these decisions were made, the rationale, and by whom. Doing so will help others not attending that meeting understand why certain decisions were made (though note that the rationale for the decision is in part embedded in the persona and in part based on other considerations). This also makes clear that your personas are actually being used. Your persona posters and other artifacts will become important records of team decisions.

Although having personas "participate" in discussions may feel a bit forced and awkward at first, this technique ensures that you never stray too far from the customer data that is the lifeblood of good decisions. After everyone becomes comfortable in "asking personas for input," your team will probably find that the personas' presence is a relief. Decisions can be attributed to (and blamed on) personas. They are happy to take the heat—as long as their opinions are not misrepresented.

PLAN, DESIGN, EVALUATE, RELEASE: HOW TO USE PERSONAS DURING THE STAGES OF PRODUCT DEVELOPMENT

Let's look back at the traditional waterfall model of product development we briefly discussed in Chapter 2 (see Figure 6.1). You will note that in an ideal situation persona adulthood extends over the majority of the development process. In fact, persona adulthood may even continue after development is complete, beyond the release phase, providing help to marketing, sales, operations, and support.

For this chapter, we have further simplified the waterfall model into four distinct development stages (see Figure 6.2).

The rest of this chapter is organized according to these four stages. For each stage we provide several usage techniques and tools that engage your personas to the benefit of your team and product.

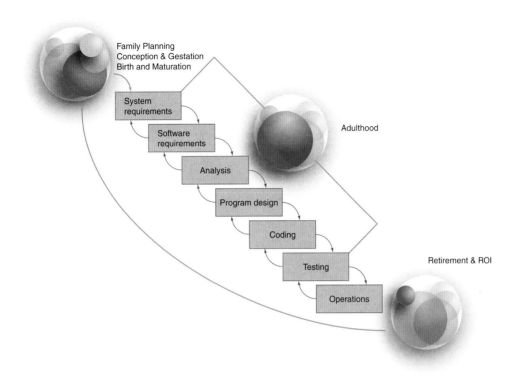

FIGURE 6.1: *The classic waterfall model of software development with persona lifecycle phases added. (Adapted from waterfall diagram from www.maxwideman.com/papers/plc-models/1990s.htm.)*

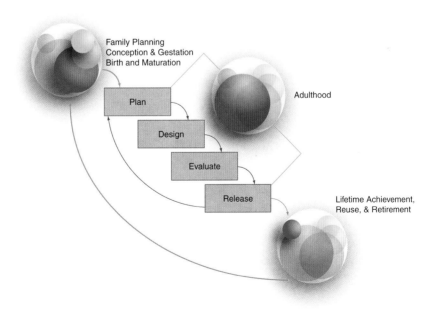

FIGURE 6.2: *Plan, design, evaluate, release. We have further simplified the waterfall process model into four stages: plan your product, design your product, evaluate your designs, and release your product.*

- ● *Stage 1:* Plan your product (system requirements, software requirements, analysis)
  - ○ Determining the product vision and functional requirements
  - ○ Competitive reviews
  - ○ Feature brainstorming, prioritization, and work planning
- ● *Stage 2:* Explore design solutions (product design)
  - ○ Scenario-based design and mapping
  - ○ Design explorations and mood boards
- ● *Stage 3:* Evaluate your design solutions (coding and testing)
  - ○ Design reviews and cognitive walkthroughs
  - ○ User testing and ongoing user research
  - ○ Quality assurance testing and bug bashes
- ● *Stage 4:* Support the release (operations)
  - ○ Documentation and product support
  - ○ Marketing and sales

Finally, note that this chapter covers only a handful of uses of personas, and we believe that personas can be used in many more ways than we have explored. Also note that the waterfall model of development is not the only model in use. Personas can be applied to any development model and design approach that lends itself to understanding users.

Story from the field

PERSONA ADULTHOOD WHEN YOU ARE A CONSULTANT

—Karen McGrane, Vice President, User Experience, Avenue A|Razorfish

Personas are a hot topic in the industry right now, and many clients come to us specifically looking for persona creation as part of the Web development lifecycle. There's a difference, though, between creating personas as one deliverable in the process and actually using the personas to drive design decisions or to change the way the business operates. Sometimes, I fear that persona creation is seen as a magic bullet, when in reality the benefits of personas arrive in using them as part of a longer process that runs throughout the project.

One challenge we face is that the client's desire to have personas doesn't necessarily mean they are prepared to take action on the personas once they are created. In our role as outside consultants, the trick is to find ways of integrating the personas throughout the project, in order to keep the client focused on the needs of the customer. The following are some of the ways in which we implement personas:

- We usually conduct some form of primary ethnographic research, and we use the personas as a way of presenting the findings from the research. Because people within the organization who are not involved with the current project want to see the research findings, the personas are a means of communicating the results of the research in an engaging way—even to people who will only interact with them through reading the final deliverable.
- Personas are used as part of a brainstorming technique to identify possible features or content for the site. We engage the client to imagine how each persona would interact with the site, and then identify site offerings that would meet that customer's needs.
- As part of a structured process for prioritizing possible features and content, we rank how well each feature would meet the needs of each persona. (We also rank each feature against other variables, such as the goals of the business, its technical complexity, and the requirements for maintenance.)
- As part of the design process, personas and scenarios can be used as a way of validating the design as it progresses. Design teams can try to look at the design through the eyes of the persona, and evaluate how well the design performs on common scenarios. This can be formal (such as a structured walkthrough) or just an informal run-through while creating.
- When it is time to lock down the designs and the specification so that development can begin, it is common for the relationship to become tense. Clients tend to get "the wedding-day jitters" when it is time to truly commit to all of the decisions they have been working toward. Personas are one tool in our toolbox we use to mitigate this response and to manage the internal politics that inevitably pop up at this point in the development process. We use the personas to gently guide the client back to thinking about their customers' needs. Of course,

personas are not the only tool we use in this situation. We also have project management tools, such as change order requests, to keep the project on track.
- We usually conduct usability testing at a couple of different points in the process. It is usually pretty easy to use the personas to help define the target users and the scenarios we are going to test. In fact, I find personas to be particularly helpful in getting market researchers at the client company to understand why we want to screen participants for criteria other than demographic variables.

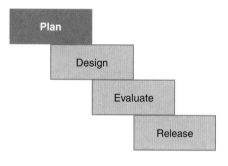

STAGE 1: USE PERSONAS TO PLAN YOUR PRODUCT

Before delving into the real work of development, your organization needs to create a vision and generate an overall development plan for your product. To do this, your leaders will want to understand both industry and market trends, customer requirements, and more technical system requirements for your product's domain. You will need to develop a big picture for your product: what it will do, how it will fit into the market, what problems it will solve, how you will approach building it, and so on.

Now that you have created your personas, you can ask the personas to "tell you their stories." The needs, goals, and contexts you so carefully included in your persona descriptions will now allow you to generate helpful stories about the way your product will be used and the actions (and reactions) it should elicit.

In this section, we explain how personas can help during this planning process, both by helping you discover important features and by helping you evaluate the relative values of each feature. You can use personas to help you understand and capture your user and system requirements through:

- Persona narratives and storytelling
- Persona-focused competitive reviews
- Persona-focused feature brainstorming
- Persona-focused evaluation of proposed features.

Persona-based approaches for understanding user requirements and envisioning your product

The personas' presence around your workplace can help you define an appropriate product for your target audience in a general fashion. The personas can also participate more directly by helping to identify specific user requirements and desires in terms of particular features and functionality.

How does your development team generate the high-level vision and then determine the key functionality and distinct features to build into your product? These decisions are often made by high-level leaders and executives in your company and are typically based on the availability of certain technologies, system architectures, and business plans/strategy ("We have the technology to do X, so let's build a product around it," or, "No one has a product that does Y; we should create it"). In other cases, your team members promote pet features, sometimes thinking of themselves as the ultimate user ("Well, I like to do Y, so the product should support doing that"). The basic requirements, functionality, and feature ideas for your product may come from any or all of the following sources:

- Executive directive
- Technological maturity (it's already built)
- Pet features ("I know what I'd like it to do.")
- Team brainstorming of ideas
- Technical or feature-based competitive reviews (keeping up with the Jones')
- Customer requests
- Support issues/costs
- Strategic partnership, key client request ("Make the sale" feature.)
- Demand from key industry influencers (e.g., John Dvorak, noted PC industry guru).

We believe it is important for you to let your target audience play a role in this process. Toward this, we examine storytelling, feature brainstorming, and competitive review using personas to help your team explore requirements and generate feature ideas. However feature ideas are generated, it is not uncommon for a product team to end up with a long list of features they are considering for the product release. We describe a two-part approach that helps bring the personas' voices (and the data they encompass) into the evaluation process—the decision-making process that determines which features and functionality end up being pursued.

Story from the field

MAPPING PERSONA DATA TO USER INTERFACE CONCEPTS

—Frank Spillers, Principal and Co-CEO, Experience Dynamics

Having a clear mental picture of what the user wants is extremely valuable in negotiating and advocating for the best user experience possible. The challenge is often to make the jump from user needs analysis data to user interface design choices. When you conduct persona research, be ready to map real-world user issues to persona design questions. The following table (Figure 6.3) outlines how user data maps directly to actual design issues as they are specified for each screen.

Persona data:	Routine Behavior
Design correlation:	Are the user's most common tasks clear and apparent in the most visible area of the screen?

Persona data:	Critical Incidents
Design correlation:	Is a recovery strategy apparent from confusion, user error, system error and navigation-related error?

Persona data:	Triggers/Touch Points
Design correlation:	What information or actions does a user refer to on this screen? What elements advance or detract from user progress on this screen?

Persona data:	Motivations
Design correlation:	Is there a justification to continue with each path? Does the user have what is important to them on this screen?

Persona data:	Habits and Expectations
Design correlation:	Does each screen have the most common elements? Is there a sense of familiarity on each screen based on the user's goal?

Persona data:	Interruptions/Disturbances
Design correlation:	Is it easy to return to the task or is concentration required? Does navigation provide effective "where you are" status?

FIGURE 6.3: *Map user data directly to specific design issues.*

When we gather user data for our personas, we try to keep in mind how real-life events will translate to the user interface or interaction design. Then, we refer back to this persona data as design issues and questions arise, and use persona data to justify or interpret our interaction design choices.

Invite personas to tell you their stories

In Chapter 9, Whitney Quesenberry includes a rich exploration of the value of stories in product design and their relationship to personas. As she says, stories:

- Communicate culture
- Organize and transmit information
- Explore new ideas
- Put personas in motion.

Putting personas into motion helps us understand behaviors, reactions, and expectations, which in turn help us design the best possible features and functionality for our products. The first stories you need to understand are the stories about the way things are done today. You can use your personas to capture and understand the problems, challenges, and pain points people encounter as they work within your product's domain *without* the help of the product you are building. Once you understand these stories, you can create new stories (scenarios, flows, use cases, and narratives) that describe the way things could work once your product is built. Whitney describes many types of stories in her chapter, each of which conveys a different level of detail and scope of context. These include:

- Springboard stories
- "Points of pain" stories
- Key scenarios
- Design Maps
- Narrative scenarios
- Flow diagrams
- Use cases.

During your product planning work, we recommend that you focus on springboard stories, "points of pain" stories, and Reality Maps (for more on Reality Maps, see Chapter 10). These "big picture" stories will set the context and motivation for your product. They will expose pain points and highlight design opportunities to your team. They can call out possible new features and clarify needed redesigns of current implementations. They show you where improvements and innovation can occur. Later, as you explore design solutions, you can use Design Maps, scenarios, flow diagrams, and use cases to design the features you have prioritized. For two interesting examples of using stories to understand the big picture and identify opportunities, see "Story from the field: Lifestyle Snapshots Help You Envision Design Opportunities" (following) by David Anderson of Microsoft Corporation and "Story from the field: Personas Help Redesign the Carnegie Library Through Storyboards and Narratives" (later in this chapter) by Heather McQuaid of MAYA Design. Heather describes the narrative

in prose and includes a chart depicting a scenario describing her persona's interactions with the various artifacts and people in her surroundings (for additional information, see [McQuaid *et al.* 2003]). Finally, see Chapter 9 for more on how persona stories can help your team craft an appropriate and tactical vision for your product.

Story from the field

LIFESTYLE SNAPSHOTS HELP YOU ENVISION DESIGN OPPORTUNITIES

—David Anderson, Visual Studio Enterprise Systems, Microsoft Corporation

With ubiquitous mobile computing devices and applications that can be accessed from Web terminals almost anywhere, it has become increasingly difficult to know in advance the context of use for an application. Without a firm context, the designer's job is difficult. Anticipation of the user's needs in any given situation is much more difficult.

This gap in contextual information can be filled by expanding the definition for each persona with a detailed "lifestyle snapshot" of how that persona lives and works for important time periods, situations, or events. A lifestyle snapshot describes a simple period in which the proposed application may be useful to that persona. It must be a sufficiently long period to provide a context for usage. Multiple lifestyle snapshots are typically generated for a given persona, though if appropriate a single snapshot could describe an entire "day in the life" of a persona.

Usage Opportunities

Lifestyle snapshots describe how the persona lives now—today—without any new technology. They come before usage scenarios, which describe how the persona might use a new application. Like anthropology, lifestyle snapshots provide us insight into the life of the persona and allow us to see the opportunities for the new application to add real value for that persona. Value might be saved time, saved money, better communication, quality improvements such as improved accuracy of information or style improvements such as improved presentation, access to previously unknown information, or faster access to stored information.

An Example

Cascade Air is a new premier service carrier operating out of SeaTac International airport near Seattle. They are determined to steal business from low-cost carriers by providing a range of personal services and quasi-luxury accoutrements. Imagine that they have asked you (as designer) to participate in the creation of a new messaging service that could enhance sales and customer satisfaction.

One of your personas is Ferdinand "Ferdie" Mosler, a 48-year-old son of German immigrants. He is fluent in German and English. He holds a degree in economics from the University of Washington and an MBA in international business affairs from IMD in Geneva, Switzerland. He works as a venture capitalist for a secretive Seattle-based firm. He lives on Mercer Island in the middle of Lake Washington.

(Story from the field, continued)

He is a frequent flyer who travels business class. He is a very desirable catch for Cascade Air and they want his business badly. The following is a lifestyle snapshot of a typical day in his life when he is traveling.

> Ferdie rises at 4:45 A.M. when his alarm clock rudely awakens him earlier than it would on a normal, non-travel day. He is traveling to San Francisco today to meet with a promising medical technology start-up company, Genogeek Incorporated. He gets up and makes coffee. On his way to the shower he checks his mobile phone to make sure it is charged and to see if there are any new overnight or early-morning messages. (Because his company does East Coast and international business, it is not unusual that there are plenty of things waiting for him.) He also fires up his laptop and starts it synchronizing his e-mail and calendar. He then showers and dresses. Before packing up his laptop, he finds a few new e-mail messages and makes sure that he has the reference material for Genogeek that he will read on the plane. He packs his laptop bag with a clean shirt and his toothbrush, just in case. He heads out, driving his Mercedes out into the darkness of the Northwestern winter. It is wet and 36 degrees outside.
>
> Ferdie pulls on to the I-90 express lanes and heads for downtown Seattle, the I-5 highway, and the road to the airport. Traffic flows smoothly despite the rain, though it is heavier on I-5 and Ferdie is denied the HOV lane. His Mercer Island privileges end at exit 1 on I-90.
>
> At the airport he pulls in to the long-term terminal parking lot, parks, and crosses the skywalk to the main terminal. He walks to the business class check-in desk. As he approaches he sees a board to his right. Flight CC003 to San Francisco is delayed by two hours.

With each lifestyle snapshot, we identify a number of candidate usage scenarios. In this example, several things pop out as interesting opportunities for innovation. Not only would Ferdie benefit from flight schedule updates but he could also use traffic and weather information. Even given his morning routine of proactively looking for information, he might not think to check traffic conditions until he is already on the road. Ferdie uses both a cell phone and a laptop, and the service could capitalize on that fact (but might need to be wary of overdoing it). The service should likely consider both push and pull technologies. Now armed with the contextual information from the lifestyle snapshot, you as the designer can determine the value proposition and develop more detailed usage scenarios.

Summary

Lifestyle snapshots work from the same assumption as personas. Rather than try to design an application that probably works most of the time, design it to be compelling for at least one specific context of use, relevant to a given persona. That way, we as designers ensure that the application is at least compelling for the user group represented by the persona on at least one real occasion in their life. The application delivers real tangible value. By identifying these opportunities to deliver value, it helps us communicate the value proposition for the application and communicate better with the target audience.

Analyze your competition through the eyes of your personas

You can use the personas to evaluate the competitive landscape into which you are going to introduce your product. You have used stories to understand your personas "in motion." Now that you know how to do that, you can project your personas into just about any situation.

Find out which existing products your new product will compete with. Your marketing team has probably already done this and they are a good source for help with this exercise. If you can, purchase a copy of each competing product. (If the products are prohibitively expensive, you can do this exercise using the marketing or collateral materials instead of the actual products. This will give you insight into the reaction of your potential customers to the messages your competitors have deemed important.) Once you have access to the products, it is relatively easy to look at them from your personas' perspectives. To conduct a competitive review using your personas:

1. Ask at least one colleague per persona—and preferably more—to help you with your competitive review. You will probably need at least one or two hours to review each product from the perspective of each persona (though you can do quicker reviews if you are extremely time pressed).

2. Convene in a meeting space and make the competitor's product as visible as possible (if it is a software product, project the interface on a wall).

3. Ask everyone to carefully review the persona and then assign a colleague to "be" the persona (in this example, let's call the persona "Sandra the Scared Shopper").

4. Conduct a simple walkthrough (or cognitive walkthrough) of the competitive product with your colleague assuming the point of view of the persona. Ask "Sandra" to talk about what she wants to do (her goal or task). Then ask her to look at the product and to talk about what she is seeing, how she feels about what she is seeing, and how she would approach her goals or tasks. Ask her what she would do (or click), and before she takes that action ask her what she would expect to happen once she does take that action.

5. Ask observers to record their ideas and observations during the walkthrough (or after, if you are recording it). Ask your "persona" (the colleague assigned to be Sandra) to try to stay in character as much as possible during the session, even if she has ideas she wants to convey.

As you observe your "persona" walking through the product, you will find aspects of the product that work well and some that do not. If members of your product design team are present, they will come up with ideas for functionality you must address in your product, as well as ideas for brand new features. If you have time, after the walkthroughs consider creating a Reality Map of each persona's experience with each product (see Chapter 10). From this walkthrough, you will be able to answer some interesting questions that will give you a unique insight into your competitors' businesses—and you will be able to avoid some customer experience mistakes they've already made.

As you do the review, ask yourself:

- Which of your personas do the competitive products seem to focus on? Do your competitors try to appeal to a persona who is missing from your "cast of characters"?

- Which of your competitors' features appeal to which of the personas? If you decide to do a persona-weighted feature matrix (see material following), this information will be very helpful.

- How do your personas react to your competitors' branding and marketing messaging?

Note that this is a great exercise to do with your marketing team. The result might be a superb new strategy for marketing your product based on differentiators from your competitors. How will you want to highlight the differences between your product and your competitors' based on the things you now know about your personas? If you decide to do persona mood boards later (see material following), you will want to find creative ways of presenting these differentiators that to appeal to your perspective customers. Later in the development cycle, you can use similar methods to conduct design reviews and cognitive walkthroughs of the features and experiences you decide to incorporate into your own product (for more information, see stage 3 later in this chapter).

G4K Meanwhile, at G4K...

G4K USES THEIR PERSONAS TO EVALUATE AND LEARN FROM THEIR COMPETITORS

The G4K team needed to get very smart very fast about the types of things on the Internet that appeal to kids and their parents. They decided to do some research about other sites that were already trying to do something similar to what they wanted to achieve with their kid's site. They looked for Web sites that seemed:

- Designed to appeal to kids Tanner's age and their parents
- Focused on children's games or on "edutainment."

They found many Web sites and decided to look at a few of them through the eyes of Tanner the Tenacious Tinkerer and Irene the Involved Parent. Two of the sites they chose to review were *www.scholastic.com* and *www.strangematter.com*. They convened the persona core and on-call teams in a conference room with a projector. The G4K core team consists of:

- *Ingrid:* An interaction design/usability person from the games group
- *Graham:* A graphics designer.

The persona "on-call" team consists of:

- *Paula:* The project lead for the new Web site
- *Michael:* A market research person
- *Theo:* A technical writer.

(Meanwhile, at G4K…, continued)

First, they made sure that everyone was still familiar with the important details of Tanner. Then Theo, the technical writer, was assigned to "be" Tanner during the review. Ingrid started by projecting *www.scholastic.com* (see Figure 6.4) and asking "Tanner" what he thought and what he would do.

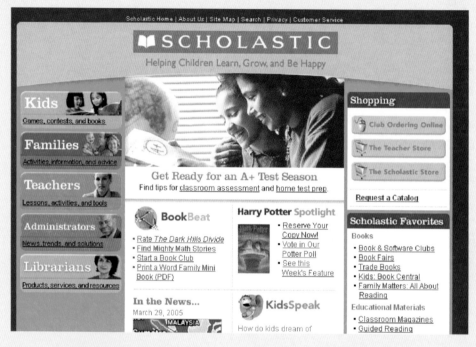

FIGURE 6.4: *The www.scholastic.com home page on March 20, 2005.*

The following is a segment of the dialog during the walkthrough at G4K.

Tanner (Theo): Well, this is kinda boring. What am I supposed to do here? Get ready for an A+ test season? What test? I hate tests. I'm outta here. But if I have to stay, let's see what else there is. Harry Potter, that's kinda cool. But I already have all those books. There's shopping stuff over here but who has money. Besides, who the heck would spend it here anyway. Maybe my mom, I guess. There's a Kids button over there with some dorky kids on it. I guess I could click that. What are the other ones? Families, Teachers, Administrators, Librarians…what*ever*. But hmmm…wonder if there is any cool secret teacher and administrator stuff behind those. Nah. I guess I'll try the Kids one.

Ingrid: What would you expect to see if you click that button?

Tanner: I don't know. I guess something for kids.

Ingrid then clicked on the Kids button, which projected the page *www.scholastic.com/kids* on the wall (see Figure 6.5).

(Meanwhile, at G4K..., continued)

FIGURE 6.5: *The www.scholastic.com/kids page on March 20, 2005.*

Tanner: Oh, this is better. Looks like it's got some cool stuff on it. I like the looks of that Deltora dinosaur thing. And there's a Harry Potter poster? I don't have one of those! There's definitely stuff I can do here.

Key findings: After the Scholastic walkthrough, the G4K team talked about what they found. They agreed that the Scholastic site was really built more for Irene than it was for Tanner, and that Tanner might even leave the site before he ever found the Kids' section because he wasn't immediately engaged by the home page. They decided this decision on Scholastic's part (to focus on parents) probably was totally in line with their own business objectives. For the G4K site, the team decided that their home page would have to be designed to engage Tanner immediately. Irene, they decided, would be willing to look a little bit harder for the area of the site dedicated to her, but if Tanner didn't like it right away their own site wouldn't succeed.

After they finished walking through the Scholastic site, they moved on to look at the Strange Matter site at *www.strangematterexhibit.com* (see Figure 6.6).

(Meanwhile, at G4K…, continued)

FIGURE 6.6: *The www.strangematterexhibit.com home page on March 20, 2005.*

Ingrid: So, Tanner, tell me about this page. What do you think? What are you going to do here?

Tanner: Those buttons in the middle are cool. I like that one that says Crush Stuff! I want to click on that one right now!

Ingrid: What would you expect to happen if you clicked that?

Tanner: I'd want to be able to crush stuff! Duh. (At this point, Theo the technical writer was really getting into being Tanner!)

Ingrid clicked on the Crush Stuff! button and the results projected on the wall (see Figure 6.7).

Tanner: Cool. Okay, I'll pick the Chipper versus Bauxer one, though I really don't know what that is. I do know that I better get to see something being crushed soon.

Ingrid clicked the "Match 3" area and the results projected on the wall (see Figure 6.8).

(Meanwhile, at G4K..., continued)

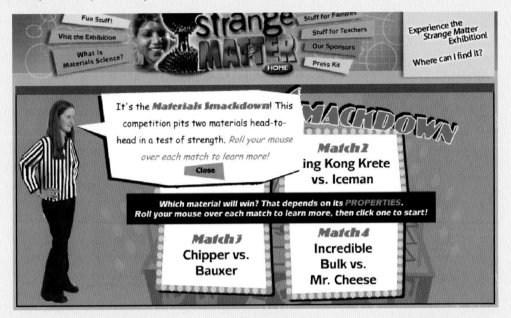

FIGURE 6.7: *The result of clicking on the Crush Stuff! button was a page called "Materials Smackdown." Each of the four "Match" areas show a set of two materials that will be "matched" against each other in a crushing machine. (From www.strangematterexhibit.com/properties.html, March 26, 2005.)*

Tanner saw Figure 6.8 and excitedly pulled the lever to start the crushing match.

Tanner: Crush it. *Crush* it! This is *cool*! I want one of those crushing things for my room.

After the match, Tanner sees an information bubble pop up on screen (see Figure 6.9).

Tanner: Oh, here's the boring teaching part. Wait a sec. There's something about airplanes.

Key findings: The G4K team got a lot of ideas for Tanner from the Strange Matter Web site. They realized that Tanner probably wouldn't do a lot of reading, but would be interested in some text if the key words were right. He would read if he had a good reason to do so. The team liked the way the Strange Matter site used carefully crafted minimal text at just the right times to capture Tanner's attention and keep him moving through the site. They were surprised to find that Tanner was totally okay with just a few options. They had assumed that sites for kids had to be like many of their G4K games—full of options and buttons on every screen. The team also liked the way the Strange Matter home page put everything in Tanner's terms and expected Irene to work around these terms. For example, Irene would have to realize that the Stuff for Families button was the best path to obtain information she would be interested in.

(Meanwhile, at G4K…, continued)

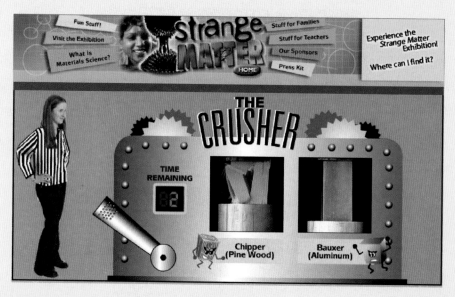

FIGURE 6.8: *The "Crusher" showing wood versus aluminum being crushed. (From www.strangematterex-hibit.com/properties.html, March 26, 2005.)*

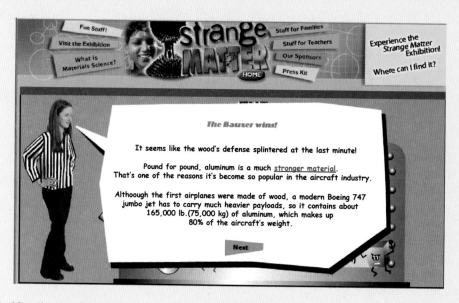

FIGURE 6.9: *After the match, the site displays an explanation of the various properties of the materials that were crushed. (From www. strangematterexhibit.com/properties.html, March 26, 2005.)*

Brainstorm possible features using your personas

Personas can help you understand user requirements and explore possible features by using them in collaborative brainstorming sessions. To conduct a persona feature brainstorm, first arrange a two-hour meeting with no more than 10 key stakeholders from your product team. Be sure to schedule the meeting in a room that has ample space for interaction and easels or whiteboards. Then, before the meeting, prime the room with any and all of the communication artifacts you have created to date and make copies of your persona foundation documents. If you don't have whiteboards and persona artifacts, put large sheets of paper around the room with the names of each persona written on them.

1. At the beginning of the meeting, have everyone browse through the persona materials to refamiliarize themselves with the personas. Remind them of the basic rules of a brainstorming session.

   a. Don't evaluate the ideas that are being explored. Evaluation will happen later. Document every idea that is expressed. At this point there are no bad ideas.

   b. Do not spend much time considering the specific implementation of any idea.

2. Before you start generating ideas, ask the participants to summarize motivations, goals, and behaviors for one primary persona (you can do this as a discussion or use sticky notes to post these on the large sheets of paper).

3. Ask the participants to think about opportunities you have for your product, given these motivations, goals, and behaviors. Ask them to think of ways your product can help each persona.

4. Repeat steps 2 and 3, spending about 15 minutes per persona.

Ideas will come in the form of new features or functionality, the acknowledgement of unnecessary or unpleasant experiences, high-level redesigns of existing solutions, and new content or domain areas that seem relevant, useful, or desirable to your personas. The meeting should end with a long list of possible features and product ideas for your team to further explore and evaluate.

Prioritize features using the persona-weighted feature matrix

If you did the previous two exercises and asked your personas to tell you their stories, you likely have a long list of possible features or services, perhaps some coming from other sources (e.g., a VP's wish list). Your team will now need to determine which are best to pursue. The process of honing in on the best features can be difficult and can sometimes feel haphazard.

G4K Meanwhile, at G4K...

G4K DOES A LITTLE FEATURE BRAINSTORMING

The G4K persona team called together several key stakeholders from the G4K kids' portal development team to hold a feature brainstorming session (about eight people in all). This included the company's VP, who had been the initiator and champion on the portal project. Ingrid reserved a meeting room for two hours and planned to hit each of the primary personas as well as the secondary personas during this session, spending no more than 20 minutes per persona.

As the session started, she reminded everyone of the brainstorming ground rules (most notably that all ideas are good and the more the better) and then reintroduced the personas. Recall that Tanner (Figure 6.10) is "The Tenacious Tinkerer." He loves to play, but he has a short attention span. He is reasonably skilled with using computers and definitely can tinker around with something until it works (or breaks). He is an active user of G4K products and has several favorite titles and characters from the G4K series.

FIGURE 6.10: *The persona Tanner the Tenacious Tinkerer.*

The 20 minutes allotted for Tanner slipped into 30 minutes—and the ideas were still flowing. Ingrid had to force the group to move on to the next persona. They generated about 30 feature, service, and experience ideas for Tanner, including:

- Braniac Bonuses (G4kids.com tokens)
- BuddyMail or "Gigantic Buddies" (a protected messaging service for registered users)
- Daily Game Hint
- E-mail reminders/notifications for kids' events
- Kids' event promotions and ticket purchasing
- G4K stories (embellishments of well-known G4K game characters)
- G4K Flash Games (simple online versions of the G4K shrink-wrapped games)
- Game feedback (ratings by users)
- Personal game score history

- Long-term teams for repeated online game play
- Meet the Idols/Stars (article column)
- Pop Polls (pop-up animated survey/polls on popular topics)
- Registration for Kids
- Search Companion (animated search helper for kids)
- Site customization (per-user content/style/layout selection)
- Toy and gizmo reviews (with "fun" ratings)
- Trial versions of G4K games for download
- *Wowzers!* E-zine (online magazine for kids)

There are a lot of forces weighing in on the decision making for your product. The persona-weighted feature matrix is a tool that will help your team make decisions based on the needs of your personas and, through them, your target customers and users. It will help you determine which features should not be included in your product—or at least which your team should focus attention on—based on the needs of your users. The persona-weighted feature matrix can also help when you (inevitably) have to triage which features you do and do not have time to include in your product. Figure 6.11 shows an abstract version of the persona-weighted feature matrix. To create a persona-weighted feature matrix, create a spreadsheet as follows:

1. List one feature per row and one persona per column.

2. Assign a weight to each persona (beneath each persona name) according to the relative importance of the persona. These weights represent the relative importance of each persona and the audience he or she represents. For example you can assign weights that add up to 100 (see Figure 6.11).

3. Assign a score for each feature to describe the value or impact of that feature on the persona:

    2: The persona loves this feature or the feature does something wonderful for the persona (even if they don't realize it).

    1: The persona receives some value, perceived or not, from the feature.

    0: The persona doesn't care about the feature one way or another.

    −1: The persona is confused, annoyed, or in some way harmed by the feature.

4. Calculate a weighted sum for each proposed feature by multiplying the score by the weight and then adding all results across each feature's row. In the example shown in Figure 6.11, the weighted sum for feature A is calculated as $(0 * 50) + (1 * 35) + (2 * 15)$, which equals 65.

	Persona 1	Persona 2	Persona 3	
Weight:	50	35	15	Weighted Sum
Feature A:	0	1	2	65
Feature B:	2	1	1	150
Feature C:	−1	1	0	−15
Feature D:	1	1	1	100
Etc.	−	−	−	−

FIGURE 6.11: *An abstract persona-weighted feature matrix. The features are listed in rows, the personas in columns. Each persona has a weight to identify its relative importance. Scores (2, 1, 0, or −1) are assigned for each feature according to how valuable or attractive it is to each persona. The weighted sums are the product of multiplying each score by each weight and then adding across the rows.*

5. Once the scores are derived and the weighted sums are calculated for each feature, sort the rows according to the weighted sum to create a prioritized list. In the example, features B and D would sort to the top of the matrix because of their high weighted sums. These features should be made a high priority for the development team. Feature C should probably be dropped.

Note that it is a good idea to leave features that *must* be included in your product out of the matrix. For example, if you are creating a transactional Web site you really can't leave out privacy and security features. Do not include these in the matrix.

The basic concept of feature-by-audience evaluation is not a new one. Geoffrey Moore, in his book *Crossing the Chasm*, describes the creation of a target customer value matrix [Moore 1991, p. 101] that employs the use of his persona-like representations (called "target customer characterizations") to evaluate the value propositions of a product in development. Mikkelson and Lee [2000] extended this basic idea toward product development by evaluating scenarios against a prioritized (weighted) set of user archetypes, much like personas. We have pushed it one step more by employing personas to evaluate product features and/or customer services. To create a persona-weighted feature matrix, you and your team must be able to:

- Assign meaningful weights to each persona that communicate their relative importance to your product
- Score each feature according to the value of that feature to each persona.

Each of these activities can be accomplished in either a rigorous "scientific" fashion or in a more casual fashion. For example, the weighting scheme can involve real measures of market size and historic revenue. Alternatively, the weighting scheme could be derived from estimates of size and predicted revenue or aligned with some notion of competitive strategy toward your target markets (e.g., your competitor doesn't attract certain audiences). At its simplest, the weighting scheme could be a simple priority rating (say, from 1 to 5, with 5 being the most important audience, or a distribution of points that total 100 across all of your personas) generated from an educated guess by your executives or market research team. You likely discussed some of this information during the prioritization of skeletons while creating personas (see Chapter 4, step 4).

It is a good idea to ask business stakeholders to participate in—or completely own—the process of assigning value ratings to the personas. Once you have these values, and once you have agreement that the values really do reflect business goals, the matrix can become a very powerful communication tool. If the values assigned to the personas really do reflect core business goals, the weighted sums in your matrix will allow your organization to discuss the merit of features according to these goals.

Scoring the features per persona within the matrix is another matter altogether. It is the more difficult of the two steps. Again, the process can range from rigorous to casual. The more rigorous approach involves recruiting groups of people that match your personas on certain critical characteristics (a topic discussed more thoroughly later in this chapter in the section on using personas in user testing and marketing research) and then having those persona representatives evaluate your features relative to one another. This can be done in focus groups, individual interviews, or through remote methods such as Web surveys. The participants can provide rating scores or you can have them allocate sums from a fixed amount of "money" to choose the features of highest value. (Note that one very important aspect of collecting this type of data is to ensure that your participants truly understand the features they are evaluating.) Once evaluations of your features are collected, it is a relatively simple process to collate, collapse, and transform your data into scores for the persona-weighted feature matrix.

On the less rigorous side, the scoring can be accomplished by committee or by individuals. When doing so, care must be taken to ensure that the scoring is done with stakeholders being fully aware of their own biases toward certain favored features. (Of course, this is not easy for any of us.) When a feature is not fully understood by the group, mark it to be reviewed later and move on to the next feature. When the group is uncertain about how a particular persona would value a feature, make note of this: it represents an area your user research team could do some investigation on. Whether done by committee or by individuals, we recommend the +2, +1, 0, −1 scoring scheme (see above) for the persona-weighted feature matrix because it is simple yet compelling, and is fairly easy to apply.

Completing the persona-weighted feature matrix almost always results in surprises. "Our top feature fell to the bottom of the list! And who had any idea that feature X would be that

CONSIDER YOUR BUSINESS STRATEGY AND BROADER MARKET

When creating the persona-weighted feature matrix, you might consider the broader audience your product has to answer to. This may go beyond your persona set. For example, is there a buyer or business decision maker, independent of the end user, who determines whether or not your product will be purchased? Is there a highly revered magazine editor or consumer advocate organization that will be reviewing your product, giving it a thumbs-up or thumbs-down. If so, consider adding a column for that person or organization to reflect their reaction, actual or estimated, to your feature set. If you have a clear non-target or anti-persona, you might experiment with what happens to your feature set when their scores are added to the equation.

important?" When this happens, it is important to remember that this matrix is simply one tool that can be used to analyze your product offering and target market. Don't allow it to dictate your feature decisions without thorough analysis and examination. The tool's value rests in its ability to bring implicit assumptions into team consciousness, providing a common understanding of your product and audience.

Treat each surprise in the matrix as a flag for further investigation. When a feature that was supposed to be your product's killer feature is shown as low priority in the matrix, begin to ask questions about the matrix itself and about that specific feature. Do you have the right audience? Why was that feature determined to be a killer feature? Perhaps your killer feature is simply the one feature your competition has over you. In that case, including the feature is a no-brainer, but the matrix can offer guidance as to how rich and complete the competitive feature needs to be. That is, if the feature simply completes a competitive checklist but your audience doesn't derive value from it, don't spend monumental development resources building all the bells and whistles into it. Allocate the most time to features that are the most valuable to your target audience.

Plot feature value versus technical feasibility

As illustrated by Dilbert and friends (Figure 6.12), determining what features are included in your product is not merely an exercise in what pleases your target audience. There are other factors you must consider. However, these need not be considered in isolation. The weighted sums generated in the persona-weighted feature matrix can be plotted against other key dimensions to help your team know how to best proceed. For example, technical feasibility (or rather, the amount of difficulty or effort required to build a feature) is an important factor to consider. Feasibility affects overall development cost, time to market, and general risk. Your team can make more precise decisions to help your overall development plan when they consider both customer value and technical feasibility. Other key dimensions might include competitive or strategic importance, or some other characteristic related to the domain or business you are in (e.g., deployability, scalability, support cost, or international appeal).

This approach was first introduced to us by one of our persona practitioner workshop participants, Damian Rees, from

FIGURE 6.12: *Product features may come and go for a variety of reasons. (Dilbert: Copyright © Scott Adams/ Dist. by United Feature Syndicate, Inc.)*

BBC New Media, in 2002. Rees suggested a color-coding method to evaluate the value of each feature versus the technical difficulty. He pointed out that this would be a great way to quickly arrive at and explain to those charged with technical scoping and to executives decisions about which features are worth development resources. We have created a variation of Rees' idea to incorporate the values generated in the persona-weighted feature matrix.

Generating a user-value versus feasibility plot is fairly simple. We have found that it is best accomplished collaboratively with your more technical staff: your development manager, system architect, and/or lead developers. It is also useful to have key stakeholders present. Schedule a one- to two-hour meeting with the appropriate people in a room that has a whiteboard or a large easel and bring along copies of the persona documentation and the final version of the persona-weighted feature matrix. To create a feature-value versus technical feasibility plot:

1. Label the Y axis "Benefit to Personas" ("User value" or "Target audience need") and the X axis "Technical Feasibility" (or some other dimension important to your product domain or organization).

2. Assign a color or symbol to each feature listed in your persona-weighted feature matrix (or write the name of each feature on its own sticky note, particularly if you have a lot of features to plot).

3. Place a colored dot (or sticky note) on the Y axis in accordance with the weighted sum of the corresponding feature (see Figure 6.13). Note that the features will probably not be evenly distributed along the Y axis, and that is fine. Also, note that the position of the X axis does not have to coincide with a score of zero in the matrix.

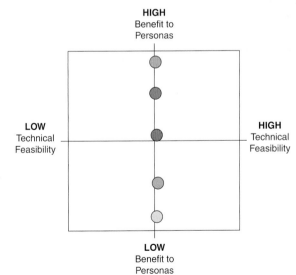

FIGURE 6.13: *The first step in a feature-value versus technical feasibility plot: assign a color to each feature and plot the weighted sum value for each along the Y axis.*

Now have the more technical folks in the meeting begin to arrange the features along the X axis (without changing their positions on the Y axis; see Figure 6.14) according to the technical feasibility of the feature.

- Will that feature be difficult to build?
- Will it take a long time?
- Will it need highly skilled developers to tackle the work?
- Is it something that has never been attempted?

You will probably have a lively discussion as you evaluate every proposed feature for your product. Make sure someone in the room is taking notes regarding the reasoning behind the placement of each feature.

Use your completed plot to further evaluate and triage the proposed feature list (also shown in Figure 6.14).

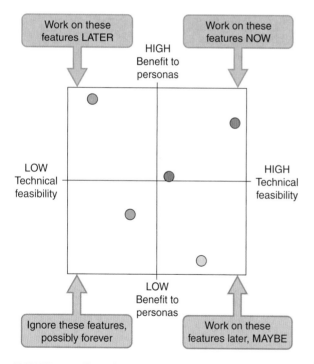

FIGURE 6.14: *Completed feature-value versus technical feasibility plot. Collaboratively arrange the features along the second axis (technical feasibility) without altering the value on the first axis (value to your target users).*

Top right-hand quadrant (high benefit to users, easy to create): These are features your team should consider high priority. Tackle these features first.

Top left-hand quadrant (high benefit to users, not so easy to create): These features are more difficult to assess. These are features that may need more resources or time committed to them if you want to ship them with your product.

Bottom right-hand quadrant (lower benefit to users, easy to create): These are "low-hanging fruit," but they are probably not that tasty to your users. We suggest that you postpone any work on these features until after the first version of your product goes out the door.

Bottom left-hand quadrant (lower benefit to users, not so easy to create): You should completely ignore these unless there are other very strong reasons to include them (e.g., a vocal and well-respected industry expert is always complaining about the lack of this feature). Generally, you will be better off spending your development dollars elsewhere.

Note that this process has not represented the fact that some features are "must have" features (i.e., you can't ship your product without them). These might be required by law, a direct request by the customer/client, or an essential

Meanwhile, at G4K...

THE G4K FEATURE PRIORITY MATRIX

The G4K kids' portal team created a persona-weighted feature matrix to help them prioritize their feature set and make a few much-needed cuts. Their first runthrough with scoring the features in the matrix (Figure 6.15) is dscribed in the following. There are clearly some "winning" features and some that will have to be de-prioritized.

Scenario/Feature Titles		Colbi Chandler			Use this column for Sorting/Ranking Your Features
	40	30	20	10	Weighted
	Score	Score	Score	Score	Sums
Registration for Kids	1	1	0	–1	60
Toy and gizmo reviews w / "fun ratings"	2	1	0	1	120
Trial version of games	2	1	2	1	160
Game feedback – rating by users	2	1	0	0	110
G4K stories – embellishments of our well known G4K characters	2	1	0	2	130
Search companion (animated search helper for kids)	1	1	–1	2	70
G4K Flash Games – simple online versions of G4K shrinkwrap games	2	1	1	2	150
Game score history	1	0	2	0	80
Join teams for game play	1	1	2	0	110
Daily Game Hint	2	0	2	0	120
BuddyMail	1	2	2	0	140
Send-Page/Send-Link to friend	0	0	1	–1	10
Back 2's (Back to school fashion, supplies, ideas)	1	2	1	0	120
Creation corner – design the world of G4K characters to roam	2	2	0	1	150

FIGURE 6.15: *The G4K persona-weighted feature matrix.*

(Meanwhile, at G4K…, continued)

Based on the weighted sums, it seems the team would be crazy not to create simple flash versions of the current G4K titles and to make available trial versions of their games on the site. BuddyMail and Creation Corner scored highly as well. At the other end of the scale, adding "send to" link capability to their site's pages seems like a bad idea now. Interestingly, the registration feature scored somewhere in the middle.

The G4K team then did a technical feasibility analysis. BuddyMail, which scored high, will require a lot of work to do properly. That feature is probably one they will put on the back burner for now. The search companion also requires some technical feats the team is not prepared to meet. Because it did not score as well in terms of user value they will also put it on the "version X" list.

Story from the field

MARY BEFORE MERELE—PERSONAS AT WORK DURING FEATURE TRIAGE

—Len Conte, BMC Software

We make a Web-based reporting system called PATROL Perceive. It is one of our products designed to help IT professionals manage the availability and performance of their servers. Perceive presented a subtle "twist" on the usual target audience. Our personas helped illuminate this difference.

Normally, our target users are performance analysts. These are the IT professionals responsible for analyzing and determining the root cause of performance problems on servers (for example, slow response time is a typical problem a performance analyst is asked to solve). The cause of the problem can be many things: slow devices, inadequate memory, network bottleneck, or whatever. The analyst's job (in this case, our analyst persona Merele Lincoln) is to analyze the problem, find the cause, and solve the problem. Unfortunately, Merele gets inundated with "drive-by" requests for reports from his customers (in this case, our customer persona Mary Trappen). In fact, Merele spends so much time obtaining reports for Mary that he doesn't have enough time to do his analysis.

To make a long persona story short, we knew that if we could make Mary happy and get her the reports she needed when she needed them she would stop bugging Merele and he could get his work done. Every feature in the product was geared to be easy to learn and use for Mary. For example, developers would say, "Well, let's add threshold lines to the CPU chart so that Mary can tell when a server is overly utilized." We would respond, "No, Mary doesn't do that type of analysis. That is Merele's job." Toward the end of the project, there were many difficult design choices to make, and many involved eliminating features. When push came to shove we always came down on Mary's side. I remember sitting in one meeting and development saying, "We have to either eliminate the one-click export for Mary or the ability of Merele to automatically generate groups of servers."

No contest—Mary before Merele.

function in a higher-level process. For a related method of feature analysis, prioritization, and selection, see the "Kano method" described by Walden [1993].

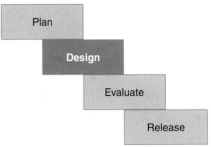

STAGE 2: USE PERSONAS TO EXPLORE DESIGN SOLUTIONS

Once your organization has a vision and overall development plan in place, it is time to design the elements of your product. Your personas helped you understand the big picture, and now they can help you make decisions about specific features and design elements. That is, your personas can help you decide what these features should look like and how they should behave. There are several methods you can use to integrate your personas into your design efforts. In this section, we discuss several of these methods:

- Scenarios and Design Mapping (a form of storyboarding)
- Mood boards and visual design explorations.

Personas and scenario-based design

"The persona is static, but the figure becomes dynamic when it is inserted into the actions of the scenario. In the scenario, the persona will be in a context, in a specific situation and have a specific goal."

—Lene Nielsen [2003a, p. 1]

Your personas can stand in for the people who are going to use your completed product to accomplish their tasks. You have gathered a great deal of information about the people

themselves, and your persona descriptions include important social and cultural context for each person. You have created stories to help understand the current experiences and pain points of your personas. Now it is time to design the features that will go into your new product. Your personas will help you explore the experiences, behaviors, and reactions your designs will elicit. These details are typically captured and illustrated in tightly scoped stories. Earlier, we referenced Whitney Quesenberry's "Storytelling and Narrative" (Chapter 9) and the broadly scoped stories that are most effective during product planning. Now that you have moved on to product design, you will need more specific stories to guide the design process.

Generally speaking, more specific stories that are to be used in guiding the design process are called scenarios. Scenarios can be long descriptions of specific tasks your personas undertake to achieve a goal or short snippets describing activities related to a specific tool. They typically refer to very specific elements of a product and an experience with that product.

As Lene Nielsen points out, "A scenario is a written story that describes the future use of a system or a Web site from a specific, and often fictitious, user's point-of-view." [Nielsen, 2002]. That is, scenarios describe in detail how your product will be used once it is built from the point of view of your persona(s). Traditional scenario-based design techniques can benefit greatly from the inclusion of personas as replacements for actors and agents. Because personas themselves include information about behaviors, skills, and expectations, these do not have to be repeated in persona-based scenarios. Scenarios written around personas tend to clearly highlight the impact of your design on your target users. Scenarios usually include:

- A specified user
- A particular task or situation
- Clearly defined desired outcome or goal for that task
- Procedure or task flow information
- A time period
- References to specific features/functionality the user will need/use.

There are many of good books and other reference materials on doing scenario-based design. John Carroll has championed the concept and has provided much of the thinking and application of it toward product design. For more information on the technique, see [Carroll 1995, 2000a, 2000b].

You will find that there are a number of types and uses for scenarios. For our purposes here, we will focus briefly on one: walkthrough scenarios. Feature specification documents (or functional "specs") are detailed descriptions of what the system is supposed to do and how it is supposed to do it. The feature spec tells the developer what to program in sufficient detail so that it is possible to proceed with coding. We believe that feature specs should always reference your personas, and this is best done by including scenarios.

A walkthrough scenario communicates and clarifies what, exactly, the feature is and does. Walkthrough scenarios are probably the most common and well-known type of scenario. They demonstrate the feature in use by the personas in a step-by-step fashion. They provide the context and actions taken to achieve a goal. Walkthrough scenarios can be written in detail or at a fairly high level. The following example is of a walkthrough scenario at a high level. Here, Colbi checks a shared calendar before purchasing concert tickets.

> Colbi wants to go to a concert with three of her friends. She is online at the G4K site, has her mom's credit card in hand, and is eager to purchase three tickets with prime seating. The only problem is that she knows that one of her friends is going on an overnight family outing sometime during that same week. Fortunately, Colbi's group of close friends have shared their G4K buddy calendars with her. Cobli clicks on the Calendar tab and selects her friend from the shared calendar pull-down menu. Her friend's overnight trip shows up in a different color on the calendar. Colbi instantly knows she can purchase the tickets for the concert that night.

See the following "Story from the field: Personas Help Redesign the Carnegie Library Through Storyboards and Narratives" by Heather McQuaid and Aradhana Goel for an excellent example of a walkthrough scenario using personas. For another interesting take on walkthrough scenarios, see "Story from the field: Use Personas to Build Your Site's 'Persuasion Architecture.'"

Keep in mind that scenarios do not have to be static text descriptions of actions and events. You can use the Reality Mapping and Design Mapping techniques described in Chapter 10. Design Maps depict the personas' experiences using your yet-to-be-built product. They are essentially long, detailed scenarios built out of sticky notes. These Maps can be broken down into shorter scenarios and augmented with wireframe design elements that deeply illustrate and complement walkthrough scenarios. Design Mapping can be a great way to create scenarios interactively with your design team. (For a detailed description of the Design Mapping process and several examples, see Chapter 10.)

Scenarios can also be illustrated graphically or even acted out live or on video. Consider creating storyboards starring your personas. This can be a great way to make your product plans and your personas come to life and to communicate the end result you are planning with your executive team and other key stakeholders. Many practitioners have recommended acting out scenarios to help make them real and comprehensible. For example,

Lynn Upshaw suggests, in *Building Brand Identity*, "Acting it out in the 'purchase theater'" [Upshaw 1995, p. 105]. Here, his user representations ("indivisualizations" of customers, which are analogous to personas) are employed to inspire dramatic enactments of users making a purchase decision. Salvador and Howells [1998] describe an interesting and related concept they call a Focus Troupe, which relies on short dramatic vignettes presented to potential end users and other stakeholders for evaluation.

Of course, scenarios for your product and its features can and will be created in various forms apart from those described here. The persona can, and likely will, be used to create scenarios that do not exist in the original persona foundation documents. To create an effective scenario based on the persona, the scenario writer needs simply to read through your persona description materials (focusing on the persona's goals, fears, aspirations, behaviors and other core characteristics) and then apply that information toward the feature or domain of interest— stepping through the actions and dialog between the user and the system. For more on personas, scenarios, and storytelling (including how to write them effectively), see Chapter 9.

Story from the field

PERSONAS HELP REDESIGN THE CARNEGIE LIBRARY THROUGH STORYBOARDS AND NARRATIVES

—Heather L. McQuaid and **Aradhana Goel,** MAYA Design, Inc.

One of our most interesting experiences with personas involved a project involving the redesign of the Carnegie Library of Pittsburgh (a large, public library). The directors of the library wanted to reinvent it—to change the public's perception of the library as a dark, forbidding place full of old dusty books to one of a bright, inviting place. To help with the reinvention, they hired an architecture firm to renovate the physical space and our firm, MAYA Design, to conduct user research, define an information architecture, and recommend design directions.

Research Phase

As part of the research phase, we interviewed and shadowed librarians, observed customers, and stepped into the shoes of customers by documenting our attempts to accomplish a common task: find and check out a book. We asked three of our own user research specialists to find books about library design using one of the following methods:

- The computer catalog system, librarians, and the physical layout of the library (the multiple resources approach)
- The library resources on the Internet (the Internet-centered approach)
- The library staff (human-centered approach)

(Story from the field, continued)

Each specialist noted what worked, what did not, what annoyed or frustrated them, and what delighted them as they attempted to complete their assigned task. When feasible, they took photographs (or screen shots) of their journey. They printed the pictures and arranged them chronologically. They then attached an acetate sheet over each and wrote their notes on them to form detailed storyboards (see Figure 6.16).

Analysis Phase

In the analysis phase, we focused on organizing and synthesizing the information collected during the research phase. Our goal was to create a coherent, manageable model of the information space (an information architecture, or IA) and a realistic embodiment of the people interacting with that space (i.e., personas). While creating the IA, we discovered that there are four basic components of the library system (see Figure 6.17).

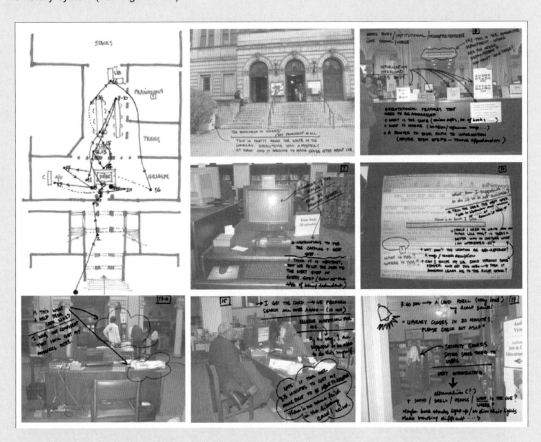

FIGURE 6.16: *A storyboard of one researcher's experience.*

(Story from the field, continued)

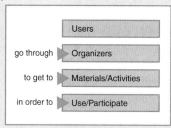

FIGURE 6.17: *The four main components of the library and how they relate to one another.*

- Customers (users): People who use the library
- Organizers: Things and systems that organize the materials (including the library's physical space, categorization schemes, and librarians)
- Materials and activities: Things customers want
- Use/participation: Customers' interaction with the materials and activities.

Relying on our understanding of users (based on interviews, observations, and walking in the customers' shoes), we created nine personas (an example is shown in Figure 6.18). Each had several general characteristics, including a primary focus (reason for using the library), age, gender, and attitude toward help-seeking (i.e., positive or negative). For each persona, we also described their current situation (e.g., job title, where they live or work, relevant hobbies or interests, comfort with technology); their current library experience, if any (e.g., what methods they use to accomplish their probable goals, where they tend to hang out); and their probable goals (e.g., check out best-sellers, use the computer to chat and play games).

We then selected four main personas and had them "walk through" one of their probable goals. Combining a persona with a specific scenario (Figure 6.19) provided a narrative that allowed people to see (and hopefully vicariously feel) what customers experience as they try to accomplish their goals.

The narrative begins with a trigger—an event that spurs Naomi to go to the library. In this case, the trigger is an advertisement for the library that compares the cost of purchasing a novel at Barnes & Noble to the cost of borrowing it from the library (free). The narrative continues with Naomi entering the library and feeling uncertain about where she should go. She is not even sure whether she should look for the card catalog (she doesn't know that it is now completely computerized), ask a librarian (which she doesn't really want to do because she likes to do things on her own), or start wandering through the space. Fortunately, she soon sees a sign for best-sellers and begins exploring that area. Unfortunately, she feels stupid because she can't figure out how the books are organized.

Naomi is mildly frustrated and decides to swallow her pride by asking for help. She looks around and is not sure where she should go for help. Eventually, she sees a man sitting at a desk. Cautiously she approaches him. He appears to be working on the computer. Naomi wonders whether she should interrupt him and whether he's even the right person to ask. And so the narrative continues, with Naomi getting increasingly bewildered and frustrated with her experience (see Figure 6.19).

(Story from the field, continued)

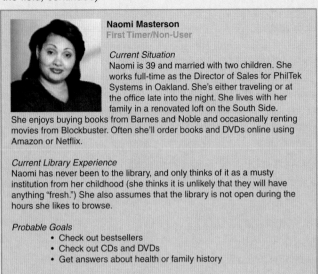

Naomi Masterson
First Timer/Non-User

Current Situation
Naomi is 39 and married with two children. She works full-time as the Director of Sales for PhilTek Systems in Oakland. She's either traveling or at the office late into the night. She lives with her family in a renovated loft on the South Side.

She enjoys buying books from Barnes and Noble and occasionally renting movies from Blockbuster. Often she'll order books and DVDs online using Amazon or Netflix.

Current Library Experience
Naomi has never been to the library, and only thinks of it as a musty institution from her childhood (she thinks it is unlikely that they will have anything "fresh.") She also assumes that the library is not open during the hours she likes to browse.

Probable Goals
- Check out bestsellers
- Check out CDs and DVDs
- Get answers about health or family history

FIGURE 6.18: *An example of a persona, Naomi.*

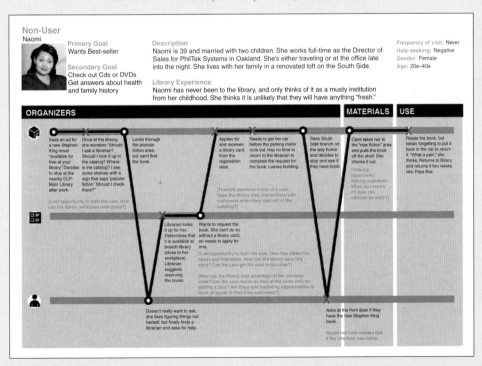

FIGURE 6.19: *An example of a narrative: a persona (Naomi) paired with a scenario (find a novel).*

(Story from the field, continued)

We then mapped the personas' experiences onto the IA to see how they interacted with the information space. Figure 6.19 shows the three organizers in the library (physical space, categorization schemes, and librarians), represented as rows, and how and when Naomi moved from one organizer (e.g., the bookshelves in the physical space) to another (e.g., a librarian). Consequently, the valleys in the diagram don't represent a negative experience, but merely the movement from one organizer to another. We represented negative experiences with an X. Each X represented a breaking point— a failure of the system to help Naomi accomplish her goal. By using an IA diagram to represent the basic components of the system, and then placing a customer into that framework, we could more clearly see how the system was failing to support its users. That is, we could easily see which parts of the system, or types of information, customers had difficulty finding, understanding, and using.

After analyzing all of the narratives, we saw a pattern of problems. Namely, many personas had difficulty understanding when and how to move from one organizer to another. We mapped these difficulties onto another information architecture diagram that summarized the problems across all personas.

Conclusions and Insights

The most effective techniques for eliciting empathy for customers were the visual storyboards that showed the steps of our specialists "walking a mile in the customers' shoes" and the narratives of select personas. However, we found the storyboards to be a more powerful tool for communicating customers' needs to stakeholders. The directors, librarians, and architects were much more engaged in discussing them than they were the narratives. Possible reasons for this preference include the realistic nature of the storyboards (real people, real pictures, and real "voices") and the fact that each step in the process was concrete and visual (in contrast to the narratives, which just described what people encountered rather than showing it). It is possible that the persona narratives could be made more powerful if we incorporated more realistic pictures of the products and systems, and showed more steps in the narrative.

Nevertheless, the narratives helped us explore and understand more tasks (compared to the storyboards, in which we focused on one task) and a broader range of customers (the personas were more diverse in age, level of comfort with technology, and their reasons for using the library).

[A continuation of this story is provided later in this chapter as MAYA's personas are used to evaluate the design solutions resulting from this project (see "Story from the field: The Librarians' Viewpoint— The Power of Personas in Evaluation").]

Story from the field

USE PERSONAS TO BUILD YOUR SITE'S "PERSUASION ARCHITECTURE"

—Bryan Eisenberg, Cofounder and Chief Persuasion Officer, Future Now, Inc.

Your company wants its online visitors to complete the action they want them to take—the one that accomplishes your company's goal. You want them to engage with your Web site, your marketing, and your brand and proceed down the path of your sales process.

However, visitors arrive with their own goals in mind. They are engaged in their own purchasing process, not your sales process. A persuasion architect's goal is to interweave your sales process with your visitors' purchasing processes—to help your site convert more visitors *and* to assist visitors with their goals. A persuasion architect is similar to an information architect. However, the goal of the persuasion architect is not to inform and create a hierarchy and taxonomy of content but to plan content that moves visitors along a path that is persuasive and engaging and helps visitors get their questions answered while moving them toward a close.

Your company's site must help visitors take action, from clicking on links, to filling in and submitting forms, to completing the transaction. Any single action that propels visitors toward completing their goals is a micro-action. The end goal—purchasing, registering, or becoming a lead—is the macro-action.

Every click represents a visitor's decision to take action. The persuasion architect's job is to convert that click—to motivate and persuade the visitor to make each of those decisions. Sometimes, though, the visitor's purchasing process gets in the way. If your company's persuasive process doesn't resolve the tension, neither the company nor the visitor will accomplish their goals. Understanding the difference between the two categories of hyperlinks can make all the difference.

Most people are familiar with hyperlinks associated with the sales process: calls to action. These links move visitors forward in the sales process. That is, they are linear. Call-to-action hyperlinks are typically labeled with a phrase consisting of an imperative verb and an implied benefit, as in, "Click here to order now."

When your company's sales process and the visitor's purchasing process don't mesh, the visitor looks to the Web site to provide a point of resolution (i.e., the answer to a question, whether explicit or implicit). The most underutilized and misunderstood hyperlinks are those that help visitors resolve the potential disconnects between your company's selling process and their purchasing processes. We compare these sets of links to a "revolving door."

The process of persuasion architecture, when well implemented, makes the optimization of these points of resolution very simple. Instead of looking at a large mess of reports generated by unintentional click streams and scenarios created by the collection of pages on the site, we "wireframe" the entire experience. Every Web site has these click streams or scenarios. The question is: Were they created intentionally?

In our version of interaction wireframing (not to be confused with traditional "page" wireframes), we take the time to plot the ideal click-through scenarios each of our prospects will take. These scenarios comprise every micro-action leading up to the ultimate business goal (leads, purchases, subscriptions, and so on), as well as all key points of resolution.

Because different people have different ways of navigating their own purchasing process, we create personas. Personas are archetypical personalities for whom we carefully map out each driving point, including where they started in the process and keyword/landing page combinations, each conversion point (the end goal or goals for this persona, spread out over time to account for latent purchasers as repeat visitors), and the key navigational points they encounter as they move through the process.

For each persona, we conduct a scenario analysis using Web analytics to pinpoint precisely which pages in the scenario are not doing their job correctly. We examine what people actually do on that page. Do they get there? Do they spend sufficient time there? What actions do they take? How do they leave the page? The information we gather allows us to optimize the page for the desired outcome: more completed scenarios and thus a more satisfied company.

Our process focuses on up-front planning to develop a powerful persuasive structure that allows us to measure intentionality rather than chance. It creates a truly measurable and manageable persuasive system.

Create a scenario collection spreadsheet

It is likely that there are already many usage scenarios of various types and quality floating around your organization. Your core team members are probably not the only ones writing and thinking about scenarios. Others across your organization may already be drafting and including scenarios in specs, vision documents, marketing plans, or other materials designed to support product development. These scenarios, all created for slightly different purposes, will differ considerably in length, content, and clarity. Some of them will reference users and perhaps your personas; some may not.

As your organization creates new scenarios, we recommend that you make an effort to collect and evaluate those scenarios. Collecting these scenarios into a single repository (preferably a spreadsheet or simple database) will help you make sense of them and allow you to do some quality control. To create a scenario collection spreadsheet, ask all of the teams working on your product to send you any scenarios they have created or to send you the documents they have created so that you can identify the scenarios they contain. Copy and paste each scenario into a spreadsheet (however long the scenario turns out to be). In another column, list the ways users and/or personas are referenced in each of the scenarios (we show an example of this in the G4K case study following). Once you have created the scenario collection spreadsheet, you can use it to do several things:

- Look for the word *user* or any other reference to the eventual users of your product.
- Look across scenarios for a single persona to make sure that the scenarios utilize the personas appropriately and consistently.
- Do a simple count of the scenarios written for each persona.

If you find references to "users" that are not stated in terms of the personas, you can contact the scenarios' owners and educate them on the personas. Consider rewriting the scenario for the document owner to demonstrate the value of using the persona names and information. When you find references to the persona names in existing scenarios, check to make sure that the personas are described consistently and accurately with respect to your persona foundation documents and other materials. For example, make sure that Tanner isn't described differently from scenario to scenario.

Finally, count the number of scenarios that refer to each of your personas. Doing this frequency count will shed light on your team's actions and focus (and this can be compared and contrasted to the overall product vision). There should be a proportional number of scenarios relative to the importance of each persona. If you find that a secondary persona appears in more scenarios than a primary persona, follow up with the scenarios' authors to make sure they understand the needs and value of the primary persona.

Story from the field

THE SEXY PERSONA PHENOMENON CAN LEAD YOU ASTRAY

—Howard Blumenthal, Director, E-Commerce & Database Management, Pfaltzgraff

As we developed our personas, some were perceived as sexier than others. Associates only wanted to work with these sexier groups. Perhaps these personas were new, or younger, or seen as "hipper." Perhaps they were simply different. Such attention can be dangerous. Do not let this phenomenon lead you astray. Yes, the sexy personas are important, but they may not be the bread and butter of your business. Right now, we have enough people at different levels of our organization who know when and how to raise the alert when they see this phenomenon. Always ensure that each persona is given the appropriate amount of attention.

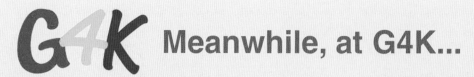 Meanwhile, at G4K...

THE G4K CORE EAM CREATES A SCENARIO COLLECTION SPREADSHEET

At G4K, the product development team is now moving fast. The core team felt like there was good buy-in for the persona effort, but everyone is now heads-down and working on their own projects and it is difficult to tell how people are using the personas (and if they are using the personas correctly). One day, Ingrid (the G4K information architect) looks through a spec for one of the product features and finds several scenarios written about Tanner the Tenacious Tinkerer, a few about Irene the Involved Parent, and one about someone named Jimmy. There is no persona named Jimmy! She begins to worry that something is going wrong.

Ingrid calls the project manager for the new Web site. They decide to create a scenario collection spread-sheet. Together, they gather all walkthrough scenarios from every existing feature specification document for the G4K portal into a single spreadsheet. This requires a lot of manual copy-and-paste from document to document, but it turns out to be worth the effort. They notice (see Figure 6.20) that one of the development managers seems to have made up his very own set of personas! They set up meetings to go over all of the "wayward" scenarios and make sure that they fit the primary personas for the project.

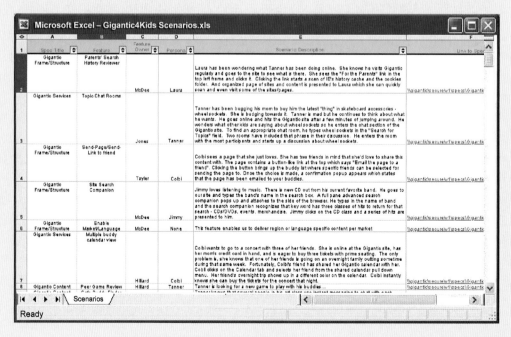

FIGURE 6.20: G4K's scenario collection spreadsheet.

(Meanwhile, at G4K…, continued)

Ingrid decides to sort the spreadsheet by persona. She looks at all scenarios for Tanner, then all scenarios for Irene, and so on. She finds that some of the Irene scenarios have taken too much liberty with Irene's ability and interest in troubleshooting. Ingrid knows she needs to review those scenarios with the feature owners.

Scenario Counting as a Rough Guide

Ingrid can now do a simple scenario count per persona and create a pie chart to illustrate the results (shown in Figure 6.21). It is *not* clear in the chart that Tanner is the most important persona. With only 36 scenarios written with Tanner as the actor/agent, Colbi overshadows him with 47 scenarios (roughly 31% of the total scenarios).

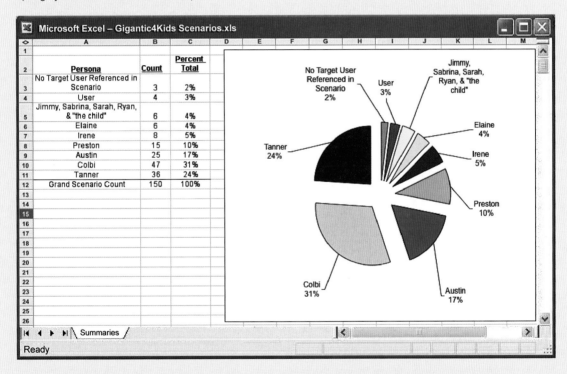

FIGURE 6.21: *The G4K scenario collection spreadsheet "scenario count per persona" view.*

Ingrid understands why this has happened. Colbi is a very cute, endearing persona! Most of the project team has a soft spot for Colbi. However, Ingrid knows that Tanner is actually more important to the product than Colbi is, so she follows up with the various development teams to make sure they are not spending time on fun features for Colbi at the expense of features for Tanner.

This scenario collection exercise highlights a tough question that many persona practitioners have come across. When you are creating scenarios for a particular feature, how do you decide which persona to use as the main user (aka, actor/agent) in that scenario? Many times, any one of your personas could reasonably serve as the actor in a scenario. If it is not clear which to use based on the goals, activities, and behaviors of your personas, the best choice is to use the primary persona (or the persona with the highest weighting in the priority matrix tool discussed previously). We have seen practitioners use the reference "all personas" in scenario descriptions in place of a single persona. We suggest that this is not a good solution, as it relinquishes the specificity and focus personas attempt to add.

Handy Detail

BEWARE OF FERAL PERSONAS!

When everybody in your organization feels free to add whatever details they want to the personas, the personas become feral, and feral personas can be dangerous. They become an excuse for people to return to the familiar comfort of the "elastic user" [Cooper 1999] because everyone feels free to describe the persona in different ways at different times. It is not enough to replace the word *user* with persona names. The persona names themselves must represent a collection of information that is stable and as data-driven as possible.

How do you know if your personas are threatening to become feral, and what can you do if this happens? The rule of thumb here is to remember that personas should not be changing much by the time they reach adulthood. True, they are "out there" in your organization and may be changing in minor ways as a result of their interactions with the people in your organizations, but like adult humans they should be solid enough to maintain their fundamental traits. If you notice that a persona seems to be a different person depending on who is talking about him or her, there is a problem. If, for example, Tanner seems to be a mild-mannered obedient school lover in one office and a tantrum-throwing, hooky-playing miscreant in another, Tanner has probably become feral.

If you find that your personas have become feral, you must regain control of them. Feral personas are a problem of ownership and communication. Although it is important that you allow your co-workers to feel some ownership of the personas, it is also critical that each persona wrangler be a solid source of information about which persona details may be malleable and which are definitely not (see Chapter 5). Visit the people who have developed the new descriptions of the personas and try to find out why. Revisit Chapter 5 and assess the ways in which your personas became feral and see if you can find solutions:

- Were people adding details? Were people hungry for more information than you initially provided and figured they could simply make up their own?
- Were they trying to simplify the personas?
- Did they fundamentally disagree with some of the data or assumptions that were contained in the personas?

Use personas to help you explore visual design solutions

How does the visual treatment of your product get specified and created? On some product teams, the developers do it themselves, possibly allowing the development environment to determine the look (e.g., Windows Forms in Visual Studio are a set of common control elements used by developers that provide a standard visual style for Windows applications). For others, there are dedicated graphic designers and artists who create a look for the product. In either case, it is useful to have a clear target user to serve as inspiration for the layout, wording, and style choices that need to be specified. Thus, personas can play a role here too. For the G4K kids' portal site, how would the home page look if it were designed solely for Tanner? How about the "support" or "contact us" pages?

Have your team begin its creative process by collaboratively creating style and branding collages on large poster boards, which we call "style" or "mood" boards. Style and mood boards consist of cut-and-paste images that "feel like" your persona. At least one collage is created per persona. As shown in Figure 6.22, style boards can include images of objects and places (such things as clothing, cars, watches, furniture, home decor, art, and even food products—anything that captures a look or style appropriate for the personas). Your team will then utilize the style boards as the basis for creating exploratory visual treatments across key areas of the product (Figure 6.23).

These design explorations can be evaluated by your product team's stakeholders or by potential users and customers (e.g., in focus group sessions). Doing so will help your team understand what aspects of the visual designs are appealing and how they work together to form a holistic style. For example, what is the preferred color palette? What should the icons and toolbar imagery look like? How do transitions and animations enhance the experience? Based on such in-depth analysis and feedback, your design team can revisit the explorations and combine the visual elements to create a single look and feel for the product.

FIGURE 6.22: *An example of a style-board collage for a teen persona.*

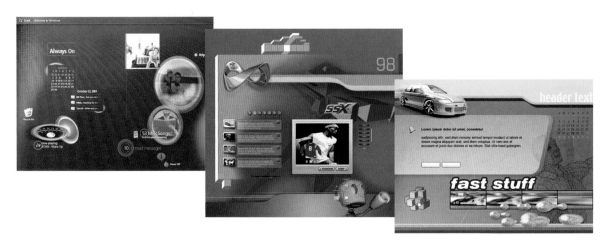

FIGURE 6.23: *An example design exploration resulting from the collage shown in Figure 6.22. (Artwork created by Jenny Lam, Greg Melander, Chuck Cummings, and Mark Ligameri.)*

Handy Detail

DATA-DRIVEN AESTHETICS—TIPS FOR CONDUCTING YOUR OWN PERSONA MOOD BOARD WORKSHOP

—Emily Henlein, Senior Customer Experience Specialist, Amazon.com

I conducted several mood board workshops using personas at Amazon.com and at the University of Washington. My goal was to explore the idea that design decisions can be data driven if designers create and use mood boards to reflect the design preferences of personas. During this exercise, I learned several valuable lessons about how to conduct an effective persona mood board workshop.

Mood Board Workshop Participants

We invited the Amazon.com designers to participate in the mood board workshop. At the time we held the workshop, most of the designers did not know very much about personas in general or the Amazon.com customer personas specifically. We arrived at the following propositions.

- *Don't use a mood board exercise to teach people about personas or to create personas.* Make sure the participants have a solid understanding of personas before creating a mood board. I recommend that you have a 30-minute persona presentation and Q&A session before you conduct the workshop (either on the same day or earlier). Take time to explain what mood boards are and how you intend to use them to influence some of the design decisions for your product. A picture is worth a thousand words: if at all possible, have examples of mood boards on hand to show your participants.
- *The persona or personas should be complete before you conduct a mood board workshop.* I was surprised to find that some of my participants thought the purpose of the mood board exercise was to add details to or otherwise enhance the personas, rather than to express their responses to various graphic design elements.
- *Schedule, supplies, and environment are important.* Finished mood boards are essentially large collaged collections of images participants believe speak to the preferences and interests of the personas. Several weeks before our workshops, we sent out e-mail messages asking people to bring in old magazines. We collected several hundred magazines from people more than happy to donate them. We also purchased basic collage supplies, including black tag board, glue sticks, scissors, and markers. We scheduled the workshop in a very large room, with big tables, to give the participants plenty of space to spread out. The workshop was comfortably completed in a 90-minute meeting.
- *Encourage Q&A and discussion.* After everyone finished their boards, we opened the floor to discussion. Surprisingly, people were very hesitant to step forward and speak about why their boards looked the way they did. Given that our goal in conducting the workshops was to create artifacts the designers could use to inform their product designs, this worried us. Even though we had two teams, and each team created very different mood boards for the same persona, people didn't readily jump in to discuss the differences. As the leader of the workshop, you should prepare thought-provoking questions for discussion:
  - Ask each team to discuss its mood board creation process. Did it feel useful? In what ways? Were there any surprises or insights they got out of the process?

- How did this process help you better understand the personas?
- How can you use these mood boards to inform your product designs?
- Did you learn something new about your company or your product through this exercise? If so, what?
- Did any aspects of your collages lead you to question some of the persona details?

After the Workshop

After the mood board workshop, decide as a group where to post the finished mood boards, and how as a group you can use them. You might also want to discuss which other groups in the company (if any) would benefit from learning about the mood boards. Mood boards can be used to "defend" or explain design decisions, and in a unique way to link these decisions back to customer data. As a group, it is a good idea to decide how you will explain the importance of the mood boards to other stakeholders.

Adult personas and developers

Before moving on to the next stage in the development process, we want to briefly discuss how you can use personas to facilitate your interaction with the most important members of your team—the developers. Developers (and development managers) are extremely powerful members of your organization. They not only hold many political cards but make thousands of decisions (of all sizes) throughout the development process that directly affect the user experience of the final product. Thus, it is critical that developers really know the personas and keep them in mind as they make these decisions. In Chapter 5, we recommended that you analyze each of the internal users of persona-related information and their various needs. In this section, we provide a few suggestions to address the issues that might arise as you communicate persona information to developers during *adulthood*.

The first step is to make sure developers buy in to the *idea* of using personas, and one of the keys to doing this is to make sure they understand that your personas are credible—that they are based on data and that the method has led to good results. Your developers do not have to understand every detail of the data behind the personas (though they will likely ask many questions to ensure that the personas are trustworthy and to be able to recognize the critical differences among them). Neither do developers have to understand all of the ways personas can be used across the organization, but they will need to see a few key uses of personas and hear a few success stories from other companies (see Chapter 7 for several compelling success stories). Finally, they will want to know exactly what they are supposed to do with the personas—preferably some easy ways to use the personas that will save them time.

Make sure that developers are fully introduced to the personas, and make sure that easy-to-use persona materials are at their fingertips. Give them persona posters to hang in their offices. Your developers have to know the basics of who the personas are and what their goals and needs are with respect to the product being built.

It is important to explain how the personas can affect feature decisions through use of the persona-weighted feature matrix, and it is critical to involve developers in the process. If you have used the matrix in your process, it is helpful to remind your developers that your personas helped the entire team make good decisions on *what* to build and that the data behind the personas is always ready to provide the *why* behind these decisions. Once the "what and why" are solid, your developers are free to work their magic on the issues surrounding *how* to build the product.

Remind developers that the personas can help them make some of their decisions. If they are trying to choose between two possible directions their code might take, they can consider the personas. Which code decision is more likely to lead to the easy addition of features the personas would like? Be sure to involve developers in the scenario creation and Design Mapping process. Make sure your developers have access to these scenarios as they do their work. Furthermore, encourage your developers to create their own walkthrough scenarios as needed to understand the experience they are creating as a result of their work.

If nothing else, personas allow developers to ruminate such things as, "When Tanner tries to initiate a download from this page, he will… ." This is a big deal! Even just using the names means that they are using the personas, and that they are relating their work decisions to a representation of the user—one that is clear, shared, and based on real data. Your developers will start being user centered instead of technology centered. Of course, your developers can use personas more explicitly by employing them in design evaluation, which we cover in the next section.

When there are changes during the course of development (and there will be), the personas can provide the objective voices that should matter most—and this is just as helpful to the development staff as it is to anyone else on the team. They are very helpful as "data-driven justifications" when difficult decisions need to be made. "Tanner needs this feature or he'll never understand how to create an account," is a much more powerful argument than, "We're just doing it."

Many of us have been in situations in which suddenly, in the middle of a project, someone decides that there needs to be a new feature added to the product. Perhaps the feature is critical to the success of the product and perhaps it is not, but without good data and personas it is usually a political and opinion-based decision whether to include the new feature. Developers often end up in the middle of these debates, having to explain schedule costs and technical difficulties related to new features. Remind developers that the personas contain a lot of detailed data about the target customers and users of the product, and encourage them to remember the needs of the personas as they participate in debates such as these. Better yet, try to get a persona representative invited to development meetings. New feature X could be a huge sprawling feature, or perhaps it could be a tiny simplified feature. Developers or the persona representative can use the persona descriptions to extrapolate the extent of new feature requirements based on the technical needs.

Finally, if you have trouble getting the development team to use the personas, remember that this is not an end in itself. Your persona effort is about getting everyone to use the personas, but it is also about changing the ways people within your organization communicate and work together. This is a long-term project that will not happen all at once.

Story from the field

PERSONAS AND EXTREME PROGRAMMING

—Holly Jamesen Carr, GreenShape LLC, formerly Usability Specialist, Attenex Corporation

We experimented with extreme programming (XP) methods for our development process. The basic idea was to code quickly and toward very specific goals. For us, the goal was a weekly demo of features that had been built the previous week. We created a weekly scenario the programmers built toward. The idea was that we would continue building on the scenarios until the product was complete (and the last scenario would essentially represent the entire set of technical requirements for the product.) In our company, each scenario was driven by the needs of one or more of the personas, and was written from his, her, or their perspectives. Everyone understood who the personas were, and shared a vision of what each persona's experience would be when the product was complete. The weekly scenarios were like chapters in the persona's stories. Even though we were moving so fast, we were all able to understand how any given week's "chapter" fit into the big picture.

STAGE 3: USE PERSONAS TO EVALUATE YOUR SOLUTIONS

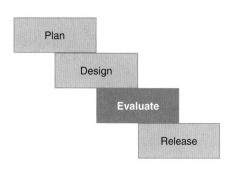

As your team settles in on the features and specific solutions it needs to embrace to create a successful product, your personas can help in honing the implementation of these features toward the very best design. In this section, we show you how to use your personas to help with evaluation of your features and solutions through:

- Cognitive walkthroughs and design reviews with personas
- User testing and ongoing user research with persona profiles
- Quality assurance (QA) testing and bug bashes.

Use personas in design reviews and cognitive walkthroughs

"If you're seeing things through the eyes of a persona, instead of the eyes of a person who's been designing Web sites, it rewires you temporarily."

—Christina Wodtke, Author of *Information Architecture: Blueprints for the Web*

Your personas are not "done" when they have finished helping specify and design the product. They are still raring to go, ready to help you ensure that the product works as it should and is not difficult to use. The personas allow you to get the perspective you need as you review designs and prototypes. Because you will never be a truly objective reviewer of your own product, the personas can help you discover and evaluate problem areas in your design, even before you do usability testing and beta releases with real users. Earlier we recommended that you conduct competitive analyses using the personas to "walk through" the user experiences of your competitors' products. You can use the same basic methods now to evaluate the designs you have come up with for your product.

There are several formal evaluation methods commonly known to UCD professionals. Two of these are heuristic evaluation and cognitive walkthrough (see Nielsen and Molich [1990],

Story from the field

PERSONAS FOCUS COGNITIVE WALKTHROUGHS ON USERS INSTEAD OF YOURSELF

—Christina Wodtke, Author of *Information Architecture: Blueprints for the Web*

Personas make for better cognitive walkthroughs. Without personas, it is easy to slip into thinking *What would I do?* Personas also help you look at the entire user experience in context, from end to end. In one project, we were helping a soda company design a promotion in which customers could find prizes listed inside the soda cap and redeem the prizes on a Web site. They had already done tons of user research and testing, and we didn't have time to do a lot of testing on our own. So, we took their research and created personas. We did cognitive walkthroughs using our personas and got some really important insights. For example, one of our personas was a 13-year-old boy who accesses the Internet at his local library. Doing a walkthrough of his experience made us realize once and for all that having music play automatically when the Web site loaded was *not* a good idea, and it wasn't enough to offer an option to turn it off once it had started playing. I'm not sure it would have been as easy to make this decision if we had done an "ordinary" heuristic review.

Wharton et al. [1994], and Spencer [2000]). Less formally, these are known as usability inspections or expert reviews [Nielsen and Mack 1994]. At the core of these techniques is the idea that someone on the development team should step through the product (or portions of the product such as individual features) and reflect on the user experience. Would the user know what to do at this point? Would they know they have made a correct choice?

Design reviews and cognitive walkthroughs are usually done through the eyes of the user, though many times the user is never made explicit or specific. This is where personas can play a part. Personas can serve as the specific user when doing an expert review or cognitive walkthrough. These walkthroughs can be done alone or in group settings. The process for conducting a walkthrough with personas is much like that described earlier in this chapter regarding competitive analysis with personas, except that the focus is your own prototypes or beta product. Rather than recreate that process here, we suggest that you revisit that section ("Analyze your competition through the eyes of your personas") and examine the example laid out by Joshua Seiden in his "Story from the field: Persona-based Expert Review" (in material to follow).

Finally, note that it can be helpful to physically act out the actions of the persona with the interface. We referred to this earlier in the chapter regarding scenario-based design. Here we

Story from the field

PERSONA WALKTHROUGHS KEEP YOUR DESIGNS CENTERED ON YOUR USER RESEARCH

—Frank Spillers, Principal and Co-CEO, Experience Dynamics

At Experience Dynamics, we use persona walkthroughs to help keep our user research close to the design. In any given scenario, a proposed design can be validated by matching it to the goals of a persona as well as their specific tasks (see Figure 6.24). We do our walkthroughs using a comprehensive list of user scenarios with the current or proposed design. As our personas interact with the designs, we note gaps, issues, and concerns and propose alternative design options.

The persona walkthrough can uncover confusion, obstacles, redundancy, and decision point issues a user would find in your proposed designs. The persona walkthrough provides sanity in a typical design room in which business, marketing, and technology needs regularly compete with that of the end user.

(Story from the field, continued)

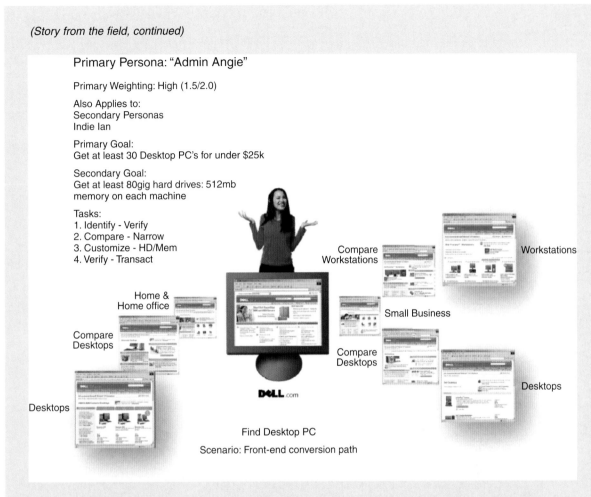

Primary Persona: "Admin Angie"

Primary Weighting: High (1.5/2.0)

Also Applies to:
Secondary Personas
Indie Ian

Primary Goal:
Get at least 30 Desktop PC's for under $25k

Secondary Goal:
Get at least 80gig hard drives: 512mb
memory on each machine

Tasks:
1. Identify - Verify
2. Compare - Narrow
3. Customize - HD/Mem
4. Verify - Transact

Compare
Workstations

Workstations

Home &
Home office

Small Business

Compare
Desktops

Compare
Desktops

Desktops

Desktops

DELL.com

Find Desktop PC

Scenario: Front-end conversion path

FIGURE 6.24: *In this illustration, the primary persona Admin Angie walks through the process of finding and identifying a desktop PC for purchase on Dell.com. This persona represents a small business user (under 100 people) and the three routes a user might take.*

are recommending it more as an aid in evaluating designs than as an exploratory tool for innovation and insight. This is along the lines of what Salvador and Howells [1998] describe as a Focus Troupe, in which dramatic vignettes are acted out for evaluation by end users and internal stakeholders. See the sidebar "Story from the field: Turn Your Teammates into Personas" by Nathalie Barthe for a brief example of the power of this approach.

Story from the field

PERSONA-BASED EXPERT REVIEW—A TECHNIQUE FOR USEFULNESS AND USABILITY EVALUATION

—Joshua Seiden, President and Founder, Thirtysix Partners

I've found that personas provide significant benefits during expert review. Personas can function to create a context for the evaluation—the context required to do a meaningful review. Personas also allow reviewers to assess the usefulness of the product, not simply its usability. Persona-based review is a relatively simple technique. You simply perform the evaluation from the personas' perspective, and make note of problems as you find them.

Typically, persona-based review can be used in three contexts. It can be used as a rapid evaluation tool. In this case, a persona-based review can take as little as an hour or two. It can be used as a more formal review tool, in which case reviewers may spend a few days researching and modeling, and another day or two performing the evaluation. Finally, it may be used as part of a larger design effort, to evaluate existing products once a significant research and modeling effort has been undertaken, or to evaluate proposed design solutions following that effort.

An Example

I used the method in a recent project—a persona-based expert review to complete a diagnostic review of a Web site used to make reservations at a popular New York hotel. On this project, my team had no research budget—typical for projects that employ "discount usability" methods. As such, all of our research consisted of a series of e-mail exchanges with project stakeholders. Through our discount research, we generated four personas:

- Our "guidebook" user, Jurgen, lives in Germany, found our hotel in a guidebook, and accessed the site over a dial-up line. And though his English is passable, he prefers using the Web to having an English-language telephone conversation, especially if he can avoid long-distance charges.
- Our "package" user, John, saw an ad in the local newspaper for a romance package the hotel offers. John lives in New Jersey, and likes the idea of bringing his fiancée to the city for a romantic weekend. He'd like to book a forthcoming weekend and is not particularly date sensitive—any weekend in the next month would work for him—but he is very concerned with the details of the room. Will it really make for the perfect romantic weekend?
- Tim is a Knicks fan who lives in the suburbs, and often stays at the hotel after seeing a game across the street at the Garden. He has the most mainstream needs: find a room on a specific night.
- Finally, Linda lives in Philadelphia, and comes to town occasionally to see long-running museum shows on the weekends. She likes to stay at the hotel because it is close to Penn Station. She's less concerned about specific dates, and more concerned with cost savings—but not concerned enough to switch to a different hotel.

We then generated between two and four basic context scenarios for each persona. Context scenarios are abstract, technology-free descriptions of a sequence of events involving the persona. They describe the setting in which the persona interacts with the system, the usage pattern, the major steps the persona takes in order to accomplish the goal, and the end result.

These scenarios were selected to give roughly 100% coverage of the functionality each persona would need. So, for example, each persona had a scenario in which they tried to book a room. But each room-booking scenario was slightly different, so as to reflect the unique needs of each persona. Tim's scenario simply involved looking for a room on a specific night for which he had Knicks tickets, whereas John's involved looking for a package, previewing dates and rooms available, and looking at the goody list that came with the package.

With our personas and scenarios in place, the evaluation was a simple matter of stepping through the scenarios from the perspective of each persona, and noting problems where we found them. To begin, we made a list of our personas and scenarios. With our four personas, we had about 12 scenarios. We selected the most representative first, but the order was not really important.

We found some problems of usefulness almost immediately. For example, package booking is not available online. Nor is it possible to modify a reservation online. Instead, users have to cancel existing reservations and create new ones. A handful of other significant features were missing that our personas would need in order to satisfy their goals. So, the technique paid off right away, identifying a certain class of problems that many usability inspection methods are incapable of finding.

As we found scenarios the reservation engine supported, however, we were able to use the personas' perspectives to identify problems. For example, none of our personas works in the hospitality industry. Yet the Web site uses industry-specific jargon (such as "run-of-house") to identify available rooms, for example. None of our personas would be likely to understand these terms.

The Benefits
Personas provide two major benefits during expert review. First, the personas function as a context for the evaluation. Personas, by their nature, are a more well-defined construct than "the user." Using personas, reviewers are better able to maintain a fixed and appropriately user-centered frame of reference during the review.

The second benefit comes from using personas during task selection. Task selection is the process of deciding which tasks to review. Because software typically supports many possible tasks, it is usually not practical to try to review every task. So, task selection becomes an important

(Story from the field, continued)

part of the review. And, as Molich and Jeffries' Competitive Usability Evaluations (CUE) studies have demonstrated, task selection has a huge impact on the results of any review [Molich and Jeffries 2003]. In this method, task selection begins not with what the application allows but with what users consider desirable. These desires are expressed in terms of the personas and scenarios. Task selection thus becomes a matter of identifying the tasks that allow the user to complete the high-level scenarios.

Story from the field

THE LIBRARIANS' VIEWPOINT: THE POWER OF PERSONAS IN EVALUATION

—Heather L. McQuaid, MAYA Design, Inc.

[The following is a continuation of "Story from the field: Personas Help Redesign the Carnegie Library Through Storyboards and Narratives" found earlier in the chapter.]

The librarians at Carnegie Library used our personas to evaluate the renovations planned for the branch of the library where they worked. They imagined the persona Naomi entering the renovated branch and trying to accomplish the "find a best-selling novel" task. In the original layout, the Best-sellers area was located near the front entrance, whereas the online catalog computers (used to search for books) were located near the back of the building. In the case in which Naomi could not find the book she wanted simply by browsing the Best-sellers area, she would need to walk all the way back to the online catalog area, conduct the search, determine that the book was in the Best-sellers area, discover its exact location, and then walk back to the front of the building to try to find the book again. By applying the persona to the new layout, the librarians discovered an inefficiency that could lead to negative experiences for their customers. They were able to use Naomi to convince the architects to place at least one computer catalog near the entrance of the building.

Story from the field

TURN YOUR TEAMMATES INTO PERSONAS

—Nathalie Barthe, Vidéotron Ltée

I organized with the product managers (Marketing) a team usability walkthrough of a prototype design. They had to "play" the persona, named Johnny, in exploring the prototype. They had all read the personas and had seen the posters, but they really had to think in the personas' roles. They were able to see the prototype from the point of view of the personas, and were able to see for the first time how our proposed changes would directly affect our personas' ability to get things done. They started saying things such as, "If we move this over here, Johnny will be able to do what he needs to do more easily." The team usability walkthrough was a success. The product managers told me that they would never look at their product marketing/development the same way as before. Through role play, they totally realized the importance of personal characteristics in the adoption/rejection/use of a technological product.

Story from the field

SOMETIMES PEOPLE ARE NOT READY TO HEAR WHAT THE PERSONAS HAVE TO SAY

—Caroline Jarrett, Effortmark Ltd

This is both a success and a failure. I used personas, in a stripped-down format, as the underlying concept in a structured walkthrough of events during the year for a major client. This walkthrough showed that there were important discontinuities: places where the details of the events didn't make sense in context. This was successful, in that it made the point very well. But it failed, because the amount of change required was too big for the client to contemplate at that time and nothing came of it. My recommendation is that this type of thinking and evaluation should happen as early in the development process as possible. Once you are past a certain point, it becomes very difficult to justify change.

Use personas as a recruiting profile for usability testing and market research

With rigorously defined personas in place, you may be tempted to sit back and enjoy the benefits they provide. Personas do bring a strong source of user centricity to your design and development process. But does this mean you no longer need to include real users in the process? Absolutely not. We strongly believe that user research, usability testing, and market research should continue throughout the development cycle if at all possible. Personas can perhaps ease the burden and cost associated with ongoing user research.

Because personas are meant to serve as your product's target audience, they can and should be used as the recruiting profile for participants in any customer research your team endeavors to complete. Interestingly, doing so not only employs the personas in a specific function but serves as a communication mechanism that can further your team's understanding of who the personas are (see Chapter 5).

Story from the field

USING PERSONAS IN THE TESTING PROCESS

—George Olsen, Principal, Interaction by Design

Your personas can be useful in determining who to recruit when testing your designs with users. Obviously, you won't find users who are identical to your personas, but you can identify aspects of the persona most relevant to the design problem being tested and try to find users who share those similarities.

The difficulty in using your personas as a recruiting profile lies in determining the "essential" qualities of your various personas. That is, your personas will have many characteristics. Some of these characteristics will be critical to the design and implementation of your product. Others will not be as critical.

You will need to develop a set of persona screener questions recruiters can use to find representative participants for your research. To do this, it is helpful to return to your original skeletons of your personas to help determine these essential qualities. Create a draft list of about 10 to 15 characteristics for each persona. Prioritize the list of characteristics and attempt to remove those that are not truly important to your business or product domain. Be prepared to make compromises in your recruiting requirements, as cost and timeliness are hugely affected by the number of questions asked when screening potential participants. Remember that with every question in your screener you will eliminate a large population of potential participants. Be willing to make decisions such as, "Tanners can be either boys or girls as long as they spend 10 hours a week playing some type of electronic game."

It is important to remember that some of your persona details relate directly to data and some are based on assumptions. It is important that you keep close track of which persona attributes are tied to data and which arose from assumptions throughout the development process. This is particularly critical as you apply the persona descriptions as test participant screeners (see "Handy Detail: Assumption Persona Users—Beware Assumption Snowballs!").

Now, turn each characteristic into a question that can be easily asked, understood by a potential candidate, and easily answered. Preferably, each question will have a bounded set of potential responses. The following is an example:

Which of the following activities have you participated in within the last 6 months?

a) Surfing the Web to compare products and prices
b) Downloading media (music, photos, video)
c) Downloading software (games, utilities, and so on)
d) Posting on an Internet bulletin board or BLOG
e) Creating a Web page

For each question, determine the criteria that qualify an answer as fitting your persona. In the previous example, a respondent doing three or more activities might indicate a moderately engaged Web surfer. (For a further example, see the following G4K case study.)

Your goal is to be able to unambiguously tell whether any potential candidate is a good match to one of your personas without taxing the recruiting process with too many questions and options. Amazingly, and even with a very reduced set of recruiting criteria, as you begin to use these participants in focus groups, user tests, field studies, survey panels, and the like, you will readily see their likeness to your personas. We have had team members observe user tests and come away saying such things as, "Wow, that person is such a Tanner!"

As part of the process, it is extremely useful to analyze, categorize, and report your findings by persona. For example, "The 'Tanners' in this study had a difficult time with the registration process, whereas the 'Colbis' breezed right through it." As mentioned earlier, doing so serves to enrich your team's knowledge of your personas and provides them a useful mechanism for understanding and interpreting complex user data.

Handy Detail

ASSUMPTION PERSONA USERS—BEWARE ASSUMPTION SNOWBALLS!

Some of you may be using assumption personas instead of data-driven personas. Assumption personas can help everyone communicate better and make good design decisions, but they should not be treated the same way as data-driven personas. For example, if you recruit usability test participants who closely match your assumption-driven personas, you may be artificially biasing your usability results. If it turns out that some of the assumptions built into your personas were wrong you will have no way of knowing this until you launch your finished product.

Assumption snowballs can still happen even if your personas *are* based on data. Consider Tanner, our tenacious tinkerer. Perhaps one of the developers notices that his own kids, who share some things in common with Tanner, talk of nothing but downloading MP3s. This developer makes the assumption that Tanner must also be obsessed with downloading music, and he begins to talk about Tanner accordingly. After several meetings, everyone begins to think that Tanner downloads a lot of music.

(Handy detail, continued)

If people start to think that Tanner likes to download music, but they don't seem to be interpreting this "extra detail" as a reason to rethink all of the product features, you may not have a problem at all. In this case, remember that the purpose of the personas is to build and maintain focus on your users and you still have that.

However, once it is time to do usability testing, what if this detail finds its way into the participant recruiting documents? You find yourself looking for nine-year-old test participants who download a lot of MP3s, and with some effort you find them. You proceed with your testing and make design changes based on the results. That is fine, right?

Not necessarily. The description of Tanner as a frequent MP3 downloader is flawed, and it could have biased your test results and therefore the design changes you recommended. As it turns out, data shows that kids don't tend to get interested in downloading music until they are a little older, and that nine-year-old boys tend to be more interested in games than they are in music. Because you tested a population of kids who download a lot of music, you may have inadvertently made design changes biased toward a very unusual group of users who are a lot less like Tanner than you would have liked them to be.

So, what do you do? You certainly cannot collect data on every aspect of your personas' personalities. However, you and your core team can keep a careful eye on the ways the personas are referenced in product-related documentation. There will inevitably be details that are added to the personas by people not on the core team. It is your job to decide whether these details are likely to veer the product off in the wrong direction. Including the MP3 detail in the usability participant recruiting requirements was a mistake because it was based entirely on assumptions. The resulting design changes would build on this initial mistake, creating a classic assumption snowball that will be difficult to undo.

If you use assumption personas, you can avoid assumption snowballs, but you and your core team have to stay on your toes. Every time you decide to use one of the tools in this book, carefully consider which persona attributes are "safe" to employ. When you create a persona-weighted feature matrix, note where there are debates on the score to give a particular feature for a particular persona and try to resolve the debate with data if at all possible. When you create a recruiting profile for usability participants, remember that you are narrowing in on a small population of potential users and stick to generic attributes of your personas (such as age and skill level). Consider creating a "value" for each of your persona attributes (according to how data driven it is) during the *conception and gestation* phase. When you see an assumption snowball forming, convene your core team and treat the situation as a communication problem. Revisit Chapter 5 for ideas on how to re-communicate the correct persona attributes.

You cannot stop your co-workers from making new assumptions that may or may not be appropriate. What you can do is carefully assess which details of your persona descriptions are data driven *enough* to drive design decisions.

Story from the field

PERSONA FRIDAYS

—Erik Goossens and **J. Vanzandbeek,** Zylom.com

[In Chapter 4, you read about the creation and validation of Zylom.com's personas (see "Story from the field: Personas at Zylom.com"). The following relates one way the Zylom personas were promoted within the company.]

At Zylom.com, our primary personas are Marie and Sophie. Because our team was small and everyone found it very easy to remember Marie and Sophie when we introduced them, we didn't create very many artifacts to communicate our personas. However, we wanted to make sure that Marie and Sophie stayed fresh in everyone's minds. More importantly, we wanted to make sure that our personas really influenced our product design. So, we decided to have "Marie and Sophie Fridays." Every Friday, we would invite users who were similar to Marie and Sophie into our offices. We would ask them to use our site and play games we had developed. We invited everyone on the team to watch, and we taped every session in case we wanted to review details later.

Our persona Fridays have helped us make many small improvements and have led to two or three "major breakthrough" ideas. For example, our purchase process was initially very complicated. In these sessions, we saw that many Maries and Sophies have trouble purchasing and/or approving the purchase agreement for our products. They simply were not comfortable with the process we had in place. Based on this, we greatly simplified the purchase process and removed the complex aspects of the purchase agreements. We noticed a major increase in completed sales almost immediately.

Marie and Sophie Fridays are inexpensive and have resulted in concrete improvements in our products. As a side effect, they have served to validate our personas and further educate our team about who they are. Not a week goes by that somebody from our technical, design, or sales teams does not walk into my office to ask me to further zoom in on a persona related to a particular element on the site they need to make a decision on. If the answer isn't clear from the persona discussion, we then decide if this element needs to be tested through a survey or on a Marie and Sophie Friday. It really fuels our innovation loops and makes the entire process of optimization and change less tedious.

[For a continuation of this case study related to the birth and maturation phase, see "Story from the field: Marie and Sophie Had a Major Impact at Zylom.com" in Chapter 7.]

Story from the field

CREATING AND USING PERSONAS TO REPORT USABILITY TEST RESULTS

—Bryan Stapp, Chief Marketing Officer, Quicken Loans

At Quicken Loans, one of our mantras is to tell things the way Forrest Gump would. In other words, keep it simple, meaningful, and to the point.

So, how do you present a two-week usability study of Quickenloans.com to senior leadership in Forrest Gump style? The 20-participant study, conducted with carefully screened target clients, produced massive amounts of data to be reviewed, indexed, and analyzed. The conventional usability report of 40-plus pages wasn't going to cut it. Our Web Marketing team needed a better way of bringing the study to life, and make it "Gump" to boot.

Personas were the answer. Rather than creating personas before the testing, the team created a set of personas *from* the study data and used them to report the findings, bring the participants' comments to life, and frame discussions about improvements to the site.

To create the personas, the team transferred all of the individual pieces of user feedback to a series of sticky notes. Next, hundreds of stickies on the wall were grouped based on the users' various goals, roles, and segments. These groups served as the basis for the four final personas.

Over a 30-day period, the personas became richly detailed. We gave each persona a name and face, as well as details on their goals, fears, and aspirations. Actual quotes from the study and enhanced demographic information were added. Finally, each had a list of usability enhancements that would improve that persona's experience on Quickenloans.com.

The personas became the centerpiece of the presentation to the leadership team. The personas made the study results seem real and easy to relate to, and provided a user-centered framework for discussing the enhancements to the site. There were no 40-page text-heavy reports and no long explanations of methodology—just clear results and next steps. Our leadership team understood the importance of the results, and supported the proposed solutions. Forrest would have been proud! With this success under our belts, we are now validating our personas and our team is using them to optimize our Web site.

Bright Idea

YOUR TEAMMATES COULD BE "OBJECTIVE" USABILITY PARTICIPANTS!

Why, that's crazy! You can't do usability tests using members of your product team! Or could you? If you ask internal people to participate in a usability study, but to take on the perspective of a persona while doing so, you just might be surprised at the usability issues you can surface. This exercise is much like the persona-based evaluations discussed earlier in this chapter.

To do this, find interested members of your team, ask them to study the persona definition documents in detail, and then schedule a usability test session just like you would with an external participant. Consider doing a round of "pilot tests" with persona-playing team members. Although you will certainly have to use professional judgment in choosing which issues should be tested with "real" participants, you will undoubtedly find a few "duh" problems your teammates would never have found without the role play.

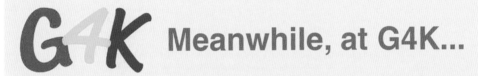 Meanwhile, at G4K...

PERSONAS HELP STRUCTURE USER RESEARCH AT G4K

The team at G4K has some prototypes of the kids' Web portal they want to test, and it is time to bring in some usability test participants. They decide they want to bring in "real" Tanners, Colbis, and Irenes to see how they like the prototypes. The core team gets together and tries to identify five key characteristics of each of these personas so that they can create screening documents to be sent to a test participant recruiter. It is a tough meeting. Everyone knows Tanner, Colbi, and Irene pretty well at this point and it is difficult to imagine broadening the description of any one of them ("How can Tanner *possibly* be a girl? He's just such a *boy!*"). It seems important that Tanners are current owners of at least one G4K game title. However, the team also knows that recruiting participants based on such a criteria will be very difficult.

There is a lot of debate, but finally everyone agrees on a set of questions they can use to screen for potential "Tanner" participants (see Figure 6.25). The team knows they can always add screener questions or revise these at a later date if these are not producing adequate participants for their usability sessions. They also know that other questions can be asked during a usability session to obtain further clarity on a participant, even if they do not screen on those responses.

(Meanwhile, at G4k..., continued)

G4K.com Persona Screener

Tanner Thompson (questions answered by parent about child)

- **Child is elementary school-aged**

  Question: How old is your child?
  Required Answer: Must be between 8–10 years of age.

- **Household has a computer at home w/Internet connection used by children**

  Question: Do you have a PC with a connection to the Internet in your home that your children use?
  Required Answer: Yes. Reject if answer is, "Yes, but I don't let the kids use it."

- **PC used by child regularly**

  Question: How often do your children use the PC? (daily, several times a week, several times a month, rarely)
  Required Answer: Several times a week or daily.

- **Child loves PC (rate the following statements as true or false)**

  Question: Which of the following statements describe your child related to the PC:

  > Statement 1: My child fights/begs for PC time (T or F)
  >
  > Statement 2: My child prefers the PC over Television (T or F)
  >
  > Statement 3: My child amazes me with their knowledge of the PC/Software (T or F)
  >
  > Statement 4: My child is continually dragging me to the PC to show me something they did or found (T or F)
  >
  > Statement 5: I have to encourage my child to do other activities than using the PC (T or F)

  Required Answer: Must answer "True" to at least two of the statements above.

- **Uses PC to play games and surf Web**

  Question: Your child uses the PC to do the following things:
  > Activity 1: Play PC games (yes or no)

FIGURE 6.25: *The G4K usability test participant screening document for "Tanners."*

As the G4K marketing team prepares the kids' portal launch effort, they can use this same set of screener questions to focus market research toward the personas. Ultimately, they will focus their advertising efforts on the media outlets they know Tanner already accesses: *SportKid* magazine, cereal boxes, and perhaps even Saturday morning television programming. They may also "harvest" lists of registered owners of G4K shrink-wrapped games.

Use personas to focus quality assurance testing and to create test cases

A major part of any development effort revolves around quality assurance (QA). Those on your team responsible for this (generally referred to as "testers" in software development) have a huge job in front of them. They make your product work as designed and intended. To do their job, testers attempt to break the product. They find bugs in the code, clarify the conditions in which those bugs occur, and partner with developers to get the bugs fixed.

QA teams are often desperate to stay in the loop as product decisions are made, and this isn't always easy to do. Like usability testing, QA is still too often seen as a final, relatively disjointed, step in the development process. Personas and scenarios can communicate critical context, summarize decisions, and clarify product requirements more clearly than most other product development materials. Therefore, they are wonderful resources for the QA team.

We recommend training the entire QA team on the persona process. They will likely see this as an extension of their skills and probably enjoy it as well as obtain information that will help make their test plans more solid. In addition, consider that in the end QA directors have the final power to hold a product up if they consider it unreliable or lacking in performance.

Provide your QA team with the complete set of personas and all supporting data materials. Help them understand that the personas not only represent expected user goals, but contain important information about the context in which the completed product will be used. For example, Tanner's persona profile contains information about the type of computer he uses, the way he accesses the Internet, and so on, and this information is based on real data about the target customer base. Such specificity can help the QA team create product- and market-appropriate test plans.

Use personas and scenarios to inform test cases

The QA team's job is huge because the possible test cases (the scenarios, paths through the product, configurations, and states in which the user could put themselves and cause the code to break) increase exponentially as the size of the code base and the product's features increase. With many software products, it is virtually impossible to test all possible scenarios and configurations. Personas, like scenario-based design techniques, can help this situation by providing testers with a mechanism for paring test cases down to a reasonable number.

Bright Idea

THE PERSONA BUG BASH

Personas can be utilized to focus less rigorous, but important, ad hoc "bug bashes." Bug bashes are loosely organized team-wide strolls through the product in search of code bugs, user experience issues, and fit-and-finish problems (typos, visual flaws, redraw issues, slow performance, and so on). They sometimes include non-test-team members (developers, tech writers, program managers, designers, and so on).

To involve the personas, simply divide the bug bash participants into teams, one team per persona. Each team then reviews the persona descriptions and related scenarios and attempts to "use" the product as if they were that persona reporting bugs as they come across them. After some period of time has elapsed (e.g., four hours on a Friday afternoon), the bugs are counted and evaluated, removing duplicates and nonreproducible issues. The results are then communicated back to the team per persona ("We found 23 Tanner bugs and 45 Colbi bugs"). Our experience in doing this has been quite positive. The bash participants enjoyed the challenge of trying to use the product as someone else and felt that the quality and types of bugs uncovered were good.

The personas serve as criteria by which to judge usage plausibility, likelihood, and frequency of occurrence—and by extension the importance of certain test cases.

The QA test scenarios can be informed or derived from the scenarios used for product design. The scenarios you have already built as part of the planning and design process contain a wealth of information about your expectations for the behavior and affordances of the final product. The QA team can create tests that will help to ensure that the product does perform as expected.

Finally, note that the persona-weighted feature matrix should be incredibly useful to the QA team. Make sure you schedule time to introduce the team to the matrix, how it was built, and how to interpret its content. Collaborate with the QA team as they decide on and build their test cases. This gives you the opportunity to ensure that the testing focus corresponds to the feature priorities expressed in the matrix.

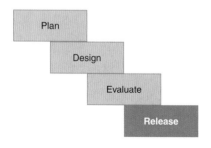

STAGE 4: USE PERSONAS TO SUPPORT THE RELEASE OF YOUR PRODUCT

Now that your product is getting close to being complete, it is time to turn your attention to details that are not directly related to product development. You have put a great deal of effort into creating and using your personas to design and build your product. Now that the product is almost complete, your personas (and all of the persona-related materials and tools you have created) can be extremely helpful to those responsible for documenting, supporting, and selling your product. In this section, we show you how to you apply your personas toward:

- Documentation, training, and product support materials
- Marketing and sales.

Personas can help focus instructional materials, guidebooks, and editorial content

The documentation and product support team is under the gun to produce highly accurate and useful materials that will help real people understand and use the features you are busy building. While the core development team is still writing code, making final decisions, and seeing changes happen, the documentation team is frantic to start writing so that they can meet their deadlines. Everyone on the development team is usually too busy to take much time to give the documentation team the detailed information they need.

Personas and their associated scenarios can help technical writers understand how a product works and who will be using it. Writers can examine the personas and determine which types of editorial, training, and support materials will be most useful to each persona. Scenarios serve as a ready-made list of tasks that need to be explained in the support materials technical writers create. Scenarios will allow writers to understand the "story" of the product and the expected behavior of features and functions long before coding is complete. Alan Cooper and his associates have also noted the role personas can play in the creation of user documentation. Their Web article on www.cooper.com, "Using Personas to Create User Documentation" by Steve Calde [2004], provides several useful tips on applying personas in this way.

Audience analysis is a well-known notion to the professional writing community (see, for example, Thralls *et al.* [1988]). Clearly, such analysis can be used to guide content selection, organization, and presentation and style. In our 2000 and 2001 workshops, we had a lively discussion on how the reader and author roles described in rhetorical theory relate to persona usage. Coney and Steehouder [2000] explored the application of rhetorical theory to persona usage in product and interaction design. They argue that not only readers but users can actually assume the role of the persona put forth in an article, Web site, or software product. In this case, personas can take on a rhetorical role.

As an example, in her book *Designing Websites for Every Audience*, Ilise Benun [2003] uses personas in a very direct and explicit fashion to organize the content of the book. Each chapter begins with a unique persona description to set the focus and tone of the subsequent materials (as shown in Figure 6.26).

USER PROFILE:
BUSINESS
BROWSERS

John Fix III

Demographic: Male, 42, married

Occupation: Retail hardware store owner

Personality traits: Friendly, inquisitive, generous

Online habits and behaviors: "I log on every day, numerous times each day for an average of about two hours per day. I have DSL at home, and a T1 connection at work. Work is noisy—it's a busy office—but at home it's quiet, because the PC is in a home office away from the television."

Web history: "I've been using the Web regularly since 1995, but using Internet e-mail since about 1992."

Favorite Web sites: www.theonion.com, ESPN.com, DejaNews.com

Usability pet peeves: Animated ads, pop-ups, code that disables the back button

How do you search? "On a Web site, I usually look for a search option if the item or information I'm looking for isn't immediately visible. I try not to get distracted by other info on the site. I use the back button all the time, usually via the mouse button (I use an MS Intellimouse Explorer)."

What are your typical online goals? "Hmmm, depends on what I'm doing. If it's something work-related, I want to get the info and then get back with my customer or employee. It's made things like finding product information for my hardware store much easier."

FIGURE 6.26: *Ilise Benun begins each chapter with a persona profile.*

In their "Story from the field: Freeler and the Freejays" (following), Marque Joosten, Marijn Pijnenborg, and Thijs Vleeers demonstrate how personas can be both applied to design and exposed directly to end users. You can use your personas to create training materials that incorporate the details of their knowledge, goals, and work habits. Imagine bringing your product into a company that has been using an older product or process for a long time. Because of your early research to inform your personas, you should know quite a bit about what how they currently get their work done. Your personas and scenarios embody the changes you are expecting in real users' work patterns now that your new product exists. In her "Story from the field: Informal Personas for Instructional Design" (following), Ariel van Spronsen demonstrates how personas can be applied in this way.

In addition, you might consider even showing your personas directly to your learners, and explain how they relate to the goals and tasks your product supports. In this way, your personas can literally show your real users what they can accomplish in relation to your product. Although we think that such direct exposure of your personas is not always appropriate or necessary, it is an interesting way to engage your target users.

Using personas in any of the ways described previously requires that your team really understand detailed aspects of how they will use your product, discover its features, and learn its interface and idiosyncrasies. You may need to expand your persona descriptions to include relevant information for your documentation team. In their "Story from the field: Personas That Learn" (in material following), Julie Nowicki and Margaret Martinez describe how they expanded their personas to include notions of learning.

Story from the field

PERSONAS ARE NOT AUTOMATICALLY THE RIGHT TOOL FOR THE JOB

—Nathalie Barthe, Vidéotron Ltée

The editorial team did not buy in or use the personas we developed for our business-to-business (B2B) portal. I think the personas were missing the information (about specific interests, reading habits, and so on) that would have helped the editors determine what content should be on the portal. The personas were too general for that.

Story from the field

FREELER AND THE FREEJAYS

—Marque Joosten, Marijn Pijnenborg, and **Thijs Vieleers,** Funda.nl

Back in mid 1999, before we had ever heard the term *personas*, we started a new Internet service provider called "Freeler" in the Netherlands. Because this ISP was free (hence the name), we expected a wide audience for the ISP portal. In order to create a relevant Web site and to anticipate how visitors would use this site, we created fictitious people. Our collective thinking led to eight characters:

- *Play:* A boy who uses the Internet to play around. His entire life is about playing and doing things for the very first time.
- *Nerd:* A boy who wants to know how things work and what the content of the Web site is, as well as search for things and topics. Loves science fiction.
- *Build:* A girl who is into building relationships, a career, and so on. She wants to create favorites, keep things in folders, and so on. Ambitious.
- *Care:* A mother who cares for her children and her own health. Watches Oprah.
- *Fun:* A young adult who just wants to have fun and party around. Really into gadgets, fashion, and latest trends.
- *Escape:* The husband of Care, who wants to escape his family and responsibility. He uses the Internet to dream away for a while. Watches sports and likes cars and do-it-yourself projects.
- *Development:* A man who is satisfied with himself but wants to develop himself culturally. Likes travel and music. Plays golf.
- *Rest:* "Empty-nest" man/woman. Money is no issue; health is. Wants to communicate via the Internet.

As we evolved our thinking about the product, we continued exploring these characters. Eventually, we dropped Play (too young) and Rest (too old) and all of the personas were given real names and representative photos (see Figure 6.27):

- Nerd (Ingmar)
- Build (Nicole)
- Care (Suzanne)
- Fun (Joost)
- Escape (Willem)
- Development (Michiel)

While building the Freeler site around these characters, considering their specific use of the Internet for navigation and design layout, we came up with the idea of making them appear real and then using them as guides for the actual visitors to our site. These were to be lifestyle guides, not topical guides such as found at *www.about.com*. We named them Freejays (see Figure 6.28).

(Story from the field, continued)

FIGURE 6.27: *Given names and photos, the Freejays started becoming more real.*

FIGURE 6.28: *The Freejays lived on our home page.*

The basic proposition to our users was: "If you are a person like me, I will show you around the Internet." We hired eight people, each of whom started a daily "column" in which they gave useful links to the visitors (sort of like blogs, but before they were invented).

From day 1 it was a big success, developing loyal fans that visited regularly. We used feedback from the specific fans to further elaborate the Web site (its design and user interface) around each group's ideas, usage, and feelings. Because of their popularity, we created other Freejays and used them in similar ways (see Figure 6.29).

(Story from the field, continued)

FIGURE 6.29: *Other Freejays were added later.*

What we noticed is that people really attach themselves to certain personas when you show them "live" on your Web site. That is good and bad. This is good because you build stickiness and certain people will visit the site just because of the persona they really like. It is bad because you characterize your audience and if people cannot recognize themselves in the personas they will discontinue visiting the site or visit it less often. So, the Web sites we have developed in the past few years have been based on personas and research (image of the Web site, user interface) done with the personas in mind. However, we do not show examples of the personas anymore—not even in advertising. This is probably more relevant to "big-audience universal-type" Web sites, but if you have a targeted niche audience Web site we believe that you can use "live" personas with success. The tremendous success of some Web blogs shows us that.

Story from the field

INFORMAL PERSONAS FOR INSTRUCTIONAL DESIGN—PERSONAS LEND A HAND IN E-LEARNING

—Ariel van Spronsen, Instructional Designer

As an instructional designer contracted to develop online art classes for a private college, I have a wide scope of responsibility (essentially managing all functions of the product effort). The development cycle is fast and intense, and shortcuts are a way of life as my team and I work to create a rich and satisfying online class experience for students. One of my most efficacious techniques is to introduce informal personas in my first meeting with the content editor and the instructor writing the class.

In that first meeting our goal is to nail out a project schedule and come to a vision for what the class will look like in an online format. To accurately develop that vision and get all team members heading in the same direction, I describe the personas I've created for the general student population based on admissions data and interviews. I then ask the instructor to add details based on his or her own experience with students in the on-ground course. The time taken to go through this simple exercise pays off almost immediately in the reduction of false starts, rewrites, and content that needs significant restructuring.

Once content production is rolling and my attention turns toward producing the actual user interface, the seemingly irrelevant details we've endowed our personas with come into play. For example, we know that Samantha, a fashion design major, was raised in a strict household that valued academic achievement. She is also on her own for the first time in a major city and is experiencing a cultural awakening. She puts a lot of creative effort into designing costumes for herself and her friends to wear to all-night dance parties, and has recently been asked to help organize a quarterly fashion show at a downtown club. We can imagine that when she sits down to take her online class she brings a commitment to obtaining her fashion degree and an academic diligence, but she may also be tired and distracted by her extracurricular projects. Samantha needs the class to keep her interest, so we may vary the tempo of the course material, incorporating video demonstrations and making the material relevant by highlighting current examples from urban culture.

By keeping personas in mind throughout the online class build cycle, we are able to quickly create courses that "speak" to students and that grow in popularity each semester. We also have a much greater chance of getting the course right the first time, preventing the time and cost of initiating rebuilds when there are low enrollments.

Story from the field

PERSONAS THAT LEARN

—Julie Nowicki, Usability Lead, Microsoft Corporation, and **Margaret Martinez,** Ph.D., President and CEO, The Training Place, Inc.

A few years prior to the release of a new version of the Microsoft Windows operating system, customer feedback on early prototypes indicated that the learning curve might be a barrier to deploying the new version, especially in large organizations where help desk, training, and support costs are considerable. The new version had a number of new features, new ways of doing existing tasks, and a redesigned user interface. User research indicated that the changes would result in significant productivity and satisfaction improvements once they were assimilated, but how to get users going smoothly and minimize business disruption?

(Story from the field, continued)

Learning materials for Windows come from a variety of divisions in the company, including the built-in Help system, our learning division (which creates e-learning products and books), and our online knowledge base. Personas had already proven to be a useful tool and a great common language for communicating across these teams. The basic Windows and Office personas were already highly recognized across many groups. So, we thought it would be good to extend these personas into the learning domain, given that there is a natural relationship between meeting persona needs and developing documentation or instructional design. In the instructional design process, understanding audience needs is an important process akin to user analysis in UCD.

Looking at the broad range of our target audience and the respective personas—from a teenager to an IT professional—it was obvious that there would be no "one size fits all" learning solution. Personas looked like a great mechanism for understanding individual differences in learning and developing a common learning framework across teams. But there was little learning data associated with the personas. How and when do they take time to learn? How much time and energy would they spend on learning? What types of educational materials would work best?

The "Personas that Learn" project augmented our personas to include individual differences in learning. We started by doing two things: (1) using existing marketing research data and (2) searching for industry or academic research that could help us. Our marketing research gave us data indicating significant differences in the extent to which users continuously engage in learning and like trying new things with their PC. Some of the marketing data was already tagged by personas. When it wasn't, we extrapolated based on the characteristics of the marketing segment and data that related personas to a marketing segment. The marketing data also helped us understand what might motivate our personas to learn. For example, many business users place a big priority on working more efficiently.

In the academic research literature, we looked at the Felder-Silverman learning style model and Kolb's learning style model. This traditional learning style research studied cognitive differences in learning, but it didn't address many of the emotional and motivational issues we believed we would be dealing with for the new version of Windows. A body of research by Dr. Margaret Martinez, called *learning orientation* research, turned out to be a good choice for us. This research explored individual differences in learning by emphasizing the role of motivation and emotion in learning, as well as traditional cognitive approaches. In addition, the learning orientation research suggested different content type and navigation structures that would work best for each learning orientation, so it had a practical application to the design of instructional materials. For example, highly motivated and autonomous learners often prefer less structured content, with the ability to explore and discover. Less motivated learners prefer structured, step-by-step content. Learning orientation research integrates the biology of learning with the more traditional psychological and educational aspects. The following extract is from the work of Margaret Martinez (see *http://www.trainingplace.com/source/research*).

(Story from the field, continued)

Based on the idea that certain individuals are inevitably more open to learning and change than others, this research examines the psychological sources that impact differences in learning and acceptance of new ideas, processes, and products. It specifically explores the important impact of emotions, values, intentions, and social factors on learning. It is no secret that tapping into what people like and value can help individuals make the connections that translate into action, progress, and achievement. Learning Orientation research explores four general learning orientations: Transforming, Performing, Conforming, and Resistant learning orientations. The learning orientations describe the extent and depth of an individual's fundamental belief about why, when, and how to use learning and how it can accomplish personal goals or change events. Those who can expertly tap into their audience's emotions and intentions have a powerful advantage, especially in addressing the fundamental needs of the learner and supporting more successful learning experiences. Developing descriptive profiles that fit your audience (as personas or some other representation) and then matching their needs is an excellent way to mass-customize your learning and performance solutions.

So, our group began collaborating with Dr. Margaret Martinez on learning orientation research. We wanted to first map our personas to learning orientations, and then to specific instructional design recommendations. To obtain more data, we decided to conduct our own learning orientation survey based on Dr. Martinez' research. From this survey we were able to classify more than 2,000 Windows users by persona and learning orientation. We found strong correlations among persona, learning orientation, and characteristics such as a tendency to ask others for assistance.

In this survey, we also asked about products used for learning, such as the Help system, Internet search, or books. An interesting result was a debunking of the common myth that "people don't use Help." Categorizing the results by persona allowed us to get beyond the blanket statement and look at what was really happening for particular classes of users.

Some of the themes that came from the Personas that Learn project applied to personas across the board. For example, being time challenged was a common learning constraint. But there were also interesting differences. Procedural, step-by-step content is not necessarily the best entry point to learning for several of our personas. Introducing an element of fun or community may appeal to some personas but not others.

We then extended our persona descriptions to include these new findings. One of the most useful Personas that Learn deliverables was a chart showing each persona, preferred modes of learning, and examples of learning tools they likely would or would not use. A simplified example of the chart is shown in Figure 6.30.

(Story from the field, continued)

"Joe"	"Ann"	"Eric"
• Loose, flexible structure • Short topics with optional links • On-demand "mentor" • Lots of choices • Background and theory	• Some structure, TOC • Mid-sized, explicit topic • Continuous "coach" • Hands-on, interactive • Fun, energizing, creative • Personal value is clear • Collaboration	• Step-by-step, highly structured, linear • Longer, more detailed topics • Constant access to guide/instructor • Simple, consistent • Less choice • Collaboration
Avoid prescriptive, highly structured	**Avoid complexity and information overload**	**Avoid flashy designs**
Appreciates: • Links to the Internet • Great search options • Cool tips and tricks May not appreciate: • Classroom tutorial • Step-by-step tutorial	Appreciates: • In-context learning • Cool tips and tricks • Short, fun, tutorial May not appreciate: • Reading a book	Appreciates: • Classroom training May not appreciate: • Self-help resources

FIGURE 6.30: *Each persona had different preferred modes of learning and learning tools they would likely use or not use.*

The results of our research and the extended personas were used by multiple teams across the company:

- One of our divisions used the findings to modify out-of-the-box training. They modified a wizard-like interface to provide more flexibility and motivation for certain personas.
- Our user assistance (Help) team gained a better understanding of the variety of learning propensities. Although they don't assume people want to spend a lot of time in Help, they understand better that people are willing to learn new things if they are presented well.
- The team that develops support materials, such as the online knowledge base, established guidelines for support content and site development to align problem types with personas and learning orientation.

Other teams at Microsoft have been inspired to create personas for specific situations. However, in general we found that a learning framework built on the existing personas was an efficient way of getting people across divisions thinking consistently about the multifaceted learning needs of our users.

Personas can tailor marketing and sales efforts

Because the marketing and sales teams are not always directly on the development team, they often have to struggle to stay in the loop. During the development process, decisions are made at such a fast pace that no one, even development team members, can keep accurate track of all of them—to say nothing of how each decision will affect the experience of the people who will have to learn about and use the product you are building. During this creative chaos, the marketing team needs to understand enough about what is being built to create materials that will help your company sell the product. These materials should neither radically over- or under-promise on the features and functionality.

The personas and their associated scenarios can provide the common language between the busy development team and the marketing team. The personas are what these teams can have in common. While developers are busy creating features for the personas, marketing teams are trying to figure out how to sell to them.

In his contributed chapter later in this book, Robert Barlow-Busch provides excellent coverage of using personas for marketing purposes. One specific approach he describes is "the brand ladder." It is a method for explicitly connecting your personas to both your product and your brand.

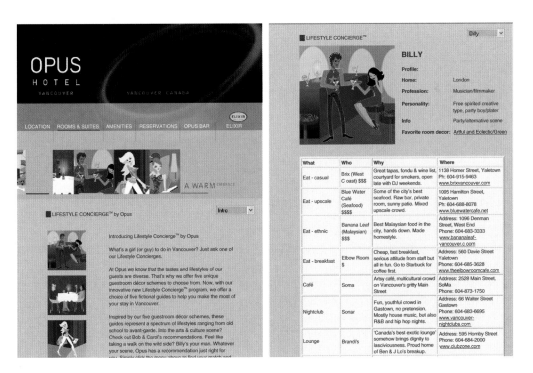

FIGURE 6.31: *Opus Hotel concierges.* (www.opushotel.com/concierge.html)

Like your documentation team, your marketing team may choose to expose the personas as part of a marketing effort. For example, as shown in Figure 6.32, the Opus Hotel Web site uses user profiles that look very much like personas directly in their user interface (as a part of their Web site front end). Visitors to the site can select from one of five personas ("Billy", "Susan", "Mike", "Dede", and a couple persona "Bob and Carol") to serve as their personal concierge (*www.opushotel.com/concierge.html*). The inclusion of these profiles helps communicate directly to potential customers who this hotel caters to while positioning itself as the hub for a wide range of activities.

Story from the field

PERSONAS "ESCAPING INTO THE WILD"

—Jess McMullin, Principal, nForm User Experience

It has been interesting over the last six months to notice personas escaping from the design team out into marketing. This is not surprising, in that personas largely derive from marketing's user archetypes. Sightings: MSN Personas and IBM print ad, and the more scenario-focused Macromedia Central Portraits and Vodafone's Future Vision. Vodafone's piece isn't just about marketing. It constitutes scenarios in the sense of prototyping the future. Most of the scenarios involve technology that only exists now as concepts or clunky prototypes, not the polished integration into everyday life of wearable mobile communications depicted in their scenarios. One of the challenges of personas being more publicly visible is that clients or other departments may start building up preconceived ideas about how personas work, what they should include, and how they should be used. The marketing scenarios and personas referenced previously are all valuable but don't have the level of detail required to be used make decisions about behavior.

Story from the field

PERSONAS CAN HELP SALES TEAMS BREAK INTO NEW MARKETS

—Howard Blumenthal, Director, E-Commerce & Database Management, Pfaltzgraff

For several years, the Pfaltzgraff sales department struggled to break into a number of targeted markets. Upon building personas, however, we discovered a disconnect between our sales efforts in these markets and our personas' interests. This discovery allowed us to refine our sales strategy. The personas helped us identify the overlaps between our consumers and the consumers within the target markets. Armed with these insights, we built a new strategy that highlights the value of our products to our wholesale partners—from our shared consumers' point of view. Our sales force now had the appropriate tools to achieve their goals.

Remember to differentiate between users and customers

Although your personas may represent both your users and your customers, there are situations in which this is not the case. Sometimes the people who will purchase your product are not the same people who will be using it on a daily basis. For example, managers and/or IT professionals in an organization often make command decisions about what software everyone in the office will use. Although these people are not the intended users of the product, they are critical to the success of the product because they make the purchasing decisions. Likewise, influencers—including market analysts, pundits, and reviewers—can make or break a product before it gets to the purchaser or customer.

Bright Idea

CREATE USER, PURCHASER, AND INFLUENCER PERSONAS FROM THE BEGINNING!

It can be very handy to create all three types of personas from the very beginning of your project. The value of having user personas is clear, but it is also important to consider the needs of the purchasers and influencers of your product. You will probably find many small ways to enhance your product in purchasers' and influencers' eyes as you make design decisions—and this can make it much easier to express the value of your product once it is ready to go on the market.
If you can, gather data and create rigorous purchaser and influencer personas. If you don't have time, create assumption personas for these roles.

Marketing professionals are usually highly sensitized to this distinction, and should be able to tell you exactly who your personas represent in this constellation of users, purchasers, and influencers. For small, highly specialized products the three roles could be occupied by the same person. For large products, the roles almost certainly could *not*. Of course, we believe that personas are a good way of representing users, and they can be a highly effective tool when you explore the differences among the users of your product, purchasers, and influencers. You now have very specific portraits of your users in your personas, and the marketers in your organization should be able to quickly create alternative assumption personas for representing purchasers and influencers.

If you don't distinguish between the users and the potential purchasers of the product, you might run into a problem we think of as the "persona identity crisis." If your organization does buy in to the personas wholeheartedly, make sure they understand that the personas can represent users and purchasers specifically. If the marketing team adopts the personas and builds all of the marketing materials to appeal to the personas, they may actually do the company a disservice—especially if the purchasers of the product are very different people with very different needs. Again, Robert Barlow-Busch provides detailed coverage of this topic that will help your team better distinguish between users and customers.

Story from the field

OUR PERSONA EFFORT NEEDED REFOCUSING AT PRODUCT LAUNCH

—Christina Wodtke, Author of *Information Architecture: Blueprints for the Web*

For a large redesign effort, we started by doing desirability testing to understand the core values our users associate with shopping. We translated the core values into goals for our personas. For example, our personas had goals such as, "I want to be able to shop safely on the Internet, no matter who I'm buying things from." The goal-based personas were great and everyone used them—during the design process. But once our new design launched, the shopping team started backsliding away from their wonderful shared vision. They all wandered off according to other forces that were acting on them, such as requests from advertisers. We quickly discovered that using personas to establish focus on users is one thing during the design process and another challenge entirely once a product is launched. We needed a way of refocusing everyone on our users' values and goals so that tweaks and "site maintenance" wouldn't undo the great experience we built for the original redesign.

We went into a full-court press with a brand new persona campaign. The personas didn't change, but the way we communicated them did. Our goal was to remind everyone else of the personas' goals, and that's just what we did. We created posters with new pictures and strong goal-based statements (e.g., "I don't say dude. Treat me like a grownup." and "I'm not a rocket scientist. Make it easy.") and hung them everywhere. We collaborated on advertising campaigns based on our personas' core goals, so that our advertising wouldn't wander off based on requests from individual advertisers.

The results were just what we had hoped: everyone's eyes got pointed back in the same direction. Everyone on the redesign team lived with our personas during the design process, so when the new posters showed up all over the walls it was an "oh, yeah" moment. It also helped our user experience team think about ways of reusing our personas as we moved on to new projects.

TRANSITIONING INTO LIFETIME ACHIEVEMENT, REUSE, AND RETIREMENT

You have done due diligence toward your persona campaign, and in return your personas have kept your product team focused and on track throughout the development cycle. As your product goes to market, adulthood for your personas is coming to a close. If your company or product team is like many companies in the industry, you are already beginning to think about the next version of your product. You may be tempted to jump right back into *adulthood* again, without re-examining your target audience. And why not just do that? You created some great personas and supporting materials, and your team knows these personas and exactly how to use them. Your team probably thought of the personas as helpful and appropriate, and are happy to just keep focusing on them. However, before diving into product version 2 and a second persona *adulthood* phase, you will need to ask yourself and your team a few questions. Was all of this time, money, and energy worth it? Was your end product good? Was your decision making better, faster? It is time to validate your efforts.

Perhaps more importantly, you will need to think again about why your team would build another version of your product. Does the current version satisfy your users? Has the market changed, or your competition? Will your target audience change? In relation to that change, will your personas retire from use? Can you reuse some of their content? These questions and many others are explored in Chapter 7.

SUMMARY

An overriding message of this chapter is that *adulthood* is key. If you have not come to this conclusion yet, you will once you attempt your first persona effort. Personas cannot just be "thrown over the wall" once *family planning, conception and gestation,* and *birth and maturation* are done. You will have to keep track of them like you would any employee. You will need to make sure they know what to do and ensure they are actually doing it. Identifying and providing specific uses for your personas goes a long way toward making that happen. Hundreds of decisions are being made every day by your product team as they plan, build, and promote your product. They can make those decisions with your target customers in mind or without them. Much of the time, such decisions are made via implicit assumptions, known only to the single decision maker. Personas can help your product team be user centered. They can take part in those decisions to make the implicit become explicit. They can help move an entire team in a user-focused direction.

How personas are used depends greatly on where you are in the development cycle, as well as on who is using them. Early on, executives are interested in the bigger picture, the product vision, as well as competitive marketplace, product marketing, messaging, and positioning. They are also interested in cost of development and time to market. Program managers and product planners are interested in defining functionality (i.e., features and user interfaces). Usability specialists are interested in scenarios and tasks, participant recruitment, interaction issues, and products that are useful, usable, fun, and good sellers. Interaction designers are interested in user interfaces, format behaviors, inflection, and style. Once things get moving, developers (programmers) are interested in architecture, implementation, and work resourcing. A little later, QA testers are interested in bugs, crashes, test scripts, and edge cases. Technical writers (user assistance/education) are interested in the documentation development process, documenting the application, and being "in the loop" with program managers, designers, and developers. And finally, once the product is nearing release, the marketing, sales, and support folks are eager to work their magic to make the product a business success.

You can use some or all of the tools presented in this chapter to ensure that your personas provide the right information to the right people at the right time—so that ultimately you end up building the right product!

Each tool provides a different utility and helps different team members at the appropriate time in the development cycle. Again, the most important thing to remember here is that you are not done once your personas have been created. The real effort and payoff occurs throughout the development cycle.

We believe there are many more persona tools out there waiting to be created or already in use. It is important to understand what your team needs and how knowledge about target users can be a part of that. Be creative and flexible in employing your personas. Your team will likely find that personas are not only useful and informative but fun and inspiring.

7

PERSONA LIFETIME ACHIEVEMENT, REUSE, AND RETIREMENT

If all has gone well, the personas have been working hard along with everyone else in your organization, and the effort is paying off. The end is in sight. You have finished testing your product and the release plan is being executed. People are starting to think about the next project.

In the development team offices, people are taking the time to sort through and clean out their e-mail in-boxes. They are shredding the mountains of versions of spec docs that have been piling up on their desks. They are cleaning their keyboards and taking long lunches and vacations. Everyone on the development team is taking a deep breath and getting ready to start the process all over again.

Product and program managers are providing materials and information to the marketing and sales teams and are, at the same time, trying to figure out the vision for the next project or product. If yours is a consumer product, the executive, marketing, and sales staffs are working full throttle on building market share. They are delivering the product message and traveling to trade shows. They are tweaking sales strategies and closing deals.

There is an odd mix of buzz and excitement around the release of the product, combined with exhaustion, regrouping, and the first glimmers of interest in the next project. Even though you and your persona team are just as worn out as everyone else, it is time for you to focus on measuring the success of your effort and figuring out what to do with your personas now that your product is launched and new development efforts are on the horizon.

WHAT IS LIFETIME ACHIEVEMENT, REUSE, AND RETIREMENT FOR PERSONAS?

The complete persona lifecycle positions your persona team as the "first in/last-out" members of the product development team. You will be first in as you collect and express data about target user populations to your executive team to support their strategic work. You will be last out as you help manage the transition from the end of one project to the beginning of the next. In this sense, this last phase of the persona lifecycle is both critical and, at present, too often ignored.

For a variety of reasons, persona efforts tend to peter out rather than end in a managed, measured, and organized manner. Consultants are usually not paid to stick around long enough to manage the personas at the end of a project and in-house teams are usually more concerned with ramping up for the next project than they are with tidying up loose ends from the previous one. Being first-in/last-out on projects means that you will probably end up with responsibilities that straddle two projects. You will be completing your work on project A even after you have begun your work on project B. That is no simple task. It is certainly easier to simply move on to project B.

G4K Meanwhile, at G4K...

G4K HAS LAUNCHED THEIR NEW WEB SITE

The G4K portal team is excited to have launched their new site. They are roughly on time and on budget, but they had to cut a few features and live with a few known bugs to make it happen. They are confident that those things will be worked out in subsequent updates and plans have already started for more significant enhancements to the site. So the persona core team will have to work fast to evaluate the appropriateness and accuracy of their current personas toward any new development.

Even though the traffic to the site is minimal right now, the executive staff believes that the effort was successful—simply because the site exists. The persona core team knows that they can lend a hand in assessing how successful the effort was and how practical site really is. Along with this, they plan to look at how useful the persona method was in this development effort.

However, we argue that an organized approach to measuring and managing the end of a project can yield significant benefits.

The final persona lifecycle phase is about measurement, regaining control of the persona effort as a whole, and preparing for the future. As the leader of your persona core team, you have two primary tasks at the end of your persona effort:

- Measure the lifetime achievement of your personas (their value), including the return on investment (ROI) of the persona effort
- Manage the organization's transition to a new project with regard to UCD and target audiences, which will involve reusing, retiring, or in some way reincarnating your personas.

In this chapter, we cover both of these topics in depth. Thus, the chapter is organized into two major sections: (1) lifetime achieve and (2) reuse and retirement.

LIFETIME ACHIEVEMENT: MEASURE THE RETURN ON INVESTMENT (ROI) OF YOUR PERSONA EFFORT

One of the most common questions we are asked about personas is if they actually work. And if they do, how can you tell if they were worth the effort? Answering these questions is difficult. What counts as proof of the method is different for different people, products, and companies. There is no single case study or research study that proves their effectiveness rigorously. However, as you have seen throughout this book, there are hundreds of little

Story from the field

PERSONAS IMPROVE MEDCOHEALTH.COM WHILE SAVING TIME AND DEVELOPMENT COST

— **Meridith Levinson,** Senior Writer, *CIO Magazine, www.cio.com* (Reproduced in part from "How to Play to Your Audience," *CIO Magazine,* November 2003)

When Medco Health Solutions undertook a redesign of its Web site, Medcohealth.com, in 2002, the pharmacy benefits manager hired a Web design company that employed the persona-based methodology [Cooper] to gear the site toward an aging population and to untangle its labyrinthine taxonomy. Steve Gold, former CIO of the Franklin Lakes, N.J.-based company, says he saw persona-based design as a way of bringing end users to life for the digital design group and pertinent business units. "We wanted the developers and workgroups to have empathy for the individuals they were building the software systems for, having them rally around somebody tangible as opposed to just building a Web site in a vacuum, which is the more conventional way of doing it."

The big payoff came when the finished prototypes were vetted with actual users in a usability testing lab. Designers had to make only minor changes to the pages, most pertaining to language. "Using this method, we consistently find fewer problems to fix after running a usability test," says Kim Goodwin, vice president and general manager of Cooper Interactive Design [the firm hired to implement the persona work].

And that saves money. "It is a more efficient way to design Web sites with fewer iterations and fewer changes because we know up front what we're designing for," says Vicente Caride, Senior Director of E-Commerce Marketing, Medco Health. "From that, you get savings."

But the really impressive numbers have shown up since the redesigned site went live in December of 2002. Medco Health has seen a 33% increase in the number of transactions and a 26% increase in the number of prescriptions ordered online. The number of abandoned shopping carts has decreased by 13%. Based on the entire number of log-ins, the number of e-mails from users to the help desk with questions about the site has decreased by 18%.

In June of 2003, ComScore Media Metrix reported that seniors 65 years and older spent more time (approximately 21 minutes) on Medcohealth.com and viewed more pages (approximately 31) there in a month than any other health Web site, including Yahoo Health, MSN Health, Drugstore.com, and AARP.com.

"The monetary reward you reap from a more efficient process, you also see in the results," says Caride. "You get savings from an efficient design once, but if you have increasing traffic and loyalty and satisfaction that, just keeps multiplying."

examples of their effectiveness and value scattered about the industry. This is why this section includes so many stories from the field describing success stories from persona practitioners.

Measuring the ROI of user experience work

Products fail for many reasons, and it is the same for their success. As Mike Kuniavsky [2003] points out, no one would argue against the assertion that in principle you should "build products with users in mind." However, how that principle is translated into reality can cause quite a bit of discussion and disagreement. Whether or not the end product does better in the marketplace because you had the user in mind is difficult to verify.

Measuring the ROI of user experience work, and particularly of personas, is tricky, but it is not impossible. There are several resources that explore how to measure the ROI of design and usability efforts (see Bias and Mayhew [1994], Brooke [1996], Donahue [2001],

Souza et al. [2001a, 2001b], and Wixon and Jones [1996] in the References section at the back of the book). Measuring ROI depends on being able to clearly express the costs and benefits of the effort, neither of which is easy to express when it comes to most user experience work.

In many cases, UCD professionals know we have done well when the solution we helped to design looks obvious to others. In a sense, we know we have done our best work when it looks like we were never involved at all—when it does not seem like the product should (or could) have been designed any other way. It is difficult to imagine, let alone measure, the problems that *might* have arisen had the design been done differently. In addition, because successful user experiences support user goals, exploit and are constrained by technology, and promote business goals, it is difficult to isolate the ROI of any one factor that influenced the final design.

Bias and Mayhew (see "Summary: A Place at the Table," in Bias and Mayhew [1994]) differentiate between trying to cost justify *any* usability work versus trying to influence *which* usability work will be the most effective. They claim that in "more enlightened" organizations the question is not whether to do usability work but "how much resource to expend and how to apply that resource (i.e., what sort of usability engineering techniques, employed when and where, will prove most cost-effective?)" [Mayhew and Bias 1994, pp. 321–322]. If you have used personas in conjunction with other UCD techniques (which we hope you have), this perspective is very helpful.

There are many good resources to help you measure the internal benefits of your entire UCD initiative. We have cited several already [e.g., Bias and Mayhew, and Kuniavsky]. For a few additional resources, check out the lists supplied at:

- *www.deyalexander.com/resources/roi.html*
- *www.rashmisinha.com/useroi.html*

Forrester Research has also published a series of reports on design and ROI that you can purchase. See, for example, the following:

- *How to Measure What Matters* [Sousa et al. 2001b]
- Get ROI from Design [Sousa et al. 2001]

As these and other resources point out, measures of product success can come from many sources. Obvious metrics include revenue or sales, abandonment rates, and completion of specific strategically defined user scenarios. However, many of the resources on usability and ROI also recommend measuring increased productivity and other benefits experienced by end users and listing these as proof of the worth of the initiative (for a list of these benefits and references to case studies, see Harrison et al. [1994]). If your organization is already dedicated to creating products that are easy to use, measurable improvements in the user experience stand on their

own as an expression of the value of your efforts. However, these measures of increased ease of use are usually much more powerful if they are related to the fiscal bottom line.

The importance of being able to measure and articulate the ROI for UCD methods will only increase as the field of UCD continues to mature. Measuring ROI is not easy in any discipline, and it is particularly challenging (and context dependent) in fields such as UCD, which produce important results that are inherently difficult to measure and quantify (e.g., communication and process improvements). We hope that the suggestions following will be useful whatever the situation you find yourself in, whether you are using personas to introduce UCD methods into your organization or attempting to change the way your organization approaches UCD.

Story from the field

CONCRETE GOALS ARE CRITICAL TO THE MEASUREMENT OF ROI

—Deborah J. Mayhew, Deborah J. Mayhew & Associates (*http://drdeb.vineyard.net*), Co-editor with Randolph G. Bias of *Cost-Justifying Usability: An Update for the Internet Age*, Morgan Kaufmann Publishers, 2005, and author of *The Usability Engineering Lifecycle*, Morgan Kaufmann Publishers, 1999.

One of the keys to being able to cost justify a usability effort (for the purpose of either winning funds for a proposed usability effort or measuring its actual impact after the fact) is to formulate quantitative usability goals early in the project, driven by user requirements analyses. Documented usability goals serve a number of useful purposes on a development project. As a definition of requirements, they (like personas) help focus and drive the design process. They (also like personas) form the basis for user sampling strategies and task definitions for usability testing. They also provide a metric for measuring the benefit of a usability effort, key to an after-the-fact cost justification or calculation of the ROI of a usability effort.

Clarifying concrete usability goals up front in a project (rather than just trying to find measures of improvement after a product has been implemented) also provides a means of ensuring that there is management buy-in to the criteria that later will be used to measure the contribution of the usability effort. You want to know that the usability goals you are striving to achieve are, in fact, the key ones in management's view before you expend the effort to achieve them.

The connection between personas and usability goals is that different specific goals can be formulated for different personas. For example, an efficiency goal might be "the persona 'Mary' should be able to perform task A in 90 seconds or less after a two-hour training session," and an ease-of-learning goal might be "the persona 'Jake' should be able to perform task B for the first time without training and without customer support within 150 seconds with a maximum of two errors." Such goals should be formulated up front based on business goals and usability requirements analyses, and then used to drive and focus design and structure usability testing.

(Story from the field, continued)

These goals can also be used to formulate a before-the-fact cost justification of the usability effort planned to achieve these goals, and ultimately to conduct an after-the-fact measure of the actual payoff of the usability effort. After-the-fact measures of payoff are key to winning support for usability across a development organization on future projects, and quantitative usability goals are key to being able to perform such an analysis of impact. Linking usability goals to personas makes them more concrete and specific and thus easier to measure.

Story from the field

USABILITY CAN AFFECT SALES

—Dennis Wixon, User Research Manager, Microsoft Game Experience Group

Wixon and Jones [1996] provide a well-cited case study from Digital Equipment Corporation about a specific product: the 4GL and database product DEC Rally. The initial version proved powerful but difficult to use. During the development of the second version, a variety of UCD techniques— including ethnographic field research, quantitative tests, prototypes, and heuristic reviews— were employed. As a result, revenues were 30 to 60% above the projected increase for Version 2. In follow-up independent surveys (conducted by a quality group), usability was considered the second most important factor in determining purchase. (The most important factor was improved database support.)

Measuring the ROI of the persona effort

The work you do during this phase to prove the ROI of the persona effort, both quantitatively and qualitatively, will empower you as you continue to introduce customer-centered methods into your organization. Now is your chance to help your organization understand why it was so critically important to understand users and their goals before diving into product design or redesign (and thus why your work as a user experience professional is valuable). In the new edition of *Cost-Justifying Usability* [Bias and Mayhew 2005], contributors Wilson and Rosenbaum [2005] refer to three distinct measures of ROI:

- External ROI: Measurable ways UCD work helped make the company money
- Internal ROI: Measurable process improvements and savings in the organization
- Social ROI: Perception that the UCD team and their methods were helpful during product development, whether or not this helpfulness is measurable.

Handy Detail

THE MANY WAYS TO MEASURE THE BENEFITS OF GOOD UCD WORK

In their chapter "Design of a Human Factors Cost–Justification Tool," Harrison et al. [1994] state that "…the benefits of UCD are a multivariate function of end-user productivity improvements, customer or company benefits, and developer productivity increases." They provide detailed lists of possible improvements and benefits, which include case studies and where possible related numbers and dollar amounts. Despite the fact that their lists were created in 1994 (and therefore some of the examples and numbers are significantly out of date), their article still provides an excellent source of examples of the potential benefits of UCD to your organization, including:

- User data results in a product that better matches user needs
- Decreased development time and costs
- Identifies and refines product ideas
- Simplified/cheaper documentation and help
- Increased product quality
- Increased customer satisfaction
- Easier decision making
- Decreased cost of providing training
- Lower support costs and decreased maintenance
- Increased productivity of developers
- Increased market share
- Increased sales volume and profits
- Decreased test time
- Identifies product problems
- Allows for shared interface code
- Allows for product differentiation.

List adapted from Harrison et al. [1994, pp. 217–223].

We think this is a helpful way of thinking about the ROI of personas, because we believe personas can help you create a product that is likely to:

- Be more successful and require fewer support costs (bottom-line improvements)
- Help you streamline your design and development efforts (process improvements)
- Improve the way your company communicates about and focuses on your users.

You will see that these three topics are major themes in this chapter.

UNDERSTANDING THE ROI OF PERSONAS

—Arnie Lund, Director of User Experience, Mobile PC Division, Microsoft

In that personas can result in improved usability, the ROI of personas can be calculated in the same way the ROI of usability is calculated. For example, the improved ease of use that comes from a coherent user model embedded in the application interface results in reductions in training time and support costs while improving user productivity and success in the market. The use of personas suggests perspectives on ROI in addition to those of the traditional approach to ROI.

For example, personas can be used to increase the usefulness and value of the product. Personas can be thought of as models of the user, and as models they can be applied to the identification of new feature opportunities and can be used to prioritize features. Although the ROI of increased value is not as easy to calculate as improvements in objective performance, it is commonly projected in business cases and assessed through market research. In rarer cases, it may be possible to document before-and-after performance, sales, and other measures that can be directly attributed to insights that came from the use of personas.

The work you did during the family planning phase will help you measure ROI

During the *family planning* phase of the persona lifecycle (see Chapter 3) we recommended that you do some "organizational introspection" to understand current product- and process-related problems you might be able to solve with your persona effort. In addition to identifying ways in which your products could be more user centered, we suggested that you ask the following questions:

- How user focused is your company?
- How does your organization think and communicate about users?
- How is user information incorporated into the product design and development process?

In the process of answering these questions, you probably collected information about how your company measures the success of its products, projects, and people. During your ROI examination you can research these questions again, now that the project is finished, to discover changes that occurred as a result of the persona effort.

You can also use aspects of your persona action plan from family planning to identify good questions to ask as you evaluate the ROI of your personas. For example, to create your action plan, you and your core team decided:

- What *resources* do we have for personas and other UCD activities?
- Which *product* problems do we want to solve with personas?
- Which *process* problems do we want to solve with personas?

You also defined the scope and goals for your persona effort by filling in the blanks to phrases such as the following:

- The personas we build will help the organization to _____.
- The personas we build will help the persona core team members by _____.
- The personas we build will be used by _____.
- The personas we build will be used for _____.
- The personas we build cannot possibly solve _____.
- We will know that the persona effort was successful if _____.

As shown in Figure 7.1, the work you did during the *family planning* phase is highly related to what you will do in to assess the *lifetime achievement* of your personas. If you can apply quantitative values to the answers, you can illustrate the ROI of your personas.

It is time to decide whether or not you satisfied the goals you established in your action plan. You will need to go a bit deeper than just stating whether or not you met your goals. If you did satisfy some (or, even better, all!) of the goals in your action plan, you can work to express

Questions you asked during *family planning*	Questions you will ask during *lifetime achievement*
What resources do we have for personas and other ucd activities?	How much did the persona affect actual cost?
What product problems do we want to solve with personas?	Has the product improved? How much, and in what ways?
What process problems do we want to solve with personas?	Has the process improved? In what ways?
How can we ensure that the personas will be accepted and used by our colleagues?	Were personas perceived as helpful? Has the company's focus on users improved? In what ways?

FIGURE 7.1: *The work you did during the family planning phase is highly related to what you will do to assess the lifetime achievement of your personas.*

the benefits of achieving these goals in quantitative and/or qualitative terms. We believe you can express the full range of persona-related ROI by answering the following questions.

- How much did your persona effort cost?
- In what measurable ways did the personas improve your product? (related to Bias and Mayhew's external ROI)
- In what measurable ways did the personas improve your design and development processes? (related to Bias and Mayhew's internal ROI)
- Is your company more user centered with personas than it was before? (related to Bias and Mayhew's social ROI)

Consider these four questions while looking back at the resources and goals your team identified for your persona effort during *family planning*. The next four sections cover these questions in depth. Our goal is to give you many ideas for determining your own plan for measuring the ROI of your persona projects. It is probably not possible to implement all of the suggestions we make, but it is possible and highly recommended to answer the four questions. We recommend that you and your core team review our suggestions related to each ROI question and together select a few of the suggestions we offer. If your efforts toward answering the ROI questions are unsuccessful, return to this chapter and try some of the other ideas until you find the measures that will work in your organization.

ROI question 1: How much did your persona effort cost?

However you describe the benefits of the persona effort, you will have to evaluate those benefits against the cost of using personas. In their chapter "A Basic Framework for Cost-justifying Usability Engineering," Mayhew and Mantei [1994] present guidelines for calculating the costs of various usability techniques. Their examples are a good place to start. They offer examples of how to break down the equipment- and labor-related costs associated with various usability methods. Most notably, they provide cost information for the related technique of user profiling. More recently, Hackos and Redish [1998, pp. 124–126] provide a detailed cost analysis for user and task analysis. Specifically, they include information on user profiling, a technique related to the use of personas. Although user profiling is a bit different from the method of personas, the Hackos and Redish measures associated with user profiling provide good general estimates of persona costs.

How much time did your personas take?

In most cases, the most expensive aspect of personas is the time it takes to create them, particularly if you executed some original research to inform your personas. A cornerstone of the theory behind personas is the hypothesis that a significant amount of user-focused work performed at the beginning of a project (to create personas) can make the remainder of the project more efficient. Measuring ROI is a way of proving or disproving this hypothesis for your own project. To create useful, effective, data-driven personas, at least two people

(and often many more) must dedicate a significant amount of time to the *family planning* and *conception and gestation* lifecycle phases. Although it does take time and effort to maintain the personas after *birth*, the lion's share of the effort should happen early in the product development cycle. If other teams feel they have to wait to get started until the personas are done, this can be seen as very expensive time indeed. There are several useful time measurements to have on hand. For the project you just finished, measure (or estimate):

- Total people-hours you and your core team dedicated to the persona effort at each phase in the lifecycle
- Calendar time dedicated to each lifecycle phase
- Time dedicated to design activities or any non-coding/building activities
- Calendar time from vision statement to the creation of a solid, actionable plan for the product (i.e., "a solid spec")
- Calendar time for the entire product development cycle from vision statement to release.

Compare these numbers to those for a previous project (one that did not use personas):

- Calendar time from vision statement to the creation of a solid, actionable plan for the product (i.e., "a solid spec")
- Calendar time for the entire product development cycle from vision statement to release
- Time dedicated to design activities or any non-coding/building activities.

It is up to you whether you map the hours spent to actual dollar amounts (easy to do if you have used consultants to help on the effort, but more complicated if the effort was in-house).

Story from the field

MAKE IT A HABIT TO TRACK YOUR TIME

—Deborah J. Mayhew, Deborah J. Mayhew & Associates (*http://drdeb.vineyard.net*), Co-editor with Randolph G. Bias of *Cost-Justifying Usability: An Update for the Internet Age*, Morgan Kaufmann Publishers, 2005, and author of *The Usability Engineering Lifecycle*, Morgan Kaufmann Publishers, 1999

Having been an external consultant for almost 20 years, I have learned to always accurately track my time on every task I do on a project. For example, if I am conducting a usability test I keep track of how much time I spend doing background research on users for sampling purposes, doing background research on tasks, developing testing materials, actually testing, analyzing data, and documenting conclusions. I need to track my time at least overall for a project for billing purposes, but the real payoff for tracking time in such detail has been that I have become very skilled at estimating the level of effort that will be required on virtually any type of project.

(Story from the field, continued)

I have typically found it very difficult, on the other hand, to get the internal usability professionals I sometimes work with to track their time so that the overall usability effort on a project I do with them can be measured. In most cases, internal management does not seem to require it, so my colleagues are not in the habit of doing it (and even though I ask them to up front, they rarely do). I highly recommend that all internal usability professionals make a habit of tracking their time in a fairly detailed way, not just by project but by subtask within a project.

The only way to calculate the cost of a usability effort is to know how much time was spent on it. And the only way to ever cost justify a usability effort is to know how much it cost. Cost justification is an invaluable tool that can help usability professionals—internal as well as external—sell their services, document their contributions to projects, and accurately estimate the time and resources needed on future projects. It is a tool every usability professional should be fluent in, whether management requires it or not. Tracking your time is the most basic first step to being able to cost justify your work and your job. Sooner or later you will want, or need, to do this.

How much did your personas cost in other ways?

In addition to time, other costs of your persona effort can include:

- Research-related costs, including the time and money required to do firsthand research and the costs of purchasing research materials from third parties.
- Costs for persona artifacts, including labor costs (if you employed a graphics designer) and costs for producing the finished artifacts.
- Opportunity costs, which can include lists of deliverables that you and your team were *not* able to provide to the product team due to your investment in the persona effort. For example, were there deliverables that were helpful in prior projects that you did *not* deliver due to your focus on the persona effort?
- The time it takes to collect and evaluate the ROI data.

You will also have to ask yourself (and other product stakeholders) more difficult questions, such as:

- Did the persona effort delay the start of product development?
- Were personas in any way a bottleneck for the rest of the organization?
- If so, was it worth it?

Once you have found a way of expressing the costs of your persona effort, turn your attention to assessing the benefits. The next three questions will help you ferret out both the obvious (i.e., obviously related to money) and not-so-obvious ways personas benefit your products, teams, and company.

Meanwhile, at G4K...

THE G4K CORE TEAM MEASURES THE ROI OF THEIR PERSONA EFFORT

During the family planning phase, the G4K core team created an action plan, which included the resources and amount of time they estimated for the persona effort and the process and product issues they hoped the personas would address (see Figure 7.2). To measure the ROI of the G4K persona effort, the G4K core team can return to each of these estimates and plans to evaluate the success of their personas. Figure 7.2 represents an excerpt from their action plan (for a full description of the G4K action plan, see Chapter 3).

Phase	Activity	Date	Related project milestones
Family Planning	• Organizational introspection • Data collection	Complete: 2 weeks from start of persona effort	Vision complete (business plan, corporate strategy)
Conception & Gestation	• Data organized • Persona creation complete, • Evaluation and prioritization by stakeholders complete, • Validation complete. • Persona team begins evangelizing persona effort around organization	1 month from start of persona effort	Requirements complete (system architecture, functional requirements)
Birth & Maturation	• Persona effort introduced to team • Initial posters and communication artifacts delivered to team. • Personas used in storyboards, scenarios, design walkthroughs, etc.	2 months from start of persona effort	Feature specification complete (Design complete) GOAL: Personas used in feature prioritization decisions
Adulthood	• User testing with personas as recruiting profile. • Personas used in Q/A test case selection. • Persona knowledge enrichment artifacts delivered.	3 months from start of persona effort	Beta 1 Complete (core features intact, but not polished)

FIGURE 7.2: *Excerpt of the G4K persona effort action plan. During the family planning phase the G4K team created this action plan, which includes elements they can use to measure the ROI of their effort at the end of the project.*

(Meanwhile, at G4K..., continued)

The G4K team can compare the time estimates they included in the action plan to the actual time it took to create and support the personas.

- Were their estimates regarding core team members' required time commitments accurate?
- Were their estimates of calendar time required for each life cycle phase accurate? They could add another column to this table to show the actual time it took to complete each task. If they missed their planned dates, what were the costs of missing the deadlines they originally set? Were some of the related project milestones completed before the personas were available to influence the decisions they contained?

These measures are important. If the persona effort was perceived as unsuccessful and you hope to use personas in another project, evaluate whether the problems were related to timing problems rather than weaknesses of the persona approach as a whole.

ROI question 2: In what measurable ways did personas improve your product?

The most powerful way of expressing the ROI of your persona effort is to associate quantitative, preferably monetary, values to features or functionality whose designs are traceable back to your personas (use of them and the data they represent). If your product improved due to your use of personas, you should be able to find ways of measuring and expressing the resulting benefits.

> *The least concrete (yet most important) link—the relationship between usability, customer satisfaction, and sales volume—is particularly elusive. It is, however, still possible to apply a cost/benefit analysis to any given project using only those variables that are identifiable and measurable.*
>
> —Mary Harrison et al. "Design of a Human Factors Cost–Justification Tool" [1994]

In this section, we provide several ideas that should help you find the specific ways your personas improved the final design of your product so that you can relate overall product success to the success of the persona effort.

Story from the field

CUSTOMER CENTRICITY—BEST BUY REVAMPS BASED ON
CUSTOMER PROFILES AND REAPS REWARDS

—Joshua Freed, Associated Press (excerpted from the *Chicago Sun Times*)

Best Buy is making a preemptive strike. It is giving itself a makeover before any problems have a chance to develop. The nation's largest electronics retailer is changing its marketing strategy and spending $50 million to redo its stores, trying to ensure that it will continue to hold off its competitors—not longtime rivals like Circuit City but a raft of newer players in the electronics market such as Wal-Mart, Dell, and eBay.

"The competitors are a diverse lot today, and for them to continue to grow they are going to have to get much better at everything they do, and define themselves in clear ways,'" said George Whalin of Retail Management Consultants. "'And I'm sure that is what this is all about."

Best Buy's plan is to revamp its stores according to the types of customers they serve, a strategy it calls customer centricity. The company came up with five prototypical customers, all of whom have been given names: "Jill," a busy suburban mom; "Buzz," a focused, active younger male; "Ray," a family man who likes his technology practical; "BB4B" (short for Best Buy for Business), a small employer; and "Barry," an affluent professional male who's likely to drop tens of thousands of dollars on a home theater system.

Over the next few years, each of Best Buy's 608 stores will focus on one or two of the five segments, with 110 stores scheduled to make the switch by February. Best Buy began testing the new strategy about a year and a half ago, eventually trying it at 32 stores.

Best Buy showed off one of the new stores in the Los Angeles suburb of Westminster earlier this month. While much of the store looked like any other Best Buy, its home theater and computer sections were tailored toward the two types of customers this store focuses on—"Barry" and "BB4B."

The store converted its old speaker display room to several model living rooms. In one, a laptop computer balanced on the arm of an overstuffed leather couch, which faced a plasma screen TV and a surround-sound system. Home theater manager Ryan Markell told of one "Barry" customer who walked in and said, "I'll take it." The man paid around $28,000 for all the equipment in the room, plus $2,000 for at-home installation, Markell said.

Best Buy stores that focus on the "Jill" segment have play areas for kids. Instead of a booming bass beat, the soundtrack at "Jill" stores is instrumental, or children's music…. "There is nobody in the category that is doing this," said Steven Roorda, an analyst with American Express.

Define product success

It is one thing to measure product sales and success; it is another to link these improvements to the use of personas during the design and development process. The challenge for you and your core team is to express the successful aspects of the product and the relationship between the use of personas and these successes. Consider the following excerpt from Hackos and Redish:

> Without a detailed understanding of user characteristics, tasks, and environments, your organization is likely to experience much greater costs in the future. Increases in customer support costs, more costly documentation and training, and last-minute changes to poorly designed interface may all result if you do not have the information you need to design effectively from the beginning [1998, p. 122].

Those of us in the UCD field read this statement by Hackos and Redish and cannot imagine how anyone could disagree, but many others in our organization need cold, hard proof. Do your best to identify specific ways in which the personas directly influenced the design and development of your product. For example:

- List the product improvements you hoped to obtain from the personas.
- Reconstruct the ways important product-related decisions were made with the help of the personas (during adulthood).
- State the value of the personas in terms of the impact they had on the final design of the product.

During the *family planning* phase, you and your core team identified product-related issues you hoped to address with personas. It is helpful to return to your family planning notes and recall how you identified the product problem and the goals of the persona effort. For example:

- Were sales below expectations?
- Were patch releases required to solve problems with your previous product that only surfaced after the initial release?
- Did the customer service group identify important support issues with a previous product that management felt should have been caught during product development?
- Were you trying to create a completely new product and were worried that existing assumptions and processes would stand in your way?

You can look at the same measurements now that your product has been released to see if the product has improved and/or the goals have been met.

Story from the field

MARIE AND SOPHIE HAD A MAJOR IMPACT AT ZYLOM.COM

—**Erik Goossens** and **J. Vanzandbeek,** Zylom.com

[In Chapter 6, you read how Zylom.com used personas as recruiting profiles for user testing (see "Story from the field: Persona Fridays"). Now you will read more about the impact their personas had.]

As you know from our other sidebars, we used two primary personas at Zylom.com, Marie and Sophie, to drive a very fast redesign and redeployment of our site. We used our personas to drive a user-centered redesign of our site. And we did further user research by bringing in actual "Maries" and "Sophies" to watch them interact with our new designs as we developed them. Through watching our Maries and Sophies, we came to further understand the goals our potential customers have when they visit our site. They visit our site to *play* games, not necessarily to *purchase* them. We knew this, of course, before we built our personas, but it was only through our persona work that we came to fully understand the design implications for our site. The personas helped us understand that encouraging our customers to purchase games as soon as they hit the site wasn't working well. We began to think that if we stopped pushing our customers to purchase before they were ready, more of them would eventually make a purchase.

Figure 7.3 shows what our site looked like before we created and used our personas, Marie and Sophie. Our design helped our visitors understand that we had many games, but it did not help them understand why they should make the decision to try and then purchase our games. Each game link took the visitor to a game page that was focused on encouraging the visitor to first download and later purchase the game.

As shown in Figure 7.4, we redesigned our site to appeal to Marie and Sophie and their goals. Marie and Sophie "told" us that our site should cater to the their most important goals: play a game online, get a version of the game I can play without being online, and get help if I need it. We redesigned our site around these three goals and the impact of these changes was swift and overwhelmingly positive.

Once their goals were satisfied, they apparently were more interested in downloading and purchasing games—so our goals were satisfied too! Without getting into details of the financial impact of our persona work, we can say that our old home page did not generate substantial traffic or sales. Today, our redesigned site generates a quite substantial part of our total number of unique visitors and is the most visited casual game site in most of the countries in which it is available. Our new purchase/registration system, which came largely from the Marie and Sophie Fridays, also had a tremendous effect on our bottom line because it positively influenced the ratio from trials to purchases. To this day, we make small and large improvements to our services and designs based on our key users, Marie and Sophie.

(Story from the field, continued)

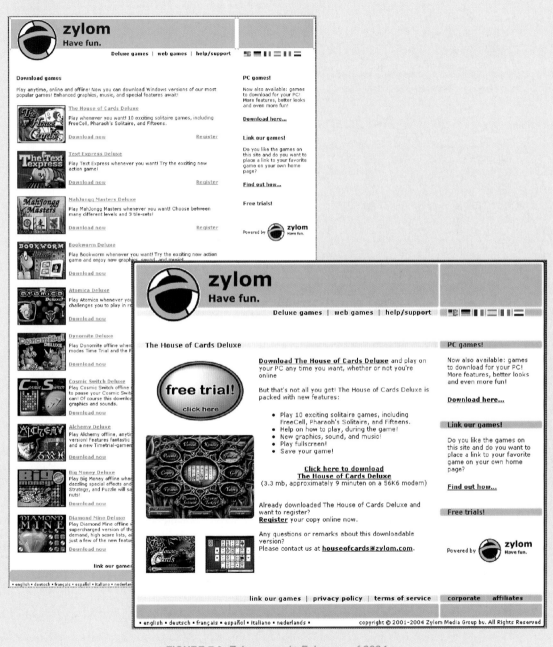

FIGURE 7.3: *Zylom.com in February of 2004.*

(Story from the field, continued)

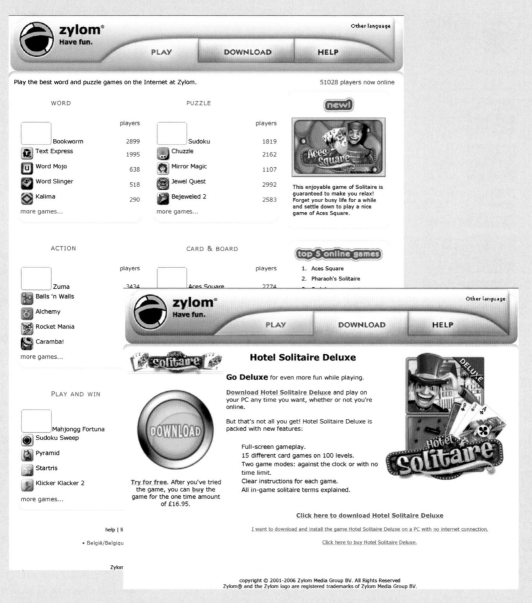

FIGURE 7.4: *Zylom.com in February of 2005, after it was redesigned for personas Marie and Sophie.*

Trace successful aspects of your product to the use of personas

In their Forrester Research report "Get ROI from Design," Souza et al. [2001] provide a simple step-by-step model for measuring and expressing ROI of design. We believe a slight variation of the model (to explicitly include personas) also works well for user experience work. Souza et al. present their model as three steps:

1. Understand the business goals.

2. Map the business goals to user (or, in this case, persona) goals.

3. Create measurable metrics to track improvements related to fulfillment and support of users achieving their goals.

If you used the persona-weighted feature matrix (see Chapter 6), you evaluated proposed product features with respect to the personas. This can be a great place to start. Look back at how various features moved up or down in priority as a result of the feature matrix and include this information with the other "design decisions made to support the personas' goals." You can look at the goal statements you included in each persona description and map them to design decisions (and in many cases to measurable improvements). You can create this type of mapping in many different ways. Figure 7.5 shows a basic table you can use to express how your persona-driven design decisions impacted the success of your product.

Business Goal	Related persona goal(s)	Design decisions made to support persona goal(s)	Measures of the design's success
Increase purchases by 25%	Buy products only after I comparison shop and ensure I get the best price	Display competition's prices along with our own	So far, 1st visit purchases have increased by X% for those products with new display!
Increase purchases by 25%	Know as much about the product as possible	• Multiple images of every product • 3-D product explorer • High-resolution fabric swatches • $10 gift certificate promotion to encourage purchasers to review products once they arrive	• Products listed with new viewing tools show X% higher conversion rate than those without • Traffic to new product viewing options increasing by X% every month • promotion success: 2,574 product owners have added reviews as result of promotion; products with reviews show X% increased conversion

FIGURE 7.5: *Identify links among business goals, persona goals, and design decisions. If you can articulate business goals, related persona goals, and design decisions made to support the persona goals, you may also be able to measure the success of each design change. It can be difficult to get the data you will need to complete the last column of this table, but this expression of the ROI of your work can be very powerful and worth the effort.*

If you want to extend your analysis, try Donoghue's "experience matrix."

In her book *Built for Use*, Karen Donoghue describes an "experience matrix" teams can use to "map business goals...through to product features and the corresponding experience requirements" [Dongohue 2002]. In creating and using your personas, you have already done a lot of this work. If your experience was similar to many practitioners we have talked to, your persona effort became a forcing factor that helped the executive staff clarify the business goals of the project with respect to consumers of the product. By creating skeleton personas and asking the executive staff to help you focus on the "right ones," you took the first steps in mapping the business goals to personas. Creating rich, fully developed personas meant adding not only demographic and personal details but detailed information about goals and needs.

Donoghue suggests that teams define an experience matrix during the product design cycle. Because the experience matrix includes metrics, testing plans, and acceptance criteria, it can also be extremely helpful as a tool to plan for and track the product ROI related to the use of personas. Although Donoghue does not specifically discuss personas and their place in the experience matrix, it is easy to see where persona work impacts the elements of her matrix (see Figure 7.6 and "Story from the field: Measure Success in Terms of User Needs and Business Goals" following).

Story from the field

MEASURE SUCCESS IN TERMS OF USER NEEDS AND BUSINESS GOALS

—Karen Donoghue, Author of *Built for Use*

In my book *Built for Use: Driving Profitability Through the User Experience* (McGraw-Hill, 2002), I argue that excellent user experiences are those that effectively satisfy both user needs and business goals.

Successful online user experiences balance the user's purposes in visiting a site with the goals of the business that offers the site. This balance is a delicate one. Customers do not appreciate an online experience focused solely on aggressive sales tactics—such as unwanted pop-ups and harassing e-mails that just won't stop—in the absence of any immediate value. On the other side of the scale, a user experience that is delivering value to the end user in the absence of any viable business model creates no revenue. Consider early Napster as an example of the latter.

To measure the success of the user experience, I believe you need to regularly measure both the quantitative and qualitative metrics that apply to the goals of both the end user and the business. Examples of quantitative metrics that track both use and business success include number of

(Story from the field, continued)

successful transactions relative to attempted ones, number of new features successfully "picked up" and adopted into a user's task flow, and number of transactions that produce voice calls to customer support. These metrics can be reported over time to track trending and to adjust aspects of the user-experience that can enhance these metrics. Examples of qualitative metrics include how much a user likes or dislikes the experience (relative to their expectations about the experience) and how a user feels about the experience relative to competitive experiences.

If your personas have been developed appropriately, there should be no gap in targeting those tasks and transactions that are specific to each user segment. Earlier stages in the design planning process—such as building an information architecture—should be able to correlate to the personas. Early user testing with paper or rough prototypes should show no "showstopper" surprises—because the tasks and transactions appropriate for the segment (as represented in the personas) have directly impacted the major architectural decisions in the design.

Later usability testing should show performance metrics indicating that users are able to find, initiate, and complete the transactions that are driving the underlying business model. If testing at this stage shows that the critical tasks are not successfully being accessed and completed, you may want to consider revisiting the personas and verifying them against the user needs and business goals for each segment the business is targeting. Doing so at this stage reduces the risk of delivering a design that misses the mark in that critical equilibrium of value delivery involving the business and the end user.

Story from the field

DIRECT FINANCIAL BENEFITS OF PERSONAS CAN SHOW UP IN UNEXPECTED PLACES

—Colin Hynes, Director of Usability, Staples.com

[The following is a continuation of the "Story from the field: Putting Real Values on Your Personas" in Chapter 4.]

In addition to the power personas brought to the design and testing process at Staples.com, they had an unexpected financial benefit. The persona survey incentives were dollars-off coupons, and the redemptions drove sales and directly added to the company's bottom line. And although most of the costs of creating personas were internal and somewhat difficult to quantify, the margin from the coupon sales alone easily covered the cost of the research.

BUSINESS DRIVER AND SUCCESS MATRIX	TASKS	PRODUCT FEATURES THAT SUPPORT BUSINESS	EXPERIENCE REQUIREMENT	BEST PRACTICES	USER INTERFACE	METRICS	TESTING PLAN AND ACCEPTANCE CRITERIA
• Increase trading activity among high-value customer segment Metric: • Increase in trading for segment	• Create Portfolio • Create new • Search for a security • Add the security • Repeat step 2	• Portfolio • Search • Add	• Rapid ability to add a security • Easy fast, and applicable search • Ease in looking up forgotten ticker symbols	• Yahoo! Finance • Midnight Trader	• Trade button prominent and pervasive in user experience • Simple, clean design that is fast-loading	• Two clicks to add security • Successful completion at first-use case • Feature used at each user session • Leads to a trade on the security • Number of securities added per session is increasing	• Quality Assurance [QA] will test each feature, and usability team will validate • Will also check usage logs every three days for behavior patterns
Increase loyalty	Personalize portal	• Customization wizard • Clear benefits statement on screen to drive push to personalize	• Ease in initiating and learning • Fast to complete, no lengthy initialization	• My Yahoo!	• Addition of a "Personalization" tab to navigation scheme	• One click to initiate personalization	• QA will test each feature, and usability team will validate interfaces • Will also check usage logs every week to calculate number of users who have customized

Callouts:
- Tasks: The goals you identified for each persona shaped the definition of individual tasks.
- Your experience requirements and UI designs were influenced by personas.
- Features: Your "Persona Weighted Feature Matrix" helped you choose and prioritize these features.
- Metrics and Testing: Measured successes can be mapped back to the influence of your personas.

FIGURE 7.6: Donoghue's experience matrix can be used to map business goals and user needs to design features and measurable metrics. Donoghue does not explicitly refer to personas in this matrix. We have highlighted the matrix elements that relate to the creation of, information in, and use of personas. (Adapted from Donoghue [2002, p. 139]).

G4K Meanwhile, at G4K...

G4K MEASURES PERSONA-RELATED PRODUCT IMPROVEMENTS

The improvements the G4K core team hoped for were stated as problems they predicted and wanted to avoid through their use of personas. These problems were reflected in several aspects of their action plan, including the G4K persona elevator pitch:

G4K Persona Effort: Elevator Pitch

G4K creates great games because we know what kids and their parents want from games. The G4K portal can only be great if we know what kids and their parents want from the Internet. We are creating specific descriptions of kids and parents—in personas—to capture everything we know and need to learn to create the G4K kids' portal. Our personas are going to allow all of our data, in the shape of real kids and real parents, to sit in on every meeting, in every office, and influence every decision we make about the portal. The following are product problems we want to solve with personas:

- Other companies have Internet portals for kids. We are behind. How can we create a product that is world class and worthy of the G4K brand in such a short time?
- How can we recreate some of the key experiences built into our G4K games into an Internet experience? The technologies are very different.

In other words, the G4K team were afraid that their unfamiliarity with the Internet would result in a product design that was difficult to build and unappealing to their intended audience. They had a small team, a short deadline, and a development staff that felt as if they already knew everything they needed to know about the intended users of the new product (i.e., the kids who play G4K games). The persona core team knew that if they relied on existing assumptions about users and traditional development processes the new G4K Internet portal might fail. They hoped that personas would allow the team to focus on the information appropriate to the portal project, whether that be information leveraged from existing knowledge or new domain specific information. The G4K team decided to look for ways to assess the impact of the personas on the product by restating the problems they wanted to solve such that the answers were in some way measurable.

From the Elevator Pitch

"The G4K portal can only be great if we know what kids and their parents want from the Internet." To construct an answer:

- How much new information did we find out about what kids and their parents want from the Internet (versus from shrink-wrapped games)?
- Can we trace how much of this information affected the design of the portal, and in what ways?
- Which are the most popular and least popular elements of the portal? Are the popular elements those for which design decisions are traceable to the data we collected?

From the Statement of Product Problems to Solve with Personas

"Other companies have Internet portals for kids. We are behind. How can we create a product that is world class and worthy of the G4K brand in such a short time?"

To construct an answer:

- Can we get measures of what parents and kids think of the G4K portal versus other portals already out there?
- How, specifically, does our portal take advantage of lessons we learned from analyzing our competitors' portals from the point of view of our personas?
- In what ways is our portal different from our competitors' portals? Can we trace the decisions to create these differences back to the data reflected in our personas?
- Do industry influencers and/or internal stakeholders think that our new portal is inferior, as good as, or superior to our competitors' sites?
- Did we meet our schedule for building and deploying our portal? Were there decisions we made as we triaged the development work that we can trace to the use of personas?
- Is the portal satisfying the business objectives that fueled the project and were reflected in the personas?

"How can we recreate some of the key experiences built into our G4K games into an Internet experience? The technologies are very different."

To construct an answer:

- What are the key experiences built into our games that we wanted to reflect in the portal?
- Did the personas help us create Internet versions of these key experiences (that are still familiar even though they are implemented differently)?

Measure the success of the end-to-end user experience

If personas really did help your entire team focus on user experience, you might find that you have to create some new (new, at least, to your team or company) definitions of product success. For example, it may no longer be helpful to evaluate the success of your Web site or features on your Web site in terms of page views, click-throughs, or conversion rates. These measures do not create a helpful picture of the overall user experience and the success of various elements of the user experience as they navigate the Web site. People come to Web sites (and products) with their own goals in mind, and you need to find ways to evaluate your site or product's success in satisfying both user and business goals.

In our example of a Web site, the fact that users click on a particular link does not necessarily mean that the link is good or effective. It is possible that many people find and click on that link, but for reasons very different from those you designed the link to address. The impact of this mismatch (in the way the link was designed versus the expectations of the user) may not show until several links or pages later in the user's experience. Users may struggle through several other pages and links before their frustration level forces them to abandon the site. If you and your team assume that the problem is on the page with the most abandonments, you may be missing critical information that could lead to a much better user experience.

If you used personas, the end-to-end user experience your product supports should be more successful in satisfying both user and business goals. To evaluate the success of the personas, you must find effective ways of evaluating the end-to-end user experience. For excellent ideas on how to do this, see the following Story from the field. See also "Story from the field: Measuring the ROI of Persona-based Copy and Navigation" in material following.

Story from the field

MEASURE SUCCESS RELATED TO CUSTOMER EXPERIENCE, NOT CLICK-THROUGHS AND PAGE VIEWS

—Jim Sterne, Target Marketing of Santa Barbara (author of *Web Metrics: Proven Methods for Measuring Web Site Success*)

One of my clients redesigned its entire Web site. They tested all changes well before implementation. They put the site through a massive traditional usability review. They addressed 90% of the issues identified in a comprehensive user satisfaction survey. Unfortunately, their conversion rate remained the same, satisfaction scores were unchanged, and there was no increase in revenue. They went back to the drawing board and identified specific goals for specific personas in specific situations. One of the modifications they made as a result was to modify eight characters in their product descriptions:

Original product descriptions:
Property 1 — Room Rates from $150
Property 2 — Room Rates from $225

Modified product descriptions:
Property 1 — Room Rates from $150 *to $350*
Property 2 — Room Rates from $225 *to $400*

This channeled to an increase in annual revenue of $20 million. How did they choose the information to change? They did this by evaluating the experience they built versus the experience (and language) that would resonate for the personas.

Rather than simply measuring click-throughs and page views, they determined the tasks each persona might perform and measured their success at completing each task. Actions such as

(Story from the field, continued)

discovering, learning, desiring, and acquiring can be divided into discrete customer experience processes. For example:

Persona: Mary Keating, VP Marketing
Task: Subscribe to Newsletter
Source: Banner ad on Yahoo
Process:
1. Click-through
2. Landing page
3. Subscription form page
4. Submit button

Some banner ads may get Mary to click through more, but others will get her to subscribe more often. If Mary repeatedly clicks through but does not make it past the subscription form page, that is where resources should be focused in order to increase subscriptions. A given process may be made up of many milestones, depending on the task at hand:

Persona: Tray Shaw, Trade Show Manager
Task: Purchase software
Source: Click from newsletter
Process:
1. Click-through
2. Landing page
3. Detail page 1
4. Detail page 2
5. Download trial package
6. Click-through to purchase pages
7. Detail page A
8. Detail page B
9. Purchase form 1: Product selection
10. Purchase form 2: Identification
11. Purchase form 3: Payment
12. Submit

If Tray typically clicks through .5% of the time, what can you do to the newsletter to up the ante and foster more interest? Try throwing in something that will help Tray decide, such as a one-liner about free tech support for 90 days. We did, and the click-through rate jumped to 2%. If you note that Tray seems to lose interest in the process on detail page 2 and downloads only 5% of the time, add a graphic that says "Money-Back Guarantee." We did something similar and saw a 12% lift in downloads. Measure the move from one milestone to the next, change something, and then measure it again. You are now on the path to continuous improvement.

Web analytics can produce voluminous reports showing click-throughs, page views, and revenues, but if you do not target specific personas who have specific needs and desires you may not be able to determine whether your Web site visitors are achieving their goals, or whether you are achieving yours. Measuring how well and how quickly different personas complete particular processes is a much more revealing gauge of a successful Web site redesign.

Story from the field

MEASURING THE ROI OF PERSONA-BASED COPY AND NAVIGATION

—Bryan Eisenberg, Future Now, Inc.

The valuable information in personas can guide the critical answers to the questions that should frame the development of your Web site.

- Who are you trying to persuade?
- What information do they need to see in order to be persuaded?
- What language most effectively engages them and motivates them further into the process?

Personas in Action: The Leo Schachter Case Study

Leo Schachter patented cut diamonds are famous for their unique brilliance. The company sells through thousands of retailers around the world, including shops on Rodeo Drive and at your local upscale retailer. Leo Schachter does not sell directly to consumers. The company's Web site had two key goals: to support brand sales by educating visitors about why a Leo Schachter diamond is different and to drive those visitors to retail locations.

When the executive VP of marketing, John Marchese, reviewed the site data last fall, the news wasn't good. Only .86% (less than 1 percent) of site visitors clicked on the link to fill out a form for finding a retailer.

No matter how impressive the site, if Leo Schachter could not persuade their online visitors to visit a local store they had not accomplished their business objective. Marchese needed to revamp the site to increase that conversion rate without sacrificing the educational impact critical to brand sales once consumers got to stores. Because you can't change how people use your site without under-standing their motivations and perspective, Leo Schachter turned to persona-based design, focus-ing less on the glory of their diamonds and more on the needs of their customers.

The Leo Schachter Personas

We developed five distinct personas for the Leo Schachter Web site, including the following.

- *David Common Sense:* He needs to learn everything about a diamond before he makes a purchase. He is methodical and logical in all decisions.
- *Natalie Gold Digger:* She's terribly fashionable, goes to the finest restaurants, and expects the best things in life. She wants to know how to keep up with the Joneses.
- *Kimberly Romance:* She's a hopeless romantic dreaming about her future engagement ring.

Creating Meaningful Navigation

With these personas in hand, we turned to mapping out every action the characters were likely to take as they progressed through their individual purchasing processes. Wireframing the structure of a Web site's interactions produces a hypertext outline that delineates proposed navigation paths, complete with feedback loops and points of intersection. Instead of assuming the needs of a generic visitor, this strategy matches a meaningful site path to each persona profile. For example:

(Story from the field, continued)

- Diamond-newbie David's wireframe path showed his first stop on a page called "How do I choose a diamond?" He was next likely to go to "What is a Leo Diamond?" and then on to "Where do I go for the fabulous diamond she deserves?"
- Fashion-conscious Natalie, on the other hand, was more likely to go to "What is a Leo Diamond?" first. From there, she would click on "Which is the most perfect diamond he could give me?" and then to "What is new, fashionable, and fabulous in diamond engagement rings?"

Every wireframed Web page addresses the following five elements:
- Which personas are likely to arrive at that page
- List of keywords and trigger words different personas use to get there
- Unspoken question the persona landing on that page needs to have answered
- Strategy the page will take to answer that question
- List of the actions each persona might take next.

Creating Engaging and Motivating Copy

Now the copywriters turned from writing the Web site's personality profiles to writing Web copy geared toward those same personas in real life. Having a clear image of any one person, imagining that person on the other end of your communication, it becomes enormously easier to "speak" directly to that person.

Some pages were written for the single persona who would be most likely to visit them. For example, when the David persona visits the Leo Diamond site he is likely to come to a page called "Diamonds and the Four Cs," which tells visitors about the carat, cut, color, and clarity of a diamond in a straightforward and methodical manner (like David himself).

David's copy reads, "Taking a few minutes now to learn about them will make your purchasing experience smarter, easier, and more enjoyable. The four Cs give you the information you need to compare the characteristics of diamonds." This is copy that will put many other people to sleep, but it is what David really wants to know before he feels comfortable making a decision.

Copy on other pages had to appeal to several personas who would be likely to visit them. For example, copy on the "Brilliance: A Diamond's Beauty" page was written for three personas: Natalie, Kimberly, and David. Because the copy could not target all of them at once and still be effective, the first couple of paragraphs were geared toward fashionable Natalie and romantic Kimberly.

Brilliant diamonds explode with light, catching people's eye inadvertently, sparkling in candle-light, adding elegance and glamour to a woman's whole being.

We assumed that methodical David would make the effort to find the information he needed, and that he would be satisfied to get the information he wanted from a (very scientific-looking) graphic.

It wasn't until the third paragraph on the page that the copy returned to the language he would appreciate.

> Diamond brilliance is defined as the reflection of a bright white light from the facets of the diamond and is determined by the artistry of the cutting and polishing.

Preliminary Results

With everything in place, the first version of the redesigned site was ready to launch. Using Web analytics—testing, measuring, and optimizing—is integral to maintaining the vitality of your online efforts. They help you refine your persona and optimize your copy and the individual navigation paths ("scenarios") for continued improvement. A Web site is never really "done."

Once the Leo Schachter site was launched, we tracked click-throughs by click path groupings and by projected persona to see if real people were following the planned scenarios. As one person on the team commented, "We're not playing and making guesses. We're setting up a scientific experiment. It is mind-numbingly tedious at times to go through our process, do not get me wrong. But it is the only way to make sure you have dotted your i's and crossed your t's."

The preliminary results have been astounding. After relaunching last fall, Leo Schachter Diamonds has increased conversions (the number of users who clicked on "Find a Jeweler" and then entered an address to search for a local retailer) from 0.86% to an unheard-of 54.1%.

That is an increase of 5,500% for a site that didn't use cutting-edge design or technology, has no Flash, no video, no taking heads, and no pop-ups. In fact, it is a site that could have been built years ago with nothing more than well-written copy, clear and meaningful navigation links, and a few graphics.

When you consider designing or redesigning a Web site, consider putting the bulk of your budget toward understanding your audience, hiring superior copywriters, and using a great metrics system to measure and optimize your results. Effective e-business is about the effective application of consumer psychology. And hasn't that really, been the backbone of exchange always?

Find out if your product reflects and supports actual user goals

Your persona descriptions should include demographic, psychographic, and goal-related information. Although no one in your actual user base will reflect any persona down to the last detail, many actual users should share important characteristics with your personas. If your company identifies itself as being customer focused, it may be powerful to show that

your persona-driven product satisfies actual user needs better than previous products. After your product has been in use for a while, you can look at the *actual* user base and their behaviors:

- Do your users' goals match the goals described in your persona documents?

- Do the paths and activities you have built into your product support the ways real people *want* to achieve these goals?

- Based on your personas, are real users most interested in and satisfied by the aspects of the product you would have predicted?

- Are the personas "showing up" in your customers' organizations? That is, are the people you built the product for those who are purchasing and using it?

- How are people using the product, and do their processes match the processes you predicted in your early design work?

To answer these questions, you will need to engage in some type of qualitative user research. This can vary from doing focus groups to site visits (and contextual inquiry) to one-on-one interviews. We suggest that you consider creating a set of Reality Maps (see the following Bright Idea). In essence, you are checking to see if your users are walking the paths you paved for them, or if they are finding workarounds and alternatives to achieve goals your product is

Bright Idea

CREATE ANOTHER SET OF REALITY MAPS

Now that your product is out there being used, you can create a new set of Reality Maps, which are flow charts that depict the actual experiences users have as they work to accomplish a goal or set of tasks (for more information on Reality Maps, see Chapter 10).When you created Reality Maps to design your product initially, you went out into the field to find people who were achieving a goal you hoped to satisfy with your product. Now that the product is completed, find people who are using your product and create a new set of Reality Maps reflecting their process *using* your product. Once you have these Maps, you can use them in several ways.

- Compare them to your Design Maps or scenarios that informed the design of the product. If these new Reality Maps are similar to the Design Maps you created in the design phase for the product, you can express this as a success in several ways, showing that
  - The Design Maps were helpful and useful to the development team (perhaps in a way that long, text-based specification documents are not)
  - You were able to successfully predict the processes that would be acceptable for your end users
- Use these new Reality Maps…as Reality Maps! You can use the new set of Reality Maps to inform the design of the next release of your product. If during the course of your Reality Mapping you find that your users are having difficulties with the current version of the product, you can create targeted support materials (or perhaps mini-releases or updates of your product).

Handy Detail

IF YOUR PERSONAS TURNED OUT TO BE HIGHLY REPRESENTATIVE, YOU CAN USE THIS TO YOUR (AND YOUR COMPANY'S) STRATEGIC ADVANTAGE

We argue that personas do not have to be accurate to be helpful in a product design project. However, if you use data to create your personas, it is entirely possible that your personas *are* representative of your most important users in ways that are important to your business. If you find that your personas do turn out to be representative of actual users of your finished product in important ways, you can use this insight to:

- Encourage the executive team to use personas earlier in their product strategy and vision process. If the personas you built for the last project really do embody your actual users, why not use similarly created personas to bring vital information about actual users and customers into the *strategic* decision-making process?
- Pique the interest of other groups in your company by asking if having embodiments of very real aspects of important user groups would be important to them. You will be able to show that the personas deliver on this promise.
- Use this to "prove" that the work you did was relevant and valid. Personas can be thought of as constructs that represent the best guesses of your team—which your colleagues may think are no better or worse than their own best guesses. Use the fact that your personas are indeed representative of real users to show your colleagues that the effort was more than an exercise in guesswork.

not supporting. If your company values the idea of incorporating information about users into the product cycle as early as possible, it is important for you to communicate that your personas *were* valid and representative—that they contained solid data and were effective in predicting various aspects of your user base.

Measure customer satisfaction

Understanding how your users feel about the quality of your product is important. There are a variety of ways to do this, including broad surveys (Web or phone), face-to-face interviews and focus groups. However, asking the question of satisfaction in a meaningful way can be difficult. Consider using one of several standard satisfaction instruments available (some for free, some for a fee). Probably the most broadly used and well-founded satisfaction measure is the Software Usability Measurement Inventory (SUMI). The SUMI "is a rigorously tested and proven method of measuring software quality from the end user's point of view" (from SUMI description, *www.ucc.ie/hfrg/questionnaires/sumi*). The SUMI (see Figure 7.7) consists of 50 statements and typically takes about 3 to 5 minutes for a participant to complete.

Handy Detail

WHAT IF YOU DISCOVER THAT YOUR PERSONAS WERE INACCURATE IN SOME IMPORTANT WAY?

It is possible that your personas turned out to be totally wrong. We have not had that experience yet, but we recognize that it is possible. More likely, you will find that your personas were "off" in some way—that the actual people who end up using your product are different in some significant way from the personas and that this difference affects their experience of the product in some negative way.

For example, assume that you created Gary, a persona for your online bookkeeping application. You collected, analyzed, and filtered the data. You created Gary, and he did his job in the organization. But now you are getting a lot of customer support calls on a set of features in the product you didn't expect to be a problem for Gary. You realize that Gary must have misrepresented the actual user population in some way, and you want to find out how.

Go back to Chapter 3 and collect data once again now that you have actual customers. Revisit all of the questions you tried to answer with your data collection, as well as the assumptions and observations that went into your personas. Create new personas that reflect the new information you have, or simply create a document that specifies the differences between the personas that were used to design the product and the people who are actually using it.

Once you understand these differences, you can act on them to both improve customer experience right now and to minimize customer support costs for the organization. In our example, you might realize that you originally created Gary as a person comfortable using a spreadsheet program such as Excel. This was based on market research suggesting that people wanted more robust features for bookkeeping, and that there were many complaints about basic spreadsheet programs such as Excel when they were used for bookkeeping. You start selling your bookkeeping application, and find out that the people most interested in signing up for it are signing up in part because they *don't like* spreadsheet programs such as Excel and actually do *not* know how to use them very well. You have probably built in some features and functionality that capitalize on the spreadsheet UI standards used in Excel, and now you have a problem because a lot of users are getting in touch with customer support to ask or complain about those very features. What do you do?

Although it is too late to redesign the features of the released product, there is a lot you can do. Of course, you can note this new information for the next version, and you certainly should. But once you identify the root of the problem (wow, it really is true that these folks do not know Excel!) you can create outreach materials to solve the problem right now, for the actual users of your product. Gather customer service representatives in a meeting so that you can capture the core problems being expressed in the customer service contacts. Create online training materials that address the particular set of features causing the problems. Invite users to join an online community or listserv that is moderated by someone trained on your application and on Excel. Create help materials that are linked directly to the problematic features. Send an e-mail to all of your customers announcing that new support materials are available.

The SUMI is referenced in the ISO 9241 standard as a recognized method of testing user satisfaction and is available for a reasonable fee directly from the SUMI Web site (as of December of 2004, prices were listed at under 1,000 Euros). The Web Site Analysis and Measurement Inventory (WAMMI) is another commercially available, similarly priced questionnaire (see *www.wammi.com*).

Item	Item wording
1	This software responds too slowly to inputs.
3	The instructions and prompts are helpful.
13	The way that system information is presented is clear and understandable.
22	I would not like to use this software every day.

FIGURE 7.7: *Example of SUMI questionnaire statements. For each statement, the user is asked to reply that they agree, disagree, or do not know. These examples (and more information about the SUMI method and materials) can be found at www.ucc.ie/hfrg/ questionnaires/sumi/ whatis.html.*

Other well-known (and free) instruments for measuring satisfaction include the After-Scenario Questionnaire, the Post-Study System Usability Questionnaire, and the Computer System Usability Questionnaire (see Lewis [1995]). These are all significantly shorter than the SUMI (3, 19, and 19 statements, respectively) and are available for free. Finally, the System Usability Scale [Brooke 1996] is a 10-statement scale that is quick to use and easy to analyze and understand (it also is free). If you are interested in more information on these and other usability questionnaires, we recommend checking out the article "Questionnaires in Usability Engineering: A List of Frequently Asked Questions," (*www.ucc.ie/hfrg/resources/qfaq1.html*).

All of the scales mentioned here attempt to tap into the perceived quality and satisfaction with the user experience of the product. They have all been rigorously derived and validated, using principles and analyses of psychometrics. When used appropriately to assess a product (e.g., with a decent sample size), they will provide a reliable and meaningful metric of customer satisfaction you can correlate to ROI. We recommend that you consider administering one of the scales on existing products (or your product prior to the current redesign) as well as your latest version so that you can get a sense of progress or regression.

Measure decreased support and maintenance costs

Personas should help maintain your entire team's focus on the end-to-end user experience and therefore enable you to create a product that makes sense to the people who use it. An indirect measure of this effect can be made through evaluating the amount of support and documentation your product requires:

- Does this version of the product require less per-user support than previous versions? (Note that it is worth investigating the changes in support costs even if you hear that the overall support requirements for the new product have increased. If your product is good, it might gain a much larger number of users. Thus, your support effort per customer might be lower. However, the total might be larger because of the much larger market.)

- Do your new users require a different type of support? Do current users have the same types of problems as previous users? Can you qualify (or quantify) the severity of the current customer issues?

- How much time does it take to train the support personnel now versus the previous product release?
- How much documentation was required for your product? Were the documentation specialists able to create effective documentation more efficiently using the personas?
- Were there fewer usability-related bugs in the released version of your product?

For all of these questions, you will need to understand exactly how to measure the answers. For example, defining what counts as less support might be the raw number of support calls or it might be the amount of time and level of escalation required to solve user problems. You will also need to have had measured it for your previous product and over time so that a trend can be observed related to the product just developed. What is more interesting and compelling would be to categorize the types of calls and associate those with your personas. Knowing that support issues for your primary persona were reduced relative to secondary personas would be tremendously valuable.

Story from the field

REGISTRY PERSONAS HELP BOOST SALES AND DECREASE SUPPORT COSTS

—Rhiannon Gallagher, Thomson Micromedex

I came into an online wedding registry company about five years ago, when that industry was just getting started. At the time, all of the sites in the industry were geared toward the couples themselves. They provided a lot of content and supporting tools for the couples, but had not really addressed the needs of the guests that were supposed to be making the actual purchases. We did some research and concluded that, particularly in 1997, this was likely to be the guests' first online purchasing experience. Although the couples themselves were savvy, the guests were insecure and uncomfortable. We created separate points of entries for the personas, and a more novice-oriented workflow for the guests. After putting this in place, purchases increased dramatically, and calls for technical support went down.

ROI question 3: In what measurable ways did personas improve your design and development processes?

Persona efforts do not just change products; they change the way products are designed and developed. Do not underestimate the value of process improvements. If you can help your organization streamline design and development work, and show clearly that you have done so, you will be in a better position to prove the value of the persona effort to your company's bottom line. In fact, Wilson and Rosenbaum "contend that UCD practitioners must be perceived as contributing to internal ROI before they can contribute to measurable, external ROI" [Wilson and Rosenbaum 2005]. Measuring the effect you had on the design and development process will also allow you to express the value of the persona effort in terms of internal cost savings.

Again, the work you did during the *family planning* phase will be invaluable as you work to measure and communicate process improvements. Create a before-and-after description of the design and development process (and its problems) for the products you worked on before using personas and the design and development process you just completed. Find out if anything has changed as a result of your introduction and support of the personas. Once you find out what has changed, you can assess the impact of the change on the overall design and development process.

Look for increased efficiency in the design and development processes

There is an adage that it is always more effective to "design twice, build once" (which is, of course, easier said than done). Iteration during product design is good, but iteration on real code is costly. Understanding the amount of late-cycle UI iteration can be quite telling. A quick calculation at this point can show you whether the percentage of project time devoted to design activities increased or decreased with the use of personas in many cases. The personas save at least as much time and work as they require (starting to code three weeks late is not a bad thing if it is due to a process improvement that helps you deliver a better product and/or enables you to finish five weeks early). You can also use these numbers later to map the benefits of personas to the time required for their creation. Note that collecting quantitative data like this can be quite difficult (it is difficult to track the time the product team spends in meetings). If you cannot collect this type of data, all is not lost. Often, the actual money spent on the personas may not be as important as the perceived benefits of the personas. In "Scenario Design Depends on Personas," Harley Manning and Moira Dorsey [2001] state that personas help you:

- Serve the most important market segments
- Simplify design decisions
- Help avoid costly rework

Look for specific examples of these benefits in your own project. Consider the following questions in comparison to previous projects that did not employ personas in the process:

- Was this process faster?
- Did important decisions get made earlier or more quickly?

● Were important decisions more "stable" once they were made? In other words, were important decisions changed as much or as frequently as they were in previous projects?

● Was inter- and intra-team communication easier and more efficient?

These benefits do not necessarily map to bottom-line financial return on investment, but they certainly make it easier to create, market, and support a great product. Personas enhance your ability to focus everyone on the most important customers and users, communicate more effectively, make decisions based on data, and build your product the right way (with the right features for the right users).

Measure the value of avoiding unnecessary work

We already recommended that you measure the value of features that were prioritized in the persona-weighted feature matrix. Identifying the resource *savings* realized due to the de-prioritization of some features is also important. Work to identify features or design elements that were excluded from the product as a direct result of persona-related prioritization (see the following Story from the field).

Story from the field

REALIZE THE BENEFITS OF AVOIDING WORK

—Robert Barlow-Busch, Practice Director of Interaction Design Quarry Integrated Communications, Inc.

The initial research performed in our client's market category resulted in the requirement for a "very high throughput" product. One of our user groups, scientists, would need to process many thousands of samples per day. Once we hit the ground and visited labs around the world, though, we were puzzled: where is everyone who's actually running this many samples? We could not find them. And nobody we spoke with could identify anyone for us, either. Strange.

We continued our investigations and ultimately realized that this immediate need for very high throughput was a myth. The myth was based on a shared assumption that "Yes, *somebody* is running this many samples, so I may want to someday as well." And in the press, the market category had been compared to a similar market in which the need for high throughput had in fact grown dramatically—which led to the assumption that this market would develop similarly. However, our on-the-ground research uncovered some bottlenecks in our customer's workflow, with products in different markets than ours. Until these bottlenecks were overcome, there would be no need for the throughput numbers we had been planning.

The happy outcome for our client: they delayed a planned component of the product and saved an estimated half-million dollars in development. Would the component ever be needed? Only the future will tell. In the meantime, they are delivering a product that people need *today*.

Find out if personas improved communication—especially across teams

In Chapter 3, we recommended that you collect assumptions and generally held knowledge about your users from various people in your organization, including members of your design and development team. Without your persona effort, these varying descriptions of "the user" would have lived, unchallenged, in the minds of your colleagues (and possibly in the design documents related to your product). During the *family planning* phase, you and your core team answered "how is user information incorporated into the design and development process" by looking in product-related documents to find:

- What is the language used to refer to users?
- How are users' characteristics, goals, needs, and behavior described?
- How are users distinguished from customers, if at all?
- How is knowledge about users communicated (research reports, segmentation analyses, presentations, or other artifacts)?

Now that you have completed a project using personas, you can examine the product-related documents to look for the same types of information.

- Did the language used to refer to users change?
- Did references to users become more specific and concrete?
- Were descriptions of users, their goals, and their tasks more consistent across various product-related documents?

Story from the field

PERSONAS IMPROVE INTRA-TEAM COMMUNICATION

—Lisa Battle, Social Security Administration, Lockheed Martin

As a team of usability practitioners who work on different projects, we have not always done a great job of sharing information among ourselves. The one real exception is our sharing of personas. We have created personas on most of our projects, and have frequently shared them with one another. Any results of our user analysis that are captured in the personas are the most likely things to be shared. So, it can be said that personas are an effective knowledge sharing approach for a team of usability practitioners.

In addition, we have done a better job of making information about UCD available to other project teams. A new do-it-yourself UCD Web site I designed at Social Security includes examples of personas from real projects and templates for people who want to create personas. We have received good feedback from our internal customers about the persona examples.

USE THE SAME RESEARCH METHODS YOU USED DURING THE FAMILY PLANNING PHASE

In Chapter 3, we recommended that you distribute a user focus survey to your colleagues (see "Story from the field: Using a Questionnaire to Find Out How User Centered Your Organization *Really* Is"). If you re-administer the same survey now, you will be able to measure the changes that resulted (at least in part) from the use of personas. You can also convene your colleagues to create another set of assumption personas: gather everyone in a room (do not tell them why in advance) and ask them to describe the users of the product they just completed. Essentially, ask them to describe the personas to you. If you find that your colleagues are able to recall and describe important aspects of your personas, you will know that your persona effort was at least partly successful and valuable.

- Were the different needs of users versus customers delineated (e.g., were marketing requirements handled separately from product requirements)?
- What new documents and artifacts appeared (e.g., persona-related materials)? Did these replace any other materials?

You can also look for ways in which user data was incorporated into design and development decisions. Your personas provided an effective medium for consolidating and ensuring the use of user research. Your personas probably had a staying power and a "stickiness" that far outlasted other reports you previously used to convey user research. Was there a perception

PERSONAS DEPERSONALIZED OUR DISCUSSIONS

—Damian Rees, Usability Engineer (formerly at BBC)

The first time I introduced them to the BBC was on a large project a lot of people had their eye on. We worked with an incredibly difficult team suffering from internal politics. By using personas, all discussions that started turning nasty were immediately pulled back and problems were depersonalized by making everyone talk about an idea, problem, or issue in reference to what a persona needs, likes, can use, and so on. I also feel it succeeded in a different way in that the use of personas was noticed by many decision makers, and now most projects I see when walking around have personas assigned to them.

(The described work was written by Damian Rees and reproduced by permission of the BBC. Copyright © BBC 2001.)

among your teammates that communication was eased or more efficient related to target users because of the use of personas?

Trace process improvements to the use of personas

As you find ways of measuring and describing the process improvements that resulted from the use of personas, try to be as specific as possible when you describe the value of each change. If you identified aspects of your processes that needed improvement as part of your action plan, you should be able to map each of these to:

- The reasons you felt improvement was needed
- The ways you have been able to measure changes resulting from the use of personas
- Quantitative or qualitative process improvements you can trace to the use of personas.

Figure 7.8 shows an example of this type of mapping.

Want to improve:	"Before personas" measure	"After personas" measure	Conclusions (process improvements)
Current process doesn't incorporate data about our users.	Review of vision and specification documents for previous projects showed 16 different terms for 'user' and differing definitions of user needs in every document.	• Project documentation for this project referred to our five persona names. Only one 'final' document still contained a non-persona reference to a 'user.' • UCD questionnaire before the project vs. after the project showed more consistent understanding of who our target users are, how they relate to our business goals, etc. (include specifics!)	• We've built a better way to communicate and maintain focus on the needs of a well-defined set of target users. • References to users and their needs are more explicit and actionable • We can trace good (and bad!) product decisions back to the data that led to the decision, which will help us improve our decision-making process for our next products.
Current process isn't allowing us to catch and fix critical issues and bugs before release. Current process assumes that we need at least two quick 'point releases' after every project.	12 issues (including 3 'show-stopper' issues) identified in usability testing. Release delayed 2 weeks to fix 2 of 3 'show-stoppers'; product released with 10 known usability issues.	20 minor usability issues (most related to text choices) discovered in usability testing. All fixed within 2 days; release on schedule.	Major usability issues are being avoided or being detected early enough to fix them and meet product schedules. Persona-driven product design was iterated many times, but earlier in product cycle.

FIGURE 7.8: *Mapping process improvements to the use of personas. If you included aspects of your process that needed improvement during the family planning phase, you should be able to relate each change you have observed back to the use of the personas.*

Story from the field

MEASURING ROI AT PFALTZGRAFF

—Howard Blumenthal, Director, E-Commerce & Database Management, Pfaltzgraff

For us, the effort is not just about creating a persona. It is about understanding the entire customer experience, which is multifaceted. We cannot measure the true effectiveness and ROI until we have all of the facets aligned. But already we see important changes. The personas are allowing everyone at our company to focus our attention, which has a lot of value almost immediately. For example, once we had the personas we were able to very quickly identify projects that were not in line with the needs of the personas and thus act accordingly.

We have had a new marketing initiative and have made some changes in our brand positioning, and we are learning what promotions excite the personas we are focusing on. Personas have also triggered design explorations to make our Web presence more appealing to our target customers. (See Figures 7.9 to 7.13.) But there is also value to be realized in the form of savings. For example, we discovered that some of our existing promotions were essentially a waste because they weren't relevant to our personas. We have been working to identify what measurement tools we have that can help us continue to evaluate the value of the persona effort.

For now, we already see changes, and the effort looks very promising. Personas are changing the way we think, and that is all good!

FIGURE 7.9: *Before our persona effort, the pfaltzgraff.com home page was designed to please everyone. This page has options for everyone, but the multiple navigational elements and destination images made it difficult to know where to start.*

(Story from the field, continued)

FIGURE 7.10: *We designed a new home page to attract our personas Carol and Laurie. We radically simplified the design to meet Carol and Laurie's goals. We created an elegant graphic design to attract the personas and express our new brand direction. We thought carefully about every element of this page.*

FIGURE 7.11: *We designed the 'pfz custom' area of our site to attract our persona Jennifer. The call to action to 'click a plate to begin' is clear and synchronizes nicely with our new 'custom dinnerware you design' product lines.*

2001   2005

FIGURE 7.12: *The Pfaltzgraff Web site wasn't the only thing that changed as a result of our persona work. The changes in our brand positioning and the impact of persona-driven design are clear in the differences between our 2001 and 2005 Bridal Catalogs.*

2003   2004

FIGURE 7.13: *We redesigned some of the catalog page layouts to attract the persona who was most likely to be interested in the particular product line. These two pages show the same "Sphere" product line as displayed in the 2003 (pre-personas) and 2004 (persona-driven) catalogs. The 2004 example shows one of eight pages we designed to appeal to our persona Jennifer.*

G4K Meanwhile, at G4K...

G4K EVALUATES PERSONA-RELATED PROCESS IMPROVEMENTS

The G4K team was highly invested in making the new Web portal a success, but they were worried about the intense schedule and lack of resources. The persona core team knew that intense schedules were likely to cause flare-ups and turf wars in the team, because everyone would be trying to work quickly under a great deal of pressure. The G4K core team hoped the personas would allow the team to be both focused and highly collaborative. In their action plan, the G4K team listed several process-related challenges they hoped to mitigate with the personas:

- Deal with incredibly fast turnaround required for online portal development (unlike game development schedules)
- Leverage the efforts of our very small team
- Leverage the efforts of people not directly on our team but whose help and expertise is needed.

The G4K core team decided to measure the impact of the personas on the design and development process by surveying the portal team to ask them questions such as the following:

- What, if anything, helped us meet (or caused us to miss) important milestones in the project schedule?
- How did you make decisions when there was no time to meet with the entire team?
- Were there more or fewer last-minute changes than in other projects you have worked on? What were they?
- What are you most proud of in our finished portal?
- What do you wish we could change?
- What would you do differently if we were creating another version of the portal?

They also surveyed the resources borrowed from other teams. They asked these people to describe the target users of the Internet portal. Through these surveys the G4K team knew they would collect information they could use to assess whether the personas:

- Helped the team meet the tight deadline, and in what ways
- Helped coordinate the efforts of the main team and of the borrowed resources (without having them get in each others' way)
- Communicated and maintained focus on the goals and needs of the targeted users of the portal (and the ways they were different from users of other G4K products).

ROI question 4: Is your company more user-centered with personas than it was before?

This book assumes that user focus and UCD are good for business and good for products, and that personas help to increase the user focus of entire organizations. Now it is time to measure these effects: is your company more user centered with personas than it was before?

During the *family planning* phase, you and your core team assessed how user focused your company was before you started your persona effort. You did organizational introspection to find out if your company described the products it produced in terms of how easy they are to use and/or in terms of how well they satisfy customer needs. This was also done to discover how integrated user focus was in your corporate culture. To measure the changes that resulted from the use of personas, try to answer the following questions:

- Did your company's commitment to UCD improve? Find out if your company measures the success of the product in new ways. For example, do people now talk about the product in terms of how easy it is to use?

- Did other UCD activities occur in addition to, and perhaps as a result of, the personas? Did you employ additional UCD methods to a greater degree in this project than you had in others? For example, did you use scenarios in a new way, or do a heuristic review of your product design from the point of view of the personas?

- Were more people talking and thinking about end users, not just about technology? Did you hear the persona names used in conversations related to the product?

- Were opinions and assumptions about end users shared by more people? Were these opinions and assumptions based on the personas you created (and therefore on data)? Did everyone, from key developers to quality assurance professionals to documentation specialists, know the personas and consider their needs before making any product-related decisions?

- Are visions for new products and features being expressed in customer-centric terms? Are stakeholders asking for persona-related information earlier in the process for the next product?

- Are people asking for more help from you and your team? Do you perceive an increased interest in user-related information?

Note that there is no one way to find the answers to these questions. In a general sense, you will be trying to quantify and qualify the ways your entire organization has changed as a result of the persona effort, and this is not easy to do. Even if your organization has changed in obvious ways (and organizational changes are often so slow to come about that they are not obvious), it is difficult to trace the "root" of any change as being any one factor.

Suggestions for measuring organizational changes

In their chapter "Organizational Inhibitors and Facilitators," Mayhew and Bias [1994] remind us that UCD professionals often function as organizational change agents. They list the inhibitors to organizational changes (everything from attitudes to organizational structures) and discuss the ways in which usability methods help to facilitate change. Their discussion is a reminder that even 10 years later we still face many of the same inhibitors in our day-to-day work and must take our jobs as change agents seriously (especially as we gain seniority and the influence that comes with experience).

As we discussed in reference to family planning, influencing change in an established organization is not an easy task, and measuring these changes is also difficult. Personas address several of the change motivators and measures of success Mayhew and Bias list in their chapter. The material that follows explores how personas relate to one example of each of the following:

> **Change motivator example:** *A need for an objective means of resolving conflicts* [Mayhew and Bias 1994, p. 302]. Because personas are usually based primarily on data, they can serve as apolitical contributors to conflict resolution. As user-centered designers become more integrated into more projects, our opinions and contributions can become as politically charged (and biased) as those of any other member of the team. Personas stand in as user advocates and allow for data-driven decision making.

> **Success factor example:** *Produce well-defined work products* [Mayhew and Bias 1994, p. 307]. Mayhew and Bias describe the difficulty of contributing opinions based on the "specialized knowledge and skills" we bring as UCD professionals, especially in early design meetings. Personas are concrete deliverables we can produce before or during the earliest explorations of a new product. The fact that the personas are rich, narrative, and easy to use by the rest of the product team demonstrates "in a powerful" way the skills and value we bring as user-centered designers.

Building accessible, data-driven personas and supporting their use during the design and development process should help you overcome some of the organizational change-inhibitors you face. The analysis you did during the *family planning* phase may have surfaced organizational change-inhibitors at play in your company. To help evaluate how things have changed with the introduction of the personas, if you did a formal UCD survey (as suggested in reference to *family planning*), you should consider administering that same survey again (see "Bright Idea: Use the Same Research Methods You Used During the *Family Planning Phase*," earlier in this chapter). Keep your eye open for inhibitors still at play even after the persona effort. Perhaps you can target these in your next project.

Bright Idea

SHOW HOW PERSONAS CHANGED ASSUMPTIONS ABOUT USERS

During the *family planning* phase, you asked various people in your organization who they thought they were building the product for. Now that the project is complete, ask the same people who they actually *did* build the product for. Create a presentation showing how the assumptions everyone started out with were different from the data-driven personas, and that the use of personas ensured that the original assumptions were replaced with data-driven persona details. You can take this one step further by evaluating how the original assumptions could have led to design decisions that may have significantly altered or harmed the product.

Was the desire for a cultural shift one of the reasons for trying personas?

Kuniavsky [2003] also provides an interesting and useful perspective on the topic of changing organizational culture. In his chapter "Creating a User-centered Corporate Culture," Kuniavsky highlights the difficulties and provides specific suggestions for moving your organization toward user centricity. He cites five reasons for arguing this approach [Kuniavsky 2003, pp. 516–517]:

- Efficiency
- Reputation
- Competitive advantage
- Trust
- Profit

Many companies (if not all) have a need for being efficient in their design and development process. (That is part of the reason UCD is not embraced uniformly across the industry. It requires some real or perceived additional effort and cost.) As a result, practitioners have developed an array of "discount" usability methods (e.g., heuristic evaluation, paper prototyping, scenario-based design). Such methods have had fairly broad acceptance and application. Personas can serve as one of these discount approaches.

Jakob Nielsen describes an evolution of acceptance of and reliance on UCD in organizations in which usability permeates the product development life cycle [Nielsen 1994a, pp. 267–269]. Discount usability techniques—including the use of ad hoc, assumption, or otherwise low-effort personas—can play a major role in driving this evolution. In fact, we have witnessed personas do exactly that in multiple organizations. Personas can engage the development team in a meaningful and exciting way.

Because personas are a concrete deliverable you own and maintain, the persona effort may have helped to establish and define your role as a user-centered designer, and therefore as a critical player in the cultural change toward user centrism. Success with your personas can serve as a catalyst to the introduction of other user-centered techniques into your organization and can serve as a milestone on your company's path toward a user-centric culture.

Find a way of measuring "social ROI"

As Wilson and Rosenbaum define it, internal social ROI "…deals with the perceptions of stakeholders in an organization that UCD practitioners add value to the development process, even in the absence of specific supporting data," [Wilson and

Rosenbaum 2005]. Consider creating a short survey or conducting a "postmortem" meeting to find out what your colleagues thought of the personas:

- How did the personas help?
- Were they worth the effort it took to use them?
- In what ways did your team feel the personas got in the way of development efforts?
- How did the personas change the design and development process from the perspective of your colleagues?

Use the results of this investigation to both express the value of the persona effort and to consider improvements for your next persona effort. As illustrated in "Story from the field: I Hate Personas," not everyone will have a positive outlook on the method. Understanding their perspective is important in improving your process and organizational culture.

Although we do recommend that you find out what your colleagues thought of the personas, we do *not* recommend that you use the results as your only measure of the social ROI of your persona effort. As usability testing professionals are well aware, people are remarkably bad at self-reporting after an experience. The personas may have had a far greater impact than the design and development teams realized.

- Your personas may have replaced assumptions your colleagues did not even realize they had. Not many people stop to think about how much influence assumptions can have on a product. If your colleagues have not considered the impact of assumptions, they may not realize the impact of replacing assumptions with data-driven personas.

● Personas are not "job one" for your colleagues. Although personas may be one of the most important deliverables for you and your core team, personas are simply glorified reference materials to the other members of the design and development teams. Asking about the value of the personas may be similar to asking a writer about the impact of a particular dictionary on a finished novel.

Although you may not be able to collect social ROI data directly from your colleagues, you can look for examples that show the impact of the personas on their day-to-day work. See the following "Story from the field: No, We Didn't Use Mavis."

Look closely at failures of the personas

It is unlikely that your persona effort went exactly as you hoped it would. It is impossible to predict all of the internal and external factors that will exert themselves on a product design and development process, and it is impossible to create a foolproof persona lifecycle plan that is immune to all of the unforeseeable pressures you and your team will experience.

Story from the field

NO, WE DIDN'T USE MAVIS

—Holly Jamesen Carr, GreenShape LLC, formerly Usability Specialist, Attenex Corporation

At Netpodium we used four primary personas, one of whom was "Mavis the Conference Call Operator." The entire design and development team sat in one large room, so we often overheard development meetings and knew that the persona names were mentioned frequently by the developers as they discussed various aspects of the product.

After the product was launched, we asked the developers what they thought about the personas. To our surprise, many of the developers said that the personas weren't all that useful during the development process. Some felt that the names of the personas provided a useful shorthand for communication but little else.

Other developers saw personas as so integral to the development process that their utility was nearly transparent. "It is such a simple and obvious tool. The persona vocabulary became so entrenched in the developers' minds that its benefits were taken for granted," says Lynne Evans, a developer on the product team.

Not only did Mavis provide a one-word encapsulation of a user, her skills, and her product needs, but she implicitly helped to define and constrain the features in the product by concretely separating the developer from the user. "Sometimes developers think of themselves as the users of the product, making feature decisions based on what *they* want the product to do," says Evans. Mavis reminds developers that, whereas they *build* the product, *she* uses it.

Even the authors of this book are not immune to persona failures. In John's first persona effort at Microsoft, the personas were not used widely by the team. There was scattered discussion of the personas in design and development meetings, but they were not broadly incorporated in scenarios across the product and team. They were generally only used by design, usability, and program management. After the fact, we found there were two reasons for this:

- We were not timely in developing and delivering the personas.
- We did not know we needed to actively promote them or define explicit uses for them.

In Tamara's first persona effort at Amazon.com, it was difficult to figure out how to use the vast internal data sources to create helpful personas. This made the first persona effort very time consuming and the first personas turned out to be of limited use. Through this experience, she learned how to balance the collection and use of data with the time pressures on many projects. She also discovered that project-specific personas would be more helpful than global personas, at least initially.

Although complete success is difficult to attain, most persona efforts are successful in some ways even as they fail in others. Even if your persona effort seems to have failed, take time to carefully analyze the perceived failure. You can use the information you find to extract and express small successes in the effort and to codify lessons learned for your next project.

Story from the field

PERSONAS CAN BOTH FAIL AND SUCCEED IN THE SAME PROJECT

—**Åsa Blomquist,** Designer, Skatteverket IT (IT Division, Swedish National Tax Board)

We used personas for one of our larger projects (one that stretched over two years) at The Swedish National Tax Board. The usability team there did field studies at local branches around Sweden, sent out questionnaires, and created a number of personas during a series of workshops. The resulting personas were introduced at the project kickoff and they were pinned up on the walls in the office. The usability team also created larger documents describing office environments and other contextual information. Everybody in the project seemed to embrace the personas, and some developers even put persona posters on the walls of their own workspaces.

However, a year into the project the personas started to blend into the environment and nobody saw them anymore. Whereas other documents grew and developed as the process went on (sketches became interactive prototypes, screen shots changed every week), the personas stayed the same. At the end of the project the personas did not contain enough information to base design decisions on as the design challenges became more and more complex.

(Story from the field, continued)

The personas were, however, very useful when someone new joined the project staff. The new team members could use the personas to understand who to design for and how the product would be used. Overall, the personas were an excellent communication tool, and creating the personas helped the usability team fully understand the user base.

Story from the field

I HATE PERSONAS

—Andrei Herasimchuk, www.designbyfire.com (quoted in part from "The Persona Crutch")

I'm going to go out on a limb on this one. I'm going to go on record and say publicly that I personally dislike personas. In fact, I'd have to be honest and say I really hate using them, I hate writing them, and I seriously hate how popular they've become. There, I said it. Shoot me.

However, I dislike personas more for personal reasons as a designer than for anything having to do with the usefulness or function of personas or the lack thereof. I fully understand the value personas bring to the table on a project for many people in the entire business organization. I also fully understand how useful they can be as a tool for creating more focused feature specifications with teams, especially teams that contain nondesigners representing every business unit inside a corporation. I also know how personas can help ground conversations toward a more UCD focus, where none had existed before.

But the reason I hate personas is more personal for me as a designer. I feel whenever I use personas I tend to become detached emotionally and less engaged with a project. Maybe that is just me, but the one thing I've seen with personas that can be a slippery slope for designers is when the persona becomes a replacement for what I feel is a crucial practice in which every designer must actively engage: becoming the user.

Story from the field

PERSONAS CAN BE PERCEIVED AS BOTH HELPFUL AND DISEMPOWERING

—Rhiannon Gallagher, Thomson Micromedex

I know from past experience that the development team appreciates the user insights and finds it easier to develop for clearly defined and separate personas than to try to encompass all needs and aspects of the user community at once. However, the method can be seen by some developers as disempowerment, because it brings with it a very user-centered approach that takes some of the eleventh-hour decision making away from the developers themselves.

Use your successes to build a case for your next project

Finally, once you have assessed the ROI of your persona effort, use that information to market your team, your processes, and your plans for future projects. Make sure that people know the success came from a concerted, long-term, organized process that you want to repeat. Do not let people walk away thinking that just names and pictures are what caused the success. Ask for a pilot project opportunity with another team or partner with a "process improvement" group (if there is one in your organization) to introduce new UCD methods. If you can show that the personas were a success, you can ask for more resources and the opportunity to get involved earlier in the development process.

REUSE AND RETIREMENT: DECIDE HOW TO MANAGE THE TRANSITION TO THE NEXT PROJECT

During the final phase of the persona lifecycle, you will not only measure the value of your personas but also decide what to do with them as you move on to your next project. So far, most of the content of this book has been about how to create personas and keep them alive. Now it is time to reconsider the personas you have created as you transition to a new project, which could mean helping your colleagues to *forget* the personas. Personas are easy to remember and easy to empathize with, which makes them great when you need them and tough to send packing when the time comes to move on to a new project.

In most cases, you will decide to use some combination of direct *reuse* (using them again without alteration), *reincarnation* (reusing some their content and related data), and *retirement* (discarding or completely replacing some of the personas). If your persona effort has been a success, retirement and reincarnation can be a bit tricky. To make room for the next set of personas, you will need to help your organization let go of the personas they have come to know so well.

Step 1: Reclaim ownership and control of your personas

During the *adulthood* phase, you relinquished control of your personas to a certain extent. You sent them out into your organization to do the work they were born to do. People have been using (or not using) them, and your ownership of the personas has probably become a bit hazy. It is a good thing to allow and encourage others to feel ownership of the personas during *adulthood*, but it is time for you to step in again as your product is completed and you begin the transition to the next project.

As your product development cycle progressed, your colleagues used the personas during the *adulthood* phase to help make important decisions about the product you were building.

Now that your product is nearly complete there are very few decisions left to be made about its design. Although the personas can and should continue to be useful for the QA, marketing, and sales teams, the design and development teams do not really need them anymore. Even if people on these teams felt a great deal of ownership over the personas during *adulthood*, you probably will not encounter a great deal of resistance as you "rein in" and ask for ownership of the personas in preparation for the next project. To do this:

- Collect all of the persona artifacts from around your offices.
- Let your colleagues know that the core team is going to work on, and possibly change, the personas for the next project.

If a particular person or group is highly attached to the personas and is not willing to let go of them, it is important to understand why:

- *Do they feel that the current product does not fully satisfy the needs of the personas, and want to work on new features for another release?* If this is the case, and if this is exactly what the team should be doing, support this. Reevaluate the data in the personas (see material following), make any necessary updates, and communicate important changes as quickly as possible so that the team can continue the work they are doing.
- *Are they simply used to having the personas around?* If so, invite the team to participate in the next persona effort. Invite them to help you find and evaluate data sources relevant to the next project or product, and participate in the evaluation of whether the "'old" personas should be reused, reincarnated, or retired before the next project. This will help them let go of the previous personas because they are directly involved in addressing the issues with them.
- *Are they already working on the next product, and using the personas in the documents they are producing because that is what they have to work with?* If you find this to be the case, you can use this as an example of how the persona effort changed the way you communicate about users in your company as you create your ROI argument. However, it is important that the personas reflect the data relevant to the new product. If the new product is not a new version of the product you have just completed, it is possible that the personas should be significantly different, and you are going to have to work quickly to replace the old personas. If you can, encourage the team to temporarily replace the names of the personas with names of the abstract roles, goals, or segments (e.g., replace references to the old persona Sally with "Mother" or "Fast Shopper" or "Neophyte") until you have an appropriate set of personas for the new project.

Note that if your persona effort has been successful you may have created a real demand for information about users in the form of personas, and now you and your core team are going to have to work quickly to deliver updated or new personas. To do this, you will need to evaluate the data you have already used and any new data you collect and make a decision to reuse, reincarnate, or retire the old personas.

Step 2: Evaluate your data. Is it still valid for the next project?

Before you decide what to do with your personas, you need to revisit the data sources you used to create them. If you are about to start work on the next version of the product you have just released, it is likely that many (but probably not all) of your data sources are still relevant and you can reuse entire personas or some of the information in the personas. If you are moving on to create a completely different product or if there have been major shifts in strategy, perhaps only a few of the data sources (e.g., those that relate to your company or to the general product space in which you work) may still be relevant. Review your original data sources to determine:

- Is the data still up to date? As a rule of thumb, if the research you conducted to inform your personas is more than a few years old you should consider collecting new data.
- Has your product or customer domain changed so much that the data is no longer relevant?
- What *portions* of the existing data are still relevant?

As you review your data sources, also keep an eye out for factoids you did not use originally but which may be relevant in your next project. In addition, take the time to see what new information is available since you created the personas, and work with your team to integrate the new data into the existing personas.

Step 3: Decide to reuse, reincarnate, or retire your personas

Once you have decided how much of your old data is appropriate for your new project, you are ready to decide how to retire or reuse your personas. In our experience, there are three possibilities:

- Reuse existing personas intact and promote or demote them (from primary to secondary, and vice versa) as appropriate for your next project
- Reincarnate your personas by reusing some or all of the data, incorporating new data, and creating new or significantly updated personas
- Retire your personas and start over.

Reusing your personas

If you are building a new version of your product, or a new product for the same audience, you might find that many of your personas can be reused. Your personas could be reused by the same team that used them originally, by a new design and development team, or perhaps by a team in some other part of your company, such as marketing, sales, or product support.

Handy Detail

SCHEDULE TIMES FOR "CHECKING IN ON YOUR DATA"

If your development cycle is long (and therefore your personas will be around for over a year) or if you plan to reuse some or all your personas, schedule times for checking in on your data sources. Revisit your original data sources about once a year to make sure they are still relevant and to see if there have been any major updates.

Handy Detail

UNDERSTAND HOW MUCH YOU CAN CHANGE AN EXIST-ING PERSONA BEFORE IT IS NOT THE SAME PERSONA ANYMORE

You will find that there is a fine line when it comes to how much data you can add or alter without creating a completely new persona. If you find yourself changing more than a few details, consider creating a new persona rather than reusing an old one. As a rule of thumb, if it would take more than a few sentences to describe how your persona has changed since the last project, you should create a new persona instead. Consider also how well your team knows the information you are changing. If the details you want to change are relatively unknown and/or subtle, there is no reason to create an entirely new persona.

When you created your personas, you assimilated your data, created persona skeletons, prioritized the skeletons, and built some or all of the skeletons into full personas. When you move on to the next version of your product, you can reevaluate the primary versus secondary classification for each of your original personas. You might decide to demote one of your primary personas and promote one of your secondary personas. This promotion/demotion is especially useful if you are building a new version of the same project but your company has decided to focus on a slightly different user base. In addition, you can revisit some of the persona skeletons you created but never developed for the first project. It is possible that one of these would be just right for the new project. If so, you have a tremendous head start and can simply build up the skeleton into a full persona.

Your personas might be happier in a new home

If the personas are no longer relevant to design or development, they could still be highly useful to other parts of the organization, such as marketing, sales, and support. Think of this as the personas "moving" to live in another part of the organization. For example:

- The support team can use the personas in creating strategies for streamlining support tasks. In addition, you can assign a member of your core team to check in regularly with a support team manager to find out what types of support issues are arising. If the support team does use the personas, they may be able to report support issues in terms of the personas (e.g., "We're getting a lot of calls from the Sarahs. They seem to be having trouble with the installation.").

- The marketing team can use the personas to understand the end user of the product (who may not be the same person as the purchaser of the product).

- The sales engineering team can use the personas to understand how to communicate product features and benefits to the end user. The personas can also become a great source of information on the IT and organizational setups of your target users.

The people who use the personas you have created are your internal customers, but they are also great sources of information and data for keeping your personas up to date. Be sure to ask these new users of your personas to evaluate their appropriateness and accuracy (i.e., get a sense of your personas' perceived or face validity by having the new users do an expert review).

Create a persona library

We have often been asked whether it is appropriate to create a collection of personas from a variety of different persona efforts—to create a "persona library," if you will. Such a collection of personas could be used as needed for various projects. At first blush, the answer seems to be an emphatic *no*. Personas are defined as highly specific archetypal users that reflect particular goals and needs relevant to your product. The data that goes into them and the questions they are meant to answer must relate to the domain of your product. Personas for communications products (such as telephony, e-mail, instant messaging, or text messaging) would require different types of information than personas for digital photography products. If personas really are this specific, creating a library of personas that can be reused in many contexts is counterintuitive (how can you create a persona that is both highly specific and targeted and at the same time reusable in many contexts?).

However, there are a few cases in which it is possible to create a set of personas that can be stored in a "library" and reused as the need arises. For example, if your company is focused on providing many products for the same niche audience, you may be able to create a bank of personas that embodies a wide range of goals and abilities and select sets of these personas for your various projects. If you do decide to create a library of personas, it is a good idea to define goals in general terms. Some aspects of the narrative and story line in a persona (the more fictional components) are easy to reuse as well as change.

Several different product teams may need a "mom" or a "small business owner." Sharing the core story line for a consumer user who is a parent among various products does not seem problematic, as long as the critical characteristics

Story from the field

THE BIRTH OF A "PERSONA LIBRARY"

—Lisa Battle, Social Security Administration, Lockheed Martin

We have had positive experiences with successfully reusing personas from one project to another (the projects were for online services targeted to the same audience). For example, we created personas of retired beneficiaries, which were reused in several different projects targeted to retired people. We also created personas of disability claimants when we were working on the design of an online application for benefits, and we reused those personas in a later project for an online service for people whose claim had been denied. We are now working on creating a persona library that can be used by other software development teams and operational groups, not just the usability team.

related to the product are present and unadulterated. Similarly, you could create the personas in such a way that there are "core" characteristics and domain-specific characteristics that can be added or swapped out depending on the needs of the product. That way, when each persona is "checked out" of the library for use on a project, there is room to assign more specific, product-related goals as appropriate.

Manage the reuse of personas

No matter how your personas will be reused, it is your job to ensure that the personas are reused appropriately. If the personas are going to be reused by the design and development team that used them originally, you should still plan to regain control and ownership of the personas, review the original data sources, find any new and relevant data sources, and reintroduce the personas and any new information they contain (including information you gathered during usability testing, reviews of the released product, and so on). If the changes are important (i.e., highly relevant to the design of your new product), you will want to really highlight that information in the new communication artifacts you create.

If the personas are going to be reused by a different design and development team working in a related product domain, consider collecting quotes, examples of usage (e.g., key scenarios that included the personas), and ideas from the original team to help you evangelize the personas and process to the new team. You might also want to ask one of the developers or designers who has already used the personas to help you introduce them to the new team. If you make changes to the personas between their first and second use, make sure you publicize these changes to everyone, including anyone who has used the personas in the past but may not be using them in the current project.

Reincarnating your personas (reusing some or all of your data)

Even if your original set of personas is no longer relevant as you move onto your next project, some of the original data are often reusable. We like to think of this data reuse as either *reincarnating* or *evolving* your personas. Reincarnation describes the reuse of key data in a new persona. Evolution describes significant changes to existing personas, usually in logical, meaningful ways.

Reincarnating personas

If some of the data in your personas is still relevant, but the personas you originally created are not, you can create reincarnated personas by reusing some "old" data in new personas. If the products you develop serve users in a specific market segment or industry, you will find many data sources that stay relevant no matter what project you are working on. If the data sources are still relevant but the particular personas you have created are not, it is important to do some research and find some additional data sources.

Once you have collected the appropriate set of data (which will include sources you have already used), you can revisit the processes described in Chapter 4 and re-assimilate data points according to the issues you are finding related to your new project.

As you create your reincarnated set of personas, be aware that many of the people who used the original set of personas probably did not have a thorough knowledge of all details in the foundation documents. Some of your colleagues may only know the persona names and a few basic details about each.

If the new personas you create out of data you are reusing are different only in very particular details, it might be difficult for your colleagues to understand why you are using new personas at all. On the other hand, if your colleagues did not know the first set of personas very well, they may not be aware that many of the details in the two persona sets are similar. As you introduce your new set of personas, try to find ways of making them more engaging and of clearly communicating the details critical to the product design. In addition, make sure that the important differences between the reincarnated personas and the original personas are clearly communicated, and not just in the long foundation documents. Even summaries of personas built from reincarnated data sources usually benefit from statements such as, "Unlike Mary [the original persona], Ginny never telecommutes. Her boss simply won't let her."

Evolving versus reincarnating your personas

How do personas change over time? In many cases, they do not. The persona you create today will likely be the same age and have the same issues, goals, and concerns two years from now. So, how do we deal with the fact that real people change over time? For example:

● What if it is important (for our product) to understand the realistic development of a teenager, and the ways in which their interests and abilities change over the years?

● What if your product changed the world (or a very small part of the world) so much that the same people are now behaving in very different ways?

Story from the field

LEARNING FROM EXPERIENCE—USING PERSONAS TO HELP US USE DATA

—Lisa Battle, Social Security Administration, Lockheed Martin

We are using personas to contribute to the dialogue between the usability team and business decision makers. We need to do a better job of capturing the results of our user analysis and usability testing and make sure that these results are fed back into the process of identifying and prioritizing new project ideas. Personas may be one good way of doing this. In a new collaborative effort with the Agency's "Customer Insight Program" we are working to share this type of information. The manager of the Customer Insight Program attended our class on personas and is excited about the possibility of working together to augment our current collection of personas through focus groups, surveys, and other activities he will sponsor.

- What if your product was new on the market and thus none of your personas were represented as actual users of your product? For version 2, several of your initial personas may have purchased, adopted, or otherwise experienced your product.

- What if Philip gets older? Or MaryAnn gets more adept at surfing the Internet? Or Renee gets promoted?

It is possible that your product changed the world enough that your target audience has changed along with it. If it is important to your product that you understand and design for the changes being experienced by your users, you will need a plan to handle this. In most cases, these changes involve aging and/or learning effects. You can choose to create different personas to represent different stages of development, or you can create a plan to describe the changes with respect to a single persona. If you decide to evolve a persona, do so carefully.

If your product needs to support the needs of people of various ages and abilities, it probably makes more sense to create different personas to represent these differences. If your product is designed to evolve with your users, you can consider re-describing your persona as he or she achieves various milestones. Keep in mind that an evolving persona can easily confuse the product team if you are not careful. You must make sure that the particular "state" of your personas is clear to them (e.g., Sarah is 82 now, so her needs and concerns are different from those she had when she was 65).

When you reintroduce any personas that have evolved, introduce the changes in the personas explicitly. For example, if you are working on a corporate intranet, you might want to evolve a new employee into one who has new concerns now that she's been at the company for a while. For example:

> Remember Kerri? The last time we introduced Kerri to you, she was a new employee who was trying to become acclimated to our company as quickly as she could. Her goals when using the intranet included such things as trying to find information about benefits, locating the offices of people she had to meet with, and understanding the history of the projects she was assigned to work on. Well, Kerri is no longer new. As we build our next version of the intranet, we are going to have to think about some of Kerri's new goals. She's been at the company for two years now and she feels very comfortable with her department, with the people she deals with on a daily basis, and with some parts of the intranet. On the other hand, Kerri is facing some new challenges. She has been assigned to figure out ways of reusing some of the work her team has done in different departments, she's been having a bit of trouble with a co-worker, and she's also about to be married.

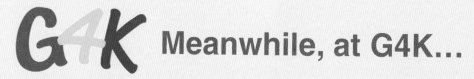 Meanwhile, at G4K...

THE G4K CORE TEAM PREPARES THEIR PERSONAS FOR THEIR NEXT PROJECT

As mentioned earlier, the G4K portal team launched their portal, but not without some compromises. Generally speaking, the project was considered a big success by the broader company and key stakeholders. After evaluating some aspects of ROI and gathering feedback on the method from colleagues, the G4K persona core team deems the persona effort a success. Now some of the other groups in the company are starting to ask, "How did you do that?" and, "Can we use your personas for our next game?"

Because of this, the core team has already been looking at ways of reincarnating their kid personas and of creating a couple more appropriate for other projects not specifically about Web/Internet delivery of content. Further, they plan to reuse and extend the parent and teacher personas for the next version of the site because they feel smarter about the domain now. They know they didn't do much for educators in their current release, so they hope to strengthen this aspect of their site without decreasing the focus on kids. In the meantime, they are using the existing personas to get new team members up to speed, as the new portal is successful enough to inspire their executive team to assign more people to the Web portal team.

Retiring your personas

You might decide that you do not want to reuse or reincarnate your personas or their underlying data at all. There are many reasons to *retire* personas before moving on to the next project:

● The current project is significantly different from the last project.

● The users' goals have changed.

- Your company adopted a new strategy or targeting a different user base.

- There are significant changes to the environment in which your product will be used, such as new technologies or new competitive products that have "changed the landscape" (e.g., the advent of streaming media and broadband in the home, or Bluetooth technology for computing).

When you determine that a persona or set of personas is no longer relevant, it is a good idea to officially retire the personas before moving on. Why officially? Why not just take down the posters and start working on a new set of personas? Because if you have done your job well, you have made the personas incredibly memorable and all your work has paid off. People in your organization have absorbed various amounts of information about the primary personas and are accustomed to thinking about them. If you try to introduce a new set of personas on top of an old set you run the risk of confusing your team, which will destroy the clarity personas are supposed to provide.

You cannot reach into your colleagues' heads and erase everything they know about the personas you have been using, but you have to find a way of helping them move past the old personas and let go of the (no longer relevant) information they contain. This can be as simple as an e-mail announcement that the old set of personas is retiring (including why). If you are moving on to a totally different product or a new strategy, most of your colleagues would know about the switch and the retirement announcement will make sense to them. Use this as an opportunity to invite feedback from the team on the ways personas helped or did not help them do their jobs. You can use this feedback to tweak your customized persona lifecycle the next time around.

Alternatively, you could plan for a richer persona retirement experience. Consider persona *retirement* an opportunity and excuse to celebrate the end of the project with your team. Create new posters that describe the ways the personas are using the newly completed product. You might even want to bring your persona models so that you can take pictures of them using the product, or even invite them in person to a retirement celebration. Plan to follow up over the following months with short updates from the old personas, describing their use of the product and perhaps even the problems they are having with it (which you can easily gather from your product support team). If there are other celebratory activities at the end of the project (such as a team dinner or some other activity), you can include some fun persona-related activities, including:

- Give prizes to colleagues who gave up "pet features" for the sake of personas.

- Reward developers who have said things such as, "I did it for Helen!" or, "Bob would never use that."

- Recognize the people who suggested or implemented a successful new feature based on a persona's needs.

- Describe product successes based on personas. ("We have had over 100 e-mails from Lauras who love these new features.")

Invite your team to self-congratulate for using personas (self-congratulation is very motivating!) and end the project and persona effort with a flourish. Help your colleagues remember the persona-related work as fun and something to look forward to in the next project. Personas are supposed to be engaging, helpful, and perhaps even stress-relieving, so it is a good idea to associate personas with fun.

SUMMARY

User-centered designers will face the task of proving their own worth for the foreseeable future, and part of this challenge is to quantify the value of the work we do. User-centered designers have to start thinking about new projects long before anyone else does, and they have to spend some time proving the ROI of UCD methods—especially if the methods are time consuming and/or expensive. As a rule, the earlier you think about measuring and expressing ROI the better. There are ways to begin measuring ROI during every phase of the persona lifecycle, and we encourage you to use some of the ideas we have included in earlier chapters to develop your own measures.

Well-crafted and appropriately applied personas can yield product and process improvements we can identify and measure to help quantify the value of the persona effort and, more generally, of the UCD process. As you evaluate the ROI of your own efforts, take the opportunity to publicize your successes and analyze reasons for problems or process failures.

The activities we recommend at the end of one project also function to prepare you for the next project. Regaining control over the personas and evaluating the success of the effort will help you be even more successful in your next effort. The *lifetime achievement, reuse, and retirement* phase provides an excellent opportunity to touch base with your core team members and with other stakeholders to talk about how things went. As you dive back into *family planning* you will want to predict the new issues you will encounter. This final lifecycle phase is a great time to have a postmortem to talk about what improved, stayed the same, or worsened during or due to your persona effort.

Story from the field

LOOK BEYOND TODAY'S SUCCESSES TO TOMORROW'S POSSIBILITIES

—Rhiannon Gallagher, Thomson Micromedex

I know that the process, and the personas involved, created a very different user experience than the current version of these products, but we are now looking at ways to refine the personas further—to better handle more complex audiences and applications.

Whatever you do during this life phase, make an event of it. Take the opportunity to celebrate accomplishments as you prepare the team for the next project and the next set of personas.

The *lifetime achievement, reuse, and retirement* phase is the least understood of all of the persona life stages, in part because the persona method is fairly young. People are still just trying to figure out how to get started. We look forward to hearing from more practitioners on how you measure ROI, what becomes of your personas at the end of a project, and how you transition between one project and another as the persona cycle of life begins again.

Larry Constantine, IDSA
"Larry, the Relentless Revolutionary"

Roles: Designer, teacher, writer, inventor
Goals: Breakthrough products that enhance user performance and effectiveness.
Objectives: Help designers discover the power of abstraction.

Quote: "Don't make users the center of the design universe. To truly empower users, give them better tools!"

Larry Constantine is a designer and design methodologist who is happiest when he is pushing the boundaries of the possible. He likes to think of himself as a problem-solver who brings to his work a mix of engineering discipline and creative passion, blending bold departures from convention with dogged attention to detail. An award-winning designer, he prefers collaboration to isolation and is a true believer in the power of interdisciplinary teamwork. His forte is producing breakthrough designs under pressure, particularly for complex, critical applications, such as medical informatics, industrial automation, and programming tools, where dependable and efficient user performance is absolutely essential.

An innovative thinker who has been questioning received wisdom and challenging standard operating procedure since his student days at M.I.T., he has contributed original concepts and techniques in both software engineering and user interface design and holds numerous patents. Drawing on an eclectic background in management, psychotherapy, and software engineering, he has spent most of his career working in the borderlands between disciplines where the people and the technical issues commingle in messy combination.

Although he is a prolific author with over 150 papers and 17 books in several disciplines to his credit, Larry says he writes because things need to be said not because writing is either easy or fun. With Lucy Lockwood he wrote *Software for Use* (Addison-Wesley), winner of the Jolt Award for best book of 1999 and, with Ed Yourdon, wrote the software engineering classic, *Structured Design* (Prentice Hall), still on book shelves after 30 years in print. *Infinite Loop* (Miller Freeman), his anthology of science fiction by writers in the computer field, was called "quite simply one of the best anthologies to appear in recent years."

Larry unwinds by cooking up gourmet meals and stays in shape by keeping up with two young children—who sometimes even like what he cooks. In the office, he is Chief Scientist with Constantine & Lockwood, Ltd., the international design consultancy he co-founded, and in Academe, he is a Professor of Software Engineering at the University of Madeira, Portugal. He can be reached at lconstantine@foruse.com.

8

USERS, ROLES, AND PERSONAS

Larry Constantine, IDSA
Chief Scientist, Constantine & Lockwood, Ltd.

You cannot think outside the box when you are trying to represent a box on screen.

—Brian Hayes

To do effective design you need to understand your users and their needs. Although no credible school of thought in design would take serious exception, opinions vary considerably on how best to gain that understanding and how to record and communicate it once you do. Models of one form or another are the medium for the message in most design methods. Models function as intermediaries between the often ambiguous, overwhelmingly complex, reality of actual users and the more narrowly focused and specific needs of designers.

In usage-centered design (see the following Handy Detail), user roles capture and carry the essential understanding of users. User roles, one of the three core models of usage-centered design, are close cousins of personas but differ in a number of ways of potential significance to designers. In an attempt to sound a counterpoint to complement the main themes of the book, this chapter introduces user roles in the context of usage-centered design and explores the relationships between user roles and personas. Compared to typical personas as presented in this book and elsewhere, user roles are a more compact and concise representation that is more finely focused on issues with direct relevance to visual and interaction design. For these reasons, user role models can also be simpler and faster to develop. Although roles and personas can complement each other, user role models may under some circumstances and for some purposes also offer distinct advantages for designers.

The connections between user roles and personas are not entirely accidental, as usage-centered design and goal-directed design share similar (albeit not identical) philosophies of design and

Handy Detail

MAKE A DISTINCTION BETWEEN USERS AND USAGE

The distinction between usage-centered design and user-centered methods is, as the terms themselves suggest, a matter of emphasis rather than an absolute difference [Constantine and Lockwood 2002; Constantine 2004a]. Whereas user-centered design makes users per se the center of attention and seeks to promote user satisfaction with the entire user experience, usage-centered design is more narrowly focused on user performance and on the creation of tools for enhancing the efficiency and dependability of user performance. Although both approaches combine field study and user involvement with modeling, in usage-centered design the models are in the foreground with user studies and user involvement in the background. This difference in emphasis can lead to differences in outcomes. Indeed, it has been argued that in user-centered approaches over-dependence on user feedback and involvement can discourage innovation and contribute to unnecessarily conservative designs [Constantine 2004a].

The emphasis on models and modeling in usage-centered design evolved over time from the need for a design process that was on the one hand both easy to learn and practice and on the other predictably led to superior designs. From its inception, usage-centered design has been shaped by the goal of enabling ordinary user interface designers to produce extraordinary results via a process that is less dependent on the skill and artistry of a few exceptional designers than on consistent application of proven techniques. In the interest of streamlining and systematizing the design process, the models of usage-centered design are condensed, simplified, and sharply focused on those matters with greatest relevance to driving the design forward toward the best results. Because of this built-in efficiency, usage-centered design has proved particularly compatible with short development cycles and modern agile development methods [Constantine 2004b; Constantine and Lockwood 2002; Patton 2002, 2003]. At the same time, usage-centered design is a fully scalable approach that has been applied to projects ranging from upward of 50 developer-years [Windl 2002b] to massive multiyear efforts involving hundreds of developers.

a history of mutual influence [Constantine and Lockwood 1999; Cooper and Reimann 2003]. Both approaches are organized design processes that emphasize fitting the interaction design to the genuine needs of users. Although probably not as well known as goal-directed design, usage-centered design is a widely practiced alternative with a decade-long track record of producing innovation and breakthroughs in user performance, This is particularly true in its application to complex situations in which efficient and dependable user performance is critical, such as in medical informatics [Strope 2003] and industrial automation [Windl 2002b]. Usage-centered design has also been influential in shaping other methods, most notably user experience modeling [Heumann 2003] within the unified software development process [Jacobson et al. 1999; Kruchten et al. 2001], which borrows and adopts core usage-centered modeling techniques first introduced into object-oriented software engineering [Ahlqvist 1996], the methodological precursor of the unified process.

In usage-centered design, models guide the designer throughout the process. As represented schematically in Figure 8.1, the final visual and interaction design derives more or less directly from a content model or abstract prototype [Constantine 1998, 2003; Constantine et al. 2000] that models the content and organization of the user interface independently of its detailed appearance and behavior. The content model is itself based on a comprehensive task model expressed in the form of so-called essential use cases [Constantine 1995; Constantine and Lockwood 2001] or task cases. (See the following Case Study.) Task cases, in turn, support user roles as represented in the user role model. Even the initial investigation and data gathering, which provide the information and insight needed to build user roles and task models in the first place, are model-driven processes based on exploratory modeling [Windl 2002a]. In these processes, provisional modeling of user roles and tasks is used to generate questions and issues that help focus field work into a faster and more effective inquiry process.

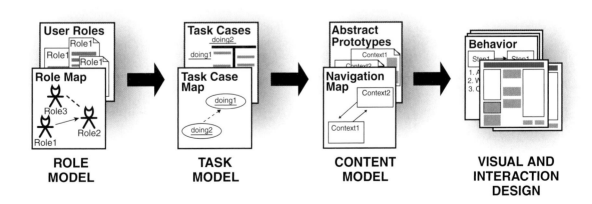

FIGURE 8.1: *Logical dependency of models in usage-centered design.*

Usage-centered design began its evolution without a name when, in 1993, the author and Lucy Lockwood formulated an improved form of use cases to help solve a user interface design problem. Use cases are one of the cornerstones of modern software engineering practice, but in their original form [Jacobson et al. 1992] were not well suited to user interface design, having too many built-in assumptions and premature decisions about the user interface being designed. The abstract, simplified form of use cases created for usage-centered design came to be known as task cases or essential use cases [Constantine 1994, 1995] and has become widely used in interaction design and requirements modeling [Constantine and Lockwood 2001; Cohn 2004]. The need to anchor the task model in an appropriate understanding of users quickly became apparent to those working with essential use cases. User roles [Constantine 1995] emerged as an elaboration of the software engineering construct of actors [Jacobson et al. 1992], which, like use cases, required adaptation to better suit the needs of user interface designers.

Use Case Essentials

Use cases, first introduced by Ivar Jacobson as the pivotal model in object-oriented software engineering [Jacobson et al. 1992], have become ubiquitous among software and Web-based applications developers but are less well known among interaction designers. A use case is simply a case of use represented in terms of the actions and variants performed by a system in interaction with external actors, which can be either users or other systems. As originally conceived, use cases were better suited for capturing systems-oriented requirements and guiding the software engineering process than for user interface design. A classic example often used to illustrate use cases is withdrawing cash from an ATM. The following is how one textbook [Kruchten 1999] represents this task.

Withdraw Money

The use case begins when the client inserts an ATM card. The system reads and validates the information on the card.

1. *System prompts for PIN. The client enters PIN. The system validates the PIN.*
2. *System asks which operation the client wishes to perform. Client selects "Cash withdrawal."*
3. *System requests amounts [sic]. Client enters amount.*
4. *System requests type. Client selects account type (checking, savings, credit).*
5. *The system communicates with the ATM network to validate account ID, PIN, and availability of the amount requested.*
6. *The system asks the client whether he or she wants a receipt. This step is performed only if there is paper left to print the receipt.*

7. *System asks the client to withdraw the card. Client withdraws card. (This is a security measure to ensure that Clients do not leave their cards in the machine.)*
8. *System dispenses the requested amount of cash.*
9. *System prints receipt.*
10. *The use case ends.*

As in this example, such conventional use cases contain many built-in assumptions about the design and implementation of the user interface. As such, they do not facilitate separating the essence of the user's task from issues of user interface design. Moreover, user interests can be lost among the systems-oriented details, as can be seen in this use case, where the user never actually takes the money withdrawn.

Lucy Lockwood and I developed essential use cases in 1993 as a technique better suited to driving visual and interaction design [Constantine 1994; Constantine 1995]. We drew on the concept of essential models introduced in a classic text on systems analysis [McMenamin and Palmer 1984]. An essential model is one expressed in abstract, simplified, and generalized form independent of explicit or implied assumptions about technology or implementation. Instead of user actions and system responses, essential use cases represent user intentions and system responsibilities. The same task of withdrawing cash when reduced to its essential form might look as shown in Figure 8.2.

Abstraction and independence of implementation enables the modeler to focus on the essence of the task from the perspective of the user without complicating the picture by jumping ahead into details of the visual and interaction design. In this example, the abstract essence of my task as a user is just to tell the system who I am, make a choice, and get my cash. Essential models challenge the designer both to understand the true nature of the problem from a user perspective and to provide a much simplified solution. Abstraction highlights opportunities for further exploration and for innovation,

Withdrawing cash from my account via ATM

User Intentions	System Responsibilities
	1. Request identification
2. Provide identification	3. Verify identification
	4. Offer choices
5. Choose	6. Give cash
7. Take cash	

FIGURE 8.2: *User intentions versus system responsibilities within a given task.*

such as making the choices that are offered reflect user intentions (e.g., withdrawing the usual amount) rather than bank policies and systems structures. If I have only one account and always withdraw $240 from it, I should not have to tell the ATM which account and reenter the amount on every withdrawal, for example.

Task models in the form of essential use cases have shown that they can help designers identify innovative solutions that better fit with genuine user needs [Constantine and Lockwood 1999, 2002; Strope 2003; Windl 2002b].

ROLES AND PERSONAS

Both user roles and personas are effective means for capturing and conveying basic understanding of users and for informing the design process, but they differ in important ways. Personas describe users, whereas user roles describe relationships between users and systems. Personas are figurative models rather than abstract models; that is, they are constructed to resemble real users, even down to photos, background information, and personal history. Verisimilitude most likely contributes to the popularity of personas. They sound like people you could know and, over the course of a project, can take on a reality that encourages empathy and facilitates thinking from the user perspective. What is more, many people find the creative process of constructing personas engaging and energizing. Personas are fun.

In contrast, user roles do not resemble real people, nor are they intended to. Roles are spartan abstractions narrowly focused on those aspects of the relationship most likely to be relevant to presentation and interaction design. Compared to personas, user roles are a more technical and formally structured model.

In the broadest sense, a user role has been defined as a collection of characteristic needs, interests, expectations, and behaviors in relation to a particular system [Wirfs-Brock 1993]. In its most compact form, the form now most commonly used, a user role is represented by its context, characteristics, and criteria; that is, the context in which it is played, the characteristics of its performance, and the criteria that must be met by the design to support successful performance of the role. Context includes the overall responsibilities of the role and the larger work and environmental context within which it is played. Characteristics refer to typical patterns of interaction, behaviors, and attitudes within the role. Criteria include any special functional facilities needed for effective support of the role, along with design objectives of particular importance to that role. Such criteria for effective support of a role are sometimes referred to as usability or user experience attributes. Checklists and templates have been developed from extensive experience to help designers think about the central issues and judge what is likely to be most relevant for user interface design. One example is shown in Figure 8.3. Others have been published elsewhere (e.g., [Constantine and Lockwood 1999]; and see *www.foruse.com/publications/templates*).

The most popular form of user role modeling is the card-based technique employed in agile usage-centered design [Constantine and Lockwood 2002; Constantine 2004b]. In this variant of usage-centered design, simplified models are constructed rapidly using ordinary index cards. The aim is to obtain a compact, easily created and managed model as quickly and painlessly as possible. The streamlined nature of the process makes it particularly suitable for software developed on tight schedules or using rapid iterative development—such as extreme programming [Jeffries et al. 2001]—but the techniques are equally effective in more formal engineering processes and have been employed with equal success even on very large and complex projects [Strope 2003; Windl 2002b].

An example of a user role card is shown in Figure 8.4, which describes the Pickup-Window-Ticket-Issuing role, one of a number of roles that might be played by ticket-window agents using ticketing software for a multi-venue arts center. As in this example, user roles are given names that highlight the core functional responsibilities of the role. A permanent identifier serves as a handle used to facilitate filing and tracking in large projects, particularly those in which tracing of requirements through the process may be required.

Each of the two views of users—roles and personas—has advantages and disadvantages. The very realism of personas that makes them so natural, appealing, and memorable means that the narrative can become complicated by potentially distracting details. In a fully fleshed-out persona, it can be difficult for the casual reader or even the well-informed designer to know what matters and what does not, what is important for user interface design and what is not, what is an accurate reflection of real user characteristics and what is mere concoction (particularly in that creative invention is encouraged in constructing personas). Although the proponents of personas would argue that properly constructed personas avoid distracting information when described with "just the right detail" suitably anchored in conscientiously collected and cataloged factoids, it might be difficult to rationalize the design relevance of such gratuitous details as that 9-year-old Tanner (an example of a persona introduced in Chapter 4) "rides his skateboard and bike, plays in the yard and nearby creek," "arrives home at 3:15," and "gives [his mother] a phone call" to reassure her.

Personas, because they are figurative models cast in concrete terms, can also easily cross the boundaries from user description into user interface design, thus subtly steering aspects of the user interface. Ogden, the "occasional user" of Chapter 4, is described as "wanting inline instructions, ToolTips," and "pre-populated fields with past values"—all of which might ultimately be good ideas but are clearly descriptions of specific solutions rather than of general features of a user perspective.

Constantine & Lockwood, Ltd.

User Role Checklist for Agile Modeling

A user role is a relationship with a system. Tasks are performed by users within roles. Tasks are about **what** users do, roles are about **how** they do it. The key to succinct characterization of user roles is **differential description**. How is this role not like other roles? What is distinctive or salient about it in comparison to other roles? Listed below are typical factors for consideration as potentially relevant and useful for characterizing a user role. They may or may not apply to a given role.

Context (within which role is played)

Is there anything special or distinguishing about this role in terms of

		Examples
❏ overall job, workflow, or **activity** within which role is played		"Follow-up of prior purchase."
❏ **physical environment** in which role is played		"Typical noisy office."
❏ **social situation** in which role is played		"With field research partners."
❏ **relationships** with indirect users in role		"Customer on telephone."
❏ **external sources** of information, such as paper forms, telephone, visual observation, in-person interview		"Phone review of packing slip."
❏ **background** of role incumbents in terms of training, education, or experience		"Cursory OTJ training."
❏ **system knowledge** expected or required within role		"Fully familiar from long use."
❏ **domain knowledge** expected or required within role		"No retail management knowledge."
❏ distribution of **user skills** in terms of novice, intermediate, or expert usage patterns		"Mostly perpetual novices."
❏ **required** or discretionary nature of role		"Part of regular job."

Left margin labels: ENVIRONMENT, INCUMBENTS

Characteristics (of performance of role)

Is there anything special or distinguishing about this role in terms of

❏ **orientation**, attitude, or emotional state typical within role	"Harried, under pressure."
❏ **frequency** with which role is played	"Less than once a month."
❏ **regularity** with which role is played	"Impulse buy after infomercial runs."
❏ **intensity** of interaction in the role	"Sporadic bursts of calls."
❏ **duration** of interaction in the role	"Full 8-hour shift."
❏ **complexity** of interaction in the role	"No-brainer."
❏ **predictability** of interaction in the role	"Scripted sales protocol."
❏ **volume** of information handled in the role	"Limited items available."
❏ **direction** of information flow to or from system	"Data entry."

Criteria (for support of role)

Are there any design objectives that are particularly important for this role, such as

❏ **ease of learning**	❏ enhancement of **proficiency**
❏ **retention** of learning	❏ user **convenience**
❏ **efficiency** of interaction	❏ **accuracy** of input
❏ **reliability** of interaction	❏ **clarity** of presentation
❏ **user satisfaction**	❏ **comprehensibility** of presentation

Are there any specific functions, features, facilities, capabilities, or content that are particularly important for this role to be performed effectively?

Contact: lconstantine@foruse.com   © 2004, Constantine & Lockwood, Ltd.

FIGURE 8.3: *Checklist of user role context, characteristics, and criteria.*

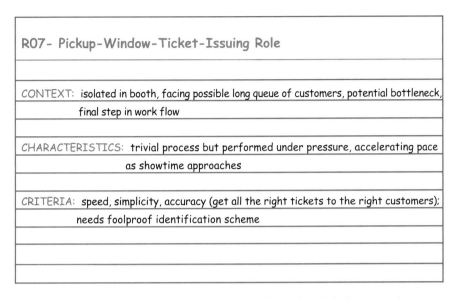

FIGURE 8.4: *Example of a condensed card-based model of a user role.*

In contrast with persona construction, the goal in user role modeling is to capture what is most salient in the most concise form. Differential description, in which each role is characterized primarily by those things that distinguish it from other roles, can also help to condense the information. Indeed, one of the operating principles of card-based modeling is that anything that does not fit on a single index card is too complicated and should be further simplified and condensed. In the interest of brevity, no attempt is made to create an interesting, engaging, or recognizable portrait of the user. The abbreviated description defining a user role is closest to the concepts of a skeleton or a résumé-style foundation document introduced in Chapter 4, but with the added twist of structuring and focusing the narrative in predefined categories deemed most likely to be of direct value in steering the design.

Portraying archetypal users as fully formed people may have a certain humanistic appeal, but users as people are complex and multifaceted, as is reflected in the elaborations needed to lend realism to personas. The relationships users have with any particular system are, by contrast, necessarily simpler and more limited. By focusing narrowly on the relationships between users and systems rather than on users more broadly, and by employing abstraction rather than elaboration, user role modeling offers designers a more precise model of users targeted more specifically to design needs.

Another difference in the two approaches is that the ideal in using personas is to fully describe a small number of archetypal users. User role modeling seeks to cover the playing field with a collection of interrelated but distinct descriptions of all of the various roles users can play in relation to the system. In most cases, then, user roles will outnumber personas but the personas will be more elaborate. Whereas descriptions of fully developed personas can often fill several pages, user roles are usually described on a single index card and seldom if ever take up more than a page.

MODELING USERS WITH ROLES

In our experience, an extra step or two that helps to reveal the broad territory or sharpen details can actually speed up the modeling process. We like to begin user modeling by mapping out all players in the story, even those who do not figure directly into shaping the user interface design. For this reason, we typically start with neither roles nor personas but with actors, the original software engineering concept that has become part of UML, the Unified Modeling Language [Fowler and Scott 1997] widely used in software engineering. In UML, actors are anything that interacts with a system.

To map out the complete context of use for a particular system and to define the requirements, you need to know all of the actors, whether or not these are people. Next, you need to distinguish user actors (people) from system actors—nonhuman systems that interact with the system. Because system actors interact through other interfaces, they are not strictly speaking part of the user interface design problem, though they are part of the problem to be solved. System actors imply requirements that shape internal and back-end design and become input to the software engineering and programming processes.

Among user actors, you need to be careful to distinguish direct user actors (who have hands-on interaction with the proposed system) from indirect (or mediated) user actors (who do not directly interact with a system but rather "use" it through intermediaries). These latter "off-stage" players are involved in the "story" of the system in use, but like extras in a movie they are really part of the context within which the interaction takes place. Often they are important stakeholders, so we do not want to forget them, but we do not normally need to model them in detail for effective usage-centered design. For example, in the ticket sales application introduced earlier, the telephone ticket agents are among the direct user actors, whereas the customers on the other end of the phone are indirect user actors whose participation is mediated by the telephone staff. We design the screens for the telephone ticket agent, the on-stage actor, but we must take into account the off-stage voice of the customer who is talking on the other end of the line. Such customers may not see the screen or touch the keyboard, but their presence as part of the context of the Telephone-Selling role can affect our design decisions. We may, for example, avoid audible prompts from the sales application to keep from distracting the customer or ticket agent or interrupting the conversation taking place over the telephone.

Exactly as on stage and screen, actors can play many different roles, so we need to identify all roles that all direct user actors can play and within which they will interact with the system. A user role, remember, is a relationship. Because the role focuses on the relationship of users with a system, it captures most closely what it is important for the designer to understand to develop the most effective visual and interaction design. Telephone ticket agents might have very different relationships to the sales support system depending on whether they are actually selling tickets or responding to telephone inquiries. We might call these the Telephone-Query-Handling role and the Telephone-Selling role. The Telephone-Query-Handling role, in turn, might be played by either regular telephone agents or by a supervisor.

Of course, actors can switch roles, so the agent on the telephone might switch among different relationships with the system even in the course of a single telephone call. An inquiry can turn into a sale, or a customer about to finalize a purchase might ask for more information. The multiple roles played by a particular actor help guide the design in terms of the flexibility and ease of navigation required to be built into the user interface.

The entire usage context can be summed up with a simple diagram called a context map, such as that shown in Figure 8.5. A rectangle represents the boundary of the system being designed.

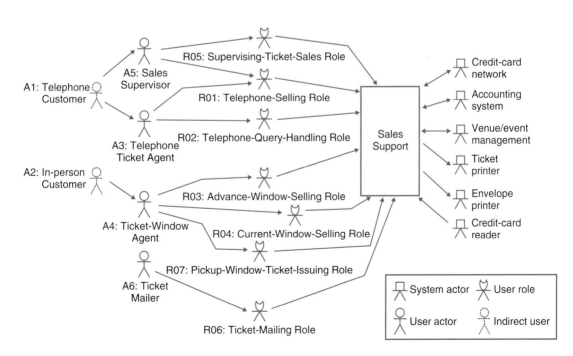

FIGURE 8.5: *Context map for the example of a ticketing application.*

System actors are shown as connected directly to that system boundary, as indeed they are. Direct actors—the on-stage players—are shown as connected to the system by way of the various roles they play. Indirect actors—the off-stage players—are shown as connected to direct actors, who serve as intermediaries through whom indirect actors are involved with the system.

For a given application, the roles in a complete catalog of user roles are typically not independent of one another. Some roles, for example, are best thought of as specialized variants of others, and some may be combinations that include two or more other roles. This interdependence makes it possible to map all roles without a lot of repetition. For the ticketing application, the Supervising-Telephone-Sales role, for instance, might be described as a specialized version of a Telephone-Selling role—characterized by additional assumptions about the incumbent, the user playing the role, and special needs in terms of functional support. Whereas the Telephone-Selling role may require only moderate training and little domain knowledge regarding the business of an arts performance center, the Supervising-Telephone-Sales role assumes greater experience and significant domain knowledge. The Supervising-Telephone-Sales role adds to the criteria the need for support of special supervisory functions, such as overriding the conditions of sale or releasing seats held for VIPs.

For complex problems, the relationships among user roles can be represented diagrammatically in a separate user role map, such as that shown in Figure 8.6. In addition to specialization and inclusion, user roles may have a workflow relationship in which one role depends on the prior performance of another. For instance, the Pickup-Window-Ticket-Issuing role in the current example is said to be preceded by the Telephone-Selling role, as shown in Figure 8.6.

Although it is useful to understand all roles users can play in relation to a system, not all roles are regarded as equally important. Some roles will be played more frequently than others and will account for a greater portion of the use of the system. Some roles may be more important than others for the practical success of a system. For example, in the ticket sales application telephone selling might happen every day, whereas ticket windows might be staffed only at performance times over the weekend. Nevertheless, the Current-Window-Selling role, which is responsible for in-person sales of tickets for today's performances, is very important for the business success of the ticketing application.

In usage-centered design, user roles are usually ranked by anticipated frequency and by business importance. The agile modeling technique for making these rankings is to sort index cards representing the roles into order [Constantine and Lockwood 2002]. On the basis of the combination of these two potentially different views of priority, a small subset of roles is distinguished as "focal" roles. Focal roles serve as a central focus for the rest of the design process, but not to the exclusion of other user roles. For the ticket-selling application, the card-sorting exercise might select the Telephone-Selling role, Current-Window-Selling role,

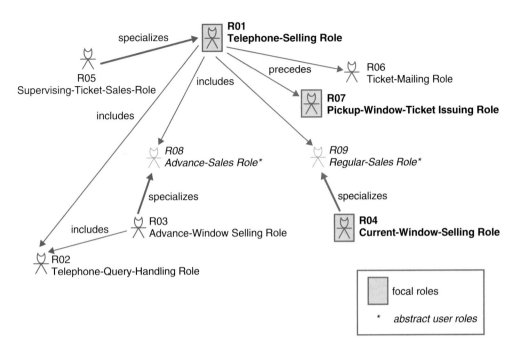

FIGURE 8.6: *User role map for the example of a ticketing application.*

and Pickup-Window-Ticket-Issuing role as focal roles. Focal roles are like primary personas in that they are recognized as particularly important for a successful design.

MODELING USER TASKS

Ultimately, the user interface must be designed to enable users to do things, which requires an understanding of users or the roles they play and a thorough understanding of the tasks users must be able to accomplish in performing those roles. Indeed, task modeling is the very core of usage-centered design in regard to its focus on user performance. Tasks are modeled with task cases, a form of the use cases introduced in object-oriented design [Jacobson et al. 1992]. A task case represents a single discrete intention carried out by a user in some role. Task cases are also called essential use cases because they are stripped down to the barest essentials of the task. Each task case is expressed as a dialogue in which user intentions and system responsibilities are abstract, simplified, and stripped of all assumptions about technology or implementation. This form of description is intended to get closer to the essence of what the task is really about from the perspective of the user in a role and to avoid making unintended or premature assumptions about the form of the user interface to be designed.

T09- issuing ticket(s) held for pickup	
USER INTENTION	SYSTEM RESPONSIBILITY
	1. ask for customer identification
2. give customer identification	
	3. give confirming details of associated ticket(s)
4. confirm tickets wanted	
	5. issue ticket(s) and inform user
6. take tickets (to give to customer)	

FIGURE 8.7: *Example of a task case expressed in essential form.*

For example, in support of the Pickup-Window-Ticket-Issuing role the task case issuing ticket(s) held for pickup might be defined as shown in Figure 8.7. Several things are worth noting about this example and about task cases in general. Unlike use cases, which are constrained always to begin with a user action, task cases can begin with a system responsibility. As shown in this example, task cases are simplified in part by focusing on the "happy case" [Cockburn 2001], the normal course of interaction in which everything goes well (i.e., the identification is valid, the desired tickets are found, and so forth). The rationale for temporarily hiding or ignoring the alternatives and exceptions is to promote an interface organized around the primary purposes as viewed from the user in a role more than around the numerous less likely alternatives and exceptions that tend to dominate in the minds of programmers.

In contrast to scenarios, which are used in goal-directed design and some other design approaches, task cases represent small pieces of the performance of a user role rather than a relatively large story that has been elaborated with extra details to make it seem real and believable. Instead, as with user roles the language is spare and abstract. This leaves open many alternative solutions for the designer to choose among. The same task case can apply whether the ticket issuer depends on credit-card verification or types the user name or scans a bar-code-imprinted confirmation form.

Task cases are identified based on the user role model in conjunction with whatever else is known about the system being designed. Many task cases follow more or less directly from the definition of roles. Among the defining criteria for the Supervising-Ticket-Sales role referred to earlier is the need to be able to override the normal selling price or to sell specially reserved seats, which leads to formulating the task cases <u>selling tickets at discounted/special prices</u> and <u>selling tickets for special seats</u>. Some task cases are implied by the purpose and overall responsibilities of a role. Successful performance of the Telephone-Selling role requires <u>selling tickets for seats for performances</u>. The Telephone-Query-Handling role requires such task cases as <u>reviewing the program/details for an event/performance</u> and <u>selecting events/performances of possible interest</u>. The Pickup-Window-Ticket Issuing role obviously requires <u>issuing tickets held for pickup</u>. Other task cases may be based on requirements that are not necessarily reflected directly in the user role model. For example, requirements specifications or other artifacts might have to be reviewed to identify the need for <u>releasing donated seats for resale</u>.

The complete task model is expressed by the narrative bodies of all individual task cases along with a task case map similar to a user role map but showing the interrelationships among task cases. The task case model can be checked against the user role model to verify that all user roles can be fully performed with the identified task cases and that every task case is genuinely needed for the performance of one or more roles. The objective is to be truly comprehensive, to cover all tasks needed to fully perform all identified roles. In principle it might seem that a complete task model is an unobtainable ideal, but in practice we have found that with well-timed and thoughtful reviews along the way it is rare to discover missing task needs late in the game. This has held true even for very large and complex applications, such as the Siemens STEP 7 Lite system [Windl 2002b], a specialized integrated development environment for automation programming that is roughly as complex as Visual Basic. In support of 25 user roles, 342 task cases were identified, which accounted for all of the functionality needed within the system.

FROM ABSTRACT TASKS TO CONCRETE INTERFACES

Many designers develop paper prototypes or page mock-ups based directly on what they understand from scenarios or other task-oriented models. In usage-centered design, content models or abstract prototypes serve as a bridge between task models and user interface designs. I am using the term *user interface design* here to cover the design of every aspect of the interface that mediates between users and systems. This includes the visual or presentation design and interaction design, by which I mean the specification of the behavior of the user interface and the means by which users interact with it.

Abstract prototypes can be distinguished from the figurative prototypes used by most designers. The latter are typically expressed as mock-ups or paper prototypes intended to look like (or more or less resemble) real user interfaces, even if only as rough sketches. Abstract prototypes are not intended to look like the real thing, but instead embody the function and organization of user interfaces divorced from details of appearance and behavior. In this way the complex and somewhat mysterious process of designing a user interface to fit the task needs of users can be broken down into two simpler and better understood steps. The content and organization of the user interface can be derived more or less directly from a well-formed task case model, and a good visual and interaction design can in turn be developed straightforwardly based on the content and organization expressed in an abstract prototype—particularly one expressed in standard form using canonical abstract components [Constantine 2003; Constantine et al. 2001].

Canonical abstract prototypes are a highly structured and standardized form of wireframe schematic that enable designers to resolve problems in layout and organization apart from details of presentation and interaction design. They use a canonical or standardized collection of abstract user interface components to model the abstract functions of the user interface as viewed from the perspective of the user. An example of a draft abstract prototype for one portion of the telephone-ticketing application is shown in Figure 8.8. For more information on abstract prototyping and canonical abstract prototypes, see the references cited above.

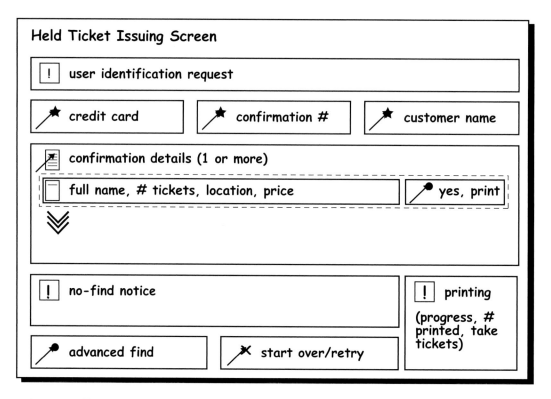

FIGURE 8.8: *Abstract prototype for ticket-issuing user interface using canonical abstract components.*

Elements of the user role model enter again in developing the final user interface design. The overall structure of a well-designed user interface that fits closely with user needs can be thought of as an elaboration of the structure of the user role model and the structure of the task model that supports it. User roles provide direct architectural guidance such as rarely can be derived from personas, in that all the parts of the interface that provide functions or information in support of a single role must form a closely interconnected set. For efficient user performance, roles that can be played by the same actor who can switch between them must be supported by parts of the user interface within easy reach of each other. Similarly, closely connected task cases must be supported together on the user interface. Conversely, roles that have little or no connection or are played by different actors can be supported through more or less distinct and separated parts of the user interface.

Although such rules may seem rather obvious, in very large and complex systems the architectural guidance provided by the user role model and the task case map are invaluable and can help designers avoid subtle mistakes that could otherwise lead to expensive changes in organization late in development. The user role model is constructed to cover all supported roles played by users, and the task case model is constructed to cover all tasks needed to support those roles. These conditions make it easier to assert that a design is complete than in a situation in which the design is based on a handful of personas or a few scenarios that are representative but not exhaustive. The user role and task models are easily validated through review by users, stakeholders, and independent auditors, and they can be cross checked using techniques such as the role support matrix [Constantine 2001]. Again, even on very large systems, it is the case that missing features or functions are rare with usage-centered designs based on full role and task modeling.

Details of the visual and interaction design, too, are shaped by insight captured in the user role model. For example, the description of the Pickup-Window-Ticket-Issuing role favors an absolutely mechanical, foolproof design in which the normal flow of interaction is trivial and the exceptions are all covered and handled in the most expeditious manner. If, for example, the customer is identified by name and the system finds more than one match, the screen can prompt the user to request a first name or ask whether the customer knows the price or seat section or whatever bit of information distinguishes the ticket instances found by the system. If the system is unable to find the tickets or there is some other problem, the user can be prompted to say, "I'm sorry, but the system is having some problem with your tickets. If you could step over to the customer service desk to your right, someone there will be able to help you." In this way, the "possible long queue of customers" referred to in the context of the role is not exacerbated.

BOTH/AND MODELING

It is possible to have it both ways—to get the precision and parsimony offered by user roles along with the richness and realism of personas—by combining them in the right way. In our experience, reinforced by that of numerous clients and the even more numerous practitioners we have trained, the disciplined abstraction of user roles make them better as the primary model for driving usage-centered design. Once a user role model covering the full range of user roles is available, it is possible to develop personas corresponding to selected roles—particularly the focal roles (that is, those most common and most important to the success of the design).

As mentioned previously, user roles are (in order to identify focal roles) ranked in terms of the anticipated frequency with which they will be played and their relative importance to the business and practical success of the system or application being designed. In a sense, focal roles are like lead roles that take center stage in driving the design to a conclusion, whereas supporting roles have significant but less central influence.

This is where personas enter the scene. For the focal user roles, one or more personas might be constructed. By waiting until all roles have been cataloged and the most frequent and important singled out for special attention, the designer can be more confident about which users to represent with personas. Personas enable us to capture the essence of the most important user roles by fleshing out roles with those elaborations that lend verisimilitude to the description. Because personas seem more "real" and are typically more recognizable than user roles, they can sometimes be more effective for engaging and drawing the attention of designers and developers.

Personas can thus become the personification of roles. One might say that a persona is about character, whereas a role is about characteristics. Characteristics focus designer attention, and character promotes identification. For the ticketing application, we might construct a couple of personas: one representing the archetypal user taking on both the Telephone-Selling and Telephone-Query-Handling roles and one for the Pickup-Window-Ticket-Issuing role.

In the final analysis, however, interaction design is about the relationship between a user and a system, which is precisely what user roles emphasize. Although other representations or user models may imply or include aspects of it, the user role model captures and features this relationship front and center in terms that are most relevant to user interface and interaction design. The combination of user roles with personas can offer designers a powerful modeling approach that is both engaging and precisely focused.

IN PRACTICE

User role modeling played a significant part in one Web design project for a network of specialty book clubs. After conducting an expert usability evaluation of the existing Web site, Constantine & Lockwood, Ltd., was retained to do a complete usage-centered redesign of the combined portal and individual club sites.

The project was kicked off with a half-day collaborative modeling workshop involving 13 participants, including developers, managers, marketing staff, and user representatives. The group began by building consensus on a vision and business priorities for the project. A list of user roles was brainstormed and the 19 user roles identified were each briefly described. The roles were then individually ranked by participants on expected frequency and business importance, and the combined rankings were used to select six roles (as follows) as focal, listed from highest to lowest ranked.

1. Confirmed-Current-Member role
2. Fence-Sitting-Current-Member role
3. Potential-New-Member role
4. Deep-and-Narrow-Information Seeker role
5. Specific-Information-Seeker role
6. Former-Member role

The prioritization and discussion of user roles yielded some unanticipated conclusions and useful insights. For example, although public relations and dealings with the media were initially considered in forming the business vision for the new site, in the context of careful comparison of frequency and business importance in relation to other roles the noncustomer roles dropped to the bottom of the list. Such modeling decisions about user roles ultimately translated directly into specific design decisions, such as using easily recognized home-page links to divert noncustomers, such as the press, to another site.

Another insight was the significance of former and ambivalent book club members for the business success of the remodeled site. The importance of retaining "fence-sitting" members and for winning back former members emerged as particularly important, suggesting the possibility of providing simple ways for former members to renew membership and making it easier for marginal participants to retain membership with minimal hassle. The importance of engaging both new and former members led to a navigation architecture in which the visitor could join a club from anywhere in the site, not just from the home page or a few "gateway" pages, which was the case in the previous design and on competitor sites.

In Figure 8.9 is a reconstructed depiction of the Fence-Sitting-Current-Member role. In principle, anything that supports members supports this role. One could say that a well-designed site that allows members to do what they want without annoyance or inconvenience is what this role needs. However, the last line of the role description suggests that there is more to the story. The design should make it possible to discontinue membership online, as this gives the company one last chance to retain the member. Online cancellation could also dissuade an ambivalent customer from simply dropping out through the expedient of refusing delivery of regular monthly selections, a costly outcome for the club. However, before the member quits,

R02- Fence-Sitting-Current-Member Role
CONTEXT: has established connection with club, possibly familiar with site; may be trying to quit or looking for reasons to either continue or bail out
CHARACTERISTICS: ambivalent or skeptical attitude; casual, unpredictable behavior; unlikely to be in role more than once or often
CRITERIA: maximal odds of good experience, minimal bad; easy, convenient operation; offer easy alternatives to quitting

FIGURE 8.9: *One user role for the book club Web site.*

the site can offer alternatives such as temporary suspension of membership for a few months or switching to the so-called positive-response option. Incentives could be offered, such as a reminder that the member would earn a free book after purchasing just one more selection.

Rather than create an exhaustive task model, the workshop focused initially on task cases needed for support of the six focal roles. The resulting list of 24 task cases was rank ordered independently by participants on expected frequency of occurrence, on importance to customers, and on importance for business success. The rankings were compared and combined to identify focal task cases, five of which were then defined in full by the group. These included the following, ranked highest priority first.

1. Joining a club
2. Ordering books
3. Browsing books by category, title, etc.
4. Viewing book-title descriptions
5. Finding books by criteria of interest

Over the eight-week project, content models and a navigation map for the site were developed by the designer and validated by the client. Then the visual and interaction design—in the form of annotated page mock-ups—was completed, inspected and refined, validated with users, and delivered to enthusiastic reception from the client. However, owing to a series of contemporaneous acquisitions and mergers in which IT functions were shifted and reorganized, the design was never implemented in its entirety, although elements and ideas from it were eventually incorporated into various Web sites that came under the newly merged corporate empire.

Although personas were not used in this project, it seems clear that quite a few might be needed to cover the members of clubs for interests as diverse as mystery and crime fiction, gardening, and computers and information science. Nevertheless, it certainly would have been possible to construct personas corresponding to focal roles, such as the Confirmed-Current-Member role or the Fence-Sitting-Current-Member role. I have little doubt that this would have appealed to the client, and it most likely would have helped make users more vivid to developers. For design purposes, however, the user roles themselves captured enough about what was essential in the relationships with the Web site to enable credible task modeling and an informed site design.

PERSONAS OR NOT

In my own work, the choice of building personas or not is made on a project-by-project basis, but the guiding principle in usage-centered design is always to model only those things for which demonstrable payoff justifies the added effort (and only to the extent payoff justifies the effort). In some cases, reification of abstract constructs is more than worth the effort and the complexities it introduces. For designers more comfortable in a world of concrete and recognizable objects than in one of abstractions, in efforts where empathetic identification with users is lacking and deemed vital, or in projects gifted with ample resources and generous timetables, there seems little reason not to augment user role models with personas. On the other hand, where time is short, resources are few, and designers are perfectly happy with succinct abstractions, user roles are most likely more than enough.

Alan Cooper, originator of the modern concept of personas, has argued that it is better to design for one user, one "real" user, than to try to be all things to all users. User role modeling, however, offers a compact way of capturing all of the essential variants in how various users can and will relate to a new system. The designer does not have to understand everything about every user to understand the essentials of those relationships.

Whitney Quesenbery
"Whitney the Storyteller"

Roles: Designer, mentor, user analyst

Goals: User centered design for every product, Web site and application

Objectives: Get everyone to listen to the stories that people tell, and use them in their designs

"The computer screen is just a very small stage"

Whitney Quesenbery is a user interface designer, design process consultant, and usability specialist with a passion for clear communication. As the principal consultant for Whitney Interactive Design (wqusability.com) she works with large and small companies to develop usable Web sites and applications. She enjoys learning how people around the world work with technology and hearing their stories.

The techniques of usability are one of her interests, and she has worked on standards and methodologies more than she cares to admit. As a result, she's spent many weekends working on articles and presentations and arguing the fine points on industry forums. She's proud that one of her articles won an award as an STC Outstanding Journal Article, and that her chapter "Dimensions of Usability" in *Content and Complexity* turns up on so many course reading lists.

An active volunteer, Whitney is President of the Usability Professionals' Association (UPA), on the Executive Council for UXnet, and manages a popular usability Web site at http://www.stcsig.org/usability. As director of the UPA Voting and Usability Project and a member of the Advisory Committee for the Elections Assistance Commission, she works to ensure the usability of voting systems.

Before she was seduced by a little beige computer into software, usability, and interface design, Whitney was a theatrical lighting designer on and off Broadway, learning about storytelling from some of the masters. The lessons from the theatre stay with her in creating user experiences. She can be reached at whitneyq@wqusability.com.

9

STORYTELLING AND NARRATIVE

Whitney Quesenbery, Whitney Interactive Design

PERSONAS WORK BECAUSE THEY TELL STORIES

A human being is nothing but a story with a skin around it.

—Fred Allen

Storytelling does not just mean the once-upon-a-time of fairy tales or the suspended disbelief of scary ghost stories. Stories are a way of explaining the real people personas are based on. In fact, it is storytelling that makes personas work, by distilling information and analysis into a character and a narrative that ignite the imagination and bring the personas to life. Personas and their stories represent a shorthand by which we can convey the world of user research discovery to everyone on the team.

If personas are the nouns, stories add the verbs, showing the personas in action over time with goals and behavior–a beginning, middle, and end. Storytelling is used throughout the persona life cycle, adding depth to the characters and connecting them to the context of the project. Every time we create a scenario or a short anecdote to imagine how our persona might interact with our product, we are creating a story that shows the persona in action and that helps us to understand that persona and how to better design for him or her.

An Experiment

DOES YOUR BRAIN MAKE UP STORIES?

Most people (even many who work on the brain) assume that what you see is pretty much what your eye sees and reports to your brain. Actually, your brain adds very substantially to the report it gets from your eye, so that a lot of what you see is actually "made up" by the brain. There is a blind spot (actually two, one for each eye), a place pretty much in the middle of what you can see where you can't see.

Instead of a big hole in the middle of our vision, the brain fills in the gap. "What you see is something the brain is making up, since the eye isn't actually telling the brain anything at all about that particular part of the picture."

If you want to see this for yourself, there is a simple experiment described on the Serendip Web site. http://serendip.brynmawr.edu/bb/blindspot1.html

Paul Grobstein, Serendip

Let's start by looking at why storytelling is such a powerful tool in our human culture, including business. We will then examine the elements that make up a story, and end with some ways of creating good stories around personas.

WE ARE WIRED FOR STORYTELLING

All human beings have an innate need to hear and tell stories and to have a story to live by.

—Harvey Cox

Stories are a very old form of communication–so old that we are wired to be receptive to learning from stories. Movies, books, TV, and even the gossip around the water cooler are all part of this basic aspect of being human. As Walt Disney imagineer Bran Ferren puts it, "Most people function in a storytelling mode. It is the way we communicate ideas richly, as well as how we structure our thoughts."

Bryn Mawr College neurobiology professor Paul Grobstein describes the brain as a "semi-autonomous, evolving, creative agent" and paints a picture of the nervous system and brain as "an exploratory device, one that is continually building and revising models of the world by generating outputs and observing the resulting inputs" [Grobstein 2002].

The concept of being hardwired for storytelling is found in the work of many people, from business storytelling expert Steve Denning to novelist Jonathan Franzen. In an article about using stories for teaching, The Turner Learning Web site says that "neuroscience is discovering that the brain is wired to organize, retain and access information *through story*." They go on to suggest that this means that stories are an effective way of teaching—that they allow students to better "remember what is taught, access that information, and apply it more readily." When we use personas and create stories for them, we tap into this deep core of human cognitive process.

SHARED STORIES CREATE CULTURE

Everyone is necessarily the hero of his own life story.

—John Barth

FIGURE 9.1: *This storyteller figure is a modern variation of a long tradition of Pueblo pottery figures, first created by Cochiti Pueblo artist Helen Cordero. They capture the sense of story as a timeless art form. [Michaelis (2004)] (Helen Cordero,"The First Storyteller," 1964 from the Girard Collection, Museum of International Folk Art (Santa Fe, NM)) (Photo by Michel Monteaux. Reprinted with permission.)*

Every culture has its stories, whether you call them folktales, myths, urban legends, or even history. One way of looking at a culture is as a group of people who share a set of stories. Some stories have survived intact for thousands of years. Epics such as *Beowulf*, *The Labors of Hercules*, *The Mahabarata*, *The Odyssey* and others are still a rich part of our culture. Other stories have been told and retold, recast to echo each culture in which they appear (see Figure 9.1). Although the details may change, the outline and strong metaphors of the story are easily recognizable. There are folktales from Europe and the Middle East, such as Briar Rose (or Sleeping Beauty), Hansel and Gretel, or Baba Yaga, which appear in hundreds of variations.

People who study stories and culture believe that there are commonalities of pattern among important types of stories. Joseph Campbell (author of *The Hero with a Thousand Faces*), for example, believed that there is a single pattern for one type of story—the heroic journey—and that all cultures share this pattern. Homer's *Odyssey* may be one version of a heroic journey, but every story of a person overcoming obstacles (and having adventures) on their way to a goal evokes this archetype. The *Odyssey* was retold in the recent movie *O Brother, Where Art Thou?* In both book and movie form, *The Lord of the Rings* is another modern telling of the story of a reluctant hero.

Still other stories evolve and change over time. They keep their basic narrative, but change their message as they travel between cultures or across time. The book *Little Red Riding Hood Uncloaked* traces the evolution of this familiar story and how it has been adapted from the original fable of sexual morals in the sixteenth-century court to a modern lesson of self-reliance in a dangerous world. Along the way, it has become a cultural icon strong enough that any image of a red cloak, hat, or hood is enough to evoke the story (as shown in Figure 9.2).

FIGURE 9.2: *These four illustrations–from the original story by Perrault in 1867 to a modern comic book, record album cover, and costume–show the enduring power of Little Red Riding Hood as a character: (a) illustration from Les Contes de Perrault, dessins par Gustave Dore, Paris, J. Hetzel, 1867, (b) cover of Classics Illustrated junior comic book downloaded from http://ksacomics.com/cj/n/510.htm (Copyright © 2004 First Classics, Inc. All rights reserved. Reprinted with permission.), (c) cover of "Sam the Sham and the Pharaohs" album downloaded from www.robert-kruse.com/samudio/pages/albums.html (courtesy of MGM records/ United Artists Corporation), (d) adult costume downloaded from www.lovethosegifts.com/prod. itml/icOid/7626.*

This ability for just a few details to stand in for an entire story and its characters is part of what makes personas work. Like characters in myths and folktales, personas are archetypes, standing in for a type or group of people. With the right details and well-chosen stories, you can create the outline of an entire life history, personal attitudes, and motivations.

STORIES ARE NOT JUST FOR BEDTIME

It is all storytelling, you know. That is what journalism is all about.

—Tom Brokaw

It is easy to dismiss stories as fiction, something just for amusement or art, just a little bit of "once upon a time." Even if you take stories seriously as an underlying cultural motif, it can be difficult to see how they apply to business. But as you will see, stories are just as powerful within a business context, serving the same purpose of communicating key elements of the culture as they do in the larger society. These stories are different from those created for entertainment, but they draw on the same traditions and power.

Knowledge management and corporate communication intersected when people such as Steve Denning and John Seeley Brown saw storytelling as a way of organizing and transmitting information. They also focused on its value as a catalyst for corporate change. A research group at IBM called this "knowledge socialization" as they focused on ways in which the strength of storytelling can be used to enable informal knowledge transfer. Three of the roles stories play in an organizational setting also explain why the story of a persona is such a powerful tool: stories allow you to (1) communicate culture, (2) organize and transmit information, and (3) explore new ideas.

Stories communicate culture

If stories are part of being human, our stories show us (and tell others) who we are. In an organization, stories create a shared history and communicate the values or issues important to the company.

Peg Neuhauser, who writes about storytelling in corporate culture in *Corporate Legends and Lore*, talks about the power of storytelling as a management tool and as a means of communicating culture and preserving a corporate history. These stories serve many purposes. They may share an event that makes people proud of their organization, help the group "let off steam," or identify the values of the group.

Neuhauser points out that any "series of events can be told as a positive story or a negative story. It all depends on the telling" [Neuhauser 1993]. Neuhauser stresses the importance of constructing a story so that people learn something from hearing it. This is the "spin" you put on a story; the point of view it communicates. For example, a story about someone having trouble using a piece of software could be about how dumb users are, or it could be about how they think differently about a task. A story does not need to have a happy ending to be one that communicates well. A good story for a persona is one that helps illustrate the persona's point of view.

Example

SAME PROBLEM, TWO CULTURES

Which story sounds like your corporate culture? Which would you like to be part of?

"Chris was leading a team design session on a part of new installation that was giving people trouble. After several hours, the team gave up, deciding that this was something that users would just have to learn to do. 'If they want to use computers, they'll just have to figure it out.'"
or
"Jason took his third call in one day from customers having trouble installing the new product. He realized that there was an easier way to explain it, and added a note to the service knowledge base.
He also sent a note to the product team, so they would know about the problem, and could make a change in the next release."

Stories organize and transmit information

One of the goals of knowledge management is to capture the information spread around the organization and make it available in a form everyone can use. There are two problems knowledge managers encounter. The first is collecting information. It is notoriously difficult to get people to contribute to knowledge management systems. The work of thinking through the lesson learned, writing it down, and fitting it into the online format becomes an extra task that is often the one put off until later. But most people tell stories naturally, especially when they are the "hero" of the story.

John Seely Brown and Paul Duguid write about this in *The Social Life of Information* [Brown and Duguid 2000], where they describe how the Xerox copier field service staff would meet at local restaurants for breakfast or after work. These sessions served a social purpose, but they also allowed the technicians to swap stories about problems they had encountered—and their solutions. Through these stories, they shared complex technical information about the difficulties of their work in a memorable way.

The second problem the knowledge manager encounters is how to make these stories available to a larger audience. The copier repair stories spread easily because they were valuable to other field service technicians. The difference between a story and a simple procedure is that the story includes context. When the reader can identify with that context, it makes it easier to know whether the story is the right answer to a problem and how to make use of the information.

Story from the field

STORIES MAKE DETAILS VIVID

This is a story from a user research session on how people look for health information online. When we asked the participant (let's call her Alicia) how she found Web sites to visit, this is what happened:

"Alicia picked up her handbag from the chair, opened it and pulled out a wad of paper. There were magazine and newspaper clippings, little note papers and wrappers with notes written on them. She said, 'My girlfriends and I are working on this together. We find these Web things—what do you call them? Earls?—everywhere and we get together to try them out. We're kind of teaching each other. It's fun.'"

We used this story to illustrate a point in our report about how the people we talked to browsed the Web with someone else. It made our point more memorable than if the report just said, "Seventy-five percent of our participants reported co-browsing activities with family members or other friends."

Another reason stories are a good way of transmitting information is that they are easy to remember and retell. (That they may add just a bit of fun to dry material does not hurt either.) When people need to know exact details, they can be included along with the story, but it is the story that makes the core information memorable by providing a context and a narrative. The message often survives long after the data has disappeared, and even if the exact story is changed or forgotten.

A good story about a persona uses details from the data you gathered and weaves them into a compelling and memorable narrative. The use of specific details grounds the narrative in a believable reality, but it is the message—the point you want the team to remember—that makes the story a useful part of the design process.

Stories explore new ideas

Stories can look back to preserve and explain the past, but they can also look forward. When you are trying to instigate change, the most difficult part can be getting everyone to see that things really can be different. Stories are a great way of exploring alternative visions of a future that does not yet exist.

When you present a new idea as a story you change the dynamic of the discussion from detailed technical discussion to one that looks at the core of the idea. Everyone in the discussion is encouraged to think about how they can contribute to making a vision come true, instead of seeing how many flaws they can find in the proposal.

Stories from the field

STORIES OPEN UP THE IMAGINATION

Saul Carliner, an expert in instructional design, created a workshop exercise that shows the power of stories in bringing ideas to life. He divided the group into small work teams and handed out project briefs. The assignment was to create a conceptual design for the online help for a new class registration system. Half of the groups were bogged down in the outline of the help file, while the other half had imaginative ideas that focused on the different people who would use the tool. When the groups swapped project briefs, they understood immediately what had happened. The first groups had been given a list of key functionality and three-line user definitions. The others had short character descriptions and stories illustrating different ways users might register for classes.

The moral of this story? Put stories into your design process and get more imaginative designs as the result.

Saul Carliner, *Presentation at STC 2003*

Video Guy :30

Jimmy adjusts himself into a more comfortable position as camera dollies back ...

V.O. (mother cont.):
...have you seen it?

5A

... revealing TU issues piled up under the cushions.

5B

Jimmy considers his situation.

ANNCR V.O.:
Hiding something ...

6

Over the shoulder shot of papers sticking out from under sofa cushions

... from your mommy?

7

2

FIGURE 9.3: *Commercial film storyboards translate the script into visual frames, showing a sketched version of a "working plot line." (Storyboard by Luis Castillo, image courtesy of Leigh Devine.)*

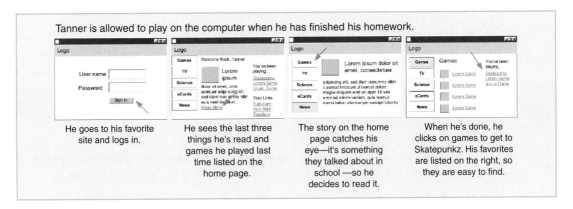

Tanner is allowed to play on the computer when he has finished his homework.

| He goes to his favorite site and logs in. | He sees the last three things he's read and games he played last time listed on the home page. | The story on the home page catches his eye—it's something they talked about in school —so he decides to read it. | When he's done, he clicks on games to get to Skatepunkz. His favorites are listed on the right, so they are easy to find. |

FIGURE 9.4: *Storyboards for software show how the persona (and eventual users) might interact with the program.*

In his article "Design as Storytelling," Tom Erickson [1996] defines a good story as one in which "people have been engaged, drawn into discussion of ideas about which–before the story–they would have had nothing to say."

In filmmaking, storyboards (see Figure 9.3) are used to map out the details of the movie and serve as a transition from the words of the script to the multimedia of the finished film.

Persona stories can be illustrated with early design sketches in a sort of storyboard (see Figure 9.4). This combination of narrative and visual presentation can help communicate a new idea, even in an early, evocative form.

Inspiration

STORIES HELP US IMAGINE

Stories have the felicitous capacity of capturing exactly those elements that formal decision methods leave out. Logic tries to generalize, to strip the decision making from the specific context, to remove it from subjective emotions. Stories capture the context, capture the emotions. Logic generalizes, stories particularize. Logic allows one to form a detached, global judgement; story-telling allows one to take the personal point of view, to understand the particular impact the decision is apt to have on the people who will be affected by it.

—**Don Norman,** *Things That Make Us Smart [1994, p. 129]*

Most techniques for user and task analysis use logical methods to carefully look at each detail of a problem. A Design Map is a detailed walkthrough of a specific scenario. Stories, in contrast, focus on the people and the situation. The story that kicks off a Design Map provides the persona and the starting context, and might include the general shape of the design solution from the point of view of the persona. We will examine the difference between scenarios and stories further as we look at how to create a good story. All three uses of corporate storytelling relate directly to personas.

- As part of communicating culture, personas' stories share their cultural history, giving them a context and a point of view communicated in a highly efficient way.
- When we need to organize and transmit information, personas are a good way of encapsulating a lot of information in a short, coherent format.
- Personas (and their stories) allow you to explore new ideas and possibilities for interaction with the new product.

THE WELL-CRAFTED STORY

A good story cannot be devised; it has to be distilled.

—Raymond Chandler

In writing stories for personas, you have to consider the purpose of each story, and then select the facts and shape the story to make the point. A complete story has to have facts, context (frame of reference), characters, plot, and resolution. In other words, something has to happen in the story. The stories created for personas show them in different situations and how the "problem" of that situation is resolved. Fragments of stories can also be used as an introduction to set the stage, introduce a situation, and connect the audience to the information that will follow.

Speechwriters (and scriptwriters) know how to use storytelling techniques to get the audience interested in the subject. A short example from the television show "The West Wing" is a good illustration of the difference between an overblown introduction and telling a story. In this episode, President Bartlett is rehearsing an introduction to a show about space exploration. He starts by reading what the agency press department has written.

> Good morning! I'm speaking to you live from the West Wing of the White House.
> Today we have a very unique opportunity to take part live in an extremely historic event which….

At this point, he stops and asks his speechwriters to do better. The version they come up with is quite different.

Good morning. Eleven months ago a 12-hundred-pound spacecraft blasted off from Cape Canaveral, Florida. Eighteen hours ago it landed on the planet Mars. You, me, and 60 thousand of your fellow students across the country along with astro-scientists and engineers from the Jet Propulsion Lab in Southern California, NASA Houston, and right here at the White House are going to be the first to see what it sees, and to chronicle an extraordinary voyage of an unmanned ship called Galileo 5.

In 81 words, they created a mini-drama with a background (a spacecraft hurtling through space), a situation (it is recently landed on Mars), characters (you, me, 60,000 students and rocket scientists), and an event about to unfold (seeing what *Galileo 5* sees). Who wouldn't want to stay tuned to see what happens?

Good stories are short

Attention spans are short, so our stories need to be short as well. The goal is to make a point quickly and effectively, not just to entertain. This compression of data is an important benefit of using personas. They boil down a lot of user research into a package that is easy to communicate. So, persona stories must be efficient, too. Stories do this very well, because they suggest data rather than spelling it out.

The examples in this chapter are all less than 350 words (about half a page) and take just a minute or so to tell. Although there are times when a story needs to be longer, the best stories are the result of ruthless editing that eliminates all unnecessary words and extraneous detail.

For example, think of what we know about Tanner, the central persona in the G4K case study (or about any of the personas in the book). If you wanted to tell someone about him, you could give them a long list of facts, but you could also tell a little story like this one:

Tanner was deep into a Skatepunkz game—all the way up to level 12—when he got a buddy message from his friend Steve with a question about his homework. He looked up with a start. Almost bedtime and his homework was still not done. Mom or Dad would be in any minute.…

Even in that short beginning of a story, we have learned a lot about Tanner.

- He is a kid (he still has homework and a bedtime).
- He is an avid computer games player, and good at it.
- Maybe he's not such a great student.
- He has friends who also use the computer.
- Getting a message is an everyday way to communicate.
- He is probably on a cable modem or some connection where it does not matter how long he stays online.

- He is probably playing in his room, or somewhere his parents cannot see him and watch exactly what he is doing.

- We might be able to infer that his family is comfortably well off.

This story is a memorable way of communicating both a long list of facts and all of the analysis that went into understanding them. The power of using stories is that they can do these things in a few words. (This example was inspired by work by the IBM Research project on knowledge socialization. [IBM 2003])

Good stories have just the right details

A good story has the right details. Too little detail and the story loses authenticity; too much and it gets bogged down in the minutiae of a single instance.

FIGURE 9.5: *What makes cartoons so appealing? Scott McCloud shows us that specificity can get in the way of universality. The more detailed an image of a face the fewer people it can represent. (Copyright © 1993, 1994 by Scott McCloud. Reprinted by permission of HarperCollins Publishers, Inc.)*

Sometimes it can be better for the details to be a little sketchy. In *Understanding Comics*, Scott McCloud talks about drawing comic book characters. He says that the less realistic the drawing style the easier it is for the audience to identify with the characters [McCloud 1994, p. 36]. "The cartoon is a vacuum… an empty shell that we inhabit, which enables us to travel in another realm. We do not just observe the cartoon, we become it." (See Figure 9.5.)

This sounds backward. Is not one of the values of personas and stories that they are specific, rather than general descriptions of "a user"? You need enough of the right details to represent what you know about users, but you need to not be so quirky or overly specific that the story can only represent one person in one situation. The trick is to make the outline, or general shape of the character, easily distinguishable, but not fill it in so much that you leave no room for each person's imagination to work. You need to make the stories unique, but neither so specific that they can be disregarded nor so generic that they could apply to anyone.

When you pick the details for a persona, you think about which pieces of information will help people understand the archetype. The same thing is true of a story. In telling a story about Tanner, it probably does not matter what color his shirt is, or even what type of shirt he is wearing. It may not matter what he ate for lunch, or who his favorite teacher in the fourth grade was. However, if you were trying to explain how technologically advanced Tanner is you might start a story this way:

> Normally it was a drag to have to wait for his kid sister to get out of her soccer practice, but his new wireless card and the discovery of a hot spot at a nearby store changed all that. Tanner was hanging out running a chat with some of his friends and playing games when….

Choose the details for your stories to provide a context or frame of reference. In as few words as possible, you want to let your audience identify with the situation. Then, you can use the events of the story to paint a picture of how the product will help the persona do something better than he could without the product.

STORIES WORK WHEN PEOPLE BELIEVE IN THEM

Storytelling reveals meaning without committing the error of defining it.

—Hannah Arendt

What makes people believe in stories, or makes stories create that "Aha!" of recognition? Stephen Denning, an advocate of storytelling as a way of instigating change, has studied what he calls the "springboard effect" [Denning 2000, 2004], which helps people get inside an idea and experience it from the inside, not just as a collection of facts. When this happens,

Example

STORIES SPARK THE IMAGINATION

Stephen Denning's example of a springboard story is the one he used to start the idea of the World Bank as a knowledge-sharing organization.

He starts, "Let me tell you what happened in Zambia.... In June, 1995, a health worker in Kamana, Zambia logged on to the Centers for Disease Control Web site in Atlanta and got the answer to a question about how to treat malaria."

In the World Bank, the point was that if this can happen in a small town in Africa, it can happen anywhere; if it can happen in the CDC, it could happen in the World Bank; and if it can happen in 1995, it can happen now.

What this story did was start the World Bankers thinking about why it wasn't happening there, and how they could make it happen. The story was the spark that turned the World Bank into a model for making their information available.

Stephen Denning, *The Springboard*

stories act as accelerators that can light a fuse. They help people connect the information they already have to create a new idea. He says that stories with the springboard effect are:

- *Understandable to the audience:* They have to show a situation that is at least familiar to the audience, and which they can identify as a problem. Persona stories that show how a known "point of pain" can be eliminated are easy for a team to understand and empathize with.

- *Told from the perspective of a single central character, the protagonist:* This is, of course, exactly what personas do: create a central character for the stories.

- *Prototypical:* Just as a persona must be a "typical" (or archetypal) person, the story must be a typical situation. You can use stories to explore unusual situations, but the stories to start with are those that would happen frequently or represent typical uses of the product.

- *Have a degree of strangeness or incongruity, but are eerily familiar:* If the story just sounds like "life as we know it today," there is not much reason to tell it. The story about the Novartis customer service worker is based on anecdotes from user research but was clearly on target as an example of a real situation.

- *Are based on a real event:* In fact, Denning suggests that your springboard stories should be based on facts or stories that have really happened. Grounding them in reality makes the inferences or results you draw from them more believable. The story of the aid worker in Zambia started as a real event.

Example

THE STORY THAT CAME TRUE

When we were introducing a new set of intranet tools at Novartis Consumer Health, we created short stories to illustrate how they might be used. This was one of them:

"February 17th. 11:23 a.m. London, England: Susan Bentley needs product information. She just received an inquiry from a pharmacist concerning a customer on vacation from San Francisco who lost his allergy medication. He needs to find a place to purchase it in the UK or to have an alternative.

Sue uses the Product Encyclopedia to access the entire consumer product database. A search by product name, ingredient and country produces three different options. She contacts the pharmacist and forwards the information."

Shortly after release, the project manager received an email with a series of messages that were almost exactly the situation we had imagined in the story. Talk about eerily familiar!

The more your stories can be based on things you have observed in user research the more compelling they will be. You may have to fill in details, or adapt them to fit precisely into the situation, but if they start from a real event they have more authenticity.

Ginny Redish [2001] has pointed out that you can make up scenarios, but when you do you are likely to "write *from* requirements rather than *for* requirements" and you miss the interesting stories because they are not the most typical.

There are two other advantages of using anecdotes from your research. One is that the "voice of the user" comes through more clearly when you do this. It keeps the personas from going feral–changing and mutating to fit into new scenarios. The other is that if you are challenged you have the data to back up your story.

It is especially important to start from a real context or event if you are using a story to illustrate a new idea. The more innovative or unexpected the idea the more it must start from a familiar context. The pattern for a new idea for a story is simple. You start by painting a picture of the situation. If the problem is not well understood, you can tell the negative story of how bad the problem is right now, which can be an effective way of making a team aware of the problem. Then, you lay out the scenario of how the new idea resolves the problem in a new and positive way. The following is an example.

> One Sunday afternoon, Jane decided to give online banking a try. In the middle of registering, she was confused by an error message. Seeing a "contact us" link in the message, she doubtfully typed in her problem and sent it off, thinking, "A lot of good that will do on a weekend." But that same day, she got a message with the name and direct number of someone to call–and got right through! The technician fixed the problem and got her account set up. She's been an online banker ever since.

This is a story that resonates well with people who use e-commerce Web sites. They immediately recognize the problem: they try new things in the evening or on weekends and can rarely get help when they need it. Their usual reaction is to begin telling their own stories about their terrible customer service experiences with online shopping or services. Think about your own reaction to this story. Did you think, "Fat chance!" or, "Yeah, that level of support would be a real winner in our marketplace." Either way, it can spark a good discussion about how and when customers will use the site, and what they might need to be successful.

When you create personas, and scenarios for them, you are making up stories. These stories must ring true—sound believable—to be compelling. It is not necessary that each story be journalistically accurate, but they will be more compelling if they are based on facts and real anecdotes. In fact, the story about Jane and the online banking service is based on a real event. Really. I could not make up something like that.

PUTTING STORIES TO WORK

It takes a thousand voices to tell a single story.

—Native American saying, tribe unknown

Until now, we have focused on stories as an efficient way of establishing context and of helping someone get to know the persona better. They set up the situation in which the persona will interact with the product. More detailed stories can also be used to explore specific tasks or interactions. These stories are sometimes called scenarios.

Example

SIMULATION SCENARIOS AS STORY

In his book about his years as a NASA flight director, Gene Kranz tells a story about how they used scenarios to plan for a flight. They ran simulations that tested the crew and their equipment under both normal and unusual circumstances. Just before the first moon landing, they ran a scenario that included an error message. In the simulation, they aborted the landing based on this error, but in debriefing, they discovered that they need not have done so. They stayed up all night to revise their procedures, so they would be able to tell a dangerous situation from a harmless warning. The best part of this story is that this scenario actually came true, with the same error occurring in the real flight. Without that simulation, Armstrong would not have landed on the moon.

Gene Kranz in "Failure Is Not an Option"

STORIES AND SCENARIOS

What's the difference between a story and a scenario? These words have been used so loosely for so many years that there is not a hard line dividing them. Both refer to techniques for creating sequential narratives, telling us what someone did (or might do), in what order, and what happened (or might happen) as a result of their actions. And both have many different variations built into common practice.

Let's start by looking at how stories and scenarios are used. A good overview of different types of scenarios used in the design process is from JoAnn Hackos' and Ginny Redish's book *User and Task Analysis for Interface Design* [Hackos and Redish 1998]. They discuss four levels of scenario: brief scenarios, vignettes, elaborated scenarios, and complete task scenarios. These scenarios grow from a brief description of a user's goals a product must handle, to a specific story of a user trying to reach a goal but without details of steps, to one that shows the details of the tasks and steps in the interactions. They grow in depth and scope, and they fill different places in a design process as they move from broad exploration of users, context, and goals to a detailed view of the task and steps in an interaction.

Another way to look at stories and scenarios is to see whether they appeal to logic or emotion for understanding a problem. There is a continuum of types of narratives that runs from the purely evocative at one end to the purely prescriptive and factual at the other. If we plotted the various types of scenarios and stories they might look as shown in Figure 9.6.

FIGURE 9.6: *A continuum of stories.*

As you move from left to right on this chart, you move from types of story (or scenario) whose purpose is to explore context and motivation to those that help explore the details of the interaction. This also maps to the progress of a design process as it moves from initial discovery and exploration to detailed interface and interaction design. To be effective, you need to use the right type of story for the right reason (and at the right point in the process).

Let's look at some examples of each type of story, using Tanner Briggs and the G4K case study. The first four are narrative stories. The last three are diagrammatic tools that can be used to look at the program structures the stories suggest.

A springboard story

These stories may be the most difficult to write. Like a haiku, they must be short and compelling, both illustrating a dilemma and hinting at the way out. They may be the spark of a new innovation, or based on an anecdote from user research. This story conveys a moment in which Tanner and his mother begin to see their home computer as more than just a games machine.

When Tanner comes home from school, he logs on to G4K and collects the essay he began during study period in school. He is usually not allowed to play games on the computer until he finishes his homework, but he tells his mother, "This is my homework."

This story sets the stage by creating a short vignette with the context and the problem revealed in just a few words. Tanner wants to spend more time on the computer. His mother wants him to do his homework. Can we provide a way to bridge this gap?

A "points of pain" story

These stories illustrate problems, and often can point forward to possible solutions that could be part of the new design. They create a vivid view of the problem from the point of view of the persona. There are many different types of pain: gaps in the process of reaching a goal, places where current solutions do not fit together, usability problems that make a task more difficult than it should be, or new needs that have no current solution at all.

Ten minutes is not enough. That is Tanner's opinion about the time limits on using the computer at school. Last Friday, he started working on a geography assignment. He used the school encyclopedia program to look up some information about the animals in Africa. He had just gotten started when his turn on the computer was up. He'd like to work on it over the weekend, but he does not have the same things on his computer at home. He prints out a few things, and figures he will retype what he's done when he gets home. What a bore.

This story shows how a reasonable-sounding rule limiting the time students can spend on the computer can be seen from another perspective. For Tanner, the rule just makes it more difficult to do his homework. The story illustrates the "point of pain" so that everyone can understand the problem from the persona's perspective, rather than arguing about what "a user might do."

A key scenario

These stories lay out more complex scenarios the design must accomodate. Where the first two types of stories are intended to be evocative, key scenarios start to move into concrete illustrations of how personas (and real people) interact with the product.

Tanner has been a member of G4K for a few months. He's been traveling (virtually) on an animal safari, along with two of his classmates. They are thinking about doing a science project that shows the various types of animals that live in their backyards, just like the program shows animals living in different parts of the world. He wants to save some of the cool pages he's been finding and then go back and look at them again later.

His mother, Laura, discovers that she can create a personal folder for him to save pages he finds. They talk about it and decide that this will be better than just using the browser bookmarks or printing out the pages. Laura uses her parent password to create the folder, and the next time Tanner signs on to G4K the folder is waiting for him in the corner of the screen.

The next day, at school, Tanner collects some great pictures of animals while his friend starts to draw out the chart of their backyard environment. That evening, at his friend's house, Tanner logs on to G4K, opens his folder, and shows all of the pictures he has found. They talk about which ones they like, and decide to print a few of them out to paste onto the chart.

This scenario begins to elaborate on how Tanner might use G4K. It not only shows how the personal folder feature might be used but puts it in a social context and shows how it supports Tanner in his task of completing a school assignment.

A narrative scenario

As the design is developed, these stories present an entire task in narrative format. The story format carries context and other environmental information to help make sure the proposed design, flow, or use case makes sense when seen from the point of view of a persona. These stories are usually longer than more evocative types of stories because they need to follow a task or scenario from beginning to end.

Laura has a busy life keeping up with her two kids, house, and job. She thinks it is important for her son, Tanner, to learn to use computers, but she worries about all the things she's read about the Internet. Tanner, on the other hand, thinks that computers are just great.

When Tanner is playing Skatepunkz, he sees a Web address on the splash screen and decides to go check it out. First he writes down the address carefully. Then he dials in to their ISP, signs on to the Internet, and types in the URL.

The G4K home page comes up, and he is immediately attracted to the Get a Hint logo he recognizes from other Gigantic games. He uses the mouse to click on the icon.

He reads the free hint, but also sees a link to get more hints if he signs up. He clicks on the link and types in his name. He's not sure about what password to use, so he enters the same one he uses to get onto the Internet.

The next thing that happens is a bummer. He sees a message that he needs to get his parents to give him permission to go into this site. He turns off the computer and waits for his mother to come home.

After dinner, he finally gets a chance to tell her about this new site. They turn on the computer together and go to the Internet. Tanner shows her the G4K page, and signs in. The same message comes up, saying he needs permission from his parents to continue.

Laura clicks on the "Information for Parents" link and takes a few minutes to read about the site. She decides that this site is okay for Tanner to visit and signs in to give him permission, setting up her own parental password.

Narrative scenarios explore how the design implements a complete task or workflow. In this example, the task of signing up for G4K includes two people and at least two different sessions on the computer. These scenarios are a good way of reviewing the overall flow of the program set in a real-world context. Do all of the features fit together? Do they support the way the persona will actually work?

A Design Map

In creating a Design Map, the team explores some of the details of an issue, either in preparation for creating a scenario or to explore one more deeply. The steps in the process are seen from the persona's point of view and may or may not involve the product.

The Design Map shown in Figure 9.7 decomposes the story into the details of the steps Tanner will take, and provides a way of exploring the questions, ideas, and assumptions that must be addressed in the final design. (For a complete view of this Design Map of the sign-up process, see Chapter 10.)

Design Maps can be used to explore a key scenario more deeply, or to look at the interaction details of a complex feature, as this illustration does. Design Maps help the team shift from the vision of motivation and inspiration of the early stories to the concrete specificity of a completed design.

A flow diagram

Flow charts are a commonly used technique for walking through the logic of a process. They can be done at a very technical level for a system design, but they can also be used as part of a user interface design process to show the different pages and ways of moving from place to place. Used this way, they are like the skeleton of a narrative scenario, mapping out the pages that have to be designed. An example is shown in Figure 9.8.

Flow diagrams allow the reader to explore possible experience paths, but are not narrative story techniques. You can use them to discover stories, or to identify points of pain that might show up in an overly complex flow. They can also be used to analyze the implications of a story and how it might be implemented in the design.

Use cases

Use cases were developed as part of UML – the Unified Modeling Language for object-oriented design. Although there are many different templates and formats for creating use cases, they are usually a sequence of actions by the "actors" (which include people, processes,

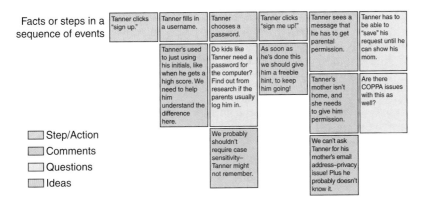

Facts or steps in a sequence of events

Tanner clicks "sign up."	Tanner fills in a username.	Tanner chooses a password.	Tanner clicks "sign me up!"	Tanner sees a message that he has to get parental permission.	Tanner has to be able to "save" his request until he can show his mom.
	Tanner's used to just using his initials, like when he gets a high score. We need to help him understand the difference here.	Do kids like Tanner need a password for the computer? Find out from research if the parents usually log him in.	As soon as he's done this we should give him a freebie hint, to keep him going!	Tanner's mother isn't home, and she needs to give him permission.	Are there COPPA issues with this as well?
		We probably shouldn't require case sensitivity–Tanner might not remember.		We can't ask Tanner for his mother's email address–privacy issue! Plus he probably doesn't know it.	

▢ Step/Action
▢ Comments
▢ Questions
▢ Ideas

FIGURE 9.7: *Example of a Design Map.*

and machines) that interact during the use of a system, mapping out what happens during a transaction. Consider the following:

Task: Log on to system, with a pending parental permission

1. *The user requests a page in the Web site.*
2. *The system looks for a saved log-in ID, and displays the log-in page if not found.*
3. *The user enters log-in name and password.*
4. *The system validates the log-in and looks for a parental permission token for this account.*

And so on.

Use cases are another way of looking at the details of the interaction. Where Design Maps focus on the human side, use cases look in more detail at how the computer system functions. If use cases are part of your development process, use them to make the bridge between your scenarios and implementation details.

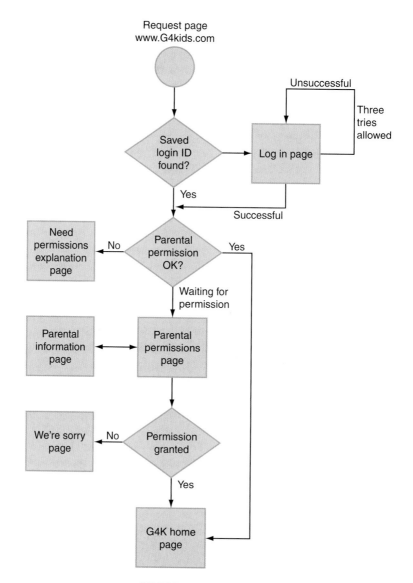

FIGURE 9.8: *Flow diagram.*

CRAFTING A STORY

The dirty secret of art is you do not have to show people your bad writing. That is what we have the delete key for.

—Robert McKee

Inspiration

WRITING EXERCISE

In college, we were given writing assignments to write "in the style of" famous authors. It's amazing how much easier is it to start writing if you've just read someone else's work and can mimic their prose voice and style.

If you are having trouble getting started, reading other stories can help you get started. They can be stories from this book, from other projects or anecdotes from user research. Just make sure you have your own goals and characters in mind as you start to adapt the stories to your own project. It sounds basic, but it's an easy way to get going.

Tamara Adlin

Let's get over writer's block first, and how difficult it can be to get past the blank page. Even people who like the idea of personas, and who understand the power of scenarios of use, can get the jitters about writing a story. They think they do not write well, are not "creative" enough to create a good story. But persona stories are not about great writing, and they are not really about creativity. This type of storytelling is a design technique, using a narrative form to make a point. The goal is to communicate what you have learned in a powerful and persuasive way.

Like the personas themselves, their stories start with a goal—a clear reason for the story to exist. The story is then structured from what you have heard or seen, details you have observed, and anecdotes or phrases that were particularly memorable.

Stories are very simple to create, with few hard and fast rules. We will cover the basics: the reason to create a story, the elements that make up a good story, and techniques for improving and refining your stories.

Reasons to write a story

Stories show personas in action and help you and the rest of the team explore how the personas might interact with your product. As you work, be clear about your goals for each story and what you are trying to communicate. You can write a story to:

- Establish a situation or context
- Illustrate a problem or a positive experience
- Propose a new solution.

Establish context

Stories that establish context help round out the personas by supplying vignettes of their lives. These stories may show problems, but more often they simply help the team understand the persona better. The action of the story may not involve the product, and the resolution may be incomplete. They can be used to help introduce a persona and may be the basis for the team's understanding of the situation in other stories. The story about Tanner works to establish context. The following story should help dispel any notion that payroll for a small company is done is a quiet, organized, and uninterrupted manner:

> Marjorie is the office manager for a small construction company. In fact, she's the only person in the office except for the owner. She manages payroll, orders supplies, pays the bills, duns the customers, and handles any correspondence. Thursday is her busiest day because it is payday. Each of the site managers drops by to turn in time cards, pick up their crew's checks, and have a little chat. It is their one chance to actually see each other during the week, and Marjorie uses it to keep in touch with "her boys" as well as take their orders for supplies. Of course, none of this stops the phone from ringing with the usual daily business. Today, everything was crazy, so it is 5:30 and she's just finishing the bookkeeping…again. It is quick and easy spaghetti for dinner again tonight!

When actors start to work on a new script, they sometimes create "back stories" for their characters. These are stories about things that happened before the action of the movie or play begins, and they help the actor understand the character better. These types of stories can help the team get to know the persona better. They provide a type of running start so that you can see what happened to the persona before any interaction with your product begins.

There is a danger in background stories. They can be seen as irrelevant, taking you off track into discussions of "what the personas ate for dinner" rather than things that have an impact on the product design. The following version of a context story about Marjorie does little to provide useful insight for a team working on a payroll program.

Marjorie is the office manager for a small construction company. She always dresses carefully for work. Her pants suit is neatly ironed, and she wears the scarf her nephew gave her for her birthday. Today, she needs to take her car to the shop, so she makes sure she wears a pair of flat shoes so that she can walk to the office after she drops it off. As she walks back to the office, she does a little window shopping. Then, she spends a hectic afternoon finishing the payroll.

If you decide to include personal details or background in a story, make sure you have a clear goal and that the story clearly relates to how the persona might use (or not use) the product.

Illustrate a problem

Stories that show a problem typically show how the current situation prevents the persona from reaching a goal or completing a task. They illustrate the points of pain by showing them in a dramatic way, and provide some explanation for how the persona behaves. These stories may end badly and seem negative, but the implication is that the new product will change the ending. You can use these stories to explain what problems the personas are encountering with the current product (or lack of one). The following version of Jane's banking adventures might be the trigger for a discussion about how to provide better customer support through a tricky registration process.

Jane had been using a home finance program for years, but had resisted online banking. While she was balancing the family checkbook one Sunday afternoon, she read a letter from her bank offering it for free. Why not join the twenty-first century, especially if they have finally met my price? she thought. In the middle of registering, she received an error message. She could not figure out how to go any further, even after calling a friend for advice and starting the entire process over. That night at dinner, she amused her family with her adventures online. She and her husband agreed that perhaps they were not ready for online banking—or maybe online banking wasn't ready for them! Jane tossed the letter in the trash.

You can also use these stories as the beginning of a conversation or to open up a design discussion. You might end them with some of the questions the persona has or that the story suggests. For example:

- Does Jane always pay her bills on the weekend? Are support staff available if she needs help?
- What are the various problems Jane might encounter? How many of them can we eliminate to be sure she gets through the initial registration?
- What would make Jane feel more comfortable, and help her get over her trepidation regarding online banking?

Propose a new solution

Finally, stories can explore new ways personas can meet their goals. These stories help explore possible new features and design approaches by showing them in action. They can be created early in a project, to propose design goals. They can also be used during the design process. For example, each story that illustrates a problem can be balanced with one that shows the personas succeeding.

Elements of a story

Once you have the goals of the story defined, there are only a few things a story needs to be complete. Whether the story is a short, evocative anecdote or a complex scenario, it starts from the basic "who, what, when, and why." All stories need characters, situation, action, and resolution.

● *Characters:* The main character will be the persona, but there may be other members of the supporting cast.

● *Situation:* What is the beginning of the story? What is the context or motivation for what will happen? What is the main character trying to do?

Inspiration

THE ANATOMY OF A SCREENPLAY

There are many theories of writing, and systems for writing well. I like Dan Decker's Character Structure as an approach to writing persona stories. He starts building a script by understanding the characters, rather than creating a plot. He defines four structural characters whose relationships and interactions are the basis for the action of the film:

• The Main Character – the person who makes the decisions that set the plot in motion
• The Objective – the person who represents the main character's goal
• The Opposition – a person whose own Objective is mutually exclusive to that of the main character
• The Window Character – the person through whom we see the changes in the main character, and who is part of the story from beginning to end.

In the movie Casablanca, Rick (the bar owner) is the main character, Ilsa (played by Ingrid Bergman) is the objective, Victor Laszlo (Ilsa's husband) is the opposition, and Capt. Louis Renault is the window character.

Dan Decker, *The Anatomy of a Screenplay*

- *Action:* Something has to happen. What is it? What influences the decisions the main character has to make?
- *Resolution:* What is the ending situation? What has changed during the story?

All of these elements must be clearly defined, but the most important thing a story needs is a reason to be told.

Putting it together

Before you start to actually write a story, make sure you have all of its elements assembled. It can be helpful to write out the answers to the questions outlined in Figure 9.9 in preparation for creating a story.

Think about the research you have for this persona and the situation or task. Are there any great observations, quotes, or anecdotes that can help bring this story to life? Next, put it all together into a short sequential narrative, starting from the opening situation and ending with the outcome. Do not worry too much about making the language elegant in your first draft. Just get it down on paper (or screen) so that you can see it take shape. Then, get ready to edit—or, as we like to say, iterate.

Element	Questions	Answers
Goals	What is your goal in writing this story?	
Character	Who is the persona in this story?	
	What other characters are involved?	
Situation	What is the situation before the story begins?	
	What is the goal of the main character?	
	What triggers the action of the story?	
Action	What happens during the story?	
Resolution	What is the outcome of the story?	

Figure 9.9: *Story element chart.*

Refining your story

Iteration is simply part of the process. Occasionally, a story will come out just right the first time, but most of us need to test and edit them to make them work. The first iteration is to edit the story yourself. Read the story out loud (or better, have someone read it to you) and listen to how it sounds. It should be "easy on the ears," using everyday speech patterns. Look for and eliminate:

Inspiration

HOW HEARING IS DIFFERENT FROM READING

In a presentation at Storycon 2002 (a conference on many uses of storytelling), Doug Lipman talked about the role of the listener in oral storytelling. He reminds us that stories are interactive; they need a speaker and a listener, and the communication takes place in what happens between them. If you tell the stories (rather than writing them down for others to read), you must imagine the events as you describe them, or you will not convey the story well.

The key, he says, is to remember that stories are not *words*, but *images.* The role of the story is to create images in the minds of the audience; the words are just the bridge to these images.

The magic of stories is that the very specific subject of the story – 1 place, 1 time, 1 character, 1 action – allows the story to be more than a summary of events, and to trigger both the message and the meta-message as the listener imagines the events unfolding.

Doug Lipman, Story Dynamics

- *Technical or insider jargon:* Use the terminology (words and phrases) of the persona's own vocabulary.
- *Passive voice:* Stories are active. The persona does things (or did them, if you are writing in the past tense). Make the language of the story active, too.
- *Lengthy explanations that are distracting or confusing:* Keep the story as short as you can, without losing critical details.
- *Judgments or conclusions:* Let the events of the story speak for themselves.
- *Technical details that focus on the product rather than on the persona's actions and motivations:* Watch for overuse of actions such as "and then he clicked on…" that focus on the computer.

Next, usability test it. Tell someone else the story and see what they hear in it.

- *What is the portrait of the persona suggested by the story?* Ask them to describe the main character. This is a good way of determining whether you have remained true to the persona or are introducing changes you may not intend.
- *Do they understand what happens in the story?* Ask them to repeat the story back to you in their own words, to see if the narrative actions are clear.

- *Do they understand the point or message of the story?* Ask them what they take away from the story. You want to be sure that the story is meeting your goals for it.

Finally, see if the story rings true, making sense both for the persona and for the person listening to the story. If the story seems unbelievable (no matter how closely it is based on a real anecdote), you will spend your time justifying it and the story itself will be lost.

Inspiration

ALL THE LITTLE STORIES ADD UP

In an interview for the New York Times, the actor Kevin Bacon was asked about his work as a director. He said:

"To me, directing is telling a story. All day long, that's all I do—in every single detail. Is she using a pencil, or is she using a pen? And what story do you want to tell with that? You see, you tell all these little stories in the course of a film, and then hopefully it all wraps up into one big story."

Kevin Bacon, quoted in
"As for Directing, It's Telling a Story"
by Dave Kehr, *New York Times,*
December 30, 2003

Finding the right details

One of the most difficult aspects of writing a good story is finding the right details, and the right level of detail. Too few specifics and the story is not grounded well enough to spark the imagination; too many and it drowns in unnecessary information. Use descriptive details to establish context, or to set expectations for the rest of the story. Consider the differences among the following descriptions of someone getting into a car:

- Mary got into her car.
- Mary slid into her brand new Audi A8.
- Mary herded her kids into the minivan.
- Mary climbed into the cab of her not-quite-antique pickup truck.

All of these tell us something about Mary through descriptions (or lack thereof) of types of cars. However, we probably do not care what color the vehicle is unless that fact will be relevant to the rest of the story in some way.

Any details you include should help reinforce the persona's character, goals, and roles. If you find yourself stretching to make up details, it is a good idea to reread your materials about the persona to keep yourself grounded. The types of details you use also place the emphasis on different aspects of the persona and the situation. The following are four descriptions of someone reading his e-mail:

- When John checked his e-mail, he had a crisis waiting for him… (emphasis on the crisis; e-mail is just setting up the context).

- John wandered around the airport until he found a WiFi hotspot so that he could check his e-mail. He liked to use flight time to answer routine messages, or prepare for anything he needed to get to right away when he landed… (emphasis on staying connected while traveling).

- John slid into his cube, and decided to check for any updates to his current support tickets before getting on the phone. He liked to keep his "in progress" cue as empty as possible… (emphasis on work patterns).

- After he got the kids to bed, John liked to disappear into his study and check his e-mail. Tonight, however, it was not for work. He wanted to see if he'd been the high bid in an online auction for… (emphasis on social context).

Finding a style and voice for the story

One of the attractive things about writing stories is that they can have a *bit* of fun to them. They can go beyond the neutral analytic language of most business reports and task analysis. In fact, they should. One of their roles is to provide a conduit for the personas' voices. All of those great quotes, quirky turns of phrase, and unexpected anecdotes help make the stories—and the personas—come alive. With that said, there are a few things to watch out for.

- Use the language and style of speech the persona uses, but be careful not to turn dialect or accents into a caricature. This is just as unacceptable in a story as in a picture of a persona. Unless you are *very* good at writing in dialect, this is best left to professionals.

- Do not use stories to poke fun at the persona, or at the product. Even if you have a direct quote from your research, remember that a story can backfire if it makes a team member too defensive.

- No matter how irate the language or behavior you observed, it is probably a good idea to keep the stories within commonly acceptable ranges, and leave out the profanity or excessive slang.

You must also decide whether to write the stories in first or third person. That is, are they being told *by* the persona or *about* the persona?. Use first-person stories if you want to let the persona speak directly to the team. These stories are good as parts of displays or when the story will be seen in print or on screen. First-person stories are also a good way of contrasting attitudes or goals among a group of personas, with each talking to the audience in his/her own words.

Use third-person stories when you will be telling the story to the team (whether in writing or orally). Unless you plan to act out the part, it is probably more natural for you to talk about the persona just as you would if you were introducing a new colleague to the group. You may also find third-person stories a little easier to write. Consider the following case study of a narrative written in first person.

Case Study

LETTING PERSONAS SPEAK FOR YOU

Back in 1995 the documentation department at AT&T wanted to convince the product teams to use online and multimedia documentation to replace the volumes of paper they created. The first version was a typical corporate presentation about the new technologies they wanted to use and how their ideas would benefit the company, which generated little enthusiasm.

We decided to create a new presentation that revolved around the needs of the many different people who use documentation. We created seven characters: sales rep, trainer, product team leader, repair technician, support center operator, customer telecommunications manager, and receptionist. For each character, we wrote a short story and created a video vignette lasting about 90 seconds. Each video showed the character in a situation in which online documentation made their work easier. We chose situations we felt were common, easily recognizable, and had a clearly identified pain point. The new presentation was a success within the company and won Best of Show in the STC International Online Communications Competition. But what made it work?

- It used seven different voices to make the point that many different people used the documentation and had different needs. As each AT&T department heard the presentation, they saw themselves portrayed sympathetically.
- The stories were short. Visual details helped create the sense of place, but the scripts relied on the beginning situations to make the point about the need, and focused on showing the solutions.
- The content was realistic and accurate. It was important not to have glaring mistakes that would annoy people who were very familiar with the products.
- The presentation was relaxed, in a style that did not get too serious and that encouraged the audience to sit back and enjoy the story. Two of the scripts even used outright humor.

The script from the Sales Rep episode (following) is written in the first person, with the character narrating the story as though she is talking to her colleagues. The music under the narration is from the theme from the TV show "Dragnet." An entire world of the sales department is evoked in just 94 seconds.

Sales Rep, working at desk in hotel room: *This is the territory. Big-time telephone sales. I'm sharp and I work for the best company in the business. But no one can know everything a customer might ask about a feature-packed system like ours. Or can they? This is the story.*

(Case study, continued)

It was 12:05 p.m. I got a last-minute appointment with a Fortune 500 bigwig at 2:00 p.m. I was hungry, and not just for food. I wanted this sale badly, but I had to work fast. My mind was racing. I remembered my successful presentation last month with another corporate hotshot. He had questions, tough ones. Thanks to the interactive documentation, I had answers. I knew what I had to do. I changed the name...and some minor details...to protect my methods. The system did the rest.

Sales Rep and Customer, in Customer's office: I showed him my stuff. How we stack up against the competition. What we can do for his bottom line. He was very impressed, but he still had doubts. He wanted proof I had what he needed, so he tossed me a live one. But I knew how to diffuse it. My secret weapon: Expert in a Box. It gets them every time. Lucky for me our competitors do not have it. He was buying, and I had a great late lunch.

It is like I always say: big-time sales take big-time sales tools. I'm glad I was armed with the powerful, fast-acting software from the documentation group.

AT&T Product Documentation Development Demo Project Team:

Jim Duyne (AT&T)

Andy Kienzle (scripts and video)

Todd Reichart (multimedia development)

Marc Reed (visual design)

Whitney Quesenbery (concept)

Practice makes perfect

If it seems uncomfortable to think about your work in terms of stories at first, stick with it. As you practice thinking about personas in action you will get better at it and stories will start to come more naturally.

Your personas do not have to start out with a full set of stories. Instead, they can evolve, with new stories added as they are needed to help the team work through design challenges. Using stories and scenarios to work through design issues is also a good way of keeping the emotional context of the personas' roles, goals, and tasks in the process. Avoid (especially in the early stages of design) constructions such as "...and then he clicks on..." This sounds more like technical documentation or a use case with names than a story that will help you understand how (and why) a persona might behave.

One way of using stories throughout the process is to employ them as aids in thinking about a problem from a different perspective. Even if you started out as an "outsider," it is easy to absorb so much information about the product or software that you start thinking like an insider. Creating on-the-fly stories can help keep the personas in the center of the process. It is a good way of banishing the generic "user" from your work.

Writing the right story

The following are a few final thoughts to keep in mind as you write your stories. A good story does not have to be long. In fact, the more the purpose of the story is to establish a context or make an evocative point the shorter it should be. Your stories should not be much longer than the examples in this chapter. Be sure you are clear about the purpose of the story, and match the style to the goal you want to achieve.

- To get your audience to think about something in a new way, start with the known facts—perhaps the bad news about problems with the current situation. Then, as briefly as possible, suggest a direction or solution that could solve the problems.

- If you are trying to explore how one of the personas might react to a new feature, consider mixing short narrative sections that establish context with bullets or other visual techniques to make the sequence easy to follow.

- Do not overload your stories with too much detail. The information you include should be just enough to make the story clear. Remember that your personas already carry a lot of context and background information.

- Be true to the personas. Do not let the stories force them into actions or decisions that are not part of their personalities, or that are inconsistent with other things you have said about them. Stories that do not make sense are one sign that the personas are going feral.

SUMMARY

Stories set the personas in motion. The personalities and characteristics you have established for the personas drive the shape of these stories, just like the characters in a film drive the plot. If they are both believable and ring true, your design ideas are probably sound as well.

The stories you write for your personas help you explore the possibilities for interaction, whether you are working on completely new feature ideas or on details of the design. Personas and their stories have a power of persuasion. They allow one person (or a small group) to reach many and to ignite the imagination of an entire development group. They are more effective than argument because they are memorable and can be easily repeated, creating a "viral marketing" effect for your ideas.

The power of storytelling may be the single most important reason why personas work. In using personas and their stories, you are not arguing or trying to convince each person on the team (one by one) that your understanding of the users is correct. You are creating a vision of the users' worlds and inviting others to enter it. If you do the work well–if the stories are compelling and convincing—not only will your personas be accepted but others will be able to use the information embedded in them to create new products that are useful and usable.

Tamara Adlin
"Tamara the Process Addict"

Roles: Co-author, Consultant
Goals: To make products that make sense.
Objectives: Find ways to help people see the structural elements of just about everything.

Quote: "If you can't see it, you can't fix it."

Holly Jamesen Carr
"Holly the Happy Hiker"

Roles: Sustainability Consultant, Usability Specialist, Outdoor Enthusiast.
Goals: To make it easier for people to do good in the world.
Objectives: To support organizations and businesses that work for environmental and social justice.

Quote: "It should be easy to do good."

Holly is still amazed by the power of the Internet. Intrigued with making this resource more accessible to non-techies like herself (she was a French major in college), she has advocated for users of software and Web-based products for over six years. She earned a Masters in Communication at the University of Washington, where she focused on online learning communities. At software startups Netpodium, Akamai, and Attenex, Holly worked closely with Tamara Adlin. Together they Mapped workflows, ran usability tests, created personas, designed interfaces for innovative new products, and had a darn good time.

Today, Holly directs her user experience skills to help design teams construct usable earth-friendly buildings. Holly lives in Washington, D.C.

10

REALITY AND DESIGN MAPS

Tamara Adlin and **Holly Jamesen Carr**

MAPS COMPLEMENT THE CREATION AND USE OF PERSONAS

This chapter is about Reality Maps and Design Maps, which are artifacts that help you understand and communicate information about the ways people achieve their goals and the ways they *could* achieve their goals with new tools. Maps are similar to other participatory design tools, but are useful in ways we have not found other tools to be. Reality Maps tell the story that is being experienced today by real people. Design Maps tell stories about the experiences of personas in the future.

As user experience professionals, we constantly have to learn about detailed and complex processes in order to design new solutions. We work to translate between the world of users and the world of developers. We try to observe people doing their actual jobs, but all too often find ourselves with no time or no access to actual users. If we do manage to collect information about how people get things done, we have to figure out how to communicate our findings at the right level of detail so that we can help information architects, graphic designers, product and program managers, developers, and even executives do their jobs. This is just not easy.

Maps can help us create and use personas. Reality Mapping is a way of collecting information we can use to create our personas. Once the personas are created, Design Maps help us understand the goals, scenarios, and tasks associated with our designs for new products—all from the

Family Planning
Use **Reality Maps** to capture and communicate information about your target users' goals and tasks

Retirement & ROI

Concept & Gestation
Harvest **Reality Maps** for data to use in your personas

Adulthood
Create
Design Maps
to explore the goals and tasks of your personas

Birth & Maturation

FIGURE 10.1: *When (and how) Reality and Design Maps fit into the persona life cycle.*

personas' points of view. We recommend that you try Reality Mapping as part of your *family planning* work and employ Design Mapping during the *adulthood* phase (see Figure 10.1). This chapter includes a description of exactly what Maps are, how to create them, how to use Reality Maps and Design Maps together, and how both kinds of Maps enhance and are enhanced by personas.

WHAT EXACTLY ARE MAPS?

Maps help you visualize and comprehend end-to-end user experiences. Mapping is the process of creating flow charts in collaboration with the users and/or members of your product design and development team.

Maps show steps in a process or experience sequentially, with any questions, comments, or ideas regarding these steps arrayed underneath (see Figure 10.2). Finished Reality and Design Maps are large sheets of paper covered with color-coded sticky notes that describe the use experiences related to your product. Reality Maps are created by a facilitator during a structured conversation or interview with current users. Design Maps are created by the design team without the participation of users.

Maps are helpful information-gathering and design tools because they are easy to create, iterate, and read. If they are kept in public spaces, they can become an accessible source of insights into user experiences (either as they exist today or as they are envisioned to become). Unlike prose documents or complex flow charts, Maps make it easy to quickly extract and understand the end-to-end user experience and/or focus on details of interest. Used together, Reality Maps and Design Maps can help you understand the current experiences related to your product space and design and help you test new experiences before you build a new product.

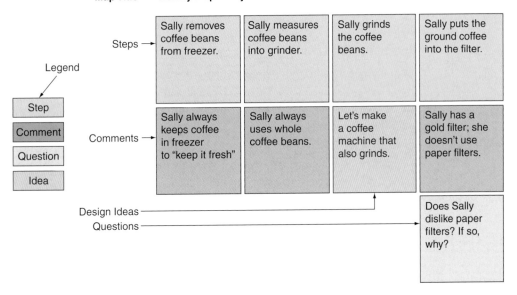

FIGURE 10.2: *Steps, questions, comments, and design ideas in a Reality Map. If you were creating a new coffee maker, you would schedule Reality Mapping meetings with one or more coffee drinkers (in this case, a real person named Sally) who make their own coffee. Reality Mapping is effective whether or not you are familiar with the product domain.*

If you need more qualitative data to create your personas, and you have access to people who are using a current version of your product or are accomplishing the tasks related to your product in some other way, you can create Reality Maps to collect this data. If you have already created personas and want to quickly describe and evaluate experiences you *could* support with your new product, Design Maps will help.

Elements of every Map: titles, steps, questions, comments, and design ideas

All Maps have five basic building blocks: titles, steps, questions, comments, and design ideas. Titles should identify the type of Map (Reality or Design) and identify the goals or tasks the Map depicts. Steps should be arrayed horizontally, with related comments, questions, and design ideas arranged under the steps they reference. You can read across the row of steps to get a sense of the process from end to end (i.e., the steps in a task taken to reach a goal), or you can focus on a subset of the steps and read down the columns to understand related questions and ideas (see Figure 10.2).

Steps (blue sticky notes)

Steps are the "verbs" (or the "backbone") of the process. The facilitator of the Mapping exercise places steps horizontally across the Map. For example, if you were Mapping the process of making coffee your steps might look like the top row of blue squares in Figure 10.2. A good way to elicit steps is to ask, "What do you do next?" Steps are the building blocks of tasks.

Comments (green sticky notes)

Comments are qualifying statements about steps. They are the most flexible elements on a Map. Comments can describe behaviors, habits, awareness or lack of awareness of features or alternative actions, or even qualities of objects. If you hear an important piece of information but it is not a step, question, or design idea, record it as a green comment.

For example, in our Sally Makes Coffee Map (Figure 10.2), the comment "Sally always uses whole coffee beans" is a note about this particular person's actions that could be significant with respect to the rest of the experience. The comment is not a step, but it relates to the step listed above it: "Sally measures coffee beans into grinder." The comment, in this example, serves to remind the facilitator and Map readers that "always using whole beans" does not necessarily indicate the standard behavior of everyone undertaking this task.

Questions (yellow sticky notes)

Yellow "questions" are the most useful interview management tool of the Reality Mapper. When you first start Mapping any process, you will identify many questions—some indicating areas where you need clarification and some that express your Mapping participants' issues. In fact, you will probably encounter so many questions that the sheer volume and importance of them will threaten to derail your attempt to Map the entire process. Listing the questions on the Map allows you to record and move past them quickly so that you can capture as much of the process as possible without being derailed. Once you create a Map that captures most of an end-to-end process you can loop back and track down answers to the questions you have identified.

Questions can either come from the facilitator or the Mapping participants. For example, in our Sally Makes Coffee Map, questions include, "The coffee is usually perfect, but once in a while it tastes sour. Why?" (asked by Sally) and, "Do many people dislike paper filters? If so, why?" (asked by the Mapper).

Create a yellow question when:

- You have questions about the process
- The Mapping participant expresses confusion, concern, or ignorance related to part of the process
- Anyone participating in the Mapping session begins to belabor a point.

Design Ideas (pink sticky notes)

As you create your Reality Map, you will inevitably think of, or be presented with, an assortment of ideas on how to improve the process. Your Reality Mapping goal is to create a solid picture of the experience as it is today. Although you do not want to allow your Reality Mapping session to turn into a discussion of potential new features, you also should not discard good ideas just because they come up at the "wrong time." For example, in Figure 10.3 there is a pink sticky that says "Let's make a coffee maker that also grinds." This is an interesting idea and worth capturing. Ask anyone who comes up with a design idea to record it on a pink sticky note, place it on the Map, and move on.

Why use Maps?

Reality and Design Maps are interesting not because they are radical departures from existing methods but because they work well with both creating personas and using them to create new designs. Used with personas, Maps can help you understand the experience-related changes (both good and bad) your new product will demand. The primary advantages of Mapping as a tool for experience observation are:

● *Reality Maps are created in conversation with real users.* Reality Maps focus on the way real people think about their experiences and can be used to fill in some of the qualitative information in persona descriptions. The Reality Mapping process also allows user researchers to explore nuances of users' work flow and thought processes that are not easy to understand from pure observation. People do not just use products; they also *think* about the products they use. Your product will probably both have to *work within* and *change* the current context of tasks and goals. Maps will help you understand both the cognitive and physical landscapes of activities into which you will be introducing your product. As they help you create Reality Maps, users will identify processes that are problematic, important to maintain, confusing, or in need of obvious improvements.

● *Reality Maps enable researchers to quickly explore and understand their users' task domain.* Reality Maps require no preparation by either the researcher or the users being Mapped. A single Reality Mapping session will provide enough information about the task domain to help you plan your remaining user research needs.

● *If you can't see it, you can't fix it.* If the best way to create great user experiences is to look at and design for them holistically, the best way to understand flawed experiences, or to even identify the ways certain experiences *are* flawed, is to look at and analyze them holistically. Reality Maps give you a much-needed overview of today's experiences. They allow you to have a bird's-eye view of the chaos of everyday activities and annoyances. From above, you and your team will be able to find problem areas and create a plan to fix the entire experience as a whole.

● *Design Maps foster creativity while maintaining focus on user experience.* Design Maps focus designers on the holistic experiences that could be built for the personas, rather than on individual tools or features. Because Design Maps and Reality Maps share the same format, they encourage designers to return to "reality" even as they design (e.g., to consult the information they have on current work flow even as they innovate). Design Maps allow product designers to create solutions that will work well for users, applying their expertise to the problems they used Reality Maps to understand.

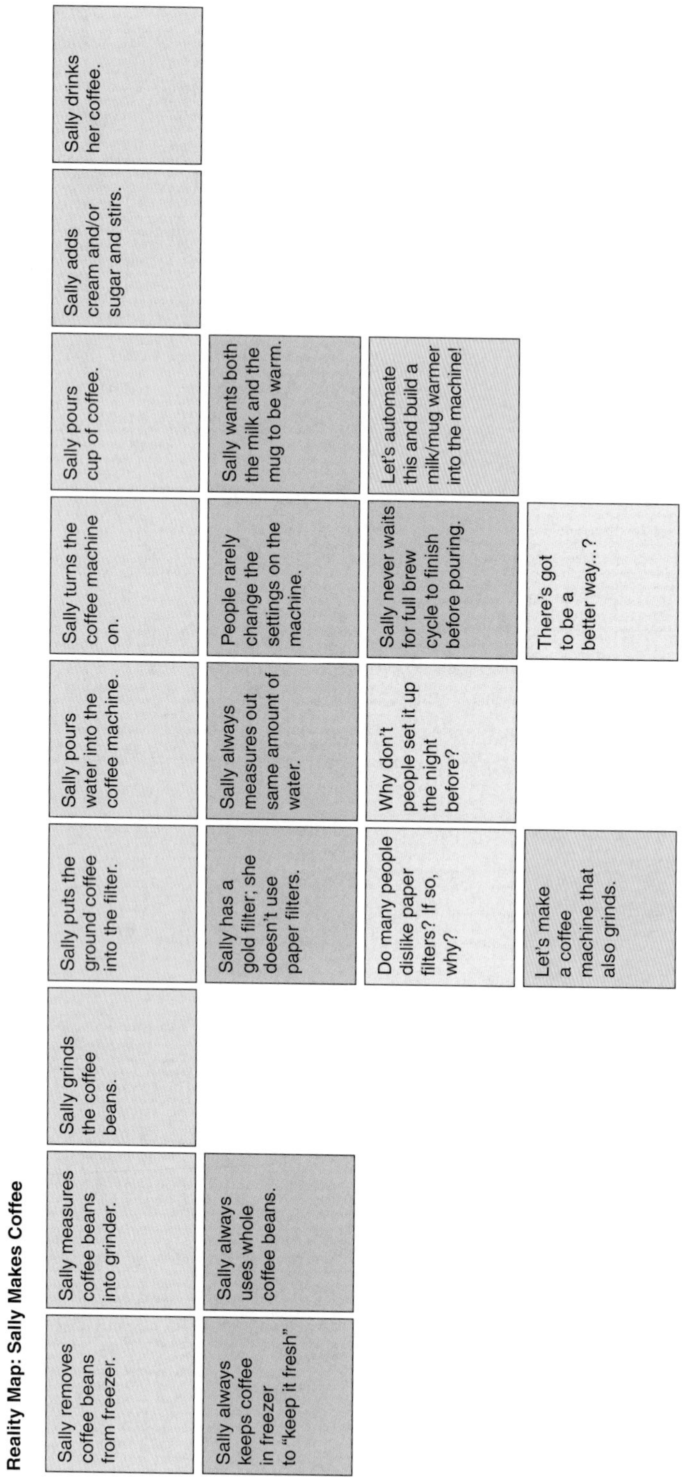

Reality Map: Sally Makes Coffee

Sally removes coffee beans from freezer.	Sally measures coffee beans into grinder.	Sally grinds the coffee beans.	Sally puts the ground coffee into the filter.	Sally pours water into the coffee machine.	Sally turns the coffee machine on.	Sally pours cup of coffee.	Sally adds cream and/or sugar and stirs.	Sally drinks her coffee.

Sally always keeps coffee in freezer to "keep it fresh"

Sally always uses whole coffee beans.

Sally has a gold filter; she doesn't use paper filters.

Sally always measures out same amount of water.

People rarely change the settings on the machine.

Sally wants both the milk and the mug/cup to be warm.

Do many people dislike paper filters? If so, why?

Why don't people set it up the night before?

Sally never waits for full brew cycle to finish before pouring.

Let's make a coffee machine that also grinds.

There's got to be a better way...?

Let's automate this and build a milk/mug warmer into the machine!

FIGURE 10.3: *Reality Map for "Sally Makes Coffee."*

● *Maps are valuable communication and collaboration tools.* Maps depict both the big picture and important details of current user experiences in an accessible format. They allow *everyone* on a design and development team to understand the user experience as distinct from the system supporting that experience. When you have Maps hanging on your walls, it is impossible to lose sight of the big picture of your users' experiences.

Handy Detail

MAPPING IN CONTEXT—HOW REALITY AND DESIGN MAPPING DIFFER FROM SIMILAR UCD METHODS

There are many methods in the user-centered designer's toolbox. The purpose of this sidebar is to describe these similarities (and interesting differences) and to place Mapping in context with other techniques that have similar methods or purposes.

User Analysis, Task Analysis, and Contextual Inquiry

To understand precisely how a user completes a task, it is imperative to actually observe that user at work in the context of his or her natural environment. Task, job, and process analysis are the methods of observing users at work and describing the actual activities that constitute the collection of tasks that make up a job or a process. The following excerpt is from Hackos and Redish [1998, p. 7]:

> User and task analysis is the process of learning about ordinary users by observing them in action. It is different from asking them questions in focus groups outside the users' typical environments and away from their work…. In fact, experience has shown that users themselves do not know how to articulate what they do, especially if they are very familiar with the task they perform.

In their book *Contextual Design*, Beyer and Holtzblatt provide detailed suggestions for UCD professionals who want to observe people doing what they normally do in the places they normally do it and "make unarticulated knowledge about work explicit" [Beyer and Holtzblatt 1998a, p. 37]. During or after these observations, Beyer and Holtzblatt recommend communicating findings in one or more of their five "work model" diagrams (Flow, Sequence, Artifact, Cultural, and Physical). Each model (Figure 10.4) describes and allows researchers to analyze a different aspect of the current work and task environment of real users.

Reality Maps are very similar to Beyer and Holtzblatt's sequence work models (Figure 10.4) and they share some qualities with each of the other models as well. Sequence models include users' intent, a trigger to the sequence, steps, order of steps (including loops and branches), and breakdowns or problems. They, like Maps, are linear descriptions of work from the point of view of users. Unlike task analysis and contextual inquiry, which require direct observation of the user completing tasks, Reality Maps can be created in conversation with users and domain experts. Actual observation and modeling is critically important in good UCD, and there are many methods you can choose from.

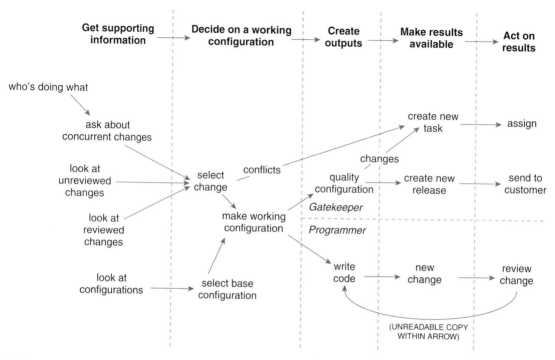

FIGURE 10.4: *A sequence work model for the development of a software system. (Adapted from InContext Enterprise, 1995.)*

The Bridge methodology

The Bridge is a three-part process for understanding the big picture of user tasks, translating that task flow into a series of "task objects" and then creating GUI elements to enable the completion of the identified tasks [Dayton et al. 1998]. The method "bridges" user tasks and GUIs by translating task flows into task objects that include attributes, actions, and containments. GUI "objects" can then be designed for each task object.

In a sense, the Bridge method combines aspects of Reality and Design Mapping. Bridge participants collaborate in a single meeting to capture the existing task flow and then work to rearrange or otherwise improve it to create a "blue sky" task flow. However, the Bridge always reduces experiences into task objects and interfaces, which may or may not capture the big picture of the user's experience (see Figure 10.5).

(Handy detail, continued)

Task Objects

Grocery List	Grocery Store	Grocery Item	Identity
Grocery items	Name Location Grocery items	Name Number Max price	Attributes
Create Edit	Pay	Add Delete Check off	Actions
I' m in | In Me Grocery items	I' m in | In Me Grocery items	I' m in | In Me Grocery store	Containment Relations

A

MyGrocery - [Grocery List 6/3/01.mgr] ☐ ▣ ⊠
File Edit Window Help

Item	Number	Max Price	Purchased?
Oranges	12	$.99/lb.	☐
Bananas	6	$.79/lb.	☐

B

FIGURE 10.5: *The Bridge methodology identifies task objects and then creates interfaces to bridge the identified tasks and the user experience. (Adapted from Participatory Design, 2003.)*

Like the Bridge, Mapping can be used to both understand current experiences and design new systems. However, whereas the Bridge asks users to rearrange and improve task flows and objects, Design Maps rely on the skills of product designers and the user information contained in personas. Product designers can use Design Maps to describe new task flows from the point of view of the personas. Users are still involved, but as *testers* or *reviewers* of the Design Map, not as *authors*.

CARD and CUTA

CARD (Collaborative Analysis of Requirements and Design [Tudor et al. 1993]) and CUTA (Collaborative Users' Task Analysis [Lafreniere 1996]) are both card-based methods for collaborating with users to understand current experiences and design new experiences. Both methods require the practitioner to create cards that capture current tasks and events (CARD) or objects, people, and work situations (CUTA) specific to a particular environment or work flow. Once the cards are created, users can describe their experiences by interacting with and arranging the cards. In the case of CARD, users can collaborate with designers to create new task flows or work flows and new interactions (see Figure 10.6).

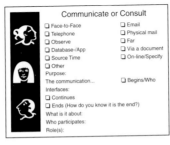
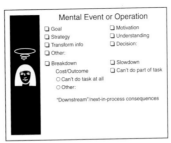

FIGURE 10.6: *Two examples of cards used in the CARD methodology. (Adapted from Muller [2003].)*

(Handy detail, continued)

Mapping, like CARD and CUTA, invites direct participation from users (who often enjoy the process of describing their activities in a new way), but this participation takes different forms. In CARD and CUTA, users collaborate with each other to arrange cards such that they describe a work process. In Reality Mapping, a user researcher facilitates a structured conversation with users to explore the task space. The discussion format actively involves the facilitator and allows her to focus on areas she thinks are important to the design of a new product. In CARD, users participate in the design process. Design Mapping works well whether or not users are involved in the creation of the new designs.

Experience prototyping

Buchenau and Suri [2000] define experience prototypes as "any kind of representation, in any medium, that is designed to understand, explore or communicate what it might be like to engage with the product, space or system we are designing." Experience prototypes should actively engage users to elicit behaviors and reactions similar to those the product might elicit, so that the designers of new technology can learn from participating in these simulations. Experience prototyping is particularly interesting for designers of products that will create unusual experiences (Buchenau and Suri include examples of remote defibrillators and underwater remote vehicles).

According to Buchenau and Suri's definitions, Design Maps are a type of experience prototype, despite the fact that they do not provide the hands-on sensory experiences of the prototypes described in the article. For many software and Web applications and experiences, Design Maps provide representations of actual experiences sufficient to supply many of the benefits of other, more immersive, experience prototypes. In addition, Design Maps are certainly much easier to create.

THE REALITY MAPPING PROCESS

To get the most out of Reality Mapping you can approach the proccess in four steps:

1. Create a Mapping plan.
2. Create the Maps.
3. Analyze the Maps.
4. Harvest the Maps for information to use in your personas.

Step 1: Create a Mapping plan

The purpose of Reality Maps is to capture and communicate the entire end-to-end user experience from the user's point of view. Once you have captured the end-to-end experience at a high level, you can iterate to fill in important or relevant details until you feel that you understand the user experience and/or have no more questions.

Let's return to the fictitious company used for case studies elsewhere in this book: G4K and their *www.G4kids.com* kids' destination site. The G4K team might have identified various processes or questions to explore through Reality Mapping, including:

- How do parents set up Web access for their kids today?
- How do parents monitor their kids' activity on the Internet?
- What do kids of various ages do on the Web today?
- How do teachers integrate the Web into their classes?

The number (and complexity) of Reality Maps you create will depend on the number of experiences you want to understand. You do not need a detailed plan to start Mapping.

Your process for getting started with Reality Mapping depends on how well you understand the domain and the Design challenges in the domain. If you understand the domain and the design challenges well, you will be able to readily identify which processes to Map and can dive right in (see the following Story from the field). If you are Mapping an unfamiliar domain, you can use the Reality Mapping process to identify the process and people you want to Map (see "Story from the field: Sometimes You will Face a Completely Unfamiliar Domain" in material following).

Story from the field

SOMETIMES YOU WILL KNOW EXACTLY WHERE TO START MAPPING

Netpodium was a start-up software company that built an online interactive broadcasting tool set. The idea was to create software that would allow a presenter to create a slide presentation, upload it, and invite audience members to a live "event" on the Web. During the event, the presenter would control the slides during his presentation and the audience would hear the presenter via a streaming media connection. The presenter would also be able to answer written questions sent in by the audience members via an instant messenger-type interface. In this case, our team knew exactly which experiences we needed to Reality Map.

- *The administrator experience:* What was the current experience of organizing and hosting a streaming media presentation, especially a live one, on the Internet?
- *The presenter experience:* What was the current experience of creating a presentation, coordinating a live in-person "event," and managing audience questions?
- *The audience experience:* What do audience members expect at various times during a presentation? How do they communicate with the presenter before, during, and after the presentation?

After we created Reality Maps, we understood much more about the current experience of delivering presentations and the needs of the people involved in putting on events. We went on to create personas and Design Maps to describe the new experiences our software would enable.

Story from the field

SOMETIMES YOU WILL FACE A COMPLETELY UNFAMILIAR DOMAIN

Several years after our Netpodium days, the Netpodium team found ourselves together again at another start-up company. This company, Attenex, builds document management software for legal services. Suddenly, we had to learn about a completely different (and quite complicated) set of goals, tasks, activities, environment, and artifacts. In this case, we simply picked one person who knew about part of the overall document management process (a consultant who had been working in the field) and started Mapping.

By the time we had completed our first Mapping session (which lasted a little less than two hours), we knew exactly how to progress. Our first participant had helped us Map—in considerable detail—the part of the process he understood. He also told us who "owned" the other parts of the end-to-end process. Over the next few weeks we continued to "quilt" what turned out to be a very long and detailed Map of the entire process (when printed, it was over 20 feet long!). Each Mapping session left us knowing exactly who we needed to talk to, and about what, in our next session.

If you can readily identify experiences you need to Map in order to understand current experiences related to your product domain, that is great. If you cannot, simply identify a single experience—or even a single user or subject matter expert—and start Mapping.

Identify Mapping participants who you feel will shed light on existing processes. In general, when recruiting for Reality Mapping sessions, look for people who:

- Are frequent users of a product or process
- Are subject matter experts
- Depend on a product or process to achieve a different or related goal
- Have identifiable roles, goals, or tasks related to the product or process.

Usually, it is easiest to conduct Mapping sessions that include more than one subject matter expert if both share similar responsibilities (e.g., in the G4K Reality Map example you might want to talk to both parents together but schedule separate Mapping sessions for parents and kids).

Try to identify several people with overlapping or identical responsibilities. You can either create a Map during a single session with both experts or schedule separate sessions and plan to iterate and reality check your first Map with the second participant. You can also use Maps to bring together observations from different observers who have had the opportunity to watch real users.

Create a schedule

Mapping meetings work best if they are between two and three hours long. In our experience, less than two hours is usually too short (because it takes a while for participants to understand the Mapping process and to create a Map that captures all of their knowledge about a set of tasks). Three hours gets long and exhausting for everyone involved. Remember that you can always ask to come back to get additional details later.

Schedule Reality Mapping meetings and invite one or two task or subject matter experts to each Mapping meeting. Trying to keep more than three subject matter experts on track and on task can be a bit like trying to herd kittens—but it certainly can be done. Ask a colleague or two to take notes while you manage the session. Although it is possible to conduct a Mapping session and simultaneously record observations on sticky notes, it is not easy, and it is likely that you will miss important bits of information in your rush to write things down. The following is an example of a schedule that allows the Mapping facilitator to take advantage of the different perspectives of several Mapping participants over several sessions.

Reality Map: Parents monitor their kids' activities on the Internet. Participants:

- Anne and Philip Jones (parents of one fourth-grader and one sixth-grader)
- Albert Brown (single dad)
- Candace and John Smith (parents of one third-grader)

Mapping schedule:

- Monday, 9:00 to 11:00: Mapping with Anne and Philip
- Monday, 1:00 to 3:00: Mapping with Albert to add his process to the Map
- Tuesday, 9:00 to 11:00: Mapping with Candace and John to add their process to the Map
- Tuesday afternoon: Create an electronic version of the "Parental Controls" Map and print it
- Wednesday, 9:00 to 11:00: Follow-up Mapping with Anne, Philip, and Albert (to review the "Parental Controls" Map)
- Wednesday afternoon: Incorporate changes from morning session
- Thursday, 9:00 to 11:00: Follow-up Mapping with Candace and John to review latest draft of Map
- Thursday afternoon/Friday morning: Create "reviewed" version of "Parental Controls" Map and post it.

If you want to conduct several Mapping sessions, you can save time by having multiple members of your team creating Maps with different participants concurrently.

Handy Detail

MAPPING SUPPLIES

If you want to try your hand at Mapping, make sure you have supplies that won't let you down. There is nothing worse than having to stop a Mapping session because you have the wrong types of supplies.

Mapping Paper

Not all Mapping paper is created equal, and you will always run out. Invest in a large roll of white paper. We usually use a 3-foot by 8-foot sheet for each Mapping session. The paper does not need to be high quality or expensive. However, when you are puchasing paper for Mapping, bring a pad of sticky notes with you to the store. Make sure you get paper the sticky notes stick well to! We have found that brown butcher paper does *not* work well for Mapping because sticky notes do not stick very well to it.

For a Mapping meeting, measure out a piece of the paper you think is far too big, add 20%, and then double it. You will be surprised how many sticky notes the meeting will generate, and running out of paper is a pain.

Preserve Your Maps

Maps are meant to be big and covered with sticky notes. This makes them inherently difficult to manage as artifacts. Bring tape to your Mapping sessions. If you ever try to move a Map, or even if you just leave it hanging on a wall, it will shed sticky notes. Take some time at the end of your Mapping sessions to reinforce your sticky notes by taping them to the large sheet of paper.

When the Map is complete, and it is not changing much any more, consider transferring it into an electronic medium. This can range from taking digital photos of your Maps to transcribing all of the sticky notes to create an electronic version. We use Microsoft Visio to create electronic versions of our Maps, and print them on large-format printers. You can also use Adobe Illustrator, Macromedia Freehand, or Omnigraffle. As a general rule, pick vector-based software for your electronic Mapping.

If your company does not own a large-format printer or plotter and you want to create electronic versions of your Maps, you have several options. Print the Maps on standard-size paper and tape the pages together to create a large Map. It is worth it to see the entire process on the wall. If your company sees enough of these Maps, you just may convince someone to invest in a plotter. Alternatively, you can contact your local copy center. Printing on a large-format printer is usually quite expensive, but talk to the manager. Ask if they will give you a better price because your Maps will not use as much ink as most large-format, full-color posters and because you will use their services frequently.

Step 2: Create the Maps

Now that you have identified your Mapping participants, it is time to get them in a room with a facilitator (you or a colleague), a large sheet of paper, sticky notes, and markers. Label the large sheet of paper with the name of the role and the description of the goal (example: "Anne (Mom) monitors her child (Bobby's) Web use"). Create a color key/legend by putting four sticky notes with their code written on them on the wall in a visible place. If you have asked another member of your core team to help during the session, agree in advance that one of you will facilitate while the other helps to record the sticky notes.

Get people talking

When you describe the Mapping process to your participants, focus on the idea that this exercise is supposed to be easy and fun. They are there to help you understand what they do every day, but you are not there to judge their actions in any way (see the following Handy Detail).

Handy Detail

SAMPLE SCRIPT FOR YOUR FIRST REALITY MAPPING MEETING

Welcome, everyone! Thank you so much for making time in your schedule to participate in this activity. We are going to get started in just a minute, but first I want to explain what we are going to do today and why it is so important to us.

Today we are going to create a Reality Map. A Reality Map is really just a big flow chart that describes how people get things done. The Mapping process is simply the process of me asking you questions about the work you do, writing down your answers on sticky notes, and putting them up on this big sheet of paper. There are four colors of sticky notes, and each is for a different type of information.

- Blue sticky notes are for steps. For example, if we were Mapping the process of making toast one of the blue sticky notes might say something like "I open the bag of bread."
- Pink sticky notes are for design ideas. For example, "Let's make a toaster that automatically applies butter!"
- Yellow sticky notes are the most important color of all. They are for questions. Anytime we come across any type of question or confusion we will create a yellow sticky note and move on.
- Green sticky notes are for comments. These are comments that are not steps, not questions, and not design ideas. In our toast example, a green comment might say "I never change the settings on the toaster."

Today we are going to create a Map for process X. We are going to try to Map the entire process from end to end, so we may end up leaving out some important details. If that happens, it is okay. We can always come back and talk about the details later.

I want you to help me understand how you get work assignments, what you do, and how you know you are finished. I will ask you to tell me details about the tasks that are a part of process X, what you have to think about or understand to do the tasks properly, who you depend on, what types of artifacts you create, and so on. No detail is too small, no assumption or comment is too insignificant, and no question needs to be answered during this session. Just two more comments before we get started:

- This is probably going to feel pretty basic and maybe even a little bit silly at first. That is okay. Even details that seem silly or basic should go on the Map. We will do our best to use the information we collect today to build products that will make your lives easier.
- Sometimes, when we come across an important topic (such as a complex, difficult, or problematic aspect of your work) we may say "yellow sticky" and skip over the details for now. We are going to try to capture the big picture first and come back to explore the details.

Okay, let's get started Mapping process X. What's the first thing you do when you get started?

Once you get your participants talking, your job is to translate the Mapping participants' comments into steps, questions, comments, and ideas. This is tricky at first, but you will find you quickly get used to it. Consider the following comment you might hear from Anne, one of the moms in our example Reality Map:

> Well, yes, I know I can look at the History feature of the browser to see what pages people have visited, so I do that a lot. But I do not know who went to which Web site, and it is not arranged to make it easy to find bad sites. I wish they were marked or something.

You will need to ask Anne to talk about what her step-by-step process and experience was and what she was trying to accomplish. In this case, it would be fairly easy to walk through the process with her. As you discuss her original comment in more detail and "unpack" it, you could create the sticky notes shown in Figure 10.7.

You will also find that your Mapping participants will help categorize their own comments as they get used to the process.

Do not be afraid to move sticky notes around, but always keep your eye on the big picture. Continue to add steps until you feel you have completely captured the end-to-end process (see Figure 10.8). You might discover that your original definitions of the goals were wrong or incomplete (e.g., Anne might divulge an additional goal regarding privacy of her family members: "Actually, it is really important to me not to invade my family members' privacy. I do not like spying but I get very worried about what Bobby could find on the Net."). This is fine. Move sticky notes or add sticky notes as needed, and move on.

Keep Mapping sessions focused and productive

Mapping meetings can stray off track if the facilitator does not manage the session carefully. As a facilitator, it is your job to encourage your participants to talk and to describe what they do, but it is equally important to keep them from diving into too much detail or churning on a single step or aspect of a process. For example, if you find yourself creating a separate blue sticky note for every form-field entry required of current users, you are probably delving too deeply. However, if you have Mapped a process you know to be complex with only ten blue steps you are probably not asking for enough detail. During a Reality Mapping session, ask questions such as the following:

> **Bright Idea**
>
> *LET PARTICIPANTS CREATE THEIR OWN STICKY NOTES*
>
> Leave an assortment of sticky notes and pens on a table. You will find that Mapping participants quickly understand the rules and that many will create their own sticky notes to add to the Map.

- Who asks you to do this activity?
- What information do you have to have before you can get started? Where do you find it? Do you always find the info you need there?
- At what point do you have to bring someone else into the process? Is that person always available? What happens if not?
- Where does your work tend to break down? What about your work is particularly difficult or complicated?
- Is there a point at which you are waiting for someone else to do something before you can continue?
- Is there a point when you are under pressure because someone else is waiting for you to provide something they need?
- Is there anything special you have to know in order to do this?
- Do you need any extra tools or documents to do this?

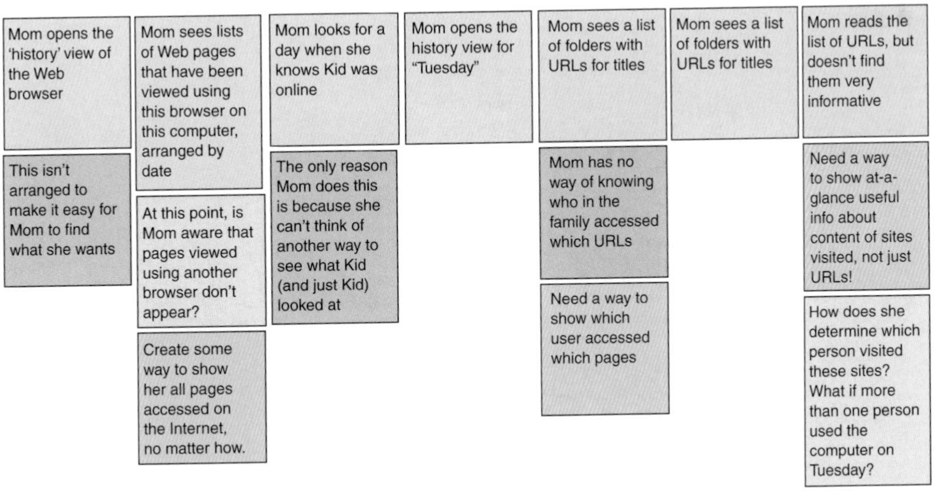

FIGURE 10.7: *Reality Map sticky notes that could come out of a deeper discussion of Anne's comment about her use of a browser history feature.*

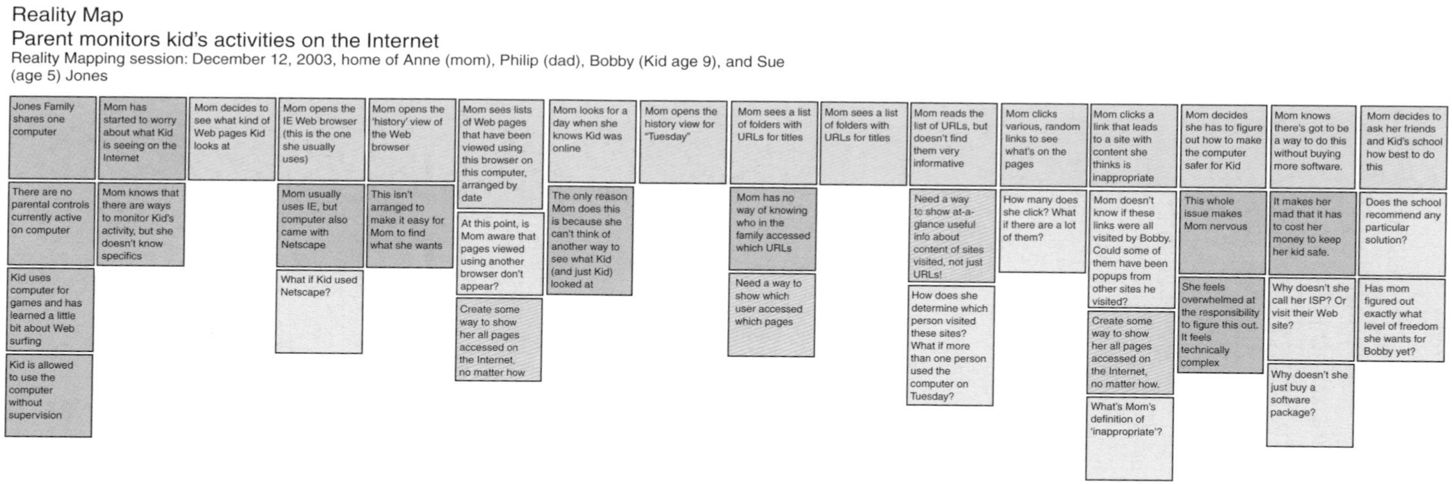

Reality Map
Parent monitors kid's activities on the Internet
Reality Mapping session: December 12, 2003, home of Anne (mom), Philip (dad), Bobby (Kid age 9), and Sue (age 5) Jones

- Jones Family shares one computer
- There are no parental controls currently active on computer
- Kid uses computer for games and has learned a little bit about Web surfing
- Kid is allowed to use the computer without supervision

Mom has started to worry about what Kid is seeing on the Internet
- Mom knows that there are ways to monitor Kid's activity, but she doesn't know specifics

Mom decides to see what kind of Web pages Kid looks at

Mom opens the IE Web browser (this is the one she usually uses)
- Mom usually uses IE, but computer also came with Netscape
- What if Kid used Netscape?

Mom opens the "history" view of the Web browser
- This isn't arranged to make it easy for Mom to find what she wants

Mom sees lists of Web pages that have been viewed using this browser on this computer, arranged by date
- At this point, is Mom aware that pages viewed using another browser don't appear?
- Create some way to show her all pages accessed on the Internet, no matter how

Mom looks for a day when she knows Kid was online
- The only reason Mom does this is because she can't think of another way to see what Kid (and just Kid) looked at

Mom opens the history view for "Tuesday"

Mom sees a list of folders with URLs for titles
- Mom has no way of knowing who in the family accessed which URLs
- Need a way to show which user accessed which pages

Mom sees a list of folders with URLs for titles

Mom reads the list of URLs, but doesn't find them very informative
- Need a way to show at-a-glance useful info about content of sites visited, not just URLs!
- How does she determine which person visited these sites? What if more than one person used the computer on Tuesday?

Mom clicks various, random links to see what's on the pages
- How many does she click? What if there are a lot of them?

Mom clicks a link that leads to a site with content she thinks is inappropriate
- Mom doesn't know if these links were all visited by Bobby. Could some of them have been popups from other sites he visited?
- Create some way to show her all pages accessed on the Internet, no matter how.
- What's Mom's definition of 'inappropriate'?

Mom decides she has to figure out how to make the computer safer for Kid
- This whole issue makes Mom nervous
- She feels overwhelmed at the responsibility to figure this out. It feels technically complex

Mom knows there's got to be a way to do this without buying more software.
- It makes her mad that it has to cost her money to keep her kid safe.
- Why doesn't she call her ISP? Or visit their Web site?
- Why doesn't she just buy a software package?

Mom decides to ask her friends and Kid's school how best to do this
- Does the school recommend any particular solution?
- Has mom figured out exactly what level of freedom she wants for Bobby yet?

FIGURE 10.8: *Reality Map "Parent monitors kids' activity on the Internet." Note that this Reality Map begins with a series of comments. Many Reality Maps start with comments that describe motivations or activities that precede those described in the Map.*

If the session starts to derail

Do not allow questions to derail the session. In our Mapping sessions, we distribute yellow sticky notes to everyone in the room. If a tangential discussion arises, someone will say, "Halt! Yellow Sticky!" to stop the "churning." This is a cue for someone to record the question or issue on a yellow sticky note and place it on the Map. Yellow sticky notes can and should be handled after the big picture is complete. For example, you might have a participant who is very worried about security features for an existing or yet-to-be-designed product:

> Participant: We have got to talk about network security before we talk about these other issues. Bill in IT and I were having a conversation the other day about this and we agree it is critical.

> Facilitator: I understand that network security is a big issue, and will affect the entire process. Can you summarize the issue so that I can put it on a sticky?

> Participant: Well, you cannot really summarize it. It is a huge issue across the entire product.

> Facilitator: Okay. So I am going to create a yellow sticky that says, "Network security is a huge issue across the entire project," or do you think, "How can we fix our major network security problems?" captures it more effectively? Before we leave today I'd like to schedule some time with you and Bill to go over the details of the network security issues as people experience them.

If you encounter situations such as these, focus on reassuring the participant that he or she is being heard. You might ask the participant to create a sticky note or series of sticky notes themselves and place them on the Reality Map. Remind the group that your goal for today is to get as much of the big picture Mapped as possible, and that you will schedule follow-up sessions to explore the issues that arise.

Handy Detail

IF YOU FEEL STUPID, YOU ARE DOING SOMETHING RIGHT

When you first start Reality Mapping, it is going to feel a bit odd. To create a useful Reality Map, you must be willing to walk task and subject matter experts through their processes in a step-by-step progression. It is difficult to sit in a room with someone who has a lot of expertise in a particular area and ask them to step you through their work processes in bite-size chunks. It often feels as though the information you are collecting is overly simplified, and in some cases obvious. If you have these feelings, you are doing something right.

Keep reminding yourself of your Reality Mapping goal, which is to create a solid end-to-end Map of the current user experience for the processes you are investigating. Also remember our experience: there have been many times when we have created Reality Maps with participants who start out grumpy or annoyed about the Mapping process but who wouldn't walk out of the room without a promise that we will send them their own printout of the Map to hang on their wall!

Why does this happen? Because Maps recast familiar experiences in a fresh, unusual, and thorough way, Mapping participants may find ways they can use the completed Maps to train others or to otherwise explain how they do what they do.

Develop your Maps iteratively

After you finish a Mapping session, take some time to evaluate your Map. First, put the Map up on a wall and look at it from far away. A Map on a wall in your office can give you an at-a-glance progress indicator. The more yellow the Map, the more work you have to do to fully understand the process (see Figure 10.9).

You can continue to develop your Maps in several ways:

- *Keep working with a participant until they do not feel they have any more to tell you.* Schedule another meeting with the same participant or participants. If you feel your original participants still have a lot of good information you have not captured, this is a good next step. (See "How do you know you are done?" following.)

- *Find a new participant with new insights about an existing Map.* Schedule a meeting with a different participant who has (or has expertise related to) the same role you Mapped originally. (See material following for ideas on layering Maps to capture different opinions.)

- *Build out the big picture by Mapping new parts of the process.* If the overall process you are Mapping includes many people and/or happens in stages, work to create an overview of the end-to-end process before you explore details (see "Story from the field: Sometimes You Will Face a Completely Unfamiliar Domain" previously).

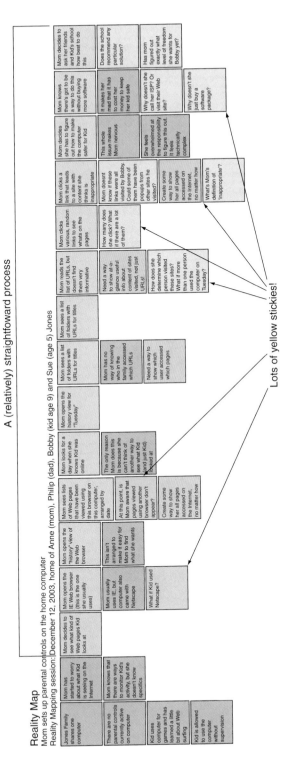

FIGURE 10.9: An "early" Reality Map. Even though this example may be too small to read, it conveys a lot of information, and you will find that many of your "early" Reality Maps look a lot like this one. Note that the steps on the Map look like they describe a clear and linear process and that the Map is covered with many yellow "question" sticky notes. Already it is clear that some aspects of the process are probably less complex than others. Note that the end of the Map (the right-hand side) has a many questions and a few pink ideas. This probably indicates that there is more confusion (and thus opportunity for improvement) in the later phases of the current process.

- Look for "puddles" of sticky notes. If you notice a large cluster of yellow and/or green sticky notes, you probably have some work to do. Puddles of yellow or green sticky notes (clusters of questions or assumptions) usually indicate:
  ○ An aspect of the process you have not fully explored yet
  ○ An aspect of the process that is very complex and perhaps no one knows how it works in detail
  ○ An aspect of the process that changes quite a bit from user to user.

As you continue to iterate your Map, it will probably contain fewer yellow sticky notes (questions tend to metamorphose into steps, comments, or ideas). It will probably also start to look more complex and messier (see Figure 10.10). Comments can also change. If in the course of iterating your Map you change any comment, you will need to review everything "downstream" (i.e., to the right) of the comment to see if the change affects anything else on the Map. In our Sally Makes Coffee Map, one of the comments describes the fact that Sally uses whole coffee beans. If you discover that most other people in your target user group use pre-ground coffee, this difference may be noted as a small branch in the Map and the steps you originally created with Sally might need to be adjusted.

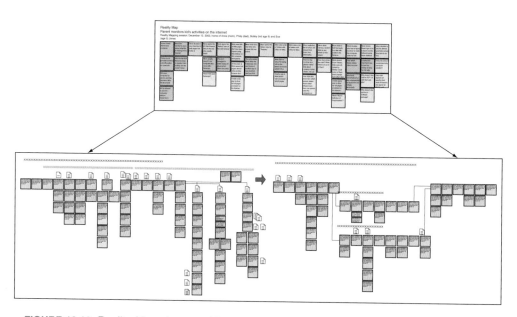

FIGURE 10.10: *Reality Maps become bigger, more complex, and less "yellow" as they evolve.*

Step 3: Analyze the Maps

During analysis you will add labels, compare different user Maps, add branches and/or layers, and evaluate the processes you have captured in the Maps. As you analyze your Maps, you will also find areas in them that would benefit from further iteration. You will also find aspects of the process that are ripe for improvements.

Identify and label interesting aspects of the Map

As you work on your Map, you will probably start to discover some important aspects of the process that are not steps, questions, comments, or ideas. As you learn more about the process, you and your team can add symbols to your Maps to capture your observations. It's also helpful to keep additional sticky note colors handy in case you decide to capture some of the following information during a Mapping exercise. In my experience, it is helpful to enrich Reality Maps with symbols (see Figure 10.11) that represent:

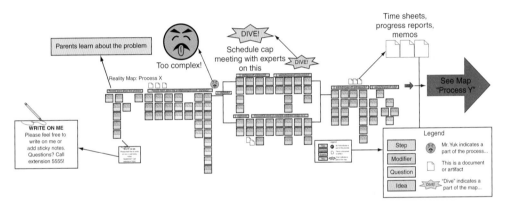

FIGURE 10.11: *Additional Mapping symbols. Additional symbols can help you highlight requests for contributions, phases in the overall process, problem areas in the process, areas you need to delve for more information, artifacts related to the process, and how the Map connects to other Maps.*

- Distinct phases of the process (see Figure 10.12)
- Artifacts or documents that support or are generated by the process
- Problem areas
- Areas that need further exploration
- Places where the process branches or connects to another process you need (or plan to) Map.

Phase labels

During early Mapping sessions, you focus on individual steps. As your Map evolves, you may find that your Mapping participants have named some of the phases of the process. These phases are collections of individual steps, and the fact that they are seen as cohesive

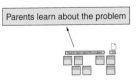

FIGURE 10.12: *Phase labels.*

phases of effort can be important as you develop your designs. For example, you may find that many parents describe some of the phases of implementing online parental controls as:

- Learning about the problem or researching solutions
- Purchasing and installing a solution
- Managing and monitoring access.

Record these phases by drawing a line over the series of steps each encompasses and labeling the line (see Figure 10.12).

Artifact indicators

FIGURE 10.13: *Artifact indicators.*

During Mapping sessions, your participants may describe various artifacts or documents that support or otherwise relate to their tasks. As we suggested in the section on field studies, you should try to get versions of the artifacts or documents to study (make sure you have permission to obtain copies of any corporate artifact you want to study). It is also helpful to note them on the Map. You can use a document symbol (a rectangle with a "dog-ear" on one corner) to indicate the step in the Mapped process where the artifact or document is used (see Figure 10.13). In Figure 10.13, you will note that there are many document icons sprinkled on the Reality Map. If you notice that there are quite a few documents required to complete a task that should be relatively automated, you may have found an aspect of the process that is ripe for improvement. If you want to a capture information about artifacts during a Mapping session, choose sticky notes in a new color (not blue, green, yellow, or pink) and write the name of each artifact on its own sticky note. You can place these directly on the Map near the appropriate step artifacts.

"Mr. Yuk" indicators

FIGURE 10.14: *Mr. Yuk indicator to highlight complexity.*

Almost every Map identifies aspects of a process that could use improvement. A great way to find these areas is to look for stubborn clusters of yellow sticky notes. If you find a series of questions that are clustered and are resistant to "being answered," you have probably found a process problem. If you find an aspect of the process that is not in question, but that everyone has ideas about or all Mapping participants seem to dislike, you have probably also found a problem area. For internal versions of your Map, it is handy to create and use a symbol to highlight that area. In our Maps, we use a hand-drawn frowning face that reminds us of the "Mr. Yuk" sticker that used to be applied to indicate the presence of poisons in household cleaners (see Figure 10.14). The Mr. Yuk sticker indicates an area of the Map that needs attention during later Design Mapping sessions. Note, however, that you may want to create versions of your Map that contain less incendiary symbols. Subject matter experts do not always appreciate being told that parts of their processes are "yucky." Find a nicer (and more specific) way of indicating a problem in the process on these versions of your Maps. If you want to capture "Mr. Yuk" aspects of a process during a Mapping session, assign "Mr. Yuk" a sticky note color.

"Deep dive" indicators

You will identify aspects of the process you are Mapping that will need more attention, or a "deep dive." If you find a part of the process you want to "take offline" or create another Mapping session to explore, note this part by placing a "deep dive" sticker (see Figure 10.15) on the Map. You can use another color of sticky note or create your own symbol. Think of "deep dive" stickers as similar to the indicators on street maps that tell the reader to refer to a detailed map in some other area. Like densely crisscrossed downtown streetscapes, some phases of some processes require their own detailed Maps. Anytime you find yourself creating many "yellow" questions, consider adding a deep dive indicator to remind yourself to come back and explore that area of the process in depth.

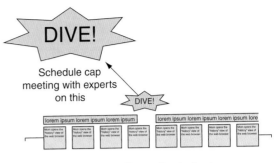

FIGURE 10.15: *Deep dive indicator.*

Map connection arrows

You will create different Maps for various user roles and/or goals. It is helpful to indicate how the Maps "fit together" in an end-to-end experience. Use arrows or notes on the Maps to show the reader how the Maps precede and follow each other to depict the entire experience (see Figure 10.16).

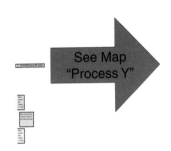

Map legend

Add a legend to your Maps so that people can read and interpret them without your help. Include short definitions of each symbol and what it stands for on your Map (see Figure 10.17). If you create your own Mapping symbols, make sure you add them to your legend.

FIGURE 10.16: *Map connection arrow.*

Look for shared—and unique—approaches to similar tasks

Every time you create a Reality Map, you run the risk of capturing a process that is heavily influenced by the personal preferences or skill and experience levels of the Mapping participant. For example, Anne's process may be very different from Albert's or Candace's. Perhaps Candace is very computer savvy and has set up her own system using several commercially available Internet childproofing software packages. Who is doing the process the "right" way? Which process should you pay more attention to? In other words, how do you know if you are Mapping the "right" person and the "right" way of accomplishing the goal? The truth is that you cannot know.

When we create Reality Maps, we try to understand the end-to-end flow of tasks and activities real people use to accomplish a goal. We try to capture the process from more than one person so that we can identify aspects of the overall process that vary according to the individual.

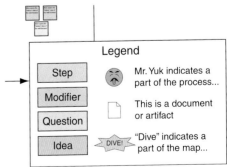

FIGURE 10.17: *Map legend.*

Most of the time, it is easy to identify the major milestones of any process, and most of the time these major milestones are the same (even if the ways different individuals reach these milestones are quite different). In the Internet childproofing case, if we went on to talk to more parents we would probably find that the major milestones (e.g., learn about security issues and research methods to improve the childproofing, set up a childproofing system, regularly monitor child's activities using available tools, and so on) are very similar and occur in the same order.

So, why not just identify the major milestones? Because understanding the specific ways in which people approach and organize themselves around tasks can help you make good decisions about the design of your new product. Different Mapping participants who have similar goals will be able to tell you which parts of the process are shared by everyone, and which vary according to personal knowledge or preferences.

Together, Anne, Philip, Albert, Candace, and John will help you understand how parents tend to think about and behave regarding online security for their children. Individually, they will help you understand how different people have tried to solve this issue for themselves. Both types of information can be helpful. When you look at the contributions of each parent to your Maps, you will probably find that each approach inspires ideas for process improvements and that their differences help illuminate the complexities you will want to analyze when you create your Design Maps. In this way, Reality Maps function much like usability tests. The insights you get from them are not statistically significant and are not guaranteed to be unbiased, but they do uncover experiences and difficulties many of your users are likely to share.

Explore complex processes and interactions with branches and layers

Although we do believe that most experiences can be expressed in a relatively linear fashion, it is also true that many processes branch and/or depend on very specific interactions among various subprocesses. You can use branching and layering to explore these aspects of your task domain.

Maps tend to look more complex and messier as you add more details to them, as you talk to more people, and as you learn more about existing processes. This makes sense. If there is a good business case for your product, it is probably because someone understood that the current process needed improvement. Your goal should not be to work on the Maps until there is nothing left to learn about the process. Rather, your goal should be to continue Mapping until you believe you have built a solid understanding of the task domain.

Branching

All processes include decision points. Many of these decision points are relatively minor and do not affect the overall process significantly (e.g., Tanner deciding to find a clue for the Skatepunkz game versus the Moneybags game). However, there are some decisions that

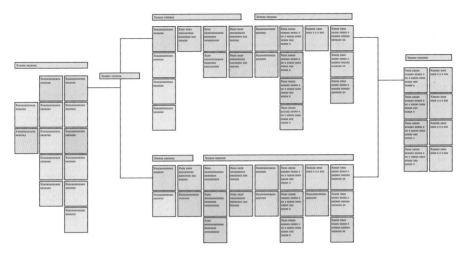

FIGURE 10.18: *Map with branches.*

radically affect the user experience (e.g., whether the child registering is old enough to do so independently or not). When you encounter this type of decision and its consequences, you can:

- Create a new Map to express the differences in user experience associated with each choice (or, if there are many, a representative subset of choices). This is a good idea if you think the choice leads to completely divergent experiences.

- Branch your existing Map to express the differences in user experience (see Figure 10.18). This is good idea if you think the choice leads to experiences that diverge in the short term and that converge later in the process.

Layering

Branches allow you to depict major decision points and their experiential ramifications for the user. Layers allow you to show disagreement among Mapping participants and/or the flow of experiences among various players in the process. In other words, layered Maps can:

- Highlight differences in experiences among users with *the same* roles and goals
- Highlight differences in experiences among users with *different* roles and goals.

Layered Maps for users with the same roles and goals

Consider Figure 10.19. In this example, the two layers correspond to two different Mapping participants. You might create a Map like this if you first Map with Herbert and then Map with Phyllis, who disagrees with the process Herbert described. Note that the major phases in the process are distinguished. Wherever there are sticky notes for both Herbert and Phyllis, the readers of the Map can assume that Herbert and Phyllis disagree on the process. When there

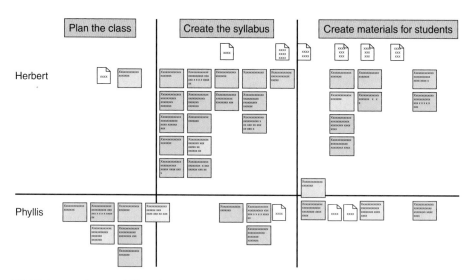

FIGURE 10.19: *Layered Map showing disagreement between two teachers describing what they believe to be the same process.*

are no sticky notes in Phyllis' layer, the reader can assume that her description of the process matches Herbert's. For example, Herbert and Phyllis disagree on aspects of Planning the Class and Creating Materials for Students, but agree on the process for Creating the Syllabus. If Herbert and Phyllis approached the tasks in the same—or similar—ways, the Maps would appear to "line up" more, with fewer differences between the Herbert process and the Phyllis process. Even at a distance, a layered Map makes it easy to see when different users' processes diverge.

When you have finished creating a layered Map to illustrate disagreement between Mapping participants, your next step should be to explore the ways in which the two participants disagreed:

● Can you identify another person who can shed light on the two different processes?

● Do Herbert and Phyllis really have the same goals and responsibilities?

● Do the differences highlight a problem, or are they simply two equally efficient ways of getting the same thing done?

● Do the participants believe that both processes must be supported, or at least addressed, in your new product?

When you create a layered Map (for any reason), it is particularly valuable to include artifact indicators and to list the name of the artifacts (usually documents) described to you by the

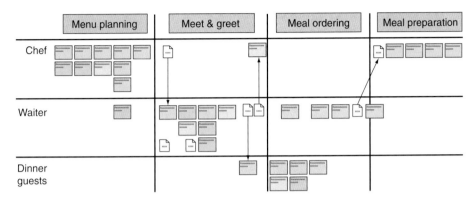

FIGURE 10.20: *Layered Map showing the experience flow that might occur among a chef, a waiter, and a dinner guest at a restaurant.*

Mapping participants. We often find that differences in opinion about the "right" way to accomplish a particular goal or set of tasks can be traced back to, or illuminated by, the documents that are part of the existing process. For example, in figure 10.19, the artifacts each teacher describes might shed some light on these differences. Perhaps the first document in Herbert's row includes his planning notes from the many previous years he has taught this class. Phyllis's definition of a syllabus might be very different from Herbert's. Examining the various artifacts in the Maps can help you solve the "mystery" behind differences.

Layered Maps for users with different roles and goals

Layered Maps can also highlight the flow of experience as it moves from one person to the next. For example, examine Figure 10.20. Unlike Figure 10.19, the layers in this Map correspond to users with different roles and goals.

This type of layered Map can illustrate how responsibilities are handed off among various people. If you create a Map like this one, pay special attention to *how* the various people communicate with and depend on one another. These are often experiences that are rich with opportunities for improvement.

Analyze Maps for repetitiveness, complexity, and overall flow

Once you identify aspects of the current process that could use improvement, you can analyze the root causes and begin the redesign process. Some of the problems with the current process may even have obvious solutions (and the solutions may have already been suggested by one or more of your Mapping participants, as illustrated in Figure 10.21). Even if you see obvious localized improvements you can make, it is worth completing a more thorough analysis to see if there are holistic changes that could improve the end-to-end experience.

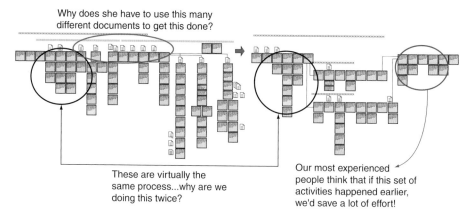

Why does she have to use this many different documents to get this done?

These are virtually the same process...why are we doing this twice?

Our most experienced people think that if this set of activities happened earlier, we'd save a lot of effort!

FIGURE 10.21: *Reality informs Design. When you have created your Reality Maps, evaluate them carefully to identify potential process improvements.*

"Perform" your Reality Maps

Walk through the experiences depicted in your Reality Maps with your core team. If you have personas (even if they are just skeletons or collections of assumptions at this point), have one of your core team members read through the Reality Map from the point of view of the Mapping participants. The rest of your core team can observe as the reader "performs" the Reality Map and reacts to the tasks. Your walkthrough will help you identify aspects of the process that are confusing, irritating, or difficult. When you find an area of the process that is ripe for improvements, you can move on to analyze why and how the current process is broken so that you can redesign it. You can use insights from this exercise to get started with the Design Maps you will use to build a new experience for your personas.

When you and your team have evaluated the Reality Maps and have some ideas for improvements, you can create Design Maps to explore the effects of changes you would like to make. Design Maps will allow you to quickly (and inexpensively) visualize new end-to-end experiences before you create wireframes, prototypes, or mock-ups.

How do you know when a Reality Map is "done" and when you have created enough Reality Maps?

Whatever you do, do not allow Reality Mapping to become an endless process. Your job is not to create a perfectly complete set of Reality Maps; it is to collect enough information about your target users and what they do today to help you design a new product. To do this, it is not necessary to make sure the Maps are absolutely complete down to the last detail. It is also not necessary to interview every single person who might be able to add insights to the Map. The purpose is to understand the big picture and provide a venue for exploration of subsections of existing processes. Think of Maps as being similar to prototypes:

- You do not need to (and probably should not) create an exhaustive set of them to get the value.
- You are looking for big insights and obvious problem areas.
- When you start to see repeated experiences and information, it means it is time to stop.

As they near completion, Maps:

- Look a lot less yellow.
- Acquire new sticky notes far less often.
- Need to be printed less often.
- Are in high demand. Mapping participants ask you to give them copies of the Maps.
  - ○ "I've never seen my whole world in front of me like this!"
  - ○ "I can use this for training."
  - ○ "I just want to put it on my wall! It is cool!"

Step 4: Harvest the Reality Maps for information to use in your personas

Personas should describe not only characteristics of people but behaviors related to your product domain. Your Maps will be good sources of information about the scope of particular roles and the ways different roles and goals overlap with one another. Your Maps will also expose the particularly good and particularly bad aspects of current experiences you can use to enrich your personas. During the *adulthood* phase, it is useful to provide detailed examples of real experiences to help designers and developers identify with the personas you have created. Maps allow you to do this based on data you have gathered rather than on assumptions. You can 'ask' your Maps the following questions:

- What is the basic outline of the task or job?
- If you hired someone to do this job or set of tasks, and had to give them a sense of the entire process end-to-end, how would you do it?
- What are the most important tasks in the Map?
- What are the results of this process?
- Is this process done alone?
- Is this process part of a bigger process? Where does it fit in?
- How do people *think* about this task domain?

If your project ever changes, or if for any reason you have to revisit or partially recreate your personas, your Maps will be helpful. Because Reality Maps describe entire experiences, they can be "reharvested." Because the Maps convey the way users think about what they do, they often provide answers to questions you did not think about when Mapping and/or that come up long after the Mapping has been completed. This means that you can return to Reality Maps to answer questions as they come up, often without revisiting the users.

WHAT ARE DESIGN MAPS?

Design Maps tell stories that look into the future. These stories describe how your personas will behave once your new product is built. Design Maps are created by your team based on their understanding of several important design factors. First, thanks to your Reality Maps, your team is familiar with the existing process. With the help of your persona set, they now share an understanding of the roles, existing and imagined, needed to carry out your task. Your team also has a very strong knowledge of the technologies that can be incorporated into your new product to make users' lives easier.

Those familiar with scenario-based design will recognize that Design Maps have a distinct similarity to scenarios, and Whitney Quesenbery's chapter on personas and storytelling describes Maps as a type of story (see Chapter 9). Scenarios are short prose stories that describe how aspects of your product will be—or should be—used. Design Maps are both a special type of scenario and a process by which to create scenarios and modify them. Design Maps are flowchart versions of many scenarios strung together to create a big picture of the experience your product will support. Design Maps are inexpensive (both in terms of time and materials) and are most helpful when built before paper prototypes and certainly before any code is written.

The process for creating Design Maps is largely the same as the process for creating Reality Maps. You will still use the same color codes for the four colors of sticky notes and you will still create a row of steps with associated questions, comments, and design ideas arrayed beneath. Just as you did for your Reality Maps, you will identify major goals and explore the start-to-finish tasks required to achieve those goals. Reality Maps describe goals and their associated tasks, as do Design Maps. While the goals described in Reality Maps and Design Maps will probably be very similar, the tasks may be markedly different (see Figure 10.22).

Reality Maps describe the present; Design Maps explore the future

The Reality Maps you built described the roles and tasks for a process in the present. Your Design Maps will describe a future process your software will support. Because Design Maps

Reality Maps	Design Maps
Describe the present	Describe the future
Describe the activities of real people	Describe the activities of personas
Created in cooperation with users	Created with your internal team
Have a right answer (they either accurately describe the present or they don't)	Don't have a single right answer (they explore possible futures)

FIGURE 10.22: *Differences between Reality Maps and Design Maps.*

are experiments, you may build more than one to test out different ideas and see which one makes the most sense *before* you write code or even create paper prototypes.

Reality Maps analyze the tasks and experiences of real people; Design Maps are the bridge between task analysis and design

By referring to your personas instead of real users when you start building your Design Maps, you immediately begin to reap all of the benefits personas offer your team. First, with everyone talking about personas the team stops focusing on the quirks of individual users and starts thinking about the commonalities among users. Second, when your team shares a vision of the users you are working to help, they can make design decisions based on this vision.

Sometimes in redesigning a process, an entirely new role emerges for whom there was no "real" person in your Reality Maps. In building a software product to help law firms complete the electronic discovery process for very large cases, we realized that, where documents were previously printed out for attorney review by hand, our Design Map called for software that would run a series of processes on the electronic documents before they were ever printed. Loading the electronic documents and running these processes required a new role, a new person who had not existed in the Reality Map. In this case we could not talk about real people because there was no one doing this work in the real world yet. We created a persona, Simon, to take on these tasks in the Design Map.

Design Maps can be created with or without real users

Design Maps allow you to explore innovative processes and methods, and it is important that you be free from current users' habits and biases as you explore the potential for your product. Design Maps are a designer's tool, and users should only be involved if they are part of the design team. Design Maps should be built using the birds-eye view of the problem. This view encompasses the problems current users have *and* the potential of new technologies.

Often someone peering into a situation from the outside (you) has the advantage of a fresh perspective and new ideas that users just do not see. The users you work with will have clever ideas that will make even the most seasoned designer say, "Duh, why didn't I think of that!?" Luckily, you have already captured many of these ideas as pink sticky notes on your Reality Map. Don't worry; the personas you have developed will speak for your users. You have also left the communication channels open with the real people who informed your personas so that they can contact you if they have additional ideas after your Reality Mapping sessions. In addition, once you have built a Design Map (or series of alternative Design Maps) you can bring users and stakeholders back in to give feedback. It is generally easier for users to give feedback on your design ideas than to ask them to start with a blank slate.

Design Maps will help you create materials for supporting the development process

Design Maps aren't just an interesting exercise. Once you have created your Design Maps, there are some very practical ways you can use them to support the product development process. In step 3, below, we describe how you can use your Design Maps to:

- Create additional scenarios and use cases for exploration and comparison
- Conduct walkthroughs of your new design before a line of code is written
- Track design changes during the development process
- Streamline the communication between the product design and development team and other groups in your organization.

Story from the field

FORGET EVANGELISM. SHOW RESULTS AND NEW METHODS WILL SPREAD LIKE WILDFIRE.

Sylvia Olveda and **Raina Brody,** Usability Specialists, Amazon.com

Persona development and Reality and Design Mapping sessions were introduced over a year ago by a single usability specialist at Amazon.com. Initially, just a few teams tried Reality Maps and personas to help with new projects and redesigns of existing features. These teams then cautiously began to use their personas as the 'characters' in Design Maps. They used the Design Maps to explore key processes and discover problematic experiences related to their projects.

How did we get from a few isolated projects to the persona and Mapping "mania" we have today? The truth is, we didn't do a thing. We tried to evangelize these new methods, but acceptance and interest only built momentum via word of mouth among the designers. One or two designers realized that personas and Maps made it easier to get from ideas to designs and helped them build better products. Other designers asked how they got the good results and soon many designers were approaching us to determine if personas and Mapping were appropriate for their projects. We even had designers asking us to convince the rest of their teams to come to us earlier in the design process because it would help make requirements gathering and product definition easier.

Recently, teams have started coming to us with their personas already drafted. These teams are ready to dive right into a Mapping exercise. We knew persona and Mapping mania were in full force when we started to hear developers we had not even met talk about these processes in hallways and in the cafeteria. Persona development and Mapping have become services offered by all members of the usability team at Amazon.com—it's the only way we can keep up with the demand! Now when we introduce additional new methods, we don't do as much active evangelizing. Instead, we use the new methods in a few projects and let the results speak for themselves.

THE DESIGN MAPPING PROCESS

Design Maps show the experiences your personas *might* have given various designs for your future product or process. Design Maps are experiments in process reengineering. They use the same linear format and allow designers to "prototype" new experiences, from the perspective of the personas, using the same basic elements they used when creating the Reality Maps. Design Maps are built by your team based on their:

● Knowledge of existing processes (captured in Reality Maps)

● Understanding of the personas

● Understanding of the technologies available to incorporate into the product

● Ability to streamline work processes.

 Meanwhile, at G4K...

MAPPING AT G4K

Reality Maps have given the G4K team a clear sense of how real kids, parents, and teachers approach the Internet and the satisfactions, frustrations, and fears they encounter. G4K also has their cast of personas:

- *Tanner Thompson (the tenacious tinkerer):* An intense nine-year-old boy who loves computers, games, and gadgets of all types
- *Colbi Chandler (the creative child):* A charming seven-year-old elementary school girl who loves to do anything imaginative, crafty, or fun
- *Austin Chandler (the active competitor):* An athletic 13-year-old boy who is interested in anything competitive or challenging
- *Preston Pasquez (a precocious preschooler):* A bright-eyed and inquisitive three-year-old boy who is intrigued by anything new
- *Irene Pasquez (the involved parent):* Mother of Preston who is, in one word, *engaged* (regarding her child)
- *Elaine Evans (the enlightened elementary school teacher):* A young and relatively new elementary school teacher who loves what she does and takes it very seriously.

With these personas in mind, the G4K team can now create Design Maps to explore the features and services the G4K site will contain. They have ideas about how their personas are likely to respond to the idea of a new destination site for kids, and have a good idea about what their expectations and initial biases will be. They also know all about the technologies available to design into G4kids.com, and know the goals the company has for the site. They hopefully know which of their competitors' sites

(Meanwhile, at G4K..., continued)

are working well and which are not, and know what types of features kids, parents, and teachers would love to see in their product.

What they do not immediately know is how to build a product out of all of this information. They do not know exactly what will make the site exciting for Tanner and Colbi, acceptable for Irene, and useful for Elaine. They know that successful products must solve real problems for real people, and offer alternatives to the "old" ways of doing things that are attractive enough to be worth learning. Design Maps allow them to experiment with ways of putting these puzzle pieces together on one big sheet of paper and reorganizing them until they fit together perfectly. Design Maps will merge the lessons learned in Reality Maps and the potential of technology to change things for the better. Equipped with this information and a lot of sticky notes, the G4K team can get started.

Step 1: Decide which processes you want to Map

When you created your Reality Maps, you focused on capturing the big picture before diving into details. You will do the same thing as you create your Design Maps. You can try to create Design Maps for all of the experiences your product will support, but this may prove to be a daunting task. When we create Design Maps, we create them as follows:

- *Design a Map for the big picture:* This Map shows the entire experience end to end, and therefore describes activities in very broad terms. Think of this overview Design Map as analogous to a map of the United States with a line drawn on it to show the route of a cross-country driving trip. The overview Map should give the reader a general sense of direction and the order of progression, but should not contain details. For example, the G4K team could create a high-level Design Map for Tanner's entire experience with G4K.com, from getting an account to logging on and navigating, to activities and playing games.

- *Design Maps for achieving major milestones:* These Maps should "fit into" the overall Map, but should explore individual goals and tasks more specifically. In the cross-country trip example, a "major milestone" Map would be the equivalent of a highway map showing the roads you used to traverse a single state. For example, the G4K team could dive to a more detailed level in Mapping the singular process of Tanner getting a G4kids.com account.

- *Design Maps for critical details:* These Maps should fit into the milestone Maps much as the milestones fit into the big picture. These Maps explore very specific details of particular tasks, the way an enlargement of a downtown area shows the specific details of the way streets crisscross a city. At this level of detail, the G4K team could Map the navigational process that Tanner would follow to choose a specific activity.

The Design Maps you create should explore the ways your personas achieve the goals you have established for them. Remember that their roles and goals may change in your new designs. In the G4K example, the team might decide to use Design Maps to explore the following experiences:

- Tanner gets a G4kids.com account and visits G4K.com a couple of times a week.
- Colbi uses G4kids.com to finish an assignment created by Elaine.
- Preston plays on G4kids.com with Irene's help.

Step 2: Create the Maps

Gather the appropriate stakeholders from your team and start creating your Design Maps. Let the Design Mapping participants know what you expect of them. The purpose of a Design Mapping session is to explore and record one end-to-end experience you could create for your Personas. For the G4K example, the team started the Mapping exercise by asking themselves, "Knowing what we do about the way things are done today and the possibilities that are available, how is Tanner going to interact with G4kids.com?"

The process for creating a Design Map looks just like the process for a Reality Map. However, instead of interviewing a real participant you consult with one or more of your personas. Figure 10.23 shows a Design Map of Tanner's registration process on G4K's yet-to-be-built Web portal.

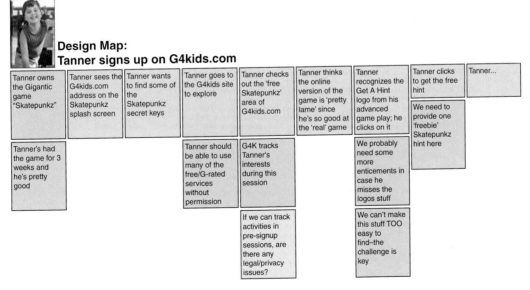

FIGURE 10.23: *A Design Map exploring how Tanner registers himself on the G4K site. Design Maps are created by your team and explore the new experiences you are going to build into your product.*

Handy Detail

SAMPLE SCRIPT FOR THE FIRST DESIGN MAPPING SESSION

Welcome, everyone! Thanks for making the time to participate in our Design Mapping session today. A lot of work has gone into preparing for these sessions. Interviews have been conducted with a number of people who will use our product in different ways. From these interviews, Reality Maps have been built to describe the way people are doing X today. Personas were also developed to describe the major roles as they are envisioned for people using our new product. We have determined that people have difficulty with X in the products currently available. In the new product, we will work to solve this problem for users. You are all familiar with the Reality Maps and personas and we're ready to create a delightful new product for X users everywhere!

For those of you who participated in Reality Mapping, the process is very similar. We will be creating a giant flow chart, but instead of charting how users do X now, this time we will record a possibility for how our personas will be able to do X with our new product. We will still use sticky notes with the same color codes: blue for steps, green for comments (anything that tells us more about a step), yellow for questions, and pink for ideas.

We are going to start with a single persona and a single goal and describe what it might feel like to use our software to achieve that goal. Remember, there is not necessarily a right answer. In fact, we may build several Design Maps that describe different ways a persona can achieve a certain goal. Also, keep in mind that we won't dive into the details during this exercise. This is not the time to decide what color certain buttons should be. Stick to fairly broad brush stokes and we will settle details in the specifications for each feature that will be informed by this Map. As we move to Design new experiences, please keep the following questions in mind:

- Are we furthering the goals of the persona with this Design?
- Do the tasks the personas perform match their stated skills or skills they are likely to be willing to learn?
- Does the new process we are building provide clear advantages over the old way?

If we can answer yes to these questions as we move through the Mapping process, we will be on the right track. Okay, let's get started. Let's begin by describing the experience of persona X as he makes coffee for himself and his wife. Are there any assumptions we need to start out with?

Managing Design Mapping sessions

Encourage Mapping participants to focus on the *experience*, not on the *tool*. The goal is not to have a Map that tells you "the serial number registration tracking database will feed the score records to the page via ASP," but one that says, "Tanner can see his Skatepunkz high scores on G4kids.com."

During Design Mapping sessions, remind your team to consider the following:

- Do the tasks assigned to personas in the Design Map correspond to your personas' skills? For example, if Preston the preschooler is expected to type in a URL address to access the site, he is not being well served by the new design. If Tanner's Design Map allows him to invite his buddies to come play games with him online with just a couple of mouse clicks, you are on the right track.

- Does this new process being constructed in the Map offer undeniable advantages to the personas over the old way of doing things?

- Are we assuming things have to be done a certain way just because that is the way they are done now?

As you move through a Mapping session, remember to table questions that might sidetrack your work by providing everyone with yellow sticky notes and encouraging participants to write down difficult questions and issues and post them on the Map. During your Design Mapping session, you might hear a comment such as, "Well, if we're assuming Tanner uses the Internet at school all the time, can we assume he's pretty good at navigating Web sites? If he is, that would make things a lot easier. We would not have to dedicate part of the site to teaching him how to use links." This is a good opportunity to refer to your personas. Do you have information about Tanner's level of Web experience? How long will it take him to learn the differences between doing things online versus doing things on a PC? Your personas will be able to immediately answer some of these questions. Others will have to go onto to the Map to be answered later.

Sometimes you will want to move fairly quickly, placing blue steps across the top of the Map and filling in details later. Other times your team might find it most effective to hash out the details under each step before moving to the next one. In either case, you will want to limit Mapping sessions to two to three hours each.

After each session, follow up on any questions or issues raised and add answers to the Map. As with Reality Maps, it can be useful to convert the sticky-note paper versions of your Maps into electronic versions in Microsoft Visio, Omnigraffle, or a similar tool. This makes it easy for participants to review progress and quickly scan for new material. The electronic versions are useful for printing in various formats and sending to stakeholders for review at a distance. An example of a completed Design Map is shown in Figure 10.24.

Use Design Maps to create wireframes

Wireframes tend to evolve naturally from Design Maps (see Figure 10.25). Once you and your team have agreed on the experience you want to facilitate for your personas, it is relatively easy to use the steps, assumptions, questions, and design ideas in the Maps to create wireframes of the product's UI.

With your team, identify the columns of the Design Map that "go together" and should be grouped on a single interface. At this point, the user interface designer or graphic designer

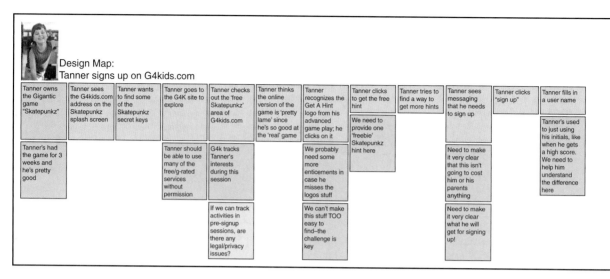

Design Map:
Tanner signs up on G4kids.com

Tanner owns the Gigantic game "Skatepunkz"	Tanner sees the G4kids.com address on the Skatepunkz splash screen	Tanner wants to find some of the Skatepunkz secret keys	Tanner goes to the G4K site to explore	Tanner checks out the 'free Skatepunkz' area of G4kids.com	Tanner thinks the online version of the game is 'pretty lame' since he's so good at the 'real' game	Tanner recognizes the Get A Hint logo from his advanced game play; he clicks on it	Tanner clicks to get the free hint	Tanner tries to find a way to get more hints	Tanner sees messaging that he needs to sign up	Tanner clicks "sign up"	Tanner fills in a user name
Tanner's had the game for 3 weeks and he's pretty good		Tanner should be able to use many of the free/g-rated services without permission	G4k tracks Tanner's interests during this session			We probably need some more enticements in case he misses the logos stuff	We need to provide one 'freebie' Skatepunkz hint here		Need to make it very clear that this isn't going to cost him or his parents anything		Tanner's used to just using his initials, like when he gets a high score. We need to help him understand the difference here
				If we can track activities in pre-signup sessions, are there any legal/privacy issues?		We can't make this stuff TOO easy to find—the challenge is key			Need to make it very clear what he will get for signing up!		

FIGURE 10.24: *A completed Design Map for "Tanner signs up on G4K.com."*

should be heavily involved. Consider what information you are collecting from the personas, and when you are collecting it, so that you can plan to display it on the UI at the right times (e.g., if you have not asked the persona for their name yet, you cannot create a wireframe for a personalized interface).

In Figure 10.25, you can see that the G4K team created very basic wireframes of the G4K.com pages based on the activities they described in the Design Map "Tanner signs up on G4K.com." As they created the wireframes, they identified a few more questions (note the yellow sticky on one of the early wireframes). As they evolved the wireframes, they continued to reference the original Design Map to make sure the site design supported the experience design in the Design Map.

Step 3: Evaluate and communicate your solutions

Perhaps the most important benefit of Design Maps (and wireframes) is that they hold and communicate a shared vision of the project for your entire team. Seeing the big picture early on in the project helps motivate everyone toward the common goal of making it real. Design Maps enable your entire team to see the product from the personas' points of view, giving the architects of the product the opportunity to understand and empathize with users. A deeper understanding of the planned product and personas early on in the development process can enhance each team member's work on your product—whether they are coding, marketing, managing, testing, funding, or selling it.

Use Design Maps to get different views of your product in action

Remember that you can continue to make Design Maps to explore various solutions your product could support. It is very useful to be able to take these variations to stakeholders for

Design Map:
Tanner signs up on G4K.com *(continued)*

Tanner chooses a password	Tanner clicks "sign me up"	Tanner sees a message that he has to get parental permission	Tanner has to be able to 'save' his request until he can show permission	Until Tanner gets permission, he can still play with G-rated stuff (if no COPPA issues)	Can Tanner log off and log back on much later to get permission?	Tanner tells Mom he wants permission for G4K.com	Tanner returns to G4K and puts in his name and pwd	Tanner and mom see a big message 'waiting for permission'	Tanner's mom clicks the 'parents' link to read about G4K.com	→
Do kids like Tanner need a password for the computer? Find out from research if the parents usually log him in	As soon as he's done this we should give him a freebie hint, to keep him going!		Are there COPPA issues with this as well?	Tanner should see a reminder that we're waiting for permission	Are there COPPA issues with this as well?	Mom probably has no idea what G4K.com is		We should have easy 'parental' links on every page, with a wizard for parental setup	Need to find out what we have to post re: COPPA for mom!	See 'Irene sets up an account for her kid'
We probably shouldn't require case sensitivity–Tanner might not remember		Tanner's mother isn't home, and she needs to give him permission						Parental setup should NOT totally reset Tanner's account. He shouldn't lose preferences he's set up so far. It should just add functionality		
		We can't ask Tanner for his mother's email address–privacy issue! Plus he probably doesn't know it								

feedback. For example, you could create one Design Map that shows Tanner getting an account on G4kids.com himself, and another showing what the experience would be like if his mother got the account for him. Comparing these two Maps could help development managers understand the resources required to build each option in light of the persona's experience. You may also choose to create a single Design Map that covers the interactions

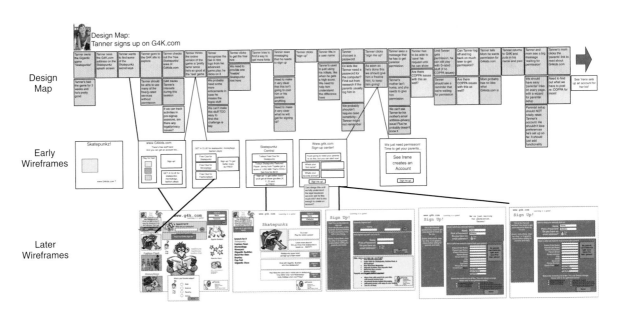

FIGURE 10.25: *Wireframes evolve naturally from Design Maps. You and your Mapping team can evaluate which process steps belong together and design the interface flow accordingly.*

Handy Detail

USE YOUR MAPS TO INTRIGUE (AND INVITE PARTICIPATION FROM) YOUR CO-WORKERS

Maps are intriguing artifacts. They are colorful, and the paper versions that still have sticky notes all over them tend to "flutter" as people walk by. Use these attention-getting aspects of the Maps to your advantage. Anyone who stops and reads a portion of the Map will begin to understand how real people experience real tasks and have real goals related to your company's product space. Your colleagues may begin to cluster around the Maps, and discussions will sprout. People will come into your office to ask you what the heck the big things in the hallway are, and you will be able to tell them that the Maps are "windows into the world of our real users." Later, when you create Design Maps that describe the experiences you want your personas to have, your colleagues will be somewhat familiar with the format and understand what the Maps are trying to convey. If you do post the Reality Maps in your company, make sure that you carefully and very visibly note:

- What draft the Map is, and whether you consider it complete
- The experience it depicts.

We have also found it helpful to make new material very visible on the Maps. We do this by placing red borders around the notes added from the most recent session (or since the last printing). In this way, interested parties can scan a posted Map and quickly see what has been changed or added recently.

Note: Share with Care!

If you choose to share your Map, do it carefully. You will have to decide for yourself whether it is appropriate to post your Maps in a publicly accessible area, and if so what Mapping symbols should be removed before doing so. For example, before you post them, take real names out of the Reality Maps. Later, when you launch your completed personas into your organization, you do not want colleagues to *already* be talking about the real people (Anne, Albert, John) you have Mapped with. Consider using the name of the role instead; in this case, "the parent." You might also want to remove any notations that are critical of the current process. You can certainly note areas that are ripe for improvement without posting a version of your Map with a "Mr. Yuk" on it.

Invite Participation

If you hang your Maps in visible places—especially Design Maps—invite passersby to participate by adding comments, questions, or design ideas (see Figure 10.26). Leave a pile of colored sticky notes and pens for this very purpose. If you are inviting participation on a sticky-note version of the Map (in other words, not a digitized version), make sure the sticky notes you leave out are a color different from those already on the Map so that new comments are not confused with original Map elements.

WRITE ON ME
Please feel free to
write on me or add
sticky notes.
Questions? Call
extension 5555!

FIGURE 10.26: *Invite participation when you hang your Maps.*

of all of the personas. This type of Map can be very helpful, especially for illuminating communication patterns and getting an overview of "who does what when" across a lengthy process.

Use Design Maps to support walkthroughs and to create scenarios and use cases

Design Maps (and their associated wireframes) are a perfect document to work from when communicating project plans to stakeholders. Once your Design Maps are completed, you can use them to perform design walkthroughs of your product with other team members. Have someone read through the Map, and another person check the prototype or the product to make sure the Mapped process is supported by the product's design.

Your Design Maps will become official historical documents, much like a formal specification document. You can use your Maps (and the assumptions they contain about how you think your product should be experienced by the personas) to make sure your product is not swerving in the wrong direction as those inevitable compromises are made during development.

You can use Design Maps to help communicate and clarify what, exactly, a given feature is. This is accomplished via *walkthrough scenarios* that demonstrate the feature in use by the personas in a step-by-step fashion. Design Maps show the persona's experience using your yet-to-be-built product from end to end. They are long scenarios, and they are a wonderful source of use cases. After you have decided which Design Map you are going to follow to build your product, you can pull individual scenarios and use cases out of the Maps. Because you have created the Maps first, you know that the scenarios you pull out of them fit together seamlessly.

For example, when preparing to write the interface specification for the kid's registration interface of G4kids.com, the product manager can focus in on the "Tanner signs up on G4kids.com" Design Map. He or she can use subsets of the sticky notes to create an interface document or technical specification document. Using this portion of the Design Map for reference, the project manager can create a section of the specification document that addresses the technical underpinnings required to support the experiences.

Use Design Maps to evaluate design changes during development

Even the best and most thorough designs evolve and change during the development process. As your development team begins coding your new product, check in frequently to evaluate what they are building against what you *thought* they were going to build. Use the Design Maps to "test" the emerging product. Does the product being built actually support the experience you have designed?

If for some reason the product cannot be created as designed, return to your Design Maps and evaluate the effect of the changes on your personas' experiences. If you find yourself changing elements of the Map to accommodate unexpected design changes, do not despair. It is much better to know sooner than later about these changes and the potential problems they will cause. Reconvene your Mapping team—and members of the development staff—to analyze the effects of changes and to tweak the design accordingly. If you cannot solve experience problems with code (perhaps it is too late to fix something you discovered to be broken), you can at the very least create support materials to mitigate the impact on the personas (or, rather, the end users they represent).

Story from the field

A PICTURE OF A DESIGN MAP COULD SAVE YOU HOURS

—Whitney Quesenbery, Whitney Interactive Design (*wqusability.com*)

I was asked to review an early version of this chapter and as a result was carrying this chapter around with me for a short period. In a meeting with a new partner, we were struggling to find a way to bring together some very incoherent Design ideas from our client. After almost 15 minutes of hand waving, I threw caution to the wind and showed them a complete Map as illustrated in this chapter. They immediately got excited— and saw instantly what it would do for us and how it would help us collaborate. It saved me hours.

Use Design Maps to communicate with other departments

Teams responsible for product launch and post-launch activities and materials love Design Maps—especially if they are kept up to date and do actually reflect the experiences your product will support. Documentation teams can use Design Maps as outlines for documentation, testing teams can extract use cases and test cases, marketing teams can build materials that express the value of the new experiences you have created, and so on.

SUMMARY

Reality and Design Maps will not build your product for you, but they can help. The most difficult part of Mapping is the courage it takes to stand up in front of a lot of experts and ask them to essentially "dumb down" the processes they undertake every day. But if you can drum up the courage to do this, you will find yourself—and your product team—in possession of a clear picture of the problems you need to fix with your new product.

The best thing about Reality and Design Maps is that they break down barriers. Sticky notes are not intimidating and function as a sort of equalizer. If people who hold very different positions in hierarchies and job roles can all agree to work on a Map together, they usually find themselves communicating more clearly than they ever could before. It is almost as if the Mapper's willingness to ask for a basic explanation of a complex set of tasks releases everyone to talk openly with one another. Like personas, Maps are, if nothing else, excellent communication tools.

Together, Reality and Design Maps help you understand the bridge you are asking your future users to cross: from the familiar shores of what they do today to the unknown terrain of the new processes supported by your product. The real people who helped you create your Reality Maps will purchase your product, and as they change the way they accomplish their goals, they will have more and more in common with your personas.

Robert Barlow-Busch
"Bob the Builder"

Roles: Interaction designer, Usability specialist, Instructor

Goals:

Build stuff. Robert delights in creating products that people find useful and enjoyable, whether he's working with invisible "bits" (such as designing a Web application) or with very real "bolts" (such as restoring his Victorian-era home).

Build stuff better. Robert frequently turns a critical eye to the process of design, and especially enjoys learning from and sharing ideas with similarly-inclined people.

Eat sushi. His friends have simply given up asking what he feels like eating today, as the answer never changes.

Classic quote:

"Stop playing catch-up with the competition. Instead, figure out what makes you different from them — then make those differences a distinguishing feature of your customer experience."

Almost daily, Robert cringes as someone pushes the wrong button in his office building's elevator — one of the slowest in the city — and wishes he could simply press it once again to cancel the selection. He would also have appreciated a simple cancel mechanism last winter when his daughter discovered the "panic" button on his rental car's keychain — at five o'clock in the morning. What was the thinking behind these devices? How could they behave more appropriately? Robert puzzles at such questions almost constantly.

Though it borders on a preoccupation, this way of seeing the world serves Robert well in his work in Interaction Design and Usability. For 14 years, Robert has lent his designer's eye to teams building technology products in a range of industries such as logistics, scientific research, corporate real estate, and consumer electronics. Today, he's the Practice Director of Interaction Design at Quarry Integrated Communications, working with clients to build their business through user experience design. "I'm excited by the recent publicity around contributions of user experience to the bottom line," Robert says. "I remember several years ago how companies would say they focused on the customer, but when probed, could explain nothing about what that actually meant. That's changed now."

In an effort to further explore what it actually means to "focus on the customer," Robert introduced personas to Quarry in 2001 and pioneered their use in client projects. He now shares Quarry's experience in building personas with other design, usability, and marketing professionals through presentations and workshops, and with students at the University of Waterloo. His efforts caught the attention of Forrester Research in early 2005, when they listed Quarry as a source of expertise in their report, "Where To Get Help With Persona Projects."

Although Robert's work keeps him busy, nothing can compare to the action at his home. Three young children challenge him and his wife to keep up with their energy and curiosity. And Robert's proud to report that, perhaps unlike the myriad products in our world, his kids *always* behave appropriately. (Well, perhaps.)

11

MARKETING VERSUS DESIGN PERSONAS

Robert Barlow-Busch, *Quarry Integrated Communications*

At a restaurant near the edge of a picturesque canal in downtown Copenhagen, the sound of lapping water mingled with our conversation as we reflected on our trip. That afternoon, we had just completed the last interview with more than 30 potential users of my client's new product. Abruptly, John, my client's technology marketing manager, put down his glass and frowned.

"Let me tell you something. When I learned that our first step in this project would be to visit customers and create these made-up characters called 'personas,' I figured it would be a waste of time and money."

Uh-oh. Was that a sudden chill in the air?

"My team had already spent a year talking to customers. What could we learn that we didn't already know?" Then he grinned. "So, I must admit, I'm surprised how valuable this exercise has been after all."

Whew!

Over the past five years, I have had the opportunity to introduce personas to people in a variety of roles, and their initial reactions are usually quite strong for or against the idea. I work in the

Interaction Design and Usability group at a brand experience agency called Quarry Integrated Communications. As a consequence of this mix, our group often finds itself acting as a bridge between the worlds of marketing and product development. Thus, we have gained some experience with using personas in both contexts.

This chapter explores the relationship of personas to the practice of marketing. We will focus primarily on how to get the most from personas you have created to inform product design (*design personas*) by looking for ways they can contribute to marketing as well, although I will also share some thoughts on creating personas specifically for marketing purposes (*marketing personas*). We have experienced our share of ups and downs with personas at Quarry, but feel that overall they are a terrific tool for adding value across a variety of project work.

PERSONAS ALWAYS HAVE ONE FOOT IN THE WORLD OF MARKETING

Marketing is about customers.

—Allen Weiss

Although those of us in other professions may sometimes hold a more cynical view, it is a fact: *marketing is about customers.* It is about understanding their values, their behaviors, and their attitudes. "Without having this knowledge," we are told by Allen Weiss, founder and publisher of MarketingProfs.com, "the tactics of marketing are just blowing in the wind" [Weiss 2002].

Sound familiar? That is the same issue we tackle through the personas described in this book, except that so far we have been primarily concerned about preventing product *design* from blowing in the wind, rather than marketing.

Before going any further, let's clarify what is meant by this term *marketing,* beyond simply claiming that it's about customers. Marketing is a discipline that analyzes customers, competitors, and industry trends to create an overall understanding of a marketplace. This understanding then fuels two primary activities: strategy and communications.

Marketing *strategy* answers the question of how we maximize our ability to compete successfully and generate revenue. It identifies the most profitable groups of customers for our products or services (through a process called *segmentation*) and formulates a plan for how to understand ourselves in relation to the competition (called *positioning*).

With a strategy in place, marketing then shifts into its other primary activity: *communications.* The strategy comes to life through a host of communications tactics such as advertising, public relations, Web site content, consumer or trade shows, publications, and so on.

Although the popular use of personas in product design is still relatively new, personas may at first glance look strangely familiar to people in marketing: over the years, marketers have developed an extensive library of methods and tools to assist with strategy and communications, some of which involve creating customer profiles or character sketches that echo the form of personas. Chapter 1 of this book includes examples such as Moore's "target customer characterizations," Upshaw's "indivisualization," and Mello's "customer image statements."

Indeed, the personas we create for product design share a common basis—both practically and ideologically—with some central ideas in marketing. Thus, even if we intend them to act in a purely design-related role, personas always have one foot in the marketing world.

Personas are a form of segmentation

> *"This Web application will be perfect for the desk of a CEO!"*
> *"Yeah, but what about for a Grandma, who wants to send cookies to her granddaughter at college?"*
>
> —Overheard in a design review at
> a Fortune 100 client

Segmentation is the process of breaking down the universe of potential customers into smaller, meaningful, more useful chunks. This is a necessary step in marketing because without the focus brought by a description of who we would specifically like to purchase our products, we might attempt to build and sell a product for everybody—which can be a recipe for satisfying nobody.

Any discussion of marketing invariably leads to, or springs from, questions of segmentation. A segmentation model forms the very underpinning of marketing strategy and communications, as it provides the means by which you identify customers, even prescribing the language by which you refer to them. That is exactly what a persona does for designers.

When you show off your personas to the folks in marketing, they see you waving yet another segmentation model. Generally, this will not win you a round of cheers and hearty congratulations. The selection of a segmentation model is a critical step in the formulation of a marketing strategy and is a decision neither made nor changed lightly.

The good news is that although personas are a form of segmentation they need not sit in opposition to market segments. Design personas divide the market according to people's goals and behaviors in the specific context of using a product. Marketing usually segments along different dimensions and is traditionally concerned with predicting behaviors in the context of purchasing a product. These models complement each other and paint a more complete

Segmentation Approach	Description of the Same Customer
Demographic	35-year-old married male with two daughters under age 5. Has a university Bachelor's degree. Annual income of $90,000.
Industry	Radiologist in a private medical clinic.
Psychographic	Aggressive achiever. Confident, success-oriented, motivated by praise.
Market maturity	Early majority. Interested in increasing the effectiveness of tools and processes. Adopts technology once it has proven itself.

FIGURE 11.1: *Examples of how segmentation models provide different perspectives on the same customer.*

picture of the customer, helping us craft better-informed strategies for both design and marketing. They help us build the right product for the right market. Common approaches to segmenting markets include (see Figure 11.1):

- *Demographics:* What are the gender, age, income level, and other socioeconomic traits of customers?
- *Industry:* Common in business-to-business markets, this model chunks customers into industry niches, organization types, and job roles.
- *Psychographics:* This approach assumes that psychological factors drive our behavior and identifies segments based on personality traits, beliefs, ideology, and so on.
- *Market maturity:* Although psychographic in nature, this particular approach gets a lot of attention in high-tech markets. A classic example is the technology adoption life cycle, marked by a progression through innovators, early adopters, early majority, late majority, and laggards.

Segments and personas answer different information needs

Marketers could hardly imagine devising a marketing plan without an appropriate segmentation model. Otherwise, their efforts are just "blowing in the wind." Designers feel the same way when building a product or Web site. However, it is uncommon for one model of the customer to serve both groups equally well, as the groups have distinct information needs. At Quarry, we call this *recognizing the differences that make a difference.* Sometimes these differences are … well, quite different. Let's consider an example.

One of our clients was entering a business-to-business (B2B) market niche in scientific research with a product based on some exciting new technology. The market segmentation model described industry slices, organizations, and job roles. It identified customers such as scientist, lab manager, technician, and IT support in industries such as biotechnology, pharmaceutical, and academic research—a familiar model to anyone who has worked in B2B markets, even if the exact titles are not. This client engaged Quarry to design the user interface of their product and to formulate its launch and marketing strategy.

To begin, we generated a cast of six personas through a research and analysis process very similar to the life cycle described in this book. Two of our resulting personas, Marcus and Tracy, played a key role in guiding the design. They are scientists with similar jobs, but very different mind-sets.

> Marcus is highly motivated by his to-do list and measures his success according to the number of samples he analyzes each week. Tracy, on the other hand, thinks of herself as a detective piecing together a puzzle from hidden clues and is unconcerned with (even unapologetic about) the number of samples she completes. Tracy measures success by discovering the unexpected, often found when combing through the scientific details that Marcus does not take time to investigate. These two people have essentially the same jobs, but their goals in using the product are quite different.

The surprise from this example came when we realized that Marcus and Tracy were in similar market segments. Earlier research had not captured this important distinction in the way people *used* the product. This is because it was not a *difference that made a difference* to the marketing strategy at the time. The segmentation model created for marketing played a vital role in identifying who we needed to design for—and would again play a key role in the product's sales and marketing plans—but clearly fell short in informing how to approach the design. Marcus and Tracy were practically the same person, from a marketing perspective.

Not so for design. We optimized the user interface for Marcus, our primary persona. It allowed him to start working within seconds, to quickly process large numbers of samples, and to automate repetitive actions. We accommodated Tracy's goals by providing tools that let her dive deep into the data and search for hidden clues, and although these tools were conveniently at Tracy's fingertips we kept them entirely out of Marcus' way—who would have found them distracting, at best.

The result? A potential customer summed it up after working with our final prototype for a while: "I can really tell that you have spent time with scientists *before* you designed this." Had we proceeded without the insights captured in our personas, the resulting software would not have acknowledged the two distinct working patterns of Tracy and Marcus. The design would have felt like a compromise to *both* types of users.

As you can see from this example, design personas segment your world of potential users according to the differences that make a difference to design. If you build a product or Web site relying only on market segmentation models, you will target the right market but you might deliver a product that behaves inappropriately for the people in that market. Geoffrey Moore, a respected author and marketing consultant for the technology industry, describes these resulting products as often having something for everybody, "but *everything* for nobody" [Moore 1995, p. 21]. Still, let's not forget: customer segmentation models are absolutely critical in defining who your organization believes are the most important (read "profitable") customers. If you proceed to create personas without first understanding how marketing has segmented your customers, you might experience the reverse scenario: building an absolutely terrific product but for the entirely wrong people.

A PLACE FOR PERSONAS IN TODAY'S MARKETING REVOLUTION

We are in the middle of a revolution. A revolution that will render the principles and models of traditional marketing obsolete. A revolution that will change the face of marketing forever.

—Bernd Schmitt, *Experiential Marketing*
[Schmitt 1999, p. 3]

Which type of car do you drive (see Figure 11.2): a manual transmission or an automatic? Many years ago, I worked as a driving instructor. Even today, the memory of adrenalin coursing through my body reaffirms a conclusion I reached during that experience: manual transmissions can be *really* difficult for people to learn.

From a usability engineering perspective, the automatic transmission is clearly superior. It is far simpler—and not just to learn, but to use. The manual transmission, for instance, requires you to engage two extra limbs on your body just to change gears while accelerating. That same action in an automatic involves nothing more than a slight twitch in one foot. You can even sip a coffee while doing so. Then why do many people prefer manual transmissions—often passionately so? I sometimes ask this question when teaching design workshops. People typically respond with answers such as:

● "I have more control in a manual transmission."
● "It's more engaging. It forces me to pay attention."
● "It's cheaper to purchase. And it's more fuel efficient."
● "It's much more fun!"

FIGURE 11.2: *Which do you prefer? For what reasons?*

- "I'd be embarrassed to drive an automatic. It's like a sign that you are not a good driver."
- "It just doesn't feel like driving if it's an automatic."

As these answers demonstrate, our reactions to a product or technology are based on a wide range of factors, both rational and emotional. This observation underlies a revolution that has hit both the design and marketing worlds: what matters is the *customer experience*.

The customer experience revolution

The question of whether a product is easy to use receives almost fanatical attention from usability practitioners, but—and this is difficult to admit, as a practitioner myself—it may have little effect on the bottom line. In their book *The 22 Immutable Laws of Branding*, Al and Laura Ries present the "Law of Quality," in which they illustrate this uncomfortable reality through numerous examples. "You can build quality into your product, but that has little to do with your success in the marketplace," they conclude [Ries and Ries 1998, p. 58]. Success may be determined by other factors in your competitive environment or in your customers' minds. Sometimes, for instance, we are happy to overcome difficult challenges if we feel we are making progress toward an important goal. In these situations, the quality of a tool may seem trivial, overshadowed by the fact that we can achieve the goal at all.

The term *customer experience* has come to represent our understanding that people form opinions based on their overall experience with a product or service, as opposed to judging it on any one dimension alone (such as "usability"). The idea has particularly taken hold in organizations involved with e-commerce, though it is by no means confined to that industry. And importantly for personas, the customer experience movement coincides with a broader revolution in the world of marketing—away from the shouting of messages to the nurturing of relationships.

Experiential marketing

We take those funds that might otherwise be used to shout about our service and put those funds instead into improving the service. That is the philosophy we have taken from the beginning.

—Jeff Bezos, CEO of Amazon.com
(*BusinessWeek* Online, August 2, 2004)

Traditional theories of marketing are based on a broadcast model of communication, meaning that organizations decide upon a "message" that will persuade "targets" to purchase their product. Targets are then bombarded with the message repeatedly over time. This theory of marketing gained prominence in the period after World War II in which a pent-up desire for consumption generated mass consumer demand, which could for the first time in history be satisfied by mass production and fueled by mass communication. In this environment, the broadcast model seemed to work quite well: tell people over and over that your product is great and after enough time they believe it is true and will purchase it. This theory has its roots in the propaganda campaigns staged during the war.

Today, these ideas about marketing are changing. Our cultural values have shifted, we have developed a healthy skepticism of advertising, and our access to information has increased. In the end, as consumers we have become tough nuts to crack. Consequently, a movement is afoot to discard the broadcast model in favor of a *dialog* model. Many companies now worry about how to build meaningful relationships with their customers, not how to hit them with a message in the hopes of persuading them to make a purchase.

For instance, the old wisdom called for companies to develop a *unique selling proposition* to guide their marketing efforts. The customer experience revolution rejects this idea in favor of the unique *buying* proposition. This shift in emphasis leads to different questions. Rather than, "What should we say?" we are inclined to ask, "What do our customers really care about?" Rather than, "What should our Web site look like?" we are more interested in, "What are people trying to accomplish on our site?"

These new questions affect not just the delivery of marketing, products, or services but cut right to the core of an organization's values. Starbucks, for example, thinks of their business less as selling coffee than of becoming a "third place" between home and work—an extension of people's front porch and home office. As a result, the customer's experience in the store becomes just as important as the coffee itself [Overholt 2004, p. 1]. Howard Schultz, CEO of Starbucks, proudly relates a story about how he "beamed with pride" when an employee made the discovery that "we are not, as he once thought, in the coffee business serving people. He said we are in the people business serving coffee" [Bedbury 2002, p. 50].

Where traditional approaches to marketing were largely analytical, rational, and product oriented, the approaches required for marketing customer experiences are decidedly more people oriented and emotional. This makes personas a potentially attractive tool for marketing, as their rich descriptions are useful in guiding decisions. Let's explore some related trends that present further opportunities for personas to play a role in your organization's marketing efforts.

An increased desire for customer intimacy

There is a great story about a consumer electronics manufacturer who held a focus group with teenagers to explore the idea of making portable stereos, or "ghetto blasters," in a range of colors. "Great idea!" came the feedback. Hot colors would be all the rage according to the kids in this group. As payment for participating, the manufacturer let everyone choose a stereo on their way out the door. And although many different colors were available, everyone chose black.

What went wrong here? Gerald Zaltman, in *How Customers Think*, criticizes research such as this as inadequate because its assumptions are wrong. "Consumers have far less access to their own mental activities than marketers give them credit for. Ninety-five percent of thinking takes place in our unconscious minds—that wonderful, if messy, stew of memories, emotions, thoughts, and other cognitive processes we're not aware of or that we can't articulate" [Zaltman 2003, p. 9]. Yet the market research industry is based on assumptions that people are rational and linear and able to explain (and predict) their thinking and behavior—and hence the popularity of third-party survey-based quantitative studies.

If we are unable to articulate 95% of our thinking, studies that occur outside the context of actually using or purchasing a product—especially those that rely on self-reported data— are clearly insufficient. Bernd Schmitt, author of *Experiential Marketing*, proclaims that customers want us to "dazzle their senses, touch their hearts, and stimulate their minds" [Schmitt 1999, p. 22]. To achieve this, we need to get close to our customers—to learn about them and from them. At Quarry, we call this *experiencing your customer's experience*. However, that is just the first step. Once you have experienced your customer's experience, it is critical that the resulting insights percolate throughout your organization so that everyone can act upon them in concert. Personas can be a useful tool in achieving this goal.

All of the characteristics that make personas so powerful in design make them equally so in marketing: portraying customers as *people* and not just *targets*; communicating insights in a distinctly human form, to build empathy; and bringing customers alive through the telling and sharing of stories, to aid collaboration across multidisciplinary teams. No, this approach to marketing is not as simple as broadcasting your unique selling proposition over and over again. This is about getting it right that one time someone opens your product's package or attempts to make a purchase on your Web site. Dazzling your customers requires getting close to the action, getting to know them intimately. To design and market a customer experience, we need rich, multidimensional models of the people who will enjoy it.

A need for richer descriptions of customers

Statistics alone do as much good describing people as a ruler does measuring a beach ball... . Statistics simply don't encompass the whole picture.

— Lisa Fortini-Campbell, *Hitting the Sweet Spot*
[Fortini-Campbell 1992, p. 27]

Maurice Allin, Vice-President of Customer Insight at Quarry, has for years posed a five-question quiz to his market research class at the Institute of Communications and Advertising. His quiz is depicted in Figure 11.3.

Maurice collects answers from each of the 25 people in his class, calculates the average response for each question, and plots the results on a board for everyone to see. Often to the surprise of his students, nobody in the room has selected answers that exactly match the class average. In fact, in all of the years he has taught this course Maurice has *never* found a student who matched his or her class's average. It is a matter of mathematics: there are a possible 3,125 combinations in these five simple questions.

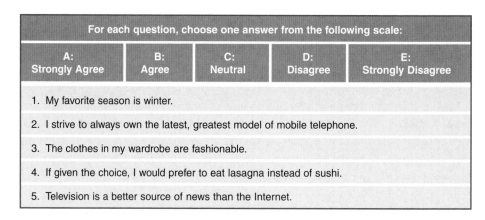

For each question, choose one answer from the following scale:				
A: Strongly Agree	B: Agree	C: Neutral	D: Disagree	E: Strongly Disagree
1. My favorite season is winter.				
2. I strive to always own the latest, greatest model of mobile telephone.				
3. The clothes in my wardrobe are fashionable.				
4. If given the choice, I would prefer to eat lasagna instead of sushi.				
5. Television is a better source of news than the Internet.				

FIGURE 11.3: *Five-question market research questionnaire.*

The point of this exercise is to illustrate that averages can be problematic and misleading. An average may in fact *never exist* in reality. How many families do you know with 2.4 children? Would you be surprised that the average age of a person who wears diapers (total population taken into account) is probably somewhere in the teen years? This is called the *fallacy of the average.* It's like saying, "Put one hand in boiling water and the other in ice; you should be comfortable because, on average, you're the right temperature!"

Although quantitative and statistically valid research makes important contributions to strategy, there is an increasing recognition that it is often applied inappropriately, particularly when used to inform the design and marketing of customer experiences. Quantitative research assumes that you know what questions even *need* to be asked, which may not be the case. When talking with someone in person, it is often a probing question made up on the spot that uncovers the real insight. Most important, though, is the fact that people are emotional creatures, often difficult to analyze and describe through statistical mechanisms.

Personas, like people, are multidimensional

> *It's hard to see emotion in a table or a chart, but it's written all over the face of an individual respondent.*
>
> —Lynn Upshaw, *Building Brand Identity*
> [Upshaw 1995, p. 84]

Traditional market research is quantitative and analytical. It is reported in tables, plotted in grids, and mapped in charts. Through techniques such as regression models and conjoint analysis, it attempts to predict people's behaviors by statistically correlating significant criteria. For example, a report might suggest that certain people base their decisions on a comparison of cost to color range, others on convenience to durability. These criteria are indexed to a hierarchy based on a segmentation model, frequently demographic. For example, high-level categories such as age range are analyzed and broken down into subcategories such as young, middle-age, and old, which are then mapped to particular characteristics and behaviors.

Sound challenging? It is. "Hmm, young people base their decisions on color; old people on cost. West coast professionals prefer style, whereas folks on the east coast tend toward function—except when they are purchasing gifts." We are looking through different lenses constantly. Our viewpoint shifts frequently as we explore the data at our fingertips. Not to suggest this type of analysis is a waste of time. It can reveal relationships we would otherwise never see. However, it takes an expert to make sense of the data, to recognize which patterns are meaningful—to spot the differences that make a difference. But most importantly for our discussion on personas: *we are using few dimensions of a person, perhaps only one, to explain their behavior.*

Quantitative research is reductive in nature, meaning that it attempts to boil down descriptions of customers to a bare minimum set of characteristics. In traditional marketing, this may be inadequate, as it oversimplifies the complex nature of the human character. However, when designing a customer experience it completely fails the job. We need something rich, something that dives deep into our customers' lives—a multidimensional model that embraces the complexity and brings it together in an illuminating form. This need makes personas a promising tool for communicating customer research.

Personas offer the distinct advantage of being substantive, not reductive. They present many characteristics of our customers all at once, in a narrative form we are naturally skilled at interpreting, assessing (no 16-year-olds in diapers, right?), and remembering. Personas tell a complete story that holds together and illustrates how a wide variety of relevant dimensions interact in a realistic way. This type of tool can help us plan an effective *experience*-based product and marketing strategy.

As the marketing world embraces the idea of customer experience, it loosens its grip on quantitative, statistical, numbers-driven research and reaches out for other tools. The advantages of personas should make them increasingly appealing to marketers in today's growing experience economy.

Story from the field

PERSONAS MUST ADDRESS A REAL-WORLD NEED

While pitching for a marketing "agency of record" relationship with a wireless communications company in the United States, Quarry briefly presented some personas we had created while designing a Web application for another client. A manager in the audience became so excited by these personas that by the end of the day she decided to hire us to make some personas for her group, regardless of whether we won the overall pitch. She had no idea what purpose they would serve. All she knew was that she wanted something as rich and descriptive of *her* customers as the personas we had shown.

We did win the business and eventually built some personas for this manager's group—but only after identifying a real-world need that would best be served by them. If you are as fortunate as us, you will find that people get very excited by the idea of personas. Just make sure the personas address a real need and can deliver real value. Otherwise, the experience may leave a bad taste in people's mouths.

An increasingly collaborative environment

...We must explore many disciplines, since the most promising knowledge frontiers typically exist at the boundaries between fields rather than at the fields' respective centers.

—Gerald Zaltman, *How Customers Think*
[Zaltman 2003, p. xii]

Working in a consulting agency, I have the opportunity to visit with people from around the world. You know what complaint everyone seems to share these days, regardless of their industry, their country, and even the size of their organization? There are never enough meeting rooms. I have even worked with a client who officially entered "East Stairwell #2" in their room-scheduling software, the need for meeting space had become so desperate.

This global shortage of meeting rooms signals a growing trend in today's business environment: the desire for collaboration. The speed of change in competitive marketplaces has grown considerably, requiring that organizations act nimbly and bring people together across professional boundaries like never before. As the marketing world reacts to the customer experience revolution, its need for collaboration grows because successfully delivering a customer experience strategy requires a diverse range of voices at the table. The Experience Design Community of the American Institute of Graphic Arts (AIGA), for example, has listed on its Web site a full 47 different job roles as making contributions to experience design. Forty-seven! The following are among this list:

- Brand management
- Consumer products marketing
- Content development
- Engineering
- Graphic design
- Information architecture
- Interface design
- Product management
- Production
- Project management
- User Research

Customer research needs to be accessible

With work occurring in increasingly collaborative environments, it is especially important that the resources supporting that work are accessible to and understandable by as many participants as possible. "What marketers need as much as the data itself is a way of packaging the information so that it can be used productively, on a daily basis if possible," Lynn Upshaw observes [Upshaw 1995, p. 95]. In her chapter "Storytelling and Narrative," Whitney Quesenbery makes a clear case that the narrative form of personas is a powerful alternative to packaging this data. We are practically hardwired to relate to personas, regardless of our professional training or cultural background.

This advantage of personas stands in marked contrast to a typical market research report, whose format is often dreadfully inaccessible. Unless you are an expert, there is a very real chance that you will misinterpret the data because it is so challenging to work with—if you manage to get through the full report in the first place. According to Maurice Allin, the first rule of market research should be: "Do no harm." We need this warning to remind us to tread carefully and to pay particular attention to our assumptions (see Figure 11.4), assuming we are even aware of them.

Do you see a young woman or an old woman in Figure 11.4? They are both visible, though it is difficult to view them at the same time. It may take a bit of work for you to identify both figures, but once you do you should be able to switch back and forth between them quite easily. (Hint: switch the ear for an eye, or vice versa.) Your perception of what is in this illustration remains stable until you deliberately look for other interpretations.

FIGURE 11.4: *Is this a picture of a young woman or an old woman?*

Similar effects can occur when analyzing market research. Different people on your team may simultaneously hold opposing views supported by the data. In a cross-disciplinary team, these disagreements are not necessarily a bad thing, as they often spark discussions that reveal insights outside any one person's experience. But if the data supporting the decision is understandable by only a few, problems arise as the discussion spirals into a conflict of opinions versus "facts." Personas help enormously in these situations by delivering customer insight in a form everyone can relate to and discuss with considerable ease, promoting smoother collaboration among the diversity of viewpoints present in today's cross-disciplinary teams.

BUILDING PERSONAS SPECIFICALLY FOR MARKETING PURPOSES

A couple of years ago, I traveled across the United States with one of our clients. We met with and evaluated a half-dozen companies to select one whose technology would power our client's new Web application. As these companies marketed themselves to us, they touted their understanding of the customer, each claiming to provide exactly what the market demanded and to offer "the best customer experience of all of our competitors." But when I asked them to describe what they had *done* to understand the market, what insights they had generated, and how this information had ultimately affected their development and marketing plans, they had no answer. They understood the need for better insight; they just did not know what to *do* about it.

Personas can make helpful contributions to this need, and not just in terms of your product's design. As we have seen, there is a revolution afoot in marketing—one that demands richer models of customers and more effective means of sharing knowledge. To this end, we have had good success at Quarry with creating personas specifically for marketing purposes.

In their book *Why They Buy*, Robert Settle and Pamela Alrick observe that "business managers and executives operate on the basis of the physical realities associated with the goods they sell. Consumers in the marketplace operate on the basis of the *psychological* and *social* images of the goods they purchase. The distance between the two is often great, and marketers have to bridge the gap" [Settle and Alrick 1986, p. 29]. We should note that this mind-set is not unique to managers and executives. Practically anyone in an organization can find themselves blinded by their product, by its "physical realities," as the development process itself demands so much energy and attention.

It is to this frenzied world of functional requirements, business objectives, and aggressive deadlines that marketing personas bring the voice of the customer—just as design personas do. They offer a concrete step in bridging the gap between a product's function and the emotional reality of the people who make the decision to purchase it.

Marketing personas versus design personas

Marketing personas assist with each of the primary activities in marketing: the formulation of strategies for positioning products against competitors, and the planning and execution of communications such as brochures, Web content, and advertisements. The main purpose of a marketing persona is to understand the factors influencing people's purchase of products in a competitive market. Thus, the primary difference between a marketing persona and a design persona is the focus of their stories: a marketing persona tells the story of someone deciding to *purchase* a product, whereas a design persona tells the story of someone actually *using* it. In other words, it is the difference between a customer and a user.

Aside from this, marketing personas are quite similar to design personas. They follow the same life cycle; they have the same strengths; they are created through the same methods and look much the same when finished. In exploring what is unique about marketing personas we will focus our attention on the first two phases in the life cycle (*family planning* and *conception and gestation*), wherein the most notable differences arise.

Story from the field

TURNING DECISION MAKERS AND INFLUENCERS ON THEIR HEADS

There is a popular theory in marketing that describes the players in a purchase decision process: the "decision maker" is the person with ultimate authority, who actually makes the final call on what product to purchase; the "influencer" is someone whose opinion on the purchase is important to consider, often because they are an expert in the subject domain.

A client asked us to research the decision process followed by their customers in the enterprise communications market. A previous research study had reinforced this idea of decision makers and influencers, and our client was requesting more in-depth information in the form of personas.

What we learned turned the models on their heads. The decision maker simply gave a "rubber stamp" to the recommendation of the influencer, feeling they did not have the expertise to make the decision themselves. The influencer, on the other hand, tailored their recommendation to the perceived needs of the decision maker, hoping in the process to increase the likelihood of their recommendation being accepted. In effect, the roles were reversed, without either side fully realizing it. Our client's personas pointed out the reality that people they had assumed were influencers were in fact decision makers, and vice versa—allowing them to respond accordingly in their marketing strategy and communications.

Family planning

The *family planning* phase of the persona life cycle is where you clarify the reasons you are creating personas, determine what you need to learn, and conduct any research required to gather the necessary data. For marketing personas, there are two primary questions that will guide your research:

- *What is the purchase decision process?* How do people decide what product to purchase? Sometimes the decision is made by a single individual; sometimes, commonly in B2B markets, it is made collaboratively by a group of people. This research is analogous to the task analysis you might perform for a design persona.

- *What needs or wants do people have that would make your product desirable?* These factors might be rational (fix this burning problem or help me achieve this specific objective) or emotional (make me feel this way). This research is analogous to digging for people's goals in using a product. Here, you are uncovering their goals in purchasing it.

The simple model shown in Figure 11.5, called the *strategic triad*, helps structure our thinking around questions of marketing. This triad shows three key perspectives for which insight

Customer

- Who participates in the purchase process?
- What initiates the process?
- How are the decisions made?
- What are everyone's roles in the process?
- What are the major influences on people's purchase decisions?
- What have they bought in the past and why?
- At what stage in the adoption cycle are customers?
- What do they hope to achieve?

Brand

- How would you describe your brand? How does this compare to what customers think?
- Does your organization share any core values with your customers?
- How relevant is your brand to customers? Does it stand for something meaningful?
- What makes your product or organization different from the competition?
- How loyal are people to your brand? To competitive brands?

Category

- What market do you compete in specifically?
- Who are your competitors? Do any come from other markets?
- How have competitors positioned themselves in the minds of customers? Are these strategies effective?
- What are the competitive products? How do customers feel about them?
- What trends do people perceive in the market?
- What is the maturity of the market as a whole?

FIGURE 11.5: *The strategic triad structures our thinking around questions of marketing. It is a helpful model in planning topic areas to address in your marketing personas.*

is absolutely required. Consequently, it is a helpful model in planning topic areas to address in your marketing personas.

Focus on customers instead of users

When performing research for marketing personas, you need to be talking with customers; in other words, the *people involved in the purchase decision*. These are not always the people who will actually use the product. For example, in enterprise organizations the responsibility for technology purchases often rests with a Chief Technology Officer (CTO) or Chief Financial

Officer (CFO), even though they may never use the technology themselves. Thus, it is critical that you understand their context and motivations.

Avoid talking about features

When investigating people's feelings about your product, focus your discussion on *benefits*. When someone says they like a certain feature, do not just accept their comment. Find out what they like about it. When you receive a request for a new feature or function, clarify what that person hopes to accomplish and why it is important to them. Customers are notoriously poor at talking about features but remarkably gifted at talking about benefits. They care about your product primarily for the benefits they can realize from it.

Experiment with scenarios

Direct questions invite direct responses. Sometimes this is exactly what you want, but if you are still finding your way around a new topic you will often learn more by asking indirect questions, as they tend to evoke more details. For example, instead of asking, "Who's responsible for replacing the toner in your laser printer?" try asking your question in the form of a scenario: "What happened the last time your printer ran out of toner?" This approach invites a more concrete response and encourages elaboration, which sets you up better to ask probing questions. In the end, it may reveal more about how decisions are actually made, and by whom.

Help people "project" their feelings

It can be difficult for people to answer direct questions about ideas they do not normally think about consciously, such as what a brand means to them or what lies at the root of their feelings toward a product. For a more effective approach, one that is often entertaining for both you and the participant, try the projective exercises described later in this chapter (in the section "Building Your Brand with Help from Personas").

With the *family of brands* exercise, discover how people perceive your brand in comparison to competitors through a description of your market as a "family." With a photo collage, identify key words or attributes people associate with your brand, and then take it further to find out if your product or Web site lives up to their expectations. Gerald Zaltman, in his book *How Customers Think*, describes a related exercise called a "metaphor elicitation interview" and provides some excellent examples of how to ask the probing questions essential to these techniques [Zaltman 2003, p. 101].

Watch it happen

Just as you would when researching design personas, get into the field and observe people in action, actually making their purchase decision. Do not rely completely on what people *say* they do; confirm it firsthand. This is easy to accomplish for consumer products, as you can recruit people in-store, or even online, as they initiate and complete the purchase process. Although more difficult for B2B products (for which the process takes a long time), it is still quite possible. Schedule interviews with people who have just begun to research their purchase, who are in the middle of the process, and who have just made the decision. Ask to see artifacts and resources that played a role in their decision, such as marketing communications and magazine articles, and learn what role other people may have played. Find out what helps and what does not—firsthand, if possible.

Conception and gestation

The *conception and gestation* phase of the persona life cycle is where you analyze and organize your data into the structure of your personas, and then fill them out with appropriate facts and narratives. Although the *process* for doing this is essentially the same for both marketing and design personas, the final *content* in your personas is not. Remember, marketing personas tell the story of how a purchase decision is made. They are less concerned with how people actually use the product, unless that happens to be an important consideration in the purchase decision.

Primary marketing personas

Another difference between marketing and design personas is how they are prioritized, or how you distinguish between primary, secondary, and so on.

> *For marketing purposes, a primary persona is someone who will have the greatest impact on your success in a segment of the market.*

Your primary persona could be an influential person to whom other customers turn for guidance. It could represent the largest group of customers—the people who will purchase the vast majority of your products. It could be a customer of your competitor—someone who has been allowed to languish and is ripe for switching loyalties. It could even be a key customer who may not be profitable to you immediately but who acts as the bowling pin that sets off a chain reaction by opening doors to other customers or markets. Which dimension identifies your primary persona depends entirely on your marketing strategy.

Identifying your primary marketing personas is critical to formulating a focused, effective strategy for positioning your product in the competitive landscape. But it is a difficult choice, perhaps even more so than in design, as giving primacy to one persona over others seems to shrink the number of potential customers. Yet sacrifice is an inherent part of any strategy. Clearly defining what you *will* do brings equal clarity to what you *won't* do. And that can be uncomfortable; it feels like you are limiting your options. Geoffrey Moore reassures us that it is an intelligent move, though, particularly just before or during the growth stage of a mainstream market. Power typically lands in the hands of the organization that leads a niche attack: "this is the company that has scoped out the target customer, understood the compelling reason to buy, and designed the whole product" [Moore 1995, p. 159]. It is difficult to create a compelling, whole product without the focus a primary persona brings.

Head office: New York City, NY
Clients in all major cities across North America

MRP Property Management Inc.
People Make the Building™

The Business

MRP's force of service providers and repair technicians are the folks who keep huge office towers operating smoothly, from monitoring security, to upgrading elevators, to fixing plugged toilets. MRP's contracts include strict performance criteria, meaning they must respond to tenant requests within a specific time, sometimes as little as 5 minutes — which can be difficult in a busy downtown building with thousands of occupants.

Employees:
4200

Portfolio:
80 million square feet

Role of Technology

MRP relies on technology to give them a competitive edge, so they rely on vendors such as Acme to keep them abreast of the latest advances. At their Call Center in Dallas, MRP operators monitor phone lines and websites for requests from tenants across the continent. Operations software provides quick access to such details as building data and service history. Work orders are sent to field technicians via cell phone.

Challenges

MRP faces some technology problems that affect their ability to deliver service. For instance, deep inside a corporate office tower, it's sometimes impossible to receive a cell phone signal, so technicians are unable to receive new work orders. If this happens often enough over the course of a month, MRP fails to earn its "performance bonus". And that bonus is the primary source of the company's profits.

"This business is a high-risk game with traditionally little loyalty. Fall behind even a bit and clients switch to the competition instead of renewing your contract."

— Industry Analyst

The Future

This industry is about to undergo a great change. Automation technology promises to revolutionize the way a building is run: smart sensors on HVAC equipment can predict breakdowns before they occur; video systems enable "virtual concierges" who can serve lobbies from anywhere in the world; and new software is allowing clients to hold property managers accountable like never before. On the one hand, MRP is excited by the future: it promises to improve their service delivery and therefore increase revenue. But the investment required to implement these new technologies is prohibitive, as MRP operates on very slim profit margins.

FIGURE 11.6: *Excerpts from a sample organizational persona created by fictional company Acme Inc., to better understand their customers in the property management business. (Photograph courtesy of Simon Gurney.)*

Identifying which personas from your collection are primary and secondary is less critical if they are intended to support only marketing communications, as opposed to positioning strategy. This is because communications, such as brochures and advertisements, are easily targeted to specific audiences. You can select a different persona for each item you produce and tailor a message for that person specifically. Unfortunately, this approach is not as practical in product design, as it is considerably more expensive to build five different products than to print five different brochures, for example.

Organizational personas

When dealing with B2B markets, you may find that it is appropriate to create an *organizational persona* for marketing purposes (see Figure 11.6). In business markets, it is uncommon for purchase decisions to be made by an individual. Instead, a group of people may collaborate and reach the decision together. In this case, your individual personas are likely to act as players in a drama, and thus an organizational persona can help to set the stage.

The organizational persona (see Figure 11.7) describes any relevant characteristics of an organization itself, such as objectives, processes, constraints, competitors, and so on. They are useful for describing the overall context in which your other personas operate, and they allow you to save space by including information that would otherwise need to be repeated in each of the other personas.

FLEXING YOUR DESIGN PERSONAS' MUSCLES FOR MARKETING PURPOSES

> *They didn't say why any one soft drink, motorcycle, service, or experience was different, better, or special. So they built it and nobody came... .*
>
> —Sergio Zyman, *The End of Marketing as We Know It* [Zyman 1999, p. 18]

Products need to be marketed. If people do not know about your product, they obviously will not purchase it. Or if the wrong people *do* know about it, they will not be interested. Also, if nobody understands what makes your product different from the other choices … well, you get the picture.

If you have gone to the effort of making personas to guide design, extract as much value from them as possible and introduce them to your marketing team. At Quarry, we frequently offer our design personas a seat at the marketing table because they contain insights into whether we are building the right product, into the competitive landscape, and into the question of how best to promote the product to our customers.

MRP Property Management Inc.
New York City, NY

Michael Anderson
Chief Technology Officer (CTO)

Age:
40

Education:
Bachelor of Engineering, MBA

*"The fully-automated office building is coming — someday. But **today**, my concern is this: what technology should I bring on board now in order to have increased our competitive advantage by this time next year?"*

Motivations

Michael has had a lifelong passion for technology. It drove him into engineering as a young student and propelled him to his current role as CTO. But to balance his enthusiasm for anything new, Michael has had to develop what he calls a "personal smoke detector": an ability to sense when the promise of a new technology is just smoke and mirrors and unlikely to offer a return on investment. His greatest satisfaction comes from rolling out technologies that have an immediate, measurable impact on their ability to run corporate office towers more effectively.

Role in Purchase Process

Michael sponsors an evaluation committee that includes Finance, IT, and at least one person who might actually use the new technology under consideration. "Too many roll-outs in large companies like ours have failed because of problems with user adoption. Before we invest in something new, we need to feel confident that people will actually use it."

Before meeting with any vendors, the committee defines their underlying needs and the criteria by which they'll make the ultimate decision. At Michael's urging, each committee this year has introduced a new criteria for every product they evaluate: a demonstrated 8-month return on investment for the vendor's previous customers.

Once the committee has selected their preferred product and vendor, they present their case to Michael. "At this point, the decision is pretty well made," he admits. "Only once in the past year have I offered criticisms that prompted them to change their recommendation."

Perceptions of Acme Inc.

Acme has been a preferred vendor at MRP for three years. In Michael's words, "Acme has proven to be flexible, responsive, and reliable. My team has come to trust their engineers completely." He's not so sure about their sales force, though, since his team dealt directly with Acme's IT group when evaluating GPS handhelds last year. "My sense is that Acme knows technology, but they're still ramping up on sales and support."

FIGURE 11.7: *Selected excerpts from a marketing persona that accompanies the organizational persona of Figure 11.6.*

Design personas are not usually created with the intention of answering questions related to marketing, and therefore the depth of their contributions will vary. However, they practically always hold clues that build upon what you already know or may suspect—though sometimes they reveal surprising insights that can change the direction of a product dramatically.

Check your requirements: Are you building the right product?

Most projects, particularly in the technology sector, begin with a list of requirements that is typically owned by the marketing department. This marks one of the very first roles of marketing in the product development process, long before anyone is thinking about how to advertise or otherwise promote the product. The intent is for this requirements list to shape the product by identifying the features and functions needed to satisfy the targeted customers. Typically, requirements themselves are gathered through a combination of means such as:

- Identifying technical problems (such as software bugs) in the existing product
- Compiling feature requests from current or potential customers
- Analyzing the competition for features and functions that might be necessary in your own product
- Performing surveys, focus groups, or other market research to determine what customers think they want.

Our clients sometimes engage Quarry to help define these requirements up front, though often we are brought in when design work actually begins—meaning that the requirements have already been set. This latter situation is also common for design and usability groups within an organization. The good news is that it is never too late for your personas to play a role in influencing a product's requirements, though it is clearly better for them to appear early in the process—especially if they suggest that a change in strategy may be appropriate. The cost of requirements errors can be staggering, likely to consume 25 to 40% of your project's budget [Leffingwell and Widrig 1999, p. 13]. Thus, whenever possible create your design personas before the requirements process is complete. And encourage them to speak up as early as possible!

Pay attention to the surprises

> *Wise executives capitalize on anomalies. They dig into them and look for ways to exploit them, asking: What's really going on? How can we learn from this? Is there an insight buried here that can move the business to a whole new level?*
>
> —Lawrence E. Shulman, "Capitalizing on Anomalies" in *Perspectives on Strategy* [Stern and Stalk 1998, p. 152]

Remember the personas I introduced earlier in this chapter, the scientists Marcus and Tracy? This same project offers my favorite example of the impact personas can have on a product's requirements when the personas contain unexpected surprises. The initial research performed by our client resulted in the requirement of a "very high throughput" product. Scientists would need to process many thousands of samples per day. Once we hit the ground and visited labs around the world, though, we were puzzled: where is everyone who is actually running this many samples? We couldn't find them. And nobody we spoke with could identify anyone for us, either. Strange.

We continued our investigations and ultimately realized that this need for very high throughput was a myth. The myth was based on a shared assumption that "Yes, *somebody* is running this many samples, and I may want to as well, someday." The press had been comparing this market to a similar industry in which the need for high throughput *had* in fact grown dramatically, which led to the assumption that events would unfold similarly here. However, our on-the-ground research uncovered some fundamental bottlenecks in our customers' work flow, which were unlikely to be addressed for a long time. Until that happened, there would be no need for the throughput numbers we had been planning. In fact, they would be impossible.

The happy outcome for our client: they delayed a planned component of the product and saved an estimated half-million dollars in development. Would the component ever be needed? Only the future will tell. In the meantime, they are delivering a product people need *today*.

The most interesting parts of your personas, and those potentially most useful to marketing, are the surprises and anomalies. If you feel you have learned something that contradicts the generally accepted wisdom, try not to hide it. Instead, bring attention to it right away. It might signal an important misperception or a waiting opportunity.

Scan the competitive landscape: Where do you sit?

One of Quarry's clients felt it owned the top end of their market, with expensive but high-performance products. Like Mercedes or BMW, they explained. Then one of their customers provided a quote that made everyone sit up and pay attention: "It's like a Mercedes. Yeah, for sure. The problem is, it's a Mercedes with the dashboard ripped out."

These are great quotes to include in personas, as they highlight key issues that affect your ability to compete effectively in the market. Would your customers rather purchase an almost-whole Mercedes or the competitor's complete Hyundai? Perhaps you should find out and let everyone know.

In the course of creating personas, you have undoubtedly uncovered insights into how people compare you to the competition. While demonstrating how your product fits into their workday, perhaps someone commented on a different product they used in a previous job; perhaps someone else told a story about their friend who works at another company loyal to your competition; or perhaps, as in the previous example, you have heard comments that speak directly to your own sense of what makes you competitive.

This information often does not make it into the text of a design persona. Insights on how someone feels about the competition may not matter to your design efforts. That is, it is not always a difference that makes a difference. Marketing activities might benefit from this information, though, so take another look through your collection of research notes and observations. Share them with your marketing team, in addition to the personas themselves.

Look for clues into technology adoption behaviors

If your organization sells technology products, its marketing strategy might be based on ideas about the *technology adoption life cycle*. Geoffrey Moore, whose work greatly influences high-tech marketing, has written extensively on how the level of a market's maturity and the product adoption behaviors of customers can signal which strategy is most likely to give you the best competitive advantage.

As a market matures, customers choose to adopt technology products for vastly different reasons, which means that organizations must be prepared to switch strategies at specific times. According to Moore, "it is imperative that organizations be able to agree on where their markets are in the life cycle"—because switching from one strategy to another is an organization's most difficult challenge [Moore 1995, p. 26]. Personas commonly contain clues that may signal the maturity level of your product's market (see Figure 11.8). How do people perceive the value of your product? Do they desire your technology for its own sake? Are they compelled by its promise to radically improve their competitive ability? Are they wary of new products yet to be adopted by similar people or organizations?

In Figure 11.8 I share a model of market maturity we use at Quarry. It was developed by Glen Drummond, a partner in the organization and VP of Innovation. This model builds upon Moore's work and on the technology adoption life cycle. Note in particular the customer goals and needs that characterize each stage; this is the type of information that you will often find in personas. If you are curious about how marketing strategies should change from stage to stage, I recommend Moore's series of books (starting with *Crossing the Chasm*).

As you can see from this model, there are times when the rich, detailed descriptions provided by personas will be particularly helpful to your organization. For instance, consider that difficult transition called "crossing the chasm," in which your product finally moves into the mainstream market. Companies want to enter this market as quickly as possible, as that is where profits are earned. But most stumble and fail during the transition. They focus on a few market segments, visit some major potential customers in each, compile a master "wish list"

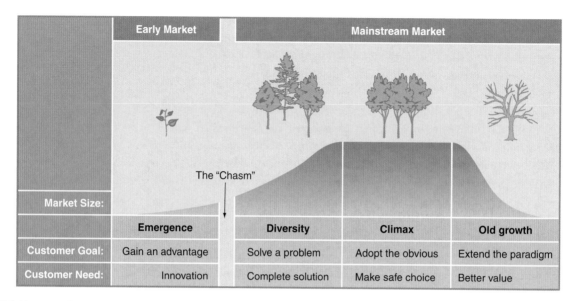

	Early Market		Mainstream Market		
Market Size:					
	Emergence	**Diversity**	**Climax**	**Old growth**	
Customer Goal:	Gain an advantage	Solve a problem	Adopt the obvious	Extend the paradigm	
Customer Need:	Innovation	Complete solution	Make safe choice	Better value	

FIGURE 11.8: *Personas often contain clues to the maturity level of your market—an important consideration in the marketing strategy for technology products.*

of requirements, and then extract the common themes and most-often requested features. The result: a broadly functional product that in fact satisfies *nobody's* needs entirely. Yet Moore tells us that a well-focused, complete product is precisely what customers insist on for new entries into the mainstream market [Moore 1995, p. 21]. So only by focusing maniacally on one key segment and fulfilling 100% of their requirements will you stand a good chance of crossing the chasm.

Here is where personas become invaluable. The principles underlying personas can help development groups focus on building a whole product for their key market. When organizations get lost in the chasm with their master wish lists, they are essentially designing one product for several primary personas. It is thus no wonder that nobody is entirely satisfied. Personas help enormously in illustrating how this one-size-fits-all approach leaves everyone wanting, and potentially nobody purchasing. They encourage the necessary discussions for exactly *which* customers will receive your maniacal focus. Moore indirectly supports the idea of selecting a primary persona when he asserts, "*the only safe way to cross the chasm is in fact to put all your eggs in one basket*" [Moore 1995, p. 22].

Plan your messaging strategy: What will grab your customer's attention?

One of Quarry's clients asked us to help investigate and design a new product for exchanging documents electronically. At the time, security was a hot issue, so it appeared as a key marketing requirement and had a real impact on the product's planned feature set and technical infrastructure. From the outset, the project was driven by an assumption that people in the

coherent set of ideas about your brand and keep the same promises. "We help you to work faster and feel smarter;" "we will simplify your job;" "we will keep you safe;" "we are a little unpredictable, but a lot of fun!"

So here's the call to action. Whether you are a usability specialist, an interaction designer, an information architect, a technical writer, a developer, a product manager, or whatever—there is always something *you* can do to help build your brand through your product or Web site. The following are a few examples from our work at Quarry, demonstrating that it takes conscious effort to make sure your product supports your brand promise:

- Our client was a national provider of financial products and services targeted at farmers. Embarking on a redesign of their Web site, we learned that although people were satisfied with its usability they clearly felt that something was not quite right. We tried a projective exercise (an exercise that abstracts people's feelings about an experience by projecting them onto an entirely different object or scenario) to help identify the root of the problem, asking customers the question: *"If this organization were a car, what type of car would it be?"*

  Not surprisingly, we heard descriptions of well-used and well-maintained pickup trucks. But when we asked the same question about the Web site itself, people described it as a new, clean, feature-loaded SUV or luxury sedan. One participant in a usability test finally identified the core issue by observing, "This Web site feels like it could belong to any Wall Street bank, not to an organization that I know lives and breathes our business out in the countryside." The Web site did not support the meaning of the brand as understood by customers. So, we helped our client adjust the site's information architecture, behavior, and visual treatment to build their brand more appropriately.

- In analyzing the Web site of a national charitable organization, we discovered a similar disconnect between the brand and the Web site. In this instance, we used a projective exercise called a photo sort, in which participants created two photo collages: one of the overall brand (conducted when they were first recruited) and one of their experience with the Web site (conducted after a usability test). Figure 11.10 shows an example of what we found.

  Participants described the brand through images that signaled values such as "inviting," "caring," and "intimate." The Web site, however, evoked a few discordant values, such as "distant" and "obscure." We discussed the images in detail with participants to determine which aspects of the Web site were responsible for these brand disconnects, and then dealt with them during the site redesign.

These examples demonstrate a point made earlier, that people make meaning from many dimensions of the customer experience. Building a great customer experience—especially one that builds your brand—requires intimate knowledge of your customers, and personas have a lot to offer to the task. They may contain insights about what promise your customers feel

FIGURE 11.10: *Images of an organization's brand (left) compared with images of their Web site (right).*

is being made by the brand (a question you can tackle directly in your research, through the projective exercises described previously). In addition, their stories provide a creative jump-start on figuring how to deliver an experience that reflects the unique qualities of your brand and lives up to its promise.

The brand ladder: connecting personas, products, and brand

Customers are uninterested whether a brand is achieving its business objectives, they care only how it might relate to their personal lives.

—Lynn Upshaw, *Building Brand Identity*
[Upshaw 1995, p. 81]

In designing for brand, the ideas, feelings, and attributes you are trying to evoke are often abstract, but the building blocks at your disposal are concrete. The challenge lies in figuring out how to devise your product's features, functions, architecture, behavior, content, and visuals to create a feeling of "comfort," "finesse," "optimization," or "connecting," for example.

To help with this challenge, at Quarry we employ a heuristic tool called the *brand ladder*. Although originally intended to assist with strategy for marketing communications, the brand ladder can help you plan how a Web site will reinforce the attributes of a brand, or how a software application will fulfill the high-level goals of its personas. The brand ladder does not generate answers; that is still up to you. It does, however, structure your thinking around how to make meaningful connections between product features and brand or customer values.

What is a brand ladder?

A brand ladder is quite simply a model that shows the relationships among features, benefits, and values. It looks as shown in Figure 11.11.

Values	A selection of attributes inherent to the brand or held by customers.
Customer benefit	An implicit or explicit benefit that supports the customer's pursuit of their goals.
Product benefit	An implicit or explicit benefit offered by the product.
Feature	An objectively observable function, detail, attribute, or quality of the product.

FIGURE 11.11: *Brand ladder.*

The relationship between rungs on the ladder is established by asking, "Why is that important?" as we look *up* the ladder and, "What's the basis for that?" as we look *down*. Figure 11.12 shows an example that illustrates the thinking behind an advertisement from Michelin Tires.

The brand ladder tells a type of story as you read it up or down. Figure 11.13 shows an example of how a company can relate its product to the idea of being a good parent. A successful brand ladder "hangs together" in that its selections at any level connect meaningfully with the other selections. You can see how the Michelin ladder hangs together in both directions, as indicated in Figure 11.14.

Reconciling brand attributes and customer values

Your personas, and particularly their goals, will contain insights to help populate the top half of a brand ladder—minimally the "customer benefit" rung but sometimes the "values" rung as well. For instance, we know from the G4K case study developed in this book that Tanner Thompson, like many "tweens," strives to identify himself and make a statement. Thus, a brand ladder for Tanner might begin as shown in Figure 11.15.

The brand ladder would be helpful at this point even without an explicit objective of building the G4K brand. It allows the design team to structure and share their thinking around how

Values	Be a good parent
Customer benefit	Safety
Product benefit	Improved traction
Feature	Shape of the tire's tread blocks

FIGURE 11.12: *Michelin Tires brand ladder. (Copyright © Michelin North America, Inc. Used by permission.)*

Another safe delivery.
Michelin. Because so much is riding on your tyres.

FIGURE 11.13: *The brand ladder helps to illustrate how a company can relate its engineering expertise to the idea of being a good parent.*

their products could offer something meaningful and relevant to Tanner. But the real value comes when you ask:

"What values are shared by our customer and our brand?"

These intersections, when you find them, provide exciting opportunities. Your customers will feel great about using your product; you will feel great about building it. And you will increase your organization's competitive edge.

The attributes of your brand and the values of your customers will probably intersect at an emotional level. This may seem odd at first, as we do not think of organizations as having emotions. But in fact they do. Brands have both rational and emotional components, as indicated in Figure 11.16.

Your marketing team should be able to provide information about your brand to help populate some rungs on a ladder. Chances are, the brand will be described through *attributes*, such as those in the previous examples. In particular, try to find out what distinguishes your brand from the competition, as you will definitely want strong brand ladders for those attributes. When customers use your product

Reading up:	Reading down:
"The tread blocks on our tires have a specific shape."	"Our tires help our customers to feel they are being good parents."
"Oh? Why is that important?"	"Really? What are you basing that claim upon?"
"Because they provide greatly improved traction."	"We keep them safe."
"Ah, I see. But why is traction important to customers?"	"What makes you able to claim that?"
"Because they are concerned about safety."	"Our tires have great traction."
"Right. And what's so important to them about safety?"	"And what's that claim based upon?"
"They are parents and want to protect their children."	"The special shape of our tread blocks."

FIGURE 11.14: *The Michelin ladder hangs together in both reading directions.*

Values	Express myself.
Customer benefit	Make a statement about my unique personality.

FIGURE 11.15: *Beginning of a brand ladder for Tanner Thompson.*

or Web site, their experience should reinforce what makes your brand unique. That is a challenge you can tackle as someone involved in product development.

We know that G4K distinguishes its games and storybooks from the competition through rich production values and emphasis on character development. It is not uncommon for brands to be described at this level—essentially the product level, the bottom two rungs of the ladder. Completing the brand ladder exercise with input from your personas often starts people talking about where the brand *could* go from there, which is good. As markets mature, people tend to make their purchasing decisions higher up the ladder. It is wise to have a plan in place for the future, a strategy for how you will compete at the level of customer benefits and values, even if you compete at the features level for now.

For the moment, production values and character development might be enough to distinguish G4K. But where will G4K go from here? The brand ladder is helpful in structuring thinking around questions such as this. For instance, we know that Tanner values fun and friendship, and G4K's products emphasize character development. Can we identify a ladder that connects these ideas in a meaningful way? If so, it is likely that G4K's current products are laying the groundwork for the future. If not, we will want to look for connections between other features and values. Figure 11.17 shows just such a ladder.

	Rational	Emotional
DISNEY	Family entertainment	Pure magic
SONY	Technical innovation	Status
Hallmark.com	Communication	Caring
Nike	Quality	Achievement
REVLON	Cosmetics	Hope

FIGURE 11.16: *Brands have both rational and emotional components.*

Values	Tanner values: Fun and friendship
Customer benefit	Can you imagine anything on this rung that makes sense and is meaningful to Tanner? Perhaps: Feeling engaged with and empathy for the game's characters.
Product benefit	G4K is distinguished by: Well-developed characters
Feature	What about G4K's products support their claim to the above benefit? Perhaps: A collection of Flash cartoons that tell stories about characters and their adventures outside the game story line.

FIGURE 11.17: *Brand ladder connecting Tanner with G4K.*

Benefits to design and communication

There is a widespread intuition among designers that good design is characterized by *integrity*—a state in which all elements of a design fit together elegantly, forming an organic whole. The brand ladder can act as a touchstone in achieving this integrity while delivering experiences that reinforce the meaning of the brand in the mind of the customer. The introduction of brand early in the design process can set up a virtuous circle of brand serving design, design serving brand, and brand serving customers by fulfilling their expectations both rationally and emotionally.

A key challenge in setting up this virtuous circle is the social context of work in product design. When people collaborate across the boundaries of an organization, they usually start out seeing things differently, understanding terms differently, and having different assumptions about what is important. Without strong leadership, this situation can deteriorate into a series of struggles about the priority of one consideration over another (such as usability over aesthetics) and of one discipline or department over another (such as marketing over engineering). In this social context, the brand ladder becomes a practical tool for discussing and sharing ideas on specific choices. Thus, the ladder supports not just design but organizational relationships.

Brand ladders help generate ideas

Brand ladders can be a lot of fun for design teams. You fill out the top rung or two of a ladder and then brainstorm for product features that could deliver on the customer or brand values. For example, consider the Virgin Atlantic brand, known for being creative and irreverent. For the drive to Heathrow airport in London, Virgin offers chauffeured motorcycles and

Values	Creativity
Customer benefit	Ability to more personally craft your travel experience
Product benefit	Make well-informed decisions about where to sit on the airplane
Feature	Identifies seats occupied by passengers with whom you share an interest

FIGURE 11.18: *Brand ladder for Virgin Atlantic connecting "creativity" to a potential feature of their seat reservation system.*

high-speed amphibious vehicles. In the air, an onboard "mixologist" creates specialty cocktails for passengers. Now imagine that you are on the Web site design team for Virgin Atlantic, working specifically on the site's seat reservation system. How could you make a contribution to the Virgin brand through your work?

Let's try a brand ladder. With "creativity" at the top rung, Figure 11.18 shows an example of what might result: an idea for allowing Virgin passengers to identify their interests online and then choose a seat beside someone with similar interests.

Note that you can branch out to different ideas at almost any rung. For instance, there are undoubtedly other ways of crafting a more personal travel experience than making informed decisions about where to sit. How about what to eat? What to read? What to watch? How long to lay over in Amsterdam's Schipol airport before catching a connecting flight? Should you enjoy the casinos? The ladder's structure does not limit your thinking; it often has the opposite effect.

Figure 11.19 shows a brand ladder inspired by the irreverence Virgin brings to an otherwise conventional industry. This ladder leads to the idea of offering a dating service on the airplane. Although this idea may seem ridiculous at first, keep in mind that great innovations often start life as ridiculous ideas. Figure 11.20 shows an actual Virgin Atlantic advertisement that makes this particular idea seem plausible.

Brand ladders help with prioritization

Brand ladders can offer a new perspective on questions of priority. You may need to decide on where to invest people's time and resources on a design project, or perhaps you need to rank the importance of some findings from a usability test. Normally we base these decisions on operational criteria such as effort required, on heuristic criteria such as "recognition not recall," or on direct feedback from customers. With the brand ladder, we have a model for assessing the potential impact of our decisions on the brand. The idea is quite simple: does the

Values	Irreverence
Customer benefit	Turn a typically boring and solitary experience into an opportunity to meet your life partner
Product benefit	Seats you next to someone who might be a good "match"
Feature	Integration of the "matching engine" from an online dating service with Virgin's seat selection system

FIGURE 11.19: *Brand ladder for Virgin Atlantic connecting "irreverence" with the idea of an on-board dating service.*

item in question (e.g., design approach, feature, or usability issue) have a strong connection to the brand? If it does, you might consider assigning it a higher priority.

Every product will contain some features that affect the brand very little and some that affect it enormously. Without the focus brought by a brand ladder, influential features might otherwise get lost in the chaos of software development. Consider the idea of allowing Virgin Atlantic passengers to choose seats based on their interests. In the crush of a tight development schedule, this feature may seem like overhead. But if Virgin's strategy is to differentiate itself based on "creativity" we can see how this feature is actually quite important. Without it, there may be nothing to distinguish the customer experience of Virgin's online reservation system from British Airways, United Airlines, or any other major carrier. This feature might deserve its share of scarce resources after all.

FIGURE 11.20: *An actual Virgin Atlantic advertisement. Could an online dating service perhaps make sense for this brand? (Copyright © Virgin Atlantic Airways, Inc. Used by permission.)*

SUMMARY

Near the end of a client project, I visited some family and caught up with a cousin I had not seen in more than 15 years. In a surprising coincidence, her current job put her squarely in the potential user community of the piece of software I was designing at the time, even though the market was highly specialized. She was naturally curious, so I showed her the primary persona that had guided our design efforts to date.

She read it over in silence, though her face registered an array of interesting expressions along the way. When finished, she put it down and gave me a sideways glance. "Whoa. This is sort of creepy," she chuckled. "It's almost a perfect description of a guy who works across the room from me. This could be him!"

It is not often you get such validation, so I was of course pleased. But it also occurred to me that this way of packaging customer insight was clearly powerful. Not only did it capture the complexities of our potential users, but it did so in an easily understood and compelling manner.

Both designers and marketers face a growing need for rich, multidimensional tools for getting to know customers more intimately. Personas have some noticeable advantages over traditional methods, as their faces and stories remind us that we are selling to real people, not nameless "targets." They can play an active role in shaping not only a product's behavior but the very relationship of its customers to the brand.

As we have seen, personas cannot help but cross the line into marketing—even if we never intend them to. Although this relationship is sometimes uneasy, both design and marketing personas can be valuable additions to the toolbox of anyone in pursuit of delivering a great customer experience.

Jonathan Grudin

"Jonathan the Psychologist"

Roles: Researcher, psychologist, use analyst

Goals: Understand the adoption, use, and effects of technologies and design methods

Objectives: Collect quantitative and qualitative data; find patterns, particularly around problems and solutions; communicate the results to people who are most likely to find them useful

Classic quote:

"Today's teenagers are the people who matter in the long run"

Jonathan Grudin has worked as a developer and researcher in industry and as an academic at several universities, but throughout quite different jobs he has focused for the past twenty years on two related topics: (i) the dynamics of groups and organizations, especially those engaged in software development; and (ii) tools to support groups and organizations more broadly. As a senior researcher at Microsoft he has worked on ways to enhance streaming media, uses of multiple displays, uses of IM and weblogs, as well as understanding persona use in design.

In 1989 he left the consortium MCC in Austin, Texas to spend two years at Aarhus University in Denmark, intrigued by the Scandinavian participatory cooperative design approach and interested in how it might be applied to the development of commercial products. Despite being a fiction writer who had studied method acting, the idea of resorting to fictional stand-ins for the user-partners of participatory design did not occur to him, but when he encountered it a decade later at Microsoft he was motivated and positioned to delve into the mechanisms by which personas work, with a Ph.D. in experimental psychology and broad experience with contextual design and other design and development approaches.

At home Jonathan has to compete for computer time with his wife and two daughters. He is never without his USB keydisk, maintains a couple work-related blogs, and has a large screen TV connected only to a DVD player. He can be reached via his Web site, research.microsoft.com/~jgrudin.

12

WHY PERSONAS WORK: THE PSYCHOLOGICAL EVIDENCE

Jonathan Grudin, *Microsoft Corporation*

INTRODUCTION

The power of personas to engage and inform team members was described in the introduction to this book. But why does engagement lead to better design? How do detailed pictures of fictional people contribute? How detailed should they be—are stereotypes enough? This chapter addresses the psychological foundations of persona use. It describes theories and findings that explain their effectiveness. We can use personas without understanding the underlying psychology. Alan Cooper has remarked on their "surprising" power without exploring the source of their effectiveness. But by understanding how they work we can design better personas, select appropriate complementary methods, and embed personas in effective processes.

A designer who envisions the way people will respond to a design is drawing on a universal skill: anticipating how another person will behave in a new situation. We exercise this skill every day when we anticipate how others will react to what we are about to do or say. The argument tying this to persona use has three assertions: (1) We find it natural to create and use models of other people. If we did not, persona construction would not make sense. (2) Our ability to engage with models of real people transfers to models of fictional people (in this case, personas). (3) Our models of other people have a certain degree of complexity and detail. If people routinely use sophisticated models to anticipate behavior, sophisticated models of potential users could better help us anticipate their reactions to designs. If the models we use are simple, expending resources on detailed or complex construction efforts might not be worthwhile.

We naturally model other people

Communication is not just attaching words and expressions to a thought. Our choices of words and intonations are guided by our sense of our audience. We explain something in different ways to a child and to an adult, to a friend and to a stranger, to a manager and to our spouse. We use context to decide whether to be frank or indirect, and whether to convey a message by e-mail, the phone, or face to face. We can better anticipate someone's responses by building an internal model of the person. The model may be detailed or sketchy. It may be accurate or inaccurate. It may be consciously accessible or something we cannot verbalize— we can think consciously about how people will react, but usually we do not.

We are social animals whose hominid ancestors lived in groups for millions of years, evolving skills that evolved to enable us to interact efficiently. In the next section, we review the origins of our fundamental ability to model other people's knowledge and mental states. Evidence points to its emergence 250,000 to 500,000 years ago, probably concurrent with larger brains, language, and complex tool construction. This indicates that the capability is deeply embedded in us, more deeply than recently acquired abilities such as reading and writing.

Models of fictional people can be as engaging as models of real people

If human interaction depended critically on pheromones or direct observation, our natural facility with people would not transfer to personas, which have no odor and cannot be observed. Fortunately, that is not the case. We project human characteristics onto people we have never met. We identify intensely with fictional characters in soap operas, *Star Trek*, or the Harry Potter series. We even project human characteristics onto pets, Furbys, tamagotchis, ink blots, and constellations of stars. When an action by a fictional character seems "out of character," we have created a predictive model of that fictional person. When we argue about what characters did after the action in a book or movie ends, we have internalized and animated the characters, just as we would like designers and team members to internalize and animate personas as a step in anticipating the behaviors of future users.

Our models are often detailed and complex

This important assumption is difficult to prove. Much of this chapter explores the psychological evidence for it. Experimental psychology takes us part of the way there, providing insight into some risks of simple personas. For less quantifiable but equally important psychological evidence, we turn to the design and production of stories, plays, and films. In her chapter, Whitney Quesenbery outlines lessons from storytelling for creating realistic and engaging personas. In contrast, I look at the arts from a different angle, seeking psychological insights into how these representations work.

This chapter is organized as follows. First, studies of human evolution and primate behavior are considered in order to shed light on the crucial question of how deeply engrained our models of other people actually are. This leads to a discussion of the conscious and unconscious models we form. Articulated, conscious representations are more easily studied, and the results of such studies are reviewed. Then I turn to our often shadowy, unconscious understandings of other people—the experimental and descriptive evidence covering such psychological constructs as stereotypes, traits, goals, plans, expectancies, scripts, specific knowledge, and holistic images. This picture is extended with psychological observations and practices of writers and actors—professionals dedicated to reproducing realistic human behavior. Implications for persona design, scenario construction, and the use of stereotypes, task analysis, ethnography, contextual design, and participatory design are considered.

UNDERSTANDING OTHER MINDS: WHERE DID THIS CAPACITY COME FROM?

Several expressions are used for our representations of other people's mental states: "theory of mind," "concept of mind," "folk psychology," and "understanding other minds." Are these representations a deeply ingrained aspect of our psychology, operating automatically below conscious awareness? Or are they an application of our general reasoning skill, operating mainly consciously, similar to scientific theories and models? One approach to answering such questions is to consider the behavior of other primates and our ancestors, drawing upon anthropological and archaeological records.

Experimental studies of theory of mind began with chimpanzees [Premack and Woodruff 1978]. Chimpanzees observe subtle cues and can predict behavior well. But do they have a model of what is in a person's or another chimp's head? This is difficult to determine. They react differently to different people, and respond appropriately to others' moods, such as good humor or anger. But this could be accomplished by combining memory of past interactions with observations of someone's current appearance and behavior. Efforts to show that primates take the additional step of creating a model of another individual's moods or knowledge and use that model generatively to anticipate future responses have been inconclusive. This stands in sharp contrast to young children, who focus intensely on the knowledge and emotional states of those around them [Repacholi and Gopnick 1997]. Morris et al. [1998] contend: "Starting at a surprising early age, children seem to instantly interpret observed action in terms of what an agent is thinking, wanting, and planning.... This penchant for making sense of others as individuals with particular beliefs, desires, goals, and traits is essential to how we navigate our social environment."

As with language, where primate competence is also debated, human abilities are either unique or of a markedly different order. We are born either with the capacity and drive to create and use models of other people or with building blocks that develop this capability through normal social interaction. We use partial knowledge of others to draw inferences, make predictions, and form expectations. When we say or do something, we anticipate others' reactions. Sometimes we think it through; often we do it effortlessly. Sometimes we miscalculate, and we learn from experience.

In an elegant essay, Mithen [2000] argues that theory of mind arose 250,000 to 500,000 years ago, coincident with the second and last increase in brain size that distanced us from other primates. This also coincided with sophisticated tool production—the manufacture of complex axes required mentoring, wherein instructor and novice had to understand one another's thinking—and language. This makes sense: Complex discourse requires an implicit model of other speakers. Children acquire language at the rate they do by grasping the goals and intentions of others. Theory of mind is logically a prerequisite for complex discourse.

Modern human beings emerged more recently, perhaps 50,000 years ago, coincident with the early cave paintings. But Mithen argues from the archaeological record that our ability to reason in sophisticated ways about the behavior of other people has been a part of our nature for much longer. Therefore, we should expect behavior that is partly unconscious, powerful, and difficult to detect.

CONSCIOUS MODELS AND UNCONSCIOUS MODELS: WHY DOES IT MATTER?

Conscious models or theories include concepts, beliefs, attributions, or explanations for the behavior of other people that can be articulated (expressed verbally). Unconscious processes can also help us anticipate reactions and choose effective words and actions. Take my Sicilian friend Sabine, for example. My saying, "Sabine is trustworthy," reveals a conscious model that could explain why I delegated a task to her. A model that is unconscious is revealed when I talk to her. I automatically slow down and simplify my vocabulary because she is not a native English speaker. I don't weigh each word consciously—my speech just shifts gears based on an internal sense that she will understand some words and not others.

If someone says, "Internet vendors can't be trusted," this consciously held stereotype may affect how they react to a sales pitch. However, conscious models can mislead. Actions don't always match words. In practice people may make frequent exceptions that reveal a more complex underlying model. People who claim not to trust Internet vendors with personal information can be observed freely supplying credit card numbers to purchase online. Conversely, behavior can reveal a bias that a person denies having and may not be aware of. Conscious and unconscious representations are not always easily distinguishable.

If representations of others are deeply ingrained, why not just study behavior? Is asking people what they think and writing down what they say a case of looking under the lamppost because the light is better? Perhaps, but people do think about their own behavior, and a consciously held model can exert influence. Once I decide that Sabine is trustworthy, I may delegate more important tasks to her. True, closer observation may reveal that I trust her with certain work tasks, but not to remember to repay small loans. I trust her to keep a secret, but not to take care of my kids. We may not work out the details consciously. Sometimes inquiry can get at them. Other times we only discover what we feel about someone when we find ourselves in an unexpected situation. Nevertheless, conscious models have been studied extensively, so it is worth considering that evidence.

STUDIES OF ARTICULATED CONSCIOUS MODELS

Most experimental studies of theory of mind focus on simple demonstrations. People are asked to provide explanations for actions or are presented with a hypothetical scenario and asked how a character would act. A common scenario involves two people, A and B, and an object. A and B hide the object in location L1. Then A leaves the room, after which B moves the object to hiding place L2. Then A returns to the room. Experimental subjects are asked, "Where will A look for the object?" The subject knows it is in L2, but also knows that A did not see it moved from L1. Pointing to L1 reveals a correct theory or model of A's state of knowledge.

Children typically do not get this right until about age 4, suggesting that a verbally accessible theory of mind develops at that age. However, far younger infants show that they sometimes know what adults know, even though they can't express it. A complication in interpreting such studies is that they presuppose that children interpret the question literally as, "Where *will* A look," rather than as the more logical question, "Where *should* A look?" Perhaps children are guided by a theory of the adult mind that includes the notion that adults ask sensible questions, not tricky questions. To summarize, the developmental literature focuses on relatively sophisticated, verbally accessible, conscious understanding.

Studies of this type reveal cultural differences [Vinden and Astington 2000]. In some cultures, people rarely discuss why others act as they do. Cultures prizing conformity may be less likely to attribute individual behavior to internal factors. Instead, they may invoke external influences such as spirits, demons, or gods, as Western cultures once did. Exorcism is rare today, but responding to a sneeze with "bless you" is a legacy of the belief that spirits act within us. The cross-cultural studies reveal a risk in relying on verbal accounts. People with sophisticated, complex social conventions, such as the Japanese, may rarely articulate explanatory models for individual behavior. Complex rules and carefully assembled knowledge guide their behavior, but the internal models may not be consciously considered.

Studies based on verbal reports also reveal individual differences. Autistic people do not express explanations for the activity of other people [Baron-Cohen et al. 2000]. Recognizing this may help in treating disorders, but leaves open whether these people have no underlying models or whether they just have no verbal access to them. People's verbal explanations for their *own* behavior often prove inaccurate in experimental studies of normal behavior, behavior under post-hypnotic suggestion, psychiatric defense mechanisms, and confabulation accompanying brain injuries.

If our underlying models go no deeper than our sketchy, inaccurate conscious models, how much time should be spent modeling potential users to shape team member understanding? If conscious models are all that we use to guide behavior, we should focus on influencing conscious models. But as outlined in the following, the evidence is to the contrary: deeper, more accurate, representations exist. They can be more difficult to understand and work with, but they are exploited by psychologists, writers, actors, and persona developers.

STUDIES OF UNCONSCIOUS MODELS

If asked to explain my behavior and that of my friends when we were 18, I would give a very different response today than I would have at the time. My explanation for past behavior changed repeatedly. I was never at a loss for models, but their accuracy was questionable. Yet at the time some internal set of representations existed and guided me to interact in reasonably appropriate, consistent ways. Inappropriate behaviors or unexpected reactions stand out in memory, but this in itself shows that I made predictions and had expectations.

Our use of deep models of people is necessary but not sufficient to motivate using them in design. Logically it might be impossible or prohibitively expensive to shape team members' models. Efforts could be counterproductive. A persona that promoted incorrect predictions could be worse than none. However, as noted in the stories from the field, personas often can contribute and the effort can pay off. Understanding of the underlying psychology should improve the odds of succeeding.

The psychological literature identifies a range of representations we form of other people that affect our behavior. Our use of them can be evident or so subtle that it goes unnoticed. Some representations are simple and static, easy to communicate, remember, and use. Some are more dynamic or complex. Is it worth the additional effort to create and communicate complex representations? The questions we face in life—how much effort should we spend getting to know other people, and what are good ways to go about it? — we also encounter in design. Let's see what psychology has learned. How do we interpret or predict another person's behavior? Possibilities, from the simplest to the most detailed, include:

- Group stereotypes
- A fixed set of traits we believe define a person
- A set of traits that can change over time

- Goals, plans, and expectancies that govern a person's behavior
- Scripts that govern behavior in specific situations, such as turn-taking in meetings or ordering food in a restaurant
- Specific knowledge that people have, their levels of sophistication, sense of formality, and so on
- A complex holistic image of a person.

The following sections cover each of these in more detail.

Stereotypes and cultural differences

A group stereotype is a fixed set of characteristics assumed to be shared by members of the group. I might acknowledge stereotyping other people, or I might stereotype without realizing it. "Stereotype" has a negative ring. "Cultural differences" is a more acceptable way to describe perceived group behaviors. We would like to know: When and how do people form stereotypes or perceptions of cultural differences and use them to predict behavior? Once formed, does a stereotype evolve to be more complex or more accurate? What happens when a stereotype is inaccurate? What are the benefits and risks of using stereotypes in design?

Bødker [2000] identifies advantages of using caricatures or stereotypes in design scenarios. Stereotypes are easier than more complex personas to create, communicate, and engage with. Cooper notes that a persona that violates a widely held stereotype (teenage computer users are nerds, nurses are women) may be less believable to team members. Djajadiningrat et al. [2000] argue that extreme or shocking caricatures are particularly effective in capturing the attention of team members. Stereotypes undoubtedly have these advantages, which is precisely why they are heavily used in films. One glimpse of the Wicked Witch of the West on her broomstick and we can confidently predict her behavior.

A surprising finding emerged from studies of prejudice and bias: stereotype formation is a natural consequence of the way human memory works. We form and maintain new stereotypes even when they have no factual basis [Stroessner and Plaks 1998]. The mechanism is simple: we remember unusual events better than typical events. This leads to illusory correlations. For example, let's say that 10 reports of spamming are reported: nine from major countries and one from Fredonia. "Fredonia?" you ask. It is memorable, in that you rarely see stories about Fredonia. Months later, after many ordinary cases of spamming, another story of a spammer from Fredonia appears. You remember the first one, and conclude that people from Fredonia are likely to be spammers. Even if no more examples emerge, the next time someone mentions Fredonia you say, "Oh, yes, the spam country." An illusory correlation has formed.

Once a stereotype is in place, evidence that contradicts it does not dislodge the stereotype from memory. Spam reports from elsewhere, or a Fredonian who is not a spammer, will not

Handy Detail

SCIENTIFIC METHOD

In the early seventeenth century, Francis Bacon identified sources of error in human reason, leading to his empirical approach, which contributed to scientific method and the scientific revolution. One error that Bacon [1625] emphasized was belief that persisted in the face of contrary evidence.

> The human understanding when it has once adopted an opinion (either as being the received opinion or as being agreeable to itself) draws all things else to support and agree with it. And though there be a greater number and weight of instances to be found on the other side, yet these it either neglects and despises, or else by some distinction sets aside and rejects; in order that by this great and pernicious predetermination the authority of its former conclusions may remain inviolate. And therefore it was a good answer that was made by one who when they showed him hanging in a temple a picture of those who had paid their vows as having escaped shipwreck, and would have him say whether he did not now acknowledge the power of the gods, "Aye," asked he again, "but where are they painted that were drowned, after their vows?" And such is the way of all superstition, whether in astrology, dreams, omens, divine judgments, or the like; wherein men, having a delight in such vanities, mark the events where they are fulfilled, but where they fail, though this happen much oftener, neglect and pass them by. But with far more subtlety does this mischief insinuate itself into philosophy and the sciences; in which the first conclusion colours and brings into conformity with itself all that come after, though far sounder and better. Besides, independently of that delight and vanity which I have described, it is the peculiar and perpetual error of human intellect to be more moved and excited by affirmatives than by negatives; whereas it ought properly to hold itself indifferently disposed towards both alike. Indeed in the establishment of any true axiom, the negative instance is the more forcible of the two.

change our perception that Fredonians are spammers. People tend to notice confirming evidence. They overlook disconfirming evidence. An individual who contradicts a stereotype may be considered an exception, while the stereotype persists. "You're a Fredonian who isn't a spammer like those we read about! I like you." For more on the phenomenon called "confirmation bias," see the Handy Detail above on the origin of the scientific method or the engaging book *How We Know What Isn't So* [Gilovich 1991].

These findings point to a risk in using stereotypes in design. Yes, a stereotype quickly identifies a persona that differs from development team members, which is good. It may give rise to empathy. But once in place, a stereotype could lead team members to ignore inconsistent evidence about real use. Stereotypes can lead to systematic, irradicable errors in predicting behavior. If the errors are small and the time available for persona development short, a stereotype may be a cost-effective compromise.

The same trade-off is evident in fiction when time is a consideration. Contrast a film and a television series. Films make heavy use of stereotyped, easily understood heroes, villians, and supporting roles to quickly introduce characters and engage viewers. A television series has more time to develop characters. A predictable, stereotyped character in a series will over time seem unreal and boring, and cease to engage the audience. Characters in successful ongoing dramas and situation comedies are (or become) more complex, more real. Archie Bunker and J. R. Ewing developed sympathetic sides. Soap opera characters are often given a dual nature, which results in less predictability, somewhat more realism, and greater engagement.

Cooper [1999] uses stereotypes if he feels it will provide more credibility. A short-lived design project or a single standalone scenario might benefit from a stereotype, but to engage team members over a longer time it seems advisable to go beyond stereotyping.

Traits

One of the major scientific approaches to personality [Idson and Mischel 2001] considers traits to be the basic units: broad dispositions that predict or explain much of people's behavior.

We often characterize people in terms of traits, such as introverted or extroverted, forward or shy, friendly or unfriendly, aggressive or timid, honest or untrustworthy. Because a set of traits is like an "individual stereotype," a quick description of someone, it raises the same questions. How accurate is it to describe a person as a set of traits? How does thinking of someone this way affect our ability to predict their behavior, and how malleable is our perception of an individual's traits? And finally, deep down, is this how we actually perceive other people?

We do readily characterize other people in terms of traits, and there is evidence that some people are born with a disposition toward shyness. On the whole, though, psychologists have shown that much social behavior is situational. Behavior can be quite easily manipulated by peers [Asch 1951], authority figures [Milgram 1963], or circumstances [Haney et al. 1973]. (Readers not familiar with the surprising social conformity studies of Solomon Asch, the shocking obedience-to-authority studies of Stanley Milgram, or the stunning Zimbardo prison study can easily learn about them on the Web.) Thus, the use of traits to characterize personas has the pros and cons of stereotypes. It is a quick way of creating an image but is likely to mislead. Team members may anticipate behavior consistent with a trait and underestimate the effects of context.

Some people regard traits as fixed; others consider traits to be dynamic or susceptible to change over time. Plaks et al. [2001] showed that people who view traits as fixed tend to ignore data that is inconsistent with an assumed trait and focus on consistent data. People who see traits as characteristics that change over time are more open to weighing evidence that is inconsistent with a trait that they assume someone has. Openness to new information is good, so if traits are used in describing personas it would be good for team members to consider traits to be dynamic. Plaks et al. have good news in that regard. In an experimental setting, they were able to manipulate people's implicit theory about traits. Encouraged to view traits as dynamic, participants responded to new information more objectively (at least for the duration of the experiment). If you use traits, educate team members to see them as dynamic, open to evolving when appropriate, rather than as describing a rigid behavior pattern.

Goals, plans, expectancies, and scripts

The second modern approach to personality focuses on situational factors (or "mediating process variables"), such as goals, plans, and expectancies. "These mediating variables are assumed to interact with each other and relevant features of situations to produce stable patterns of behavioral variability across situations" [Idson and Mischel 2001]. If we know enough about someone's goals and plans, we can anticipate their behavior in different situations.

This is a very familiar level of description for designers. Scenarios typically consist of characters with specified goals in particular situations. Cooper's formula is to create personas, give them goals, and embed them in scenarios. These personality theorists argue that if you flesh out the goals, plans, and expectancies fully you have the basic persona. "Fully" includes all life goals, not just those tied to some work tasks or technology use.

Idson and Mischel focus on conscious, verbal explanations that people give for the behavior of others. They report that when a person is more familiar we are less likely to attribute behavior to traits and more likely to mention goals, plans, and expectations. This is even more true when the other person is also important to us. We would like team members to feel that surrogate users are familiar and important, which is further support for deemphasizing stereotypes and traits and emphasizing finer-grained particulars. Whether goals, plans, and expectancies are enough is another question. These are the consciously accessible factors that people verbally report in studies. Unconscious factors may have been filtered out.

The power of situations in everyday life emerges in research on scripts that are used in many situations, often unconsciously, to guide and interpret behavior. Sets of conventions govern behavior in a formal restaurant, a fast-food restaurant, a department store, a checkout line, and so on. Scripts vary from culture to culture and evolve over time. We learn scripts through experience and may notice them only when they are violated. Scripts are particularly relevant to scenario construction. The fact that they differ according to geography, socioeconomic status, and other factors makes a case for developing personas that vary in these attributes.

Social psychology seeks explanations that capture behavioral variability. Traits are one approach; situational determinants such as scripts are another. Shoda and LeeTiernan [2002] look for greater explanatory power by merging the two, finding evidence for individual differences in patterns of behavior variation across a fixed set of situations. When closely examined, individual behavior is complex, yet in our everyday interactions we work with it naturally and easily. We are sometimes but not often surprised. This strongly suggests that our internal models are complex.

Specific knowledge of individuals: holistic images

Should we expend resources to go beyond goals, plans, tasks, and scripts to create complex characters? It requires going beyond verbal reports and most experimental evidence and offers less certainty. We have seen indications that it could be worthwhile. Our explanations for behavior are more complex for people we know and value. Abstract descriptions of people and common situations are less engaging.

As we move into the realm of our unconscious use of detailed knowledge or observation, reliable psychological data are more difficult to obtain. But there is evidence that we rely on such unconscious activity. Malle [2004] summarizes findings from conversation analysis that shows that when we converse our syntax, choice of words, and enunciation vary automatically depending on the other speakers. Subtle cues are used to infer the state of others and guide pauses, interruptions, and so on. We position ourselves depending on what we know of the others present, such as their status, friendliness, or competitiveness. We are usually unaware of these subtle influences, as noted in a recent article, "Unspoken Rules of Spoken Interaction" [Bickmore 2004].

Designers consciously think about how personas will respond to a design, or how team members will make use of new information, but unconscious mechanisms are also likely to be at work. Testers who sit down to examine an application by using it "like Colbi" should reason about Colbi the persona's attitudes and behaviors, but they can also respond in subtle unconscious ways based on their knowledge of Colbi. We make subtle distinctions in daily interactions. Subtle details in persona development may contribute.

Experimental psychology has limitations. It can address high-level constructs such as traits that can be approached through conscious or general behavior. Methods such as conversation analysis can quantify some fine-grained details. But it is less successful at addressing the necessarily idiosyncratic, qualitative elements of a model we inevitably construct for one person in our life. This is an intrinsic part of the psychological impact of a persona. To address it we expand our inquiry to include the arts. The first step is halfway between behavioral science and art—a mental construct that is amenable to scientific study while inspiring artistic invention: dreaming.

Psychological evidence from dreams

Freud (1900) said "the interpretation of dreams is the royal road to a knowledge of the unconscious activities of the mind." Freud arguably misread some of the highway signs, but dreams are indeed pure mental productions. Experimental psychology has tended to avoid dream evidence because verbal reports of past activity violate the stimulus/response and input/output paradigms. For our purposes, though, even if dream reports are created after dreamers wake up, the details include representations of people. And these representations of people are much richer than the traits, goals, and other aspects of personality that can be explored experimentally.

Behavior in dreams is complex, detailed, and generally consistent. Dream reports are strikingly assertive about the people and places present. Consider the following excerpts from a child awakened during REM sleep on different nights [Foulkes 1999]. "There was a lady and she was on the TV show *Gilligan's Island* and in a Comet commercial.... The lady is really on *Gilligan's Island*, but in the dream she was doing a Comet commercial with the plumber Josephine." "There were some ladies walking down the hall, talking.... It looked like it was in a school." "I was in school, and the teacher was up at the board, talking and writing on the blackboard, showing us something. We have some SRA things in school, and she was telling us we had to hand in one SRA thing, and talking about how we would have to do it. It was my real teacher, and my real school."

My real teacher, my real school. The child knows that dream events are fictional. The second example described unknown people, but the teacher in the third behaved in complex ways that seemed characteristic of the actual person. The following are additional examples from Domhoff [1996].

I have a recurring dream that my grandmother calls me at my house while my mother, sister, and I are preparing dinner. I answer the phone and she says, "Hi, it's me." I said, "Hi, Grandma." She asks, "How are you?" Then I want my mother to talk to her and she says, "No, I called you." When my mother comes to the phone, my grandmother hangs up. My mother replies, "Stop saying it's Grandma; she's not there."

My father died nine years ago but I often dream that he returns, especially at times of stress in my life. He looks older than he ever got to be in real life and very wise looking. I tell him problems I am having and sometimes he just listens and I feel better but usually he gives me advice, sometimes very clear, sometimes garbled. In the instances where it is clear, it is always good advice but things I already know I should do. But just seeing him and hearing it from him makes me feel better.

In this dream I was little, about 5 or 6 years old, and I was in the bathroom at my grandmother's house. She was giving me a bath in this big claw-footed tub. The old steam radiator was turned on, making it very cozy. I knew that I was dreaming and that I was getting to see my grandmother well again. After the bath, she lifted me out onto the spiral cotton rug and dried me with a blue towel. When that was done she said she had to leave now; this seemed to mean for heaven. I said, "Good-bye, Grandma. I love you." She said, "I love you too Mary." I woke up feeling wonderful. She had been delirious in the last few months of her life, so I'd never really gotten to say good-bye.

Mental representations of other people are actively elaborated in our minds. People who become blind after the age of seven or eight retain the ability to generate visual images in dreams, and create in their dreams visual images of people they meet after becoming blind [Kerr 1993].

Dream characters do not behave stereotypically. The fact that at night we generate complex, detailed representations of other people is very strong evidence that our mental representations of other people are complex and detailed. Noting that dreams have bizarre and unrealistic aspects that could suggest random fragments, Meier [1993] examined speech and thought in dream reports, including many from bilingual speakers. Would the thought and grammar be normal or disorderly? She found conclusive evidence of "the high appropriateness of language in dreams." Dream language is influenced by "the linguistic context of dream sources… . The pragmatic competence to select the appropriate language for a given dream situation… give(s) further evidence to the integrative capacity of information processing in dreams." The information being integrated includes detailed mental representations of other people.

PSYCHOLOGICAL EVIDENCE FROM WRITING

This thing happens where the characters take over and you almost want to look behind you to see who's writing your story.

—Joseph Wambaugh

Our mental representations of people guide our interactions with them. Dreams draw on aspects of daily life. What about fictional characters? Compelling evidence that fictional characters take on active roles comes from the creation and portrayal of characters in plays, stories, novels, television, and film. Authors and actors identify mechanisms and techniques developed over centuries.

Authors, including Flaubert, Dostoevsky, Henry James, Flannery O'Conner, and Alice Walker, have commented on the autonomy of their characters [Watkins 1990, cited in Grudin 1996]. Elmore Leonard, who has written novels for 50 years, comments:

Case Study

PSYCHOLOGICAL STUDIES AND ANECDOTAL ACCOUNTS—
THE NATURE OF EVIDENCE

Some years ago, on each of my annual visits, an aunt updated me on a year's activity in her favorite soap opera. One year she said "…and the Senator was shot, but you must have seen that in the newspaper." She momentarily forgot that this was not a real senator. I am reminded of this when at lunch or dinner colleagues speak matter-of-factly about personas I know nothing about: "He was a Tanner" or "They were Austins." On one occasion a team member reported grimly that a manager did not want the team focusing on a particular category of user by saying, "Hillel wants Irene dead!" (Hillel was the manager. Irene was a persona.) When I inquired later as to how it turned out, the glum answer was, "She's gone." (This Irene was not the one found in this book.)

Such experiences, like reports from authors and actors, illuminate the power of representations. Anecdotal accounts must be approached with caution, especially given the unconscious nature of the phenomena they describe. However, authors and actors devote their professional lives to character representation. They labor to produce convincing fictional representations. Similarly, no carefully controlled laboratory studies have been conducted to prove the effectiveness of persona use. Studies would be good, but the purpose would be to demonstrate beneficial effects, not to prove that personas can be engaging. We already know that personas can engage.

> I figure out from whose point of view the scene should be seen… . Then I start to write. The characters, very often, start to give me ideas. I rely on them [Leonard 1998]. I sort of let my characters audition for me. I listen to them and let them do all the talking [Leonard 1999]. I thought he'd be a good character… . So when I got him into the book and within 20 pages he's in jeopardy, his life's at risk, another character comes along and takes over. There's nothing I can do about that. I let it happen and I'm not going to force this guy to become the main character [Leonard 2002].

Laura Brewer [2003] describes one of her fictional characters coming to life thus:

> At some point in this process you will notice a change. The character will push back. Not only will they react, but they'll initiate action… . Unfortunately it does not always work out so well. The second book was moving well until one of the characters developed this little quirk. He started chasing women. For a while I ignored his activities. I let him go off

on his own when he wasn't "on stage" in the story. His little romantic adventures never made it into type. They didn't usually reach a conscious level in my planning and I didn't really notice the charisma he was developing. When he started paying attention to the Admiral's daughter I pulled him up short. I could see where this was heading. This time, he had gone too far! I rewrote the scene several times. I took the girl out of the scene. The scene, the whole chapter, didn't work. I set the project aside for a while in frustration. When I came back to it and read over the various versions of the chapter I realized the character had won this round. I did the only thing that I could do. I let the romance develop and married them two chapters later. It was the only way I could keep him from dominating every scene.

After characters "come alive" it becomes relatively effortless to anticipate their responses in new situations. If a character (or persona) named Elaine purchases a cell phone, the author (or designer) can infer how this affects her behavior and create scenarios around it. We draw such inferences about people all the time; we are skilled (though not perfect) at it. If the same data is conveyed as, "Market research shows that 20% of our target users have bought cell phones," it is less clear how a designer can use the information.

In Chapter 4, Christina Wodtke described how this process can also affect persona creation, when a persona team creates a persona who evolves into a "bad guy" and gets out of control, needing to be reined in. Mental representations that enable effortless anticipation of behavior are a powerful aid to design. However, as indicated in the novelists' accounts, power comes with risk. If a persona with a mind of its own ignores our eventual users' activities in favor of pursuing the Admiral's daughter, it will be less than fully effective, like the self-confirming stereotype that ignores disconfirming evidence. This argues for care in persona design and presentation.

There is no single path to inventing good characters, but the most consistent advice to writers after, "Write!" is, "Write about what you know." This enables drawing on knowledge of details to construct convincing situations and characters. Many fictional characters are based in part on real people. Writers often conduct extensive research into settings and occupations— observing, reading about, or interviewing people whose lives reflect aspects of their characters. The "back story" is detail that is often not used in the final product. It is intended to help authors anticipate the responses of fictional characters to events.

PSYCHOLOGICAL EVIDENCE FROM ACTING

Actors preparing to play fictional characters often engage in similar efforts to accumulate detailed knowledge about real people with similar occupations, histories, or attitudes. Actors also invent detail to flesh out a character. The following is from a chapter titled "Creating the Inner Character" in Easty's classic text *On Method Acting* [Easty 1981].

As he approaches the problems and tasks concerned with finding the Inner Character, the actor can begin by a simple and direct character analysis… to accumulate information about the character which must then be regarded as fact. I say fact because this information must be gathered objectively in much the same light as a statistician or census-taker would gather them. The actor's own relationship to the Inner Character he is portraying must be subjective only in how he will play the knowledge he has found, not what he will play as the character.

The actor's awareness of what is needed for the creation of Inner Character can be greatly stimulated by asking himself honestly, as the character, a series of questions pertinent to the life of the character… . For example, Who am I? What are my particular likes and dislikes? Do I have a hobby? Am I religious? Which religion do I believe in? What is my background? What did my father do for a living? What was my day like? On what street do I live? (Be able to describe the street.) What does my apartment look like? How many rooms do I have? (Give a full description of the type of living quarters that you as the character might inhabit. Give particular detail to the furnishings.) What did I do today? Who did I talk to? What is my basic relationship to the other characters in the play? What is my political outlook or my views on the world situation at the time of this play?… The actor can ask himself what kind of music a character such as this would enjoy. He can then listen at length to pieces of this music, deciding which passages the character would like best and, more important, why… .

With a full character analysis will come relaxation, an easy response of the senses, and concentration.

An obituary for method acting proponent Marlon Brando began [Lyman 2004], "In preparing for his first film role, as a paraplegic veteran in *The Men* (1950), he spent weeks living at a veterans' hospital; many of the film's first audiences came away perplexed, thinking that he was an actual war casualty who had been hired to be in the movie."

Real data informs fictional people. Sound familiar? Details contribute to the representation and allow one to anticipate the posture, tone, gestures, glances, and movements of a character. Knowing the history of furnishings in a character's apartment could affect the way the character will look around the set. Another method acting exercise is improvisation: a novel situation is provided without warning and actors react to it. For example, characters are asked to use unfamiliar software! How will they behave?

Not all writers research extensively, and not all actors prepare with "The Method." Some give more weight to inspiration and instinct derived from years of training. Similarly, good design can spring from invention. On the whole, though, one builds representations of fictional people whose responses one wishes to anticipate through immersion in realistic detail.

SUMMARY: PSYCHOLOGICAL ACCURACY AND FICTIONAL PREPARATION

People shout advice to fictional characters in novels, movies, and television programs. They argue over what the characters did off-screen or after a novel ends. Successful ongoing television dramas or situation comedies require believable characters—better looking or wittier than the average person on the street perhaps, but moderately complex. Stereotypes would grow boring.

Fiction based on research can communicate useful knowledge. Watching a character succumb slowly to a dementia over several episodes of *ER*, one feels one understands the disease better. If the portrayal is based on real observation and data, it could inspire the design of technology to support sufferers.

PSYCHOLOGICAL ASSESSMENTS OF OTHER DESIGN METHODS

Most techniques used alone or in conjunction with personas stress understanding users. Some stress the communication of requirements. This section does not cover all of the methods discussed in Chapter 2. It assesses, in light of the psychological research, the methods most likely to be used in place of personas.

Scenario-based design and task analysis

A scenario is a story with a setting, agents, or actors who have goals or objectives, and a plot or sequence of actions and events [Carroll 2000]. Typically used without personas, scenarios have "actors" to whom relatively little attention is paid. Consider Carroll's example:

> An accountant wishes to open a folder on a system desktop in order to access a memo on budgets. However, the folder is covered up by a budget spreadsheet that the accountant wishes to refer to while reading the memo. The spreadsheet is so large that it nearly fills the display. The accountant pauses for several seconds, resizes the spreadsheet, moves it partially out of the display, opens the folder, opens the memo, resizes and repositions the memo and continues working.

The accountant, typical of actors or agents in scenario-based design, is not well defined—no family, hobbies, or aspirations. The accountant is not engaging. Similarly, task analysis is usually directed toward formal representations. Work is decomposed into constituent elements, with less emphasis given to high-level goals and plans. A scenario can be a good description within the boundaries established for it, but it is not generative—it provides no handle for thinking about a new situation. These weaknesses were noted by Benyon and

Macauley [2002], who recommended supplementing task analysis and scenario use with detailed character sketches.

Scenarios based on data and constructed around personas are key tools, but too often scenarios are used in place of firm data. When poorly anchored in psychological or physical reality, scenarios can be created to promote any feature or to support any position. Bødker [2000] cleverly proposes turning this lemon into lemonade by constructing both utopian and nightmarish scenarios around a proposed design, as a way of stimulating reflection and discussion. A utopian location-aware mobile computing scenario could depict wonderful efficient communication; the nightmare could describe inescapable visibility, interruption, and micromanagement. A scenario, in Bødker's view, is an argument, not a depiction of a work situation.

Stereotypes and traits

Bødker [2000] also addressed stereotypes or caricatures, writing:

> It gives a better effect to create scenarios that are caricatures… . It is much easier… to relate to… . Not that they "believe" in the caricatures, indeed they do not, but it is much easier to use one's commonsense judgment when confronted with a number of extremes than when judging based on some kind of "middle ground."

Team members may consciously realize that a stereotype is exaggerated, but how are they then to anticipate real users' responses to a design? Given no concrete alternative, they may consciously or unconsciously adopt elements of the stereotype, or revert to other biases. As noted earlier, traits are similar to stereotypes. Dynamic traits are more promising, but would require an ongoing effort.

If resources permit, why not provide the team with nuanced representations through personas?

Contextual design

Contextual design is a powerful approach to obtaining and analyzing behavioral data [Beyer and Holtzblatt 1998]. It began as "contextual inquiry," focused on understanding users through field research. Data from the field is used to create flow models, sequence models, artifact models, physical models, and cultural models. These help a field researcher build an understanding of users. They also help in communicating findings to team members, which Beyer and Holtzblatt stressed more and more over time. Although powerful, this analytic decomposition, like task analysis, can be difficult to engage with and use. Personas are a natural complement and partner of contextual design, as Holtzblatt notes in a chapter in this book (see also [Blomquist and Arvola 2002]). Put the other way around, contextual methods can be useful in creating and extending personas.

Ethnography and participatory design: direct contact with specific users

In one sense, the closely observed "informants" of ethnography or descriptive anthropology are ideal personas. They can directly engage our capacity for learning about and engaging with new people. Ethnographic data are expensive to collect in terms of time and resources, and as with contextual design, ethnographers face the challenge of communicating their understanding to designers [Hughes et al. 1992; Dourish and Button 1998], but, when available, ethnographies are valuable contributions [Kiel et al. 2005].

Creating a persona effort around real individuals seems logical, but as noted in Chapter 3 it can have drawbacks. People who match a desired profile have idiosyncrasies that one might not wish to design specifically for. We also face this challenge when developers engage too enthusiastically with the first user they meet. If research shows that 8 of 10 people matching a persona profile have acquired laptops, it is easy to report that a fictional persona has a new laptop. But if you are wedded to a real person who does not have one it complicates matters.

Relying on a small number of real people can mean ignoring or dealing awkwardly with other, potentially useful, sources of information. Usability tests for successive versions cannot employ a small fixed number of people, because exposure to earlier versions will influence subsequent behavior. Reporting composite usability data through a persona is easy, reporting it alongside an ethnographic informant is more complicated. Quantitative data collected from hundreds or thousands of people present similar challenges. Of course, when it is available, ethnographic data is a terrific tool for creating and aging personas, and it can be motivating to use ethnography to introduce team members to some of the real people who underlie the personas.

Personas and ethnography have striking parallels. Each excels in the underlying psychological mechanisms of representation and engagement. Both face the twin challenges of forming and communicating a veridical understanding. Traditional ethnography relies on information obtained from a few people over a longer time to reach an understanding, which is then communicated to others through examples that show the norms and ranges of behavior. Persona design draws on information obtained from many people, over a shorter time, to reach an understanding, which is then communicated to others through examples–personas—that show the norms and ranges of behavior.

Participatory or cooperative design, in which team members and future users interact extensively and get to know each other, is also psychologically compelling. This approach is ideal for projects in which a relatively small development team develops an application for a specific or homogeneous group of users. But it does not work well with a large or distributed development team, or a diverse and distributed user population. Participatory design and persona use can be viewed as realizing the same outcome in different development contexts [Grudin 2003].

Participatory design and ethnography encounter the "tradition/transcendence trade-off" [Ehn 1993]. Prospective users often focus on the initial disruptive effects that will accompany a new technology. They do not trust that the envisioned benefits will materialize. Such fears can be well founded and should be accepted as part of the response to a product idea. However, this conservative human tendency can be softened in a persona.

FROM ENGAGEMENT TO CARING

Designers of commercial software usually avoid mixing values and design considerations. This has not been universally true of software development. Early Scandinavian participatory design efforts in particular stressed sociopolitical and "quality of life" issues [Ehn 1993]. Today, with computer use often a necessity rather than an option, value issues around security, privacy, spamming, digital property rights, viruses, and other matters are getting more attention. Nevertheless, most usability and interaction design techniques have striven to be value neutral, apart from some attention to universal access.

Persona use is different. It inevitably surfaces sociopolitical issues. Each persona has a gender, age, race, ethnicity, family or cohabitation arrangement, socioeconomic background, work and home environment. Assumptions are easy to identify and challenge. A persona set comprising only middle-age white males becomes an obvious problem. Cooper wrote, "all things being equal, I will use people of different races, genders, nationalities, and colors," noting that the central goal of being credible can limit diversity. (No geriatric hip-hop artists, please.) And that's fine.

Whatever their intentions, a team relying on usability studies, for example, is unlikely to inquire very deeply into the diversity of the participants, few or none of whom they might ever see. But teams live with their personas. A set of personas often starts out with significant diversity, but later an overlooked group is noticed: "Hey, why don't we have any international personas?" Not long afterward, when it is time to expand or change the persona set, international personas are added. This means collecting more data from international users, and as a result they receive more consistent, comprehensive attention.

SUMMARY

Data from psychological studies and artistic experience indicate that we naturally and generatively create and engage with detailed representations of people. Personas tie into this powerful human capability. Most of us do not naturally reason about extensive statistical summaries, but we do reason effortlessly about people, real or fictional. With the power of personas comes the need to be accurate in constructing them. Evidence suggests that stereo-types might suffice for short projects, but richer personas are better for longer-term use. Personas address weaknesses in some of the major methods that can be used with them. They may be useful in situations in which participatory design is not feasible. Finally, personas can reintroduce a useful discussion of values and diversity in design.

APPENDIX

G4K ORGANIZATIONAL ARCHETYPE AND SAMPLE PERSONA

ORGANIZATIONAL ARCHETYPE: GIGANTIC FOR KIDS (G4K), INCORPORATED

Gigantic for Kids (G4K) is a fictitious company that we've created to help illustrate many of the concepts presented in this book. The initial description of G4K is presented on page 68 in chapter 3. Rather than repeat that content here, we present G4K as an organizational archetype (i.e., a "persona" of a company). We created G4K so that we could give you an idea of how a persona project might work in a company from start to finish. We have also included an example persona, Tanner, that the G4K team created during their persona project.

www.G4kids.com

Gigantic for Kids (G4K) currently specializes in children's entertainment and education ("edutainment") software. Their products are distributed through traditional "brick and mortar" retail outlets as well as third party Web retailers.

Gigantic has been exploring the viability of the Internet, both to market and distribute their traditional shrink-wrap software products as well as to extend their product offerings and business/revenue model. As part of this new strategy, their corporate Web site, www.G4kids.com, is soon to become a "destination" site for kids, providing children-oriented entertainment, news and merchandise primarily related to their existing software offerings. While this is not a major departure from their normal business (the new kid's portal is seen simply as an opportunity to build stronger customer loyalty and deeper branding), they are also flirting with the possibility of partnering with other children-focused merchants, potentially offering joint promotions, advertising, and sponsorship (e.g., sponsoring children's events, promoting other non-competing brands or goods-clothing, skateboarding equipment, cola companies, and retailers).

A smallish company of 53 employees, G4K has never formally defined its development process to include user-centered design, even though they consider graphic design, branding and storytelling (essential elements of experience design) as core competencies of the company as a whole. Gigantic's modest User Experience team, consisting of two people (an interaction designer and a business analyst, who have recently been moved off of a game development team in the company) are creating personas to help with the development of the company's new portal Web site.

G4K Company Details

Financial Info

Privately Held Company
Established in 1992
FY 2002 Revenue: $8M (basically flat from $7M in FY2001)
FY 2002 Net Income: $1.2M (increased from FY2001 net income of $.8M)
53 Employees

Corporate Background

Gigantic for Kids is a privately held, independent company that produces entertainment and educational games and stories aimed at children and young teens from three to fourteen. G4K was founded in 1992, while CD-ROMs were in vogue and their popularity was still growing. The original vision for G4K was a Hollywood-style production studio that developed more traditional multimedia games and storybooks for home PCs delivered via CD-ROMs. Although the studio met with a couple of early successes, the lure and promise of the Internet pushed them towards interactive Flash technology and Web delivery. The company began seeking heavier financial backing and was pushing to go public shortly before the dot com bust. They never made it to IPO, but have remained viable even though they are only mildly profitable. More recently, Gigantic desires to build exposure and revenue through its premier portal site (really, a destination site for kids), www.G4kids.com.

G4K distinguishes their products from competitive efforts with rich production values and emphasis on character development in their games and storybooks. Both of these strengths obviously come from the company's original employee pool of talented animators, artists, writers, programmers and producers, who bring a slick finish to G4K products.

These days, G4K faces two major challenges. First, the rising cost of developing, pressing and distributing their shrink wrap game and educational titles has forced them to look for new opportunities to improve the efficiency of their development and distribution process. The company's software architects are always looking for new ways to 'genericize' and reduce code to make it more easily reusable in future projects as well as more easily delivered via Internet technologies. Second, a declining market for traditional "shrink-wrap" PC software has prompted the company to explore new sources of revenue. Within the last 2 years, G4K has launched a fledgling corporate Web site complete with subscription services, advertising and promotion revenue, and streamed distribution of G4K's various titles. G4K sees their software and Web offerings as mutually dependent and supporting.

Mission Statement

The G4K mission is to provide young consumers and their parents the most compelling and entertaining, yet enriching and educational, software and Internet content on the market.

Customers

Gigantic's customers are mostly home consumers though they do have some distribution in educational settings. Most of Gigantic's products are aimed at kids and children, aged 3-14, though the company produces a few games for teens and young adults (such as Moneybags). These "older" offerings are aimed at a broad audience and are a far cry from the products designed for "hardcore gamers" that dominate much of the gaming market segment. All Gigantic's titles are non-violent and non-sexual in nature. Most are education or learning oriented.

Key Software Products

Animated Storybooks: allow a child to explore strange landscapes and interact with interesting characters. The emphasis is always on highly interactive environments and embedding educational content into the puzzles and scenarios. The popular *Peter Plane and Hallie Helicopter* series is representative of the interactive storybook products.

Activity Centers: present a variety of arts-and-craft type activities for children to explore, all centered around a particular theme. Most Activity Center products allow the child to print pages to color with crayons, create online animated greeting cards, and put props and characters together to build their own animated scenes.

Moneybags: is a home version of the immensely popular Moneybags quiz show that appears on one of MediaGiant's cable networks. The game teaches math skills in the context of a trivia game.

Skatepunkz: is an action game built around skateboarding. There are versions of Skatepunkz for various gaming platforms. It can be played by one or multiple players. In order to reach advanced levels of the game, players must be able to comprehend basic scientific principles.

Business Overview

Historically, the vast bulk of G4K's revenue has come from the retail sale of its software products. Roughly half of these sales are through large department store and toy store chains (WalMart® and Toys 'R Us® are the company's two largest accounts) and half are through dedicated PC software and games retailers (e.g., Babbage's®, CompUSA®, Wizards of the Coast®). However, competing for distribution and shelf space with non-software products and other more well-known studios has been a challenge. In recent years, the channels with the largest revenue growth have been the large online retailers like Amazon.com. In addition to traditional retail sales, Gigantic also pulls in a very small chunk of its overall revenues through OEM sales to consumer PC manufacturers; a few PC SKUs (stock-keeping units) have shipped with Gigantic titles bundled with the system.

At retail, the typical G4K product goes through two distinct sales cycles. For the first 4-6 months of its life, the product is a "new release" with an MSRP of somewhere between $20 and $30. Then after sales begin to slow, the product is reintroduced as a "budget title" and marked down to roughly half its original price. The average product sees 95% of its sales within twelve months of its release (70% within the first six months), so products are discontinued often and have relatively short shelf lives. The company occasionally pulls in extra revenue by bundling several older titles together into "economy packs" and is considering partnering with other studios in a similar fashion.

Gigantic in a Nutshell

- Provider of children's entertainment and education software.
- Privately held, small work force.
- The market for boxed software is fading.
- Hoping to maintain profitability through Web portal with advertising, sponsorship, subscription and distribution business.

AN EXAMPLE PERSONA, TANNER THOMPSON, THE TENACIOUS TINKERER

Data-Driven Persona: Tanner Thompson

In chapters 3-7, you followed the G4K team as they conceived of and created a series of personas for their G4kids.com kid's portal project. Tanner Thompson is an example of a complete, data-driven persona created using the persona lifecycle process. Note that the G4K organizational archetype is not built on data, but the Tanner persona is. The Tanner persona, which starts on the following page, is long and richly referenced to the data sources that were used in its creation. For the purpose of presentation in this book, we have formatted the data references (factoids)

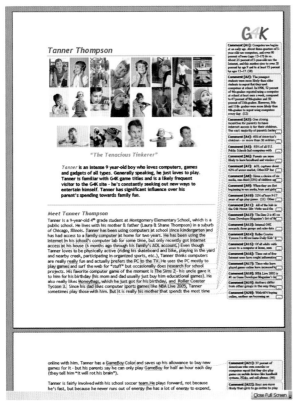

as footnotes here. However, as noted in Chapter 4, we recommend that data references be made more explicit and interactive for the reader. On the previous page are two examples of what the Tanner persona would look like using MS Word "comments" or HTML rollover hotspots. Other example personas in Appendix B show alternative persona formats and approaches. You and your team will decide how much data, and how much effort, you want and need to put into your own personas.

Tanner Thompson

"The Tenacious Tinkerer"

Tanner is an intense 9-year-old boy who loves computers, games and gadgets of all types. Generally speaking, he just loves to play. Tanner is familiar with G4K game titles and is a likely frequent visitor to the G4K site - he's constantly seeking out new ways to entertain himself. Tanner has significant influence over his parent's spending towards family fun.

Meet Tanner Thompson

Tanner is a 9-year-old 4th grade student at Montgomery Elementary School, which is a public school. He lives with his mother & father (Laura & Shane Thompson) in a suburb of Chicago, Illinois. Tanner has been using computers[1] at school since kindergarten[2] and has had

---

[1]Computer use begins at an early age. About three-quarters of 5-year-olds use computers, and over 90 percent of teens (ages 13–17) do so. About 25 percent of 5-year-olds use the Internet, and this number rises to over 50 percent by age 9 and to at least 75 percent by ages 15–17. (28)

[2]The youngest students were more likely than older students to report that they used computers at school. In 1996, 72 percent of 4th-graders reported using a computer at school at least once a week, compared to 47 percent of 8th-graders and 50 percent of 11th-graders. However, 8th- and 11th- graders were more likely than 4th-graders to report using computers every day. (12)

access to a family computer[3] at home for two years. He has been using the Internet[4] in his school's[5] computer lab for some time, but only recently got Internet access[6] at his house (6 months ago through his family's AOL account.)[7] Even though Tanner loves to be physically active (riding his skateboard and bike, playing in the yard and nearby creek, participating in organized sports, etc.), Tanner thinks computers are really really fun and actually prefers the PC[8] to the TV.[9] He uses the PC mostly to play games[10] and surf the Web for "stuff" but occasionally does research[11] for school projects. His favorite computer game of the moment is The Sims 2[12] — his uncle gave it to him for his birthday (his mom and dad usually just buy him educational games). He also really likes Moneybags[13], which he just got for his birthday, and Roller Coaster Tycoon 3.[14] Since his dad[15] likes computer sports[16] games[17] like NBA Live 2005,[18]

---

[3]One strong incentive for parents to have Internet access is for their children. The vast majority of parents believe that their children need to know about computers and the Internet in order to succeed. (20)

[4]45% of America's children – or more than 30 million of those under age 18 – have internet access. Fully 73% of those between the ages of 12 and 17 have internet access and 29% of those under 12 have been online. 82% of those living in households with more that $75,000 in income now have internet access, compared to 38% of those in households earning less then $30,000. (27)

[5]95% of all U.S. Public Schools had computers with Internet access in 1999. Within those schools, 63% of instructional rooms had computers with Internet access. (39)

[6]Parents are more likely to have broadband and wireless Internet access and are more willing to embrace these access capabilities in the future, thereby creating a lucrative market for online service providers. (26)

[7]AOL captures about 42% of access market, Other ISP has 37% - not included in other is: MSN, Earthlink, CompuServe, AT&T, and Prodigy. (41)

[8]Given a choice of six media, one-third (33%) of children aged 8 to 17 told KN/SRI that the web would be the medium they would want to have if they couldn't have any others. Television was picked by 26% of kids; telephone by 21%; and radio by 15%. (16)

[9]When they are first beginning to use media, boys and girls spend the same amount of time watching TV, reading, listening to music and using computers. They develop the same basic media-use skills, and do so at roughly the same age. By the time they are in the four- to six-year-old range, however, there is a difference between boys and girls when it comes to video games, with boys being more likely to play and to play for longer periods of time. (25)

[10]52% of boys 9-17 years of age play games. (11) Other research has claimed that 90% of U.S. households with children rented or owned a video or computer game and that U.S. children spend an average of 20 minutes a day playing video games. (33)

[11]All of the kids in the G4k Home Site Visits used the Internet for school project research. (29) Also, 29% of 9 –17 year olds use the Internet to do their homework. (11) 8.3% of 1st – 8th grade kids use a home computer for school assignments. (39)

[12]The Sims 2 is #5 on Game Developer Magazine's list of the top 20 PC First Person Action Game Titles for the week of 2/11/05. (43)

[13]Internal G4K research: focus groups and sales data shows that boys age 9-11 chose to play Moneybags over other G4K titles. (18)

[14]Roller Coaster Tycoon 3 is #2 on Game Daily Kids' list of the top 20 Children's Entertainment Software Titles for the week of 1/05/05. (42)

[15]Of all adults with access to a computer at home, men continued to exhibit marginally higher rates of use than women (72 percent versus 70 percent). Considering computer use at any location, there is no longer a gender gap. (10)

[16]Three out of four Internet users have sought information about a hobby or interest online. The number of hobby seekers increased by 40% between March 2000 and January 2002 — from 65 million to 91 million. (21)

[17]Those who have played games online have increased by 45% — from 29 million in March 2000, to 42 million in June-July 2002. (21)

[18]NBA Live 2005 is #1 on Game Developer Magazine's list of the top 20 PC Sports Game Software Titles for the week of 4/12/05. (43)

Tanner sometimes plays those with him. But[19] it is really his mother[20] that spends the most time online with him. Tanner has a GameBoy Color[21] and saves up his allowance to buy new games for it, but his parents say he can only play GameBoy for half an hour each day (they tell him "it will rot his brain").

Tanner is fairly involved with his school soccer team. He plays forward, not because he's fast, but because he never runs out of energy (he has a lot of energy to expend, all of the time). In addition to soccer and other organized school activities, he likes to build things with Legos (he wants to collect all the Star Wars Lego sets), play board games, ride his skateboard with friends, and just run around the neighborhood. He watches episodes of his favorite cartoon series as much as he can, and avidly follows the Chicago Fire[22] (the big pro soccer team) with his dad. Although his parents limit his TV time, they make a point to watch Malcolm in the Middle[23] together every week.

Tanner's Goals & Desires[24]

- Be accepted and sought out as a friend by neighborhood kids and schoolmates
  - Impress his friends with knowledge and skills[25] related to the video and PC games they play (e.g., find out new hints for Dragon Ball Z[26] before his friends do)
- Stay entertained (i.e., not be bored)
  - Please his parents and teachers, but get schoolwork[27] done fast so he can play

---

[19]Mothers differ from other groups in the way they use the internet; praising the medium because it allows them to do research or write e-mail in 5 to 10 minute chunks. (6) Time savings is one prominent reason behind increased use of the internet by parents, especially for shopping. Further, 59% of mothers regularly multitask to save time, versus only 43% of men. Still, mothers are more likely than fathers to say they "surf for the fun of it". (7)

[20]With 46% buying online, mothers are becoming an increasingly important segment of online purchasers to target. This is in comparison to 41% of all online women purchasers. Online mothers are also very loyal consumers; once they find a brand that they like, 70% find it difficult to change. (26)

[21]37 percent of Americans who own consoles or computers report that they also play games on mobile devices like handheld systems, PDAs, and cell phones. (44)

[22]Boys are more likely than girls to go online to play games (52% vs. 43%) and to get sports information or scores (40% vs. 15%). (11)

[23]Ten of the 15 households mentioned watching regularly scheduled television shows together. Among those mentioned were "Malcolm", "Seventh Heaven", "The OC", and "Americas Funniest Home Videos". (29)

[24]All goals were derived as underlying themes from the G4K site visits (29)

[25]At age 9 or 10, children begin to think in abstract terms and become more focused on interactions with others. By ages 5 to 6 years, children have already formed their identities, can play cooperatively, and have develop fine motor skills. By age 9, a child's world has expanded beyond the immediate surrounding. (3)

[26]Overall, boys are more interested in technology, seeing out game-playing resources, building web pages, downloading software, and even downloading music files. Teen boys largely use the internet for game playing and game-playing advice. (18)

[27]The number of children age 12 and under going online for entertainment and games more than tripled between 1998 and 1999, reaching 9.2 million and surpassing homework as the most popular activity in this age bracket. Growth has been exceptionally fast among boys age 12 and under. (1)

- ◯ Watch his favorite movies and TV shows, extending his interest in these things online (searching for info, chatting with others)
- ◯ Find really fun but free online games,[28] so he can have fresh experiences without having to ask for money[29] to buy stuff
- ● Have cool stuff[30] & do cool[31] things
  - ◯ Find out the best prices[32] on Nintendo 64s to show to his mom (so maybe she'll get him one for his next birthday[33])
  - ◯ Make his parents get broadband (their dialup connect is "soooo slooooow")
  - ◯ His dream is to convince his parents to go to Disney World and Universal Studies during spring vacation.[34]

What does Tanner want from G4kids.com?

- ● Tanner knows all about G4K because he already loves our games. He loved the G4K Peter Plane and Hallie Helicopter interactive book series 'when he was a kid' and now G4K Moneybags and G4K Skatepunkz are two of his favorite games. He expects G4kids.com to be very cool!
- ● He will likely seek out our site for game hints, new product information and especially direct entertainment.
- ● Tanner has a short attention span and little patience. He will leave the site if we do not quickly engage him and provide enduring fun experiences.

---

[28]The popularity of online games has risen since 1999 when only 18 percent participated. The 2003 poll revealed that more than 1/3 (37%) of frequent game players go online to play – up from 31% in 2002. (9)
[29]31% of parents would allow their child to purchase online if they could control the amount spent. Though only 11% of parents were award of services that allow parents to allocate money for kids to spend online. (2)
[30]Kids seem to be highly aware of age and age-appropriateness of the products and media content around them. Boys in particular were very vocal about not wanting to do something or use something that was clearly intended for a younger audience. (29)
[31]More than half (54%) of teens say that the Internet helps them find out what's cool in fashion and music that they like. Younger girls, 12 to 14, are the most likely (64%) to say that the Internet helps them to find fashion and music. Fifty-nine percent of frequent users (those who go online every day) are also more likely to have used the Net to find out what's cool. (17)
[32]More than eight out of ten Internet users have researched a product or service online. (21)
[33]8% of online parents who's children go online indicated that they had made purchases as a direct result of information retrieved by their kids. (7) 15% of children have retrieved information online leading to a purchase by the parent. (2)
[34]34% of online parents said their use of the Internet improves the way they plan weekend outings and family trips. 27% said it improves the way they shop for birthday and holiday gifts. 26% said it improves the way they spend time with their children. 19% said it improves the way they care for their children's health. (20)

Tanner's Computer & Internet Usage

Tanner at School

Before Tanner had a computer at home,[35] he would sign up for free time on the computer in his classroom[36] as often as he could.[37] The kids in his class get 10-minute turns and they have to use one of the teacher's choices of educational games,[38] which seem quite limited to him[39] (the computer is a Power Mac G4, and the teacher[40] keeps KidPix, HyperStudio, and a bunch of Jumpstart and Blaster math and reading stuff on it). Now that he has a computer at home, he has better games there and so doesn't fight for the classroom computer as much.

On Thursdays at school he spends an hour in the school computer lab.[41] He always has to start out practicing his typing (they use Read, Write, and Type)[42] and then most of the rest of the time is taken up with a class assignment using the Internet, HyperStudio, Word, or Excel.[43] Tanner really likes it[44] when his teacher does an Internet assignment[45] and he can go online to

---

[35]More school-age children use computers at school than have access to them at home (8). 66% of teenagers that are online have access from home while 60% have access from school. 30% have access from both home and school and only 11% have access from some other location. (2)

[36]Much like a school-issued textbook or a traditional library, students think of the Internet as the place to find primary and secondary source material for their reports, presentations, and projects. This is perhaps the most commonly used metaphor of the Internet for school—held by both students and many of their teachers alike. (24)

[37]Students think of the Internet as one way to receive instruction about material that interests them or about which they are confused. Others view the Internet as a way to complete their schoolwork as quickly and painlessly as possible, with minimal effort and minimal engagement. For some, this includes viewing the Internet as a mechanism to plagiarize material or otherwise cheat. (24)

[38]66% of public school teachers reported using computers or the Internet for instruction during class time. (19)

[39]Two-thirds of teachers agree that the internet is not well integrated into their classrooms and only 26% of them feel pressure to use it in learning activities. 44% percent of teachers cite lack of knowledge about how to use the internet as the reason for not logging on. 78% of teachers cited lack of time as the number one reason for not logging on to the internet. (14)

[40]More than eight out of 10 teachers (84 percent) believe that computers and access to the internet improve the quality of education. (14)

[41]In 1996, 79 percent of 4th-graders, 91 percent of 8thgraders, and 96 percent of 11th-graders reported using a computer at home or at school to write stories or papers, a substantial increase from 1984. The percentage of students who used a computer to learn things also increased between 1984 and 1996 for all three grades. (12)

[42]Elementary school teachers were more likely than secondary school teachers to assign students practice drills using computers (39 versus 12 percent) and to have their students use computers or the Internet to solve problems (31 versus 20 percent). Secondary school teachers, however, were more likely to assign research using the Internet (41 versus 25 percent). (19)

[43]41% of teachers reported assigning students work that involved computer applications such as word processing and spreadsheets to a moderate or large extent; 31 percent of teachers reported assigning practice drills and 30 percent reported assigning research using the Internet to a moderate or large extent. (19)

[44]Young people believe that online use benefits them in a number of ways. Forty-four percent say it has increased their interest in current events, while 36% think it has improved their writing or language skills. Altogether, 33% think that it has improved their performance as a student overall. Online use benefits kids' relationships, as well, with 39% saying it has improved the quality of their friendships. Virtually no online young people say online has negatively impacted these areas of their lives. (11)

[45]Online or PC based homework or school assignments are more common as the age of the child increases. Browsing or informal learning activities are now performed by over 5 million children age 12 and under, three times as many as were doing this in 1998. Growth has been somewhat faster among boys and children age 9 to 12. (1)

find out something. Even though the teacher says the Internet is an unlimited resource,[46] they're only allowed to go to certain sites, like PBS or Britannica, and sometimes he can't even get to those because the filter the school uses screws up.

Tanner and his friends don't[47] use Instant Messaging[48] as much as some of the girls[49] in his class do. He doesn't email[50] very often either, but mostly because he doesn't have his own email account[51] (the whole family shares one email address) but occasionally (at his mother's urging) he'll reply to notes from family[52] members.

Tanner at Play

Tanner likes using the computer at his home, because he gets to play around[53] and do what he wants.[54] He uses the computer at home to go online about 3 times a week,[55] mostly on Saturdays or Sundays and occasionally on a weekday when he doesn't have soccer practice. His mom says he has to do his homework[56] before he gets on the computer for fun on a weekday, but if he has to do some research for a report[57] or look up words he might use Encarta, or go online with his parents' AOL account to search the Web.

---

[46]75% percent of teachers said the internet is an important tool for finding new resources to meet new standards. (14)

[47]Just over 3 million children age 12 and under go online for email or chat. Email and online chat is the second most popular activity among online teenagers, surpassing entertainment and games. However, very few children age 8 and under go online for communications purposes and this number hasn't grown appreciably in the past year. This activity segment has an even split between boys and girls, with growth being faster among teenage girls over the past year. (1)

[48]Communication Tops List of Favorite Online Activities: Three out of the five activities most engaged in by young people involve communicating with friends and family — writing letters or notes to friends (59%), using instant messages (52%), and writing letters or notes to relatives (36%). Other popular activities include playing games (48%) and getting information about rock stars or music groups (35%). (11)

[49]Girls are more likely to go online to socialize than boys (68% vs. 50% in 9 -17 year olds). (11)

[50]Only 32% of 9-11 year olds email friends. (11)

[51]Almost half of all online parents share access with a spouse/partner. (7)

[52]36% of 9-17 year olds say they go online to write letters or notes to relatives "very" or "pretty often." (11) Pre-teen participants in the G4k Home Site study mentioned that they don't often inniate IM conversations and email threads, but they will reply. (29)

[53]Young people display a strong interest in a range of new online activities, including sending and receiving pictures from family and friends online (78%), downloading music or songs online (76%), having a live video conference with a friend online (70%), and watching short cartoons or video clips online (63%). (11)

[54]Younger children are more likely than older children to go online to play games (58% of 9 to 11 year olds vs. 40% of 15 to 17 year olds) and to get information about TV shows (23% vs. 13%). (11)

[55]Online Use Grows as Young People Get Older: The amount of time per week young people report spending online increases as they mature: 2.8 days per week for 9 to 11 year-olds to 4.5 days per week for 15 to17 year olds. Eight in ten young Internet users (79%) say they go online, on average, at least an hour daily. (11)

[56]Half or more of online young people say their parents have rules about going online only after home-work is completed (67%), limiting the amount of time spent online (51%), or checking with an adult before going online (50%). Younger children are most likely to say their parents set rules (76% of 9 to 11 year olds), though half (52%) of online teens between the ages of 15 and 17 also say their parents set rules for them about going online. (11)

[57]55% of 9-17 year olds say they prefer to use the Internet as a resource for homework. (11)

Not surprisingly, most of Tanner's time on the computer is spent playing PC games,[58] both online[59] and off; once he gets into a Half-Life or Sims 2 game he can stay involved with it for hours. His mom will usually have to say "that's enough" and make him go outside. Several times a week, he goes online to play instead of starting a more traditional PC game.

When Tanner goes online for fun he likes to surf around[60] for just about anything that comes to mind;[61] and he'll stay online for at least an hour[62] or so. Because of the ISP they use, he usually starts at AOL Kids and uses familiar links[63] there, or sometimes goes to Yahooligans and uses their categories to get back to favorite sites. He sometimes checks out the scores[64] and stats for the Chicago Fire and the Cubs, and he goes to links for Dragon Ball Z stuff, GameBoy games, and Half-Life 2 (to look up cheat codes that his friends have told him about). He often tries out new games[65] on Yahooligans, Nick, Disney, or Lego and has downloaded music[66] only a few times. Generally, his online[67] activity is more like a flowing stream of consciousness[68] rather than a planned event; if it catches his attention, he's off to it until something else does. His bedroom reflects this[69] disposition, the walls "littered" with posters, print outs, and other artifacts representing his varied interests.

---

[58]Boys and girls use computers almost equally, but for different activities. While 42 percent of girls use the household computer for word processing, only 36 percent of boys did. In addition, 79 percent of girls played games on the home computer compared with 87 percent of boys. (10)

[59]Younger children are most likely to go online to play games (58% of 9 to 11 year olds vs. 40% of 15 to 17 year olds) and to get information about TV shows (23% vs. 13%). (11)

[60] Young People Prefer Online to Television and Telephone: The centrality of Internet use can be seen in the degree to which it has supplanted other favorite activities. Sixty-three percent of those surveyed prefer going online to watching television, and 55% choose online over talking on the telephone. (11)

[61]The number of online Americans who say they sometimes go online for no particular reason, just to browse for fun or to pass the time, has increased by 44% since March 2000. These recreational users of the Web grew from 54 million in March 2000, to 78 million in January 2002. (21)

[62]69% of online youth access Web sites related to favorite hobbies. This compares to the 78% of adults who search for hobby information. Boys are more likely to go to hobby Web sites than girls, with 76% of boys having ever done this, compared to 62% of girls. (17)

[63]9-11 year olds spend an average of 1.15 hours online per session. (11)

[64]Kids in our site visit study around this age were less likely to add sites to favorites – they tend to just recreate the actions that got them to a specific page in the first place. For example, if they found what they wanted from their home page they'd simply try to remember the path and repeat it the next time. (29)

[65]40% of 9-17 year old boys say they go online "pretty often" to get sports information or scores. (11)

[66]The popularity of online games has risen since 1999 when only 18 percent participated. The 2003 poll revealed that more than 1/3 (37%) of frequent game players go online to play – up from 31% in 2002. (9)

[67]More than half the children (53%) in that age bracket (12 – 17) have downloaded music. It was particularly popular with online boys, some 60% of whom said they downloaded music, compared to 47% of girls. Some 73% of older boys (ages 15-17) had downloaded music. There was some evidence that the prevalence of downloading increased with age. For instance, 44% of the kids between ages 12-14 had downloaded music and fully 61% of those 15-17 had done so. (23)

[68]Forty-one percent of tweens say they do other things while surfing the net. Some split their attention between surfing and talking on the phone, eating or listening to music. Still others say they watch TV while working at their computer. (4)

[69]Both boys and girls spent significant effort making their bedroom (and sometimes playroom) personal and unique. There was clearly a need to identify themselves and make a statement. (29)

Tanner and the Family Computer

The family's 56k modem is sometimes too slow and makes surfing frustrating. Not to mention that sometimes he gets disconnected from AOL[70] (often in the middle of a game or something cool). Slow connections and getting kicked off really make him mad. He doesn't have much patience[71] for slow sites, so if a Web page is loading slowly he often clicks the "back" button or opens another browser window and finds a different link to follow.[72] In addition to broadband, Tanner really wants his parents to get a new PC for the house (secretly, so that he can get the old one for his room).[73] His parents are considering it mostly because they are tired of Tanner messing things up.[74]

Tanner knows his mom is worried[75] about what he might see on the Internet.[76] That is one reason[77] why their PC is placed in the family room.[78] He hasn't really been interested in going into chat rooms, but his mom said she wouldn't let him anyway, and he has to ask one of his parents before he can go online. He's a little worried that his parents might turn on the parental controls[79] or get some other filtering software like "the dumb one at school" but they haven't gotten around to doing it yet. He knows he's not supposed to look at anything "gross"

---

[70] Most of the families in our site visits reported being very frustrated because they were often disconnected or dropped in the middle of a session. (29)

[71] We witnessed lots of kids being impatient with slow-loading pages and many times assumed that the page was down or broken if nothing happened quickly. (29)

[72] Across our site visits, kids all of ages just don't show a lot of patience – or at least, they are highly excitable and easily distracted. Regarding internet behavior specifically, they won't wait for pages to load. Instead, they either click on a different link, type a new URL, or open a completely new browser instance and get distracted with something else. (29)

[73] As a result, only 25 of the 103 (24%) computers in the sample were located in a private space - a parent's or child's bedroom. This placement is surprising, in part, because so many of the families in the sample got their computers for their children. Families were more likely to place the computer in public spaces like the dining room, kitchen, family room, spare room, or basement (50% of computers) or in a semi-private space, like a study, which had an adult owner, but could be used by all household members (26% of computers).This made it difficult to use the computer for tasks like email, finances or word processing that require a degree of peace and quietness. (15)

[74] Parents often complained that their kids "messed up" the computer regularly, by freely tinkering with settings, downloading unknown items and installing all kinds of applications. (29)

[75] 80% of parents think that Internet filtering is a good idea. Parents worry about their kids seeing pornography (81%) or violence (74%) on the Internet. (26)

[76] Online teens as a group are generally much less concerned than parents about online content and do not feel as strongly that they need to be protected. (17)

[77] Many parents selected a public place precisely because it denied privacy to their children, as they used the Internet. By placing the computer in a public place, parents could casually inspect what their children were doing online. As they walked past, they could see what was on the screen, for example, and ask questions about their children's behavior. (15)

[78] While 75% of tweens (7 to 14 yo) have a computer at home, one-fifth of the older ones (13 and 14) have a PC in their own bedroom. (4)

[79] Another tool that parents use to control what their children see and do online is to actually sit down and surf along side their son or daughter. Close to seven in 10 parents (68%) report sitting down at the computer with their child. More mothers than fathers sit down at their computers with their children. Interestingly, 34% of parents who say that they "do not go online" say they do sit down and go online with their children. (17)

and his mom checks in periodically[80] when he's online to make sure he's not into anything bad. His mom likes to sit with him[81] when he goes online for school stuff[82] — she gives him ideas[83] on where to look for certain things,[84] and helps him type in search questions. Sometimes she even plays games[85] and online activities with him.[86] He helps his mom out sometimes[87] too; for example, he showed her[88] the Ask Jeeves site that they use at school. She really liked it.[89]

Tanner wishes he could play games[90] more often than he actually gets to. However, his mom limits his time playing PC or online games[91] as well as with the GameBoy, particularly if it is something that she thinks is not very educational or social. He has a few friends who have a Nintendo

---

[80]Some parents used the public location of the computer as a deterrent, believing that their children would be less likely to visit sexually explicit web sites or converse with strangers in chat rooms if their behavior was subject to parental oversight. Conversely, children lobbied to have the computer place in their rooms because of the privacy it afforded them. (15)

[81]A majority of young people (56%) say they go online sitting together with their parents. The younger the children, the more likely they are to say they go online together with their parents – two-thirds (67%) of 9 to 11 year olds say so, compared to half of 15 to 17 year olds (49%). (11) Nine out of 10 parents "always or sometimes" surf the net with their kids. (4)

[82]Across studies, it has been found that younger children preferred and spent more time playing education games than did older children. (13)

[83]74 % of 9-11 year olds say their parents give them new online ideas. (11)

[84]More than eight out of ten Internet users have searched the Internet to answer specific questions. (21)

[85]A range of age groups are getting in on the [gaming] action, and the activity is becoming quite popular with women. (9)

[86]Parents' use of online content is closely linked to things their kids want to do online. This is especially true for children under 12 online, [87]91% of whose parents say they supervise their kids' online session some of the time and 62% all of the time. (7)

[87]47% of 9-11 year olds say they give their parents new online ideas. (11)

[88]Young boys in this study promoted themselves as the household "computer guru". A quote from one 11 year old participant, "I sometimes have to hang out while my parents try to use the computer – just in case they get confused or something." However, observation of actual skill and knowledge indicated that parents and children are actually not that different in this regard. (29)

[89]Among adult users of home computers, 70 percent used them for word processing, the most common use. Other common uses included games (54%), email and communications (44%), bookkeeping/finances/taxes/household records (44%) and working at home (34%). (10)

[90]Use of home computers for playing games and for work on school assignments are common activities. A majority (59 percent) of 5- through 17-year-olds use home computers to play games, and over 40 percent use computers to connect to the Internet (46 percent) and to complete school assignments (44 percent). Middle-school-age and high-school-age youth (ages 11–17) use home computers to complete school assignments (57–64 percent), to connect to the Internet (54-63 percent), and to play games (60-63 percent). (28)

[91]Contention for computer time is a heated issue in many of the families we visited. Families do not sit down calmly at the beginning of the week and schedule time slots together. According to our informants, they watch the space in which the computer sits, try to read each other's plans, and fight for a seat. (15)

game console that they play with together[92] and he wants one *really badly*.[93] He talks about it all the time and points out prices and cool games[94] (even educational ones) to his parents.[95]

RESEARCH REFERENCES

1. The Internet Consumer: Online Children. (December 1999). Interactive Consumers. Cyber Dialogue. http://www.cyberdialogue.com/

2. Cyberfacts: Teenagers on the Internet (summary data sheet in PDF format; based on data from the American Internet User Survey). http://www.cyberdialogue.com/

3. Children on the Internet, http://www.otal.umd.edu/UUPractice/children/

4. Children's Internet Use (Canada). Media Awareness Network. http://www.media-awareness.ca.

5. Curiosity: Five to Eleven (R. Brooks & L Dumas). Sesame Street Workshop. http://www.sesameworkshop.org/parents/advice/article.php?contentId=75002

6. Why Net Marketers love mom. http://news.com.com/

7. The Internet Consumer Industry Brief: Families Online (February 1999 — Published by Cyber Dialogue). http://www.cyberdialogue.com/

8. Home Computers and Internet Use in the United States (August 2000). US Census Bureau. http://www.census.gov/population/www/socdemo/computer.html

9. Gamers Growing Up. The Big Picture Demographics. http://cyberatlas.internet.com/

10. Computer use in the United States (October 1997). US Census Bureau. http://www.census.gov/population/www/socdemo/computer.html

11. The America Online/Roper Starch Youth Cyberstudy 1999 (Nov. 1999). http://www.corp.aol.com/press/study/youthstudy.pdf

12. Student Computer Use - Indicator of the Month, National Center for Educational Statistics (August, 1999). http://nces.ed.gov/pubsearch/pubsinfo.asp?pubid=1999011

13. Children and Interactive Media. Wartell, Lee, and Caplovitz (Nov 2002). Markle Foundation.

14. Teachers say Internet improves quality of education. Cyberatlas. http://cyberatlas.internet.com/

15. The social context of home computing. Frohlich and Kraut (April 2002).

16. More Kids say Internet is the medium they can't live without. http://www.sriresearch.com/press/pr040402.htm

---

[92] PC gaming and general PC usage, as opposed to gaming consoles, were treated as individual activities. Game playing with dedicate consoles was more social in nature. (29)

[93] Boys in our study tended to not care about brands. They knew individual/specific products (and either loved or hated them), but they didn't particular know or care who made it. As an example, in one family, even though they had one specific gaming console that they seemed to enjoy, the two boys in the family repeatedly discussed wanting specific games made only for other platforms. Girls on the other hand tended to appreciate not just specific products but the companies that make them. They expressed interest in having other products by the same specific company/brand. (29)

[94] A majority of parents (77%) think teens who provide a very lucrative market, should be allowed to shop online. (26)

[95] Nearly two-thirds (63%) of parents plan to purchase at least one computer video game in 2003, as will 56% of all Americans under age 45. (9)

17. Teenage Life Online: The rise of the instant-message generation and the Internet's impact on friendships and family relationships. (June 20, 2001). Pew Internet & American Life Project. http://www.pewinternet.org/reports/toc.asp?Report=36

18. Targeting Teens is a gender game (August 2000). Jupiter Communications.

19. Teacher Use of Computers and the Internet in Public Schools, Education Statistics Quarterly - National Center for Education Statistics. http://nces.ed.gov/pubsearch/pubsinfo.asp?pubid=2000090

20. Parents Online. (November 17, 2002). Pew Internet & American Life Project. http://www.pewinternet.org/reports/toc.asp?Report=75

21. America's Online Pursuits: The changing picture of who's online and what they do. (December 22, 2003). Pew Internet & American Life Project. http://www.pewinternet.org/reports/toc.asp?Report=106

22. The Ever-Shifting Internet Population: A new look at Internet access and the digital divide (April 16, 2003). Pew Internet & American Life Project. http://www.pewinternet.org/reports/toc.asp?Report=88

23. The Music Downloading Deluge: 37 million American adults and youths have retrieved music files on the Internet (April 24, 2001). Pew Internet & American Life Project. http:// www.pewinternet.org/reports/toc.asp?Report=33

24. The Digital Disconnect: The widening gap between Internet-savvy students and their schools (August 14, 2002). Pew Internet & American Life Project. http://www.pewinternet.org/reports/ toc.asp?Report=67

25. Zero to Six: Electronic Media in the Lives of Infants, Toddlers and Preschoolers (Fall 2003). Kaiser Family Foundation. http://www.kff.org/entmedia/3378.cfm

26. Online Parents: Gateway to a New Generation, Cyber Dialogue, The Internet Consumer, Year 2000, Vol.7. http://www.cyberdialogue.com/index.html

27. More Online, Doing More: 16 million newcomers gain Internet access in the last half of 2000 as women, minorities, and families with modest incomes continue to surge online. (February 18, 2001). Pew Internet & American Life Project. http://www.pewinternet.org/reports/toc.asp?Report=30

28. Computer and Internet Use by Children and Adolescents in 2001 (October 2003). National Center for Education Statistics. http://nces.ed.gov/

29. G4K home site visits (Summer 2004). Visit notes for 15 homes with 1 or more children between the ages 5 and 12. \\G4K\user_research\site_visits\summer_2004

30. Internet Access in U.S. Public Schools and Classrooms: 1994-2002. (October 2003). National Center for Education Statistics. http://nces.ed.gov/pubsearch/pubsinfo.asp?pubid=2004011

31. The Internet and Education: Findings of the Pew Internet & American Life Project. (September 1, 2001). Pew Internet & American Life Project. http://www.pewinternet.org/reports/toc.asp?Report=39

32. Consumption of Information Goods and Services in the United States: There is a trendsetting technology elite in the U.S. who chart the course for the use of information goods and services. (November 23, 2003). Pew Internet & American Life Project. http://www.pewinternet.org/reports/toc.asp?Report=103

33. Let the games begin: Gaming technology and entertainment among college students. (July 6, 2003). Pew Internet & American Life Project. http://www.pewinternet.org/reports/toc.asp?Report=93

34. Cities Online: Urban Development and the Internet. (November 20, 2001). Pew Internet & American Life Project. http://www.pewinternet.org/reports/toc.asp?Report=50

35. Spam: How it is hurting email and degrading life on the Internet. (October 22, 2003). Pew Internet & American Life Project. http://www.pewinternet.org/reports/toc.asp?Report=102

36. Tracking Online Life: How Women Use the Internet to Cultivate Relationships with Family and Friends. (May 10, 2000). Pew Internet & American Life Project. http://www.pewinternet.org/reports/toc.asp?Report=11

37. Broadband Adoption at Home: A Pew Internet Project Data Memo. (May 18, 2003). Pew Internet & American Life Project. http://www.pewinternet.org/reports/toc.asp?Report=90

38. G4K Games Usability Test, \\G4K\usability\reports\03-34-2004.doc

39. Digest of Education Statistics, 2000, National Center for Education Statistics. http://nces.ed.gov/pubsearch/pubsinfo.asp?pubid=2001034, or http://nces.ed.gov/pubsearch/pubsinfo.asp?pubid=2001034

40. Online content for kids, http://www.clickz.com/experts/design/cont_dev/article.php/1381161

41. Internet Service Provider Review, 2005, G4K Marketing Group

42. Game Daily Kids. http://www.gamedaily.com/general/gdkids/

43. Game Developer Magazine. http://www.gdmag.com/

44. Games People Play, Robyn Greenspan, May 31, 2002. http://www.clickz.com/stats/sectors/software/article.php/1152221

45. Get-in-the-game News. http://www.gignews.com/

46. E3 Expo online news. http://www.e3expo.com/

47. Firing Squad - Home of the Hardcore Gamer. http://www.firingsquad.com/

48. G4K holiday usage focus groups, December 2004. \\G4K\marketresearch\reports\12-18-2004.doc

APPENDIX B

EXAMPLE PERSONAS FROM REAL PROJECTS

Quarry Integrated Communications (and RealSuite Incorporated)

Mentor Graphics

Zylom Media Group

QUARRY INTEGRATED COMMUNICATIONS & REALSUITE INCORPORATED

Robert Barlow Busch, Quarry Integrated Communications

Project Overview

Quarry Integrated Communications (www.quarry.com) is a consulting firm providing a full range of services including communications planning, advertising and communication arts, public relations, database and direct marketing, Web and digital development, and interaction design and usability. The example personas discussed here were created by Quarry Integrated Communications during a project with their client RealSuite Incorporated (www.realsuitesoftware.com). They can also be downloaded as PDFs by visiting personas.quarry.com.

RealSuite is a subsidiary of BLJC, Canada's leading outsourced provider of commercial real estate services. RealSuite offers a Web-hosted enterprise software product used by experts in leasing, facilities management, and occupancy planning.

Quarry was hired to redesign the user interface for a RealSuite software module used by project managers to coordinate work such as office renovations, moves and relocations, building repairs, and construction.

Persona creation

This project followed Quarry's Design Builder™ process, a framework for designing digital products that build brand through the user experience. A key step in the first phase of Design Builder is the creation of personas following contextual field research with current and potential users. For this project, the field research was conducted by a team of three people: Robert Barlow-Busch, Design Lead (Quarry), Emily Christofides, Customer Insight Specialist (Quarry), and Mark Mulholland, General Manager of Projects & Workspace Solutions (BLJC).

The research involved 31 participants across Canada, in cities such as Toronto, Ottawa, and Vancouver. Visits ranged from 1 to 2 hours in duration and included a mix of interview, observation, and demonstrations of tools and processes. Sessions were audiotaped for later reference.

A careful analysis of the research findings resulted in a total of five personas, two of which are presented here: Genevieve Boutroux (a Project Manager) and Jim Robinson (a Facilities Manager). Please note that these examples have been modified from the originals, to protect confidential or competitively sensitive information.

Outcome

Increased understanding of what's important to end users. "These have certainly shattered a few myths about our users!" exclaimed Herb Verma, VP Software Development at RealSuite, when the personas were first introduced. The project's executive stakeholders and the development team rallied around a new shared vision of their customers.

Confirmation of the product strategy and clarity around where to focus resources. The personas reaffirmed RealSuite's commitment to designing for the user experience, as the resulting benefits to their customers—and to their business—were made explicit by the personas. The personas also helped RealSuite to reach agreement around what aspects of the redesigned project management module deserved priority attention.

Software that project managers are excited about using. The personas captured a host of insights that helped the designers create a tool that reflects the realities of a project manager's job. For instance, an ability to set aside documents lets Genevieve Boutroux (the primary persona) recover smoothly from the many interruptions she faces every day, and a new dashboard provides a strategic view that helps her to anticipate issues, instead of reacting to them as she did previously.

Two example personas from this project:

Genevieve Boutroux | Project Manager

Primary

Delight her customers. Genevieve loves making a real difference in the lives of her customers. "It's not just about being on time and on budget. It's about thrilling people with the end result!" She likes to visit newly-completed job sites just to hear people talk with each other about how much they love their new space.

Achieve a better work/life balance. Genevieve has around 20 projects underway at all times, in various stages of completion. The work required to keep her projects "on the rails" means she's never really off the job. She feels constant pressure to keep up with her responsibilities, even when at home.

> "I'd love to actually accomplish something instead of being pulled in 500 directions. But it's the nature of the job."

Age: 42

Education: Bachelor of Interior Design, California State University (Sacramento, CA)

Employer: Providence Corporation in Boston, MA

Manages: Projects in 4 buildings in downtown Boston

Role Description

Genevieve is responsible for coordinating all the activities and people involved in completing projects for Providence Corporation's four main buildings in downtown Boston. Although her desk is in the PM group's third-floor office in the national headquarters building — a 350-thousand-square-foot tower — her projects take place either here or in three other large buildings downtown. One is within walking distance and the others are just a short drive away.

Most of Genevieve's work is with tenant service projects, meaning office or commercial relocations, painting and similar updates, or larger-scale interior renovations. Other project managers handle the more expensive and complex engineering work that occasionally arises, such as alterations or repairs to a building's structure. Genevieve's projects tend to come up throughout the year, as opposed to being planned well in advance, so they each require a separate budget to be estimated, approved, and then met. Her projects typically cost between $10,000 and $40,000 and are completed within four to ten weeks from start to finish. But she occasionally handles jobs up to $80,000, especially if it's within her area of expertise as a trained interior designer. Genevieve enjoys using those skills in her job, whether it's by recommending a lighting system for the boardroom or by editing CAD drawings to illustrate where a wall should be moved.

Genevieve works closely with Sarah, a Project Coordinator in the office who provides some much-appreciated support to Genevieve and two other PMs who handle work for Providence in the Boston area. Sarah hopes to become a PM herself someday, so Genevieve sometimes gives her small, simple projects to manage, especially when her own workload is even heavier than usual. Normally, though, Sarah's job is to help the PM's with administrative tasks such as scheduling meetings and taking minutes, plus performing data entry and reporting tasks in PC-Project (an enterprise software tool used by Providence). Genevieve relies heavily on Sarah's help in moving projects forward, as she isn't comfortable using tools such as PC-Project herself. "I've never had the time to learn them; I'd rather do my job than spend time figuring out software."

Genevieve's Day

After a long commute from her home in the outskirts of Boston, Genevieve is relieved to reach her office by around 8:30 most days. Traffic is much lighter on weekends, though, so she allows herself an extra hour of sleep. Genevieve often needs to work on weekends, as many of her projects occur outside normal business hours to minimize disruption to the building's tenants; to compensate for this, she tries to take some time off during the week, though she's often unable to do that. Monday morning is her favorite time of the week, strolling through a building and listening to people marvel at how much was accomplished since they left on Friday.

During the day, Genevieve splits her time between taking calls and responding to email at her desk, attending meetings with customers and contractors, and roaming her buildings to check up on her projects. "Because of the number of projects I'm managing, my phones are ringing almost non-stop. And my laptop is always dinging to let me know a new email has arrived. If Genevieve ever needs to focus on something for more than 30 minutes, she'll arrange to work on it at home; it's the only way to avoid the constant interruptions that plague her at the office. Most nights after dinner, she spends one or two hours dealing with these items, catching up on messages, and skimming her notebook for anything that requires a more official paper trail.

Genevieve's notebook is her primary tool. It's a 500-page 5"x 8" perfect-bound book that's always in her hand or in her bag. Throughout the day, she takes note of everything she's done, everyone she's spoken with, and anything she needs to do. She likes her notebook because it's easy to use, it's light to carry, it never crashes or runs out of batteries, and it's easy to find what she needs: she just flips to the date of interest. "Some people use PDAs or laptops for this, but I'm not interested. Paper is great. Maybe I'm impatient, but I don't care to experiment with new software and gadgets. I'm too busy staying on top of things as it is!"

The only software Genevieve has patience for is Outlook and Excel, because they're so critical to her. Email is her primary means for keeping in touch with the people involved ›››

©2005 RealSuite Inc. and Quarry Integrated Communications Inc. All rights reserved. Do not copy or distribute this document without written permission.

Genevieve Boutroux

Project Manager

in her projects, even more so than the phone; she receives over 50 emails per day. In Excel, she created some simple spreadsheets for tracking each project's commitments against its budget; she updates these every day with notes from her paper notebook and data from reports sent to her by Sarah. Genevieve doesn't use PC-Project, although she was given an account when it was first introduced. Several months ago, she tried to log in to get a report when Sarah was away, but she couldn't remember her user ID or password. "So I said forget it! I haven't touched it since."

Genevieve leaves Boston each day at 6:00, hoping the rush hour traffic tapers off during her drive home. But in the end, it feels like she's on the job 24/7. Her laptop follows her home, her cell phone follows her home — and she knows she'll be back on the job site tomorrow.

Project Processes

A fair number of Genevieve's projects initially come through her buildings' Facilities Managers. Tenants will request something that's not in the building's annual budget, so it gets implemented as a project, assuming it's big enough. Genevieve describes her relationship with the FMs as "cool," which disappoints her, as she takes pride in being able to get along with anyone. For instance, things often get tense between her and Jim, the FM for one of her downtown buildings. He expects a lot and can be demanding. "I know it's 'his' building, but I can't keep him in the loop constantly; I sometimes wish he'd back off. Once the project's in my hands, it's my responsibility. You can't have two chiefs."

Genevieve sees the formula for completing projects as fairly straightforward: first, you make the plan, which involves defining the work, setting a budget and timeline, and going to tender if over $25,000. Then you execute the work, making sure it's completed by vendors according to budget and to everyone's satisfaction. Finally, when the work is done, you close the project. But although this sounds simple, it often isn't. Because of the workload imposed upon her, Genevieve finds herself reacting to problems or issues

instead of anticipating them — which makes the situation even worse. "Problems are solved only through lots of communication, fact-checking, and reporting, which takes lots of time," she explains. "The problem is, from the amount of time I spend chasing and documenting information, you'd think I'm spending ten *million* dollars, not just ten thousand."

Genevieve complains that although her projects are fairly small, they take just as much work as the really big ones — which she feels is ridiculous, when you realize she has twenty of them on the go at once. She adds that people are often more demanding with smaller projects than with large ones, as they expect the work to be simple and fast to complete. As a result, she's under pressure to get things rolling almost immediately. But this often isn't possible, because it takes time to get the required paperwork in order and to set up the project in Providence's systems. "Sometimes it takes days just for me to get a PO number so I can get started — and by that time, the customer wanted the job done already." So, to keep her customers happy, Genevieve often works ahead of or around the official process; for instance, she might approve a scope change on the spot when talking to a contractor, then catch up the paper trail later.

Closing out a project is particularly difficult for Genevieve. The finance team at Providence is always on her back to get the paperwork in order so they can close the project in their systems. Genevieve feels the amount of time spent at this point is often disproportionate to the project's size, even small projects can involve a lot of invoices. The problem is that vendors are notorious for sending their invoices incredibly late, often months after the job is done, and it takes a lot of time to chase them down and convince them to take care of it now. "You'd figure that contractors would be eager to collect their money, but they aren't. They're so busy, they leave it until a whole bunch of invoices have piled up, then do them all at once." This is particularly stressful for Genevieve, as she is evaluated on meeting strict deadlines: she has only 20 days to close a project after it reaches the milestone of substantial completion.

Staying Organized

- Believes that, "In my head, I always have a good sense of how things are going."
- Maintains a paper folder for each project. Prints a copy of everything, including emails, and files it. Each folder has a checklist of documents required.
- Keeps every email. Organizes them in Outlook under folders for each project.
- Schedules important meetings in Outlook so there's a reminder that pops up thirty minutes beforehand.
- Post-it notes on her laptop provide reminders of major to-do's.

Tools and Technology

- Primary tools are her paper notebook and cell phone, although Outlook is also important because of the high volume of email.
- Does not use any of Providence Corporation's tools. Relies on her Project Coordinator to keep those systems up to date.
- Creates her own spreadsheets in Excel for tracking projects financially and generating reports.
- Does not use Microsoft Project, or any other PM software, as she feels there's no need for projects of the size she manages.

©2005 RealSuite Inc. and Quarry Integrated Communications Inc. All rights reserved. Do not copy or distribute this document without written permission.

Jim Robinson | Facilities Manager

> **Make good things happen for his tenants.** Jim works hard to keep his tenants happy, so he wants to know exactly what's going on in his buildings and how the occupants might be affected. Jim strives to earn high marks on his annual satisfaction survey, as he's rewarded with a substantial performance bonus.

> **Avoid a major crisis.** Although Jim enjoys his job very much, he has terrible days on occasion. "You'll feel like toast by the time you get home. You'll have a headache and will dream about the job all night." For Jim, the possibility of a major problem or a confrontation with an angry tenant is always just around the next corner.

> *"At the end of the day, it's the facilities manager who's hung out to dry when things go wrong."*

Age: 46

Education: Electrical Technology Apprenticeship Program at Michigan State University (East Lansing, MI)

Employer: Providence Corporation in Boston, MA

Manages: 35 buildings in MA

Role Description

Jim is responsible for all aspects of running 34 of Providence Corporation's buildings, a mix of field and service offices in Massachusetts. Providence owns all its buildings and rents extra space to third-party tenants in many of them; it's mostly office space, with a small mix of retail storefronts and restaurants. Jim is based in Boston, in a 200-thousand-square-foot building where he has a small office on the second floor. He is supported by a Customer Service Representative (CSR) in the call center and two technicians who are on the road servicing buildings in his region.

Jim oversees the planning and delivery of services such as cleaning, security, repairs, and small renovations. He is the prime contact for tenant requests in his Boston building, which he receives either in-person or by phone and enters into Providence's PC-Help software himself. For his 33 other buildings, Jim's CSR in the call center dispatches work orders to his technicians or, if they're not available, to a local vendor — but he'll still get a call if the request is at all unusual or urgent, or if those people can't be reached immediately. Jim figures he handles about 80 tenant requests on an average day. On those rare occasions when Jim takes a brief vacation, he forwards his office phone to the call center and physically gives his CSR his cell phone so she can take his calls.

Jim is responsible for forecasting the annual cost of managing all 34 of his buildings and for meeting that forecast throughout the year. At the end of each month, Jim checks his performance against the forecast, as he's evaluated on whether he meets the numbers. Every day, Jim logs into Oracle to approve invoices entered by his CSR, but he also keeps track of his commitments in an Excel spreadsheet. He created this spreadsheet because he knows that neither PC-Help nor Oracle has up-to-date information, which he needs for determining whether he's met his targets and if he should adjust next month's forecast.

Jim's Day

Jim's day starts by 7:00 am, when he reaches his office in Boston. He grabs his second coffee of the morning before sitting at his desk and plugging in his laptop to check email. "I'm always in Outlook," Jim explains. "I usually have about 50 unanswered emails to deal with at any given time," many of which are information requests from his manager or the finance folks at Providence. He also receives email from his tenants and occupants, who are always looking for updates and information about their retail and office spaces. Keeping everyone informed and staying on top of paperwork is a real challenge for Jim. "I try to squeeze it in between phone calls and meetings, but it's hard to keep up. I'm fighting fires most of the day, so everything else takes a back seat." He often catches up with paperwork in the evenings at his home office, where he has a high-speed Internet connection.

Jim finds himself on the road about 2 days per week. He avoids overnight trips if possible, choosing to return home each day to spend time with his family even though he doesn't arrive until late in the evening. He likes to be onsite to personally check on his buildings, especially when major work is underway; but when his workload prevents him from hitting the road, he usually asks his technicians to email digital photos instead. Face-to-face time with tenants is especially critical to Jim, as it allows him to deal with complaints that might otherwise surface only at year-end, on his satisfaction surveys. It also helps him to better understand what people really need vs. what they want. Understanding this allows him to keep them happy while still staying within his budget.

Being on the road isn't easy. He leaves his laptop at home because it's unlikely he can find a place to dial in during the day. "But this means I return home to dozens of emails. I never go more than three days on the road, because it's impossible to catch up afterwards. And the call center freaks out when they can't reach me." On days when he's in Boston, Jim gets home by 7:00 pm and spends some time with his wife and two

>>

Jim Robinson

Facilities Manager

teenage sons. But he always finds himself back on the phone or the computer for a couple hours later at night. He finally packs it in and heads to bed when one of his kids yells downstairs, "This is a reminder: your day is over!"

Project Processes

In addition to overseeing the normal operations and maintenance of his buildings, Jim also plans and manages projects. A "project" is anything that falls outside his annual financial plan and requires its own budget — or something that is particularly expensive or complex.

The projects that Jim manages range from $100 (e.g., a small cabling job for a tenant) to $10,000 (e.g., renovating a boardroom). "I know I'm supposed to follow the same process regardless of the project's size. But it drives me nuts to raise so much paperwork for only a few hundred bucks." It takes so much time for Jim to follow all the steps that he skips as many as possible; for example, he'll often set up small projects as a work order instead of asking Providence's finance team to set it up in their systems. Jim's first concern is with satisfying his tenants, so he'll work around the "official" process if it saves time and money.

Although Jim normally engages someone from Providence's Project Management group for work over $10,000, he sometimes handles much larger projects himself. For example, earlier this year, he delivered a $55K project to repair the underground parking deck at his Boston building. He knew the PM who would have been assigned and figured it'd be more work to deal with her than just to do it himself. "The jobs that require project management often have a huge impact on the people in my buildings. So my bonus is often tied to the performance of the PM." Jim complains that Project Managers aren't accountable to him because they're both employees of Providence; they don't treat him as a customer like a third-party PM would, for instance.

When Jim does engage a Project Manager, he likes to stay involved and help the PM "stickhandle" the work through to completion. He's most active at the beginning of the process, though. Typically he initiates the project by identifying work that needs to be done in the building, although tenants also approach him with projects they'd like him to handle, such as moves or furniture upgrades. These projects are sometimes frustrating, as he's expected to provide an estimate almost immediately. But meeting onsite with vendors takes time, especially if competitive bids are required. When he finally does email an estimate to the tenant, they often do nothing for two weeks — "then, of course, they call me two days before the job has to be done!" To help reduce this frustration, Jim has begun keeping records of the actual costs of his projects so he can give people a quick ballpark estimate based on historical data, perhaps buying more time in the process.

Staying Organized

- "My paper notebook is my lifeline. If I wrote it anywhere, it's in here." Keeps a record of everything he does. Refers to it frequently when tenants call with such questions as, "did you get that message"? Has gone through 20 notebooks in the last three years.

- Maintains a paper file for each of his 34 buildings. Contains copies of inspection reports, warranties, drawings, photos, project documents — anything he deems to be important. Jim feels comfortable having these files on hand, although he admits to not using them for much.

- Keeps a list of to-do's in his paper notebook, as well as phone numbers.

- In Outlook, saves emails inside a folder for each building. Creates sub-folders for any projects occurring in the building.

Tools and Technology

- Primary tools are his paper notebook, his cell phone, and his laptop.

- Is most comfortable working on paper and likes that it's always at his fingertips.

- "I'm not a computer whiz, by no way, shape, or form!" Often loses files on his computer and feels unsure about whether he's using Providence's software properly.

- Uses PC-Help to enter and monitor work orders and to identify vendors to dispatch if his technicians are unavailable.

- "I have no sense in PC-Help of what's important and what's not."

MENTOR GRAPHICS

Christine Egli, Mentor Graphics Customer Support

Project Overview

Mentor Graphics is a leading provider of Electronic Design Automation (EDA) software. We serve a diverse customer base, offering dozens of highly specialized products across the spectrum of electronic design activity:

- Integrated circuit design
- Printed circuit board design
- Wiring and cabling system design
- Design for manufacturability
- Testing and simulation of the design

Historically, most customers requested technical support via the telephone. Over the past few years we realized our support teams could become more efficient by providing solutions to technical issues via the Web. In making the transition from primarily telephone support to more Web-centric support, we created an initiative to make SupportNet, our support Web site, the first line of support.

Persona Creation

When we started building our 'SupportNet' Web site, we realized that we were going to have to think about our customers in a different way. We needed to understand how people approach solving problems on Web sites and how that differs from getting phone support.

The creation of personas was an outgrowth of our usability testing. Our SupportNet team started doing usability studies in person at our offices and at our user conferences. In an effort to better understand our various customer segments, we collected customer profile information at the beginning of our usability tests. The profile data from our usability labs formed the foundation for our first personas. To further describe customer motivations and roles, we designed an interview guide to include more detailed survey questions and conducted a series of customer visits in the US and Europe. Customers were interviewed at their desks in their environment, and asked to give examples of SupportNet use in their day to day jobs. The detailed notes from those interviews included descriptions of the customer's working environment, workgroup structure, and organizational/cultural observations, in addition to the direct responses from the customers.

We have adapted some of the traditional persona methods to our organization. Personas often have clever names to help illustrate the various types of users. In our case, we started out with some cute names, but decided to scale back to more functional, serious titles such as

"Help Desk," or "SuperUser" (provided here, below), in order to show respect for our customers and improve the chances for adoption of personas within our organization.

Outcome

Having a realistic picture of the types of customers and what they expect from SupportNet is a useful tool in shifting our focus. The descriptions of the customers in our personas are recognizable to our support engineers. They use the personas as a vehicle to communicate profile details based on daily interactions to our Web development team.

The personas have helped us make better design decisions. Like many development teams, the SupportNet team creates use cases when we develop new applications and features for our support site. The personas have made these use cases more readily useful and understandable to our team. Some team members work on SupportNet continuously while others rotate among several projects. Personas helped the entire team quickly establish a frame of reference to get a clear picture of which features will serve which customers and why.

The personas have also been useful within our support marketing team. We currently use them as a discussion tool to help describe, develop and test new support offerings for our help desk customers.

Two example personas from this project:

- **Role:** Internal help desk, provides support for 80 EDA tool users. Manages vendor relationship, licensing issues in a large organization.

- **Experience:** 10-20 years on the job

- **Measured on:** Responsiveness, avoiding showstopper tool problems, vendor response to issues and problems

- **Typical Day:** 80% of the time he's answering questions and responding to user issues. He also looks for ways to improve their processes & design flow used in development projects. Downloads latest versions of software, writes documentation of design flow and points users to existing resources from vendor.

- **Likes:** Anticipating issues before they happen. Automating repetitive tasks.

- **Dislikes:** Administrative types who don't understand EDA tools. Anyone who restricts his access to networks, utilities, resources to get his job done.

- **Uses SupportNet for:** Researching problems in software, submitting or checking up on a service request, news on new releases, downloads. Reviews license reports and downloads licenses when needed to fix a prob. Checks weekly newsletter for advance warning of known issues.

Help Desk

Improve SupportNet with: Advanced service request management features for their site and company, delegated administration (change/add/delete) of SupportNet accounts w/additional access levels. License ease-of-use and maintenance improvements

The Superuser

- **Role:** Senior designer on project, go-to person for team members, other users in a large organization.
- **Experience:** 15-20+ years on the job, has used every tool out there
- **Measured on:** Managing project scope, hitting deadlines, team performance, manufacturing yields
- **Typical Day:** Answers a lot of questions, tries to keep up on her own design work as well. Integrates various tools in the flow and works on harder import/export issues.
- **Likes:** Being the expert, solving hard problems
- **Dislikes:** Scope creep; any surprises during the last week of a design project
- **Uses SupportNet for:** checking out error messages, tool version information, finding related flow, methodology and 3rd party tool information, advanced white paper information tips/tricks

Improve SupportNet with: expert-level technical content, acknowledgement of her advanced expertise by giving her preferred access to backline technical help, no beginners please.

ZYLOM MEDIA GROUP

Erik Goossens, Zylom Media Group

Project Overview

Zylom Media Group (www.zylom.com) is a leading European developer and publisher of casual games. Zylom creates and sells its own games and localized versions of games developed by other companies. The example personas were created to help Zylom redesign their Web site to encourage more visitors to try and then buy their games.

Persona creation

Zylom's persona creation process is detailed in the sidebars on pages 258, 409, and 450 earlier in this book (these are in Chapters 4, 6, and 7). The Zylom staff created assumption personas and then validated their assumptions by administering surveys to groups of users they identified in their existing data. Throughout the site redesign process, Zylom brought in real customers who were similar to the personas for "Maria and Sophie Fridays."

Outcome

After creating and validating their personas, Zylom completed an extensive redesign of their site to simplify the process of trying and then buying games. Zylom ran surveys with their users to ask about color usage, shapes and types of content and then cross-tabbed their results to their personas; they created designs based on these insights and followed up by testing the designs with real users during their "Maria and Sophie Fridays." Zylom also found that the persona Fridays helped keep the personas fresh in everyone's minds during the design and development process and helped them identify both small and large opportunities for improvements to their site.

Though they aren't able to share before-and-after sales and conversion data, they did say they noticed very significant positive changes as a result of the persona-driven redesign process. According to Erik Goossens, none of their persona-related work was difficult—he found the whole process to be logical and feel 'natural.' The hardest part for Zylom, he says, was just to take the time to do the persona work in a logical way. Their next challenge is to explore A/B testing methods using their personas.

Two example personas from this project:

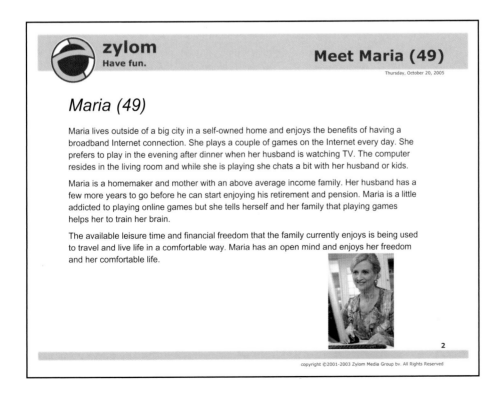

Sophie (32)

Sophie lives in one of the big cities and owns a first or second house/apartment together with her partner. She surfs the Web on a broadband connection and both the computer and the Internet play a central role in her daily life. She plays a couple of games on the Internet every week if her busy schedule permits it.

Sophie lives a busy life, combining her work and socializing with her many friends and close relatives. Her partner is also working his way up the ranks and they both have an above average education. Sophie is ambitious but she also longs to start her own family. Playing games gives her a moment of rest in a busy day.

In their spare time Sophie and her partner like to go out, preferably with friends or family.

1

C

SAMPLE IMAGE RELEASE FORM

I hereby grant permission for *Your Company Name,* including its subsidiaries, successors, assigns and affiliates and all joint ventures, partnerships and limited liability companies in which *Your Company Name* participates, to use my image and corresponding audio tape ("Recordings"), in whole or in part, for use in *Your Company Name* internal product development, internal communication and evangelism, and partner communication and evangelism.

I release *Your Company Name* from any and all claims and causes of action I may have now or in the future based upon defamation, invasion of right of privacy, publicity or personality, copyright or trademark infringement and unfair competition in connection with the Recordings and *Your Company Name* use of the Recordings. I agree not to initiate any legal action based on any of the grounds specified in this section.

Signature _____

Printed Name _____

Date _____

Consent of Parent or Guardian

(Applicable if under signatory above is 18 years of age)

I have read the foregoing Release, and I hereby give my express consent to the execution thereof.

PARENT OR GUARDIAN

_____

By

_____

Name

_____

Date

_____

Note from the authors: We recommend that you consult your company's legal representative before using this or any other legal form.

REFERENCES

Ahlqvist, S. (1996). "Objectory for GUI Intensive Systems: Extension," Kista, Sweden: Objectory Software AB.

AIGA Experience Design (2005). "Who Is AIGA Experience Design For?," *www.aiga.org/content.cfm? contentalias=who_for.*

Asch, S. E. (1951). "Effects of Group Pressure upon the Modification and Distortion of Judgments," in H. Guetzkow (ed.), *Groups, Leadership, and Men,* pp. 177–190. Pittsburgh: Carnegie Press.

Bacon, F. (1625). *First Book of Aphorisms.* Aphorism XLVI. Reprinted in *Internet Modern History Sourcebook, http://www.fordham.edu/halsall/mod/bacon-aphor.html.*

Baron-Cohen, S., H. Tager-Flusberg, and D. Cohen (eds.), (2000). *Understanding Other Minds: Perspectives from Developmental Cognitive Neuroscience* (2d ed.). Oxford: Oxford University Press, UK.

Baxley, B. (2003). *Making the Web Work: Designing Effective Web Applications.* Berkeley, CA: New Riders.

Bedbury, S. (2002). *A New Brand World: 8 Principles for Achieving Brand Leadership in the 21st Century.* New York: Viking.

Benun, I. (2003). *Designing Websites for Every Audience.* Cincinnati: How Design Books.

Benyon, D., and C. Macauley (2002). "Scenarios and the HCI-SE Design Problem," *Interacting with Computers* 14(4):397–405.

Beyer, H., and K. Holtzblatt (1998a). *Contextual Design: Defining Customer-Centered Systems.* San Francisco: Morgan Kaufmann.

Beyer, H., and K. Holtzblatt (1998b). "Contextual Inquiry and Design Methods," in *Contextual Design: Defining Customer-Centered Systems.* San Francisco: Morgan Kaufmann.

Bias, R. G., and D. J. Mayhew (eds.), (1994). *Cost-Justifying Usability.* Boston: Harcourt Brace & Co.

Bickmore, T. W. (2004). "Unspoken Rules of Spoken Interaction," *Communications of the ACM* 47(4):38–44.

Blankenship, A., G. Breen, and A. Dutka (1998). *State of the Art Marketing Research* (2nd ed.). New York: McGraw-Hill.

Blomquist, Å., and M. Arvola (2002). "Personas in Action: Ethnography in an Interaction Design Team," in *Proceedings of the Second Nordic Conference on Human-Computer Interaction,* NordiCHI, October 19–23, 2002, Aarhus, Denmark. New York: ACM Press.

Boehm, B. (1988). "A Spiral Model of Software Development and Enhancement," *IEEE Computer* 21(5):61–72.

Boyle, C. and M. Clarke (1985). "An Intelligent Mail Filter," in *Proceedings of HCI '85,* pp. 331–341. New York: Cambridge University Press.

Brewer, L. (2003). "When Characters Develop Minds of Their Own," *Vision* 13, January/February.

Brooke, J. (1996). SUS: A Quick and Dirty Usability Scale. In: P. W. Jordan, B. Thomas, B. A. Weerdmeester & I. L. McClelland (eds.), Usability Evaluation in Industry. London: Taylor & Francis.

Brown, J. S., and P. Duguid (2000). *The Social Life of Information*. Cambridge, MA: Harvard Business School Press.

Buchenau, M., and J. F. Suri (2000). "Experience Prototyping," in *Symposium on Designing Interactive Systems, Proceedings of the Conference on Designing Interactive Systems: Processes, Practices, Methods, and Techniques*, pp. 424–433. New York: ACM Press.

Bødker, S. (2000). "Scenarios in User-centered Design: Setting the Stage for Reflection and Action," *Interacting with Computers* 13(1):61–75.

Caine, R., and G. Caine (1994). *Making Connections: Teaching and the Human Brain*. Reading, MA: Addison-Wesley.

Calde, S. (2004). "Using Personas to Create User Documentation," *www.cooper.com/content/insights/ newsletters/2004_issue04/Using_personas _to_create_user_docs.asp*.

Campbell, J. (1949). *The Hero with a Thousand Faces*. Princeton, NJ: Princeton University Press (reprinted 1972).

Card, S., T. Moran, and A. Newell (1983). "GOMS (Goals, Operators, Methods, and Selection Rules)" in *The Psychology of Human/Computer Interaction*. Hillsdale: Lawrence Erlbaum.

Carliner, S. (1998). "Future Travels of the InfoWrangler," *Intercomm* 45(8):20–24.

Carroll, J. (2000a). "Five Reasons for Scenario-based Design," *Interacting with Computers* 13(1):43–60.

Carroll, J. (2000b). *Making Use: Scenario-based Design of Human-computer Interactions*. Cambridge, MA: MIT Press.

Carroll, J. (ed.), (1995). *Scenario-based Design: Envisioning Work and Technology in System Development*. New York: John Wiley and Sons.

Chiu, C., Y. Hong and C. S. Dweck (1997). "Lay Dispositionism and Implicit Theories of Personality," *Journal of Personality and Social Psychology* 73(1):19–30.

Chung, Hyejin; Hu, Yuegu; Lim, Kapin and Park, Eliot. (2004). A Study of Snack Perception and Behavior. Team project for D786: Design Research, Fall Quarter, in the Department of Industrial, Interior and Visual Communication Design at The Ohio State University.

Clancy, K., and P. Krieg (2000). *Counter-intuitive Marketing: Achieve Great Results Using Uncommon Sense*. New York: The Free Press.

Cockburn, A. (2001). *Writing Effective Use Cases*. Boston: Addison-Wesley.

Coen, J., and E. Coen (2000). *O Brother, Where Art Thou?* Universal Pictures.

Cohn, M. (2004). *User Stories Applied for Agile Software Development*. Boston: Addison-Wesley.

Coney, M. and M. Steehouder (2000). Role playing on the web: Guidelines for designing and evaluating personas online, *Technical Communication*, Vol. 47, No. 3, August, 327–340.

Constantine, L. L. (1994). "Essentially Speaking," *Software Development* 2(11). Reprinted in L. L. Constantine, *The Peopleware Papers*. Upper Saddle River, NJ: Prentice Hall.

Constantine, L. L. (1995). "Essential Modeling: Use Cases for User Interfaces," *ACM Interactions* 2(2).

Constantine, L. L. (1998). "Abstract Prototyping," Software Development, 6(10). Reprinted in S. Ambler and L. Constantine (eds.), *The Unified Process Elaboration Phase*. San Francisco: CMP Books.

Constantine, L. L. (2001). "Creative Input: From Feature Fantasies to Practical Products," in L. L. Constantine (ed.), *Beyond Chaos: The Expert Edge in Managing Software Development*. Boston: Addison-Wesley.

Constantine, L. L. (2003). "Canonical Abstract Prototypes for Abstract Visual and Interaction Design," in J. Jorge, N. Jardim Nunes, and J. Falcao e Cunha (eds.), *Interactive Systems: Design, Specification, and Verification. Proceedings, 10th International Workshop*, DSV-IS 2003, Funchal, Madeira Island, Portugal, 11–13 June 2003. *Lecture Notes in Computer Science*, vol. 2844. Berlin: Springer-Verlag.

Constantine, L. L. (2004a). "Beyond User-Centered Design and User Experience," *Cutter IT Journal* 17(2).

Constantine, L. L. (2004b). "Agility and Usability," Cutter Executive Report. *Agile Project Management*, Vol. *5*, No. 6.

Constantine, L. L., and L. A. D. Lockwood (2001). "Personas," *forUse Newsletter* 15, August. *www.foruse.com/newsletter/foruse15.htm*.

Constantine, L. L., and L. A. D. Lockwood (2002). "Modeling: Persona Popularity and Role Relationships," *forUse Newsletter* 26, October. *www.foruse.com/newsletter/foruse26.htm*.

Constantine, L. L., and L. A. D. Lockwood (1999). *Software for Use: A Practical Guide to the Models and Methods of Usage-Centered Design*. Reading, MA: Addison-Wesley.

Constantine, L. L., and L. A. D. Lockwood (2001). "Structure and Style in Use Cases for User Interfaces," in M. van Harmelan (ed.), *Object Modeling and User Interface Design*. Boston: Addison-Wesley.

Constantine, L. L., and L. A. D. Lockwood (2002). "Usage-Centered Engineering for Web Applications," *IEEE Software* 19(2).

Constantine, L. L., H. Windl, J. Noble, and L. A. D. Lockwood (2000). "From Abstraction to Realization in User Interface Design: Abstract Prototypes Based on Canonical Components," working paper, The Convergence Colloquy, July 2000. *www.foruse.com/articles/canonical.pdf*.

Cooper, A. (1995). *About Face 1.0*. Foster City, CA: IDG Books Worldwide.

Cooper, A. (1999). *The Inmates Are Running the Asylum*. New York: Macmillan.

Cooper, A., and R. M. Reimann (2003). *About Face 2.0: The Essentials of Interaction Design*. New York: John Wiley and Sons.

Cushman, W.H., and R. Derounian (1988). "Design and Testing of a Facility for Two-Way Video Teleconferencing," Proceedings, 33rd Annual Meeting of the Human Factors Society, Volume 2, pp. 224–228. Denver, CO.

Dalton, J. P., H. Manning, and M. Amato (2003). *Executive Q&A: Evaluating Design Personas.* Forrester Research Brief Series. *http://www.forrester.com/ER/Research/Brief/Excerpt/0,1317,32548,00.*

Davidson, J. P. (2001). *The Complete Idiot's Guide to Change Management.* Indianapolis: Alpha Books.

Dayton, T., A. McFarland, and J. Kramer (1988). "Bridging User Needs to Object-oriented GUI Prototype via Task Object Design," in Larry E. Wood (ed.), *User Interface Design: Bridging the Gap from User Requirements to Design,* pp. 15–56. Boca Raton, FL: CRC Press.

Decker, D. (1998). "Anatomy of a Screenplay," Screenwriters Group, 1998. Excerpts online at *www.anatomyofascreenplay.com/index.html.*

Denning, S. (2000). *The Springboard: How Storytelling Ignites Action in Knowledge-Era Organizations.* Woburn: Butterworth-Heinemann.

Denning, S. (2004). "Empathy: The Mechanism of Storytelling," Organizational and Business Storytelling in the News: Story 67, February 22, 2004. *www.stevedenning.com/SIG-67-empathy-key-to-storytelling.html.*

Djajadiningrat, J. P., W. W. Gaver, and J. W. Frens (2000). "Interaction Relabeling and Extreme Characters: Methods for Exploring Aesthetic Interactions," in *Proc. DIS 2000,* pp. 66–71. New York: ACM Press.

Domhoff, G. W. (1996). *Finding Meaning in Dreams: A Quantitative Approach.* New York: Plenum Press.

Donahue, G. M. (2001). "Usability and the Bottom Line," *IEEE Software* Vol 18, No. 1, pp. 31–37.

Donoghue, K. (2002). *Built for Use: Driving Profitability Through the User Experience.* New York: McGraw-Hill.

Dourish, P., and G. Button (1998). "On 'Technomethodology': Foundational Relationships Between Ethnomethodology and System Design," *Human–Computer Interaction,* 13(4):395–432.

Dreyfuss, H. (1955). *Designing for People* (2003 ed.). New York: Allworth Press.

Easty, E. D. (1981). *On Method Acting.* New York: Ballantine Books.

Ehn, P. (1993). "Scandinavian Design: On Participation and Skill," in D. Schuler and A. Namioka (eds.), *Participatory Design,* pp. 41–77. Hillsdale, NJ: Lawrence Erlbaum.

Erickson, T. (1996). "Design as Storytelling," *Interactions* 3(4):30–35.

FindLaw (2005). "Your Target Market." *http://smallbusiness.findlaw.com/business-operations/advertising-marketing/marketing-target-market.html.*

Flanagan, J. (1954). "The Critical Incident Technique," *Psychological Bulletin* 51:327–358.

Fortini-Campbell, L. (1992). *Hitting the Sweet Spot: How Consumer Insights Can Inspire Better Marketing and Advertising.* Chicago: The Copy Workshop.

Foulkes, D. (1999). *Children's Dreaming and the Development of Consciousness.* Cambridge, MA: Harvard University Press.

Fowler, M., and K. Scott (1997). *UML Distilled.* Reading, MA: Addison-Wesley.

Freed, J. (2004). "Best Buy Starts an Overhaul Before Its Problems Begin," Associated Press, 19 May.

Freud, S. (1900). *The Interpretation of Dreams.* New York: Macmillan.

Garreau, Joel (2001). The End-User View of Techno-Nirvana: Blink, Blink, Blink. Washington, D.C: *The Washington Post.* Monday, March 19, 2001: C01.

Garrett, J. J. (2002). *The Elements of User Experience: User-Centered Design for the Web.* Berkeley, CA: New Riders.

Gass, M. (2005). "An Introduction to the Bridge," *www.participatorydesign.com/BridgeIntro.pdf.*

Gilovich, T. (1991). *How We Know What Isn't So.* New York: Simon & Schuster.

Godin, S., and M. Gladwell (2001). Unleashing the Ideavirus. New York: Do You Zoom, Inc.

Gould, J. D., and C. Lewis (1985). "Designing for Usability: Key Principles and What Designers Think," *Communications of the ACM* 28(3):360–411.

Grobstein, P. (2004). "The Brain's Images: Co-Constructing Reality and Self," 11th Annual Usability Professionals' Association (UPA) Conference, July 2002, Orlando, Florida. *http://serendip.brynmawr.edu/ bb/reflections/upa/UPApaper.html.*

Grudin, J. (2003). "The West Wing: Fiction Can Serve Politics," *Scandinavian Journal of Information Systems* 15:73–77.

Grudin, J. and J. Pruitt (2002). "Personas, Participatory Design and Product Development: An Infrastructure for Engagement," Proc. *PDC 2002*, 144–161.

Grudin, R. (1996). *On Dialogue.* New York: Houghton Mifflin.

Gudjonsdottir, R. (2001). "Life-size Personas," Proceedings of the Usability Professionals Conference, Tenth Annual Conference. Bloomingdale, IL: The Usability Professionals' Association.

Hackos, J. T., and J. C. Redish (1998). *User and Task Analysis Techniques: User and Task Analysis for Interface Design.* New York: John Wiley and Sons.

Hague, P. N. (2002). *Market Research: A Guide to Planning, Methodology and Evaluation* (3d ed.). London: Kogan Page.

Haney, C., W. C. Banks, and P. G. Zimbardo (1973). "Interpersonal Dynamics in a Simulated Prison," *International Journal of Criminology and Penology* 1:69–97.

Harrison, M., R. Henneman, and L. Blatt (1994). "Design of a Human Factors Cost-Justification Tool," in R. G. Bias and D. J. Mayhew (eds.), *Cost-Justifying Usability,* pp. 203–242. Boston: Harcourt Brace & Co.

Heumann, J. (2003). "Use Case Storyboards: Integrating Usability with RUP and UML," in L. Constantine (ed.), *Performance by Design: Proceedings USE 2003, Second International Conference on Usage-Centered Design.* Rowley, MA: Ampersand Press.

Hiatt, J., and T. Creasey (2003). *Change Management.* Loveland, CO: Prosci Research.

Holtzblatt, K. (2002). "Personas and Contextual Design," *www.incent.com/community/design_corner/02_0913.html.*

Holtzblatt, K., J. Burns Wendell, and S. Wood (2004). *Rapid Contextual Design: A How-to Guide to Key Techniques for User-Centered Design.* San Francisco: Morgan Kauffmann.

Hoult, J. (2000). "Perfecting Your Pitch, Part One: Assume Short Buildings," Fast Company Web Exclusives, October, *www.fastcompany.com/articles/archive/act_joos1.html.*

Hughes, J. A., D. Randall, and D. Shapiro (1992). "Faltering from Ethnography to Design," in *Proc. CSCW'92*, pp. 115–122. New York: ACM.IBM.

IBM Research Knowledge Socialization Project (2003). "Why Stories," 22 August. *www.research.ibm.com/knowsoc/project_whystories.html.*

Idson, L. C., and W. Mischel (2001). "The Personality of Familiar and Significant People: The Lay Perceiver as a Social-cognitive Theorist," *Journal of Personality and Social Psychology* 80(4):585–596.

Jacobson, I. (1995). "The Use-Case Construct in Object-Oriented Software Engineering," in J. M. Carroll (ed.), *Scenario-Based Design.* New York: John Wiley and Sons.

Jacobson, I., G. Booch, and J. Rumbaugh (1999). *The Unified Software Development Process.* Reading, MA: Addison-Wesley.

Jacobson, I., M. Christerson, P. Jonsson, and G. Övergaard (1992). *Object-Oriented Software Engineering: A Use Case Driven Approach.* Reading, MA: Addison-Wesley.

Jahnek, A. (2004). "Tomorrowland: Interview with Bran Ferren," *CIO Web Business Magazine*, December 1998. *www.sio.com/archive/webbusiness/120198_qa.html.*

Jeffries, R., A. Anderson, and C. Hendrickson (2001). *Extreme Programming Installed.* Boston: Addison-Wesley.

Jensen, K. B. (ed.), (2002). *Handbook of Media and Communications Research: Qualitative and Quantitative Research Methodologies.* London: Routledge.

Kehr, D. (2003). "As for Directing, It's Telling a Story," *The New York Times*, 30 December.

Kerr, N. (1993). Mental Imagery, Dreams, and Perception," in C. Cavallero and D. Foulkes (eds.), *Dreaming as Cognition*, pp. 18–37. Hemel Hempstead, UK: Harvester Wheatsheaf.

Kiel, A. C., C. Fuson, J. Grudin, and E. Feldman (2005). "Ethnography for Software Development," in R. G. Bias and D. J. Mayhew (eds.), *Cost-Justifying Usability: An Update for the Internet Age.* Burlington, MA: Elsevier.

Kirakowski, J. (ed.), (2000). Human Factors Research Group, "Questionnaires in Usability Engineering: A List of Frequently Asked Questions," (3d ed.). *www.ucc.ie/hfrg/resources/qfaq1.html.*

Kranz, G. (2000). *Failure Is Not an Option: Mission Control from Mercury to Apollo 13 and Beyond.* New York: Simon & Schuster.

Kruchten, P., S. Ahlqvist, and S. Bylund (2001). "User Interface Design in the Rational Unified Process," in M. van Harmelan (ed.), *Object Modeling and User Interface Design.* Boston: Addison-Wesley.

Kuniavsky, M. (2003). *Observing the User Experience: A Practitioner's Guide to User Research.* San Francisco: Morgan Kaufmann.

Lafreniere, D. (1996). "CUTA: Collaborative Users' Task Analysis, A Simple, Low-cost Approach to Task Analysis," *Interactions Magazine*, Sept./Oct.

Leffingwell, D., and D. Widrig (1999). *Managing Software Requirements: A Unified Approach.* Boston: Addison-Wesley.

Leonard, E. (1998). Interview. *www.bookreporter.com/authors/au-leonard-elmore.asp.*

Leonard, E. (1999). Interview with Sean Elder. *www.salon.com/people/bc/1999/09/28/leonard/.*

Leonard, E. (2002). Interview with Simon Haupt. *www.globeandmail.ca/servlet/ArticleNews/printarticle/gam/20020204/RVLEON.*

Lewis, J. R. (1995). "IBM Computer Usability Satisfaction Questionnaire: Psychometric Evaluation and Instructions for Use," *International Journal of Human–Computer Interaction* 7(1):57–78. *http://drjim.0catch.com/usabqtr.pdf.*

Lyman, R. (2004). "Marlon Brando, Oscar-winning Actor, Is Dead at 80," *The New York Times*, 2 July.

Macdonald, Nico (2001). "Breakout Group: What's Next?" Presentation for The Advance for Design Summit 4, *http://advance.aiga.org/timeline/artifacts/Matrix.pdf.*

Malle, B. F. (2004). *How the Mind Explains Behavior: Folk Explanations, Meaning, and Social Interaction.* Cambridge, MA: MIT Press.

Manning, H., and M. Dorsey (2001). "Scenario Design Depends on Personas," Forrester Research Report, 14 August. *www.forrester.com.*

Manning, H., B. D. Temkin, and N. Belanger (2003). The Power of Design Personas. Forrester Research Report, December 2003. *www.forrester.com.*

Manning, H., B. D. Temkin, and N. Belanger (2004). Persona Best Practices From Discover Card. Forrester Research Report, January 2004. *www.forrester.com.*

Maxim, P. S. (1999). *Quantitative Research Methods in the Social Sciences.* Oxford: Oxford University Press.

Mayhew, D. (1992). *Principles and Guidelines in Software User Interface Design.* Englewood Cliffs, NJ: Prentice-Hall.

Mayhew, D. (1999). *The Usability Engineering Lifecycle: A Practitioner's Handbook for User Interface Design.* San Diego, CA: Morgan Kaufmann.

Mayhew, D., and M. Mantei (1994). "A Basic Framework for Cost-justifying Usability Engineering," in R. G. Bias and D. J. Mayhew (eds.), *Cost-Justifying Usability*, pp. 9–44. Boston: Harcourt Brace & Co.

McCloud, S. (1994). *Understanding Comics: The Invisible Art.* New York: HarperPerennial.

McGovern, (2002). *Content Critical: Gaining Competitive Advantage through High-Quality Web Content.* London: Financial Times Prentice Hall.

McQuaid, H., A. Goel, and M. McManus (2003). "When You Can't Talk to Customers: Using Storyboards and Narratives to Elicit Empathy for Users," *Proceedings of the 2003 International Conference on Designing Pleasurable Products and Interfaces.* New York: ACM Press.

Meier, B. (1993). "Speech and Thinking in Dreams," in C. Cavallero and D. Foulkes (eds.), *Dreaming as Cognition,* pp. 58–76. Hemel Hempstead, UK: Harvester Wheatsheaf.

Mello, S. (2002). *Customer-centric Product Definition: The Key to Great Product Development.* New York: AMACOM.

Michalis, P. (2004). "The First Storyteller." *www.collectorsguide.com/fa/fa014.shtml.*

Mikkelson, N., and W. O. Lee (2000). "Incorporating User Archetypes into Scenario-based Design," 9th Annual Usability Professionals' Association (UPA) Conference, Asheville, North Carolina.

Milgram, S. (1963). "Behavioral Study of Obedience," *Journal of Abnormal and Social Psychology,* 67:371–378.

Mithen, S. (2000). "Palaeoanthropological Perspectives on the Theory of Mind," in S. Baron-Cohen, H. Tager-Flusberg, and D. J. Cohen (eds.), *Understanding Other Minds: Perspectives from Developmental Cognitive Neuroscience* (2d ed.), pp. 488–502. Oxford: Oxford University Press.

Molich, R., and R. Jeffries. (2003). "Comparative Expert Reviews," Conference on Human Factors in Computing Systems, CHI '03 extended abstracts on human factors in computing systems. New York: ACM Press

Moore, G. A. (1991). *Crossing the Chasm: Marketing and Selling High-Tech Products to Mainstream Customers* (rev. ed. 2002). New York: HarperCollins Publishers.

Moore, G. A. (1995). *Inside the Tornado: Marketing Strategies from Silicon Valley's Cutting Edge.* Oxford: Capstone.

Morris, M. W., D. R. Ames, and E. D. Knowles (2001). "What We Theorize When We Theorize That We Theorize: Examining the "Implicit Theory" Construct from a Cross-disciplinary Perspective," in G. Moskowitz (ed.), *Cognitive Social Psychology: The Princeton Symposium on the Legacy and Future of Social Cognition,* pp. 143–161. Mahwah, NJ: Erlbaum.

Mourier, P., and M. Smith (2001). *Conquering Organizational Change: How to Succeed Where Most Companies Fail.* Atlanta, GA: CEP Press.

Muller, M. J. (2003). "Layered Participatory Analysis: New Developments in the CARD Technique." *http://www.research.ibm.com/compsci/spotlight/hci/p90-muller.pdf.*

Neuhauser, P. C. (1993). *Corporate Legends and Lore: The Power of Storytelling as a Management Tool.* Austin: PCN Associates.

Newburger, E. S. (2001). "Home Computers and Internet Use in the United States," U.S. Bureau of the Census. *http://www.census.gov/prod/2001pubs/p23–207.pdf.*

Nielsen, J. (1992). "The Usability Engineer Lifecycle," *Computer* Vol. 25, No. 3, pp. 12–22.

Nielsen, J. (1993). *Usability Engineering.* Boston: Academic Press. Hardcover edition.

Nielsen, J. (1994a). "Guerrilla HCI: Using Discount Usability Engineering to Penetrate the Intimidation Barrier," in R. G. Bias and D. J. Mayhew (eds.), *Cost-Justifying Usability*. Boston: Academic Press.

Nielsen, J. (1994b). *Usability Engineering*. San Diego, CA: Academic Press.

Nielsen, J., and R. Mack (eds.), (1994). *Usability Inspection Methods*. New York: John Wiley and Sons.

Nielsen, J., and R. Molich (1990). "Heuristic Evaluation of User Interfaces," in *Proceedings of the ACM CHI '90 Conference*, Seattle, WA, 1–5 April, pp. 249–256. New York: ACM Press.

Nielsen, L. (2002). From User to Character: Designing Interactive Systems — 2002. London, ACM Sigchi.

Nielsen, L. (2003a). A Model for Personas and Scenario Creation. Third Danish Human-Computer Interaction Research Symposium 2003, Roskilde, Writings in Computer Science, Roskilde University.

Nielsen, L. (2003b). Constructing the User. Human Computer Interaction International 2003 — Theory and Practice Crete: Lawrence Erlbaum Associates, Inc.

Norman, D. (1993). *Things That Make Us Smart*. New York: Perseus Publishing.

Orenstein, C. (2002). *Little Red Riding Hood Uncloaked: Sex, Morality, and the Evolution of a Fairy Tale*. New York: Basic Books.

Overholt, A. (2004). "Do You Hear What Starbucks Hears?," *Fast Company*, July, *www.fastcompany.com/magazine/84/starbucks_schultz.html*.

Patton, J. (2002). "Extreme Design: Usage-Centered Design in XP and Agile Development," in L. L. Constantine (ed.), *forUSE 2002: Proceedings of the First International Conference on Usage-Centered, Task-Centered, and Performance-Centered Design*. Rowley, MA: Ampersand Press.

Patton, J. (2003). "Improving Agility: Adding Usage-Centered Design to Agile Software Development," in L. L. Constantine (ed.), *Performance by Design: Proceedings, forUse 2003, Second International Conference on Usage-Centered Design*, Rowley, MA: Ampersand Press.

Plaks, J. E., S. J. Stroessner, C. S. Dweck, and J. W. Sherman (2001). "Person Theories and Attention Allocation: Preferences for Stereotypic vs. Counterstereotypic Information," *Journal of Personality and Social Psychology* 80:876–893.

Preece, J., H. Rogers, and H. Sharp (2002). *Interaction Design: Beyond Human–Computer Interaction*. New York: John Wiley and Sons.

Premack, D., and G. Woodruff (1978). "Does the Chimpanzee Have a Theory of Mind?" *Behavioral & Brain Sciences* 4:515–526.

Pruitt, J. and J. Grudin (2003). "Personas: Practice and Theory," Proc. DUX 2003.

Rackham, N. (1988). *SPIN Selling*. New York: McGraw-Hill.

Rao, V., and J. Steckel (1995). *The New Science of Marketing: State-of-the-Art Tools for Anticipating and Tracking the Market Forces That Will Shape Your Company's Future*. New York: McGraw-Hill.

RedHat Applications (2005). "Personas," *http://ccm.redhat.com/user-centered/personas.html*.

Redish, J. (2001). "Storytelling: The Power of Scenarios," Goldsmith Award presentation from the IEEE PCS Conference, October 2001. *www.redish.net/content/handouts/redish_Goldsmith_Oct2001.pdf.*

Repacholi, B. M., and A. Gopnick (1997). "Early Reasoning About Desires: Evidence from 14- and 18-month-olds," *Developmental Psychology* 33:12–21.

Ries, A., and L. Ries (1998). *The 22 Immutable Laws of Branding: How to Build a Product or Service Into a World-Class Brand.* New York: HarperCollins.

Rönkkö, K., M. Hellman, B. Kilander, and Y. Dittrich (2004). "Personas Is Not Applicable: Local Remedies Interpreted in a Wider Context," Proceedings of the Participatory Design Conference 2004, Toronto, Canada.

Rubinstein, R. and H. Hersh (1984). *The Human Factor: Designing Computer Systems for People.* Burlington, MA: Digital Press.

Salvador, T., and K. Howells (1998). "Focus Troupe: Using Drama to Create Common Context for New Product Concept End-user Evaluations," Proceedings of CHI 98. New York:ACM Press.

Sanders, E.B-N., and C. T. William (2001). "Harnessing People's Creativity: Ideation and Expression through Visual Communication," in J. Langford and D. McDonagh-Philp (eds.), *Focus Groups: Supporting Effective Product Development.* London: Taylor and Francis.

Sato, S., and T. Salvador (1999). "Methods & tools: Playacting and focus troupes: theater techniques for creating quick, intense, immersive, and engaging focus group sessions," *Interactions of the ACM* 6(5):35–41.

Schmitt, B. H. (1999). *Experiential Marketing: How to Get Customers to Sense, Feel, Think, Act, Relate to Your Company and Brands.* New York: The Free Press.

Schön, D. A. (1983). *The Reflective Practitioner: How Professionals Think in Action.* New York: Basic Books.

Schön, D. A. (1987). *Educating the Reflective Practitioner: Toward a New Design for Teaching and Learning in the Professions.* San Francisco, CA: Jossey-Bass Publishers.

Schwartz, B. (2004). *The Paradox of Choice: Why More Is Less.* New York: HarperCollins Publishers.

Selden, L., and G. Colvin (2003). *Angel Customers and Demon Customers: Discover Which Is Which and Turbo-Charge Your Stock.* New York: Portfolio.

Senge, P. M., A. Kleiner, C. Roberts, G. Roth, R. Ross, B. Smith (1999). *The Dance of Change: The Challenges to Sustaining Momentum in Learning Organizations.* New York: Currency.

Serendip (2004). "Seeing More Than Your Eye Does," *http://serendip.brynmawr.edu/bb/blindspot1.html.*

Settle, R. B., and P. L. Alreck (1986). *Why They Buy: American Consumers Inside and Out.* New York: John Wiley and Sons.

Shoda, Y., and S. L. Tiernan (2002). "What Remains Invariant?: Finding Order Within a Person's Thoughts, Feelings, and Behaviors Across Situations," in D. Cervone and W. Mischel, *Advances in Personality Science*, pp. 241–270. New York: Guilford.

Sinha, R. (2003). "Persona Development for Information-rich Domains," in *Proceedings of CHI 2003.* New York: ACM Press.

Sissors, J. (1966). "What Is a Market?," *Journal of Marketing* 30:17–21.

Sleeswijk-Visser, F., R. Van Der Lugt, and P. J. Stappers (2004). "The Personal Cardset: A Designer-centered Tool for Sharing Insights from User Studies," in *Proceedings of 2AD, Second International Conference on Appliance Design.* Bristol, UK: Appliance Design Network.

Sorkin, A., and K. Falls (2000). "Galileo," *The West Wing,* originally broadcast on 29 November, 2000.

Souza, R., H. Manning, P. Sonderegger, S. Roshan, and M. Dorsey (2001). "Get ROI from Design," Forrester Research Report, June 2001. *www.forrester.com.*

Spencer, R. (2000). "The Streamlined Cognitive Walkthrough Method," in *Proceedings of the ACM,* ACM-CHI 2000, 1–6 April, pp. 353–361. New York: ACM Press.

Stern, C. W., and G. Stalk Jr. (1998). *Perspectives on Strategy from the Boston Consulting Group.* New York: John Wiley and Sons.

Stroessner, S. J., and J. E. Plaks (1998). "Illusory Correlation and Stereotype Formation: Tracing the Arc of Research Over a Quarter Century," in G. Moskowitz (ed.), *Cognitive Social Psychology: The Princeton Symposium on the Legacy and Future of Social Cognition,* pp. 247–259. Mahwah, NJ: Lawrence Erlbaum.

Strope, J. (2003). "Designing for Breakthroughs in User Performance," in L. L. Constantine (ed.), *Performance by Design: Proceedings of forUse 2003, the Second International Conference on Usage-Centered Design.* Rowley, MA: Ampersand Press.

Tahir, M. F. (1997). "Who's on the Other Side of Your Software: Creating User Profiles Through Contextual Inquiry," in Proceedings of the Usability Professionals Conference '97. Bloomingdale, IL: The Usability Professionals' Association.

Temkin, B. D., J. P. Dalton, M. Dorsey, H. Manning, and P. Sonderegger (2003). "Executive Q&A: Design Personas, the Bridge Methodology." *Business Brief Series.* Sept 15. Cambridge, MA: Forrester Research, Inc.

Thralls, C., N. Blyler, and H. Ewald (1988). "Real Readers, Implied Readers, and Professional Writers: Suggested Research," *Journal of Business Communication* 25:47–65.

Tognazzini, B. (1995). *Tog on Software Design.* Reading: Addison-Wesley.

Tolkein, J. R. R. (1965). *The Lord of the Rings.* New York: Ballantine Books.

Tudor, L. G., M. J. Muller, T. Dayton, and R. W. Root (1993). "CARD: A Participatory Design Technique for High-level Task Analysis, Critique, and Redesign," in *Proceedings of HFES'93.* Seattle, WA: Human Factors and Ergonomic Society.

Turner Learning (2004). Learning Through Storytelling, "Teaching with Stories: Brain Based," Turner Learning. *http://learning.turner.com/turnersouth/storetelling/brain.html.*

Upshaw, L. (1995). *Building Brand Identity: A Strategy for Success in a Hostile Marketplace.* New York: John Wiley and Sons.

Usability Net (2003). Methods Table. *http://www.usabilitynet.org/tools/methods.htm.*

Vinden, P., and J. Astington (2000). "Culture and Understanding Other Minds," in S. Baron-Cohen, H. Tager-Flusberg, and D. Cohen (eds.), *Understanding Other Minds: Perspectives from Developmental Cognitive Neuroscience* (2d ed.), pp. 503–519. Oxford: Oxford University Press.

Vredenburg, K. (2003). "Building Ease of Use into the IBM User Experience," *IBM Systems Journal* 42(2). *www.research.ibm.com/journal/sj/424/vredenburg.html.*

Vredenburg, K., S. Isensee, and C. Righi (2001). *User-Centered Design: An Integrated Approach.* Englewood Cliffs, NJ: Prentice Hall.

Walden, D. (1993). "Kano's Methods for Understanding Customer-defined Quality: Introduction to Kano's Methods," *Center for Quality Management Journal* 2(4).

Wambaugh, J. (attributed). Quoted on Bard's Ink. *http://www.iprimus.ca/~pjduane/Sitemap.htm.*

Watkins, M. (1990). *Invisible Guests: The Development of Imaginal Dialogues.* Boston: Sigo Press.

Weerdmeester, B. A., and I. L. McClelland (eds.), (1996). *Usability Evaluation in Industry.* London: Taylor and Francis.

Weinstein, A. (1998). *Defining Your Market: Winning Strategies for High-tech, Industrial, and Service Firms.* New York: Haworth Press.

Weiss, A. (2002). "What is Marketing?" MarketingProfs.com, November 26, 2002. *http://www.marketing profs.com/2/whatismarketing.asp.*

Wenger, E. (1998). *Communities of Practice: Learning, Meaning and Identity.* Cambridge, MA: Cambridge University Press.

Wertsch, J. V. (1998). *Mind as Mediated Action.* Oxford, UK: Oxford University Press.

Wharton, C., J., Rieman, C., Lewis and P. Polson (1994). *The Cognitive Walkthrough method: A practitioner's guide.* In J. Nielsen and R. L. Mack (eds.), Usability Inspection Methods. pp. 105–141. New York: John Wiley & Sons.

Wideman, M. (2004). "The Role of the Project Life Cycle (Life Span) in Project Management: A Literature Review by R. Max Wideman," Max's Project Management Wisdom. *http://www.maxwideman.com/papers/plc-models/1990s.htm.*

Wilson, C. E., and S. Rosenbaum (2005). "Categories of ROI and their Practical Implications," in R.G. Bias and D. J. Mayhew (eds.), *Cost-Justifying Usability.* San Francisco: Morgan Kaufmann.

Windl, H. (2002a). "Usage-Centered Exploration: Speeding the Initial Design Process," in L. L. Constantine (ed.), *forUse 2002: Proceedings of the First International Conference on Usage-Centered Design.* Rowley, MA: Ampersand Press.

Windl, H. (2002b). "Designing a Winner: Creating STEP 7 Lite with Usage-Centered Design," in L. L. Constantine (ed.), *forUse 2002: Proceedings of the First International Conference on Usage-Centered Design.* Rowley, MA: Ampersand Press.

Wirfs-Brock, R. (1993). "Designing Scenarios: Making a Case for a Use Case Framework," *Smalltalk Report* Nov./Dec.

Wixon, D., and S. Jones (1996). "Usability for Fun and Profit: A Case Study of the Design of DEC Rally Version 2," in M. Rudisill, C. Lewis, P. B. Polson, and T. D. McKay (eds.), *Human-Computer Interface Design: Success Stories, Emerging Methods, and Real-World Context.* San Francisco: Morgan Kaufmann.

Wodtke, C. (2002). *Information Architecture: Blueprints for the Web.* Berkeley: New Riders.

Zaltman, G. (2003). *How Customers Think: Essential Insights into the Mind of the Market.* Boston: Harvard Business School Press.

Zyman, S. (1999). *The End of Marketing as We Know It.* New York: HarperCollins.

ADDITIONAL RESOURCES

There are many sources of persona information that can be found on the Web. The following are a few of those available at the time of writing (most are free, and some are available for a fee).

Brechin, E. (2002). "Reconciling Market Segments and Personas," Feb./March Newsletter from Cooper Interaction Design. *http://www.cooper.com/newsletters/2002_02/reconciling_market_segments_and_personas.htm.*

Calabria, T. (2004). "An Introduction to Personas and How to Create Them," *http://www.steptwo.com.ua/.*

Dalton, J., M. Dorsey, H. Manning, and P. Sonderegger (2003). "Design Personas," Forrester Research Report, 6 Aug. *www.forrester.com.*

Dalton, J., H. Manning, and M. Amato (2003). "Evaluating Design Personas," Forrester Research Report, 15 Sept. *www.forrester.com.*

Freydenson, E. (2002). "Bringing Your Personas to Life in Real Life." *http://boxesandarrows.com/archives/002343.php.*

Goodwin, K. (2001). "Perfecting Your Personas," July/Aug. Newsletter from Cooper Interaction Design. *http://www.cooper.com/newsletters/2001_07/perfecting_your_Personas.htm.*

Goodwin, K. (2002). Interview: User Interface 7 East. *http://www.uiconf.com/uie-7/goodwin_interview.htm.*

Perfetti, C. (2002). "Personas: Matching a Design to the User's Goals," User Interface Engineering. *http://world.std.com/~uieweb/Articles/Personas.htm.*

Questionnaire Resources

- SUMI: http://*www.ucc.ie/hfrg/questionnaires/sumi/whatis.html*
- WAMMI: *http://www.wammi.com*
- "Questionnaires in Usability Engineering: A List of Frequently Asked Questions" (3d ed.): *http://www.ucc.ie/hfrg/resources/qfaq1.html*

Other Sources

- http://www.oohci.org/methods/bridge/bridge.html
- http://www.incent.com/pubs/workmodeling.html
- http://www.incent.com/community/design_corner/02_0913.html

CONTRIBUTOR INDEX

SUBJECT INDEX

customers
  focus on instead of users, 619–620
  images of, 23
  increased desire for intimacy with,
      611–612
  measuring satisfaction of, 465–467
  need for richer descriptions of,
      612–613
  reconciling brand attributes and
      customer values, 635–638
  vs. users, 427–429
customer segmentation models, 608
customer service costs, 96
customer support professionals, 78

D

D'Angelo, Brenda, 117, 379, 494
data assimilation process, 177
data collection, 120–129
data-collection-by-topic spreadsheet,
    157, 159
data-driven personas, 120
data mining professionals, 77
data processing, during conception and
    gestation, 189–195
  assimilating factoids, 200–201
  describing goal and outcome of
      meeting, 196
  drawbacks of assimilation, 195
  identifying factoids in data sources,
      196–197
  labeling clusters of factoids, 201–203
  methods of, 189–194
  overview, 189
  planning assimilation meeting, 195–196
  posting user category labels around
      room, 199–200
  side benefits of collaborative
      assimilation, 194–195
  transferring factoids to sticky notes,
      197–199
data sources
  creating index for, 159–161
  identifying, 120–129

day-in-the-life toolkit, 135–137
deadlines, 113
decision points, 582–583
Decker, Dan, 546
Defining Your Market, 21–22
deliverables, list of, 115–117
Dellino, Domenick J., 313
demographics, 62, 126–128, 606
Denning, Steve, 522, 525, 533
descriptive anthropology, 661
descriptive profiles, 25
descriptors, 239
design and development processes, how
    personas improved, 468–477
  avoiding unnecessary work, 470–471
  communication improvement, 471–473
  increased efficiency, 469–470
  overview, 468–469
  process improvements, 473–477
Design Builder, Quarry's, 678
design communicators, 74
design-focused persona, 227
design ideas, as element of Maps,
    560–561
Designing for People, 21
Designing Websites for Every Audience, 415
Design Maps, 144–145, 359, 381, 464,
    540–541, 557–601
  elements of, 559–561
    comments, 560
    design ideas, 560–561
    overview, 559
    questions, 560
    steps, 559–560
  flow diagrams, 541
  overview, 540–541, 557–590
  vs. Reality Maps, 588–589
  reasons for using, 561–566
  step 1: deciding which processes you
      want to Map, 592–593
  step 2: creating Maps, 593–596
    managing Design Mapping sessions,
        594–595
    overview, 593–594

Design Maps *(Continued)*
    using Design Maps to create
        wireframes, 595–596
  step 3: evaluating and communicating
      solutions, 596–601
    communicating with other
        departments, 601
    design changes during development,
        600
    getting different views of product in
        action, 596–599
    overview, 596
    supporting walkthroughs and
        creating scenarios and use case,
        599–600
design personas, 604
  for marketing purposes, 623–629
    looking for clues into technology
        adoption behaviors, 627–628
    overview, 623–625
    paying attention to surprises, 625–626
    planning messaging strategy, 628–629
    scanning competitive landscape,
        626–627
    whether building right product, 625
design reviews, 399–405
design solutions, exploring, 379–398
  adult personas and developers, 396–398
  creating scenario collection
      spreadsheet, 388–393
  overview, 379
  scenario-based design, 379–388
  visual design solutions, 393–396
Desktop Management Services (DMS), 297
details in stories, 532–533, 548
developers, 78, 281, 396–398
development cycle, 266, 285, 363
development managers, 78
development teams, 68, 163, 274, 316,
    346, 398, 400, 425, 433
diagrams
  flow diagrams, 541
  image diagrams, 26
dialog model, 610

family planning phase (*Continued*)
    avoiding talking about features, 620
    experimenting with scenarios, 620
    focus on customers instead of users,
      619–620
    helping people "project" their
      feelings, 620
    overview, 618–619
  organizational introspection, 84–99
    incorporation of user information
      into product design and
      development process, 95–99
    overview, 84–85
    thinking and communicating about
      users, 91–94
    user-focus, 86–91
    whether personas are solutions to
      problem, 96–99
  overview, 67–71
  planning and executing own primary
    user research, 130–131
  Reality Mapping during, 558
  tracking and managing data sources as
    you collect them, 157–161
    creating data-collection-by-topic
      spreadsheet, 159
    creating data source index, 159–161
    overview, 157–158
feature-by-audience evaluation, 372
features
  avoiding talking about, 620
  brainstorming using personas, 369
  plotting feature value vs. technical
    feasibility, 374–379
  prioritizing using persona-weighted
    feature matrix, 369–374
feelings, helping people "project," 620
fictional preparation, 659
field studies, conducting to gather
    qualitative data, 131–147
  analyzing data, 147
  conducting visit, 135–146
  creating artifacts to communicate
    data, 146

field studies, conducting to gather
    qualitative data (*Continued*)
  creating list of things you want to find
    out, 132–133
  creating script for visit, 134
  deciding who you want to visit and
    train your team, 133
  overview, 131–132
  recruiting participants, 133
flow diagrams, 541
focal user roles, 510, 516
folktales, 523
Forrester Research, 19–20, 437
Fortini-Campbell, Lisa, 612
foundation documents, 220, 221–229,
    236, 246, 275, 288, 295, 309,
    329, 389
Freed, Joshua, 448
full-team review sessions, 82

G

Gadney, Max, 73
gestation, *see* conception and gestation
    phase
Gibb, Justine, 350
Gigantic for Kids (G4K), 665–676
  business overview, 668
  corporate background, 667
  customers, 667
  example persona (Tanner Thompson),
    670–679
  financial info, 666
  key software products, 668
  mission statement, 667
  overview, 665–666
gizmos, 316–318
Goal-Directed Design, 32, 38, 55, 74,
    500, 501
goals of users, 178, 179–180, 463–465,
    652–653
Goel, Aradhana, 382
Goodwin, Kim, 74, 232
Goossens, Erik, 258, 409, 450, 683
Grange, Laura, 188

graphics and interface designers,
    15, 78–79, 80, 393
grass-roots efforts, 39
Grobstein, Paul, 522
Grudin, Jonathan, 242
guidebooks, focusing, 415–424
Guðjónsdóttir, Rósa, 250, 318

H

Hackos, JoAnn, 28, 536, 563
Hackos, J.T., 28–29
handouts, 333–335
Harrison, Mary, 447
Hayes, Brian, 499
Henlein, Emily, 395
Herasimchuk, Andrei, 484
holistic images, 653
Holmes, Noel, 178, 284
Holtzblatt, Karen, 30, 563
Hourihan, Meg, 12
How Customers Think, 611, 620
human cognitive process, 523
Hynes, Colin, 169, 253, 263, 455
hypothetical archetypes, 32

I

idea maps, 141–143
idea viruses, 112
identity crisis, 427
Idson, L.C., 652
illustrating personas, 247–248
  audition illustrations, 252
  illustrations as alternative to photos,
    249–251
image collages, 138–140
image diagrams, 26
image statements, 25–26
improvement of product, 447–468
  defining product success, 449–452
  Donoghue's "experience matrix,"
    454–458
  measuring customer satisfaction,
    465–467
  measuring decreased support and
    maintenance costs, 467–468

P

psychological evidence of why personas work, 643–663
from acting, 657–658
conscious models, 646–648
from engagement to caring, 662
models of fictional people can be as engaging as models of real people, 644
our models are often detailed and complex, 644–645
overview, 643–645
psychological accuracy and fictional preparation, 659
psychological assessments of other design methods, 659–662
contextual design, 660
ethnography and participatory design, 661–662
overview, 659
scenario-based design and task analysis, 659–660
stereotypes and traits, 660
unconscious models, 646–647, 648–655
goals, plans, expectancies, and scripts, 652–653
overview, 648–649
psychological evidence from dreams, 654–655
specific knowledge of individuals: holistic images, 653
stereotypes and cultural differences, 649–651
traits, 651–652
we naturally model other people, 644
from writing, 655–657
Pyra, 12

Q

qualitative data, 121, 130, 241
qualitative research, 131, 135, 464
quality assurance (QA), 68, 274, 294, 346, 398, 413
quantitative research, 131, 196, 613–614

Quarry Integrated Communications & Realsuite Incorporated, 677–680
outcome, 678–680
overview, 677
persona creation, 678
project overview, 677–678
Quesenbery, Whitney, 251, 359, 600, 644
questionnaires, 87
questions, as element of Maps, 560

R

Rapid Contextual Design, 147
rapid user mental modeling (RUMM), 191–193
"reality check" site visits, 261
Reality Maps, 144–145, 359, 362, 464, 557–601
elements of, 559–561
comments, 560
design ideas, 560–561
overview, 559
questions, 560
steps, 559–560
overview, 557–558
reasons for using, 561–566
step 1: creating Mapping plan, 566–571
step 2: creating Maps, 571–578
developing Maps iteratively, 576–578
if session starts to derail, 575–576
keep Mapping sessions focused and productive, 573–575
overview, 571–573
step 3: analyzing Maps, 579–587
artifact indicators, 580
branching, 582–583
connection arrows, 581
"Deep dive" indicators, 581
determining when finished, 586–587
identifying and labeling interesting aspects of Maps, 579
layering, 583–585
legend, 581
"Mr. Yuk" indicators, 580

Reality Maps *(Continued)*
overview, 579
"performing" Maps, 585–586
phase labels, 579–580
for repetitiveness, complexity, and overall flow, 585
shared approaches to similar tasks, 581–582
step 4: harvest for information to use in personas, 587
toolkit, 144–145
real people posters, 146, 338
RealSuite Incorporated, 677
recruiting and visiting representative people, 262
recruiting profile for usability testing and market research, 405–412
Redish, Ginny, 28, 285, 535, 536, 563
Redish, J.C., 28–29
Rees, Damian, 207, 237, 292, 472
reference booklet, persona, 325
Reimann, Robert, 38, 170
reincarnating personas, 491–494
reports, on users needs, 8
repository, for persona artifacts, 338–340
representations of users, *see* user representations
representativeness of personas, 190–191
representative people, recruiting and visiting, 262
résumé-like documents, 329, 507
retirement, *see* reuse and retirement
retirement (ROI) deliverables, 116–117
return on investment (ROI), *see* lifetime achievement
reuse and retirement, 52, 429–431, 485–497
deliverables, 116–117
overview, 433–435, 485
retiring personas, 494–497
reusing personas, 487–494
creating persona library, 489–490
evolving personas, 492–494
managing reuse, 490–491
overview, 487–488

ABOUT THE AUTHORS

John Pruitt is the User Research Manager for the Tablet and Mobile PC Division at Microsoft Corporation, a group leading the quest toward truly mobile computing for both work and personal use. Since joining Microsoft in 1998, he has conducted user research for a number of product releases, including Windows 98SE, Windows 2000 Professional, Windows XP, Windows Vista, and MSN Explorer versions 6, 7, and 8. Prior to Microsoft, he was an invited researcher in the Human Information Processing Division of the Advanced Telecommunications Research Laboratory, in Kyoto, Japan, and worked as a civilian scientist doing simulation and training research for the U.S. Navy.

John holds a Ph.D. in experimental psychology from the University of South Florida and has published articles and chapters on usability methods, skill training, naturalistic decision making, speech perception, and second-language learning. He has been creating and using personas for more than six years, continually developing a more rigorous approach to the method and mentoring numerous product teams at Microsoft and companies worldwide in adopting the technique. John has led workshops and spoken widely on the topic at both academic and industry events.

Tamara Adlin is the founder and principal of adlin, inc., a customer experience consulting company located in Seattle, WA. Tamara has over twelve years' experience developing user-centered design and user interface design methods. Prior to starting her own company, she managed the customer experience team at Amazon Services, working holistically to create brand-, business-, and customer-centered e-commerce solutions for online and multichannel retailers. She moved to Amazon Services from Amazon.com, where she was a Senior Customer Experience Specialist working with teams across the company to invent and improve user experiences for buyers, sellers, partners, and support professionals. Previously, she was the Human-Centered Design Lead at Attenex Corporation, a legal services software company in Seattle, where she designed advanced document management interfaces. Prior to that, Tamara led teams and designed interfaces for Web applications at Akamai Technologies, INTERVU, and Netpodium Corporation, where she designed the UI for the award-winning Netpodium Interactive Broadcasting Toolset. Tamara started her user experience career as an Engineering Psychologist at the Army Research Laboratory, evaluating human factors issues associated with military systems.

Tamara holds a B.A. from Vassar College and an M.S. in Technical Communication from the University of Washington, where she focused on user interface design techniques and interdisciplinary communications. Tamara has led workshops and been invited to speak all over the world on personas and other user-centered design methods.

ABOUT THE ILLUSTRATOR

Nelson Adlin simply has to have a pen in his hand so that the creatures in his imagination have a way to escape. The illustrations in this book are just a few of the thousands of pen, ink gel-pen, and pastel "Allegories Without Words" that make up his heady zoo of characters that illustrate both his take on the human condition and his wildest dreams. When Tamara started working on this book, she quickly realized that her dad had already created the perfect illustrations of imaginary people at every stage of their development. From the hazy first glimpse of an almost-human shape emerging from a simple line through to the over-evolved creatures that personas can become, Nelson Adlin had already drawn every phase of the persona lifecycle.

Adlin is a retired professor of art who spends part of his time illustrating, sculpting, and making jewelry. He is an honors graduate of the Maryland Institute College of Art and earned an M.A. on a fellowship from Columbia University. His work has been recognized by the Art Directors' Club and galleried shows, and has been exhibited at the Maryland Institute College of Art, Peale Museum, The Baltimore Museum of Art, Columbia University, University of Maryland, The Johns Hopkins School of Medicine, Baltimore City Hall, and other area galleries. He lives, works, and continuously doodles in Baltimore, Maryland with his wife Lily. Son Josh and daughter Tamara both reside in Seattle.

For more information about Nelson Adlin and his artwork, visit www.nelsonadlin.com.